COMPARING NATIONS

THE UNITED KINGD[OM]
THE FEDE[RAL]
FRANCE FRANCE FRANC[E]
THE SOVIE[T]
NIGERIA NIGER[IA]
EGYPT EGYPT EGYPT
TANZANIA TANZANIA TAN[ZANIA]
CHILE CH[ILE]

OM THE UNITED KINGDOM
AL REPUBLIC OF GERMANY
E FRANCE FRANCE FRANCE
UNION THE SOVIET UNION
A NIGERIA NIGERIA NIGERIA
EGYPT EGYPT EGYPT EGYPT
ANIA TANZANIA TANZANIA
LE CHILE CHILE CHILE CHILE

COMPARING NATIONS
The Developed and the Developing Worlds

Vaughn F. Bishop
Emory University

J. William Meszaros
Emory University

D. C. HEATH AND COMPANY
Lexington, Massachusetts   Toronto

To Our Parents

Published simultaneously in Canada.

Printed in the United States of America.

International Standard Book Number: 0–669–01142–8

Library of Congress Catalog Card Number: 79–66852

PREFACE

Instructors face a number of important decisions in designing an introductory course in comparative politics. They must decide what countries to include and which concepts or ideas to emphasize. Finally, they must concern themselves with the best way to introduce the logic of the comparative method. *Comparing Nations* provides a comprehensive approach to handling all of these decisions.

This text surveys four *developed* nations—the United Kingdom, France, West Germany, and the Soviet Union—and four *developing* nations—Nigeria, Egypt, Tanzania, and Chile—permitting a comparison of the political institutions and political patterns. It also introduces students to nation-states that have not been traditionally treated in comparative politics courses. The nations of the developing world are becoming more important in our lives, and few American students have any understanding of the political and cultural traditions they represent, or the problems and challenges they face.

To emphasize our view that politics is a universal phenomenon and that all nations face similar problems, we have chosen not to present the material in strict nation-by-nation fashion. Each chapter deals with a topic that is of traditional concern to comparative politics and is a major problem facing nation-states, whether developed or developing. Within each chapter there are separate discussions of each country. By our organization we have sought to encourage comparison. It is our hope that students using this book will not see nation-states as isolated, unrelated entities but as different nations facing similar problems.

The text begins with chapters on the logic of comparison and on the history and cultures of the eight nations. Chapters 4 through 6 focus on political participation, the role and importance of political parties, and different means of leadership selection. The discussion then moves to important governmental institutions—those that deal with the making and implementing of policy, those that serve symbolic functions, and those whose purpose is to resolve conflict. The text concludes with an evaluation of the political performance of the eight nation-states, with emphasis on their adaptability to economic, social, and political changes.

CONTENTS

MAPS

TABLES AND FIGURES

CHAPTER 1
COMPARING NATIONS

What tools are needed to compare the politics and governments of Great Britain, West Germany, France, the Soviet Union, Nigeria, Egypt, Tanzania, and Chile?

Every day each of us is confronted with news reports from other countries, and, unfortunately, we often do not have the background to understand these news events. When reports circulate that the head of the Communist party of the Soviet Union is ill or contemplating retirement, we wonder who is likely to succeed him and by what means. When we hear that the British pound is declining in value or that there is a fresh outbreak of violence between Protestants and Catholics in Northern Ireland, we ought to ask how Great Britain, one of the world's oldest, ongoing parliamentary democracies will respond to these new crises. When the military takes over the government in Chile and Nigeria, we may ask why such a coup occurs in these two nations while in other nations the military stays out of politics. To answer these questions, we need facts.

Facts without a framework with which to put them into perspective are of little use. There are patterns that recur in politics, and we need to see how and why countries with the same basic political structure can be so different. For example, why are Britain and France, both with parliamentary traditions, so different in their political "styles"? Are there reasons why political violence is so common in some nations and rare in others? Almost all nations have political parties, but what are the differences and similarities between parties like the Labour or Conservative parties in Great Britain and the Communist party in the Soviet Union? To answer these, and other, questions we need both facts and a general understanding of politics as practiced in other nations.

This is a comparative politics textbook that will discuss the "politics" and the "political systems" of eight "foreign" nations—the United Kingdom, the Federal Republic of Germany (West Germany), France, the Soviet Union, Nigeria, Egypt, Tanzania, and Chile. They are foreign because most Americans know so little about them and also because their political systems seem so different from what we are most familiar with—our own. You will read about the history of each nation and of the events that shaped each country's political traditions. Political events do not occur in a vacuum; they occur within the context of the traditions and culture of the nation. The personality and behavior of political leaders and the organizations and framework of the political system influence how politics is played and what the outcomes of the political game are. When you complete this text, you should have a better understanding not only of why specific events occur in other nations but also what effect these events may have on the future.

Many textbooks on comparative politics focus only on the major nations of Western Europe and the Soviet Union—no doubt because these nations are most often in the news, most visible, and most familiar; however, the nations of Africa, Latin America, and the Middle East are becoming increasingly important. The political spotlight has expanded to include the developing new nations as well as the developed older ones. After World War II the international community added many new members. In 1946 there were 51 charter member states of the United Nations; today there are over 140 member states. Almost every year a new nation proclaims its independence. Comparative politics today requires an understanding of both the big and the small nations, the young and the old, the familiar and the unfamiliar.

This new age of nationalism forces us to alter radically the way in which we think about and discuss politics; the concepts and vocabulary have changed with the times. In this chapter we present some of the terms commonly used in comparative politics, the various ways in which nations are compared, and a brief introduction to the politics of the eight nations that we will study.

Political Tradition, Political Systems, and the "Art of Comparison"

Several factors confuse most political discussions and make the systematic study of politics difficult. The first is the way we use political words. In our daily lives many of us are vague and imprecise when we use political terms. Depending on how they are used, "socialism," "totalitarianism," and "democracy" can mean very different things. Many political discussions flare into arguments simply because people fail to use political terms consistently and uniformly.

The fact that our political beliefs differ from others and that our own beliefs can change compounds confusion. People may see politics as good or bad, exciting or boring, beneficial or hurtful. The politician may be a wise statesman one moment, a corrupt politician the next. For some, politics depends on whose "ox is being gored" at the time. When we achieve what we want through political activity, we are pleased and politically astute; but when our opponents win and we lose, we are not pleased.

Our definitions of politics and political activity also depend on what is being studied. When looking at the politics of personal interchange, we stress the personalities of those who are involved. At the local governmental level politics cannot be understood apart from such issues as schools, property taxes, and zoning. Parents are concerned with the quality and cost of local schools; property owners are concerned with the taxes needed to pay for public services and with preserving the value of their homes. In some communities people attempt to separate politics and government and argue that "politics" (which they view as bad) has no place in "government" (which is good). This produces a strange hybrid, "nonpartisan, good government."

At the national level the issues may appear less immediate but more important. Such tasks as protecting national security, regulating trade between nations, controlling and monitoring the economy, and developing nationwide policies are issues usually associated with the nation. A characteristic of national politics that elevates the study of government at this level is *sovereignty*. Sovereignty means there is no higher authority or power that can override or change the decisions made at this level.

In discussing politics, we use a political shorthand. We do not, for example, describe every detail of a nation when we analyze its politics; we classify and categorize. Countries are classified as "democratic," "authoritarian," or "totalitarian." With reference to their economies they are "capitalist," "socialist," or "communist." In addition, countries may be categorized as "traditional" or "modern," "developed" or "developing." Whatever the distinction drawn, the goal is to give us clues about how the system operates. Sometimes the category also conveys value judgements as to which systems are "good" and which are "bad."

A third level of politics is international, and involves the relationship between nations and groups of nations. Here the concerns focus on trade and cooperation between nations, attempts to provide worldwide security and order, and the need for cooperation between countries. Organizations like the United Nations seek to promote cooperation among nations and prevent violent conflict in the international community. It is unrealistic, however, to expect (or necessarily even desire) that national boundaries will disappear in the near future.

Most commentators agree that, although it may be an appealing thought at times, the game of politics is not going to disappear. To understand more about politics, we study politics within various nations; and our understanding of each nation is increased because we have a basis for comparison.

Understanding politics then requires studying what the rules of the game are, how they develop, how the rules differ from nation to nation, and what the effects of the political game are on individuals and groups in the nation.

Demands, Decisions, and Power: The Primacy of Politics

Individuals and groups within society have certain specific expectations and demands. They expect certain things to occur and others not to occur; they expect to be provided certain benefits and services. Labor unions want higher pay and shorter working hours. Civil servants expect that their performance will be judged on how well they do their job and not on political concerns. Some religious groups lobby that their values be reflected in government policy, while other groups argue with equal force that religion and government need to be separate.

Individual and group expectations are often translated into demands. People with similar interests join together in interest groups to press for what they want in the political arena. When these groups make demands, political leaders must make decisions. For example, labor unions may demand that the government establish a minimum wage for all workers and limit the number of hours that can be worked per week. Leaders must respond to these demands, demands that sometimes conflict with the interests of another group. The interests of labor, for example, must be balanced against those of business.

This is the business of politics. Politics is the allocation of values, goods, and services; it is the making of decisions concerning "who gets what, when, and how."[1] The political contest involves choosing between different demands and deciding what can be delivered in what situations. If someone were to ask a politician to define utopia, the reply might well be, "A situation where all the demands of all citizens are met all of the time." Perhaps an even more perfect utopia (if that is possible) would be a situation in which there were no new demands.

Unfortunately for the politician, he or she does not operate in an imaginary or visionary world but in the real world. This means that political leaders must make choices. They must choose between alternatives.

---

[1] Harold Laswell, *Politics: Who Gets What, When, and How* (New York: World Publishing, 1958).

If workers demand more, that may mean that others must settle for less. If one group's demands are met, another group's may have to be sacrificed.

Responding to demands is made doubly difficult because demands do not remain constant. People's expectations change. In developing nations, such as Nigeria and Tanzania, people expect that their economic well-being will improve. They expect, and demand, that their children have access to education, that they have steady jobs, and that health care be available. Other demands include the right to participate in the decision-making process and the right to voice opinions.

Demands made in developed nations are similar, although the most important issues may differ. In post-World War II Great Britain, for example, Britons demanded increased social services. The introduction of a national health service to provide care for all patients was one response to these demands. Minority groups in Britain, many from former colonies in Asia and Africa, are now demanding the right to full participation in the political system. These more recent demands regarding minority rights must be acted on as well.

Utopia then will never exist. The resources of the nation are limited and expectations can never be fully realized. When one demand is met, others arise. To understand the politics of other nations requires studying the conflicting demands and interests of individuals and groups within the society. These interests and demands become *cleavages* when they are the most important distinguishing characteristics between individuals. In some nations cleavages may be drawn along religious, ethnic, linguistic, or regional lines. In other nations class divisions—the rich, the middle, and the poor—may be the most significant. Great Britain, one of the most homogeneous nations in terms of race, religion, and language, has a sharp class cleavage between the upper and the lower classes. The Soviet Union, Nigeria, and Tanzania are nations faced with ethnic and linguistic cleavages. In Nigeria well over 250 different language groups coexist within the national boundaries, while in the Soviet Union there are 15 republics based on ethnic/linguistic criteria. France is characterized by rural/urban splits, regional differences, and religious divisions between the clerical and anti-clerical. West Germany has a regional cleavage (the north and the south), class divisions, and divisions between Catholic and Protestant.

Depending on the situation, cleavages may be politically important or unimportant. In Tanzania, for example, ethnic or tribal differences are not as important as they are in Nigeria. The question of the relationship between church and state in England was resolved in the sixteenth century during the rule of Henry VIII, but differences between Catholic and Protestant are very important in one part of the United Kingdom, Northern Ireland. There are some indications that class distinctions in France are becoming more important while traditionally important distinctions such as the one between rural and urban France are becoming less so.

Whatever the type of cleavage, conflicting interests and demands require political leaders to make decisions concerning the allocation and the distribution of goods, services, and values. To make and enforce decisions, leaders need *power*—the power to influence others and to have the capability of enforcing that influence if need be. Political powerholders are the men and women making decisions; the people and groups with which they constantly deal are the political participants. When participants view the exercise of power as legitimate or just, it becomes *political authority*. An individual, a group, or an institution has *legitimate authority* when the population of that community accepts the right of an individual, group, or institution to make decisions concerning their fate and the allocation of values. Only those over whom the power is being exercised can grant legitimacy.

For the political leader, or the would-be leader, power is needed to make and enforce decisions. Many potential resources are available and can be used for political purposes. One of the most common resources is physical coercion. Those individuals or groups in society that control the weapons of force can use them to make decisions, and to make sure that once the decisions are made they are carried out. In Nigeria in 1966 and in Chile in 1973 soldiers in the army used force to end civilian governments. All political systems, if they are to continue to make decisions, possess at least the potential threat of coercion. Where there is a general acceptance by the citizenry of the decision-makers' right to make decisions, coercion remains only a potential weapon; during periods of crisis or where there is a general nonacceptance of the decision-makers' right to make decisions, coercion may be used.

The rather tired maxim "knowledge is power" suggests a second resource of political power. The civil servant, the bureaucrat, the administrator, and the expert all have potential political power. They may have power because they have knowledge that few others possess. Specialized knowledge of nuclear physics, education, foreign affairs, or agriculture gives some potential political power in specific areas. Others may have power because of their ability to control and manipulate the administrative apparatus of the state. How many times, in how many different societies, have people complained that it is not the elected officials who make decisions, but faceless bureaucrats? The relationship between the "expert" and the political leader often leads to conflict, a conflict between those who possess knowledge and those who seek to control its application.

Economic power may be transformed into political power. Those individuals or groups who control the distribution or the allocation of economic resources may seek, if they so choose, to transform their economic wealth into political wealth—the power to make decisions. Economic power is important because it is convertible· to other resources of power. It may be used to buy individuals, institutions, knowledge, or access to influence. Wealth may be used to protect the wealthy, to ensure the more equal distribution of economic resources, or to control and influence the political leaders and decision-makers.

A specific individual can possess political power much greater than that conferred by office. A very few unique men and women may exercise control through the force of their personalities. *Charisma* is the term used to characterize political leaders who derive their power from the force of their personality. The leader becomes a living political symbol. Several examples are discussed in later chapters. General Charles de Gaulle in 1958 created the Fifth French Republic, a political system that represented General De Gaulle's political beliefs and which, for over ten years, was dominated by his presence. Likewise, the modern political history of Egypt has been shaped and influenced by the personal power of Gamal Abdul Nasser. In the Soviet Union, the symbol of Lenin continues to provide support and legitimacy for the system created after the 1917 revolution.

Finally, political power may be derived from a higher authority. People may be willing to accept decisions made by others because they feel that the powerholders possess a special authority. Some religious leaders exercise power in part because their followers think that they are the best equipped and qualified to provide for and interpret spiritual needs. Monarchs often ruled because of "the divine right of kings." In more secular and modern cases, power may rest with those who have won election to specific offices. In this case the vote, as sanctioned by the higher authority of a constitution, becomes the mandate to make decisions. In still other cases, individuals or in some cases political parties (such as the Communist party of the Soviet Union) have political power because they have developed and control the ideology that sets the goals of the nation.

In the following chapters the various resources of power available to and used by people and groups are discussed. Power is a complex concept, and its discussion raises several questions. Why, for example, is power centralized in one person or institution in some systems, while in others it is distributed among several different individuals and institutions? Why are some leaders more effective in exercising power than others? What causes changes in who has power and who does not? Studying power requires not only the analysis of resources of power, but also of how resources are transformed into political power, how power is used to make and enforce decisions, and how political power can change hands.

There are still other questions raised concerning power and its use. What, for example, causes the military in some nations to transform its *potential* coercive power to *active* power by intervening in the political arena? How can an individual with personal or charismatic power transform that power into other resources of political power? Under what circumstances can a charismatic leader lose his personal power? These questions, and others, illustrate the complexity of the concept of political power.

Thus far we have concentrated on those who possess and exercise political power. To understand power and politics completely, however, requires studying those over whom power is being exercised. We need to know not only how these participants behave politically, but also how they think they ought to behave, what they view as their primary political role, and under what circumstances that role changes.

Although we may not think about them often, we all have political values—things we think are politically important. These values and beliefs differ from group to group in the society and from nation to nation. Civil servants, for example, value expertise over politics; soldiers in some societies are taught to value an apolitical role, while in others they think they should actively participate; legislators tend to believe that conflict should be resolved through debate rather than violence.

There are also differences between nations. Soviet citizens have different views of politics than do British and French citizens. A West German and a Nigerian might find that they do not think at all alike when it comes to politics. Differences between nations are the result, in part, of different historical and cultural experiences. France and the Soviet Union both underwent violent revolutions. Although the impact in each case was different, the revolutionary experience colors the way citizens in each nation think about politics. The experience of colonial rule changed the way Nigerians, Egyptians, and Tanzanians look at politics.

What is important to understand is that there are certain values, attitudes, and behaviors associated with nations. The process by which societal members learn their political values and what political behavior is expected is referred to as *political socialization*. Socialization includes both the values and the way they are learned. Friends, family, schools, and the media are examples of socialization agents. From a very early age future "citizens" begin to learn about politics, what is good and bad, what should be done, and what should not be done. Although the values and the specifics of the process differ from nation to nation, all peoples seek to ensure that the traditions and beliefs of the nation are passed from generation to generation.

To summarize, politics involves the allocation of goods, services, and values. Within the nation people with similar interests often join together in interest groups or political parties to make demands. These demands of various groups are sometimes conflicting. When there are sharp or severe divisions within a nation, these are referred to as "cleavages." The political leaders are responsible for making decisions concerning the allocation of goods, services, and values, and for managing conflict among the groups and interests in the nation. To make and enforce these decisions, the leaders need power. Political power is derived from many different sources and can be used in different ways. Leaders and participants can be studied by analyzing their political behavior (how they act) and their political values (what they believe).

The Political System

Until now we have examined only part of the complex game of politics. Our concern has been with demands and interests, cleavages and conflicts, decisions and power, behavior and attitudes. To more fully compare nations, we also must compare each nation's *political system*. The institutions and structures of government in which the political decisions are made comprise the political system. In some nations these institutions are easily identifiable, highly regularized and stable, and exhibit well-defined patterns of interaction. In the United States we normally speak of legislative institutions that formulate policy and make decisions, executive institutions that administer and enforce policy, and judicial institutions that adjudicate conflicts between alternatives—three separate sets of institutions, each with specific functions. In Great Britain where "Parliament is supreme," the legislative institution is also ultimately responsible for the administration and execution of policy. In the Soviet Union the relationship between the Communist party and the administrative government is critical. In each case it is possible to distinguish specific institutions and structures characterized by ongoing, regularized patterns of interaction and behavior.

In other nations the institutions may be less easily identifiable, more fluid, and less regularized. They are constantly changing and evolving. This may be the case in nations undergoing severe crises or strain, or in nations where there is little general agreement on what institutions should be established. The Fourth French Republic, which collapsed under the weight of the Indochina and Algerian colonial wars in the 1950s, and the interwar Weimar German government, which led to the rise of Adolf Hitler and the National Socialists, were both political systems that had performance problems. The legitimacy of each regime sharply decreased as governmental performance faltered. People began to look for new answers and new structures and institutions that could meet their demands and protect their interests. The coup against the Chilean government of Salvadore Allende in 1973, the 1967 civil war in Nigeria, and the revolution that destroyed the tsarist government in Russia in 1917 are examples of crises of performance that faced three nations in our study.

The political system is the arena in which leaders and participants act. The roles political actors play are determined by their position in the network, by their patterns of interactions with others, and by the tasks and functions assigned each role—citizen, politician, bureaucrat, judge, soldier, legislator, executive.

Four different types of political institutions are of central concern. The first, and most readily recognizable, are those institutions and structures designed for making policy. How is the policy made? What types of policies and decisions are taken? Who are the political actors making the political decisions and policies within the institutions? In our study executive/presidential structures, parliaments, and military regimes are the most common policy-making institutions.

Second, there are institutions responsible for enforcing political decisions. If politics involves the making of decisions, the choosing between alternatives, and the allocating of resources, it also involves the ability to enforce and administer those decisions once made. The bureaucracy, and in some cases, the military, the police, and certain political parties normally have the responsibility for implementing policy. The resources available to these institutions vary. At one extreme, enforcement can be assured by force or coercion; at the other extreme, people may voluntarily comply with the decisions.

Third, there are institutions that provide symbolic support for the political system and the nation. These institutions are important because they help to give leaders legitimacy and authority. They also provide the pomp and circumstance of the nation, and ensure representation, participation, and accountability. The British monarch Queen Elizabeth II, for example, has little real political power but does symbolize British heritage and political tradition. As the head of state she also performs important ceremonial functions like welcoming visiting dignitaries.

Finally, there are institutions responsible for managing the conflicts that occur in society. In many systems the judiciary has primary responsibility for resolving conflict between disputants, while in others the same responsibility may fall to the military, the police, or political parties. Conflicts arise over the allocation and distribution of goods and services and over political values and behavior. The performance of these conflict-resolving institutions is assessed in part by how independent they are from outside influence and the scope of conflicts with which they deal. Some judiciaries, for example, are free from outside political pressure, while others are subject to much interference from politicians. Judiciaries also vary in the number and types of issues they act upon; some hear all types of cases from the political to the nonpolitical, while others may not be charged with deciding purely political issues.

Chapters 7 through 10 describe the institutions and structures that make policy, enforce policy, provide symbolic support to the system, and resolve conflicts in society. The political system is the whole of these parts, and the institutional arrangements found in each of the eight nations vary widely. Why?

Political Culture and Tradition

If these are functions that must be performed by all political systems, it should be easy to determine how they could be accomplished most efficiently. The best-performing system could then provide a universal model. Were it that simple, many political scientists and commentators would quickly find themselves looking for new jobs.

The reason for radically different political systems is that nations have radically different goals. In some systems people value and demand representation and political responsiveness; in others they value the equal distribution of resources, while in still others they desire economic growth. Both the goals and values determine the type of political system. When political goals change, the system must change and respond to the new goals. In short, it adapts to the new environment.

The political tradition, history, and culture of a country also influence its political system. *Political culture* is the sum of the shared history, shared values, and shared experiences of a community. The history of the nation provides the core of the political culture. Specific experiences, images, and symbols distinguish one nation from another. A nation's political culture is the cement that holds the nation together; it separates the "we" from the "they," "them" from "us." The political culture (or cultures) of the nation also establish the setting in which the political drama is played.

Chapters 2 and 3 discuss the political cultures and traditions of the eight nations in our study. The intent is to show how political cultures and traditions influence present-day politics. In Nigeria, Tanzania, and Egypt, for example, the nationalist struggle against Great Britain symbolized the movement toward national independence. The 1917 Soviet revolution, which marked the beginning of the new era in the U.S.S.R., provided legitimacy for actions taken by Soviet leaders. In Great Britain the gradual transformation of the absolutist monarchy to a representative parliamentary government influenced political activity and the roles of the various participants. Every nation's history influences the present-day practice of politics.

Often within a nation groups are characterized by different political cultures and traditions. These cultural cleavages may be politically significant or insignificant; they may create conflict or provide a basis for unity. In cases where there is severe conflict between groups there may in fact be no basis for the continuation of a unified state. Nigeria from 1967 to 1970 faced the prospect of the dissolution of the nation, and a civil war was fought to prevent the Eastern Region from seceding and forming a new, independent nation. We can classify nations according to the types of cultural cleavages found in the nation and the importance of these cleavages for the political system. Some nations, such as Great Britain, are relatively homogeneous in terms of religion, race, and language, while others, such as Nigeria and Tanzania, are highly diverse and heterogeneous. Different languages, religions, and tribal groups coexist, often uneasily, within the national boundaries.

Our study of the politics of eight nations concentrates on three major concerns: (1) the political culture and traditions of each nation; (2) the behavior and values of leaders and participants in the political arena; and (3) the nation's political institutions and structures. In each area we are concerned with the similarities and differences among the eight nations. Ultimately, most political systems are evaluated on how well they perform and how well they adapt to new situations and environments. To make these judgments and to practice the "art of comparison" requires studying all three areas, and how they interact with each other. Before describing these areas in detail, however, it is necessary to look at the various ways nations can be compared.

Comparing Political Systems: Established Perspectives

The earliest attempts at comparison involved classifying types of governments. Early students of comparative politics, notably Aristotle, struggled with a basic set of comparative questions.

What do political systems have in common regardless of external trappings?

What are the essential differences between political forms and political practices?

What difference does it make that politics is organized differently from place to place?

Classifiers of political systems were motivated in great part by a desire to find a good or perfect form of government—an ambition certainly doomed to failure. Most eventually settled for generalization about what seemed to work given peculiar local conditions.

Thus, Aristotle is considered the first practitioner of the systematic study of politics from a comparative perspective. His study of 158 constitutions of the Greek city-states was conducted very much in the spirit of modern comparative research. The "arrangement of offices" of these constitutions in his scheme varied according to the distribution of *power* and *authority* in a society. Political arrangements were said to be monarchical, oligarchical, or democratic according to the extent of participation in political decisions. The "best" form depended upon the economies and societies of each state. In particular, Aristotle emphasized the pattern of political cleavages in a given system. In states where the rich and poor were sharply divided, instability would result, whatever the constitution. Aristotle felt that a broadly based oligarchy performed better if a substantial middle class was present. The mass of the people would have the wisdom to defer to their betters while retaining a secondary role in the process of government with this social and political arrangement.

Later political theorists used similar classifications. These classifications differed according to what were considered to be "important" political differences—that is, those that were thought to make a difference in how political systems perform. Many classifications, like Aristotle's, distinguish among political arrangements according to how authority is distributed. This is the most common basis for classifying political systems. In this way democratic, authoritarian, and totalitarian forms are distinguished. Others classify political systems according to the relationship between government and the economy. The capitalist, socialist, and communist distinctions are made in this way. Other important classifications are based on the nature of a society's political values—traditional or modern—and strength and complexity of political institutions—developed or developing.

Each method of classification results in the artificial creation of perfect or pure political forms. Thus, Aristotle defined democracy, oligarchy, and monarchy as, respectively, rule by all, rule of the few, and one-person rule. He categorized real governments according to how closely they approached the defining features of the governmental types. Few real-world political arrangements perfectly matched these definitions. The classifications and distinctions commonly used in comparing political systems are all subject to this discrepancy between the carefully defined pure form and the more complex real-life approximations. From this perspective, the art of comparison involves generalizations that are more or less useful in understanding complex forms of politics.

How Authority Is Distributed:
Democracy, Authoritarianism, and Totalitarianism

DEMOCRACY

Few governmental arrangements perfectly match the definitions advanced by scholars and thinkers. The "idea of democracy" has changed over the centuries. In Aristotle's definition, democracy meant *direct democracy* in which all citizens actually participated in debate and decision-making on all issues of importance. The modern meaning is modified to account for the size and complexity of the modern nation-states. Modern democracy is based on several related principles: (1) the equality of citizens, (2) a defined area of liberty retained by all citizens, and (3) representation based on elections and majority rule. Most political scientists would accept this definition of democracy, but it is not without controversy among students and practitioners of politics. Certainly, Communist political actors in democratic republics and people's republics would want to be included in democratic categories, whatever the opinions of American scholars.

Some standard of equality is required in a democratic polity. Democracy at least implies that governments will encourage economic and social equality as well as "equality of opportunity." Most governments that are considered democratic, however, tolerate a good bit of disparity on these standards of equality, and some seem to completely ignore them. Political equality and equality before the law seem closer to defining attributes.

Political equality can also mean equality of opportunity. This aspect of equality demands that all citizens should have the same formal opportunities to participate in elections and public deliberations as well as have the same opportunity to hold public office. This means that the rules of the political game should not systematically favor one group or type of individual over another.

Equality of opportunity is violated when race, sex, religion, wealth, or similar criteria are used to determine who can play a role in politics and who is excluded. In the United States, a country with a long history of democratic politics, individuals have been denied the vote because of their race, sex, or the amount of property they owned. For these reasons less than 5 percent of the adult population elected America's first presidents. Nations in our study are struggling with this issue today. Catholics in Northern Ireland, Jews and nationality groups in the Soviet Union, leftists in post-1973 Chile are all denied the political opportunities granted their fellow countrymen.

The democratic value of *liberty* refers to freedom from governmental actions. Basic liberties are guaranteed in most democratic systems and are referred to as the *rights* of citizens. In many democratic systems traditional and customary rights are formalized by their inclusion in a constitutional document. The English and German constitutions provide such guarantees. Lists of rights invoke higher law in terms of either natural or God-given rights. Thus, the rights of British citizens are protected by the British Common Law as articulated in a 300-year-old document, while the rights of Germans are included in a written constitutional document that is above ordinary law.

Liberty as a political value often contradicts other political values. Liberty, for example, implies an individual's freedom to set himself above his fellow citizens by standards of merit or wealth, and makes real equality a difficult commodity to obtain in many democratic systems. Liberty also conflicts often with the values supporting majority rule. The expertise or resources of the few may outweigh the preferences of the many when decisions are made.

Since modern democracies are large and complex, the direct democracy of the ancient Greek city-states is out of the question. Ordinary decisions involving public policy must be made by representative bodies. In the decision of the electorate regarding who shall be their representatives and in the deliberations of the representatives themselves a decision-rule is required. There must be a clear and unambiguous determination of exactly who are the winners and who are the losers. Majority rule is the accepted democratic standard for both elections and other forms of democratic decision-making, although it is often only approximated by more easily attainable rules based on plurality and proportionality.

"Rule by the majority" flows from democratic values such as equality and is modified by other values such as liberty. Majority rule assumes equality in the sense of "one man, one vote." If all are equal, each vote should have the same weight, and outcomes should be determined by the simple computation of individual preferences. The notion of liberty, however, modifies the application of majority rule. Specifically, the rights of the minority are protected in most democratic systems. Strict majority rule may result in arbitrary action against minority groups—defined in terms of race, ethnicity, region, wealth, or other standards.

Rule by the majority is an unattainable goal for many societies. This democratic value assumes a consensus that does not characterize many societies. The social divisions present in France, for example, have made modifications of strict majority rule necessary in the election of parliamentary representatives. The cleavages that characterize Nigerian social and political life have led to the suspension of the democratic forms that require majority rule. In some societies, then, there simply is no majority sharing common interests and beliefs. Examples of this sort suggest one reason for the emphasis on political cleavages—they can help explain the success or failure of democratic institutions as defined above.

Democracy, then, requires that institutions promote political equality, provide an area of individual freedom or liberty, and supply the mechanisms by which majority preferences and demands are acted on. The ability to develop and maintain these kinds of institutions is very sensitive to political cleavages. Societies with few important cleavages are characterized by a wide area of agreement on political values and beliefs. *Political consensus* prevails in such systems and democratic principles are more easily acted on. In divided societies made up of dissatisfied minorities each with unsatisfied demands, government may function only by the use of *coercion* against dissident groups. Political systems lacking political consensus must rely on the use of coercion. Political authority is concentrated in the hands of a small group of political actors who at least agree on the necessity of wielding power based on coercion.

AUTHORITARIANISM AND TOTALITARIANISM

Authoritarianism implies a narrow distribution of authority. Authority, as defined earlier, is power legitimized or justified by a political belief. Monarchies in their traditional form are the best examples of authoritarian regimes. Monarchical authority was based on birth, and often reinforced by religious beliefs. Authority was exercised by the monarch and the advisers selected for particular tasks. Most traditional monarchs had unlimited authority conferred on them, and they exercised that authority through advisers and the governmental apparatus. That authority was unchecked by other political bodies, higher law, or the preferences and demands of subjects.

The monarch, unencumbered by a constitution, had full control over the nation's instruments of coercion, the police and the army. These elements enforced the monarch's will against opposition, which by definition was illegitimate. Monarchs relied on the police and the army when particular policies and actions proved unpopular. For example, from time to time the Russian tsars decided to promote the Russian language, customs, and traditions on the many nationality groups under their jurisdiction. If opposition developed among these groups, coercion was relied upon to ensure compliance.

The monarchs' power rested on two impressive power resources—control of the instruments of coercion and the normative resources associated with their positions. The normative resources stemmed from monarchs' special positions as national symbols. This usually ensured a fairly widespread willingness to respond to their commands. Where willingness was not forthcoming, coercion was applied. The tsars, for example, generated a considerable willingness on the part of their subjects to comply with royal commands because of their special role as defenders and symbols of the national religion and as a living embodiment of Russian history. Where this power resource failed, they relied on the secret police.

In an era of premodern technology, however, the power was limited in its application. Poor communications made it difficult to make a monarch's wishes known throughout society and allowed officials outside the capital some leeway in carrying out royal commands. Poor transportation limited the monarch's ability to use his instruments of coercion against parochial resistance. Premodern techniques of information-gathering limited one possible source of power—the monarch often did not have sufficient information to understand the opposition and to make plans to overcome it.

These considerations of scope of power and available technology provide the distinction between authoritarian and totalitarian regimes. Totalitarian political systems can be considered authoritarian systems that employ modern technology to extend the scope of governmental power and influence to a much greater portion of society. Fascist and Communist totalitarian regimes, although differing in the nature of the political beliefs supporting them, share a similar concentration of political authority and make use of similar technological innovations in extending the power of government over every important social and economic group. Fascist concentration of authority is legitimized by the leadership principle—the necessity for a single, inspired leader, while Communist authoritarianism is based on the idea of the indispensable revolutionary vanguard who understand the laws of history.

Totalitarian control over society depends upon modern technology—communications, transportation, information-handling, and political organization. The last-named element has proven to be the most important modern innovation of totalitarian regimes. Totalitarian systems rely on a highly disciplined, pyramidal political party to control other groups and organizations. Adolf Hitler was able to use his National Socialist party (Nazi party) to make his power felt in every German social and economic unit. Hitler's first acts involved what he called *Gleichshaltung,* or coordination of all groups. Labor unions, business associations, and the news media were put under party supervision. In addition, special groups were created under direct party control, such as the youth branch of the party—the Hitler *Jugend.*

Totalitarian and authoritarian systems differ from democratic systems on several dimensions. First of all, democratic systems are characterized by much wider participation in decision-making, and therefore political power and authority are less concentrated. Totalitarian systems do not permit the existence of autonomous political groups. These groups are "coordinated" and controlled by the party. Totalitarian regimes also do not allow an organized political opposition capable of criticizing the government and competing for the control of the government. A final distinction involves the area of freedom or liberty that is reserved for individual and group action. Democratic systems tend to identify and protect substantial areas where individuals and groups are free of governmental interference, while totalitarian systems are defined by the extent of their power over individual and group activities and functions. This last distinction is related to another basis of classification—one based on governmental intervention in the nation's economic life.

The Economic Role of the Government: Capitalism, Socialism, and Communism

Political systems may also be classified by the nature of their economic organization—in particular the role of government in the control or regulation of the economy. It is helpful to ask the following questions:

How extensive is governmental regulation of economic practices?

How great a share does government have in basic economic decisions?

How much does government regulate day-to-day management of the economy?

By this standard, capitalism involves the minimal level of governmental control while Communist economies are characterized by a very high degree of state control. This way of classifying political systems should be viewed apart from questions of democratic principles. Advocates of the different forms of economic organization each justify their belief on the basis of democratic principles. Advocates of capitalism justify their preferred system primarily in terms of political liberty and individualism. Advocates of socialism and communism point to economic equality as a major purpose of their way of economic organization.

CAPITALISM

Like most political forms, capitalism is often defined by an ideal form— as "pure" capitalism. Early nineteenth-century Great Britain, for example, approached the pure model. Capitalism can be defined as a system characterized by (1) private ownership of property, (2) unlimited accumulation of property, and (3) absence of governmental interference in the economy —the free market system.

This definition approximates the earliest capitalist system but must be modified to meet modern conditions. With modern technology, many capitalist enterprises have become large and complex and require massive capital investment to operate. Most people see a need to regulate the economic power of such modern economic giants. As a result, capitalist governments intervene extensively in the economies of their countries; however, they do so in a way intended to strengthen the essential features of capitalism. For example, extreme accumulation of property by a very few individuals would greatly restrict the realm of private property and be self-defeating to the purposes of a capitalist system—widespread property-holding and individual liberty. Only the government can prevent extreme accumulations of wealth and property, and most capitalists see the necessity for governmental intervention for this purpose. Governmental regulation is seen as essential for preserving competition as a mechanism of the free market and protecting a broad base of capitalist ownership.

SOCIALISM

There are many varieties of socialism. By the broadest definition socialism would include everything from tiny communal sects to modern socialist nation-states such as Sweden. But socialism is best defined by its most widespread modern form labeled "democratic socialism." Democratic socialism exists as a political-economic type in much of Western Europe. Many new nations of Asia and Africa are considered democratic-socialist systems as well. The model most often mentioned, however, is based on the Western European experience. Its essential features include a large sector of publicly held property that is supervised and managed by a democratically elected government. Major industries such as the coal and steel industries, the transportation industry, and major utilities are managed in this way. Democratic socialism also implies strict measures to promote equality in income and avoid the accumulation of wealth in a few hands. Finally, extensive welfare services in the realm of health care and social security are provided in democratic-socialist systems.

Britain is perhaps the best example of a democratic-socialist system.

The government owns and operates the coal, iron, and steel industries, and substantial parts of the transportation and communications industries. The government names the managing board members of these industries and has a final say on industry policy. The British have a sharply graduated income tax and steep inheritance taxes to promote equality of income. Finally, they provide a great variety of social services, most notably, free medical treatment in the nationwide system of public hospitals and clinics.

The active role of political authorities and institutions in democratic-socialist systems is based on well-defined sets of political goals and values. Socialists value substantial economic and social equality. They expand the definition of political equality to include the reduction of individual differences in class, income, and living standards. The management of the public sector and the regulation of the private sector promotes a balanced concern for both individual and societal interests. Democratic socialists can be considered individualists in the sense that concern is with individual equality and individual quality of life. This concern includes all individuals, not only the economic sector as is the case in the pure capitalist model.

COMMUNISM

Communist economic systems differ from those previously discussed by their rejection of individualism and by the extent of governmental control of the economy. The philosophy of Karl Marx was based on the relationship between economic forces and politics. Politics, for Marx, was a part of a nation's "superstructure," which was absolutely determined by the economic structure. For Marxists then, political change depends on forceful economic change. By this view, the economy must be thoroughly controlled and directed by political leadership that understands the laws of history revealed in Marx's writings. This is the only way to bring about change in political values and institutions.

All Communist nations are in a transitional stage of communism which Marx called the period of the "dictatorship of the proletariat." Communist leaders in this stage strive to promote the disappearance of classes, increase equality and productivity, and achieve a distribution of income based on work performed. These goals are brought about by state management of the economy. Nothing can be left to chance if the final goal is to be reached—a society that no longer requires a state. The state's economic planning is designed to ensure that there will be no need in the future for powerful state institutions, described by Marx as "the withering away of the state."

Communist economic systems are organized by extensive and elaborate economic plans. The Soviet Five Year Plan serves as a model for most newer national varieties of communism. Planners analyze resources, labor supply, and society's needs in order to decide what should be produced. Each productive sector of the economy—each agricultural, manufacturing, and industrial unit—is told what to produce and how much. The distribution of products is also controlled. Goods are directed to regions and localities on the basis of the planners' estimate of need and demand. The distribution of income is controlled as well, and in the current transition period it is used to stimulate production rather than to promote industrial economic equality. These features of Communist economies clearly suggest why these systems are called "command economies." Raw materials, finished goods, and economic incentives move at the command of the state machinery.

The command economy, like pure capitalism, and the Western democratic-socialist model, represents a comparative scholar's ideal or perfect form from which he/she measures real-world cases. Individual incentives and some free-market activity characterize those political systems that we label Communist, just as government regulation occurs in those systems we categorize as capitalist. Similarly, democratic-socialist regimes vary a good deal on the basis of the specific mix between the public and the private sectors. Nevertheless, the extent of governmental control of the economy is an important characteristic of political systems, and much can be gained by placing political systems in categories according to this criterion.

Political Values: Traditional and Modern Political Systems

Most of the distinctions among nations we have introduced thus far are related to aspects of "modern" political systems. For example, all of the economic differences discussed apply to political attitudes and values that are "modern." The concepts and distinctions associated with these classifications are not helpful in understanding those political systems that are based on "traditional" views of political and social life.

In traditional systems, authority is based on ascriptive standards—on considerations of birth, lineage, age, or similar attribute. Traditional politics tend to be highly stratified and characterized by stable, fixed patterns of interaction. An individual's relationship to other individuals and to the state is defined by characteristics over which he or she has no control—particularly familial relationships. Political values and attitudes tend to be stable and unchanging. These last features suggest that political and social change or innovation are difficult in traditional systems.

A modern system is distinguished by its focus on the value of achievement. Individuals are defined by their achievement in the social, economic, or political realms. The stratification pattern with its emphasis on individual merit is fluid and flexible; an individual's mobility is dependent on talent and initiative. Political attitudes, values, and beliefs assume that human control of the environment is possible. All modern systems—from democratic to totalitarian—reflect the belief, perhaps illusory, that progress, change, and positive action are meaningful.

Most political systems include both traditional and modern elements producing conflict and tension. For example, French politics often reflects a struggle between a modern urban society and a traditional rural society. The rural France of small family shops and farms resists changes emanating from Paris—governmental regulations that punish small inefficient enterprises. Similar tensions are present in African countries where groups with a modern perspective meet strong resistance from those in the traditional sector.

The traditional/modern distinction relates most directly to the ability and willingness of individuals to change and adapt. Performance, however, must be judged in the context of political circumstances and by the nature of political demands. If demands do not require drastic changes in the relationships among political actors or change in political values, traditional systems are just as likely to perform satisfactorily as their modern counterparts.

Developed and Developing Systems

Political development refers to the creation of strong political institutions. In order to "cope" with changing circumstances and increasing demands for governmental action, political systems must be organized so that they are able to make decisions, lay plans, and take decisive action. Institutions must be organized so that they can take advantage of specialized knowledge and expertise. Governmental institutions become able to concentrate authority and expertise on the problems of the day in the course of political development. Development also implies that institutions are able to organize and control mass participation in politics rather than be overwhelmed by popular movements and political unrest.

In concrete terms political development first of all means the creation of bureaucratic institutions and institutions charged with maintaining order, the police and the army. Bureaucracies are rationally organized structures designed for problem-solving. Bureaucracies are organized to promote clear lines of authority and specialization by task, features that are helpful in dealing with the complex problems associated with modern demands for governmental action. The police and the army are created to control the violence and disorder that might occur if problems are not solved and demands are not met.

Another important institution in developed systems is that which channels and organizes political participation. The most important institutions of this kind are political parties. Parties may organize political actors by offering alternative programs for governmental action and by presenting rival candidates pledged to their respective programs in democratic elections. This is one important way to deal with popular demands, which we will observe in politically developed Britain, France, and Germany. Another type of party and another means of organizing participation is demonstrated by the Communist party of the Soviet Union. This highly developed institution publicizes and promotes governmental policy in order to get active public support for programs such as land reclamation or industrial development. In this case participants are organized to carry out plans that they had no voice in shaping.

The eight nation-states to be studied were selected first of all to provide a balance between developed and developing political systems. In addition, the eight nations represent the different "types" discussed above. Some class themselves as Communist, some as socialist, some as capitalist. Authoritarian, totalitarian, and democratic nations are included as well. A wide range of political solutions to universal problems is represented in this small group of nation-states.

Overview of the Eight Nation-States

All nations face similar problems involving change and performance, but for some, specific problems may be more severe or pressing than in others. Some nations, for example, face severe problems because of ethnic cleavages, while others face severe problems of class cleavage. Some nations must confront problems of economic growth, while others face problems of economic distribution. In this section the eight nations are briefly introduced, and special attention is given to the problems each faces.

▪ THE UNITED KINGDOM ▪

The United Kingdom is usually chosen to represent a nation in which a homogeneous people are ruled by pragmatic leaders in highly adaptable tradition-based institutions. It is contrasted with developing nations marked by deep cleavages and new, relatively weak institutions. The United Kingdom is pictured as having a society that is easy to govern because societal divisions are not deep or marked. Political extremism is absent; most conflicts have been resolved, and emotional issues have been removed from the agenda of politics. Questions of religion, urban or rural divisions, and nationality issues were thought settled. Britain's parliamentary system has been the envy of the world, a system that blends majority power and responsibility with respect for the necessity of political opposition.

In many ways this romantic view of the British constitution and people still holds true, but it must be revised in several important ways. The parliamentary institution is a unique blend of tradition and pragmatic political power. Taken as a whole, the British public shares many basic political beliefs and values. However, the present-day United Kingdom is a nation facing serious problems. These problems are difficult challenges to the government's highly developed institutions. The crisis has taken two forms—one economic, the other cultural. Both aspects have implications for how Britons will be governed in the future.

The United Kingdom faces a persistent set of economic problems. There are many suspected causes for these economic ills. One involves the loss of empire and a reorientation of British trade from the Commonwealth to the European community. Another is that Britain is the world's oldest industrial power and therefore tends to have older machinery and methods than its competitors. Some observers suggest that Britain's postwar priorities emphasized welfare and social services at the expense of economic growth. The problem is complex, and no doubt all of these factors have an impact. Whatever the causes, the United Kingdom lags behind several European neighbors—most notably West Germany and France.

A second major problem is a nationality problem. The United Kingdom is a multinational political system. The major nationality groups are the English, the Welsh, the Scots, and the Irish. The British Crown gradually incorporated these nationality areas over centuries of conquest and political struggle. The Welsh were the first to be effectively brought under the British Crown, and they remain more closely tied to the English center of power than other groups. Scotland has been governed from Westminster for 270 years. Like the Welsh, the Scots have been an integral part of British society and politics for centuries. The bonds between these peoples are strong—both the Welsh and the Scots, for example, are still proud of their roles in Britain's former worldwide empire. Both, however, have become centers of demands for more regional autonomy. Ireland was always a source of nationality unrest, but that problem was for a long time mitigated by the independence granted to Catholic Ireland in 1922. Only in the last 10 years has the "loyal" North of Ireland become a center of national and religious conflict.

Currently, Scottish nationalism is a major issue in British politics. The Scottish Nationalist party, dedicated to Scottish independence, has scored impressive successes at the polls, forcing the major British parties to support a plan for increased autonomy for Scotland, including the creation of a Scottish parliament with limited powers. It is not yet clear whether this will satisfy the political demands of the Scots.

Both problems have rather important consequences for the way the United Kingdom is governed. The long-term economic difficulties raise the question of how well institutions and authorities can persist in the face of apparent failure of performance. People judge leaders and institutions in part on how well they deliver in the economic realm. If leaders consistently perform poorly relative to the leaders of similar neighboring systems, institutions may be blamed as well as leaders. The question becomes more interesting when the political institutions involved are the world's oldest democratic specimens—the British Crown and the Westminster Parliament.

The nationality question has a number of compelling features also. The strong drive for Scottish nationalism, which has taken both legal and extra-legal forms, is fascinating. National feelings, long dormant, are coming to life under the influence of changing circumstances. The discovery of oil in the North Sea in particular brought visions of economic independence. Whatever the practical considerations, feelings of a national separateness are important in the current dispute. It will be interesting to compare this sort of fundamental political cleavage in a developed country with similar cleavages in developing political systems.

■ THE FEDERAL REPUBLIC OF GERMANY ■

The Federal Republic of Germany has demonstrated a remarkable capacity for political change. Unlike the United Kingdom, the challenge in studying West Germany lies in understanding performance—the ability of Germans to function so well within a democratic framework. As Germans in the Federal Republic emerged from Allied occupation in 1949, few observers were optimistic about the prospects of the new regime. Germany's last brief experiment with democracy had been a disaster. In the democratic

Chancellor Helmut Schmidt addressing the West German Parliament (Bundestag) in 1976. Courtesy, Presse und Informationsamt der Bundesregierung.

regime of the 1920s the military and the bureaucrats held power, while democratic politicians bickered and evaded responsibility. The net result was the ascendancy of Adolf Hitler and his National Socialist regime.

The German political culture in the 1950s seemed no more congenial to democratic institutions than it had in the 1920s. Society was still divided on the basis of class, religion, and region. Antidemocratic views and beliefs were common, and there were few democratic leaders with experience in national politics. When the victorious powers of World War II forced an unfamiliar set of democratic institutions on a reluctant German populace, it was expected that there would be a return to instability and violent patterns of politics.

The transition to democratic forms, however, was aided by a remarkable economic recovery following the founding of the new republic. With considerable aid from their World War II enemies the Germans of the Federal Republic performed an "economic miracle." The rapid improvement in living standards no doubt bought time and tolerance for the leaders and institutions of the new regime.

The economic miracle paralleled a political miracle. The unfamiliar democratic institutions proved to be stable and efficient. Old political patterns changed remarkably. Radical political parties and leaders disappeared, and the moderate democratic parties prospered. The Federal Republic made a serious attempt to regain a respected international position. At a formal or legal level the government of the Federal Republic has attempted to come to terms with the German responsibility stemming from the criminal excesses of Hitler's era.

This kind of dramatic political change is almost unique to Germany. Rapid change, even if it appears successful, usually is followed by serious problems. For example, there is little doubt that Germans have very high expectations of governmental performance. In particular, they seem to expect that their living standards will continue to improve as they have in the last 25 years. Few German politicians believe that this is possible. Since failure in performance is relative to expectations of performance, politicians in West Germany are very concerned. If future German leaders cannot meet the persistent demand for economic growth, the attachment of West German citizens to democratic institutions and values will again be tested. This is not an insignificant problem if one remembers that the institutions are new and not yet viewed as fully legitimate by many Germans.

▪ FRANCE ▪

France presents an interesting case because it represents a developed political system that has felt the profound influence of a single exceptional leader. Even after his death, General De Gaulle remains a very real presence in French politics. He left a constitution, a political philosophy, and a political movement as his legacy. Each has greatly affected the pattern of French politics in a fundamental and perhaps permanent way. In the course of the discussion on France we will be concerned with both the durability of "Gaullism" and its long-range impact on French politics.

Charles De Gaulle was a remarkable figure who possessed charisma if one follows the general's own definition of "communicated self-confidence." A true leader, De Gaulle maintained, must possess a great vision that can be communicated to the people and that will move them to action. De Gaulle's confidence was apparent when he promoted himself as the leader of Free France during World War II—without a political or military base of power. De Gaulle used his postwar prominence to promote his vision. He wanted to reform the French political order so that a strong leader could lead the French back to their historic role as the leading civilized nation of the Western World.

When the French rejected De Gaulle's constitutional vision in 1946, he retired to his estate but remained a rallying point for those who were frustrated with France's postwar position. French defeat in the guerrilla wars of Indochina and Algeria and the resultant loss of the French colonial empire thrust De Gaulle forward as the only alternative to anarchy and total collapse of the civil order. In 1958 De Gaulle returned to restructure French institutions to fit his requirements. For many, the heroic return signified the political salvation of France; De Gaulle became a living symbol of French "grandeur."

Of course, not all political actors or participants welcomed De Gaulle's return or De Gaulle's constitution with its powerful presidency tailored to the needs of its first incumbent. Politically, the French are divided by religion, class, and by urban/rural distinctions. The parties and politicians that represented distinct cultural groups refused to bury their differences in the face of the General's attempts to bridge the divisions.

France is interesting then on a second count. The 1958 constitution was largely designed to lend strong leadership and political direction to a society fragmented by deep political cleavages. As such, France provides an experiment in constitutional engineering. Can institutions be designed to reduce the political importance of societal divisions? Can essentially democratic institutions maintain political order and stability in a society characterized by intense group conflict, mistrust, and hostility? De Gaulle's constitution may be a lasting legacy that changes the nature of French politics, it may fail like the thirteen previous political regimes of France, or it may evolve over time into a different form.

A final reason for including the study of France is that it affords the opportunity to analyze another political trend—the role of European Communist parties in the democratic regimes of Western Europe. The French Communist party has had great success in the last 10 years. The party came close to electing a left-wing presidential candidate in 1974 and has increased the size of the leftist forces in the French Parliament. The revival of the French Communist party reflects the trend toward more independence by Communist parties of both Eastern and Western Europe and the desire of these parties to assert their independence from Soviet influence.

The presence of a powerful Communist party in a democratic political system may represent a problem or a solution depending on the perspective of the observer. Most observers can agree that the viability of the Communist party challenge increases the stakes of French politics and the intensity of political conflict.

▪ THE SOVIET UNION ▪

The Soviet Union represents a political system that is the result of almost 60 years of state-directed change. Society, economy, and political culture reflect the conscious policies of political actors to an extent unparalleled in any other system. The Soviet case presents an opportunity to study forced or planned change. Can the political attitudes, values and beliefs of a citizenry be shaped within several generations by state plan? Does near total control by state and party permit superior problem-solving, and at what cost? What blend of coercion and consensus is implied at each stage of political and social change?

The Soviet Union is also, by earlier definition, perhaps the most "developed" of all political systems. Both state and party are massive bureaucratic hierarchies designed to promote political control and efficiency. The political system is designed to encourage widespread political participation so that Soviet citizens participate by the millions in party, state, and allied organizations that channel and direct such political activity. Because the Soviet system is "highly developed" and based on modern scientific-rational principles, it has been chosen as a model for some new nations that feel they must force change.

A political system organized in a hierarchical fashion may become rigid with age—that is, it may not be able to adapt to external and internal changes beyond its control. In fact, such systems become "conservative" in the sense that institutions and actors become resistant to change. Newer Communist nations have made this charge with regard to the Soviet Union. A system geared to forcing change may not be able to change itself when circumstances require adaptive behavior. The Soviet case allows an investigation of a mature Communist system facing this problem.

The Soviet Union also represents a very "different" political system— the only totalitarian system in our study. In this sense it provides a great

Statue of Lenin in Moscow. Henri Cartier-Bresson, Magnum Photos, Inc.

challenge to our ability to compare and generalize across political systems. Just how different is the Soviet system? There is a political party in the Soviet Union, a bicameral popular assembly, a system of elections, and a judicial system. How are these similar to corresponding institutions in other political systems? Do they involve the same kinds of political activities? Are the participants similar to their counterparts in other nations? Do they have a similar impact on the larger political and social systems?

The Soviet Union shares many problems that face the other political systems in the study. Soviet leaders must provide necessary services and pay some attention to the living standards of Soviet citizens. Presumably, failure in this regard will have consequences for even totalitarian leaders. Leaders in the Soviet Union also must deal with political conflict. They need to determine which of society's groups get their way and which groups must give in on particular issues. Since leaders in all systems have alliances with important social and economic groups, leaders must resolve or manage conflict among themselves. Which leader's policies are

promoted? Which leader's ambitions are satisfied? Ultimately, this involves the question of how leaders are selected at each level of responsibility. The selection of Brezhnev's successor will represent the culmination
of a long-standing struggle among leaders and groups. How, for example,
is the struggle different from the politics of conflict and succession in other
systems?

▪ NIGERIA ▪

In the early 1960s, shortly after its independence, it was popular to refer
to Nigeria as the sleeping giant of Africa; it was characterized by its un-
tapped, enormous potential. With the largest population in Africa, it has
a large manpower pool, and large reserves of mineral and natural resources. Unlike many other African states, it is both economically and
politically viable in terms of its size and resources. Nigeria achieved its
independence through a nonviolent, complex constitutional process that
established a multi-party system based on the traditions given them by the
British colonial administration.

Nigeria's potential must be balanced against the problems Nigerians
face. Nigeria is one of the world's most diverse nations. The conflicts that
arose as a result of the sharp cleavages were not resolved during the decolonization process. Once the umbrella of colonial protection was
removed, conflict spilled over into the political arena. There were splits
between ethnic, linguistic, religious groups, and class groups. The political
system inherited by Nigeria's new civilian leaders existed from independence in 1960 to January 1966. In 1966 the military violently intervened
and ended the first period of civilian rule. Since then Nigeria has been
governed by a series of military regimes. The denouement of the crisis in
Nigeria came in May 1967. The Eastern Region attempted to secede from
the federal government and create a new nation, Biafra.

Nigeria is an interesting case because of its diversity and its wealth. At
the time of independence it met few of the criteria normally associated
with nation-states; it had no common language, no common political
traditions and culture, no set of mutually accepted national symbols
around which individuals and groups could rally, and it had few mutually
accepted rules of the political game. Much of modern Nigerian political
history is the attempt to develop political institutions that are responsive
to the Nigerian environment, and to create a national set of symbols and
values that can form the core of a national political tradition and culture;
in short, Nigerians are attempting to build both a state and a nation.

The discussion of Nigeria in the following chapters focuses on how
Nigeria's diversity influences and affects the political system, both in terms
of its style and performance. Nigeria has moved from civilian to military

Providing greater access to education is a goal of all developing nations. Pictured here is a primary school in Kano, Nigeria. Marc Riboud, Magnum Photos, Inc.

government and weathered one of the severest crises possible for a political system—the dissolution of the state through civil war.

An understanding of Nigeria is not complete without a realization of its great potential wealth. Oil reserves make Nigeria one of the largest oil suppliers in the world; both civilian and military leaders make decisions concerning the distribution and allocation of the oil revenues. For example, they must decide how the revenues will be distributed among different groups and regions, and how the revenues will be used to modernize and transform the society.

One must also understand the relationship between cleavage and conflict, and the various methods, structures, and institutions that may be used to resolve or manage societal conflicts. Nigerian politics is characterized by the attempts to develop sets of structures that can allocate values and resources between groups that have little in common, and are in some cases, violently antagonistic to each other.

Nigeria offers one example of a political system undergoing rapid change. It is a nation in transition. First there was the transition from civilian, parliamentary rule to military rule, then the transition from war-torn state to a nation seeking reconstruction and reconciliation. Since

1976–1977 Nigerians have been attempting yet another transition. This time Nigeria's military leaders are seeking to return power to constitutionally elected civilians. It is not an easy transition to make.

▪ EGYPT ▪

In each of the case studies one of our primary concerns is how the leaders and citizens of a nation respond to change. Leaders who continually fail to perform or meet the challenges presented them may soon find themselves out of power. King Farouk, monarch of Egypt, was just such a leader. In 1952 he was deposed by a group of young military officers. Very quickly, one officer among the "Free Officers" came to dominate the group. It is difficult to separate the history of modern Egypt from that man. Gamal Abdul Nasser, like Charles de Gaulle in France, created a political system tailored to his needs and values.

Any initial discussion of present-day Egypt must begin with the personality of President Nasser and the role he created for himself. Even after his death in 1970 the legacy lived on. His successor, President Anwar

Vice President Anwar Sadat became Egypt's president following the death of President Nasser in 1970. René Burri, Magnum Photos, Inc.

Sadat (also a member of the Free Officers) found that succeeding a hero and legend was not an easy task.

Both Sadat and Nasser faced a bewildering array of problems. Among the most serious of these is Egypt's precarious economic position. The problem begins with the relationship between Egypt's land and population. Almost 95 percent of Egypt's land total is arid and unsuitable for agriculture. The fertile lands beside the Nile must feed and support a rapidly growing population. While the habitable land remains fixed (or relatively fixed), the population continues to increase in size, often at an annual rate of over 2 percent. More citizens create more demands and new problems. The resources available to meet demands and solve problems, however, are limited.

Complicating the internal dilemma is an external one. The conflict between Israel and the Arab nations directly influences domestic Egyptian politics. Since 1952 Egypt has found itself at war with Israel on three separate occasions—the Sinai war in 1956, the June war in 1967, and the October war in 1973. The need to maintain a large military force places a strain on the Egyptian economy. Revenues that might otherwise be expended on development projects must go to support the military services.

Our study of Egypt raises several important questions. For example, how effectively has the post-1952 Egyptian political system performed? What is the precise relationship between economic change and political change? In a political system that was dominated by one central figure, President Nasser, what problems are likely to face a successor? And finally, what are the options open to Egyptian decision-makers for resolving the many problems of Egypt?

Egypt may properly be classified as a developing nation. It is a nation, however, rich in political, social, and cultural traditions. Understanding politics in present-day Egypt requires that we look at the setting that led to the 1952 revolution, as well as postrevolutionary events.

■ TANZANIA ■

Tanzania, in East Africa, is made up of the former British mainland colony of Tanganyika and the island of Zanzibar. In 1961 Tanganyika gained its independence from Britain and joined together with Zanzibar in 1964 to form the United Republic of Tanzania. Like most African countries, Tanzania is a diverse nation. There are differences between the island and mainland peoples, but also differences among ethnic, religious, and linguistic groups on the mainland. Unlike Nigeria, however, where three major ethnic groups traditionally dominate politics, there are no dominant groups in Tanzania. The major groups are all relatively the same size. As we shall see, this is an important political fact.

Tanzanians have faced relatively little political instability since independence. Despite its diversity, Tanzanian leaders have been successful in developing a strong sense of national unity. This appears to be a case that is an exception to the rule that severe cleavages lead to political instability. To understand why this is so requires studying the role of the Tanzanian African National Union, the leadership of President Julius Nyerere, and the importance of Tanzania's political ideology.

A common distinction drawn in political science is between the role of the political party in one-party states and its role in multi-party systems. One-party states generally are characterized as states that inhibit political participation, strive for the mobilization of the population, and both formulate and implement the goals of the political leadership. Multi-party systems are viewed as competitive systems—systems that respond to the changing demands of the citizenry and that represent the diverse interests and demands within the society. Tanzania, a one-party state, is attempting to bridge the gap between these two types. The Tanzanian African National Union (TANU) attempts to combine the characteristics of the one-party and the multi-party system. It seeks, for example, to institutionalize competition, not between parties, but within the party. Thus, while there is only one party listed on the ballot, there may be more than one TANU candidate standing for election. Tanzania and TANU merit attention precisely because the party system runs counter to commonly held assumptions.

Leadership also plays an important role in Tanzanian politics. The head of state and the head of government, Julius Nyerere, is attempting to lessen the impact of the oft-drawn distinction between participant and leader. Tanzania's elite, at least in theory, is expected not only to lead, but also to follow. The goal is to eliminate or narrow the gap between the political haves (the politicians) and the political have-nots (the citizenry).

A third area of interest is the role of ideology in the process of nation-building. Tanzania's leaders have made a conscious effort to develop an ideology of political and economic action that transcends subnational loyalties and traditions. Emphasis has been placed on adapting the philosophy of socialism to African conditions and on improving agricultural productivity before launching into industrial development.

Finally, Tanzania is developing symbols that are national in perspective and orientation. For example, the national language, Swahili, is an African rather than a colonial European language. Throughout the nation Tanzanians make a special effort to build a national identity both uniquely African and Tanzanian. Local village/community projects are encouraged as long as they do not conflict with the national objectives established by the leaders and the party.

Certain crucial questions emerge from this initial description. Are there unique factors or forces that have allowed Tanzanians to develop a sense of nationhood while others have apparently been less successful? To answer this, one must study the political traditions and political culture of Tanzania. Even more pressing is how well the system itself performs.

Has, for example, TANU been effective in creating competition within the structure of the party? Has the party been able to balance the need to mobilize the population for the achievement of specific goals, and yet still allow for discussion and dissension? How effective has the leadership been in lessening the gap between themselves and those they serve? What are the implications for the future for a political system so clearly dependent on one man, President Nyerere?

Tanzania often is cited as a model for other African and developing nations. Many argue that it is an applicable and realistic model because it balances the modern with the traditional and the possible with the ideal. To judge such a bold generalization requires not only an analysis of the Tanzanian political environment, but also an analysis of the performance of the political system.

▪ CHILE ▪

Chile, like the other nations in the study, is a nation of contrasts. Whereas Nigeria is a nation whose new, untested parliamentary government gave way to military rule, Chile is a nation whose well-established, highly institutionalized constitutional government was violently overturned by the military. A study of Chile provides another case of military intervention, but in another setting and involving other factors and forces.

Chile exhibits characteristics of both developed and developing nations. On the one hand, like many developed nations a majority of the population is literate, industrialized, and urbanized. Chile also has a relatively homogeneous population; it is predominantly Spanish-speaking and Roman Catholic. On the other hand, Chile is plagued by many of the problems facing developing nations. Poor economic performance and unstable political institutions are two of the most pressing of these problems.

Since Chileans won their independence from Spain in the early nineteenth century they have experimented with a variety of forms of government. These include federal and unitary systems, as well as parliamentary, presidential, and military regimes. Between 1925 and 1973 Chile was governed under a constitution that called for the direct and popular election of an executive president and a legislative congress. During this period it was one of Latin America's most stable democracies.

Like many of the states of Western Europe, political parties dominated Chilean politics. Parties ranged from the Communist and Socialist parties on the far left to the Christian Democratic party in the center to the conservative parties on the far right. In 1970 Salvadore Allende became the first Marxist to be freely elected president. Allende called for sweeping political, economic, and social changes. He demanded agrarian reform, redistribution of wealth, the nationalization of industry, and wider and

The Chilean presidential palace under attack during 1973 military coup d'état.
UPI Photo.

more open opportunity for all Chileans. As a minority president who received less than 40 percent of the vote during the election, Allende and his followers met stiff resistance once they took office. His election provoked a crisis for the political system; the rules of the game changed and many groups, both in and out of government, called for extra-constitutional action.

Salvadore Allende's presidency ended with a violent military coup d'état in 1973. President Allende was killed, many of his followers imprisoned or exiled, and a conservative military government installed in power. The new leaders have sought to reverse much of what was carried out during the tumultuous 1970–1973 period. The economic problems that plagued the Allende government also plague the military government. General Augusto Pinochet's government appears to be willing and prepared to hold power for the foreseeable future. How effective this regime will be in solving Chile's problems remains to be seen.

In many respects Chile serves as a bridge between the developed and developing nations. It exhibits characteristics of the developed nations of Western Europe but faces many of the problems associated with the developing areas of Africa and the Middle East. In Chile we can see how different political systems cope with similar problems but reach different solutions.

CHAPTER 2
THE DEVELOPMENT OF THE NATION-STATE

How does history influence the modern
nation-state?

Modern nation-state building is a complex process. Nation-building requires the development of political values and traditions which unite
peoples. Values and cultures unite peoples by giving them a common
identity, common shared experiences, and a common political and historical outlook. But the same values that unite Germans, Britons, the
French, Russians, Chileans, Nigerians, Tanzanians, and Egyptians also separate them. Traditions and histories distinguish between "us" and "them,"
between "we" and "they." Much of modern political history revolves
around attempts to create and maintain national unity and loyalty. Nationalism is the dominant unifying symbol of the twentieth century.

State-building, closely related to nation-building, requires the development of centralized political institutions and structures. These structures
institutionalize and regularize the pattern of politics within the nation.
This process allows political leaders, operating within the political system, to make and enforce their decisions. State-building involves the
exercise of political power, the maintenance of political authority, and the
establishment of political legitimacy.

Nation-state building is a dynamic process, strongly influenced by the weight of history. While some nation-states may claim to have more highly developed and stable patterns of politics, and a more clearly defined sense of nationhood, no nation can claim to have completed the process. The nation-state faces continuing challenges to its identity and sovereignty and to the authority and legitimacy of its institutions and leaders. To meet these challenges, leaders and participants alike must have the ability and willingness to adapt to new situations and environments.

The Historical Process of Nation-State Building

Europe in 1500 included over five hundred independent or semi-indepen-dent political units; by 1900 that number had decreased to about twenty political units. The change was not merely in numbers. Beginning in the sixteenth century, and gaining pace with the French Revolution, Europe's political complexion and organization was transformed radically. Nine-teenth-century Europe witnessed the decline, and set the stage for the eventual collapse, of the "old world order." To be sure, many of the great, multinational empires such as Austria-Hungary of the Hapsburgs and the Ottoman Empire of the sultans continued to rule, in one form or an-other, until World War I. Others, like the autocratic Hohenzollerns in Prussia and the tsars in Russia, continued to attempt to exercise absolute power. But the political trends were clear—new political ideas were challenging the old notions about the organization of society and the dis-tribution of authority.

As the new European nation-states industrialized, became more urban, and altered their economic and political organization, their vision and interest expanded beyond Europe. Raw materials were needed to make new products. In turn, new products needed new markets. The nineteenth century ushered in the era of the nation-state in Europe, while in the rest of the world it ushered in the era of imperial conquest and colonization. The multinational empires of Europe were replaced with worldwide, multinational imperial empires. The world was colonized in the name of economic expansion, national and strategic security, and cultural superior-ity. Great Britain officially annexed Egypt in 1882 in part to protect the vital Suez sea link between Great Britain and the pearl of her empire, India. Nigeria, in West Africa, became a British possession in 1900. Tan-ganyika after a short period of imperial German colonial rule passed to Britain as a "spoil of war" following World War I. Few areas in the world were left untouched by the colonial and imperial experience.

In Europe the nation-state building process occurred over a period of three centuries. The British experience, while often violent in the seven-teenth century, tended to be evolutionary; in Chile (strongly influenced by European traditions), France, and Russia the process was partially evo-lutionary but capped by periods of intense violence, revolution, and civil war. For new nations like West Germany, Nigeria, Egypt, and Tanzania, the process is telescoped. Evolution is replaced by planned growth and development designed to shorten the time required for the creation of a national identity and national political institutions. Whatever the age of the nation, nation-states face two kinds of problems: there are certain problems that all nations face, regardless of their stage or level of development; other problems are unique to each nation, areas that ultimately define and give character to the nation. To understand the complex process of nation-state building, we must focus on both the problems common to all of the eight nations that we will study and also on those problems that are unique to each country.

The Idea of the Nation

The new political ideas that began to emerge in the nineteenth century challenged the traditional political order. Most monarchs recognized the challenge and resisted it; a few were wise enough to recognize the challenge and adapt to the new circumstances. Tsar Nicholas II of Russia resisted. In the early part of this century the advisers of the tsar cautioned him to make an attempt at understanding the needs and desires of "his peoples." In true imperial fashion the tsar responded that it was not his responsibility to understand the people, but their responsibility to understand him and to ask his forgiveness for their actions. The tsar was expressing the divine and absolute power of the monarch over his subjects. His authority and power came from coercion, from his role of tsar as the embodiment and symbol of Russia, and his position as head of the Russian Orthodox church. While many of "his" peasants and workers began to question his authority as Russia approached 1917 and the Revolution, the tsar held fast to the centuries-old tradition of tsarist rule. The tsar and his family paid for their intransigence with their lives.

Tsarist Russia, like many of the other great European empires, was characterized by its diversity. Different ethnic and language groups were bound together by their allegiance to the monarch. The legitimacy of the empire was based on acceptance by the subjects of the absolute power and authority of the monarch.

The new nation-states that replaced the multinational empires were characterized by a greater homogeneity and a new relation between the ruler and the ruled. The foundations of the state and the political rules of the game were altered. The heterogeneity of the empire was replaced by the homogeneity of the nation. The ideal nation was

a single people, traditionally fixed on a well-defined territory, speaking the same language all its own, possessing a distinctive culture, and shaped to a common mold by many generations of shared historical experience.[1]

---

[1] Rupert Emerson, *From Empire to Nation* (Boston: Beacon Press, 1962), p. 103.

Although this ideal rarely existed in reality, it provided a new model for the nation-states of Europe. The legitimacy of the nation changed from one based on the divine right of kings and emperors to one derived from the citizenry of a defined geographical area. Legitimacy was granted the ruler and the state by the people over whom he sought to exercise his authority.

Nation-building unified and consolidated peoples under the national banner. Individuals and groups gradually came to view others as either similar or different from themselves. Religion, language, race, or definition of community membership united one group and separated it from others. It was no longer possible for the state, in the person of the monarch, to simply assert his right to rule; he had to justify it. His right to rule was allied closely with his relation to his people; and his people increasingly began to demand the right to participate and make demands—a revolutionary idea. The nation, then, became the "terminal community":

It is the largest community which, when the chips are down, effectively commands men's loyalty, . . . a community of people who feel that they belong together in the double sense that they share deeply significant elements of a common heritage and they have a common destiny for the future.[2]

The nation is the bedrock on which the state institutions and structures are built. Among the factors that influence a nation's characteristics are the diversity of peoples within its boundaries, the depth and types of shared experiences of the members of the nation, and their unique historical development. Together these comprise the political cultures and traditions of the nation. The political culture and traditions of Great Britain, a nation with a relatively high degree of homogeneity and with long-cherished, shared experiences, differs considerably from newer nations, created where none had existed before, with few shared experiences and traditions, and with little unifying history.

One of the best places to begin comparing nations is with the different historical experiences nations have undergone. Individuals and groups constantly refer back to "their history"—those events, crises, triumphs, and failures that shape and influence modern politics.

The Concept of the State

Just as new political ideas and values arose to challenge and replace old political values in organizing the nation, new political institutions developed to challenge and replace old governing structures. In this case political leaders sought to harness and control the nation by using these new state institutions. The state transforms the legitimacy provided it by the citizenry into authority—the justified right and power to make and

---

[2] Ibid., pp. 95–96.

enforce decisions. In the European case, this meant the centralization of power and control under the monarch. Later it involved the changing relationship between the monarch, the nobility, and the people over whom power was being exercised. Ultimately, power passed from the monarch to the nobility, from the nobility to the representative institutions of the citizenry. More and more individuals and groups began to participate in politics.

Closest to the monarch were his council of advisers usually made up of the most powerful and influential nobles of the realm. These councils were the forerunners of modern legislative institutions. In Great Britain, for example, the modern, powerful Parliament is derived from the earlier less powerful advisory bodies. The monarch's chief adviser served as his prime minister; and eventually the prime minister replaced the monarch as the most powerful political figure. As the state expanded and became more complex, specialized bureaucracies were created. Taxes needed to be collected, justice dispensed, and records kept. State-building required specific institutions performing specific jobs.

The state sought the power necessary to make decisions and to coordinate the distribution and allocation of goods and services. Political power was centralized in political institutions rather than in individuals. People participated and made demands, were protected and controlled by the state.

The complexity of the relationship between state and nation can be seen in the diversity of patterns and forms that exist today. In Chapter 1 several of these forms and patterns were introduced. Democratic, authoritarian, and totalitarian political systems and capitalist, socialist, and Communist economic systems are different nation-state patterns. Each of the forms and types, as well as variations, emerged and developed within the context of the general sequence of political development, but affected by unique cultural and historical factors.

Nation-states that underwent the transformation during the seventeenth, eighteenth, and nineteenth centuries exhibit very different patterns of development than those states undergoing the process in the twentieth century. In early nation-state building the nation, or the idea of the nation, appeared first and was followed by the development of the state. For example, the assertion (by Otto von Bismarck) of Prussian authority, and the eventual German unification, was aided by the emerging sense of German nationhood and German culture. By the time that Bismarck governed, the number of independent German principalities had shrunk considerably from over 300 that had existed in the seventeenth century.

In many new nation-states a sense of national identity and loyalty has yet to emerge. Territorial boundaries are often marked not by their cultural, linguistic, ethnic, or religious homogeneity but by political considerations beyond their control. The "natural" evolutionary sequence of European nation-state building is replaced by an "artificial" imposed sequence.

Nation and state must form at the same time. To cite only two examples, Nigeria and Tanganyika as nations did not exist before European colonialism. National boundaries joining together diverse peoples with little in common were drawn by Europeans not "Nigerians" or "Tanganyikans."

One way to compare nations is to compare their historical experiences. Leaders and citizens alike constantly refer to their past and to the experiences they all share. The shared experience of evolutionary political change in Great Britain, for example, influences the way the British politically think and behave. Likewise, the French and Russian revolutions color French and Russian political perceptions. History provides the milieu in which political decisions are made. It is impossible to understand modern political institutions without understanding how they developed. How the game of politics is played today is influenced by the unique political traditions and cultures of the nation. The weight of history defines and limits what is politically acceptable and unacceptable, as well as providing continuity from regime to regime, from leader to leader, from election to election.

Political Socialization

The stability and continuation of the nation makes it essential that the national values, beliefs, and experiences be passed from generation to generation. Citizens must both know and accept these traditions and histories. The process by which the rules of the game, the political traditions, and the political culture are passed from generation to generation is referred to as political socialization.

Political socialization involves both the content of the political messages and the agents and methods used to transmit them. In traditional societies, for example, the responsibility of storing and recounting the societal history rests with older generations. It is their responsibility to see that the legends, the folklore, the beliefs, and the values of the community are not lost, and that they are effectively passed to younger generations. In some societies without written languages, oral history replaces written history. Individuals are trained to remember and pass on the histories and lessons of their ancestors.

The socialization process tends to be more diversified and complex in modern nation-states. The family, peer groups, the media, and the schools are primary agents of political socialization. Each, operating in different ways, provides individuals with cues of what is acceptable and not acceptable, what is right and wrong, what is to be valued and what is to be avoided. These agents teach individuals what their roles as citizens and subjects are, and they provide the necessary skills and training for these roles.

There are important differences in the socialization process between democratic and more totalitarian systems. In democratic systems the agents may work independently from each other, and provide groups with different information and cues. For example, someone who watches only television for political news will have a different outlook from someone who reads several newspapers of differing political perspective, watches television, and discusses politics frequently with family and friends. In more totalitarian systems where the goal is to create a uniform set of beliefs and values, the socialization process is more rigid, formalized, and characterized by mutually reinforcing cues and information. Television, newspapers, and schools are expected to provide the same message.

Whatever the means, all political systems seek to train and educate their citizenry to play certain political roles and behave in certain defined ways. To understand why political leaders and participants act the way they do in other nations requires first an understanding of the historical trends that shape the political institutions of the modern nation-state. We must search for similar patterns in nations but also recognize the differences and unique factors that influence modern politics. All nations look to and are influenced by their history.

▪ THE UNITED KINGDOM ▪

The development of national unity and state authority in the United Kingdom is often described as evolutionary. The development of institutions and political rules was marked by few discontinuities in Britain, unlike its neighbors Germany and France. The contemporary British monarchy, Parliament, and legal system are direct descendants of their thirteenth-century counterparts. Long-range trends such as increased parliamentary power and democratization have seldom been reversed—never for long. National unity developed gradually but has not yet been accomplished; the English have not succeeded in spreading their culture to Scotland, Wales, and Northern Ireland.

Development of National Feeling

By comparative standards the peoples of the British Isles are culturally distinct groups. The nationality groups—the Scots, Welsh, and Irish—are descendants of Celtic tribes. Each represents a distinctive Celtic group that was occupying the Isles when the Romans arrived in 43 A.D. The Romans and subsequent invaders drove the Celtic population to the mountainous west (Wales) and north (Scotland) and across the Irish Sea. In these remote and isolated corners the groups survived as related but increasingly distinct cultural groups with different languages, customs, and political traditions.

That part of the British Isles more accessible to European peoples, modern England, was subject to a greater cultural mixture. Norse invaders mixed with remnants of the Celtic and Roman groups. By the year 1000 the differences among the ethnic groups in England largely disappeared and the inhabitants shared a common language and customs. A loose political structure also developed under a confederation of warrior chieftains, some of whom aspired to the title king.

The British Isles were invaded in 1066 by William I (the Conqueror). William's kingdom had been in northwest France, or Normandy, and his people were the French-speaking Normans. William set up a feudal social and economic system and a stronger political structure than England had ever known. He divided the land and granted it to Norman lords. William extracted taxes, tribute, and military personnel from his subordinates in return. With these resources he began to build a strong monarchical system.

William's feudal system made the Normans lords over the native population, called Anglo-Saxons by this time. Over the next several centuries differences in language and customs diminished between the rulers and the ruled. The shared institutions of feudal England had begun to forge the common cultural groups we now refer to as the English people or nation.

Development of State Institutions: Early Period

The growth of state authority and the development of state institutions began from the English national core as defined by William's conquest. The monarch stood at the top of the social order. His authority was based on feudal, military, and economic obligations. The authority was checked, if only feebly, by two embryonic political institutions—the common law courts and a representative assembly. Political development from 1200 to the present is largely one of the growth in importance of these institutions and of the gradual refinement of their powers and duties through custom and precedent.

The English common law goes back to the twelfth century. Monarchs of this period began to send judges invested with state authority to the various localities to settle disputes. By collecting a fee for their efforts these judges raised important revenue and extended the king's influence. Local traditions and customs supplied the basis for rulings—a strategy that encouraged local acceptance of the judgement and of the judge. Gradually, the accumulated judgments and the customs supporting them took on the sanctity of "higher law." Such law based on the shared experience of a national group eventually limited the power of the Crown.

Parliamentary development followed a similar path from modest almost accidental beginnings to a position of great importance. The 750-year history of the British Parliament is usually traced to thirteenth-century efforts of British monarchs to extend their taxation to new groups of nobles and townsmen. Representatives were summoned by the monarch to inform them that new taxes would be levied. This repeated fundraising expedient led to several unprecedented ideas. First, it suggested

Chronology of Events

UNITED KINGDOM

43 A.D.	Roman invasion of the British Isles.
1066	Norman invasion of Britain. William the Conqueror defeats Saxon king. Feudal social system established.
1213	King John convenes the forerunner of Parliament. Representatives of the knights of the realm approve new taxation.
1413	Accession of Henry V. Origins of legislative process in the form of written petitions for Crown action.
1649	Successful rebellion against Stuart absolutism. Charles I executed. Republican government established by Oliver Cromwell.
1688	The Glorious Revolution. James II of the Stuarts is driven from the throne. William and Mary are offered the throne by victorious Parliament. Bill of Rights.
1701	Act of Settlement. Limits on monarch's power are formalized in act of Parliament.
1832	First Reform Bill. Franchise is extended to middle or propertied classes. Elimination of "rotten boroughs."
1867	Second Reform Bill. Franchise is extended to include working-class men.
1911	House of Commons limits the powers of the hereditary House of Lords. The superiority of the lower house is formally established.

that individuals should be selected to represent the recognized components of the political community in matters affecting the welfare of these groups. Second, it suggested that extraordinary taxation or other important actions were not legitimate without consultation with recognized representatives of the monarch's subjects. The ideas of representation and the popular basis of legitimacy were not understood or accepted then, but a trend had begun which would not be reversed.

Parliament gradually expanded its powers through a basically cooperative relationship with the Crown. In fact, the early and currently legal meaning of Parliament is the meeting of Crown, Lords, and Commons (these last are representatives of communities). The earliest parliamentary assertion of power provides the classic example of the process—that of control over new taxes. Government expenses originally were paid by revenue generated by Crown properties, from customs duties, and the fees and fines collected by legal officers of the Crown. In normal times under the more prudent monarchs these sources of income were sufficient. As governmental expenditures grew and as individual monarchs began to use Crown property revenue solely to finance the considerable royal household, new tax sources were necessary. Parliaments were called to approve new taxes and as early as the fourteenth century claimed the exclusive prerogative of approving new sources of governmental revenue. The special parliaments of the early period always demanded the redress of particular grievances as a condition for agreeing to royal requests. They therefore gained some measure of influence in other areas of government and administration. By the reign of Henry V (1413–1422) written petitions were submitted in this spirit and in a way which foreshadowed modern legislative procedures.

Throughout the Tudor dynasty (1485–1603), Parliament quietly expanded and solidified its powers. Although the Tudors are justly remembered as strong and even despotic rulers, they had a keen appreciation for political reality. Political reality included a landed gentry and urban merchants who became very interested in political issues in this period and who sat in the lower house of Parliament, the House of Commons. Their support was particularly crucial for the Tudor monarchy for two practical reasons, which accounted for the increased importance of the Commons. First, a number of the great aristocratic landowners were discredited from the period of the War of the Roses (1455–1485)—the dynastic struggle for the English Crown between the houses of York and Lancaster. The Tudor monarchs reduced the influence of the noble families which had opposed them during the War of the Roses. The great families' political influence was limited to the upper house of Parliament, which was then emerging as a separate body.

The second reason that elements of the House of Commons became more important stemmed from the English Reformation engineered by the Tudor monarchy to consolidate the power and authority of the Crown. Henry VIII confiscated the property of the old Catholic church establishment and made a break with the papacy. This Tudor monarch created the Church of England, which he and all later English monarchs have served as temporal head. Unlike the Protestant Reformation on the continent of Europe, in Great Britain matters of church doctrine were unimportant in the break, and the masses did not become directly involved in the religious upheaval. With ecclesiastical opposition removed and with the neutralization of the great aristocratic houses, Henry sought support from the House of Commons for these sweeping changes.

Although the assembly that had become known as Parliament was important by the end of the Tudor period in 1603, it was not at all like the institution we know today. Meetings were not regular, and members were not popularly elected. The House of Commons, which is currently the powerful or "efficient" part of the modern Parliament, held an ambiguous position. The commoners did not sit with the monarch and the Lords for many important activities—as when the Lords acted as a judicial or administrative body. Monarchs skillfully used one house against the other as demonstrated by Henry VIII when he used Commons support in reforming the church. The powers of the House of Commons were limited to control of the raising and disbursement of revenues.

The Seventeenth-Century Constitutional Settlement

The test of parliamentary power and authority came in England's turbulent seventeenth century. A new royal dynasty, the Stuarts, challenged the limits placed on them by custom and tradition. The constitutional struggle of the seventeenth century produced two aberrant forms of English government—a monarch ruling without Parliament and a Parliament ruling without the Crown. Charles I asserted that his authority was ordained by God and as such was indivisible. He claimed that sovereignty was vested in the Crown and that sovereignty could not be divided, delegated, or checked. Charles did not call a Parliament into session from 1629 to 1640. The price Charles paid for this breach of English custom and precedent was his life; he was beheaded. The monarchy was dissolved for a brief period when General Oliver Cromwell presided over a brief and less than satisfactory experiment with "republican" government—that is, government by Parliament without the monarchy.

Cromwell's brief reign as Protector of Britain suggests that custom and precedent had already established important principles of British government by the midseventeenth century. Cromwell executed "that man of blood, Charles Stuart"[3] for ignoring the prerogatives of the already ancient institution, Parliament. Having achieved power through the instrument of the army, Cromwell was forced to constitute a new Parliament, which was nominated by the army. The result was a failure because it defied all of the traditions of the English parliamentary institution. Frustrated, Cromwell on his deathbed in 1658 named his son Richard as heir to the title of Protector. Oliver Cromwell's protectorate collapsed soon after his death, and the monarchy was restored under Charles II.

Cromwell fought a civil war to protect the prerogatives of Parliament. The unintended result was the creation of an illegitimate form of the parliamentary institution. By the seventeenth century, informed Britons knew the difference between legitimate and illegitimate institutions. Cromwell's protectorate also demonstrated that Britons wanted a monarchy—the British found that they were not comfortable as republicans during Cromwell's brief rule.

Once the monarchy was restored, a second challenge was made to the power and authority of Parliament. James II, a Catholic, raised again the conflict between English Protestantism and the Catholic church when he came to the throne in 1685. Fears of Catholic influence led to a bloodless revolution in which Parliament decided the succession to the English throne. James's daughter Mary and her husband William of Orange were

---

[3] Ivan Roots, ed., *Cromwell* (New York: Hill and Wang, 1973), p. 18.

invited to be the English monarchs, and their acceptance finally signified the supremacy of Parliament. Future monarchs had to acknowledge that they ruled by the grace of Parliament.

The accession of William and Mary and the defeat of James II was termed the "Glorious Revolution." Two documents established a new relationship between Parliament and the Crown. The first, the Bill of Rights of 1689 (the year of the accession to the throne of William and Mary) specified actions of the Stuart monarchs that infringed on the powers of the courts and Parliament that had been established by custom. (The language in fact served to inspire the American colonists as they wrote their Declaration of Independence.) Monarchs were expressly forbidden to raise standing armies, suspend the laws, or levy money without parliamentary grants of authority. The Act of Settlement (1701) formally subjected English monarchs to the will of Parliament. The act makes it clear that monarchs rule only through the acts of Parliament and that ultimately Parliament's actions are deciding.

The Glorious Revolution returned essential governmental relationships back to those of the Tudor era. A balance was restored between the executive responsibility of the Crown and the legislative power of Parliament. The traditional power of the Commons in public finance was underlined, yet in other ways the Commons had no more power than the Lords. Kings such as George III could wield substantial and real power depending on the agenda of politics and their alliances. Political alliances or relations with Parliament were critical in monarchical influence. The king's men in Parliament became crucial, and of necessity the king's advisers were drawn in part from his parliamentary allies. These allies were bound to the Crown by patronage, political interest, or ties based on the forerunners of modern political parties—the Tories and the Whigs.

The Modern Parliament: Adapting to Democraticization

A series of ineffectual monarchs after George III (reigned from 1760–1820) led to a gradual transference of power to the king's ministers who had long been referred to as the cabinet. The need for leadership and governmental direction led to the emergence of a leader of the cabinet or prime minister. The efforts of the prime ministers and cabinets of the late eighteenth and early nineteenth centuries were alternately aided and confounded by the growth of the importance of political parties. The Whigs came to strongly represent the claims of the rising business class. The Tories stood for the landed aristocracy. As the issues sharpened, loyalty to party increased among members of Parliament so that the management of parliamentary business required the development of links between cabinet and party, and the king had less and less real choice in his ministers if he cared about their effectiveness.

The development of a cabinet and prime minister with a partisan parliamentary base of support was reinforced by the major nineteenth-century electoral reforms. The Reform Act of 1832 enfranchised the middle classes and eliminated rotten boroughs, the virtually unpopulated voting districts controlled by major landlords. The Reform Act made it clear that popular support was the source of a government's legitimacy. The cabinet depended, from that date on, on electoral outcomes to justify its authority, and political party fortunes became the standard for evaluating the mandate of any given cabinet. The democratic reforms (1867, 1918, 1928, 1948) which gradually increased the popular base of politics led to cabinet and responsible party government. It also finally tipped the balance of parliamentary power away from the hereditary House of Lords and toward the democratic Commons.

The evolution of the British constitution over 750 years has resulted in a remarkable blend of old and new institutions. The monarchy and House of Lords have survived to serve useful—if rather ceremonial—functions. The lower house has adapted itself to modern democratic and partisan politics. All of the developments, with the exception of the seventeenth-century experiments with different forms, flowed naturally from one another and so reflect national traditions and customs. Few nations have had the time or isolation required for this sort of evolution, and Britain no doubt is the least realistic model for new nation-states. The new states cannot expect isolation from the modern world. Nor can they be comforted by the fact that separate national identities have persisted in this ancient kingdom.

▪ THE FEDERAL REPUBLIC OF GERMANY ▪

Few nation-states have had a history that so clearly separates the development of national feelings and the development of state institutions as has Germany. The beginnings of a sense of German national feeling can be traced as far back as the Germanic tribes of Roman times described in the accounts of the historian Tacitus. A powerful German state, however, did not develop until 1871. In these centuries German nationalism was not strong enough to unite those people who by language, culture, and tradition considered themselves German. Failure in building a German state was the result of great historical events beyond the control of the Germans themselves.

Development of National Feeling

The first tangible tradition of German national identity dates from the period of the Holy Roman Empire, or First Reich. German princes during this time ruled as heirs to the old Roman Empire. This very weak premodern political entity was a federation of small German states in which the imperial mantle was passed from German prince to German prince.

By the time the imperial office was permanently bestowed on the Austrian Hapsburgs in the fifteenth century, it was little more than an honorary title. Germans remained divided into numerous small states for centuries to come.

The First Reich was not a serious or important attempt at state-building, but it was very important in forging a sense of German identity. This period strengthened the cultural bonds that could have dissolved after the collapse of the old empire. It solidified the inheritance of Roman law, the Christian religion, and left a mark on the German language. The period placed Germany in an evolving European culture and helped to delineate what was distinctively German.

Barriers to State-Building

The shared historical experience and the cultural distinctiveness that developed in this period might have slowly evolved into a modern centralized state were it not for massive historical crises. The first was the social and religious upheaval that was the Reformation. Misreading Martin Luther's intent, German peasants in large areas of Germany attempted to not only cut the ties with Rome but to expand their freedom from local princes. Luther and his followers were appalled; Luther himself reacted violently, "The peasants are murderers and robbers who must be stabbed, smashed, or strangled, and should be killed as mad dogs."[4] German Protestantism henceforward was closely tied to such political authorities as existed in Germany. The Protestant establishment in Germany had begun to promote the longing for a strong state to maintain order in German-speaking Europe.

The legacy of the Reformation included problems beyond the religious division of Germans into Catholic and Protestant states. Germany became a battleground as ambitious rulers of France and Sweden attempted to take advantage of the weakness and division of the German principalities. Unification of the German peoples was frustrated by the invading armies of the seventeenth century. Ironically, a nineteenth-century conqueror helped unify Germany. Napoleon's invasion served to consolidate the small German states by forcing the people to band together to resist Napoleon's mass citizen army. Ordinary people became important, and means were needed to move them to action—ancient "national" feelings were stirred.

German Unification and State-Building

After Napoleon's defeat in 1814, one German state began to unite the other German states under its state machinery. Brandenburg-Prussia

---

[4] Arnold Heidenheimer, *The Governments of Germany* (New York: Thomas Y. Crowell, 1971), p. 6.

Chronology of Events

THE FEDERAL REPUBLIC OF GERMANY

1648	Peace of Westphalia, end of Thirty Years' War. Germany is weak and divided. High point of political fragmentation.
1740	Frederick the Great is crowned king of Prussia. Beginning of the growth of Prussian state power.
1815	Congress of Vienna. New German confederation is established after Napoleon's defeat. Rivalry between Austria and Prussia for supremacy in German-speaking Europe.
1848	Abortive democratic rebellion. Defeat of German liberalism. Increased emigration of German liberals to the United States.
1871	The German empire is proclaimed. German states are unified under the Prussian monarch. Catholic Austria remains outside the Second Reich.
1890	Wilhelm II accedes to the throne. Chancellor Otto von Bismarck—the "Iron Chancellor"—retires.
1918–1919	Defeat in World War I. The "November Revolution" forces the Kaiser's abdication. Weimar Republic constitution establishes parliamentary democracy.
1933	Adolf Hitler subverts the Weimar regime. Enabling Act passed by Reichstag. Beginning of National Socialist regime.
1945	Defeat of National Socialist Germany. Beginning of Allied Occupation and "De-Nazification."
1949	Democracy is reintroduced in West Germany. First elections are held under the Federal Republic of Germany's new constitution.

strengthened and modernized its state institutions for the task. The emphasis, by necessity, was on the instruments of coercion and control. The military came to a preeminent position in the state, and in some minds *was* the state. In the words of a general of the Prussian tradition: "The army in serving the state merges with it and becomes the purest image of the state. The army serves the state and only the state, for it is the state."[5] Prussian militarism stemmed in large part from its task of unifying the existing German national groups—a task it performed in three wars between 1864 and 1871. The Prussian state administration was similarly rigorously prepared for the task of homogenizing the regionally and religiously fragmented nation it was to govern.

---

[5] General Hans von Seeckt, quoted in F. L. Carsten, *The Reichswehr and Politics* (Berkeley: University of California Press, 1973), p. 400.

The bureaucratic-militaristic Prussian state in 1871 came to control all the major German-speaking areas except Catholic Austria. The king of Prussia became the Kaiser—or emperor—of the Second Reich and his closest adviser became the prime minister—or chancellor—of the new empire. Authority was centralized and enforced through impressive instruments of coercion. All of the new Germany was subjected to the Prussian-dominated army and a relentlessly efficient bureaucracy.

The first prime minister of the empire was Otto von Bismarck, who "by blood and iron" had engineered the unification. Bismarck, as chancellor from 1871 to 1890, faced a serious problem of establishing the legitimacy of the new order. He could try to associate the new regime with the ancient German Reich and suggest that the Prussian king had been elected by the German princes just as had emperors of the First Reich. However, mass involvement in public life was inevitable after the War of National Liberation against Napoleon and new means of justifying the authority of the state were necessary.

Bismarck essentially had two other strategies for establishing the legitimacy of the empire's institutions and actions. The first was essentially negative in that it involved an attack on rival sources of authority. Bismarck's government moved first against the influence of the Catholic church. He launched a *Kulturkampf,* or struggle for civilization, against the church and its affiliated social and political organizations. Having just defeated Catholic Austria and Catholic France in his drive for unification, he mistrusted the political loyalties of Catholic Germans. Anti-Catholic laws were passed that confiscated church property, undermined fundamental Catholic rites such as marriage, and forbade the activities of the more active Catholic religious orders.

Later Bismarck attacked socialist parties and associations for the same reason. The socialist ideal of a worker's international undermined the authority of the new regime. Severe limits were placed on the socialist press and socialist associations. The activities of the German Social Democratic party were curtailed for a time. Like the Catholics, Bismarck feared the Socialists were serious about their talk of a "socialist state within a state"—a network of social service associations and political groups.

Bismarck also had a more positive strategy for increasing the legitimacy of the new regime. The chancellor tried to justify state power by providing outlets for political participation and by providing advanced social services. He permitted the illusion of mass democratic participation by introducing universal suffrage for the powerless lower house of Parliament, the *Reichstag.* Since the body could do nothing but complain and criticize Bismarck's government, it soon acquired a derisive nickname, the "chatterbox of the empire." The powerful upper house, the *Reichsrat,* was made up of instructed delegates from the component states of the empire with Prussia having a controlling number in its delegation. By allowing parties

Otto von Bismarck, chancellor of the German empire from 1871 to 1890. Brown Brothers.

and elections, Bismarck developed a popular base for legitimacy at considerable risk. Eventually, the Catholic and Socialist parties were the largest in the Reichstag.

The legitimacy of the empire was probably more enhanced by the provision of advanced welfare and social services than by the other strategies. The Second German Empire introduced social security legislation before the turn of the century, and played on a paternalistic theme in German culture. The government achieved legitimacy by protecting people and providing them with personal economic security. Bismark's government was a "people's" government in the sense that it did a large number of things for people.

The most severe test of authority for a nation occurs in a crisis such as war. From this point of view the authority of the empire's institutions ultimately proved insufficient. The unsuccessful conclusion of World War I brought down the institutions of the Second Reich. However, during the war the authority marshaled by the empire was impressive. The war effort was supported widely. Even the Catholics and Socialists did not openly criticize the Kaiser's dictum—"I no longer recognize parties, only

Germans."[6] Popular support was not sufficient, however, in the face of military defeat and the attendant social and political disruption.

Weimar Germany: Failure of Democratic Institutions

In the wake of the German defeat the democratic political parties had the opportunity to establish liberal democratic institutions modeled on the Western European tradition. A republic was established and named after the German center of humanism, the city of Weimar. The institutions included a Reichstag with impressive powers checked by a potentially powerful president. The president's power rested in part on his ability to nominate candidates for the prime minister's office in times of governmental crisis, and his ability to dissolve Parliament and call for new elections. These familiar powers were augmented with the power to declare a state of emergency and to rule through the army in the face of any domestic or foreign threat. The broad powers of this famous Article 48 of the Weimar constitution were ultimately important in Adolf Hitler's seizure of power.

The Weimar failure was only superficially a result of the president's extraordinary powers, since presidential constitutional powers came into play in periods of parliamentary crisis, when the democratic parties of Weimar could not govern. The parties dedicated to parliamentary democracy failed in their responsibilities in part because of their inexperience in democratic politics. Under the empire they had no power of responsibility, and their experience was limited to criticism and often nonconstructive debate. In another sense the failure of the Weimar parties was beyond their control—a product of a deeply divided society. Germans were divided politically by religion, region, class, and urban-rural traditions. Many parties contested the elections. Few of them had much in common with rival political groupings. The result was predictable. The fourteen years of Weimar were marked by twenty changes in cabinet leadership.

National Socialism, War, and Occupation

The economic crisis of the 1930s brought a sudden end to the parliamentary experiment in Germany. The fragile legitimacy of the new institutions quickly dissolved. Economic failures and international humiliation produced a longing for strong state authority and leadership among many, but by no means all, Germans. Authoritarian traditions based on the Prussian and empire experiences were easily reactivated by Hitler's National Socialist movement, which was the best organized of many flourishing nationalist groups.

Hitler's rise to power was aided by a clever manipulation of political

---

[6] Quoted in Alfred Grosser, *Germany in Our Time* (New York: Praeger, 1971), p. 5.

issues and ideological appeals. One set of issues were "national"—those stemming from Germany's defeat and humiliation in World War I. Germany's war reparations payments were scheduled to last until 1984. Hitler's first important political success was to join with "respectable" political conservatives, former aristocrats, and newly rich industrialists in urging the unilateral repeal of these measures. In addition, Hitler pledged to rebuild Germany's army that was reduced to 4,000 officers and 96,000 enlisted men by the Versailles Treaty. These positions had broad popular appeal, and even the political left was anxious to appear soundly "national" in this sense.

Ideological appeals centered on Hitler's particular brand of biological racism. Germans were said to be not only superior in culture but also "by blood." Germany's external enemies, the Slavs or Russians, were inferior, and German *Lebensraum* or "living space" could be gained by the conquest of their lands. Germany's internal enemy, the Jews, Hitler referred to as the "cancer of the body politic." Hitler, a convinced anti-Semite, was not delicate in his imagery, "As soon as you cut even cautiously into such a cancer, you found a maggot in a rotting body, often quite dazzled by the sudden light—a little Jew."[7] Jewish treachery was used to explain all of Germany's domestic problems, and the small German Jewish population served as a group which the insecure Germans of the depression could look down on. Hitler tried to build the unity of the German *Volk*, or people, on hatred or resentment of Germany's Jews.

Hitler's totalitarian regime quickly attracted support from two sources. The conservative or monarchical nationalists were attracted by Hitler's dedication to undoing the World War I humiliation of reparations and military limitations. They were moved by Hitler's allusion to traditional German greatness and to the symbols of Germany's two historical empires.

A second source of support were the Germans who had suffered personal economic disaster. This accounts for the support accorded Hitler by the "middle classes." They had lost their valued status in the depression and were desperate for a return to economic security. Hitler's massive militaristic state doubled industrial production by the mid-1930s and greatly reduced unemployment. Allusion to the myth of the German past and successful economic performance no doubt led to widespread feelings that Hitler's authority was indeed legitimate—until that legitimacy was shattered by war and the postwar revelations of massive barbarity committed in the name of the German state.

The victorious powers of World War II left nothing to chance following the second outbreak of twentieth-century German nationalism. In a four-year transition period (1945–1949), they oversaw the selection of new German leaders and the drafting of a new democratic constitution. The

---

[7] Quoted in J. P. Stern, *The Führer and the People* (Berkeley: University of California Press, 1975), p. 51.

new constitution reinstituted parliamentary government but provided for only a ceremonial president. The occupying powers built into the constitution measures that would limit the number of parties, decentralize the government, and provide increased protection for individual and group rights. They were powerless, however, to erase the traditional political hostilities out of which arise political parties and conflict. The Allies were equally helpless in changing the political attitudes born in earlier regimes, which have been passed on through political socialization—paternalism, authoritarianism, and anti-parliamentarism. These problems were left to the new leaders of democratic Germany.

▪ FRANCE ▪

France's political development began with a very early national unification under centralizing political authorities. With an ethnic mixture of Celtic, Germanic, and Latin strains, the sense of nationality derived more from centuries of shared history than from ethnic heritage. The centralizing French monarchy set the boundaries of the political realm and was an important force in integrating and, to some extent, homogenizing the peoples within the Old Regime.

The Old Regime

The French monarchy established the legitimacy of its rule on religious grounds. The monarch was closely identified with the French Catholic church and used church symbols and doctrine to support his own actions. This relationship was perhaps most clearly seen in the era of the Crusades in which the French monarchy insisted that the French people had a divinely ordained mission in the Holy Land.

The first acts of state-building by the French monarchy further increased the French sense of nation. The Old Regime was based on one of the world's first truly bureaucratic systems of government. The administration was centralized, hierarchical in organization, and characterized by the specialization of tasks. The king's personal secretaries acted as his liaison to the governmental machinery. The administrative system of France reached its most rigid form during the long reign of Louis XIV (1643–1715). The advanced and modern form of government proved to be a powerful monarchical instrument against political rivals. In particular, it avoided regional rivalry as well as opposition from the religious leaders or the rising economic classes.

The strength of the bureaucratic institutions prevented a smooth evolution to parliamentary government as had occurred in Britain. The French forerunners of representative assemblies fared rather poorly against the power of administrative institutions. The *Estates General*, which emerged in the fourteenth century, was abandoned as an ongoing institution in the

Chronology of Events

FRANCE

1789	French Revolution. Louis XVI is deposed and revolutionary government is established. End of the Old Regime.
1804	Napoleon Bonaparte is proclaimed emperor. The First Empire is established.
1814	Napoleon is defeated. Bourbon monarchy is reintroduced.
1830	Bourbon monarchy is overthrown. The business-oriented "July monarchy" is introduced.
1848	July monarchy is dislodged by republican forces. The Second Republic is proclaimed.
1852	Louis Napoleon declares himself emperor. French electorate approves in plebiscite. Second Empire established.
1875	Third Republic begins after the Franco-Prussian War. Provisional Assembly opts for extreme republican solution.
1940	German invasion of France. Vichy regime is established to collaborate with Germany. Authoritarian tradition resumed.
1946	Divided constituent assembly recommends republican constitution. French public approves in closely contested referendum. Republican institutions reintroduced. Fourth French Republic begins.
1958	Charles de Gaulle returns to draft new constitution after prolonged Algerian crisis. Constitution introduces a strong presidential institution. French electorate overwhelmingly approves. Fifth French Republic begins.

---

early seventeenth century. Other institutions that might have countered royal power were the *parlements,* or law courts which proclaimed the king's laws in the important cities. At times the parlements became focal points for criticism of the monarchy. When the parlements took on a revolutionary posture, the monarchs of the Old Regime wasted little time in disbanding them. After a confrontation with the monarchy in 1788, these bodies were suspended, a prelude to the Revolution.

The French Revolution and Problems of State-Building

The French Revolution led to experiments with democratic forms. The first efforts at establishing a new political framework were directed toward the creation of a parliamentary, representative democracy. The first popular assembly was not capable of containing the social and political forces set loose by the Revolution, and the attempt at democracy was doomed by political demands and revolutionary rhetoric. With virtually no experience the apprentice parliamentarians faced a most fantastic and intense variety of popular demands. They also were attempting to deal with an

Nouvelle Méthode pour faire prêter Serment aux Curés

Scene from the French Revolution. The caption reads, "New way to make a priest give his sermon." © Arch. Phot. Paris/S.P.A.D.E.M.

influential political idea put forth by Jean Jacques Rousseau—the ideal of direct democracy.

Rousseau and other French political philosophers rejected representative institutions because they felt that the people's representatives would frustrate the "General Will." Representatives were unnecessary intermediaries between the people and the government. Indeed, one of the pre-Napoleonic experiments was an abortive attempt to approach the ideal of direct democracy by holding frequent elections and referenda. It was hoped that the public could constantly intervene in deciding the important issues of politics without the interference of professional politicians. In fact, Napoleon, only 15 years after the French Revolution, used some of the ideas of direct democracy and popular sovereignty to establish himself as a "people's emperor."

The defeat of Napoleon in 1814 led to the restoration of the Bourbon monarchy and a repetition of the cycle of instability: authoritarian monarchy overthrown by representative republican institutions which, in turn, are usurped by a people's emperor. Like the Bourbons, the French people seemed to have learned nothing and forgotten nothing. The Bourbon and July monarchies, which lasted from 1814 to 1848, were very much in the tradition of French authoritarianism, most evident in the Old Regime, although its spirit was diluted in the July monarchy with its elections. The alliance of church, aristocracy, and monarchy was reinstated along with distinctions of birth and rigid social hierarchy.

The rigid monarchy and its social system could not survive the revolutionary year of 1848. The Second Republic lasted exactly four years until Louis Napoleon was elected president of the Republic. He declared himself emperor and gained overwhelming popular approval in a plebiscite reminiscent of those staged by his uncle. The Second Empire again justified the centralization and abuse of state power by the special relationship between a leader and the people.

The Triumph of Republicanism

France's military defeat of 1871 by the Prussian army led to the first prolonged republican regime—the Third Republic. This attempt at pure parliamentarism and small government proved to be remarkably enduring. The republican regime lasted until the devastating defeat of 1940 by Hitler's forces. The ideal of representative government was closely followed in the 65 years of the Republic. Executive power was carefully checked, and constituency interests were defended. The price, however, was often political stalemate. Fears of flamboyant leadership and demagoguery were almost an obsession among these parliamentarians. The Third Republic was, in balance, successful judged against the expectations and political demands of the times, although it is doubtful that the Republic would have survived if political change demanded a new governmental activism—for French republicanism rejects large-scale action.

Vichy France

The small-government orientation of the Third Republic drew strongest criticism from the advocates of the French authoritarian tradition. The most extreme of these adherents, like the *Action Francaise,* were attracted to Hitler's example during the 1930s. With the defeat of 1940 the authoritarian groups got a chance to put their ideas into practice in the collaborationist Vichy regime (1940–1944) under the 84-year-old Marshal Petain. (Vichy France took its name from the rural southern town that served as its capital.) All vestiges of popular participation were eliminated, as were the rights guaranteed under the Third Republic. The revolutionary motto "Liberty, Equality, and Fraternity" was officially replaced with a new motto—"Work, Family, Country." Petain, while he still had his faculties, conducted himself in the style of a traditional monarch as sole repository of political authority.

The collapse of France in 1940 and Petain's military reputation probably induced many of the bewildered French public to support the aging soldier's regime with its bizarre collection of monarchists, fascists, and bureaucrats. The support derived from two ideas—that Vichy meant a truly French government drawing on French political traditions and that the task of this government would be to protect the lives and property of French citizens. These ideas did not stand up long in the face of the day-to-day business of collaboration with the Germans. The Vichy government offered protection to some French citizens, but was quick to hand over French Communists and leftists. The Vichy government also had to handle quotas established for the delivery of Jews and candidates for forced labor to the Nazis. The lives of some French Jews were saved but at the cost of actively seeking out Jewish refugees from other countries to take their places on the rolls. These kinds of actions quickly alienated most French citizens when coupled with the obvious infirmities of Marshal Petain.

Postwar France

During the crises of World War II two sources of national pride were the Resistance groups that pressured the German occupying forces and the French government in exile established by Charles de Gaulle in London. These groups came to dominate postwar French politics. The Communists were the most visible and organized of the resistance forces and could lay claim to the title of the "party of the 10,000 shot." This distinction they owed to both the authoritarian elements of Vichy and the Nazis who sought out French Communists for summary execution. General De Gaulle used skillful diplomatic pressure to gain a place for French forces in the liberation of France and later in the occupation of Germany. It was largely through his efforts that France regained its place among the Allies. In the era of postwar disillusionment and guilt, the Resistance and De Gaulle became symbols of the "real France"—or that France of which one need not be ashamed.

The task of restructuring French politics fell to De Gaulle's supporters, the Communist party of France, the Socialists, and representatives of the new Europeanwide Christian Democratic movement. There was little agreement about what shape the new governmental institutions should take among either politicians or the public at large. The public voted overwhelmingly (96 percent) to replace the Third Republic constitution but rejected a draft constitution submitted to them by a constituent assembly representing the major parties. The political left eventually won the day with their insistence on a purely republican, parliamentary-dominated regime with a weak executive. The public eventually approved a republican constitution similar to the prewar model. The vote was not, however, very comforting to French republicans—36 percent of the eligible voters voted "yes," 32 percent voted "no," and 32 percent abstained.

The Fourth Republic Parliament produced a very mixed record of performance. Governmental instability was pronounced; cabinets in the multi-party parliaments fell even more frequently than under the notorious Third Republic. On balance, it is fair to say, however, that the French Parliament did not match the foreign stereotype of "a cross between a comic opera and a beer-garden where every month rival groups of excitable fanatics brought down a government in their passionate devotion to incomprehensible principles." The French public's view was equally at variance with the facts. The Fourth Republic Parliament was not quite an "exchange mart for crafty and crooked careerists."[8] It was merely a political institution that could not generate enough political authority and executive direction to cope with the dissolution of the French colonial empire. The trials of Indochina, Tunisia, Morocco, and most of all Algeria wore out all of the formulas and expedients that the Fourth Republic institutions and leaders could devise to deal with the agonizing and divisive task of liquidating an empire in a period of very low national morale.

The failure of the Fourth Republic can be explained in part in terms of the fragile legitimacy of these institutions. It is doubtful whether there ever was more than a third of the French public who supported the regime. After 12 years of colonial wars and 20 consecutive years of war, dating from 1939, the support dwindled even farther. By 1958, large sections of the French military were in open mutiny, and mass unrest gripped French and Algerian cities over the colonial question. No important political actors felt that the Fourth Republic institutions could cope with the challenge.

It was in this spirit that the leaders of the Fourth Republic turned to the only viable alternative, Charles de Gaulle. De Gaulle had consistently opposed the republican formula, insisting that strong leadership was required to restore French grandeur. The model he favored was in the Bonapartist tradition, a charismatic president who would lead through his special relationship with the people. The intermediaries between the leader and his people were done away with by De Gaulle's Fifth Republic constitution. The republican ideal of representative government was rejected in favor of direct democracy. The French returned to that which was promoted by Napoleon and his nephew. De Gaulle may have finally settled France's last major constitutional controversy when his new regime supplanted its republican predecessor.

■ THE SOVIET UNION ■

The growth of the Soviet state and nation was not evolutionary as was the case with Britain and did not involve series of experiments with governmental forms as was the case in continental Europe. Soviet state and

---

[8] Phillip M. Williams, *French Politicians and Elections* (Cambridge: Cambridge University Press, 1970), p. 34.

nation-building were conscious efforts undertaken by the Communist leadership. Efforts to unify the Russian people under the vast state machinery were influenced by two historical traditions. The first was the inescapable weight of Russian history, especially the legacy of tsarist Russia. The other impact on contemporary political development was the Revolution of 1917.

Background of Nation-Building

The Russian people are descended from the major language group of Eastern Europe, the Slavs. Ethnic mixture, however, was inevitable given the free movement of early peoples over the broad Eurasian plain. Later Russian rulers conquered neighboring peoples, inhabiting vast tracts of territory, in order to protect the core of the Russian state and nation. This accounts for the multinational character of Russia under both the tsars and the current regime.

The conquest of European Russia by the Mongols in 1240 and the subsequent 250 years of Mongol rule left a great mark on the future Russian state. The Russian rulers treated subject nationalities as the Mongols had treated the Russians. The Mongols exacted tribute and taxes without directly meddling with the Russian way of life, with ultimate control maintained by the threat of military coercion.

The Mongols also had a hand in deciding which of the Russian princes would participate in building the future Russian state. The Mongols in 1340 recognized the preeminent position of the princes of Moscow, who for some time had enhanced their position by their loyalty and obedience to the foreign conqueror. The position of the Russian nobles of Moscow also resulted from the close ties that had developed between the Moscow nobility and officials of the Orthodox church. The dramatic increase in the power of Moscow's rulers was instrumental in reducing the power of the Mongols.

Growth of State Power

The unification of the Russian people under a centralized authority occurred under Tsar Ivan IV also known as Ivan the Terrible. Ivan drew on the despotic tradition of the Mongols. He eliminated all nobles who were not absolutely loyal to his rule and in effect built a new class of nobles. The new nobility, many of whom came from his own household, were totally dependent on Ivan. They were just as much slaves—to the tsar—as were the Russian peasantry.

The nobles attempted to reverse the trend toward tsarist absolutism after Ivan's death in 1584. The nobles used controversies over succession to the throne to weaken the central authority established by Ivan. A foreign threat, however, that of the Poles and Lithuanians, led to new support for

Chronology of Events

THE SOVIET UNION

1240	The Tartar invasion. Russian principalities are subjected to Eastern despotism.
1340	The Prince of Moscow is designated the "Great Prince" of Russia. Moscow becomes center for Russian unification.
1533	Reign of Ivan IV "the Terrible," begins. Principles of tsarist autocracy are established.
1613	Zemsky Sobor elects Michael Romanov tsar. Romanov dynasty established. Beginning of 300-year reign of Romanov tsars.
1682	Reign of Peter the Great. Westernization is attempted. Nobility is subjected to tsarist rule.
1825	The Decembrist Revolt. First major revolt against tsarist authoritarianism. Beginning of era of revolution.
1855	The reign of Alexander II. Major reforms introduced including the liberation of Russian serfs.
1881	Alexander II assassinated. Reforms associated with constitutionalism are deferred.
1905	Revolutionary violence. "Bloody Sunday"—September 22—leads to the creation of a popular assembly, or *Duma*.
1917	The Russian Revolution. Tsar Nicholas II abdicates in favor of a Provisional Government composed of the Duma and workers/soldiers' Soviets. Lenin's Bolshevik faction establishes its leadership of the Revolution.

the tsarist system. A broad-based group of landowners met in the *Zemsky Sobor,* or Congregation of the Lands, to elect a new tsar and establish a new dynasty, the Romanovs. The new royal family drew on Ivan's harsh principles of government and established an autocratic system on those lines that lasted until 1917.

The 300-year reign of the Romanovs was marked by territorial expansion and the perfection of tsarist authoritarianism traditionally referred to as the Russian "autocracy." The most notable Romanovs were Peter the Great (Peter I) and Catherine II. Both were "Westernizers" who introduced Western methods to enhance Russia's power. Both, however, were dedicated to territorial expansion and to the autocracy. The traditional policies of the dynasty, Peter's in particular, solidified the tsar's control over the nobility and in so doing perfected the autocrat's power. In addition to building St. Petersburg, Russia's window to the West, Peter the Great did away with the hereditary privileges of the nobility. Peter's "nobility of service" carefully placed all of the nobles in ranks or levels of status depending on the noble's usefulness to the tsar autocrat. Peter's work was so successful that an important nineteenth-century noble exclaimed: "I wish someone would point out that the authority that the sovereign wields over the landlords is in no way different from the power the landlord has over his peasants. . . . I find in Russia only two estates: the slaves of the sovereign and the slaves of the landlords."[9]

If the nobility's freedom was no greater than that of the peasants, they were indeed slaves. About three-fourths of the population were peasants, serfs who were legally bound to the land they worked. Almost half of them worked the tsar's land. Serfdom also meant that one could be sold as property and punished as the owner saw fit. Serfdom formally lasted from the midseventeenth century to the midnineteenth century, although conditions for peasants before and after these dates were not appreciably different from those of formal serfdom.

In the absence of an independent nobility, church, or peasantry there was no effective counter to tsarist power and authority. Over time the tsar's authority increasingly was exercised through the massive bureaucracy in the capital, St. Petersburg, and by the governors of the administrative districts and city governments into which Russia was divided. The governor was the tsar's prefect, and he ruled his area, often somewhat independently, through police lieutenants. Direct lines of authority ran from the tsar's private chancery to the governors. The third section of the chancery, the secret police, performed an important function in linking the administrative units to the central power. It was in this sense that the secret police were the "eyes and ears of the tsar." Needless to say, this system choked off any institutions resembling Western parliaments.

The Revolutionary Challenge

This sort of absolute authority, almost unique in nineteenth-century Europe, came under increased pressure for reform. The pressure was resisted by Alexander I (reigned 1801–1825) and Nicholas I (reigned 1825–1855). The administration of Nicholas I began with a bloody attempt to overthrow the autocracy, but the military mutiny led by conspiring officers and nobles was quickly broken on the first day of the tsar's reign. Nicholas I placed a high priority on increasing the importance and efficiency of his secret police. It was left to Alexander II (reigned 1855–1881) to handle the backlog of modern reform proposals suggested by the tsarist bureaucracy. Alexander freed the serfs in 1861, and in the same decade reformed local government, which included provisions for elected local assemblies, or Zemstvos. The creation of the Zemstvos along with tsarist decrees establishing greater intellectual freedom in the universities allowed the free

---

[9] Edward Crankshaw, *The Shadow of the Winter Palace* (New York: The Viking Press, 1976), p. 80.

expression of ideas and opened new avenues for dissent. The assassination of Alexander II by underground terrorists cut short the possibility of further reforms. The "tsar-liberator" was assassinated on the day he approved reform proposals that included a disguised representative assembly.

The remaining years of the tsarist regime were characterized by continued erosion of the tsar's authority and by the growth of revolutionary activism. The erosion of tsarist authority resulted from failures of the tsarist government. The most notable was the debacle of the Russo-Japanese war (1904–1905) in which Russian lives were squandered by governmental incompetence and during which the Russian populace suffered economic privations. The proponents of democratic reform in the Zemstvos and among the Constitutional Democrats increased their demands for civil liberties and for a popular assembly. The latter was finally granted after hundreds of peaceful demonstrators were slaughtered near the Winter Palace as they carried their portraits of the tsar and their petitions to Nicholas II. Bloody Sunday, September 22, 1905, made Nicholas II a reluctant constitutional monarch as he soon approved the creation of a nationally elected popular assembly, or *Duma*. The fact that

Tsar Nicholas II (reigned 1894-1917) and his family. Brown Brothers.

Nicholas did not understand the significance of his own "October Manifesto" which created the Duma is clear. The manifesto did not, in his mind, alter the fundamental laws: "To the emperor of all the Russias belongs the supreme autocratic power."

The Duma of 1905–1917 offered the moderate democratic politicians an opportunity to limit the tsar's power; however, their inexperience with democratic politics and the Russian public's ignorance of politics reduced their importance to that of a debating society with a very small audience. The trappings of manhood suffrage, legislative initiative, and a bill of rights did not limit the tsar's power.

The Duma further diminished its public support with its patriotic adherence to the government's goals in World War I. The tsarist system was not any more capable of waging a major war that it had been in the Crimea (1854–1856) or against the Japanese (1904–1905). Corruption, economic collapse, and military reverses sealed the fate of tsarist Russia. Nicholas II, against all reasonable advice, took field command of the dispirited Russian army while the German princess who had become the tsarina, Alexandra Federovna, exercised disastrous judgment in St. Petersburg. The tsarina allowed government positions to fall to the favorites of a mystical cleric, Gregor Rasputin. Rasputin's reputed ability to heal the hemophiliac heir to the throne was to prove very costly to the last members of the Romanov line.

The Revolution and Consolidation of Soviet Power

Food riots and other forms of civil disturbance broke out in March 1917. The tsarist regime, too weak to cope with major disorders, collapsed. Initially, the revolutionary forces had no clear leadership. The Duma attempted to take control and assert its authority. It succeeded in obtaining the tsar's house arrest and abdication, but could not control the revolutionaries. The authority of the Duma leaders was undermined by their insistence on continuing the unpopular and devastating war. The power fell to the more ruthless and organized of the revolutionary groups.

The forces of revolution were represented by workers' and soldiers' revolutionary committees called "Soviets." The Petrograd (the new name for the capital) Soviet soon came to share power with the Duma and was later joined by the Soviets of Moscow and other major cities. An extreme group of Marxists, the Bolsheviks, who were led by Lenin, became very influential among these groups. By November 6–8 they had seized the major public buildings in Petrograd in league with the military elements in the Soviets. On November 8 the authority of Lenin and the Bolsheviks was established by the acknowledgment of the Congress of Soviets.

Lenin faced severe obstacles in establishing the authority of the new government. The society and economy were totally disorganized and dispirited, civil war was imminent, and foreign intervention by Russia's former military allies was soon to follow. Lenin first of all relied on coercion in the form of the new Red Army and the secret police. Marxist doctrine allowed for the gradual building of the regime's legitimacy. Marxism justified the rule of a revolutionary elite who understood the laws of history. This vanguard would form a dictatorship in order to establish a workers' state that would reject class and privilege. Rewards of status and power awaited those who understood the revolutionary message.

Lenin's successor, Joseph Stalin, perfected the technique of control through coercion, terror, and purge. Dissident groups, such as the landholding peasantry, were ruthlessly suppressed. At the same time the state and schools were teaching a new generation the essential qualities of the "New Soviet Man." The twin instruments of coercion and ideological justification gradually established the authority of the new regime. The final product, ironically, was in the tsarist tradition. A single glorified leader was bolstered by the secular religion of Marxism and ruled through the secret police and extensive state bureaucracy. The single greatest difference lay in the efficiency and technological sophistication of the Soviet system.

▪ NIGERIA ▪

Compared to the nations of Europe, the history of the Nigerian nation is short. Before 1900 there were no "Nigerians" because there was no "Nigeria." Different ethnic groups (sometimes referred to as tribes) co-existed but did not think of themselves as members of the same nation. Only after 1900 and the imposition of British rule did the idea of Nigeria begin to emerge.

Nigerian history centers on attempts to join together in one nation different ethnic groups, different language groups, and different religious groups. This joining together has been a difficult, and sometimes violent, process. Nigeria epitomizes the problems associated with nation-building in new states.

Before Nigeria—The Pre-Colonial Period

Three major ethnic groups are most commonly associated with Nigeria. Before the British created the colonial protectorates of Nigeria, the Hausa-Fulani, the Yoruba, and the Ibo, as well as many numerically smaller groups, formed distinct political communities, with clearly defined boundaries. Each was concentrated in a specific region, and each group had its own language and traditions.

The Hausa-Fulani empire in the north looked to the larger Islamic world.

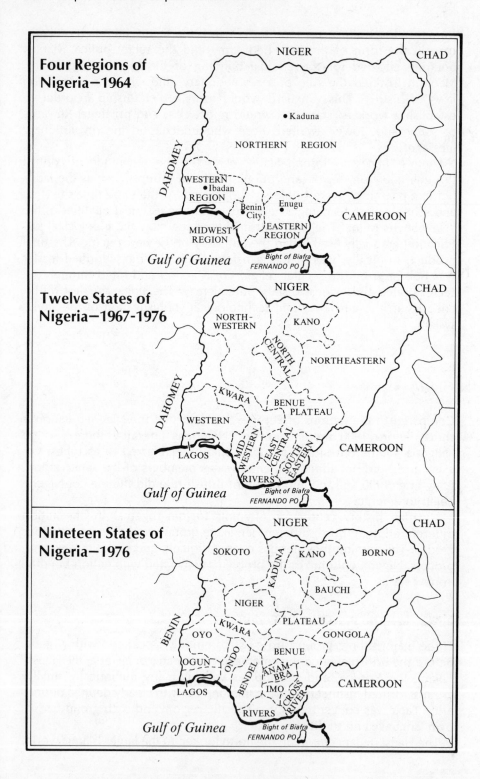

Four Regions of Nigeria—1964

NIGER

CHAD

• Kaduna

NORTHERN REGION

DAHOMEY

WESTERN REGION
• Ibadan

Benin City •

Enugu •

CAMEROON

MIDWEST REGION

EASTERN REGION

Gulf of Guinea

Bight of Biafra
FERNANDO PO

Twelve States of Nigeria—1967-1976

NIGER

CHAD

NORTH-WESTERN

KANO

NORTH CENTRAL

NORTHEASTERN

DAHOMEY

KWARA

BENUE PLATEAU

WESTERN

MID-WESTERN

EAST CENTRAL

SOUTH EASTERN

CAMEROON

LAGOS

RIVERS

Gulf of Guinea

Bight of Biafra
FERNANDO PO

Nineteen States of Nigeria—1976

NIGER

CHAD

SOKOTO

KADUNA

KANO

BORNO

BAUCHI

NIGER

BENIN

KWARA

PLATEAU

OYO

GONGOLA

ONDO

BENDEL

BENUE

OGUN

ANAM-BRA

IMO

CROSS RIVER

LAGOS

CAMEROON

RIVERS

Gulf of Guinea

Bight of Biafra
FERNANDO PO

As Islam spread from North Africa to West Africa in the fourteenth and fifteenth centuries, the seven Hausa states gradually adopted the new religion, although they continued many traditional religious practices. The expansion of Islam was closely tied to economics. The Hausa were important partners in the trans-Saharan trade between black Africa and Arab Africa; important cities, like Kano, were southern terminals for caravans coming from the Islamic north. Already united by a common myth of origin, by the Hausa language, and by similar types of political patterns, Islam added to the growing sense of Hausa identity.

In 1804, however, the Fulani peoples took control from the weakened Hausa rulers. Uthman dan Fodio, a religious teacher and political activist, declared a *jihad* or holy war against the Hausa rulers. His goal was the establishment of a new state founded on strict adherence to Islamic tradition and practice. Political and religious power in this new state were vested in the *sultan* (supreme secular power). Descendants of Uthman dan Fodio ruled from the city of Sokoto and assumed the title, Sultan of Sokoto. With the assistance of their *emirs* (princes), the Fulani aristocracy governed autocratically. When the British arrived in the late nineteenth century, they found and were challenged by a well-established political system.

The political development of the Yoruba peoples in what is now western Nigeria differed considerably from the Hausa-Fulani in northern Nigeria. The most common political institution of the Yoruba peoples was the city-state. There were fifty city-states, each ruled by an *oba* or king. The oba's office was hereditary, and occupants of the office were responsible for the ceremony and ritual of politics. Day-to-day administration was often carried out by a chief whose position was based on merit, not birth. The Yoruba were highly urbanized, and during the nineteenth century the city of Ibadan replaced the more traditional Yoruba capital of Oyo as the most important political and military city in Yorubaland. While political power was not centralized in Yorubaland, the Yoruba, like the Hausa-Fulani to the north, shared a common language and a common myth of origin.

The Ibo peoples in eastern Nigeria had the least centralized political system of the three major groups. There was not the hierarchical administration of the Hausa-Fulani, nor the urbanization of the Yoruba. Political power and authority rested with the family or in the village. In most cases the largest political organization was the village, which consisted of several extended families. Usually only during times of crisis would a larger Ibo organization form.

Early contact between Europe and West Africa was limited to explorers, missionaries, and traders. Portuguese traders began trading with the peoples along the coast of West Africa in the mid-1400s. The major commodities were ivory, gold, and later, slaves. The early Portuguese monopoly on trade was challenged by Dutch, British, and French concerns.

Europe's interest in Africa increased as trade became more profitable and as European explorers began to move into the interior of Africa. Merchants sought to protect their sources of supply and open up new markets, while missionaries hoped to spread their word in areas untouched by Christianity. Because of Britain's abolition of slavery in 1807, new markets had to be developed to replace the lost markets in slaves. Enforcement of the new edict required constant vigilance. Permanent settlements began to appear in and around the major trading and ex-slaving areas. The most important areas were the site of present-day Lagos and the Niger river delta.

British interest in the soon-to-be Nigeria evolved slowly and with little coordinated planning. Great Britain claimed Lagos in 1861 and governed the settlement first from their colony of Sierra Leone and then from the Gold Coast (later Ghana). Trade on the Niger River was the exclusive monopoly of the newly formed Royal Niger Company. Great trading companies, like the Royal Niger Company, not only controlled trade but became the government and law for their areas.

The Colonial Period

In 1884–1885, partly in response to the increased interest in Africa, the great powers of Europe met in Berlin to divide Africa into spheres of influence. What was to become Nigeria fell to Great Britain. Britain created the Niger Coast Protectorate in 1893, and in 1900 relieved the Royal Niger Company of its administrative duties on the Niger River by creating the Protectorate of Southern Nigeria. In 1906 the British joined the Lagos Colony to the Protectorate of Southern Nigeria to form the Colony and Protectorate of Southern Nigeria (later divided into the Western and Eastern Regions). Further to the north, Frederick Lugard, British colonial officer and soldier, defeated the Fulani states with a small military force and proclaimed the Protectorate of Northern Nigeria (later the Northern Region) in 1900. Unbeknownst to a majority of the inhabitants of the areas, they had become members of the growing British Empire.

In a very short space of time the British found themselves responsible for the administration and development of two vast areas. To complicate the task, the people from these areas had little in common. In many cases groups had expressed a long-standing animosity toward each other. Administratively, wherever possible, the British attempted to govern through the already existing political structures. Indirect rule, as envisioned by its prime advocate Lord Lugard, had one very large advantage—it allowed the British to control large areas with minimal resources and few British personnel.

Indirect rule was applied most consistently in the Northern Region. Rather than replacing the Fulani political structures and leaders, British district officers administered the Region through them. The sultan and the emirs continued to hold their titles, and succession continued to be hereditary, but much of their power was gone. The emirs collected taxes, Islamic justice and law were upheld when not in conflict with British practice, and the traditional, religious educational systems continued to function. Now, however, the emirs were ultimately responsible to and derived their authority from the colonial administration.

In some areas, like much of the eastern region of the Southern Protectorate, indirect rule was not possible. The traditional political structures in these areas did not lend themselves to the centralized administration of a modern colony. In these cases the British rule and administration were more direct. Colonial administration was pragmatic, and administrators often experimented trying to find the most suitable way of governing.

Colonialism in Nigeria produced fundamental social and economic changes. In southern Nigeria new government and mission schools were opened. More and more Africans received Western educations and took positions in the modern economic sector. Africans became teachers, civil servants, businessmen, and government workers. In the North the process tended to be much slower. Rather than risk the delicate balance between the conservative emirs and British officers, the British attempted to shield and protect the North from any of the changes occurring in southern areas. For example, missionaries, so active and important in the spread of Western education among the Ibo and Yoruba, were prevented from opening new schools and seeking converts among the Islamic Hausa-Fulani.

Indirect rule has often been referred to as "divide and rule." Although Northern and Southern Nigeria were amalgamated into one protectorate in 1914, administration continued to be exercised by two separate colonial structures, with markedly different rates of modernization and growth in the two areas. The first demands for increased participation and then independence were first voiced in the more "modern" South. Beginning in the 1930s some of the more educated, politically active Ibos and Yorubas began to organize and make demands on the colonial administration. These interest groups and protective societies formed the nucleus for future Nigerian political parties.

Despite the fact that Nigerians were taking an increasingly active role in politics, there still did not exist a unique Nigerian identity that could unite the different groups in Nigeria. As demands for participation and independence increased following World War II, attention focused on the shape of political structures most suited to an independent Nigeria, rather than on the much more difficult task of building national unity. Throughout the 1950s various constitutions were introduced. Each constitution attempted to provide a pattern for politics that would be acceptable to the various factions.

The British favored the creation of a federal system based on the British example. This "Westminster model" included a lower House of Assembly and an upper House of Chiefs (similar to the House of Lords). The prime

Chronology of Events

NIGERIA

1861	British government assumes control of Lagos Colony.
1886	Royal Niger Company granted charter over Niger River area.
1900–1901	British create Protectorates of Northern and Southern Nigeria and assume direct colonial control.
1914	British amalgamate Northern and Southern Protectorates and Lagos Colony to form the Protectorate of Nigeria.
1960 (October)	Nigeria achieves independence. Prime Minister Sir Abubakar Tafawa Balewa leads a multiparty parliamentary democracy.
1966 (January)	First military coup d'état. Prime Minister Balewa and others are killed. Major General Johnson Aguiyi-Ironsi heads a military government.
1966 (July)	Second military coup d'état. Major General Ironsi and others are killed. Colonel Yakubu Gowon heads a new military government.
1967 (May)	Eastern Region of Nigeria secedes from the Federal Republic and declares itself the independent state of Biafra. War between Biafra and Nigeria begins.
1970 (January)	Biafra surrenders and is reunited with Nigeria.
1975 (July)	General Yakubu Gowon removed from power in a nonviolent coup d'état. General Murtala Mohammed becomes new military head of state.
1976 (January)	General Murtala Mohammed killed in an unsuccessful coup d'état. General Olusegun Obasanjo, second in command, becomes new military head of state.
1979 (October)	Scheduled return to civilian rule. Executive presidential system scheduled to replace military government.

minister was selected from the House of Assembly and had the right to select his cabinet. In addition, there was an appointed head of state, or president, at the national level. In each of the three regions, the North, the West, and the East, there were regional legislatures and premiers.

The only way the Westminster model could succeed was if all of the political parties and various interests would play by the same political rules and agree to accept the results of elections. As Nigeria approached its first elections in 1959, the political contest centered on three political parties representing the three different Regions. Each party sought to "run strong" in its own area first, and then attempt to pick up a few seats in other Regions. These regional parties viewed it as their duty to protect their members and to help their followers in the scramble for jobs and power. Political parties appealed to regional, ethnic, and linguistic loyalties, not to national loyalties.

The Independence Period

The political patterns that emerged in the immediate pre-independence period intensified following independence in 1960. "Ethnic politics" and "ethnic arithmetic" were the dominant political games. Political activity centered on preserving and protecting regional and ethnic interests. Now, however, the protective authority and power of the British were removed.

The government became more and more corrupt and inefficient. Chinua Achebe, a Nigerian author, cited a William Butler Yeats poem to describe Nigeria and Nigerians during this period:

> *Turning and turning in the widening gyre*
> *The falcon cannot hear the falconer;*
> *Things fall apart; the centre cannot hold;*
> *Mere anarchy is loosed upon the world.*[10]

In January 1966 a frustrated group of military officers, primarily of Ibo origin, violently ended parliamentary rule. The prime minister, the Western and the Northern regional premiers, and several army officers from both areas were killed. The officers intended to end the corruption of the civilian regime, reestablish effective political authority, and provide a new foundation for national political activity. Tragically, however, the splits and divisions that characterized the civilian regime now appeared in the military. An officer's ethnicity, not his rank, became his most distinguishing and important characteristic. In July 1966 a second coup occurred led by a group of officers primarily from the North. This time most of the victims were Ibo.

The new regime, headed by Colonel Yakubu Gowon, attempted to preserve the fragile unity of Nigeria. By 1967, however, the situation deteriorated to such a degree that the federation could not hold. In May 1967 the Eastern Region, led by Colonel Odemegwu Ojukwu, seceded from the Federal Republic and declared the creation of the new independent state of Biafra. The civil war lasted from 1967 to 1970, when the Biafran forces were defeated and reunited with the Federal Republic. The cost in terms of national unity, loss of life, and destruction of property was enormous. Reconciliation and reconstruction proved difficult.

Since independence Nigerians have experimented with many different forms of government. Old regions have been broken up into new states.

---

[10] W. B. Yeats, "The Second Coming," cited by Chinua Achebe, *Things Fall Apart* (London: Heinemann Educational Books, 1958), Introductory Citation. These lines are reprinted by permission of Macmillan Publishing Co. and Mr. M. B. Yeats from *Collected Poems* of William Butler Yeats (copyright 1924 by Macmillan Publishing Co., Inc., renewed 1952 by Bertha Georgie Yeats).

Depending on the situation, central authority has been strong and the regions weak, or vice versa. Questions of the distribution of power and authority have not been resolved.

The process of nation-building is still going on in Nigeria. The political, social, ethnic, and cultural splits have made the development of a national set of values and symbols difficult. Subnational loyalties have taken precedence over national loyalties. The problems of developing ongoing, regularized, and efficient national political institutions is complicated by this lack of national consensus.

▪ EGYPT ▪

The Mediterranean world of the nineteenth century was one of rapid political, economic, and cultural change. New political ideas conflicted with centuries-old political practices. Islam, the dominant religion of the eastern Mediterranean and long in a state of decline, experienced a period of renewal and reform. New ideas, both religious and secular, asserted a new and unique nationalism. In this period of turmoil Egyptian nationalism began to develop; the culmination of the development of the idea of Egyptian nationhood came in 1952 with the Egyptian revolution.

Early Nineteenth-Century Egypt

Egypt, and the peoples of the Nile, have been governed by a bewildering assortment of political systems and leaders. Pharaohs, religious *caliphs* ("successors" to the political and religious leadership of Islam), kings, military dictators, descendants of slaves, and landed aristocrats have all at one time or another attempted to assert their control and authority over Egypt. In some cases they have been Egyptian, in other cases foreigners. In most respects, however, these different forms left the life of the Egyptian *fellahin* (peasant) largely untouched. For the fellahin, life continued much as it always had, regardless of who was nominally in control.

The sultans of the Ottoman Empire dominated the Mediterranean from the fifteenth century. By the nineteenth century much of their control and authority had been dissipated, and over large portions of their empire they ruled in name only. The legitimacy of the empire was challenged by religious reformers who questioned the political authority of the sultans as well as their religious piety. Nationalist groups demanded greater control over their own affairs and more autonomy within the framework of the empire. The Ottoman response to these demands vacillated between reform and repression.

At the same time that the empire faced an internal crisis, it also faced an international threat—European expansion. As the power of the Ottomans waned, European powers moved into the vacuum. England, France,

Chronology of Events

EGYPT

1805	Muhammad Ali establishes an Albanian monarchy to rule Egypt. The modernization of Egypt begins.
1869	Suez Canal opened.
1882	Colonel Ahmed Arabi leads an Egyptian nationalist revolt against foreign domination. Great Britain militarily intervenes, defeats Arabi, and assumes direct colonial control over Egypt.
1922	End of the direct British protectorate and the establishment of a strong Egyptian monarchy and a weak parliament.
1952	Free Officer movement within the military overthrows King Farouk and ends the monarchy. General Muhammad Neguib is made figurehead head of state.
1954	Colonel Gamal Abdul Nasser becomes president of Egypt.
1956	"Suez War" with Great Britain, France, and Israel.
1967 (June)	"Six-Day War" between Arab states and Israel.
1970 (September)	Gamal Abdul Nasser dies. Anwar Sadat becomes new president of Egypt.
1973 (October)	"Yom Kippur" or "Ramadan" war between Arab states and Israel.
1977	President Sadat makes first visit to Israel. Beginning of peace negotiations between Egypt and Israel.

Germany, and Russia began to assert claims to parts of the decaying empire. The Ottoman Empire was the "Sick Man of Europe."

Egypt was at the center of this world, both economically and politically. Although under the nominal authority of the sultans in Constantinople, Egypt for hundreds of years had been ruled and dominated by different powers. In 1798 Napoleon invaded the Egyptian province but was soon forced to withdraw for military and diplomatic reasons. Muhammad Ali, the Albanian commander of the sultan's troops, was appointed governor of the province. Although his power and authority were theoretically derived from the sultan, he was in fact an independent ruler. He created a system in which he, and hopefully his descendants, would be absolute rulers. This required the elimination and the control of all possible rivals to his power.

Once assured of his own control, Muhammad Ali began the modernization of Egypt. His goal was nothing short of the complete transformation of Egypt and the creation of a modern state based on the Western example. New crops (most notably cotton) were introduced. The amount of cultivable land was increased by the use of new irrigation methods. New industrial and commercial operations opened new markets to both Egyptian and foreign entrepreneurs. New railroads and communications links made these new markets more accessible. This economic transformation continued under Muhammad Ali's successors.

Modernization required technical capabilities, educational skills, and massive financing that Egypt was unable to provide. The gaps were filled by European educators, technicians, and bankers. As more and more Egyptians acquired educations and technical skills, and as the economy continued to grow, the financial debt of Egypt to her European creditors mounted. As this debt increased, the freedom of action of the monarch and his absolute authority became more and more circumscribed.

The opening of the Suez Canal in 1869 dramatically changed the economy as well as the political/strategic importance of Egypt. For Great Britain the route to India became quicker, more profitable, and more vulnerable. Shortly after the opening of the canal the Egyptian debt grew to such a level that the Egyptian monarch was placed in the rather unenviable position of being forced to sell Egypt's shares in the canal to Great Britain. In addition, he was forced to grant special concessions to Europeans, and to accept the advice of a growing number of European advisers. By 1879 Egypt and the monarchy were close to economic and political bankruptcy.

Muhammad Ali's modernization policies eventually cost Egypt its political and economic independence. The new landed aristocracy that replaced the one destroyed by Muhammad Ali and the prosperous middle class created by the industrialization and commercialization policies found that they had little political power. The monarch's modernization policy did not include increased, popular political participation. Many Egyptians began to challenge both the monarchy and the increased British presence in Egypt.

In the late 1870s and early 1880s the situation reached a crisis. The European creditors deposed Khedive (an ancient Persian title) Ismail in 1879 and replaced him with his son, Twefik. The authority of the monarch now rested with his European bankers and creditors. In response to this crisis the first truly Egyptian national revolt occurred. Colonel Ahmed Arabi representing disenfranchised and powerless Egyptians revolted against both the corrupt and indebted monarchy and their increasingly powerful British advisers. Arabi and his followers presented a serious threat to the authority and power of the monarch and to the stability of the political system. In 1882 the British military intervened and crushed the revolt, but it remained a symbol of nationalist feeling, one of the earliest manifestations of specifically Egyptian political feelings.

The Colonial Period

The crushing of the nationalist revolt led to a new period in Egypt's political development. From the defeat of Arabi in 1882 until 1919, Great Britain directly administered Egypt. The British sought the economic reorganization and recovery of Egypt. The key was efficient and effective administration. In an attempt to provide this stability and efficiency few efforts were made to expand social and welfare services, to encourage economic growth, or to change the unbalanced distribution of economic rewards. On the political front there was equally little effort made to involve Egyptians in the decision-making process.

Nationalists, excluded from active participation in the political arena, increasingly focused their attention and discontent on the British presence. "Egypt for the Egyptians" became their powerful new slogan. Organizations that were forerunners to political parties emerged to focus and articulate the nationalist demands.

Following World War I the demands for independence became more frequent and intense. These demands were now expressed through a new political party, the *Wafd* (delegation). Said Zaghlul, the leader of the party, demanded that Egypt be represented at the Paris peace talks so that he could present the Egyptian case for independence. Great Britain, hoping to reassert firm control over Egypt, refused the request. Rioting, strikes, and a general uprising spread throughout Egypt. Unlike the nationalist revolt of 1882, however, the 1919 movement forced the British to make concessions.

Both the monarchy and the British sought a compromise that would satisfy the nationalists, yet not fundamentally alter the political pattern or the distribution of authority. The initial response was to abolish the protectorate and create an "independent" monarchy under King Ahmed Fuad. Despite the nationalist rejection of this plan, the British proceeded unilaterally and in 1922 ended the protectorate, created a reformed monarchy, and drafted a new constitution.

The 1923 constitution called for a strong executive in the person of the monarch. The king had the power to appoint cabinet ministers and to dismiss Parliament and rule by decree. Although Egypt was now nominally independent, Great Britain continued to exercise the dominant power. Zaghlul until his death in 1927 and then Mustafa Nahas sought to establish a base of power for the Wafd in the Parliament. King Fuad until his death in 1936 and then King Farouk sought to exercise power through the executive monarchy. The issues in this three-cornered conflict were the continued presence of British troops in Egypt and the claims of Egypt to the Sudan.

From the perspective of the Wafd and the more militant nationalists this solution was highly unsatisfactory and frustrating. Although the Wafd won all free elections in Egypt from 1922 to 1952, they governed for less than eight years. The normal pattern of events was for the Wafd to win an election, form a government, and then watch helplessly as it was dismissed by the king. This prevented the nationalists from implementing reforms and establishing continuity in government.

The Wafd leadership found itself in an untenable position. They were not a radical party in the sense of calling for violence and violent protest, nor were they a mass party that hoped to mobilize the entire population for political action. Instinctively, when violence occurred, such as that between 1919 and 1922, they pulled back from the brink. They were, however, opposed to the British domination of Egyptian affairs and the role the monarch played in "independent" Egypt.

The increasing threat of world war in the 1930s altered the relationship between Great Britain and Egypt. The importance of Egypt to the Allied war effort was immense. To assure the support of Egypt and to maintain political stability during the war, a new alliance was negotiated between Egypt and Britain. The 1936 agreement ended many of the special privileges held by foreigners in Egypt, and permitted Egypt to join the League of Nations. In return, Great Britain was given military rights in Egypt, and was allowed to station 10,000 troops in the canal area.

The end of the war brought an almost immediate Egyptian demand for the renegotiation of the 1936 agreement. New issues were added to the already existing ones of British troops on Egyptian soil and who should control the Sudan. Among the most important were Egypt's opposition to the creation of Israel and the dismal performance of the Egyptian army in the 1948 war that established Israel. The poor performance of the army took on added significance when it was discovered that King Farouk and the palace had supplied the army with inferior and defective weapons. Both King Farouk and the Wafd were discredited—the king because of his dependence on the British and the corruption of the palace, and the Wafd because they were unable to change the situation. The Wafd appeared to many to have become a special interest group more interested in the preservation of politicians. It did not resemble the active, nationalist political party that increasing numbers of Egyptians wanted.

Old demands were now being expressed by new groups. One new group was the Muslim Brotherhood, founded in 1928. Hassan al-Banna, the leader, called for a state based not on Western, secular traditions, but on Islamic principles and cultures. He clearly stated his view of Egypt's decline in the 1920s:

Young men were lost, and the educated were in a state of doubt and confusion. . .
I saw that the social life of the beloved Egyptian nation was oscillating between her dear and precious Islamism which she had inherited, defended, lived with and become accustomed to, and made powerful during thirteen centuries, and this severe Western invasion which is armed and equipped with all the destructive and degenerative influences of money, wealth, prestige, ostentation, material enjoyment, power, and means of propaganda.[11]

Hassan al-Banna's movement struck a chord among many Egyptians, especially among those less politically "sophisticated." By the 1930s and

---

[11] Quoted in Christina Phelps Harris, *Nationalism and Revolution in Egypt* (The Hague: Mouton, 1964), p. 146.

1940s the movement had widespread popular support and presented the authorities with a real threat. Had it not been for his assassination in 1949, Hassan al-Banna and the Muslim Brotherhood might have exercised even greater political importance.

A second political force was less ideological than the Muslim Brotherhood, but equally dissatisfied. Junior military officers, many from lower- and middle-class backgrounds, organized a secret society within the military. The Free Officers, whose membership included Gamal Abdul Nasser and Anwar Sadat, opposed the British military presence, the corruption of the old regime, and favored the establishment of a truly independent Egyptian nation. The defeat of the Egyptian army in 1948 and the subsequent arms scandal magnified their discontent.

Gamal Nasser, like many of his fellow members in the Free Officers, fought in the 1948 war that led to the establishment of Israel. The Palestine experience helped to focus Nasser's discontent and clarify his goals. While Israel was one enemy, the major enemies of Egypt were the monarchy and the British military presence. He wrote:

When I now try to recall the details of our experience in Palestine, I find a curious thing: we were fighting in Palestine, but our dreams were centered in Egypt. Our bullets were aimed at the enemy before us, but our hearts hovered over our distant country, which we had left to the care of wolves.[12]

Political discontent became more violent. Neither the monarchy nor the Wafd were able to reestablish order and control. In January 1952 widespread burning and rioting in Cairo resulted in many deaths. Finally, on July 23, 1952, the Free Officers intervened and deposed King Farouk. Shortly thereafter the monarchy was abolished, the Wafd banned, the power of the potential rival Muslim Brotherhood broken, and the British forced to remove all troops from Egyptian territory.

The Free Officer movement and the political ideas they represented were influenced by the long nationalist struggle in Egypt. The universal goal, stated clearly and unequivocally, was: "All of us dream of an Egypt free and strong."[13] In order to achieve this goal, Egyptians needed to create and assert a strong Egyptian nationalism. This nationalism developed in response to the rule of a foreign and corrupt monarchy and the imposition of colonial rule. The revolts of 1882 and 1919 both had their genesis in the growing demands by Egyptians for control over their own political fate. The success of the 1952 revolution forced Egypt's new Egyptian leaders to consider not only problems of nation-building but also those of institution-building.

---

[12] Gamal Abdul Nasser, *Egypt's Liberation: The Philosophy of the Revolution* (Washington, D.C.: Public Affairs Press, 1955), p. 21.

[13] Ibid., p. 49.

General Muhammad Neguib (right) and Colonel Gamal Abdul Nasser (left) shortly after the 1952 revolution that ended the Egyptian monarchy. Keystone Press.

■ TANZANIA ■

Tanzania is a young nation. It represents the diversity and complexity of nation-building in the twentieth century. Many of the nation-state building patterns that occurred in Europe from the sixteenth to the nineteenth century are now being repeated in newly independent states like Tanzania.

However, there are important differences between the nation-building sequences in Europe and more modern nations like Tanzania. New factors influence the development process and in many ways make it more difficult. For one, Tanzania, like many other new nations, must create both a new nation and a new state at the same time; new political values that stress national identity and loyalty must develop alongside and reinforce new political structures. The development process also has been collapsed in time. What took centuries to evolve in Europe must now be accomplished in a much shorter period. This telescoping of the development process results in directed, rather than evolutionary, change. Finally, Tanzanian leaders are limited in their freedom and action. They operate within a complex web of international political and economic relations.

No nation in the world can any longer operate totally independently from others.

The Pre-Colonial Period—Before "Tanzania"

The idea of a geographically definable area known as Tanzania is a recent one; the related concepts of a Tanzanian community and culture are even more recent. From the late nineteenth century until the defeat of Germany in World War I, East Africa was the colonial holding of imperial Germany. From the end of World War I until 1961 the former German territory was known as Tanganyika and administered by Great Britain. Tanzania was born in 1964 with the merger of independent mainland Tanganyika and the island of Zanzibar.

The history of the area, however, goes back much farther than colonization by the Germans. Before the age of imperialism and colonialism, East Africa was made up of many city-states on the coast, a few large, well-organized, politically sophisticated political kingdoms in the interior, and many smaller, highly decentralized tribal groups. The coastal cities, under the control of Arabs from the Persian Gulf, dominated the area. Their primary economic activity was trade in gold and ivory.

Interaction between Arab and African created a new culture and a new language, Swahili. Both the Swahili language and culture were influenced strongly by Islamic law, political traditions, and customs. The new culture, concentrated along the East African coast, was a unique combination of Arab and African civilizations.

During the sixteenth century, the Portuguese challenged the Arab and Swahili domination of the profitable trade routes. The explorer Vasco da Gama rounded the Cape of Good Hope in 1498, and soon after Portuguese explorers and traders followed. They dominated the coastal trade for almost a century until their defeat by the Arabs from Oman. Trade now involved not only gold and ivory but also slaves.

Slaving radically altered the relationship between the coast and the interior. Contact increased as slavers pushed inward, depleting the population of many parts of the interior in massive slave raids, in order to meet the growing world demand.

During this period there were few, if any, permanent European settlers or residents in East Africa. At the turn of the nineteenth century, Omani Arabs were the dominant political and economic force, and the sultan of Oman, Sayyid Said, was primarily concerned with the protection of his economic empire. He was little concerned with the political, social, or cultural unification of the diverse peoples of East Africa. The importance of this area to the Omani Arabs was symbolized by Sayyid Said's decision in 1840 to officially move his capital and his entourage from Oman to the island of Zanzibar. From here he could more effectively manage the growing clove plantations on the island and his coastal trading empire.

During the early nineteenth century the Sultan of Zanzibar, pictured here with his entourage, dominated the political and economic life in East Africa. Radio Times Hulton Picture Library.

The general lack of European interest in East Africa did not last. By the middle of the nineteenth century a series of events combined to produce a new European interest. Previously, the major contacts between East Africa, Zanzibar, and Europe were based on relatively low levels of trade. Political contact was the responsibility of powerful British consuls stationed in the city of Zanzibar.

The abolition of slavery by the British in 1807, and thereafter by the French and Dutch, focused new attention on one of the major slaving areas in the world. The mere abolition of slavery was not enough to end so lucrative a concern; abolition had to be followed by enforcement. The sultan continued to trade in slaves, and as reports of his cruel treatment of slaves reached Europe, European abolitionists called for more direct intervention. In many eyes, the root of all trouble in East Africa was the continued presence in the area of Arab slavers.

A new age of European exploration spurred new interest in Africa. Legendary explorers like Henry Stanley, David Livingston, Sir Richard Burton, and Samuel Baker, among others, explored the interior of East Africa and freely published their exploits. The search for the headwaters of the Nile led to European "discovery" of new political kingdoms, potential new resources, and a competition for strategic control.

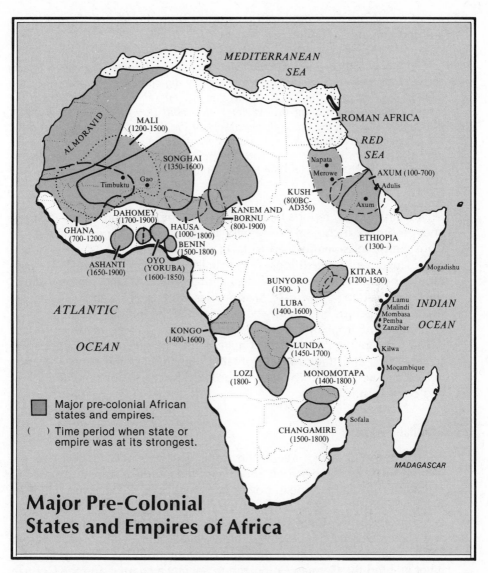

MEDITERRANEAN
SEA

ROMAN AFRICA

MALI
(1200-1500)

ALMORAVID

RED
SEA

SONGHAI
(1350-1600)

Napata

Merowe

AXUM (100-700)

Adulis

Timbuktu   Gao

KUSH
(800BC-
AD350)

Axum

DAHOMEY
(1700-1900)

KANEM AND
BORNU
(800-1900)

GHANA
(700-1200)

HAUSA
(1000-1800)

BENIN
(1500-1800)

ETHIOPIA
(1300-)

Mogadishu

ASHANTI
(1650-1900)

OYO
(YORUBA)
(1600-1850)

KITARA
(1200-1500)

BUNYORO
(1500-)

ATLANTIC

LUBA
(1400-1600)

Lamu
Malindi
Mombasa
Pemba
Zanzibar

INDIAN

OCEAN

OCEAN

KONGO
(1400-1600)

LUNDA
(1450-1700)

Kilwa

Moçambique

LOZI
(1800-)

MONOMOTAPA
(1400-1800)

Major pre-colonial African
states and empires.

( ) Time period when state or
empire was at its strongest.

Sofala

CHANGAMIRE
(1500-1800)

MADAGASCAR

Major Pre-Colonial
States and Empires of Africa

Source: John N. Paden and Edward W. Soja, eds., *The African Experience,* Vol. 1 (Evanston, Ill.: Northwestern University Press, 1970), p. 178. Reprinted by permission.

Henry Stanley, explorer, controversial author, and newspaperman for the *New York Herald* initially achieved fame when he successfully carried out his charge: "Seek out Livingston and ascertain from him what discoveries he had made."[14] Reports on uncharted Africa captured the inter-

---

[14] Norman R. Bennett, *Stanley's Despatches to the New York Herald 1871–1872, 1874–1877* (Boston: Boston University Press, 1970), p. 4.

est of many. Stanley's description captures both the fear of the unknown and the romance of adventure:

Fatal Africa! One after another, travellers drop away. It is such a huge continent, and each of its secrets is environed by so many difficulties,—the torrid heat, the miasma exhaled from the soil, the noisome vapours enveloping every path, the giant cane-grass suffocating the wayfarer, the rabid fury of the native guarding every entry and exit, the unspeakable misery of the life within the wild continent, the utter absence of every comfort, the bitterness which each day heaps upon the poor white man's head, in that land of blackness, the sombrous solemnity pervading every feature of it, and the little—too little—promise of success which one feels on entering it.[15]

Not surprisingly, reports like this attracted the attention of missionaries, and produced increased missionary activity. To gain new converts to Christianity, missionaries had to face, according to one, "slavery, polygamy, sanguinary superstition, and sensual habits, some of which are promoted through the sanction of rites and ceremonies, and others through universal custom."[16] By 1878 missionaries were well on their way to establishing missions both along the coast and in the interior.

Gradually, European leaders became more and more involved in East Africa. The opening of the Suez Canal in 1869 made communications and travel easier, and trade more profitable. Zanzibari domination was challenged by a new and more powerful political force—European imperialism and colonialism.

The Colonial Period

The European powers, meeting in Berlin in 1884–1885, established the ground rules for the partition and the colonization of Africa. In order to claim a territory, a European power had to occupy it. Once the rules had been established, the "scramble for Africa" began. In 1884 the German explorer and adventurer Carl Peters entered the interior of Tanganyika and signed several treaties, of dubious legal claim, with African chiefs. These treaties gave Germany the right of protection. The German government granted the German Colonization Society a charter, and the German East African Company was established. By 1888 the Germans had formally occupied the coast, and in 1890 the German government formally took complete control. The new colony was named German East Africa. The sultan protested his loss, but there was little that he could do without

---

[15] Dorthy Stanley, ed., *The Autobiography of Sir Henry Morton Stanley* (Boston: Houghton Mifflin, 1909), pp. 296–297.

[16] M. A. Pringle, *A Journey in East Africa: Towards the Mountains of the Moon* (Freeport, N.Y.: Books for Libraries Press, 1972), p. xv. Originally published in 1884 as *Towards the Mountains of the Moon.*

British support and assistance. However, in return for recognition of several of their claims in Africa, the former protectors of the sultan agreed to the German claim of a "sphere of influence."

The creation of the German colony began the formal period of colonization and, at the same time, the initial phases of decolonization. Prior to this time there was no sense of Tanganyikan nationhood or nationalism. The establishment of fixed territorial boundaries, the creation of a colonial administrative structure, and the development of territory-wide communication and transportation systems structured the pattern of political activity. It defined the new arena of politics. For better or worse, it united diverse peoples and tribes, often with nothing in common, under one administration.

Before they could administer their new territory, the Germans had to pacify it. The early period of German rule was characterized by harshness and repression as various African tribes challenged the supremacy of the Germans. The most violent of these resistances occurred in 1905–1906 when many different southern tribes joined together to fight German control. The Maji-Maji rebellion resulted in the death of over 100,000 Africans, and represented one of the earliest attempts of Africans of different tribes to unite together in a common cause.

German administration of the colony was based on local units. Because there were so few Germans in the territory and because of the diversity of the population, strong, centralized administration proved difficult. Different policies were required for different areas and different peoples. This diversity had the effect of giving the local district officer wide latitude in the exercise of his office. In some cases, Muslim Arab or African *akidas* (administrators) were employed to carry out the day-to-day tasks of administration.

Colonial power and administration passed to Great Britain after Germany's defeat in World War I. Britain renamed her new mandate Tanganyika. Colonial administration, at its peak, sought to govern through indirect rule. Both philosophical reasons and practical concerns led the British, where possible, to maintain traditional patterns of authority. By preserving existing structures of government, usually chieftainship, administrators were able to cut costs, and hopefully minimize the need for coercion. The chief maintained his position, but his authority was derived from the colonial system. In cases where it was difficult or impossible to locate or administer through a traditional structure, the British attempted to create a traditional structure, or, in the last resort, rule directly.

This policy had the practical effect of preserving traditional African institutions and cultural patterns. One of the primary targets of nationalist leaders was the system of indirect rule. They argued that indirect rule fragmented and divided the population, making territory-wide political and social movements difficult. Indirect rule was "divide and rule." Nationalists also argued that traditional rule gave undue power to the con-

servative chiefs. The young, the newly educated, and the "modern" elements of society were frozen out of the system. In short, the policy hindered the realization of the nationalists' goals—the development of
territory-wide values regardless of tribe and the development of a national,
centralized political movement.

The Nationalist Movement and Independence

The nationalist movement gained steam gradually. Nationalists seeking
greater participation first needed to form organizations that would cut
across the established divisions in the territory. The Tanganyikan African
Association (TAA) was one of the first such movements. Established in
1930, its early aims were not specifically political but the protection and
the promotion of the small number of educated, urban Africans in Tanganyika. As the number of educated Africans increased, the small and
narrow base from which the TAA could draw began to expand.

The colonial system in its purest form was an administrative, rather than
a political, system. It was designed to administer efficiently a territory, not
provide means for political participation. The members of the Legislative
Council in Tanganyika were not popularly elected, and until 1945 there
were no African members. The major role of the council was to assist the
colonial governor in the task of administration. Only after World War II
when Africans demanded the right to participate did the Legislative Council begin to resemble a truly representative institution.

Following the war the British introduced a series of gradual reforms
designed to allow for the evolutionary development of democratic political institutions and the creation of a positive, national identity. The aim
was disengagement through reform. At the same time that the colonial
authorities began to "allow" greater African participation, the Africans
themselves began making demands not only for participation within the
colonial system, but for independence itself. The debate centered on the
nature of the proposed reforms, and on the pace of decolonization. The
British favored a "go-slow," gradual approach, the Africans a more rapid,
radical one. The Legislative Council was transformed from a body that
represented European and Asian opinion and was subordinate to the will
of the colonial governor to a body that represented African, European, and
Asian opinion, and increasingly challenged the authority of the governor.

More and more Africans became politically conscious and active during
this period. They were receptive to new political ideas, like nationalism
and independence, and they became more willing to join modern political institutions like the Tanganyikan African National Union (TANU). In
part, this was a response to educational and social changes occurring in
Tanzania. For example, in 1913 it was estimated that only 9 percent of
school-age children were receiving any type of education (and less than
2 percent of these children were receiving government or government-

Chronology of Events

TANZANIA

1840	Sultan Sayyid Said moves his court from Oman to Zanzibar, and exercises control over much of East Africa.
1884–1885	German explorers claim much of East Africa.
1890	German government establishes and assumes control over German East Africa.
1919	Great Britain assumes control of colony of German East Africa. Colony renamed Tanganyika.
1959–1961	The Tanganyikan African National Union (TANU) achieves large electoral victories in a series of pre-independence elections.
1961 (December)	Tanganyika achieves independence. Julius Nyerere, leader of TANU, becomes head of government.
1963 (December)	Zanzibar achieves independence.
1964 (April)	Tanganyika and Zanzibar merge to form Tanzania.
1965 (September)	General election. TANU, the only political party, offers competing slates of candidates.
1967	TANU issues the Arusha Declaration outlining the development plans of Tanzania.
1970 (October) 1975 (October)	General elections. TANU, the only party, offers competing slates of candidates.
1977	TANU and the Afro-Shirazi party of Zanzibar officially merge to form *Chama cha Mapinduzi* (Revolutionary party). New constitution making party supreme is introduced.

---

aided education).[17] By 1948, 15.5 percent of school-age children were enrolled in primary school, and by 1965 the figure had grown to 42.4 percent.[18] In Tanzanian society in general the literacy rate rose from 3.1 percent in 1940 to 8.7 percent in 1954, and to 16 percent in 1961.[19] As newly educated young people grew to adulthood, they served as active members of the emerging political organizations.

Increased educational opportunities and literacy were not the only major changes. For better or worse, the colonial experience increased the

---

[17] Hugh W. Stephens, *The Political Transformation of Tanganyika: 1920–1967* (New York: Praeger, 1968), p. 49.

[18] David R. Morrison, *Education and Politics in Africa: The Tanzanian Case* (London: C. Hurst, 1976), p. 322.

[19] Stephens, *The Political Transformation of Tanganyika: 1920–1967*, pp. 63, 108.

number of Tanganyikans employed in the modern cash economy and the number of people exposed to modernity. Many of these people provided the core of early support for TANU. They saw that their lives could be improved, and they were willing to organize to change their circumstances. TANU very effectively tapped this discontent.

The presence of European and Asian communities in Tanganyika complicated the decolonization process. Although not numerically large when compared with the African population, the 23,000 Europeans and the 87,000 Asians held a disproportionate share of the economic and political power. The colonial governor responded to demands for greater participation by expanding the size of the Legislative Council and allowing a certain percentage of its members to be elected. Representation was based on multi-racialism and parity. Parity meant that regardless of the African, European, and Asian populations, each group would have the same number of seats on the Legislative Council. Thus, despite their numerical majority, Africans were to be left a permanent legislative minority.

Not surprisingly, most Africans were opposed to this plan. Julius Nyerere, a schoolteacher recently returned from studying in Great Britain, transformed the Tanganyikan African Association in 1954 from an interest and protective organization into a political party. The demands that Nyerere incorporated into the party platform of the Tanganyikan African National Union were reformist, yet much more radical and sweeping than any made previously. Nyerere called for a nationwide movement not restricted to specific African tribes, language groups, or regions. TANU demanded democratic elections to democratic institutions, African majorities, independence, and an end to racialism and parity. Nyerere mobilized not only the educated and urban Africans but also, for the first time, the rural masses.

The new political organizations faced their first tests in the scheduled elections for the Legislative Council in 1958 and 1959. Despite the attempts of the colonial administration to frustrate and control TANU, and despite voting restrictions that limited the number of Africans who could vote, TANU candidates won sweeping majorities. TANU won even greater victories in the 1960 elections. TANU candidates won 70 or 71 seats, and for 58 of these there was no opposition. It was clear to all that TANU had emerged as the dominant political institution in Tanganyika, and that Nyerere was the dominant, national political leader. In October 1960 Nyerere became chief minister of the newly formed cabinet, and the following May Tanganyika achieved internal self-government. Complete independence came in December 1961.

Many of the problems that faced pre-independent Tanganyika and TANU face independent Tanzania and TANU. Problems of economic underdevelopment and foreign dependence, cultural diversity, the complexity of building new political institutions that effectively perform and are responsive, and the need to create and maintain national loyalties did not disappear with the end of colonialism. In some respects the problems have become more acute with the removal of the common colonial enemy.

Nation-building in Tanzania occurred relatively recently and developed quickly. African and Tanzanian nationalism was, on the one hand, a response to colonial control and racial domination. On the other hand, it involved the positive creation of a new identity and a new, national culture. Unlike the Nigerian experience, the nationalist struggle in Tanzania was a unifying one, representing the efforts of the entire population. At independence, Tanzania leaders turned their attention to maintaining the new political and cultural identity and to the problems of creating new, national political institutions.

▪ CHILE ▪

Chile's long history is witness to many different patterns of politics. Chileans have been governed by strong parliamentary governments, strong executive governments, and military governments. Since independence, Chile has undergone significant social, economic, and cultural changes. These forces have led to a gradual increase in participation by new groups and classes and to the placing of new issues on the agenda of politics. Despite these many changes, prior to the coup d'état against the late President Salvadore Allende in 1973, Chile was considered to be one of the most politically stable and democratic of the Latin American nations. Recent Chilean history has been strongly influenced by the Chilean colonial experience and early attempts at nation-building.

The Colonial Period

The first Spanish explorers and conquistadors arrived in Chile from Peru in the early sixteenth century. Members of the army of the legendary Francisco Pizarro established the city of Santiago in the central region of present-day Chile in 1541. Almost immediately these early settlers found themselves at war with the indigenous Indian population concentrated south of the first early settlements. As the colony expanded, the conflict between Spaniard and Indian became more severe. The War of Arauco, the general name given to the Indian wars, began in 1553 and lasted well into the seventeenth century. These wars resulted in the subjugation and defeat of the Indian population and the development of an early sense of separateness and uniqueness among the Spanish colonialists. The early wars and the privations facing the colonialists began the process of forming a separate Chilean identity later manifested as Chilean nationalism.

Chronology of Events

CHILE

1535	First Spanish conquistadors arrive in Chile from Peru.
1818	Chile achieves independence from Spain. Bernardo O'Higgins, a military hero, becomes first president.
1823–1830	Conflict between Liberal and Conservative aristocrats over the nature of the new political system.
1833	Conservative constitution creates a presidential-congressional political system. Government dominated by conservative, aristocratic elite.
1879	"War of the Pacific" with Peru and Bolivia begins. Chile increases in land size by one-third.
1891	Civil war between those favoring and those opposing reform. Conservative congressional forces triumph over Liberal presidential forces. Strong parliamentary system created.
1925	Period of strong parliamentary government ends. New constitution creates a strong president and limits the power of Congress.
1964	Eduardo Frei of the Christian Democratic party elected president. Christian Democratic platform calls for democratic reform.
1970	Communist/Socialist coalition candidate Salvadore Allende elected president. Coalition calls for radical reform of Chilean society and economy.
1973	Allende government overthrown in a violent military coup d'état and President Allende killed. New military junta, headed by General Augusto Pinochet.

The early political and social organization of the new colony was based on a modified Spanish colonial system. Large landed estates, or *latafundia,* were worked by the subjugated Indians. The government consisted of a governor, provincial governors (increasingly important as the colony expanded), and town councils. There was also an *Audiencia* (Supreme Court of the colony) that ultimately was responsible for making policy as well as arbitrating disputes. The great distance between crown and colony allowed the colonialists much greater independence and control than might otherwise have been the case. The geographical isolation reinforced the separateness of the settlers, gave power to the growing landed aristocracy, and began the process of creating a unique Chilean culture and Chilean people.

In 1810 Napoleon conquered Spain. Spain no longer was the invincible colonial power. Between 1810 and 1814 Bernardo O'Higgins, a Chilean living in Argentina, took advantage of the weakened Spain and organized an army to fight for Chilean independence. O'Higgins, whose father was an Irish immigrant, joined with the South American liberator, San Martin, to defeat the Chilean Spanish loyalists in 1817.

O'Higgins' tenure as the first Chilean president or Supreme Director from 1817 to 1823 was stormy. Although only those of the aristocratic class were actively engaged in politics, they were sharply divided. When O'Higgins attempted to introduce a series of reforms, the conservative land-owning classes resisted. Attempts to raise taxes, abolish titles, and exercise greater government control over the church eventually led to revolt, and O'Higgins' resignation. He died in Peruvian exile in 1842.

O'Higgins' exile did not resolve the conflict between the conservatives and the reformists. Between 1823 and 1829 both groups struggled for power. The conservative land-owning classes were referred to as *pelucones* or "bigwigs" after the popular wigs they wore. The liberals or *pipiolos* were "novices" or "beginners." Both groups represented the upper aristocratic classes but differed on the form of politics they thought most desirable for Chile. The temporary victory of the pipiolos ended in 1829 with the decisive military victory of the bigwigs.

Bigwig victory ushered in a 30-year period of unchallenged conservative supremacy. Independence from Spain did not bring with it a social or political revolution. Many of the colonial institutions remained intact. The period following independence has been described as "the Spanish mon-

Bernardo O'Higgins (born 1778, died 1842) was Chile's national liberator and the first leader of an independent Chile. He was forced to resign from office in 1823 and died in Peruvian exile. Radio Times Hulton Picture Library.

archy in republican dress."[20] The landed aristocracy jealously guarded their privileges.

The political system created by the pelucones was designed to protect their position. Political participation was limited. The constitution of 1833 limited the franchise to males over 25 (if single), who were literate, and who held property. Only 10 percent of the population qualified. Diego Portales, the architect of the constitution and one of the most important political figures during this period, favored a strong central government that protected the position and privilege of the landowners and encouraged economic development. This is not surprising from a man who had been granted monopolies on tobacco, tea, and liquor in Chile. In short, the oligarchic regime emphasized political stability, and was not dissimilar from many of the European governments of the same period.

The conservative, aristocratic, autocratic regime established by Portales gave Chile 30 years of political stability, economic growth, and educational expansion. The powers of the president were relatively unchecked by the Congress. It is difficult, however, to maintain political stability during periods of rapid economic change. Chile was being transformed from a feudal or semi-feudal society to an increasingly modern, capitalist, market-oriented economy competing for world markets; as these changes occurred, challenges to conservative control became more frequent.

As education and urbanization increased and as the economy prospered, the once relatively homogeneous upper class was fragmented. New political ideas, strongly influenced by current British and French political philosophies, emerged. Chileans began to demand reform and the right to participate. Political parties became important organizations for representing these new interests. The Liberals, reformists not revolutionaries, wanted wider political participation and greater governmental control over the activities of the Catholic church. The moderates supported the president over the Congress and drew most of their members from the more conservative Nationalists. The Nationalists represented the traditional, conservative old guard that had held power since 1830.

One area where the dispute was particularly intense was over who would control the increasing number of political offices. From 1860 to 1890 the Liberals controlled the office of the president. This was made possible when more and more Chileans were allowed to vote. The property requirement for voters was dropped in 1884, and in 1888 all males over age 21 were given the vote.

During this same period the Nationalists controlled the Congress. As presidents initiated and recommended more and more reforms, the Congress became more intransigent. The outcome, civil war, appeared inevitable. Only an external threat, the War of the Pacific (1879–1883)

---

[20] Harry Kantor, *Patterns of Politics and Political Systems in Latin America* (Chicago: Rand McNally, 1969), p. 543.

between Chile, Peru, and Bolivia postponed resolution of the crisis. The war temporarily united the nation against Bolivia and Peru and increased the size of Chile by a third (the nitrate-rich northern provinces added both to the size and the economy of Chile); it did not, however, resolve the internal political crisis.

The crisis between Liberals and Conservatives peaked in 1891. Once again as in 1829 the Conservatives defeated the disorganized and fragmented Liberals. This time the victors sought to ensure that the power of a Liberal president would never again challenge the power of a Conservative Congress.

The Parliamentary Period

The power of the president was curbed by the establishment of a strong parliamentary government, which removed some of the president's political authority and made it difficult for him to act. New political parties emerged to contest the congressional elections.

The political stability that characterized earlier Conservative governments was replaced with instability. From 1831 to 1886 there were 31 different Chilean cabinets; from 1891 to 1925 there were 121 cabinets with over 530 different ministers.[21] No one political party was able to achieve a clear parliamentary majority, and there were shifting coalitions among the various parties. Parties and legislators were concerned more with playing parliamentary politics than with governing the country.

One reason for the increased instability and number of political parties was Chile's continuing economic growth. During the parliamentary period the rapidly growing mining industry helped to industrialize Chile. The demands for participation now spread to the middle and lower classes. Classes that were previously politically inactive became more politicized and organized new parties. Labor unions and socialist political parties stressed that growth was not enough; what was needed was more equal distribution of society's economic rewards.

As long as the economy continued to grow, albeit unevenly, the parliamentary system muddled through. However, the collapse of the nitrate market following World War I, the rapidly increasing inflation, and general economic stagnation focused attention on parliamentary inactivity and the inability of the parliamentarians to solve the nation's increasingly severe economic ills.

In 1920 Arturo Alessandri, combining political astuteness and personal charisma, united the Liberals and the Socialists, and captured the presidency. Once in office, he and his followers attempted a sweeping series of reforms that met with congressional resistance. The bickering ended temporarily when the Congress refused to pass reforms but did have time

---

[21] Federico G. Gil, *The Political System of Chile* (Boston: Houghton Mifflin, 1966), p. 49–50.

to pass themselves a pay raise; the military intervened, and the focus of power shifted back to the office of president.

The Modern Constitutional Period

The new constitution of 1925 (which remained in effect until the 1973 coup d'état) created a strong executive rather than a strong Congress. The president was elected by direct vote for a six-year term (but not allowed to succeed himself). Congress could no longer issue a vote of no confidence and bring down the government. The constitution called for a republican government that protected the rights of individual citizens and groups. The church, so powerful under previous constitutions, lost much of its special status.

The most pressing crisis facing the politicians and the new system was the economy. Throughout the 1920s and 1930s governments rose and fell based on their ability to manage economic problems. Presidents were temporarily replaced by military dictators, who were then replaced by newly elected presidents. The politics of the presidents during this period ranged from conservative to Popular Front coalitions (during the late 1930s) which included Communist, Socialist, and middle-of-the-road parties.

There was a political party to represent every shade of political opinion. The tendency, however, was for political parties to coalesce into identifiable blocs. Parties of the left, center, and right joined together at election time to form coalitions. Often these coalitions would collapse after the election was over, but they did provide voters with clear-cut alternatives. A voter could vote for a candidate of the left, center, or right coalition.

It was also clear that the mood of the electorate had changed. The Conservatives continued to win their share of electoral victories, but power slowly shifted from the conservative upper class to the Socialists and the reformers who represented the middle and lower classes. The political arena expanded to include not only the wealthy and the landowners but the more militant middle and lower classes. More and more Chileans became politically active and made political demands. The question was not whether change and reform were necessary, but how best to implement change for the benefit of most people.

Conservative dominance collapsed in the 1964 presidential election. The election was a contest between two reform parties. Eduardo Frei and the Christian Democratic party campaigned for major reform through democratic means. Salvadore Allende and the Socialist and Communist coalition campaigned for more radical and far-reaching change. With the support of the right and the center, the Christian Democratic candidate, Frei, won the election. In the 1970 election the Christian Democrats were defeated by a more radical coalition led by Allende. In 1973 the military intervened, ended the rule of Allende, and suspended the 1925 constitution.

Prior to the coup d'état in 1973, Chilean history was characterized by evolutionary change. More and more Chileans won the right to vote and to participate. New groups formed new political parties that made new demands on leaders. Power gradually passed from a small, aristocratic, land-owning elite, to the growing commercial classes, and finally to the middle and lower classes. To respond to these new situations, Chilean leaders experimented with both parliamentary and presidential government. Since 1973 the military has offered yet another form of government.

CONCLUSION

The history of these eight nation-states has offered a variety of political patterns and problems. The first observation that can be made is quite obvious. First, these nations are not equally "nations." Second, they are not equally "states" insofar as they vary greatly in their ability to marshal state power to cope with their problems.

The differences in national unity and institutional strength among the eight nation-states are products of their histories. Among developed nations, France and Germany had disruptive histories strewn with wars and domestic unrest. As a result these nations have developed a weaker sense of national community and more fragile political institutions than those of the British whose history was less troubled.

The Soviet Union is the product of forced revolutionary change. The stagnant and static system of the tsars delayed evolutionary change and ensured that drastic solutions would follow. The Communist party elite has transformed Russian social, economic, and political life by coercion and by channeling all resources to the task of building state power. Creating a national sense of community has received a lower priority. Ethnic groups and dissident groups have been controlled through coercion.

All of the developing nations are currently struggling to strengthen their institutions and create national communities. Tanzania and Nigeria have only recently emerged from colonial status. The boundaries drawn by the colonial powers left each with multiethnic societies. The long period of colonial administration also left them at independence without trained personnel or institutions that grew out of their own traditions.

Egypt and Chile do not share the ethnic confusion of the other developing nations, but do have serious difficulties with creating effective political institutions. The problem of state-building in these countries is the result of a lack of the resources needed to build state power. Deficiencies in the economic realm are reflected in the skills of their public officials and the resources that can be brought to bear in solving problems and meeting demands.

This chapter has given us the necessary groundwork for understanding the political divisions and group life of these eight nations. The origins of political differences between groups have been introduced. This chapter has also provided information on the capacities of the eight nation-states to handle group differences as expressed in political demands. Chapter 3 is devoted to the group life of the nations in our study.

CHAPTER 3
GROUP LIFE

Why do cleavages make politics difficult?

For the citizen in the modern nation-state the nation is the most important object of his or her political loyalty. The nation-state is the ultimate source of political authority. In many nations there is little question that leaders and citizens alike have a deep affection for and loyalty to the national political institutions; however, in other political systems, there may be more than one object of political loyalty. When this occurs, the result is often political conflict.

In Chapter 2 the historical evolution and development of each of the eight nation-states was described and compared. Attention was focused on those factors that separate one nation from another. Another way to compare nations is to study the differences that separate people within the nation. The political boundaries of the nation often include individuals and groups that do not share the same characteristics or political values. Chapter 3 discusses the various patterns of group life within nations, and assesses the potential political importance of these groups.

Cleavages—Forces That Divide the Nation

A society can be looked at in terms of the groups that comprise it. Groups may be formed because people share similar characteristics such as language, race, ethnicity, or religion. Other groups may be formed on the basis of similar interests, values, or goals. Whatever the foundation for the group, the members share a set of characteristics, values, interests, or goals that distinguish them from others within the society.

Cleavages are those critical, distinguishing divisions within a society. In some nations the differences between groups may have little or no political significance, while in other nations the same cleavages may provoke sharp disagreement and conflict. In order to understand the domestic politics of the nation-state, it is important to describe and determine the importance of the most common political cleavages.

Certain cleavages appear to be more important than others to the political life of the nation. Among the most important are primordial ties. *Primordial cleavages* are those fundamental and basic differences between peoples that are either impossible or very difficult to change. Distinctions based on kinship, race, ethnicity, language, religion, or historical experience may be thought of as primordial cleavages. These ties are often much stronger than the ties individuals or groups have to their nation. People would rather join together on the basis of one or more of these traits than on the basis of loyalty to the nation.

Nigeria provides a good example of a nation made up of many different primordial groups. The three major groups, the Hausa-Fulani, the Yoruba, and the Ibo, each have their own language, historical traditions, and sense of ethnic identity. These bonds hold each group together, but they make it difficult for the groups to work together as a single nation. The civil war in Nigeria from 1967 to 1970 is evidence of just how difficult it can sometimes be for different groups to work together.

In most cases groups are separated by several distinguishing characteristics; these characteristics tend to reinforce and strengthen the group's "separateness." Language, for example, is both a means of communication between speakers and a storehouse for the culture and traditions of the language group. Different language groups have a problem understanding each other because they do not speak the same language and because they may not understand the culture associated with a foreign language. Language barriers are among the most difficult barriers to cross. Nations with more than one language must make several difficult choices; they must choose a national official language acceptable to all groups, a language to be used in schools, and a *lingua franca* or language that can be used to communicate between different groups. These are difficult political decisions since few groups in the world willingly give up their language for another.

Religious differences also divide peoples. Religion provides a way of organizing one's life, and in many cases influences political thought and action. There are two common patterns of potential religious conflict. Conflict may occur between different religions or religious traditions, or it may occur over the role of the church in the political arena.

France and Chile, for example, have experienced severe conflicts over the proper role of the Roman Catholic church in politics; some people favor a strong relationship between church and state, while others argue just as forcibly for a strict separation of church and state. In Germany the conflict was not so much over the relationship between church and state as the relationship between Protestant and Catholic. Whatever the pattern, religious differences provide the potential for political conflict.

In many African societies the most important cleavages affecting political life are ethnic or tribal. Ethnic groups have unique social and political institutions, unique myths of common origin, different definitions for membership in the community, and oftentimes, specific religious traditions, languages, and regional locations. "Tribal conflict" is not, however, unique to Africa. Differences between the Welsh, the English, and the Scots often appear, at least on the surface, to bear a remarkable resemblance to conflicts between Hausa, Ibo, and Yoruba in Nigeria.

Cleavages other than primordial ones also can strongly influence the political life of a nation. Depending on the issues, these cleavages may be just as important, or more so, than those described above. One of the most powerful divisions is that between the rural and urban populations, a cleavage found in almost all nation-states. In this circumstance differences are based not so much on shared individual characteristics, but on shared perspectives, perceptions, and interests. The problems facing the farmer are different from those facing the factory worker in a large city. People growing up in rural areas experience different patterns of socialization and undergo different experiences than those growing up in an urban environment. As a result, these two groups often have very different values and expectations about life and politics.

Class is another cleavage that divides many nation-states. Relatively stable, evolutionary systems such as Great Britain and France, as well as rapidly changing systems such as those in Nigeria and Chile, must face political conflicts and issues caused by class. Supposedly classless societies like the Soviet Union even admit that the problem of class has yet to be fully resolved. Divisions between the upper, middle, and lower classes often reinforce other cleavages such as those between the educated and the uneducated, between the rural and the urban, and between ethnic or racial groups. Liza Doolittle and Professor Henry Higgins in *My Fair Lady* epitomize many of the class distinctions found in Great Britain. In many nations a person's class is his or her most important label and characteristic; it is also the most important factor in explaining a person's political outlook and behavior.

Each of the eight nations in our study exhibits a different pattern of group life. Relationships among different groups are influenced by historical tradition, by the policies of the political leaders, and by the values and actions of the political participants. We can, however, make several useful generalizations about group life.

First, and perhaps most important, cleavage patterns do not remain stable. Economic, political, and social developments, as well as specific events such as wars or revolutions, alter relationships among groups. In older nations the sharpest conflicts between different groups may already have been resolved and their importance receded with the passage of time. Issues that may have led to war, revolution, or rioting a hundred years ago have been relegated to the history books.

The relationship between church and state in many nations is a good example. Although the question still evokes debate in Great Britain, France, Chile, and Germany it has been resolved as a major issue either in favor of one side or the other. In the Soviet Union, which is avowedly atheistic, the Russian Orthodox church continues to exist but is state controlled. In other nations, however, the religious issue may still be current and politically explosive. Differences between Muslims and Christians in Nigeria, for example, came to the surface during the 1967–1970 civil war.

A second general point is that similar cleavages may produce different effects in different nations. Cleavages need not necessarily produce conflict. Different races, different language groups, and different classes may accept the established order and work together. In another nation, however, racial, linguistic or class differences may produce violent conflict. To assess the significance of group differences requires both describing the distinguishing characteristics of groups and the relationship among groups.

A third point is that just as the relationship among groups does not remain constant, so too, the significance and the importance of the group's own identity may change. In the United States, for example, the descendants of immigrants who came to this country very early may not now feel a particularly strong sense of ethnic or national identity. In times of crisis, however, a group's distinctiveness may become important. When threatened by another group, members may stress those common characteristics and bonds that separate them from others.

This suggests that during periods of crisis, of rapid political and economic change, or when new factors are introduced into the political equation, the importance of group differences may increase. The discovery of oil on the east shores of Scotland appears to be altering the traditional relationship between Scotland and England. Indications are that the discovery of oil may increase Scottish nationalism, as well as making Scottish economic and political independence more feasible. The rapid economic inflation in Chile during the 1970–1973 period provides another example. The relationship between rural and urban Chileans, and between upper, middle, and lower class Chileans was radically transformed during this century. The economic crises of the Allende presidency magnified the differences separating groups and made it more difficult to resolve conflicts among them.

Finally, cleavages either may reinforce or cut across other cleavages. In some societies different ethnic groups have their own languages, their own religious traditions, and their own territories or regions. When cleavages reinforce other cleavages, differences among peoples are strengthened, and the possibility of severe political conflict increases. In other situations different ethnic groups may share the same language or the same religion; different classes may share the same language or the same religion and hence have a stronger basis for developing a stronger sense of common identity. Tanzanians, for example, although they are divided by ethnicity and religion, share a common language, Swahili. The potential for conflict remains, but takes on a different political significance.

Interest Groups

Peoples who share common interests, characteristics, or values and beliefs normally form organizations to protect and further their positions. In most nations interest groups and political parties (discussed in Chapter 5) are the most common organizations performing these tasks. Interest groups perform important functions and are an integral part of the political process in all nations. In Wales there are groups to protect the heritage of the Welsh language. Ibos in Nigeria join together in "progressive unions" and self-help societies. Middle-class women in Chile form groups to protest high food costs and consumer shortages. French students demand changes in the educational system. And in almost all nations workers join together in unions to protect their interests.

The relationship between interest groups and government is determined in part by the attitudes of the political leadership toward various groups and by the nation's historical experiences. Political leaders respond in different ways to such issues as the representation of various interests in the government, what avenues and opportunities should be open to interest groups, and how much influence interest groups should have in the decision-making process. Soviet party leaders, for example, have a considerably different attitude toward independent interest groups than do the leaders of France and Great Britain. Likewise, Nigerian and Chilean military leaders have responded differently than the civilians they replaced to the demands of various interest groups. Sometimes, as we will see, interest groups may be used to support the political system, while in other cases the relationship between interest groups and the government is a much more adversary one.

The distinct pattern of group life in each nation of our study exerts a strong influence on that nation's political life. The number of groups politically involved, the political significance of the issues that separate groups, and the responses of the political leadership to the continuing challenges posed by groups need to be studied in some detail because these factors oftentimes present political leaders with their most difficult problems.

▪ THE UNITED KINGDOM ▪

The group life of the United Kingdom is characterized by a substantial degree of homogeneity and political consensus when compared with other political systems. The homogeneity is particularly marked in the most populous part of the United Kingdom—England. Even though this is true, there are some very real and important group differences. The population of the United Kingdom is divided by nationality, language, religion, and race. Groups also are separated by social and class distinctions. All of these differences have some political importance. Currently, nationality and class seem particularly relevant to politics.

Nationality

The official name of the political entity that we normally call Britain or Great Britain is the United Kingdom of Great Britain and Northern Ireland. The name suggests the multinational character of the political system. The island of Great Britain includes England, Wales, and Scotland, each of which has somewhat distinct national traditions and histories. Wales became part of the English state in 1536 through dynastic inheritance. Scotland was added in the same fashion with the formal merger of the English and Scottish Crowns in 1707. The island of Ireland contains the other major nationality group in the British Isles. British claims and military intervention in Ireland stem from the twelfth century but attempts at effective control did not occur until the seventeenth century, and common Anglo-Irish institutions were not established for 200 years after colonization. Since 1921 only the six counties of Northern Ireland have been fully integrated into the United Kingdom.

Each national group clearly demonstrates a well-established sense of nationality. For members of each component area of the United Kingdom national identification is important.[1] Scots, for example, see themselves as having a separate identity based on history and institutions of which they are quite proud. Some Scots will go so far as to suggest that they are more compatible and comfortable with Scandinavians than their English neighbors.

Language is one important element in this kind of national feeling. Welsh nationalism to an extent is based on the survival of the Welsh language in the face of English attempts to discourage multilingual edu-

---

[1] Richard Rose, *Governing Without Consensus* (Boston: Beacon Press, 1972), pp. 207–209.

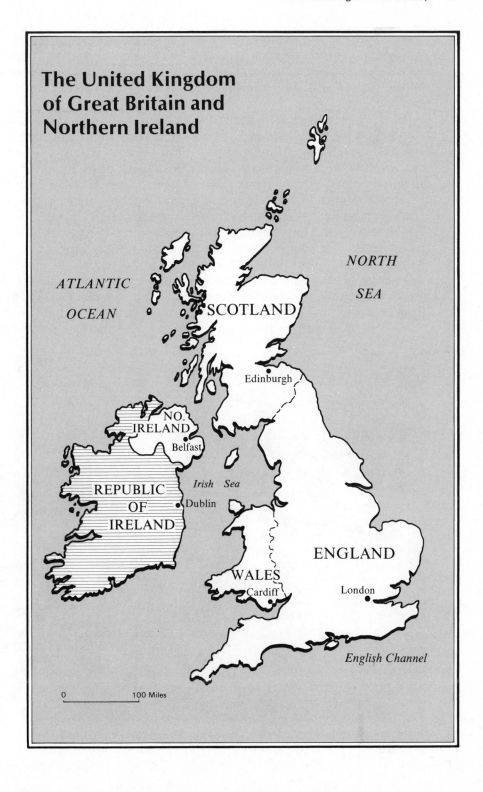

The United Kingdom
of Great Britain and
Northern Ireland

ATLANTIC

OCEAN

NORTH

SEA

SCOTLAND

Edinburgh

NO.
IRELAND

Belfast

REPUBLIC

OF

IRELAND

Dublin

Irish Sea

WALES

Cardiff

ENGLAND

London

English Channel

0   100 Miles

cation. Today over a quarter of the people of Wales can truly be called Welsh-speaking—a declining but substantial proportion of the population. The proportion of native Gaelic-speakers in Scotland and Northern Ireland is much smaller. However, language revival has been an important part of the nationalism in these areas as well.

Religious differences form a part of national identification in the United Kingdom. Most people in England belong to the established Church of England—a high-church or Episcopalian form of Protestantism. Very few of these nominal members are active churchgoers, probably fewer than 10 percent. Scotland has its own national church, the Church of Scotland, which is Presbyterian. Churchgoers in Wales are drawn largely to the nonconformist Protestant sects such as the Baptist and Methodist churches.

Northern Ireland has the most distinctive and the most politically significant religious heritage. First of all, citizens of Northern Ireland regardless of faith are much more actively religious than people in the other national areas. They are also much more religiously conservative in the sense of being fundamentalist—their religion is a very real guide to their daily lives and their political lives. Religion in Northern Ireland is much more entangled with politics than is the case elsewhere in the United

Protestant "Orangemen" marching in Belfast, Northern Ireland. Alan Band Associates.

Kingdom. Finally, of course, Northern Ireland is the only area of the United Kingdom where serious Catholic-Protestant conflict persists. The Protestant two-thirds of Northern Ireland exists in a very unstable and dangerous relationship with the Catholic minority.

The nationality groups maintain a variety of independent institutional and political arrangements that help nurture national feelings. At one extreme, Northern Ireland had a virtually autonomous Parliament at Stormont from 1921 until its suspension during the political violence of 1972. Since that time the government in London has attempted to develop another constitution for Northern Ireland, which would be drafted by the Catholic and Protestant political leaders and which would guarantee minority participation in government. The new constitution, if it can be produced, would no doubt provide for considerable autonomy. Scotland maintains a separate administration for health, housing, economic development, and agriculture in Edinburgh. Scotland also has a separate and distinct legal system based on Roman legal traditions and a separate educational system. These sorts of institutional-political differences are both a reflection of historical differences and a source of contemporary national feelings.

Religion

Traditionally religion has been an important factor in British politics. The political left and right were defined by political differences associated with the Church of England–nonconformist split in religion. To an extent this pattern still holds. Regular attenders of the Church of England are more likely to vote for and support the Conservative party, while nonconformists disproportionately support the Labour party and the political left.

Religion's impact must be understood in the light of two related factors, however. As we have seen, religion tends to be an important aspect of national feelings, and it is difficult to separate the weight of religion and national feeling. Second, religious differences also follow class lines. Middle-class Britons tend to be active members of the Church of England, while workers tend to be either nonconformist or irreligious. Political science research suggests that class identifications have become more important in this century and that religion has lost most of its independent importance for British politics.[2]

Race

Until recently racial differences were unimportant in the United Kingdom. However, in the last 20 years over a million and a half nonwhite immi-

---

[2] David Butler and Donald Stokes, *Political Change in Britain* (New York: St. Martin's Press, 1972), Ch. 7.

grants have come to the United Kingdom from Britain's former colonial areas. The largest and most easily identifiable groups come from Pakistan, India, and the West Indies. Although nonwhites represent less than 3 percent of the population, their problems and presence have been accentuated by their concentration in urban centers and by the fact that the British are inexperienced in domestic race relations.

Nonwhite immigration and minority rights became an issue in British politics with the immigration restriction bill passed in 1962. In subsequent elections the issue has been raised by prominent politicians. For example, Enoch Powell, a conservative politician, rapidly made a name for himself by resisting a liberal immigration policy with his dramatic rhetoric. Powell advocated a course that he referred to as a "white England" policy. In his most famous speech the skilled orator implied that England would drown in a "river of blood" if nonwhite immigration were not stopped. Powell intoned that "like the Roman I seem to see the River Tiber foaming with much blood." Powell also warned in this 1968 speech that "in this country in fifteen or twenty years' time the black man will have the whip hand over the white man."[3]

The racial issue is currently being exploited by the frankly neo-fascist National Front party. The National Front has staged a number of rallies and parades to promote its version of the white England policy. Several of these have led to serious racial rioting. The Front has made dramatic gains in voting strength, although it has yet to gain a foothold in Parliament.

The power of race as a political issue was demonstrated in a speech made by Conservative party leader Margaret Thatcher in February 1978. Thatcher called for a "clear end to immigration." She suggested that nonwhite immigration threatened to damage British culture and society. "Every country can take small minorities," Thatcher observed, "and in many ways they add to the richness and variety of the country. The moment the minority threatens to become a big one, people are frightened." Large minorities might dilute "fundamental British characteristics."[4] For the first time a major party took a hard line against immigration and based the stand on racial and cultural grounds. Race became a more prominent issue with the opposition leader's speech.

Class

There is little doubt that in this century differences in economic class have become the most fundamentally important political cleavage in the United Kingdom. Britons are highly conscious of class distinctions and feel that class criteria can and should guide important aspects of their

---

[3] Quoted in Stephen Haseler, *The Death of British Democracy* (London: Elek Books, 1976), p. 90.

[4] *Christian Science Monitor,* 2 February 1978, p. 22.

social and political behavior. This sensitivity to class extends to the nuances of accent and style of speech, type of dress, general appearance, and manners. These criteria reflect a nationally accepted social stratification system recognized in all regions.

Occupation and income form the objective basis of class distinctions in the United Kingdom as they do in most other modern nations. The most important occupational distinction is between manual and nonmanual workers. This separates groups that differ substantially in life-style— even beyond that which could be predicted by differences in income.

The manual-nonmanual distinction separates those who perceive themselves to be middle class from those who perceive themselves to be working class. Skilled manual workers may earn more than a low-level white-collar supervisor, but their life-style will be more similar to their unskilled co-workers than to nonmanual workers with middle-class manners. These perceptions of class also shape political attitudes and actions. The skilled workers are likely to vote and work for the Labour party, while the low-level white-collar workers will likely support the Conservative party.

The British educational system has tended to solidify these class lines and enhance the role of class in politics. Despite several attempts at educational reform since World War II, the English educational system is elitist in nature. A smaller proportion of British college-age adults attend a college or university than in any comparable industrial country.[5] Further, British secondary schools and colleges differ sharply in their status and in their utility for social and economic advancement. "Public schools"—or college preparatory schools on the model of Eton and Harrow still virtually guarantee success. Other secondary schools vary greatly according to the proportion of their students who go on to higher education from less than 1 percent (for so-called secondary modern schools designed to "staff the lower echelons of Britain's industrial machines . . . with unskilled and semi-skilled workers")[6] to over 25 percent for the college-track state grammar schools. Since workers' children are likely to predominate in the former and middle-class children in the latter, the system perpetuates the basic class division.

The Pattern of Consensus and Cleavage

The dominant political cleavage is the nationwide division between middle-class and working-class Britons. This vertical cleavage holds in all regions and areas. It is relevant for politics in that it has proven to be a guide for party loyalties and political attitudes. Religious differences reinforce this basic cleavage and are hard to separate from class differences.

---

[5] Graeme C. Moodie, *The Government of Great Britain* (New York: Crowell, 1971), p. 48.
[6] Ibid., p. 47.

Nationality and race cleavages have shown some potential for altering the dominant cleavage pattern. For example, a large number of Scottish workers have been drawn from their traditional Labour party political home to support the Scottish Nationalist party. Their national identification overcame their class feeling, and so on the whole the class cleavage applies less to Scotland than it did a decade ago. Nonwhite manual workers similarly are separated from their white co-workers and racial identification often precludes the normal class solidarity in politics. The nationality cleavage clearly is the most important of the two primordial distinctions, if only because of the proportion of the population involved— 17 percent of the population of the United Kingdom live in Wales, Scotland and Northern Ireland.

Group Structure

The group structure of British political life reflects the dominant class cleavage. Large interest groups representing owners and managers of British business and industry compete with the large trade unions on matters of public policy and conflicting demands. Indeed, British politics can be viewed simply as a contest between powerful interest groups.

If, for example, the British government were considering a major change in economic policies—such as those related to trade or currency revaluation—the major representatives of British business and labor would be mobilized and brought into the policy-making process. The Confederation of British Industry (CBI) represents the most important business firms and trade associations. Industrial firms, commercial and banking firms, and allied enterprises are all organized under this large umbrella association. The CBI would be opposed in any basic dispute by the Trade Unions Congress (TUC), which represents over 150 unions and more than 80 percent of Britain's union members. On more specific matters the individual unions representing a particular segment of the economy would act independently of these national business and union confederations.

The British political system is very receptive to interest group activity. Civil servants regularly make use of the expertise of interest group representatives in the drafting of legislation. The British cabinet, which is the policy-making center of the government, permits or rather requires interest group participation in policy deliberations within special cabinet committees. Interest group advice is also sought out as policy decisions are implemented in the ministries and in Britain's public enterprises.

The importance of economic interest groups is underlined by several political relationships between interest groups and political actors that would be considered highly irregular in a number of political systems. First of all, it has been accepted practice for British members of Parliament (MPs) to be in the pay of interest groups. The term "interested MP" is a euphemism for this relationship. The other, more significant, relationship is the formal organizational ties between the Trades Union Congress and the Labour party. The TUC elects members to Labour's Executive Committee, sends delegates to Labour's Annual Conference, and funnels union money into the Labour party treasury as party "membership dues."

The close relationship and easy access to power permitted economic interest groups is not granted other sorts of interest groups that cannot claim to represent functional elements of Britain's economy. Groups representing social, cultural, or minority ethnic groups are at a distinct disadvantage. The political parties are tied to groups which like themselves have been organized to handle the demands generated by class-based politics. The centralized, unitary British political system allows for close collaboration between the natural allies in the economic interest groups and in public office. This means that groups recently organized to present demands for national autonomy for Scotland or against racial discrimination are bucking existing power relationships and long-standing political traditions without much success.

British group politics are changing, but change is difficult because a particular pattern of group politics has been so well established and successful. The challenges of nationality and to a lesser extent racial groups will severely test Britain's leaders and its system of government.

▪ THE FEDERAL REPUBLIC OF GERMANY ▪

Contemporary West German politics are influenced by the full range of political cleavages that traditionally define European politics. Germans are divided from one another by religion, region, and urban-rural residence. Like most industrial societies class differences are quite important in determining the agenda of politics as well as political alignments. By comparative standards, however, the political cleavages of the Federal Republic are not particularly deep or productive of conflict.

The relatively mild nature of political divisions is a very recent development in German history. The society of the Weimar Republic (1919–1933) was divided along the lines that characterize today's Federal Republic, but the cleavages were critically relevant to all aspects of politics. Group attachments often dictated whether an individual favored or opposed the very existence of the regime. A person's religion, region, or class situation was an important factor in whether he or she was a liberal democrat (pro-Weimar), a monarchist (anti-Weimar), a Communist (anti-Weimar), or an exponent of regional separatism (anti-Weimar).

Shortly after the restoration of democratic politics in Germany in 1949 and certainly by the third Federal election in 1957, dramatic changes were evident. The old political cleavages were still present, but social and economic divisions seemed less important for deciding both fundamental political issues and day-to-day decisions. Economic growth and prosperity lessened the differences in life-style between the working class and the middle class. The life-style changes seemed to foreshadow a lessening in political differences. Similar developments reduced differences between urban and rural Germans—for example, the number of German farmers drastically declined with the postwar emphasis on industrial growth and foreign trade.

A second far less subtle change involved the massive population dislocations that occurred in the war and occupation years. Germans were uprooted during Hitler's era to settle the "Eastern Territories" of conquered Poland and Russia. After the war Germany lost not only these Eastern Territories but much prewar German territory—primarily to Poland. The Soviets expelled large numbers of German settlers as well as the native German-speaking population. Nearly 30 percent of the Federal Republic's population in 1950 consisted of refugees and expellees from Soviet-occupied Eastern Europe (including the Soviet occupation zone of Germany). Such a massive relocation of individuals could not help but make local, regional, and urban/rural attachments less significant.[7]

Another war-related change was the change in West Germany's religious composition. Before the war only one-third of the German population was Catholic. The postwar figures show that Catholics became almost equal in strength to the Protestant majority. This change made the Catholics full partners in the new regime rather than an isolated minority as was the case during the empire and Weimar periods.

The reduction in group differences and in group conflict does not mean of course that political cleavages can be ignored or that Germany is without political conflict. Political demands and political organization reflect the old cleavages. As in the past, religion is perhaps the most significant political division.

Religion

German history is filled with events that have led to the politicization of religious differences. The Protestant Reformation is much more "real" to Germans than it is to other peoples. The bloodshed and geographic division of the Reformation period are still felt in areas that were most affected. Catholics in Germany are very aware of the insecure position of German Catholicism in the regimes that preceded the Federal Republic. They understand the defensive attitude of the German Catholic church in the context of such events as Bismarck's "struggle for civilization" against German Catholicism.

These historical events help explain why German Catholics have traditionally had their own political organizations emphasizing self-defense

---

[7] David Childs, *Germany Since 1918* (New York: Harper & Row, 1970), p. 114.

against state power. In the empire and during the Weimar Republic German Catholics supported the Center party. This party was liberal democratic in orientation and belonged to the "small government" liberal tradition. The organization resisted all governmental interference in cultural, religious, social, and economic life. The Center party's political viability was ended by its concern for protection of Catholic religious life. The party's leadership in 1933 supported Hitler's consolidation of power to further its traditional goals of self-protection. The Center party voted for the Enabling Act which transferred the powers of Weimar's Parliament to Adolf Hitler. They did so because Hitler gave them assurance of his noninterference in church matters. Today Catholics disproportionately support the Christian Democratic Union (CDU), considering it an heir of the Center party.

Catholics also have had a tradition of independent group life. Catholic organizations traditionally supplied a full range of social and welfare services normally provided by the state. In this way, Catholics could be protected regardless of the current government's attitude toward the church. The notion of a self-sufficient Catholic subculture was very strong well into the era of the Federal Republic.

In the early years of the Federal Republic, Catholic political action largely occurred within the CDU. This nondenominational Christian political organization was part of a large Catholic and Christian reformist movement in Europe. The CDU drew overwhelming support from Catholics partly in its role as heir to the Center party and partly because the major opposition party—the Social Democrats (SPD)—represented a truly socialist tradition.

The importance of the religious implications of the CDU-SPD rivalry was plain in the 1950s. Catholic clergy denounced the Socialist Democrats from the pulpit on election days and sent out pastoral letters warning parishioners of the socialist threat. The Social Democrats retained until 1959 all of the Marxist rhetoric guaranteed to upset Catholic sensibilities.

The predictable result of this type of religious antagonism was felt in politics. Catholics tended to vote, work, and participate within the Christian Democratic Union, while the non-Catholic working classes supported the Social Democrats. Beyond this, the groups that represented economic interests were divided by religion as well. The German working class was divided by religion as were other economic groupings. The weakness of the Social Democratic minority in the 1950s could be partially traced to the inability to mobilize Catholic workers to their class's "natural" political home.

Since 1959 the Social Democrats have managed to defuse the religious issue by their political moderation and by their efforts in supporting important aspects of the Catholic church's social and cultural role. The Social Democrats have in some cases gone farther than their CDU rivals in supporting Catholic education and Catholic social services since 1959. The

Catholic church in Germany has responded by greatly reducing its overtly political activity.

The result has been that Germans are much less guided in politics by their religious identity than they were 10 or 15 years ago. Working-class Catholics are voting and participating more according to their class and economic interests. Conversely, the Christian Democrats are consolidating their conservative base by drawing a greater vote share from rural and small-town Protestants.

Region and Place of Residence

Regionalism and urban-rural residence remain important aspects of the German political culture. Regionalism is strongest in Germany's southern *Land* (state) of Bavaria. Urban-rural distinctions still separate Germans along modern-traditional conservative lines.

Bavaria has always been a bastion of conservative Catholicism and separatist nationalism. Bavaria has been independent or relatively autonomous for long periods of its history, and even after unification (1871) retained special rights such as the right to have relations with foreign nation-states. The separatist tradition carries over to this day in many forms. Perhaps the most important is that the Bavarian wing of the Christian Democrats—the Christian Socialist Union—maintains its own identity and leadership. The proper designation of the Christian Democratic party in Bavaria therefore is CDU/CSU. The Bavarian contingent to Parliament has always had a separate identity and since early 1977 the CSU under its "political boss," Franz Joseph Strauss, maintains a separate caucus in Parliament.

The rural-urban distinction is still important in Germany. Because of Germany's late industrialization rural and agricultural values survived longer than elsewhere. Rural German parochialism has led to a genuine and distinctive conservatism, which has some affinity for authoritarianism and rigid social distinctions.

Class

As in most industrial societies, class feelings are important in German politics. The German working class has long been marked by a distinctive "political consciousness." The Social Democratic party is the oldest socialist party in the world, and socialist group life has been quite intensely organized. Consciousness, or at least a sense of unique identity, was heightened because German workers were long excluded from meaningful participation in political life. Under the empire their organizations were persecuted and ignored, and during the Weimar regime their political party often declined to take governmental responsibility when they could and should have. Under the Third Reich, working-class organizations were

The States of the Federal Republic of Germany and Their Capitals

regimented and "coordinated" as were all other social and economic groups.

Class distinctions have been reinforced by the educational system and by anti-egalitarian governmental policies. The German education system is as class-based as any modern society's. Governmental policy has encouraged or permitted substantial economic inequality as well. The gap between the poorest and richest Germans is greater than it is in France, Britain, or the United States, and the gap has grown considerably in the postwar years.

Despite the history of class antagonism and the record of class inequality, militant class conflict is quite low in contemporary West Germany. This can be seen in the low rate of strikes and work stoppages as well as in the style in which political campaigns are conducted. Two explanations are offered for the low level of class conflict in a society in which class distinctions are real and widely perceived. One is that West Germany is an affluent society in which the standard of living of workers is higher than it is for workers in most other European countries. A second reason involves the German labor movement and the techniques and style of German trade unions.

Group Life and Interest Group Politics

The style of German group politics is one of compromise and accommodation. The leaders of the large trade unions, the representatives of business and industry, and the government work closely to minimize open conflict. There seems to be widespread agreement that the interests of workers, managers, corporate shareholders, and owners are best served by minimizing class-based strife.

The keystone of this system is a German managerial technique known as "codetermination." By the German codetermination law, public corporations have union and worker representatives on their boards. Workers have direct access to decisions of both general policy and day-to-day management. (By the German laws of incorporation two separate boards are established for these purposes.) Codetermination has been followed for over 25 years and seems to reduce open confrontation on issues sensitive to labor.

Labor is organized under the German Federation of Trade Unions (*Deutscher Gewerkschaftsbund,* DGB). The federation coordinates 16 industry-wide unions with memberships totaling 7.4 million workers. For most purposes the federation acts as labor's spokesman before government and within the codetermination system. The federation has openly sympathized with the German Social Democratic party, and most union leaders are Social Democrats; however, there are no formal ties, and the federation strives to maintain a nonpartisan stance.

Business, industry, and commercial enterprises are represented by two large umbrella organizations that represent the main subdivisions of German business. The first is the Federation of German Employers' Associations (*Bundesvereinigung der deutschen Arbeitgeberverbände*, BDA). This important organization is particularly strong in defending business interests as they relate to labor relations and social policy. The other important business organization is the Federation of German Industry (*Bundesverband der deutschen Industry,* BDI). This organization represents over 90 percent of West Germany's industrial concerns. It is quite active in placing demands for governmental action on issues involving industrial development and in public relations work aimed at providing a "good climate for industry."

Other German interest groups follow the moderate style of the class-based groups. Particularly noteworthy are the changes that have taken place in the political activities of the Catholic church and the major Protestant interest group (which coordinates over 20 separate and autonomous churches). After a period of intense political activity in the first decade of the Federal Republic, religious controversy has abated. The major issues of Catholic education and of the relationship between church groups and state and federal governments have been settled. The Catholic church has generally reduced the number of its major demands, and the growing moderation of the Social Democratic party has eliminated old conflicts between Catholics and Socialists.

Interest group politics in the Federal Republic seem to suggest the possibility that political, economic, and social elites can reduce conflict by conscious action. One important aspect of the growing moderation of German politics is found in the political style of interest group leaders and the politicians with whom they interact. Their attitude of accommodation affects rank-and-file followers and the broader public.

▪ FRANCE ▪

France is among the most seriously divided developed political systems. Political cleavages are intense and numerous. This is a result of the difficult history of French political, economic, and social development. Group conflict and unsettled political issues are the legacies of that unsettled history. Religion, urban-rural residence, region, and class are politically relevant barriers dividing the French.

Religion

The most significant political cleavage in France involves the conflict between "clericalism" and "anti-clericalism." The issue is not between people with different religious attachments but between believers and nonbelievers. Although over 90 percent of the French population is nominally Catholic, a much smaller number are practicing or active Catholics. A substantial element of the population (anti-clericals) are firmly opposed to Catholic doctrine and the Catholic church as an institution. The division between clericals and anti-clericals defines the division between political right and political left.

The origin of the conflict is in the French revolutionary period and is associated with the conflict between French authoritarians and republicans. The church was closely associated with the old monarchy and its stratified social system. The revolution against the Crown was simultaneously a revolution against the church. Revolutionaries and republicans viewed the church as a bastion for traditional authoritarian beliefs and medieval superstition. They preferred the rational religion of the Enlightenment known as "deism."

As French regimes changed, the role of the church also changed. In regimes in which the traditional right was strong, such as the Bourbon Restoration (1814–1830) or the early Vichy regime (1940–1944), the Catholic church had a privileged position. In periods of intense republicanism, such as the period following the founding of the Third Republic, the church's privileges regarding Catholic education and social policy were revoked. Periodically, the issue has been revived and has taken on great political meaning.

The political significance of the clerical issue has not lessened appreciably for 200 years, although there are some recent signs of change. Since World War II the concrete manifestation of the clerical issue of state subsidies for Catholic schools has been handled without great conflict. In 1951 educational laws were passed permitting state support for Catholic schools under specified guidelines. Despite the removal of the problematic education issue, the French still think and act politically according to their religious views.

The continued importance of religion is seen in political attitudes, voting behavior, and in interest group politics. The French people have difficulty in forming attachments to particular parties, but they are able to distinguish among the dominant political tendencies of left and right. The importance of the left-right distinction has increased since the founding of the Fifth Republic with its powerful presidency. Politics centers on the efforts of the partisan alliances of the left and of the right to capture this central locus of power. As in the past, clericalism and anti-clericalism help determine identification with the two major tendencies.

The clerical issue divides other types of political organizations as well. Within each major economic and social interest separate organizations for clericals and anti-clericals have been established. Catholics workers, farmers, and businessmen prefer not to join interest groups dominated by anti-clericals. This issue has proven to be the master political cleavage that can divide members of the same class, region, or rural/urban area.

Class

The French political culture is characterized by strong feelings of class consciousness and by widespread belief in the existence and necessity of class conflict.[8] Class differences are seen in manners, dress, and taste so that daily personal encounters are regulated by rituals associated with class distinctions. Working-class people are to a large degree residentially segregated from middle-class individuals and have strong community and neighborhood roots that limit interclass contact. In such a setting fear and mistrust are easily generated.

There is a fairly high level of working-class militancy in France, far surpassing the militancy of British or German workers. The reason for these

Workers' protest in Paris, May 1968. Wide World Photos, Inc.

---

[8] Henry W. Ehrmann, *Politics in France* (Boston: Little, Brown, 1976), pp. 57–58.

attitudes is historical. France has traditionally been a rural and agricultural country. Workers' problems, therefore, were not high on the list of the dominant political elite before World War II. After the war millions of workers who voted for the Communist party of France (PCF) were disenfranchised in effect by the isolation of the workers' party in electoral and parliamentary politics. Until recently, when the Socialists formed an alliance with the PCF, cooperation with the Communists was the "persistent taboo" of French politics.

The frustration of workers caused by delayed social legislation and the French political system's bias against Communist participation has resulted in violent strikes, demonstrations, and other forms of "street politics." Workers draw inspiration from the symbols and martyrs of earlier proletarian uprisings, such as the uprising of the Paris Commune of 1871. The red workers' flag has a good deal of meaning for many French workers. Like other symbols of working-class solidarity, the flag dates from decades before France—or Russia for that matter—had a Communist party.

The militancy of the French working class was dramatized during what has become known as the Events of May 1968. Approximately half of the French labor force joined in a general strike touched off by the actions of student radicals. Approximately 7 million workers participated in this general strike for better wages and working conditions. The demands were radical and far-reaching, as was the violently anti-capitalist tone of the rebellion. The highly emotional symbols and beliefs of the French working class clearly retain their potency in "modern" France.

Rural vs. Urban Differences

France has been a predominantly rural and small-town nation until quite recently. The traditions, customs, and attitudes of the French countryside are still quite relevant to politics. Before World War II, 48 percent of the French population lived in communities of less than two thousand, and there were only a handful of cities of any size. Today rural dwellers comprise less than a third of the population, but this is still quite a high figure relative to Germany and the United Kingdom.[9]

Paris has always dominated French cities in terms of both population, wealth, and modernization. Roughly 20 percent of the population of France currently reside in Paris, and these persons draw a disproportionate share of the available income and amenities of life. It would take a city of 40 to 50 million Americans to dominate the United States in a way that Paris dominates France. In part, the urban-rural distinction is a distinction then between Paris and "the provinces."

The conflict between urban and rural France can be described as a conflict between traditional and modern values. Traditional elites in the

---

[9] Ibid., p. 22.

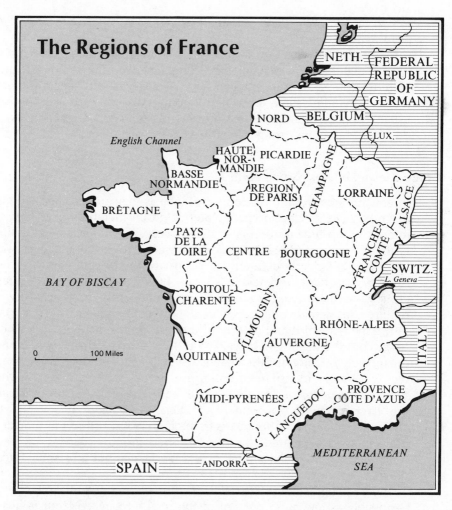

The Regions of France

NETH.
FEDERAL REPUBLIC OF GERMANY
NORD
BELGIUM
LUX.
English Channel
HAUTE NOR-MANDIE
PICARDIE
CHAMPAGNE
LORRAINE
ALSACE
BASSE NORMANDIE
REGION DE PARIS
BRÊTAGNE
PAYS DE LA LOIRE
CENTRE
BOURGOGNE
FRANCHE-COMTÉ
SWITZ.
L. Geneva
BAY OF BISCAY
POITOU-CHARENTE
LIMOUSIN
RHÔNE-ALPES
ITALY
AUVERGNE
AQUITAINE
MIDI-PYRÉNÉES
LANGUEDOC
PROVENCE CÔTE D'AZUR
0   100 Miles
MEDITERRANEAN SEA
SPAIN
ANDORRA

French countryside and small-town areas seem to instinctively oppose innovation in family relations, business practices, or political customs and practices. They prefer families that are father-dominated and close-knit. They prefer businesses that are small and family-run. They decidedly prefer local politics to national.

Above all, the economic and political influence of Paris is resisted in the countryside of rural France. Traditionally, elements in rural France do not recognize the legitimacy of certain laws and decrees of the central government and have therefore not obeyed them. Notable examples are found in the realm of tax laws where rural businessmen are appalled at the government's implied right to look into their books. A more recent example involves the French-Italian "wine war," in which indignant French peasants blocked shipments of "inferior Italian wines" to French markets. The government was acting according to treaty obligations but was forced to back down and violate agreements with Italy and other European nations.

The rural-urban cleavage is closely related to French regionalism. Several French regions have maintained strong feelings of a separate cultural identity. Some, such as Brittany, have evolved serious separatist movements demanding some form of autonomy. As is the case with the rural-urban conflict, these separatist movements tend to be reactions to the directing and modernizing role of Paris.

Group Life and Interest Group Politics

Interest groups are not as strong in France as they are in other nations at a similar level of development. Interest group membership is low, and interest group organization is relatively weak. This reflects a cultural distaste for "pressure" organizations and the art of lobbying. In France words like these are clearly pejorative for most of the people who use them. Another reason for weakness may be the highly political nature of interest groups—particularly labor unions. Joining an interest group may very well require considerable political or ideological commitment.

The memberships and activity of interest groups fluctuate greatly over time, contributing to their weakness. In the mid-1950s Pierre Poujade organized the Union for the Defense of Shopkeepers and Artisans to protect small and old-fashioned enterprises from the threats of modernization. The activities of this group included the storming of tax offices and the harassment of government politicians. Poujade in several years claimed several million followers in the mid-1950s, and just as quickly his movement disintegrated. More established groups, such as the major trade unions, have been subject to less spectacular but substantial fluctuations in support.

The trade unions organize only a fraction of their potential membership—possibly as few as 15 percent of the total. Organized labor is divided among Communist, anti-Communist, and Catholic trade unions. All of these organizations have declined greatly in membership since their postwar highs in 1946 and 1947.

The largest trade union organization is the Communist-controlled Federation of Workers (*Confédération Générale du Travail*, CGT). This organization has a large staff that provides members with a wide variety of services in the tradition of the French labor movement. The organization is highly ideological and is committed to class struggle and an overturning of the capitalist economic system. The division and ideological style of French trade unions have no doubt impaired their effectiveness in both labor relations and in politics.

Similar divisions are found in other economic sectors. Traditionally, French agriculture was divided between clerical and anti-clerical groups. After World War II an attempt was made to broaden the organization of farmers' interests. While a large federation has been established (*Fédération nationale des syndicats d'exploitants agricoles*), its active component parts reflect the political cleavages of France. For example, younger more modern farmers have organized to oppose the outworn methods of traditionalists. Several Communist trade unions are active in organizing farmers, and therefore class divisions are relevant to agriculture as well.

French interest groups maximize their influence by informal contacts with the government and senior civil servants. These contacts are quite frequent between the agricultural and business groups (particularly the *Conseil national du patronat Française,* CNPF) and the appropriate ministries. This informal contact is enhanced by a considerable interchange of personnel between these particular interest groups and government. Individuals move from jobs with the government to interest group positions and from interest groups to government service.

A second opportunity for influence lies in France's extensive network of economic planning bodies. Interest groups play formal roles in the economic planning system by making recommendations about investment priorities and techniques of modernization. Influence on government spending and investment policies can be substantial.

Regardless of formal and informal access to areas of policy-making, French interest groups speak with a "weak and divided voice." Each economic interest is represented by a variety of interest groups reflecting the dominant political cleavages of France. The ideological stance of many groups discourages membership as does the low level of acceptance by the French of interest group activity.

▪ THE SOVIET UNION ▪

The Soviet Union is plagued by many of the same cleavages that complicate the politics of the liberal-democratic nation-states of Western Europe. Citizens of the Soviet system may be distinguished on the basis of their class or socioeconomic status, urban or rural residence, nationality and religion. Each of these divisions has considerable political importance, and each receives a good deal of attention from the Soviet leadership. The importance of the cleavages is magnified by the fact that Soviet ideology puts a premium on "socialist unity" and because the groups produced by these divisions are sometimes difficult to control.

Class

The Soviet leadership is particularly sensitive to socioeconomic and class differences. A central element of the Marxist-Leninist ideology is the utopian ideal of the classless society. Since the Revolution, the Communist party of the Soviet Union has affirmed and reaffirmed its devotion to this political goal. The ultimate Communist society will operate on the principle "from each according to his ability, to each according to his need." Living standards and "class differences" will disappear as they are separated from the criteria of talent and birth.

The Communist party elite states that they have not yet reached the ideal—but have reached the important intermediary stage of mature socialism. At this stage some differences between socioeconomic groups remain because of the necessity of keeping incentives to work and because of individual contribution. Nevertheless, the official Soviet view is that there now exist only two cooperative classes—the workers and the peasants.

The claims of the party aside, 60 years of economic development have created a much more complex socioeconomic structure. Since 1917 the Soviet Union has changed from a rural agriculture-based society to a modern, urban industrial society. Education has expanded dramatically. Now over 80 percent of the population gets a full secondary education while almost 10 million Soviet citizens have higher educations.[10]

One result of these social and economic developments has been the creation of a large, diversified, and important Soviet "intelligentsia." This group includes all those elites familiar to a modern society. Scientists, managers, and engineers make up the technical intelligentsia. Scholars, journalists, writers, and artists are members of the creative intelligentsia. These "mental workers," as they are sometimes called, are a rapidly growing segment of the Soviet population. It's been estimated that this group includes some 35 million people, or roughly 15 percent of the total population.

In many ways the members of the educated class of nonmanual workers are privileged. They are rewarded for their special contributions and live comfortably compared to their fellow countrymen. At the highest level of each of the arts and sciences individuals emerge to enjoy great status and prosperity. Rewards include coveted country homes—or *dachas*—automobiles, the ability to purchase imported "luxury goods," and foreign travel. The number of individuals who attain these rewards is quite small, but they are envied.

Even the Communist party is highly concerned with questions of the appropriate rewards for party service. Incentives for party service are carefully graded and distributed in accordance with strict rules. A *Politburo* member, the highest party body, may expect to be given a luxury chauffeur-driven limousine. Normally, this would be a Soviet-made Zil, which resembles an elongated Lincoln Continental worth about 75,000 U.S. dollars. The Politburo member will receive a country house and a Moscow apartment, often those of the person he is replacing. He will be

---

[10] Frederick C. Barghoorn, *Politics in the U.S.S.R.* (Boston: Little, Brown, 1972), p. 50.

able to buy imported foodstuffs at the most exclusive private party stores. A party member who ranks below the highest level, perhaps in the Central Committee of the party, will receive ample, but less extensive, rewards. He will probably drive his own Chaika, which has been described as a "pregnant Packard" and is valued at 13,000 U.S. dollars. The party clearly operates on the basis of individual incentive and motivation.

The more specialized branches of the intelligentsia such as scientists, industrial managers, or creative writers and performers develop distinctive attitudes and outlooks based on similar background, training, and work experience. It is only natural that they develop a sense of having special or unique interests that should receive a hearing by those who make political and economic decisions. Attempts at influence of this sort seem to be increasing whether through informal channels or through the existing interest group structure which is closely tied to and regulated by the Communist party of the Soviet Union.[11]

A second major political implication of the growth in the size and influence of the intelligentsia is the possibility of individual and group protest against official governmental policy. The Soviet "dissidents" who have become so prominent in the last 20 years represent a prominent handful of the creative and technical elites of the Soviet Union. The Nobel Prize–winning novelist Alexander Solzhenitsyn and the internationally known physicist Andrei Sakharov are the two best-known members of this select society. Their international reputations no doubt have allowed them to conduct their activities against censorship and in support of human rights.

The policy of the Soviet leadership reflects uncertainty with regard to the proper mix of coercion and forbearance toward dissidents. Nikita Khrushchev allowed a good deal of freedom of expression in the period of de-Stalinization. His policy encouraged the publication of Solzhenitsyn's *One Day in the Life of Ivan Denisovich,* which depicted life in a Stalinist prison camp. After Khrushchev's ouster in 1964, the leadership under Leonid Brezhnev began a policy of selective repression. This policy was an attempt to contain the criticism of dissidents without returning to the violent excesses of Stalinist police actions. Some dissident thinkers were arbitrarily selected for harassment, confinement in mental institutions, or arrest. During this period Andrei Sakharov has been a focal point of protest against these actions, a clearinghouse for information about the violation of human rights in the Soviet Union, and a liaison to the foreign media.

Nationality

Class cleavages and dissident problems are the concerns of the modern Soviet Union. Other political cleavages are holdovers from tsarist Russia;

---

[11] Darrell P. Hammer, *U.S.S.R.: The Politics of Oligarchy* (Hinsdale, Ill.: The Dryden Press, 1974), Ch. 8.

they represent cultural divisions that the Soviet political elite has been unable to overcome or make less relevant to politics.

The major traditional or premodern cleavage is based on nationality. The Soviet Union contains approximately 100 distinct language groups. Twenty-one of these groups have as many as a million members. Many also are different in religion and customs from the Great Russian Slavic majority.

The largest nationality group is the Slavs, who include the Great Russians (129 million), the Ukrainians or "Little Russians" (40 million), and the Belorussians or "White Russians" (9 million). The religious tradition of the Slavs is Orthodox Christianity, although an affiliate of Roman Catholicism has been important in the Ukraine.

A second set of nationality groups is the Turko-Tatar ethnic family (totaling 27.2 million), which is located in an area between the Caspian Sea on the west and Mongolia on the east. The Uzbeks (9.2 million), Tatars (5.9 million), and the Kazakhs are the largest of these national groups. These are Muslim peoples whose culture is very different from the Great Russian majority.

A third ethnic group consists of the Transcaucasian peoples. The Georgians, Armenians, and Azerbaidzhans make up the 7 million members of this group. The Georgians and Armenians share a Christian heritage similar to that of the Slavic majority; however, their traditions and customs are quite different from the Slavs. For example, the Armenians and Georgians have their own alphabets, which are very different from the dominant Russian Cyrillic alphabet.

The other major set of nationalities is the Baltic group (5 million), including the Lithuanians, Latvians, and Estonians. The Baltic languages are primarily Indo-European. The Estonian language is Finno-Ugrian, which is related to the language of the Hungarians, Finns, and Turks. Religious traditions are mixed in the Baltic area. Roman Catholicism has been important in Lithuania, while Lutheranism has been influential in Latvia and Estonia.

The plight of "nonterritorial" groups such as Soviet Germans and Jews often depends on external or international events. Both groups have been suspected of having loyalties to foreign powers—Germany and Israel. During World War II the Volga Germans were shipped away from their homes and stripped of their political rights. This action was based on suspicion rather than on any real act or threat. The rights of these Germans were not restored until the 1960s, and their lands were never restored.[12]

Soviet Jews have often been repressed because of developments in the Middle East or because of the actions of Israel's chief international sponsor, the United States. Major official anti-Jewish campaigns occurred at the time that Israel was established in 1948 and during the 1967 Six-Day War.

---

[12] Barghoorn, *Politics in the U.S.S.R.*, p. 77.

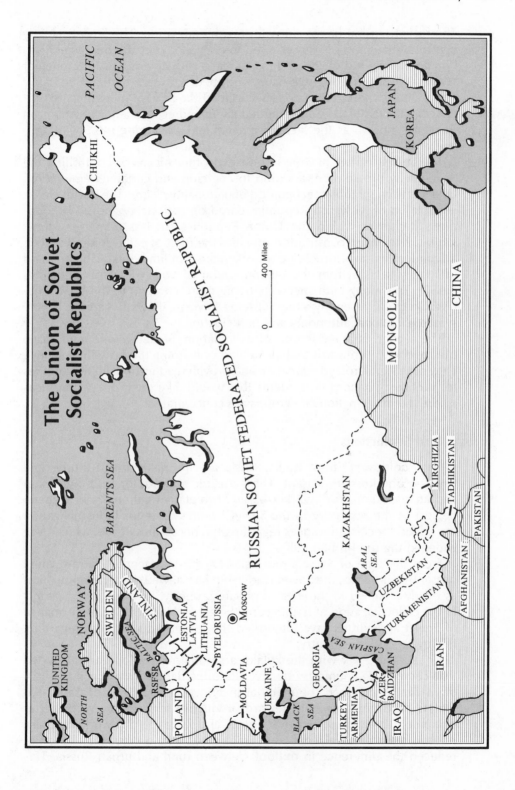

The Union of Soviet Socialist Republics

PACIFIC OCEAN

BARENTS SEA

NORTH SEA

UNITED KINGDOM

NORWAY

SWEDEN

FINLAND

BALTIC SEA

RSFSR

POLAND

ESTONIA

LATVIA

LITHUANIA

BYELORUSSIA

MOLDAVIA

UKRAINE

BLACK SEA

Moscow

RUSSIAN SOVIET FEDERATED SOCIALIST REPUBLIC

CHUKHI

KAZAKHSTAN

ARAL SEA

UZBEKISTAN

TURKMENISTAN

CASPIAN SEA

GEORGIA

AZERBAIDZHAN

ARMENIA

TURKEY

IRAQ

IRAN

AFGHANISTAN

PAKISTAN

KIRGHIZIA

TADHIKISTAN

MONGOLIA

CHINA

KOREA

JAPAN

400 Miles

0

The recent tension has to do with Jewish emigration. The Soviets closely control the number of Jews allowed to emigrate. They discourage emigration by making it difficult for Jews to leave with any significant money or property. These restrictions have worsened with international criticism. For example, the Soviets severely curtailed the flow of emigrants in 1974 after the United States Senate added an amendment to a Soviet-American trade bill, known as the Jackson amendment, criticizing the Soviet emigration policy.

The Soviet leaders have relied on two other means of controlling the "nationality problem" in addition to coercion and curtailing emigration. One has been symbolic recognition of nationality claims. The Soviet Union is made up of 15 Union Republics based on nationality and 20 Autonomous Republics within the Union Republics for less populous ethnic groups. The Soviet constitution specifies the right of each Union Republic to conduct its own foreign policy, maintain a military establishment, and ultimately secede from the federal Union of Soviet Socialist Republics (USSR). This along with special national representation in the USSR's national popular assembly—the Supreme Soviet—allows for ample if only symbolic national autonomy and participation.

The second strategy is one of assimilation. Soviet governments have tried a variety of rewards and incentives for learning the Russian language. They have standardized education and provided educational opportunities for promising nationality students that would take them out of the areas where the major nationality groups are concentrated.

Urban-Rural Distinctions

Other "holdovers" from tsarist Russia are the distinctive attitudes and values of the Russian peasant. These include a desire for land-ownership and an alienation from worker-based "proletarian culture." The general neglect of the peasantry in the Soviet Union's drive for industrialization has added specific grievances regarding the necessities of life, which have widened the rural-urban gulf.

From the time of Stalin's repression of the independent land-owning peasantry, or *kulaks,* the Soviet leadership has viewed the farm population as overly attached to the idea of private property. Resistance of peasants to the collectivization of farming and the general low level of performance of Soviet agriculture have intensified the leadership's concern regarding the loyalty of the peasantry.

Since Stalin's war with the kulaks, a gradual realization has developed that coercion is counterproductive. Reforms dating from the mid-1960s dramatically increased the material incentives available to peasants. Attempts have been made to reward productive farm groups with better equipment, greater use of private plots, and wages for the workers. These reforms seem to have reduced peasant dissatisfaction, but they have not reduced the difference in outlook between rural and urban Russia. This difference is particularly important since the rural population of the Soviet Union constitutes 45 percent of the population—one of the largest agricultural sectors in a developed political system.

Group Life

The Soviet Union has the full complement of interest groups characteristic of a modern industrial society. Labor unions, associations of managers, professional associations, and other groups have large memberships and are relatively active. The difference is that all of these formal interest groups are linked to or are auxiliaries of the Communist party of the Soviet Union. As such, they are responsible for carrying out party policy. This includes informing the membership of changes in policy, disseminating propaganda, and promoting work-group goals such as industrial productivity. In the creative fields of endeavor the professional groups are responsible for producing the "right" sort of literature, film, or drama.

The official party-dominated interest groups also provide some information about the attitudes, needs, and demands of economic and professional groups. Although this does not involve political pressure or influence, it does serve to articulate some of the views of rank-and-file members. It also serves the information needs of the leadership.

This kind of group pressure and influence familiar to Westerners is conducted by informal groups of specialists and experts. The distinctive views of scientists, managers, engineers, and the creative intelligentsia are expressed in their relations with state and party elites. The informal groups have some of the familiar interest group resources in this game. In particular, they have the resource of expertise which puts them at a great advantage in confrontations with bureaucratic and political adversaries.

The Soviet political culture clearly is marked by important political cleavages and a great variety of economic and social group life. There is no reason to suggest that this group life does not generate conflicting demands, which competing groups present to the appropriate political authorities for decision. The rules are different, and group politics are less visible and formalized. These are the major differences between group politics in the Soviet Union and what exists in other developed nations.

▪ NIGERIA ▪

Almost one of every seven persons living in Africa is a Nigerian. This huge manpower resource, coupled with vast oil and mineral wealth, makes Nigeria one of the richest nations in Africa. Its gross national product is greater than all of the other independent, tropical African states combined. Nigeria is also one of the world's most diverse nations. No nation in our study is as diverse or has as complex a pattern of pluralism.

These patterns strongly influence the political development of the Nigerian state and nation. The difficulty of establishing a national Nigerian identity and national unity that transcend subnational loyalties continues to affect the politics of independent Nigeria. The two important factors that should be understood about Nigeria are its potential for growth and development and the cleavages and divisions that characterize its society.

Cleavage Patterns

Initial descriptions of Nigeria best begin by describing Nigeria's diverse peoples. While differences among ethnic groups or "tribes" are normally considered to be the most important and significant divisions, there are many other cleavage patterns. The most important are religious, linguistic, cultural, and regional differences.

There are several important general points about the cleavages in Nigeria. First, and perhaps most important, is that the cleavages and the cleavage patterns are constantly changing. Cleavages mark boundaries between groups and interests, but these boundaries change as the people who are included in the group change and as the group's importance to political activity changes. Depending on the situation and specific events different criteria or rules may be established that define the boundaries between groups. By the same token, cleavages that in the past may not have had political significance may become politically more important as a result of a new situation.

A second important characteristic of cleavage patterns is that they may cut across or reinforce other cleavages. For example, different ethnic groups may unite on certain issues because they share a common religion or a common regional interest. In other cases each ethnic group may have its own language, its own religious traditions, and its own specific regional interests. Achieving a base for national unity is difficult in this situation. Groups may feel that little is to be gained by compromising or respecting the traditions of others.

Finally, subnational loyalties need not necessarily conflict with national loyalties. Individuals and groups may have multiple loyalties. Individuals, for example, may feel loyalty to and have affection for their ethnic group, their language group, their religion, as well as their nation. In most modern nation-states, however, one's primary political loyalty is to the nation.

The most important cleavages in Nigeria are ethnic, linguistic, religious, and regional. Ethnic groups, or more imprecisely "tribes," are groups that share a common set of values about who belongs and should belong to the community and a common set of values about the distribution of authority and power within the group.[13]

---

[13] Donald G. Morrison, Robert C. Mitchell, John N. Paden, and Hugh M. Stevenson, *Black Africa: A Comparative Handbook* (New York: The Free Press, 1972), p. 415.

Ethnic politics in Nigeria centers on three major groups, each associated with a specific region. These three groups because of their size have dominated the political scene since independence. The Hausa-Fulani in northern Nigeria comprise about 21 percent of the total population, the Yoruba in western Nigeria about 20 percent, and the Ibo in eastern Nigeria about 17 percent. The remaining third of the population is composed of

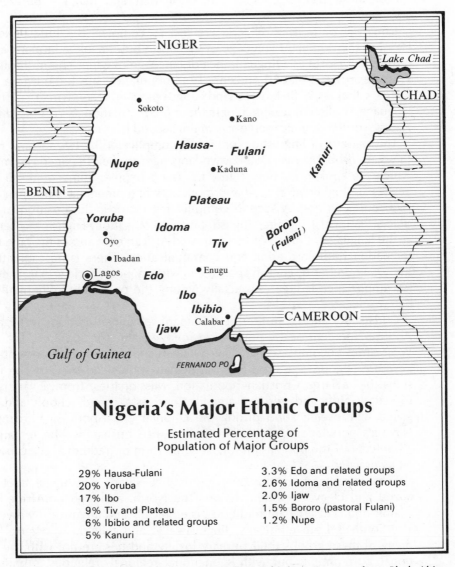

Nigeria's Major Ethnic Groups

Estimated Percentage of
Population of Major Groups

29% Hausa-Fulani
20% Yoruba
17% Ibo
9% Tiv and Plateau
6% Ibibio and related groups
5% Kanuri

3.3% Edo and related groups
2.6% Idoma and related groups
2.0% Ijaw
1.5% Bororo (pastoral Fulani)
1.2% Nupe

smaller groups that play crucial political roles during periods of crisis. Groups such as the Tiv, Kanuri, Nupe, Idoma, Ibibio, and Edo have acted as balances or counters to the dominance of the three major groups.

Besides sharing a core set of political values, each ethnic group has other factors that distinguish them from other groups. Ethnic groups normally share a common myth of origin, a set of political institutions and structures, and often distinct languages and religious traditions and practices. All of these factors combine to strengthen and magnify differences among groups.

Language patterns in Nigeria are just as complex as ethnic patterns. Hausa is the dominant language of the North but is spoken in many areas outside the North as a lingua franca or language of wider communication. Estimates suggest that 50 percent of the population speak the Hausa language either as a first or second language. The second major African language, spoken by about 20 percent of the population, is Yoruba. Unlike Hausa, Yoruba does not serve as a major second language.

This pattern of linguistic pluralism is complicated by two factors. First, there are probably over 250 known languages spoken in Nigeria, some of which are spoken by only a few thousand people. Some of these languages are highly developed and modern, while others have not yet been reduced to writing. A second complicating factor is the position of the official national language, English. Since colonization, English has served as the language of much of the educated African elite and as the language for national administration and communication. There is no estimate of the total number of English speakers in Nigeria, but it is clear that its political importance is great, especially among the politically influential and better educated.

Christianity and Islam are the dominant religious traditions in Nigeria. About 52 percent of the population follow Islam. The spread of Islam in West Africa encompassed the Hausa-Fulani and most areas in present-day northern Nigeria. Southern Nigeria, heavily influenced by Christian missions, has a large Christian population. Missionaries, from a variety of Christian faiths and mission organizations, established schools and engaged in proselytization during the colonial era. About 35 percent of Nigeria's population practice some form of Christianity. The remaining 13 percent of the population follow some form of traditional African religious practices.

What emerges from this overview is that Nigeria is a highly fractionalized and cleavage-ridden nation. The North, although dominated by Islamic and Hausa-Fulani traditions, is ethnically and linguistically diverse. The South is both ethnically, linguistically, and religiously diverse. For many of these groups their primary loyalty and ties are not with the national government, but with subnational regional, religious, ethnic, or linguistic groups.

Class Differences

Colonial control and administration did little to bridge the gap and unite these various groups. Nigeria initially was divided during the colonial period into a Northern and Southern Protectorate and later into Northern, Eastern, and Western Regions. These regional divisions solidified and reinforced existing differences among groups. Regional interests often were more important and politically significant than national interests. Political parties were organized around and appealed primarily to regional interests. The contests for jobs, favors, and the limited resources of the national government were defined in terms of regional or ethnic goals and interests rather than national ones.

Colonial control and the impact of colonialism were uneven. Some groups were more strongly influenced and affected by the colonial experience than others. The strong Islamic tradition of the North and the emphasis on indirect rule slowed the rate of change in the region. In the South change was more rapid. Various factors led to differential rates of modernization and Westernization, which in turn created real and potential political conflicts once the British left Nigeria.

In rapidly changing societies special importance is often attached to education. The acquisition of an education, and in the Nigerian case the acquisition of English, is a key to increased economic and social mobility. One of the effects of the colonial system was to introduce a new educational system to Nigeria. Western education and English language training, for those fortunate enough to receive them, set them apart, giving them both economic and political mobility. A new elite, with special training and skills, was created. A 1965 estimate that only 17 percent of the population is literate (either in English or other languages) is probably low; the percentage has certainly increased since then. In 1976 the military government introduced universal primary education so that all Nigerian children would be assured of at least a primary education. At present, there is a sharp distinction between those with an education and those without.

The effect of education varied markedly between the northern and southern areas. Islamic areas in general, and northern Nigeria in particular, have long traditions of comprehensive religious education. The traditional educational system supported the values of the Hausa-Fulani culture and the authority patterns of their state. Western education, or more precisely missionary Western education, was viewed by many, British and Nigerian alike, as a direct threat to the existing political values and institutions of the North. The prohibition against missionary education meant that the number of Northerners with Western educations lagged far behind the number of Southerners.

The impact of education, from both the missionaries and the government was much greater in the Western and Eastern Regions. More and more individuals received educations and took new jobs in the modern sectors of the economy. As the protective cover of British colonial authority and control was removed, many Northerners began to fear that they would be at a disadvantage in competition with Southerners for jobs and opportunities in an independent Nigeria. This created a new cleavage between Nigerians, resulting in rapid increases in Western education in the Northern Region.

Interest Groups

Many types of interest groups developed in Nigeria to represent group interests and values. In many cases the rapid changes occurring in Nigeria reinforce and make more important traditional institutions and structures. While this may not at first appear logical, it is best illustrated using the example of urbanization.

Nigeria is fast becoming an urban society. While only about 14 percent of the population live in cities with populations over 20,000, more and more individuals are leaving rural areas seeking new opportunities in large cities. Urbanization places strains on traditional structures and traditional value sets. Old answers and solutions are no longer suited to the new

Like all modern cities, Lagos, Nigeria, suffers from many urban ills—overcrowding, pollution, and inadequate public transportation. Courtesy, United Nations.

problems. This is especially true in multi-ethnic urban areas where different groups, with different interests, find themselves in constant contact.

Many Nigerian cities are divided residentially on the basis of ethnicity. In northern cities there are sections of the city where Ibo or Yoruba migrants live and sections where migrants from other northern areas live. In the famous walled city of Kano most of the inhabitants living within the walled city are indigenous to Kano. Living immediately outside the walls are migrants from other areas. Likewise, in southern cities such as Ibadan there are well-defined areas where northern Hausa migrants live.

A type of organization that is common in Nigerian cities is the protective or self-help society. These organizations preserve some aspects of traditional life yet at the same time meet modern needs. Societies can be based on ethnic ties, or in some cases, on regional or village ties. They provide assistance and help for people of similar backgrounds. For example, in northern and western Nigerian cities with sizable Ibo populations there are normally "Ibo Unions." These unions, and similar unions for other groups, help newcomers to the city find work and housing, enroll their children in schools, give loans, and provide some continuity for those moving from rural to urban environments. As service organizations, they provide very real material assistance; as cultural organizations, they preserve traditional social patterns, languages, and cultures.

Chinua Achebe describes the importance of these organizations in his novel *No Longer at Ease*. Obi, a student just returned from study in Britain on a scholarship provided by the Umofia Progressive Union (Lagos Branch), is both an object of pride and a valuable resource for the future. The secretary of the Union declares:

The importance of having one of our sons in the vanguard of this march of progress is nothing short of axiomatic. Our people have a saying "Ours is ours, but mine is mine." Every town and village struggles at this momentous epoch in our political evolution to possess that of which it can say: "This is mine." We are happy that today we have such an invaluable possession in the person of our illustrious son and guest of honor.[14]

Obi is expected not only to repay his scholarship, but also, now that he is educated, to help others from his home village gain success.

Organizations such as these often exist side by side with more "modern" interest groups. Labor unions, teacher unions, commerce organizations, and the like all seek to represent various interests. In some cases these organizations limit membership to specific groups, or they may bridge certain cleavages and include members from many groups. In some cases they are nationwide organizations; in others they are limited to specific regions or areas.

Nigeria as a developing nation is undergoing radical and rapid change.

---

[14] Chinua Achebe, *No Longer at Ease* (Greenwich, Conn.: Fawcett, 1961), p. 37. Reprinted by permission of author and William Heinemann, Ltd.

Patterns of group interaction are constantly changing. The civil war in Nigeria from 1967 to 1970 was a direct outgrowth of conflicts between different groups. The end of the war, however, has lessened the importance of certain cleavages and increased the importance of others. It is logical to expect that as Nigeria continues to develop ethnic, religious, and linguistic cleavages may become less important, while differences between classes and economic and social groups will increase in importance. As a greater sense of national identity and loyalty develops, primordial distinctions will not necessarily disappear but may complement and support a new, wider national loyalty. The process of managing conflict between cleavage groups, however, remains one of the most severe tests facing Nigerian political actors. In Chapter 4 the first attempted solution to this problem, the multiparty system of the first republic, is described.

▪ EGYPT ▪

The July 1952 revolution overthrowing the monarchy of King Farouk had many different causes and many different goals. The young Free Officers, led by men such as Gamal Abdul Nasser and Anwar Sadat, sought to end the corruption of the old regime, to remove the stigma of the military's defeat in the 1948 war, and to make sweeping changes within Egypt. Their immediate goal was the acquisition of political power, their long-term goal was revolution. According to the Free Officers, achieving these goals required the consolidation of their political power within Egypt, the removal of the foreign British presence and influence, and the economic and social transformation of Egyptian society. President Nassar, in writing on the philosophy of the revolution, focused on what he perceived the problem to be:

We are going through two revolutions, not one revolution. Every people on earth goes through two revolutions: a political revolution by which it wrests the right to govern itself from the hand of tyranny, or from the army stationed upon its soil against its will; and a social revolution, involving the conflict of classes, which settles down when justice is secured for the citizens of the united nation.

.... For us, the terrible experience through which our people are going is that we are having both revolutions at the same time.[15]

These goals could only be accomplished by changing the traditional social, economic, and political patterns that characterized pre-1952 Egypt. A series of related factors made this process especially difficult. First and

---

[15] Gamal Abdul Nasser, *Egypt's Liberation: The Philosophy of the Revolution* (Washington, D.C.: Public Affairs Press, 1955), pp. 39–40.

foremost, Egypt has a population problem. The population is too large for the available, arable land area, and is growing much more rapidly than the ability of the government to reclaim land. As a result of this unfavorable population/land balance, and a general lack of natural resources, Egypt is forced to depend on external assistance. This aid from other nations is often in the form of long-term loans or development capital for specific projects. Much of the aid, however, has been diverted from domestic use to use by the military. The state of belligerency between Egypt and Israel since 1948 forced Egypt to build and maintain a large and expensive military force. Internal and external factors have combined to retard the process of social and economic change first proposed by President Nasser and now continued by President Sadat.

The goals of economic development and social change have not, however, been abandoned. The process of change has begun. As is often the case, the revolution that sought to make fundamental changes in the traditional patterns of life and divisions within society has created new divisions and new cleavage patterns. These new patterns strongly influence the nature of domestic politics in Egypt and the development of new political institutions.

The Egyptian Population

The Egyptian population is unified racially, religiously, and linguistically. Racially, the Egyptian people are primarily of Mediterranean origin. The position of Egypt at the crossroads of Europe, the Middle East, and Africa and thousands of years of contact with other groups have produced racial characteristics that are distinctively Egyptian. There also exist in Egypt foreign communities, of varying sizes and importance, which have influenced the political and social development of Egypt. Many of these, such as the Greek, Lebanese, and Armenian communities, are intimately involved in the commercial life of Egypt. To the south, in Upper Egypt, there is also a relatively small Nubian community with it own language and physical characteristics.

Islam has been the dominant religious tradition in Egypt since the early eighth century when it replaced Christianity. Probably close to 90 percent of the Egyptian population follow Islam. The 1971 constitution proclaims that "Egypt is an Arab Republic with a democratic, socialist system based on an alliance of the working people and derived from the country's historical heritage and the spirit of Islam." It further states that "Islam is the religion of the State" but "safeguards the freedom of worship and of performing rights for all religions."[16]

The largest and most influential religious minority in Egypt are the

---

[16] Cited in *The Middle East and North Africa, 1975–1976* (London: Europa Publications, 1975), p. 307.

Coptic Christians. Numbering about 3 million, these Egyptians are descended from the original Christian community which existed prior to the spread of Islam. They continue to exert a significant political and social influence in Egypt.

Arabic is the official language of Egypt and the language spoken by almost all Egyptians. Although English and French are sometimes used by the elites, and although there is a strong tradition of higher education in English and French, Arabic is clearly the most important language. There is a specific Egyptian dialect of colloquial Arabic, a strong literary tradition in classical Arabic, and an emerging middle Arabic, which lessens some of the more pronounced differences between standard, classical Arabic and spoken Arabic.

The most important characteristic of the Egyptian population is its size and growth. It is estimated that at the time of the modernization begun by Muhammad Ali in the nineteenth century the population of Egypt was approximately 3 million; by the 1952 revolution the population had increased to almost 20 million. In 1975 the population was estimated to be almost 37 million. This rapid growth is the result of better health and sanitary conditions in Egypt, which increase the life expectancy of Egyptians, and to a high birth rate. Although great emphasis is placed on limiting the size of Egyptian families through family planning, the birth rate continues to be one of the highest in the world. From 1965 to 1972 the population was growing at a rate of 2.5 percent per year.

The problem of population growth is compounded by the inability to rapidly increase the amount of arable land. About 96 percent of Egypt's total area is desert. The Aswan Dam, built in the 1960s, increased the amount of arable land, as have land reclamation schemes such as the Liberation Province scheme in the western desert. The cost, however, is extremely high, and requires massive technical and financial aid from foreign nations.

The ever-increasing Egyptian population strains Egypt's financial capabilities. The effectiveness of many development projects is negated by the increased population. Making the situation even more complex and volatile has been the desire of the government since the revolution to make a radical transformation in the economic and social life of the average Egyptian. New groups produce new demands, which the government often finds hard to meet.

Cleavages

It has often been remarked that while Egypt has been invaded many times and ruled by many different conquerors, the life of the peasant, the fellahin, has remained relatively unchanged. The constants are poverty, disease, illiteracy, and a short life expectancy. Before the revolution most Egyptians were tied to, but did not own, their land. There was little opportunity or hope for social or economic mobility.

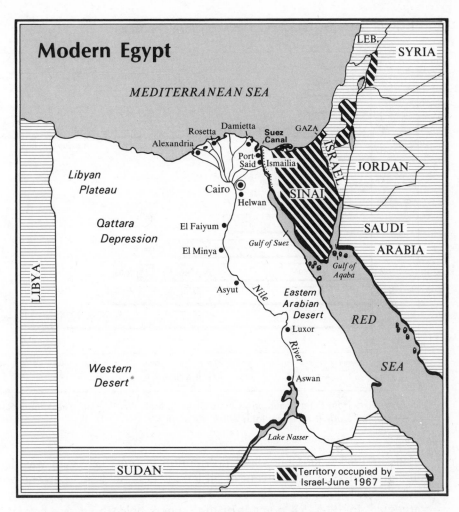

Modern Egypt

MEDITERRANEAN SEA

LEB.
SYRIA
Damietta
Rosetta   Suez   GAZA
Alexandria   Canal
                Port
                Said   Ismailia   ISRAEL   JORDAN
Libyan
Plateau   Cairo
                Helwan   SINAI
Qattara   El Faiyum
Depression   Gulf of Suez   SAUDI
             El Minya   ARABIA
                                    Gulf of
                                    Aqaba
             Asyut   Eastern
                        Arabian
                        Desert   RED
                         Luxor
Western
Desert   SEA
                         Aswan

                    Lake Nasser

SUDAN   Territory occupied by
                         Israel-June 1967

The 1952 revolution aimed to alter this pattern and break the cycle. In 1962, ten years after the revolution, President Nasser issued a charter to the National People's Congress that summarized the goals of the political leadership: "Justice . . . cannot be an expensive commodity beyond the reach of the citizen. Medicine must be cheap and available to everyone. Educational curricula must be reviewed 'in a revolutionary manner.' Laws must be redrafted to serve the new social relationship of political democracy."[17] The aim was the rapid development of Egypt and the creation of a new political and social order.

One of the first areas of interest for the new political actors after the revolution was land reform. A 1952 land reform bill limited the amount of land that could be held by an individual to 200 *feddans* (1 feddan = 1.038 acres); this was reduced to 100 feddans in 1961 and then to 50 fed-

---

[17] Cited in Tom Little, *Modern Egypt* (London: Ernest Benn, 1967), pp. 238–239.

FIGURE 3–1   The Rapidly Changing Egyptian Population

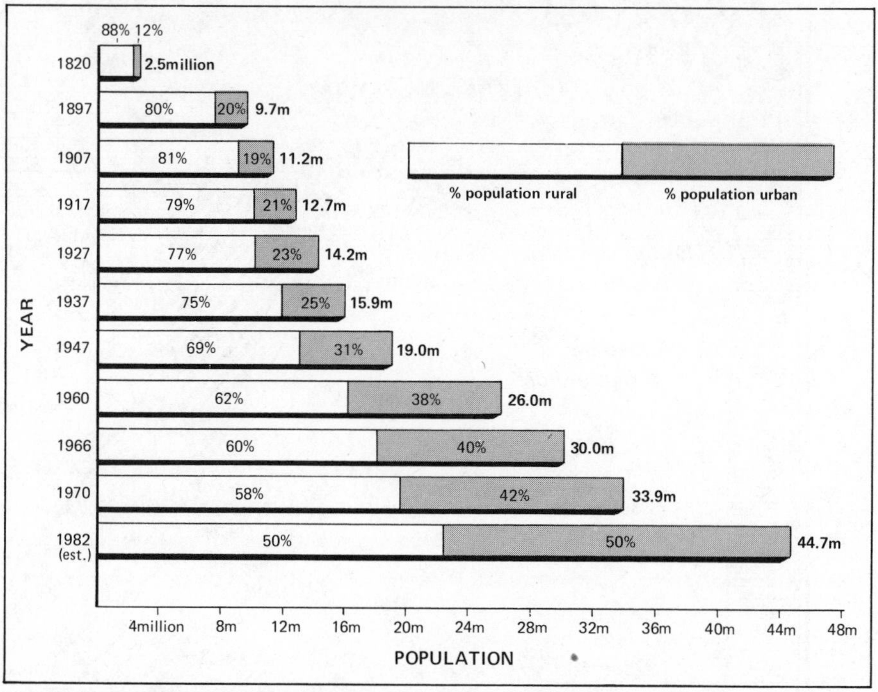

Source: Data from Peter Beaumont, Gerald Blake, J. Malcolm Flagstaff, *The Middle East: A Geographical Study* (New York: John Wiley, 1976), p. 476.

dans in 1969. Like Chile, land distribution in pre-1952 Egypt was highly unequal. In 1952, 5.5 percent of all landowners held 64.5 percent of the total area. Figures for 1965 reveal that the land distribution pattern is still unequal. In 1965, 5.4 percent of the owners held about one-half of the land while 94.6 percent held the remaining half. The average holding for the 5 percent was about 18 feddans, while that for the remaining 95 percent was about 2 feddans.

Reform in agriculture was also designed to provide the peasant with security and to increase productivity. Rent control and the regulation of land tenure were introduced. Cooperatives were established to help agricultural workers financially and to increase productivity. The number of cooperatives grew from 1,727 in 1952 to 4,897 in 1963, with loans made to almost a million borrowers.

Although attempts are being made to improve the living conditions of the rural Egyptian and to increase the productivity of the agricultural sector, more and more Egyptians are leaving the rural areas for the large cities. They seek jobs in the rapidly expanding industrial sector of the economy or in service areas. In terms of contributions to the gross domestic product, agriculture contributes about 30 percent, industry about 20 percent, and service related areas about 20 percent. Increasing industrialization and urbanization have created new classes of skilled, semi-skilled, and un-skilled workers.

Most of these new workers live in urban areas. The population for the greater Cairo area was estimated to be 6.5 million in 1974. The second largest urban area, around Alexandria, had a population of 2.25 million. While many of these new urban residents seek to maintain many of their traditional patterns of interaction, they face new demands and have new expectations. Rapid urban growth creates problems for city planners, edu-cators, health officials, and most of all, for the new residents of the cities.

The changes inaugurated by post-1952 Egyptian governments have pro-duced new groups with diverse interests. Small landholders, workers in urban areas, and new managerial and technocratic elites have developed. New and more-established groups are not always pleased with govern-ment policies. For example, the wealthy aristocracy that dominated Egyptian economic and political life before 1952 lost much of their power during the Nasser presidency. Many of these people went into exile after 1952, while many of those who stayed found their wealth heavily taxed or

Egyptian farmers, dependent on the Nile, continue to use many traditional— but efficient—farming practices. Courtesy, United Nations.

confiscated. The rapid and sweeping nationalization of industries in the 1961–1962 period also created dissatisfaction among much of the middle class. For the lower classes, both urban and rural, rapid inflation and the general shortage of consumer goods often make increases in income less significant than might first appear. Although President Sadat has reversed many of Nasser's economic policies in the 1970s, the Nasser period dramatically altered group life. New cleavage patterns now mix with centuries-old patterns, with implications for the structure of politics as well as for the economic sphere.

Interest Groups

The trend in post-1952 Egypt has been to limit the growth and control the influence of independent interest groups. One of the first acts of the new regime from 1952 to 1954 was to control active opposition to the government. The conservative Muslim Brotherhood, which presented perhaps the most serious challenge, found its influence limited by the arrest of its major leaders and thousands of its members in 1954. This action followed the attempted assassination of President Nasser. Likewise, political parties from the nationalist Wafd to the Communist party of Egypt were outlawed.

The decision of the Nasser government to take a more active role in the economy changed the relationship of business and labor groups to the government. The new leaders established a policy of allowing the formation of interest groups, but making sure at the same time that the government and the political organizations of the day could exercise considerable control over them. For example, the number of unionized workers climbed from 125,000 in 1952 to 600,000 in 1965. The freedom of these unions and newly unionized workers to challenge the government, however, was limited. The Egyptian Federation of Labor, formed in 1957, has been the major labor interest group. It is composed of 16 affiliate unions and claims a membership of 2.5 million persons.

The nationalizations carried out in the early 1960s also influenced business and industry. The government took a more active role in managing existing industries and in creating new ones. This changed the influence of organizations like the Federation of Egyptian Industries. Founded in 1922, this organization traditionally has been one of the most important groups representing Egyptian industry.

Since 1975 President Sadat gradually, and cautiously, has removed several of the restrictions interest groups operated under during the Nasser presidency. There remains, however, a limit to the freedom of action and independence granted certain groups. For example, the rioting in late 1976 and early 1977 over increased food prices resulted in emergency legislation restricting the freedom of action of certain opposition groups and giving the president emergency powers (see Chapters 10 and 11).

The 1952 revolution created new economic and social groups and altered the relationships among existing groups. By the admission of the leaders of the revolution, the revolution begun in 1952 is not yet complete. Some of these new groups are an important influence on political life in Egypt, but it is clear that their power to act independently of the government is limited. Rapid population growth, urbanization, industrialization, and the changed life-styles in rural areas have all combined to produce a society in change, both in terms of its composition and of the demands these groups make on the political leadership of Egypt.

▪ TANZANIA ▪

Tanzania, like many other African nations, is a highly pluralistic and fractionalized nation-state. Different ethnic, language, and religious groups, as well as different economic and social classes, coexist in the same polity. However, unlike many developing nations, Tanzania has been politically stable since independence, and has suffered relatively little political violence. The questions we must begin to ask are: Why do two nations such as Tanzania and Nigeria, each characterized by diversity, exhibit such different political histories? and, Why has Nigeria suffered a civil war and several coup d'états, while Tanzania has remained stable?

There are no easy or simple answers to these questions. A clue is found in the nature of the differences that characterize the Tanzanian population and in the response of the government to these differences. In this section we describe Tanzanian society, and explore the factors that make Tanzania unique among African and developing nations.

Cleavages

Cleavage patterns in Tanzania present an interesting contrast to those found in Nigeria. Differences among groups are much more sharply drawn in Nigeria than in Tanzania. As described earlier, the Hausa-Fulani, Yoruba, and Ibo in Nigeria have distinct languages, political traditions, and political structures. Since independence, Nigerian politics has been dominated by the changing relationships among these three dominant groups.

Tanzania is also an ethnically diverse nation, but the relationships among groups are considerably different. Group differences are not as clear-cut or as mutually reinforcing as those in Nigeria; major identity groups in Tanzania share similar linguistic and cultural backgrounds. Given these similarities, it is more correct to speak of Tanzanian identity groups rather than distinct ethnic or tribal groups. Identity groups recognize those factors uniting them, as well as those separating them.

Thousands of years ago, for reasons that remain unclear, Bantu-speaking peoples in Central Africa began a great migration. This migration took them to almost all parts of Africa, but especially to southern and eastern

Africa. Over time many of these Bantu-speaking groups came to view themselves as distinct from other Bantu-speaking groups, but in many cases they continued to share similar linguistic and cultural origins. Scholars disagree on the reasons for the migration, but most do agree that the technological advances of the iron age and the introduction of new crops allowed for a great population increase.

Most of the major groups in present-day Tanzania are related by this Bantu-speaking connection. Although distinguishing between groups is complex and difficult, it is possible to isolate different identity groups based on their regional locations. The geography and topography of Tanzania separate groups, often by long distances. Traditionally, this has made communication and interaction among groups difficult.

The Nyamwezi, who occupy the central area of Tanzania, are the largest numerical grouping, comprise about 19 percent of the population. Around the rim of Tanzania, the Lakes Bantu, Northeast Coastal Bantu, Central Bantu, and Rift Cluster Bantu each make up between 10 and 14 percent of the population. The remaining population is divided between smaller Bantu-speaking and non-Bantu groups.

No group is so large that they can dominate other smaller groups. This diversity and relative numerical parity among groups lessens the possibility of violent conflicts arising among groups. Unlike Nigeria where southern groups feared domination by the Hausa-Fulani in the North, there is no one group in Tanzania that can "win the political game" based solely on its numerical size. Some groups complain that others receive a disproportional share of the rewards and opportunities, but the conflict has not reached the state it did in Nigeria.

There are other differences in Tanzanian society that present at least potential threats to the political system. Three major religious traditions are present in Tanzania: about 40 percent of the population profess faith in Islam, about 37 percent follow indigenous African religious traditions, and about 23 percent are Christian (both Protestant and Roman Catholic).

There are also differences between the rural and urban populations. Most Tanzanians do continue to live in rural settings. Less than 10 percent of the population live in cities of over 20,000 persons. Dar es Saalam, the capital and largest city, has a population of only about 300,000. The lure of the city is strong, however, and many young Tanzanians flock to urban areas. Many of those with an education express no desire to live in rural, "backward" areas. Although the government attempts to prevent unplanned urbanization, the city acts as a magnet, drawing the young to the "land of opportunity."

Unifying Factors

Clearly, group differences are not as strong in Tanzania as in Nigeria, but they do provide potential sources for political conflict. Balancing the

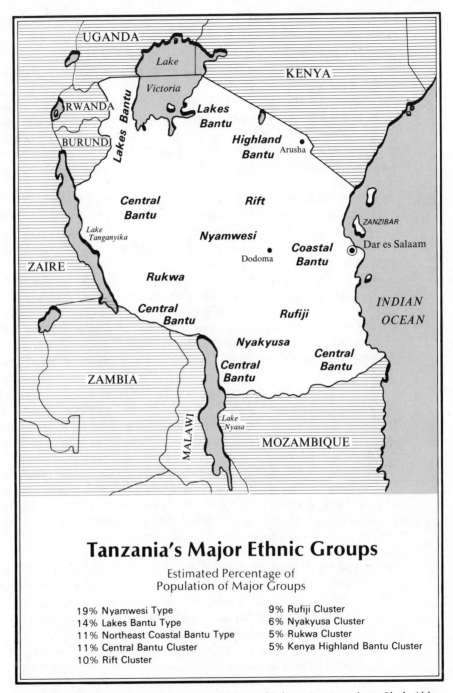

Tanzania's Major Ethnic Groups

Estimated Percentage of
Population of Major Groups

19% Nyamwesi Type
14% Lakes Bantu Type
11% Northeast Coastal Bantu Type
11% Central Bantu Cluster
10% Rift Cluster

9% Rufiji Cluster
6% Nyakyusa Cluster
5% Rukwa Cluster
5% Kenya Highland Bantu Cluster

Source: Reprinted with permission of Macmillan Publishing Co., Inc., from *Black Africa;*
A Comparative Handbook by Donald Morrison, R. C. Mitchell, J. N. Paden, and H. M.
Stevenson. Copyright © The Free Press, a division of the Macmillan Company.

factors dividing Tanzanians are the factors uniting them. Two are of special interest. The first is the important role played by Swahili, the national language. The second is the development of a national ideology designed to unify all Tanzanians under the banner of economic, social, cultural, and political progress.

Swahili plays a dual role in Tanzania. It is the national official language, and it is the dominant lingua franca among different language groups. Probably close to 90 percent of the population speak and understand Swahili either as a first or second language. Increasingly, Swahili is viewed as one of the most important factors in developing and preserving national unity.

Several factors combine to magnify the importance of Swahili in Tanzania. First, the language developed as a mixture of Bantu and Arabic in the coastal areas of East Africa, and so is not associated with specific ethnic groups in Tanzania. One ethnic group did not have to give up its language for the language of another group.

Contrast this with the complex situation in Nigeria. Yoruba and Ibo peoples certainly would resist and resent being forced to abandon their mother tongues were Hausa chosen as the Nigerian national language. Likewise, the Hausa would resist and resent any attempt to impose Yoruba or Ibo as the national language. Swahili does not provoke these emotional responses, and acts as a "neutral" language, acceptable to most all groups.

Swahili is also an African language, not associated with the colonial experience. Unlike French and English, the official national languages of most African states, Swahili does not carry with it a suspect colonial past. Because it is a common language among many different groups in Tanzania, nationalist politicians could use it to appeal to and address these groups.

Finally, Swahili is a highly developed language. It is rapidly developing a rich and diverse literary tradition. Works from other languages are being translated into Swahili and, more important, original works are being written in Swahili expressing Tanzanian themes. To cite only one example, President Nyerere has translated Shakespeare's *Julius Caesar* into Swahili, as well as writing many original works in Swahili.

Since the 1960s government policy, where feasible, has supported the use of Swahili over English, the former colonial language. Although English is still widely used, Swahili is now intimately associated with the concept of a wider Tanzanian culture and identity. It is increasingly being used as the medium of instruction in the educational system, in the mass media, and where possible in government service. The Ministry of Community Development and National Culture emphasizes this relationship between Swahili and the evolution of a national, unifying political culture:

The role played by Swahili language in Tanzania is immense. Almost everybody in Tanzania can speak the language: and, therefore, it has become a useful medium of communication. Since the language has now become the national language, we feel we must do something to widen its scope so that it may be sufficiently useful in all Government activities, in schools, and commercial circles. We want to rid the language of bad influences and to guide it to grow along the proper road. We want to standardise its orthography and usage, and to encourage all our people to learn to speak and write properly grammatical Swahili.[18]

Swahili also plays an important role in the developing of the national ideology. This ideology is the outgrowth of the political thought and experiences of President Julius Nyerere and the ruling, and only official, political party, the Tanzanian African National Union (TANU). The ideology serves as both a justification for the exercise of political power by TANU and establishes the short- and long-term goals of the political leaders.

Ujamaa is the core concept of the Tanzanian ideology. Ujamaa means socialism or familyhood. African socialism incorporates certain characteristics common to most traditional African societies as well as more modern political values. President Nyerere describes this mix:

By the use of the word "ujamaa," therefore, we state that for us socialism involves building on the foundation of our past, and building also to our own design. We are not importing a foreign ideology into Tanzania and trying to smother our distinct social patterns with it. We have deliberately decided to grow, as a society, out of our own roots, but in a particular direction and towards a particular kind of objective. We are doing this by emphasizing certain characteristics of our traditional organization, and extending them so that they can embrace the possibilities of modern technology and enable us to meet the challenge of life in the twentieth century world.[19]

Special attention is paid to the development of cooperative agricultural villages. These ujamaa villages eventually are to be self-sufficient. Each individual is expected to provide labor for the common fields, but, each family is given a small plot on which to grow what they like and dispose of as they see fit. Emphasis in both theory and application is on working for the common good, self-reliance, equality, and common production (see Chapter 11).

Estimates suggest that as many as 9 million Tanzanians now live in ujamaa villages. Some clearly are more developed and self-sufficient than others, and the overall assessments of the efficiency and productivity of the villages vary. There is some resistance to the creation of these cooperative enterprises, but in general, it appears as if the ideological goals, if not the practical implementation, are fairly widely accepted.

---

[18] Cited in Wilfred Whiteley, *Swahili: The Rise of a National Language* (London: Methuen and Co., Ltd., 1969), p. 104.

[19] Julius K. Nyerere, *Freedom and Socialism* (London: Oxford University Press, 1968), p. 2. This and other quotes in this book are reprinted by permission of the author.

Tanzania's ideological leaders have also given considerable attention to the relationship between the rulers and the ruled. All political systems face the potential problem of the political leaders losing touch with those over whom they exercise power and authority. TANU attempts to prevent the development of a gap between the elite and the participants by emphasizing the responsibility of the political leaders to the political participants. The most stringent guidelines were laid down in the Arusha Declaration of 1967.

The Arusha Declaration (named after the town in which the policy was formulated) establishes the rights and duties of TANU and government leaders. Leaders must be either peasants or workers, should not hold shares in companies or serve as directors of companies, and should not receive salaries other than their government one. The declaration is designed to make political leaders more responsive and to control growing corruption in both government and party circles.

The party, the leader, and the national ideology are central to Tanzanian political life. They dominate both the government and the bureaucracy. Little politics occurs that is not directly related to or controlled by one of them. This being the case, to understand and evaluate politics in Tanzania, we must study the relationships among the leader (President Nyerere), the party (the Tanzanian African National Union), and the ideology (ujamaa or African socialism).

We have suggested that Tanzania is blessed with a national language that serves as both a unifying symbol and an effective means of communication and that there is a fairly widespread acceptance of the national values formulated by the president and the party. This does not mean that the differences in Tanzania will remain unimportant. Societies undergoing rapid economic, political, and social change often find that differences that are unimportant today become vitally important tomorrow. Ethnic differences, urban/rural differences, religious differences, or differences between social and economic classes present developing political systems with an awesome array of potential problems.

▪ CHILE ▪

The protection afforded by the Andes Mountains to the east and the Pacific Ocean to the west has given Chileans a unique political culture. Chile's relative isolation led to the early development of a strong sense of national unity and identity. Many of the ethnic, religious, and linguistic divisions that plague other nations are not as important in modern-day Chile. Sharp economic and social divisions, however, strongly influence Chilean politics. Many of the current political conflicts and crises stem from these cleavages.

The two major issues that dominate Chilean politics are the perpetually rising rate of inflation, which has accompanied general economic instability, and conflicts over the role of the government in the management of the economy. Since World War II the political spectrum has been divided into three distinct political blocs—left, center, and right—each bloc competing for political power in the electoral arena. Each of the three blocs, before 1973, appealed for support to specific sections and classes within the Chilean population. In order to better understand the growth and collapse of political parties and political coalitions, it is first important to describe the divisions that characterize Chilean society.

The Setting and the Population

Geographically, Chile is diverse. Its long length (over 2,600 miles) and narrow width (average 110 miles) span a wide range of geographical and climatic patterns. Northern Chile is arid and semi-arid, relatively unpopulated, but economically rich in copper and nitrate. Southern Chile, by contrast, is tropical in climate and heavily forested. It too is relatively unpopulated.

It is in central Chile that political and economic power are concentrated. The majority (over 60 percent) of Chileans live and work in this fertile and rich central region. Santiago, the capital and dominant urban center, is located in this area, but also in this region are the richest and most profitable agricultural lands. Since early settlement, the central region has dominated political life in Chile, and it is here that the struggles between competing political forces have been most intense.

A profile of the Chilean population must stress both those factors supporting national unity and identity and those factors dividing the population. In many respects Chile appears to be a homogeneous nation—95 percent Roman Catholic, predominantly Spanish-speaking, ethnically homogeneous, highly literate, and highly urbanized. Estimates suggest that 80 percent of the population is literate and that by 1980 75 percent of the population will live in urban areas. Certainly, when compared to the complex patterns of religious, ethnic, and linguistic diversity in Nigeria and Tanzania, Chile on the surface appears to be a more cohesive nation.

Many of the factors that help to unify can also, however, separate Chileans. Like other nations dominated by one religious tradition, political actors and participants in Chile have struggled over the role of the church in state affairs. The 1833 constitution established Roman Catholicism as the state religion; the 1925 constitution reversed this and separated church and state. Within the church there are liberal and conservative factions that differ fundamentally on political, economic, and social issues, and on the role of the church in politics and government; and in the larger society there are those who seek to involve the church in the processes of social and economic change and those who seek the support of the church in

Modern Chile

preserving the existing institutions and patterns of behavior. The popularity of the Christian Democratic movement during the 1960s (see Chapter 5) points to this widespread division of opinion.

The lack of educational opportunities further divides Chilean society. Although there is free, compulsory primary education for grades one through six, there is a sharp decline in the number of students who go beyond primary school to secondary school, and an even sharper drop in those who go on to university. Thus, while 80 percent of the population is literate, there are sharp distinctions in terms of levels of literacy, educational skills, and educational opportunities. This results in frustration for many who would like to continue their education but are unable to do so for economic reasons and for those who are educated but unable to translate their education into better jobs or a better living condition.

Likewise, urbanization produces new demands and expectations, and has led to new divisions. Rapid urbanization usually means unplanned urbanization. Between 1960 and 1966 Santiago's population grew from approximately 1.9 million to 2.5 million. This rapid increase resulted in housing shortages, unemployment, and general discontent. It created a new class of urban poor, many of whom had migrated from rural, agricultural settings seeking new opportunities. An added burden was placed on the already strained, inflationary budget, in the form of increased welfare services and demands for assistance.

The general picture that emerges thus far is of a nation with strong unifying traits, but also one undergoing rapid changes. Changes have produced and are producing politically important cleavages. These cleavages represent different political traditions and outlooks, and offer different solutions to similar problems. Two of the most important of these in recent years are the split between the rural and urban populations and the emergence of clear-cut economic classes.

Rural/Urban Split

Although Chile is an urban society, it is highly dependent on its agricultural sector; 30 percent of the population are engaged in some form of agricultural occupation. Of the remaining population 25 percent are engaged in service or utility related occupations, 18 percent in manufacturing, 10 percent in trade, and about 4 percent in mining and related industries. What develops is a split between the rural and urban sectors over budgetary allocations and the distribution of political power and influence.

Traditionally, political power was concentrated in the hands of the large landowners. These men, along with the emerging commercial and industrial elite, dominated the political scene and determined the political agenda. In many cases those who worked the land and provided labor were tied directly to and under the control of the landed aristocracy. They depended on them for their livelihoods, their housing, their educations, and their security. They voted the way they were told, and they did not organize to press for more rights or better conditions. The system in many ways was a feudal one.

Land distribution was highly unequal. Most of the argicultural land was concentrated in the hands of a few wealthy owners. In 1925, for example, 10 percent of the farms and ranches in Chile had 90 percent of the agricultural land.[20] This meant that a majority of the agricultural workers, by economic necessity, were forced to work for the rich and powerful few.

Unequal distribution combined with the paternalistic attitudes of owners to produce a relatively stable, apathetic, and passive rural population. The land tenure system was not agriculturally efficient or productive, for the large haciendas were not, by and large, profitable operations. Agricultural equipment, farming techniques, and labor relations were traditional and backward. As the population increased, agricultural production lagged behind. This had the dual effect of forcing the government to buy foodstuffs from overseas and of forcing rural workers to migrate to urban areas to look for employment.

In present-day Chile the economy is affected by rural-urban differences. For example, while the mining industry employs a relatively small percentage of the entire work force (about 4 percent), it produces over 80 percent of Chile's exports. Much of the revenue generated from the export of copper must be used to buy imported foodstuffs. A more efficient and productive agricultural sector might well be able to meet Chile's needs without having to import. Money spent to buy imported foodstuffs decreases the amount that can be spent on other social and economic problems; many of the most severe problems are found in urban areas. There is a keen competition between groups for the limited resources available to the government.

Class Structure

Educational expansion, industrialization, and urbanization have created new economic classes. During the twentieth century these classes have been represented by political parties and other interest groups. One indicator of the conflict and competition between these new groups was labor unrest. Betwen 1849 and 1884 there were only 9 major strikes reported. From 1885 to 1910 there were 290 reported, while from 1911 to 1925 there were 747 major strikes.[21]

---

[20] Brian Lovemen, "The Transformation of the Chilean Countryside," in Arturo Valenzuela and J. Samuel Valenzuela, eds., *Chile: Politics and Society* (New Bruswick, N.J.: Transaction Books, 1976), p. 243.

[21] Julio Samuel Valenzuela, "The Chilean Labor Movement: The Institutionalization of Conflict," in Valenzuela and Valenzuela, eds., *Chile*, p. 138.

Unionization was an important factor in the changing political scene. Although the government at times sought to exercise strict control over union finances, bylaws, and elections, unionization became an increasingly important political fact in the early part of this century. The Chilean Workers' Federation (*Federation Obererea de Chile,* FOCh) was formed in 1909 and had over 100,000 members by 1920. In 1920 the FOCh switched its allegiance from the Socialist party to the Communist party. Various unions united in 1936 to form the Chilean Workers' Confederation (*Confederation de Trabajadores de Chile,* CTCh), which during the Popular Front movement in the late 1930s became a major supporter of the government.

Rural workers were much slower to organize and press for better conditions. The control the hacienda owners exercised over their day-to-day existence placed the rural Chileans in a precarious position. Despite this tradition of passivity, land questions and specifically those issues dealing with the redistribution of land on a more equitable basis became central in postwar politics. Both the Frei government (1964–1969) and the Allende government (1970–1973) initiated land reform and land redistribution schemes. The goals were to break the power and the monopoly of the landed aristocracy, to distribute land on a more equitable basis, and to organize the rural workers in effective and responsive organizations. While the success of these movements was not as great as was at first hoped, a start was made.

Middle- and upper-class groups also organized. Middle-class and center groups organized organizations such as teachers' groups to represent their positions. Upper-class groups organized employers' associations, which sought to protect middle- and upper-class interests and to counter the growing power of the trade union movement and the demands being made by rural workers.

Most developing nations have undergone or are undergoing economic and social changes similar to those that have occurred in Chile. However, unlike many developing nations, Chile has a long, well-established history of popular participation in politics and political stability. Because it had a strong, viable set of political institutions, much of the debate between classes occurred within the political system. Political parties of the left, center, and right mobilized and harnessed the support and power of these movements. The left associated itself with the unions; the center political parties, with the moderate and reform oriented groups; and the right, with the conservative, wealthy classes. In cases where groups had not yet organized, such as among rural workers, political parties sought to create organizations that would mobilize them.

The growing complexity of the Chilean political scene is in part due to the rapid politicization of certain previous "nonpolitical" issues and to the rapid increase in the number of individuals participating in the political arena. Differences between rural and urban groups and between various economic classes are manifest in the large number of political parties that contested elections during the 1950s and 1960s. The upper classes, generally conservative and traditional, sought to protect their position and privilege; the center and middle sought change through democratic reform; the left, increasingly radical, sought change through revolution. The successive election victories of the right, center, and left in the 1958, 1964, and 1969 presidential elections point to the intense competition among these groups.

CONCLUSION

The seriousness of the problems posed by the existence of political cleavages for a nation-state depends first on their number and intensity. The number of cleavages refers to the number of societal divisions that have real political importance. Today in Britain, for example, society is divided politically on the basis of class, nationality, and race. Only a few years ago class was the only political cleavage of importance. As the number of political cleavages of importance increased from one to three, the problems facing British governments increased accordingly. Increased violence and political instability accompanied the addition of new intensive divisions.

Britain's recent troubles regarding group conflict and instability are similar to the traditional problems of French and German governments. The politics of continental countries are typically complicated by a number of intense cleavages, notably those associated with class, religion, and urban/rural differences.

The most extreme cases of cleavage-based violence and instability are found in the developing areas. The case of Nigeria is particularly striking. The tribal and regional cleavages are numerous and intense, a fact that has made this nation difficult to govern.

Our discussion in this chapter has suggested several ways that governments may reduce the impact of political cleavages. Soviet authorities have relied on a blend of coercion and state-directed socialization to reduce or control group differences. President Nyerere of Tanzania has sponsored language and community development programs to achieve the same end. Major party leaders in West Germany have avoided controversial group-related issues and dropped ideological appeals in order to emphasize the things that most Germans have in common. All leaders, however, realize that group antagonism of this sort is persistent even in the face of concentrated efforts at reconciliation.

The group life described in this chapter represents the raw material of politics. A nation's group life determines the competing forces engaged in politics and the nature of their demands. Group life also greatly influences the pattern of participation in a nation—the subject of Chapter 4.

CHAPTER 4
POLITICAL PARTICIPATION

Who participates? How do they participate?
Why do they participate?

People's meaningful participation in politics differs according to the countries they live in. In some, the opportunities are widespread and diverse; in others, only a few important political jobs—elective, appointive, or volunteer—are available. A person's likelihood of participating is also affected by the nation's history and political culture. Nations vary considerably according to how important it is for citizens to participate. Systems also differ in the rewards and risks that political participants face. Some nations offer rewards: personal satisfaction, the ability to influence decisions, and the opportunity to hold political office. In other nations the risks of participating and losing are high; losers may find themselves not only out of office, but even imprisoned or executed.

History and Culture

History and culture influence who participates, the value placed on participation, and the types of participation encouraged. Not all individuals or groups in a political system have the same chance to participate. The culture of a nation determines in part who participates and who is allowed to play the political game. In some nations wealth, education, family background, or a particular type of education may be important. For example, Britain's political elite before World War I was dominated by the aristocratic landowning class who shared the experience of a classical Oxford or Cambridge education. In the Soviet Union a working class or proletarian background is helpful because the USSR places a cultural value on labor.

Culture also influences the type of participation valued. Some nations admire representative institutions, while others are more impressed by administrative institutions. Germans, strongly influenced by a history and culture that value efficient administration, have higher regard for bureaucrats than for politicians. On the other hand, the British associate politics with the parliamentary institution and with members of Parliament.

In some cultures political participation is largely a ritual associated with the myths of the nation. The massive turnout of Soviet voters every four years to elect representatives does not significantly influence who makes decisions in the Soviet Union or what decisions are made. The heritage of the 1917 revolution, however, stresses the need for mass participation by all citizens, especially peasants and workers previously not allowed to participate. In Tanzania participation has both symbolic and instrumental impact. The Tanzanian African National Union seeks to build national unity and purpose by consulting with and listening to Tanzanians in all walks of life. This view of African socialism stresses members of the village, town, or city discussing their problems and reaching solutions together.

Participation can have an effective input into decision-making and policy implementation. Where effective participation is valued, citizens have a real role in settling disputes over leadership and policy—normally through elections. Once decisions are made, citizens may become involved in realizing the policy goals through political work. Community work projects in Africa, production quotas in the Soviet Union, and voluntary energy conservation programs in Britain are examples of participation after the decision has been made.

Rewards and Incentives

Not all people have the same motivation to participate. The psychological drives associated with political activity vary widely. The most basic drive seems to be desire for political power—to enforce one's will on others. Other drives include the need to associate with others in groups and altruism—the need to do things for others. There is no particular reason to suppose that nations differ dramatically in their proportion of power-seekers or do-gooders. Within a given nation psychological factors help to explain differences in participation.

People are also motivated to participate in politics because of potential rewards. In the United Kingdom participation has a public service, nonprofit orientation. Though members of Parliament receive low salaries, political careers are considered high-status occupations. Politicians are generally respected and may also have the personal satisfaction of performing essential public tasks. Members of Parliament often maintain part-time employment after election.

In developing nations with weak economies—like Nigeria and Egypt—political salaries are much above the national average. In some cases, political jobs also may offer a lucrative, second income derived from corruption. Graft, bribery, and other illegal operations are not, however, unique to the developing world; examples are found in all nations.

Rewards, then, are both real and symbolic. Nonmaterial rewards include status, prestige, and recognition, depending on how the public views politicians. Material rewards include obvious financial benefit as well as increased future opportunities. Many politicians leave politics for lucrative careers in other fields.

Political Risks

The rewards, however, must be balanced against the risks. In most systems political success is rewarded in some fashion, but how political failure is punished varies. In some systems those who fail simply sit out until they are re-elected and re-enter the game. In other cases failure results in loss of status or money. French political losers, operating in a system that encourages political entrepreneurship, face both these risks. Would-be office seekers in France may commit their personal resources gambling that political success will return a profit. This individual, however, is on his or her own, win or lose. As we shall see, political parties and institutions in France are not strong enough to control the selection process.

In other political systems risk involves loss of life and liberty. Where politics is not regularized and predictable, some may be tempted to seek total success by using extralegal means to gain power. Plotting against the existing authorities is a relatively common occurrence in many nations. The rewards are great, but so are the risks. Chile in 1973 was a system torn between rival factions; by September the military made the momentous decision to intervene and end civilian rule. Hundreds were killed; thousands were exiled or imprisoned.

In the Soviet Union, political risk is unusually high. Since authority is concentrated in a political hierarchy, it is tempting to gamble all to reach the higher party levels. However, since leadership selection is not institutionalized and predictable, miscalculations are costly. During Stalin's rule the cost of failure was your life; in more recent times exile and imprisonment in Siberia or forced retirement are more likely punishments.

Political Opportunity

A nation's history, culture, and pattern of political reward and risk influence its citizens' participation in politics. The populations of different

political systems differ in their desire, interest, and motivation to participate. Whether or not there is adequate outlet for these varying drives to
participate depends on the political structures of the nation and the nature of political institutions.

Opportunities depend on the raw number of positions available. Is the
system unitary, or is its authority divided on the basis of some federal
arrangement? In unitary systems like Chile and the United Kingdom, there
is only one important level of government—the national. The Soviet Union
is organized at four levels: the Union level, the Republic level, the provinces, and the localities. This fourfold division multiplies political offices,
party offices, and necessary volunteer and support positions.

The institutions responsible for recruiting people to political roles also
greatly affect participatory opportunities. In most nations the political
party is the most important institution recruiting new people into the
political system. The party screens the pool of people interested in participation, selecting some and rejecting others. In strong party systems the
organization imposes its standards on anyone eager to become involved.
Parties train activists to socialize newcomers to the political process—to
influence their attitudes and actions. In this way opportunities are restricted to potential "party people" who possess attributes the parties
view as desirable.

How effective the party is in screening potential recruits depends on
how well it can control political opportunities. To be successful a party
must demonstrate to potential activists that it can gratify or deny their
political ambitions; it must be able to deliver the "political goods" in the
form of jobs. This task is made easier when the political opportunities are
limited and therefore, more valuable.

In studying the distinctive patterns of participation in the eight nations,
we should keep in mind that the drive to participate must be balanced with
the opportunities for participation. In the United Kingdom people are encouraged to participate in politics and the steps to follow are clear and
unambiguous. Because of the strength of political parties and interest
groups, participation is likely to be highly institutionalized, regularized,
and predictable. The political jobs available, however, are few, and the
competition for them keen.

This is only one pattern, however. In France and some developing nations the drive to participate is weak, even though the opportunities for
participation are fairly broad. Participation is guaranteed to virtually
anyone interested enough to get involved in politics. Unlike the situation
in the United Kingdom, fewer people are competing for the available
opportunities. This permits greater individualism and reduces the role of
political parties in selecting and screening potential candidates.

Participation patterns change. This is especially true in developing nations. Groups that never participated in politics or that were prevented
from doing so may begin to demand the right to participate. Groups that

have traditionally held power may find themselves challenged and their authority questioned. In Nigeria and Chile, for example, military officers, trained not to intervene in civilian politics, decided that they must break this rule. In both cases they became active participants in politics. In many developing nations the military has become one of the most significant institutions for channeling participation.

Studying the active political community helps explain the types of political leaders found in different political systems and why they act as they do. Before we can study political parties and elections, we need to ask three important questions: Who participates? Why do they participate? How do they participate?

▪ THE UNITED KINGDOM ▪

The political system of the United Kingdom both encourages and channels widespread political participation. Britain's historical and cultural heritage promotes political activism. The institutions and political structures provide considerable rewards for activists—largely in terms of status and influence. People involved in politics need have few fears if their adventures in the political realm are less than successful. Opportunities are limited in scope and variety, but highly motivated individuals of widely differing backgrounds can participate meaningfully.

Historical and Cultural Factors

In some political systems—particularly in continental Europe—history discourages political activism as futile or dangerous. In Britain, though, gradual democratization made political activity safe as well as meaningful. The British system has accommodated itself to new groups and new group demands. The landed gentry, the commercial middle class, the industrial entrepreneurs and, finally, working Britons were all gradually admitted to full partnership in the political community. As a result, members of each group developed positive feelings about the political process. There was little need for militant movements, ideological postures, and inflexible stands.

The historical pattern of group accommodation is reflected in the political attitudes, values, and beliefs of citizens of the United Kingdom. The most important political attitude influencing political participation is the celebrated British pragmatism. Inspired by sixteenth and seventeenth-century empiricists—John Locke, David Hume, and George Berkeley—and grounded in Britain's role as a commercial nation, pragmatism sets the tone of politics. Uncomfortable debating political theories, Britons prefer to compare likely tangible results, thus they avoid dogmatism and emotionalism. The political style of political bargaining and accommodation defuses the explosive aspects of politics and make political life safe and potentially rewarding.

British respect for tradition and custom also contributes to wider participation in politics. The central institutions of British politics—Crown, Lords, and Commons—are more than seven hundred years old. Most Britons mention politics, political institutions, and politicians as special objects of their national pride. Other European peoples, notably the French and Germans, exhibit more pride in national art, culture, and science than in political institutions or practices.[1] The British feel added enjoyment and pleasure from voting, campaigning, or debating politics because these activities make them feel a part of a great political tradition.

Perhaps people's greatest incentive to participate is their belief that their material interests and well-being are tied to the struggle between the leading political parties. Most Britons, particularly the large number who identify with a political party, see each party as standing for particular class interests and that each party can make a real impact on the distribution of wealth, privilege, and power within the nation.[2] The overwhelming majority of Britons identify themselves simply as either middle class or working class and see a clear connection between class and party. People who work for the Labour party, for example, feel that their work will better the material position of working-class Britons.

Reward vs. Risk

Participation in British politics offers the full complement of political rewards available in a political system—status, influence, and financial rewards. The status incentive is more important in the United Kingdom than in many other nations. A political career is honorable, a gentleman's profession. The "best families" provide a son in each generation to help govern the realm. (His elite education at a private boarding school, called a public school in England, helps his political career greatly.) British parents do not recoil in horror when a child announces an intention to get involved in politics; rather, they see a career that will reflect well upon the family. Participating individuals themselves are directly rewarded by a substantial amount of respect and the opportunity to associate with highly regarded colleagues.

A desire for power may motivate serious political activists and professionals. With patience and persistence an individual may attain a position of very great influence during the course of a long political career.

---

[1] Gabriel A. Almond and Sidney Verba, *The Civic Culture* (Boston: Little, Brown, 1965), pp. 64–68.

[2] David Butler and Donald Stokes, *Political Change in Britain* (New York: St. Martin's Press, 1971), pp. 53–70.

The relatively few important political positions in the United Kingdom are powerful and highly coveted.

Direct financial reward is seldom a motivation for a career in British politics, as members of Parliament are poorly paid, earning the equivalent of $11,000 a year. Members of the House of Lords get no salary but can collect $21.50 in expenses for each day's session attended. In the past, low salaries meant that most MPs needed a large private income or a second job. Today more depend on their parliamentary salary, but "moonlighting" is still common.

Political Opportunity

Political opportunity in the United Kingdom ranges from merely voting to serving in the most important entity in the system—the cabinet. Each step from casually participant citizen to national leader requires greater commitment and greater skill. Few citizens of the United Kingdom get beyond the lowest rungs of the ladder of political involvement.

Since World War II approximately three-quarters of the eligible British public have elected to vote. The two figures given in Table 4–1 represent the usual range between elections with high interest and those with low interest. British citizens also exercise the opportunity to affiliate with organized interest groups; over three-fifths are "joiners."

The more difficult test of commitment to participation quickly weeds out most citizens. Twenty percent of Britain's public are members of political parties; but this number includes members of British trade unions, who automatically become members of the Labour party and whose party dues are paid through the union. Only 5 percent of the public are indi-

TABLE 4–1   Political Participation in Great Britain

Level	Number	Percent
Total Electorate	39,800,000	100
Voters (1974 Feb.)	31,333,226	78.70
Voters (1974 Oct.)	29,188,606	72.80
Organization Members	24,000,000	61.00
Voters/Local Election	16,800,000	42.00
Party Members	8,000,000	20.00
Official Post	5,500,000	14.00
Activists	2,750,000	7.00
Individual Party Members	2,000,000	5.00
MPs and Senior Civil Servants	4,000	0.01

Sources: Howard R. Penniman, ed., *Britain at the Polls* (Washington, D.C.: American Enterprise Institute for Public Policy Research, 1975), p. 241; and Richard Rose, *Politics in England Today* (London: Faber, 1974), p. 179.

vidual party members and, as such, have initiated the contact and borne the expense personally. Only a tiny fraction reach the powerful positions in Parliament and the civil service. It is in these institutions that effective political power—the power to make and enforce decisions—is wielded.

The Actives

Most political activists in the United Kingdom work through the constituency organizations of the major parties. Others work permanently with the national party organizations and are involved in questions of strategy and organization. Understanding the background of these activists gives us a clue as to who participates most intensely and who the system rewards.

Local party activists are those who carry out the basic day-to-day tasks of the party. Most importantly, they have a say in the nomination of candidates to Parliament, are involved in campaigning, and through attendance at the national party conferences help to formulate party programs. They are, in short, those one in twenty Britons intimately involved in politics.

In terms of education and occupation, party workers are not that different from the public at large. Over 60 percent of the activists left school by age 14—the age when most Britons leave school.[3] Over half of the local core of participants are either clerical white-collar workers or industrial workers within the Conservative party.[4] The corresponding figure for the Labour party exceeds three-quarters of the pool. In short, both parties provide meaningful participation for "average" citizens. The basic requirements seem to be interest and a sufficient knowledge of politics.

At the very top rung participation seems to be limited to individuals with particular advantages, especially that of education. Roughly 45 percent of candidates for Parliament have some higher education (compared with about 10 percent for other politically active Britons), and 70 percent of the *successful* parliamentary candidates have some higher education.[5] Roughly 30 percent, including over half of those on the Conservative benches, have prestigious public school backgrounds. The absence of university experience seems to be a major barrier to the highest level of participation.

Occupational status is also important. The professions are the largest single source of livelihood for members of Parliament, even for those in the trade union and welfare-oriented Labour party. In recent Parliaments over half of the members for Labour have been in professions such as law or education.

Beyond these background characteristics, members of Parliament tend

---

[3] E. G. Janosic, *Constituency Labour Parties in Britain* (London: Pall Mall, 1968), p. 82.

[4] A. H. Birch, *Small Town Politics* (London: Oxford University Press, 1959), p. 1.

[5] Janosic, *Constituency Labour Parties,* p. 82.

The Speakers' Corner in Hyde Park, London. Courtesy, Central Office of Information, London.

to be individuals with experience in local government and in local party politics, although these are not absolutely necessary. Their prior experience differs from other activists in their desire and willingness to stand for office. A number of successful MPs began their careers as losing candidates—often in hopeless districts. Since there is no requirement for a candidate to live or work in his district, some move around in search of a promising constituency; in fact, only 40 percent of winning MPs have business or residential ties with their constituency.[6] Sheer desire for office manifested in an early commitment to becoming a "professional candidate" seems to separate those at the peak of British politics from those on lower rungs.

Desire and persistence seem to be all-important at the very top level—the step to cabinet membership or party leadership. In Britain over two-thirds of cabinet members serve over 10 years in the House of Commons—a much higher proportion than for other parliamentary systems.[7] The long

---

[6] Howard R. Penniman, ed., *Britain at the Polls* (Washington, D.C.: American Enterprise Institute for Public Policy Research, 1975), pp. 47–53.

[7] Richard Rose, *Politics in England Today* (London: Faber, 1974), p. 190.

period of apprenticeship includes substantial service in minor positions in party and administration.

The Pattern of Participation

There is widespread participation in the United Kingdom in the least taxing and meaningful political activities. Britain's history and culture encourage the basic citizen duties of voting and group membership, and the public seems to find these activities to be rewarding.

Compared to other countries, partisan activism is open to a large number of people. Local party constituency organizations have the crucial nominating function and thus are at the vital center of British political life. Since these party groups are membership based, all functions must be carried out by committed partisans in the localities. This opportunity is available for a wide cross-section of the public.

The great barrier to political involvement comes at the level of elective national office and high-level civil service, mainly because there are so few really important offices in the system. If we include the 635 seats in the House of Commons, the 200 active members of the House of Lords, and the several thousand key administrative positions, we are describing a very small political elite. The general public must be content to guard the gateways of power rather than to enter them.

▪ THE FEDERAL REPUBLIC OF GERMANY ▪

Observers of the new West German democracy are concerned that Germans lack the drive to participate in politics and to attempt to influence governmental decisions. This concern is often called the problem of the "unpolitical German." Motivation to participate has been low because historically there have been few opportunities and because participation has involved considerable risk. German institutions and leaders have generally been interested in doing things for people rather than encouraging citizens to do things for themselves. The result is a tendency for Germans to pay attention to the results of political action (outputs) and to ignore the political process itself (inputs).

Historical and Cultural Factors

German history contains traditions that strongly oppose widespread political participation. The delayed unification of the German people prompted strong, distinctly authoritarian state development and promoted "national" issues rather than questions of individual rights and responsibilities. Collective goals and needs were stressed at the expense of full citizen development.

The extreme manifestation of German authoritarianism was the German Empire or Second Reich (1871–1918). All men could vote, but the vote was meaningless because the *Reichstag,* the lower house of Parliament, was so weak. Participation was further mocked by the voting system in the dominant German state, Prussia. In Prussia the votes of 3 percent, 12 percent, and 85 percent of the population were weighted equally to reflect the power of the wealthy. Voting was a meaningless but socially approved citizen duty.

The empire period also established a strong tradition of state paternalism. Though antidemocratic, the regime provided many services and welfare goods for the mass of the people. The profoundly conservative Otto von Bismarck, chancellor of the empire, introduced a social security and health care program long before these ideas gained currency in more liberal systems—forty years, for example, before Americans began to get similar benefits. Germany's early leaders were showing that direct citizen action was not necessary for securing material benefits from government: the political elite would do what they were trained to do—discovering and delivering the things that people needed.

The ill-fated experiment with democratic institutions in the 1920s did little to change the prevalent authoritarian flavor of German politics. Unable to deliver economic and personal security, the representatives of the people came to rely on the old experts in the civil service and the army. The nonparticipatory institutions "worked," while those based on participation provided only a tiresome, empty show.

Traditional German cultural themes, then, included authoritarianism, paternalism, and a preference for administrative rather than representative government. In the course of 30 years' experience with democracy, these attitudes have gradually been modified. Today, however, it is still fair to say that Germans tend to defer to authority and to value order and obedience as personal traits. Moreover, they still focus on the outputs of governmental action—on the material benefits—rather than on the politics of influence. The belief continues that the executive and bureaucratic elements of government are much more important than Parliament, political parties, and interest groups.

Reward vs. Risk

Political participation in Germany has financial and psychological rewards but—unlike Britain—not a status reward. Participation through parties and interest groups has never been entirely respectable, although this is probably changing. People generally are suspicious of politicians, of the political enterprise, and particularly of partisan politics.

The prejudice against partisan activity is largely based on the German view of political conflict and division. German society has been so seriously divided in the past that special interests seemed threatening to the good of the whole. In particular, the motives of religious minorities and workers were once questioned and the threat of hostile "un-German" minorities seemed real. Conflict could not be contained, and most traumatic periods of violence and instability are associated with parties, interest groups, and the groups they represent. Standing out in contrast are the forces of order and security—the military and the administrative units of government.

Today much of the stigma has been removed from political activism because of the moderation of politics and the low conflict level of the current West German political process. Attitudes, however, often lag behind real-world political change; Germans have been slow to acknowledge that it is safe to discuss, participate, and become emotionally involved in politics.

Each family has a member who lost his or her life or freedom because of political belief during the Hitler era. Socialists, Communists, and liberal democrats, much of the 57 percent of the electorate who never voted for Hitler before 1933, were all in considerable fear or under stress for the subsequent 12 years. That generation is not convinced that political involvement is risk-free, and it has in some degree influenced subsequent generations.

Political Opportunity

Opportunities for electoral participation are much broader in West Germany than they are in the United Kingdom and most other parliamentary systems. This is true in part because of the federal nature of the regime. Opportunities exist in the 10 state governments, each with their own Parliament and administrative agencies, as well as in the federal institutions. Another source of opportunity is the rather loose and decentralized nature of party organization. In a way familiar to Americans, decentralized parties in Germany allow for greater chances for political novices who desire participation.

Table 4–2 reflects the broad opportunities available to Germans interested in participating in political activities. In terms of voting, group activity, and low-level activism the figures compare favorably with the United Kingdom and other major democracies. However, the opportunities at the level of the political professional are much wider than Britain's, largely because of the greater localism of German politics and the resulting number of state and local opportunities.

The Actives

In Germany participants are much like active citizens in other developed nation-states. First of all, middle- and upper-class individuals are more active in politics than those less fortunate. In Germany the class base of activism is more striking than it is for the United Kingdom. Occupation, income, and education as reflections of social and economic status are

TABLE 4–2   Political Participation in the Federal Republic of Germany

Level	Number	Percent
Registered Voters (Federal)	39,000,000	
Actual Voters	34,000,000	80
Group Membership	18,000,000	46
Active Group Members	5,000,000	13
Party Members	1,500,000	0.5
Local Office Holders	220,000	—
Parliamentarians	1,600	—
(State and Federal)		

Source: Karl Deutsch, *Politics and Government,* 2nd ed. (Boston: Houghton Mifflin, 1974), p. 56. Copyright © 1974 by Houghton Mifflin Company. Reprinted by permission.

notable in separating those who are active from those who are not.[8] This is what can be expected in a political culture that tends to downplay political and economic equality as important values.

As in other political systems, activists are set apart by their knowledge and interest in political matters and by their conviction that individual efforts do affect political outcomes. Since the Federal Republic is still relatively new and unfamiliar and since many German traditions discourage this kind of activist outlook, the core of participants is rather small. Remembering the long stretches of German history when voting and party action were meaningless, many Germans resist the notion that participation brings about specific accomplishments. Many contemporary Germans also lack confidence because governments consist of parties in coalition and therefore political outcomes are blurred. The current apparent absence of important party differences also makes participation seem less important.

The relatively weak impulse to participate is seen when the membership of the major parties is analyzed. The Social Democratic party has roughly 800,000 members, only 5 percent of the total vote cast for the party in elections. The Christian Democratic Union (CDU/CSU) has over 400,000 members, or less than 3 percent of its total vote received in elections. Membership dues do not go very far toward financing the parties. Dues make up 40 percent of the SPD income and only 12 percent of the Christian Democrats'. Thus, party politics must be subsidized by the state.

Parties try to generate participation through their affiliated organizations, such as the important youth wings. The Social Democrats' Young Socialists (abbreviated in German to *Jusos*) is particularly influential. The

---

[8] Kendall L. Baker, "Political Participation, Political Efficacy and Socialization in Germany," *Comparative Politics* 6 (October 1973), pp. 73–98.

A woman votes in the 1972 West German federal elections. Courtesy, German Information Center.

Jusos include nearly 200,000 activists under 30 years of age. Ideology sparks recruitment to the Jusos much more than it does for regular SPD actives. The Jusos, who view themselves as the incubator for fresh ideas, are relatively radical. They have embarrassed their elders with policy pronouncements on disarmament, redistribution of income, and human rights. The smaller (120,000) *Junge Union* of the CDU, although more docile than the Jusos, offers similar issue-oriented challenges.

The greatest opportunity for meaningful participation short of political office involves nominating members to stand for the *Bundestag*—or Federal Parliament. This process is quite decentralized at the constituency and *Land* (state) levels. Since Germans share the European preference for selection by loyal party members and reject the values inherent in an American primary system, few are involved. One estimate is that as few as 20,000 Social Democrats have a say in their parties' parliamentary nominations. This means that a core of average rank-and-file members have considerable power and influence.

The Pattern of Participation

Germans participate in political activities that do not take much time or effort; they vote consistently at just below the 90 percent level. Relatively few, however, muster sufficient interest and motivation to become party members. As we have seen, this is a historical-cultural phenomenon; it certainly is not the result of party policy or strategy. All parties try to stimulate membership, as they benefit from the resultant dues and manpower.

In this system with its broad opportunities and relatively low impulse to participate, parties are less important in channeling participation than in a low-opportunity system like the United Kingdom. Motivated individuals have many options for attractive political positions and therefore depend less on parties. Once involved in politics, they are less in need of party help for their political advancement. West Germany is characterized by the decentralized nature of its politics and the individualism of its political activists.

▪ FRANCE ▪

France offers many opportunities for participation—largely because of its tradition of political localism. There are many local government units, each with political offices of some importance. There are also wider opportunities at the national level than there are for a pure parliamentary system because there is a separation between the effective executive unit—the presidency—and the Parliament. This effectively increases the size of the national bureaucracy by duplication of efforts. Recruitment to these positions usually comes through weak, divided, and often decentralized political parties; thus, political participation is not directed by strong organizations (as in the case of Britain).

Historical and Cultural Factors

French history—with its frequent changes in regimes, governmental instability, and political violence—has not encouraged the French to participate in politics. Another influence on current patterns of participation is the importance of rural, small-town, and traditional values in French political culture.

The effects of regime changes are subtle yet important. First of all, the simple fact that the rules for participation change frequently makes it difficult for people to become politically involved because of the time and effort needed to become familiar with new institutions. Second, many people who are loyal to previous regimes boycott or sabotage contemporary institutions. Finally, changes in regime entail risks for political activists. For example, the change from the Third Republic to the authoritarian-fascist Vichy regime made life very much more dangerous for supporters of the Communist party, just as the change to the Fourth Republic endangered those who collaborated with the Germans.

Governmental instability and the tendency for cabinets and governmental ministers to change frequently have a deadening effect on political activism as well. The frequent crisis atmosphere in Parliament (largely in the Third and Fourth Republics) gave the impression of political incompetence and impotence. The picture of Parliament as a "tragic circus" made participation considerably less meaningful to many Frenchmen.

People's perspectives on politics are shaped by these historical experiences. Cynicism about political institutions and politicians discourages activism because "the politicians are going to have their own way anyway and they do not care about me." Lack of a feeling that participation satisfies an important value—playing the part of the good citizen—also weakens the impulse to participate.

The French political culture is most often described in terms of cynicism and absence of civic duty (incivisme). The French mistrust of groups is part of the legendary French individualism. French children are taught to avoid strangers and face-to-face relationships with others—or "les autres" as they are ominously described. As a result, a majority of French people polled in 1969 said it was best to mistrust any stranger as a matter of course.[9] Related to this cultural tendency to mistrust others is the French view of collective action. Many Frenchmen do not see any benefit in cooperation. There is a definite pejorative connotation to the idea of compromise and a preference for inflexible attachment to an individual position.

The French incivisme makes matters worse. In a recent survey 87 percent of French respondents said they had "no confidence at all" that their representatives in the two houses of Parliament would defend their interests. Over three-fourths felt that their representatives had no interest in "serving their fellow citizens." In some French minds these feelings suggest a positive duty not to participate or cooperate with these politicians.[10]

Some of the most dramatic examples of incivisme involve tax evasion—a favorite pastime in France. Evidently many Frenchmen feel that they do not owe the government their cooperation even in this basic citizen duty. It is estimated, for example, that French professionals declare as little as 35 percent of their income to the tax authorities. The practice of merchants' keeping two sets of books, one for the tax man and an accurate personal record, is reportedly common. Public opinion polls show that barely half of the French public think that it's "normal" to declare all of your income.[11]

Reward vs. Risk

The rewards of participation appear to be largely material for what is often called France's "political class." Since cynicism extends to individual

---

[9] John S. Ambler, *The Government and Politics of France* (Boston: Houghton Mifflin, 1971), p. 52.
[10] Ibid., pp. 52–54.
[11] Ibid.

politicians as well as to institutions, little status is gained through political activism. That mistrust is considerably greater for national institutions and politicians than the more close-to-home variety. Community-based activists may, in fact, receive respect and prestige from their positions.

The practice of "double office-holding" attracts some individuals motivated by the desire for political power. Since the founding of the Fourth Republic, over 40 percent of members of the National Assembly, or lower house of Parliament, have simultaneously held local office. The proportion is even higher for the upper house, or Senate.

Although the risks of activism are relatively unimportant under the Fifth Republic, the French are still reluctant to get involved and to identify themselves politically. Their refusal to affiliate with a party or to discuss politics is probably related to the fact that being on the wrong political side was once fatal in France and not so long ago. For example, during the German occupation leftists were executed. After 1946 rightists who cooperated with the Germans were assaulted or imprisoned.

Political Opportunity

Opportunities for political participation are broad. At the national level there are the standard administrative positions as well as parliamentary positions. At the local level the basic offices are municipal councillor, departmental councillor, and member of the senatorial electoral colleges responsible for the election of members of the Senate.

The local positions offer a remarkable number of political opportunities. There are 470,000 locally elected municipal councillors representing 38,000 *communes* (cities and towns of all sizes). Another 3,000 people serve as departmental councillors in the next higher level of local administration. Around 100,000 individuals act as the electoral college for the Senate, but most of these are already municipal councillors (90 percent). Put another way, almost 2 percent of France's eligible voters are local officials. Table 4–3 summarizes the political opportunities of France and the proportion of Frenchmen who take advantage of them.

We have examined the reasons why the French motivation to participate is weak and why party memberships are strikingly lower than in other European nations. The effective barrier to participation seems to be reluctance to become associated with any sort of organized group—not a very demanding test.

The Actives

Activists in France include party members, local officeholders, and candidates for the national Parliament. The fact that so few Frenchmen are party members makes membership itself a stiff test for activism. Local officeholding, largely in the municipal councils, is so widespread that it repre-

TABLE 4–3   Political Participation in France

Level	Number	Percent
Eligible Voters	32,000,000	100
Registered Voters	30,000,000	91
Actual Voters	20,000,000	63
(1970 Parliamentary Election)		
Group Members	11,200,000	35
Party Members	750,000	2.5
Local Officials	500,000	2.0
Political Elite	20,000	.5

Sources: Karl Deutsch, *Politics and Government* (Boston: Houghton Mifflin, 1974), p. 56; Roy Pierce, *French Politics and Political Institutions* (New York: Harper & Row, 1973), p. 245; and Henry W. Ehrmann, *Politics in France* (Boston: Little, Brown, 1971), p. 128.

sents little more of an elite position than simple party membership. Beyond this core of activists, candidates to the national Parliament, successful or otherwise, represent an important activist element. The highest level for activists includes the double officeholders with both local and national office and successful legislators and civil servants.

In distinguishing activists from less active citizens, sex is perhaps the best guideline. Participation has been largely a male preserve in France. Women did not get the vote until 1944. In 1958 only 6 of 465 members of the National Assembly (lower house of Parliament) were women. The figures have not changed much at the national level. At the local level only 2 to 5 percent of postwar officeholders have been women.[12]

Attributes other than sex that separate the politically active from the politically indifferent in other countries do not help explain activism in France. Occupation is not a good guide for several reasons. First, the Communist party of France has the largest membership of any political party, and its members are disproportionately from working-class and clerical occupation categories. Second, the rural base of French politics means that farmers are among the most politically active Frenchmen. These facts explain why education, income, and related characteristics are not so important in France as they are in most other developed countries.

Party activists come predominantly from the parties of the left. Of the estimated 750,000 members of French parties, at least 400,000 are members of the Communist or Socialist parties. The actual number of party "militants" among these is small; only 10 percent of the Communist membership is deeply involved in party matters.

The local officeholders similarly vary greatly in their commitment to politics. A large proportion of these people are interested only in local concerns. They are drawn from groups with specific material interests

---

[12] Ibid., p. 245.

A French polling station with ballots for presidential candidates. Bruno Barbey, Magnum Photos, Inc.

associated with the localities—such as farmers and shopkeepers. A fraction of the local government officers have used their local base to become involved in national politics. These are the traditional "twenty thousand" of France's political elite.

The local activists provide a pool of potential national officeholders, as well as representing behind-the-scenes influentials. National office-holders, parliamentarians, and top civil servants overwhelmingly are drawn from professional circles. Intellectuals—professors, journalists, doctors, and technical experts—always have been important in French politics. In this sense, France has not changed greatly since a leading observer called Third Republic France "the Republic of the Professors."[13] Recent trends, particularly associated with the Fifth Republic, have favored technical experts or "technocrats." In any case, the national political elite of France continues to be elite.

The Pattern of Participation

Cultural and historical factors, then, have led to a very low level of political participation in France, despite the sheer number of offices available.

---

[13] Henry W. Ehrmann, *Politics in France* (Boston: Little, Brown, 1971), p. 147.

The weakness of the political parties resulted in a recruitment pattern that seems less guided by political forces than by social forces. Activists in France recruit themselves and pick their own opportunities. As a consequence, most activists are not socialized, homogenized, party men. This fits rather nicely with the cultural tendency toward individuality.

It is only at the highest level of activism, in national office-holding, that selection seems restricted to a particular type of Frenchmen—the professional or the expert. This barrier to participation by the average citizen is not a partisan or political policy but a social and cultural preference. Regimes have come and gone, but the nature of the top elite has remained remarkably consistent—at least over the last four regimes.

In sum, short of the very highest office, most Frenchmen are limited only by their desire to participate. Those with greater ambitions are limited by their own talents and by society's standards for public service. French individualism is not defeated by partisan politics.

▪ THE SOVIET UNION ▪

The Soviet Union is unique in its combination of party control of participation with the provision of widespread and diverse political opportunities. A major task of the Communist party of the Soviet Union is to inspire, but also to control, the participatory urge of Soviet citizens. This, of course, requires a massive bureaucratic organization, but the world's most highly developed and densely organized political party is equal to the task.

Historical and Cultural Factors

The backwardness of prerevolutionary Russia can be traced partly to the passive role intended for the mass of the citizenry. Russians of all classes were "subjects" by temperament, training, and preference. In tsarist Russia individuals viewed themselves as subject to political actions and rules that they must obey as God-ordained and given.

Soviet leaders have tried to make every Russian a politically active citizen. Only an all-out effort, with no wasted labor, could attain the great performance goals that the Soviets set for themselves in modernization and industrialization. The party uses ideological terms like the "need for collective action," the "political basis of labor," and the "necessity for each individual to help build socialism." The nature of the work to be performed is set by the party, and participation is required to implement these tasks and goals. Participation is guided by a desire for the mass of

Soviet society to carry out policies and plans made in the party hierarchy. Participation is not geared to making demands for governmental action or becoming involved in selection of leaders.

The party has devoted a great deal of attention to building this "New Soviet Man" through its control of political socialization. The schools and the youth auxiliaries of the Communist party are the major organizational foci for preparing youngsters for Soviet citizenship. Since both are controlled by the party, children do not receive conflicting messages that can undermine the learning process. Some dissonance, however, is unavoidable, and most Communist officials suspect that family teaching practices often conflict with the party's.

Schools influence young children by discouraging individualism and praising contribution to the group effort. The youngest play simple games stressing group solidarity—dancing and singing in unison. Older pupils learn that school units—such as rooms or grades—are considered as collectives with collective tasks and goals. Rewards go to the units, not to the individual.

School training is seen as a necessary corrective to individualism taught in the home. Parents, it is believed, stress the special worth and ambitions of their children, which will lead to "careerism"—an undue concern for success, status, and career ambitions. For this reason periodically the party leadership favors boarding schools in order to reduce family contacts. The current leadership is emphasizing boarding schools, but only for a relatively small proportion of gifted or "special" children.

The youth organization of the party, the *Komsomol,* plays a particularly important role in developing the proper views toward participating in politics. The Komsomol has separate organizations for young children as well as its university and young adult organization. The Pioneers are for children 7 through 9; the Octoberists, for those 10 through 13. Members of the Komsomol may be up to 30 years of age.

Adult education and socialization occurs at the work place as well, for the party is organized in part on the basis of work units. Political education and political discussion are encouraged here. In particular, party units try to explain the connection between production targets and party policy so that workers become involved in the implementation of party policy.

Reward vs. Risk

The Soviet Union has a "high-risk" political system. Rewards can be substantial in terms of status, prestige, power, and material benefits, but the cost of failure is often very high. The party has close control over political rewards, and failure means deprivation, if not punishment, for poor performance or "anti-party" attitude. Most people today have little to fear from a party purge or a campaign against a particular profession. There is, however, thorough screening of individuals for advancement in the party or in party-controlled areas of employment.

Political Opportunities

The Soviet Union offers many opportunities for people to participate in politics. Some are largely symbolic, while others provide instrumental participation. Both party and state have a large number of activist roles that must be filled (see Table 4–4).

Almost every Soviet citizen votes in elections for the state's representative assemblies, the Soviets; in fact, 97 percent can be counted on to vote in any election. Voting is given a good deal of encouragement by the party and by work supervisors, who give workers time off to vote. A large number of people act as volunteer "political assistants" particularly in the system of Soviets. Brezhnev in a 1971 address to the Central Committee of the party estimated that 25 million individuals acted as assistants for the Soviets alone.

The real test of activism is membership in the Communist party or its auxiliary organizations. Since the party views itself as an elite vanguard party, membership is restricted; it fluctuates between 5 and 10 percent of the adult population, depending on party policy. A slightly larger group is affiliated through the Komsomol. Membership imposes fairly heavy obligations in terms of time and work. It would be fair then to say that by including adult-age individuals in the Komsomol and the party, the Soviet Union has a very high percentage of activists—approximately 24 percent—compared with Western European nations, where only 1 to 7 percent are active.

TABLE 4–4   Political Participation in the Soviet Union

Level	Number	Percent
Voting-Age Population	158,000,000	100
Voters	153,000,000	97
Political Volunteers	40,000,000	25
Members—Komsomol Youth Organization	28,000,000	16
Members—CPSU	14,000,000	8
Members of Soviets	2,000,000	1.5

Sources: Karl Deutsch, *Politics and Government* (Boston: Houghton Mifflin, 1974), p. 56; John A. Armstrong, *Ideology, Politics and Government in the Soviet Union* (New York: Praeger, 1974), p. 67; and Frederick C. Barghoorn, *Politics in the USSR* (Boston: Little, Brown, 1972), p. 245.

The system of popular assemblies or Soviets also provide opportunities for symbolic participation in state representative institutions. The Soviets are organized at four levels—national, Union Republic, province (*oblast*), and city/district (*rayon*). In all, there are over 4,700 assemblies with 2 million members. Since terms are short (usually two years below the national level, which has four-year terms) and turnover in membership is high, a great many people can participate. The odds of a given citizen serving in his lifetime are fairly good—certainly much better than the chances that a citizen enjoys in other countries.

The Actives

Political activism is limited mostly to party members. Nonmembers can certainly have political influence through their professional affiliation, but their political role is indirect. (Few members are of the political elite, although party membership is a necessary condition.) What all members share is fairly intense, if routine, political activity. The activities for the average member involve ongoing study, indoctrination tasks, a large number of meetings, and an occasional special job or task.

Party members are above average in education. Over half have at least completed secondary school, compared to 32 percent of the general populace. Party members are three times as likely to have a university degree than the average citizen. Education is not a strong requirement, however, for fully 20 percent of the party members have only an elementary school education.

In terms of occupation the party is supposed to mirror the occupational distribution in the full population; however, high-status groups are overrepresented. Professional people—teachers and physicians—have three times the representation one might expect by their proportion in the population; and a particularly sensitive elite group like the military is vastly overrepresented. By occupation, roughly 40 percent are industrial workers, 15 percent farmers, and the rest "mental workers" or "the toiling intelligentsia." These last are euphemisms for white-collar and professional types.

The really influential party members are a narrow band of the full membership. At the national level, these would include the approximately three hundred members of the party's Central Committee, Politburo, and Secretariat. Many would be found in the state bureaucracy and among the 100,000 professionals of the nationwide party apparatus.

This top elite stratum of the party usually follows one of two routes to power. The first is through the party bureaucracy or apparatus. About half of the people from the Central Committee came up from the party apparatus; they have always been full-time professional party men. Another route is through the state's administrative bureaucracy. Most of these in-dividuals have some special expertise in an important governmental area—economics or foreign relations, for example.

The Pattern of Participation

Soviet leaders have been remarkably successful in transforming the role of the average citizen in politics. Through intensive political socialization they have produced an activist political culture. The Communist party of the Soviet Union effectively controls this growing citizen participation by limiting it to symbolic participation as in the Soviets.

Activism is a possibility to all Soviet citizens who have the proper views toward politics. The composition of the party includes members from all major occupational groups. Top leadership positions require special talent and experience. For party professionals advancement is carefully screened by superior bodies. Party men rise level by level, undergoing tests of loyalty and skill as they go. For experts and administrators the process is matched in the state bureaucracy. As the leadership has intended, only a special type of person reaches the top, usually an experienced party-oriented individual.

▪ NIGERIA ▪

The ways that Nigerians participate have changed dramatically since in-dependence in 1960. These changes have been caused by economic and social changes, and by military coups such as the one in January 1966 that formally ended parliamentary government and electoral politics. Questions of who participates, how they participate, and the role of partic-ipation in the political life of Nigeria are among the most troublesome questions facing both civilian and military political leaders.

Political participation was different in each of the three distinct periods of modern Nigeria. During the first period—from the end of World War II until independence in October 1960—representative political institu-tions gradually developed, providing new opportunities for participation. Political power gradually shifted from the colonial administrators to Nigerian administrators and politicians. The second period (October 1960–January 1966) spans the life of the first Federal Republic, when participation centered on the competition for elected and appointed offices at both national and regional levels. New patterns of participation emerged with the end of the civilian regime in 1966 and the establishment of the first of several military governments. The announced plans of the military government to return to civilian rule in 1979 will presumably begin a fourth period and introduce still new forms of political participation.

Political Participation During the Colonial Period

The colonial administration at the height of its power was a bureaucratic system, little concerned with Nigerians' participation but valuing efficiency, economy, and stability. As Nigerians increased their demands for participation and representation, colonial officials faced a series of important political decisions. All agreed with the broad goals of creating a political system that would represent the diverse interests and values of Nigerians, but at the same time would be stable and efficient. What differed was how quickly changes should be made and how best to achieve the broad, long-term goals.

The British hoped to leave Nigeria with a political system that closely resembled their own Westminster model: political parties to compete in national and regional elections, a bicameral parliament, a prime minister appointed from the majority party in the lower house, and an appointed president to serve as head of state. Most Nigerian politicians active during the nationalist movement had been educated in England; they agreed on the desirability of establishing this type of parliamentary system.

However, despite agreement on the general goal, there were sharp disagreements on specifics. One important question concerned where ultimate power should rest. Some favored a strong central national government, while others preferred a weak central government and strong regional governments. Those who favored strong regional governments argued, persuasively, that the differences between the Eastern, Western, and Northern Regions were so great that there was little hope of agreement between peoples so diverse. Those who favored a strong central government argued, just as persuasively, that with strong regions there would not be one Nigeria, but three Nigerias.

A closely related issue concerned who should participate in the political game. The preindependence election laws gave the franchise to all Nigerian residents 21 years or older who were British subjects or protected by Britain. The one important exception to this rule was in the Northern Region, where the franchise was restricted to males because of the North's traditional social and religious values. This exception is indicative of the strong differences between regions.

Questions arose not only about who should participate but also about the qualifications and qualities the new politicians should possess. In the North the still powerful grip traditional leaders held on the population meant that many of the new politicians were also traditional leaders. Ahmadu Bello, the Sardauna of Sokoto (killed in the January 1966 coup d'état), coupled the traditional authority of the emirate system with the skills of the modern politician. Many traditional leaders skillfully bridged the gap between traditional and modern political practices. The mixing of traditional authority and modern politics helped to ensure the dominance of the Northern People's Congress in any regional elections.

In the Eastern and Western Regions, traditional authorities continued to exercise influence, but there also developed a new elite whose base of support was not traditional. Leaders such as Obafemi Awolowo in the Western Region and Nnamdi Azikiwe in the Eastern Region created more modern political parties like the Action Group and the National Council of Nigerian Citizens, formulated more radical nationalist demands, and generally operated in the modern, electoral arena. These men, and others like them, were more strongly influenced by Western European political practices and educations. Less concerned with tradition than were their counterparts in the North, they worked at harnessing and controlling the new governmental machinery.

The first nationwide test of this new system was the 1959 election. Although solutions to the regional/federal dilemma and the ultimate nature of the new system had not been fully resolved, the election proceeded nonetheless. The registration figures for all three regions indicate that relatively few Nigerians registered. Figures vary from region to region, but in most districts between 30 and 70 percent of those eligible registered.[14] Although registration was low, those who did register voted in the election. In all three regions and the federal territory of Lagos, almost 80 percent of those eligible voted in the election.[15]

The period between the end of the war and the achievement of independence was a transition period. Gradually at first, and then more rapidly, power and authority were transferred from British to Nigerian hands. Making their own decisions was a new experience for Nigerians. The politicians faced pressures and demands that were especially intense and divisive during the six years of parliamentary government from 1960 to 1966.

Participation During the First Federal Republic

To succeed with the parliamentary government and electoral machinery bequeathed them at independence, Nigerian politicians and participants alike needed to accept the political rules of the game. But an important rule—that of accepting the outcome of the electoral contests—was continually violated. From 1960 to 1966, and especially from the 1964 federal election to the first coup d'état in 1966, Nigerians questioned both national and regional election returns.

---

[14] Kenneth Post, *The Nigerian Federal Election of 1959* (London: Oxford University Press, 1963), pp. 204–207.

[15] Ibid., p. 350.

Participation during this period was strongly influenced by the pattern of group life in Nigeria. Politics and elections centered not only on winning seats to the parliaments but also on protecting cultural and regional interests. The political parties representing the interests of the Hausa-Fulani, the Yoruba, and the Ibo, as well as a multitude of smaller parties, sought to dominate national politics and at the same time assure their control of their respective regions. Coalitions between different parties and regions were matters of convenience rather than compatibility.

Different perspectives and expectations concerning participation affected electoral politics. All individuals did not participate equally or with the same expectations. For many Nigerians, politics and elections were very remote. The national government and even the regional governments had little effect on their day-to-day, tradition-oriented lives. Many of these people lived in rural areas, had little formal schooling, and were outside the modern economic sector. Their social obligations were with their kinship or cultural groups rather than the more modern political institutions and activities.

Others did participate. More politically aware and mobilized, these individuals formed the core of the political participants' pool in Nigeria. They registered to vote, attended political rallies, and joined political parties. The political parties in Nigeria were the major channels for participation during this period, usually stressing group or regional interests over national interests.

The interaction between group life and parliamentary politics fractionalized Nigerian political life. The Northern Region feared southern domination because it lagged behind the Western and Eastern Regions in modern education; consequently, Northerners banded together to protect their interests. On the other hand, many Southerners feared northern domination because of the large northern population and what was viewed by many Southerners as the conservative traditionalism of northern political leaders.

The conflicts were not simply between North and South. Minority groups in all areas feared the domination of the three major groups. Conflicts between the Eastern Region and the Western Region were often as intense, or more so, than those between the North and South. Coupled with this fear and mistrust was the fact that although there was an elaborate electoral machinery, the conduct of the elections led to the questioning of the results. Corruption and thuggery were often the rule rather than the exception. The 1964 federal election (the first since the 1959 pre-independence election) and the 1965 western regional election cast many doubts about the honesty of the electoral process and the results.

While politicians often mistrusted their counterparts from other regions, many were united by their desire to preserve their position in the new, emerging elite. In this sense they shared a similar interest—self-preservation. As bureaucrats, civil servants, and politicians competed for the spoils of office, corruption became flagrant. To many, it appeared that politicians were more concerned with protecting and improving their own positions than in representing their constituents' interests.

The collapse of parliamentary government in 1966 evoked little outward dismay. The obvious corruption, questionable election results, and general political malaise outweighed for many the loss of parliamentary, representative government. Public opinion generally favored the military officers who ended parliamentary government. The end was not, however, without its omens. Tragically, the violent end of parliamentary government and the backgrounds of both the leaders of the coup and those who were killed, set the stage for the rapid slide to the civil war of 1967–1970.

Participation During the Military Period

The military coup d'état in January 1966 officially ended electoral politics and representative government in Nigeria. Political parties were banned and political activity restricted. The military's stated goal was to end divisive ethnic politics and to provide a stable political setting that would allow an eventual return to civilian politics. Initially, however, the military stressed national unity and national identity.

Traditionally, military officers viewed themselves as apolitical and above politics. The military was a national institution, not an ethnic or regional one; its role was to provide for the national defense. Many of the officers in the higher ranks were trained at the military academy at Sandhurst, England, and conceived of themselves as professional soldiers, not politicians. When the military assumed control in January 1966, there was an expectation, or at least a hope, that the divisive influences of the past might be controlled.

Once in power, though, the officer corps experienced many of the ethnic splits that characterized the old civilian regime. The fact that most of the officers who carried out the January coup were Ibo and that most of those politicians (including the prime minister) who were killed were Northerners or Westerners, raised new fears of Ibo domination. The July 1966 coup d'état, which was conducted primarily by Northerners and in which mainly Easterners were killed, produced a fear in the South of northern domination.

Participation during the military period involved not only the increasingly politicized officer corps but also the bureaucrats and the civil servants. Soldiers soon found that there was much about governing and administering that they did not know. Civil servants provided much needed technical and administrative expertise. In some cases the new military leaders were even forced to call for help from the politicians they had just removed from office and discredited.

Since assuming power in 1966 military leaders in Nigeria have stressed governmental efficiency and stability over popular participation and representation. They have attempted to create a political system that can effectively make decisions and prepare the nation for the return to civilian rule and elected representation. The problem is how to do this without destroying the fragile unity of the nation. Participation involves potential conflict, which in the Nigerian case has been frequent and violent.

▪ EGYPT ▪

Popular political participation in Egypt is not a well-established tradition. Throughout most of their history Egyptians have not been given many opportunities to either participate as citizens or hold government office. Access to positions of power has been restricted. Since the 1952 revolution political leaders have attempted to create institutions that allow for popular participation but do not challenge those in power.

Traditions of Participation in Egypt

Very early in the colonial period Egyptian nationalists began to demand a greater share of power in the Egyptian political system. They demanded the right to be heard and to influence decision-makers. Political parties, labor unions, business federations, and religious organizations developed and began to press for the right to participate. Each, in different ways, stressed the need for Egyptians to have a say in the political affairs of Egypt.

The demands for participation intensified following World War I, but the pool of participants remained small. With the exception of the 1919 nationalist uprising, which had widespread support throughout Egypt, there was little mass activity or mass popular participation. Political power was concentrated in the hands of a relatively small elite that included the king and his court retainers, members of various minority groups like the Copts, the Islamic religious hierarchy *(ulama),* and the rich landowners. Ultimately, on many issues the British had the final word.

The most important political party during the interwar period was the Wafd. The Wafd appealed to the moderate middle-class and rural land-owning populations that were becoming nationalistic. It was not a political party that encouraged widespread participation by all groups in Egyptian society. The Muslim Brotherhood, formed in the 1920s, provided a second opportunity for participation and appealed to those favoring the creation of a conservative, theocratic state based on strict Islamic practice. Likewise, labor unions, business organizations and federations, and other interest groups began to press for the realization of their specific goals and to demand an end to British control.

One result of the creation of these different groups was that a nationalist party with a mass base did not develop. Unlike the Tanzanian situation (where the Tanzanian African National Union was the prime mover against colonialism), no one party or movement was able to mobilize the entire population for the long period of time needed to win independence. The small, secret group of Free Officers (headed by Gamal Abdul Nasser) that eventually overthrew the monarchy initially did not seek to rally widespread public support. Their primary goal was to gain power; attempts to gain public support and loyalty came only after that.

Other factors worked against the development of participatory institutions and attitudes in Egypt. Centuries of foreign domination produced a situation that emphasized the paternalistic attitude of the rulers and the responsibility of the ruled to suffer in silence. For most Egyptians the family and the kinship groups were the most important organizations in their lives. These groups were centered in small, rural villages. They had little experience in participating, and most probably had little desire to do so either.

Participation During the Nasser Period

One of the most startling aspects of the 1952 change of power was the "Egyptianness" of the new leaders. The Free Officers, while they differed among themselves in their political values and goals, were united by the fact that they were Egyptian officers and nationalists. Their immediate aims were to rid Egypt of the British presence, to secure their position of power in Egypt, and then to transform the economic and social foundations of Egypt. Their initial aims did not include the establishment of a political system based on mass political participation.

The 1952–1954 period witnessed the consolidation of power by Nasser. The new leaders banned the Wafd and other political parties, abolished the monarchy, and effectively curtailed the Muslim Brotherhood by arresting and imprisoning many of its leaders. General Neguib, the popular figurehead leader of the Free Officers, soon found himself a leader with no real power. At the top of the new pyramid of power, ruling in part through his charisma, was Gamal Abdul Nasser.

The Charter of National Action presented in 1962 represents the public and official thoughts of President Nasser on the subject of political participation. A section entitled "True Democracy" encouraged participation:

The value of a true revolution lies in its degree of popularity, in the extent to which it is an expression of the vast masses, in the extent to which it mobilizes their forces to rebuild the future, and also in the extent to which it enables these masses to impose their will on life.

True revolutionary action ... would not be possible unless it possessed these two attributes:

(1) popularity
(2) progressiveness.[16]

---

[16] *The Charter* (Cairo, U.A.R.: Information Administration, no date, c. 1962), p. 20.

If participation was to be encouraged and if old institutions for participation, such as the Wafd, were banned, then new channels for participation needed to be developed. Once secure in power the new leaders needed popular support, loyalty, and legitimacy. Three new organizations, one following the other, were created in an attempt to institutionalize and control political participation. The first of these, the Liberation Rally, existed from 1955 to 1957 but never really became an effective organization either in terms of its ideology or structure. The second, the National Union, lasted from 1957 to 1961. During this period Egypt and Syria were joined in the stormy marriage of the United Arab Republic. The collapse of the union in 1961 also led to the end of the effectiveness of the National Union.

The Liberation Rally and the National Union were not ringing successes, but from them new guidelines emerged as to who should participate and how that participation should be controlled. Despite the fact that all Egyptians of age were eligible for membership in the National Union, it was clear that the considerable power of the old elites remained strong. President Nasser, in a 1961 speech, listed six classes that had the right to participate—laborers, farmers, intellectuals, professionals, owners of property not based on exploitation, and military officers sympathetic and loyal to the revolution.

The third experiment in directing political participation began with the formation of the Arab Socialist Union (ASU) in 1962. From 1962 until President Sadat's liberalization in the mid-1970s the ASU was the only legal political party and the most important institution for channeling the popular political participation of the groups listed above. The initial membership of the ASU was reported to be 6 million Egyptians out of a potential participant pool of 7 million (probably an overestimation). By 1964 membership fell to about 4.8 million, only to rise again to about 5 million in 1968. Of this number about half were considered, by various changing definitions, to be either "peasants" or "workers." About 250,000 members were women.[17]

Following the trauma of the June 1967 war with Israel and the massive Egyptian defeat, President Nasser re-evaluated not only his own political role but also the relationships among various branches of government—the representative National Assembly, the military, and the Arab Socialist Union. The general trend during this postwar period was to allow for different interests to emerge under the umbrella of the ASU. The movement continued to stress the need for the mobilization of the population within limits and the need for national unity, but it also now began to emphasize the need for responsiveness and representation of different interests.

---

[17] R. Hrair Dekmejian, *Egypt Under Nasir* (Albany: State University of New York Press, 1971), p. 146.

ASU elections of 1968 show the results of the new guidelines. Over 180,000 candidates sought about 76,000 local committee seats in about 7,500 election units. Five million Egyptians voted. Locally elected officials selected 1,648 members to the National Congress. As in the past, the aim was to ensure that at least half of these positions were held by either peasants or workers. Other members included a broad range of Egyptians who represented various governmental and nongovernmental interests.[18] Smaller groups were then chosen and appointed to determine the political agenda of the ASU.

Another way to evaluate participation within the ASU is to examine those members who were active and those who were listed simply as members. (It is safe to assume that the organization never intended for all members of the organization to become active.) In the early period (1964) the ASU probably had about half a million active members, and plans for intensive training of a very active cadre of 20,000,[19] who were to provide both the organization and the structure necessary to make the ASU an efficient and effective party. Figures for 1968 indicate that only about 40 percent of the membership had paid their dues, and many of these were either workers or peasants whose dues were automatically deducted from their wages.[20]

Participation During the Sadat Presidency

Patterns of political participation changed when Vice President Sadat became president on the death of President Nasser in 1970. Sadat won an overwhelming mandate to his office through referendums in 1971 and 1976. Of the 9 million voting in the 1976 referendum, fully 99.94 percent voted for the president; and over 90 percent of those eligible to vote in the referendum did so.[21]

Given his mandate, President Sadat changed the ways that Egyptians participate in the ASU. During the 1975–1976 period, feminist and youth sections were added. More important was the decision in 1976 to allow the formation of political platforms as contending positions within the ASU. By the end of October almost 30 groups had applied for platforms within the ASU; the dominant groups were those representing traditional positions on the right, left, and center. The one important group prohibited from forming a platform were military officers.

Shortly after the 1976 elections for the ASU positions, the president went further in his reorganization by announcing that new parties could

---

[18] Ibid., p. 271.
[19] Ibid., p. 146.
[20] Ibid., p. 153.
[21] *African Research Bulletin*, Vol. 13, No. 9, p. 4154.

now exist alongside the ASU. Once again the major contestants were representatives of the right, center, and left. This decision was not made public until after the elections for the People's Assembly; thus there was no open conflict between competing organizations during the election.

The Pattern of Participation

Participation patterns in Egypt have changed substantially since the 1952 revolution. Groups that previously did not participate are now allowed and encouraged to do so. Egyptian leaders, however, face a dilemma similar to the one that faces most leaders in developing nations when they begin to encourage participation. On the one hand, widespread public support is needed to achieve their social, economic, and political goals; the transformation of Egypt means that Egyptians in all walks of life must be mobilized. On the other hand, Egyptian leaders want to ensure that their power and authority will not be seriously challenged by "uncontrolled" participation.

As a result, political participation in post-1952 Egypt has tended to be more symbolic than instrumental. As we shall see in Chapters 5 and 6, most of the important political decision-makers have not "worked their way up through the ranks" of the party. One of the most important functions of the party is to build popular support for decisions that have already been made. The Liberation Rally, the National Union, the Arab Socialist Union, and the "multi-party" system instituted by President Sadat in the mid-1970s represent the attempts of the Egyptian leadership to balance the need for participation with the need for the regime to maintain firm control.

■ TANZANIA ■

Tanzanian leaders, like their counterparts in Egypt and Nigeria, are seeking to balance the need for widespread popular participation with the need to preserve and build national unity. Most popular participation in Tanzania, since independence, has occurred under the broad umbrella of the Tanzanian African National Union (TANU). As the only legal political party, TANU has the responsibility for encouraging, guiding, and controlling citizen participation. This is not an easy job in so diverse a nation as Tanzania.

Participation During the Colonial Period

Since the 1950s almost all African political participation has been directed by TANU. During the nationalist struggle many individuals and groups that previously had not been politically active joined the party, paid party dues, voted for party candidates in the elections, and provided services for the local party organizations. Many leaders of the party were urban, educated, and politically conscious; but rural, traditional, and illiterate Tanzanians also became politically active and provided strong support for the movement.

The success of TANU during the colonial and early independence periods is a testament to the power and appeal of the party and its leader, Julius Nyerere. By focusing on a common opponent—the British colonial authorities—the party gained a unity of purpose. Although there were opposition parties that rejected TANU leadership, the preindependence election, in which TANU won all but one of the contested seats in the newly formed Parliament, clearly indicated the central role the party was to play following independence.

Postindependence Participation in TANU

Throughout the nationalist period TANU never lost sight of its major goal—independence. With independence, however, the new party and government leaders needed to reassess their respective roles. What responsibilities would fall to the party, and which to the government? President Nyerere referred to this changed situation:

The job of our political parties is much more difficult now than it was when we were struggling for independence. Then, we called mass meetings: we shouted "Uhuru" (freedom); we abused the colonialists—who, I may add, richly deserved it! But now we are building nations. If we have mass meetings we cannot abuse the government—for we are the government, and the people are the government. Our job now is to educate, to explain, and to build. We have to lead the people in the constructive work of development, we have to listen to them, co-operate with them, and work with them.[22]

The problem stated by Nyerere was not easily resolved. The results of the first post-independence election indicated growing voter apathy. Although President Nyerere won the election by an overwhelming margin (about 97 percent of the vote), only about 20 percent of those eligible to vote did so; this is compared with the 50 percent of the eligible voters who voted in the 1960 elections. Party membership included about 1.25 million out of a population of 10 million, but many of these party members did not pay their dues, were inactive, and showed little interest in party affairs.[23]

---

[22] Julius K. Nyerere, *Man and Development* (London: Oxford University Press, 1974), p. 16.

[23] Raymond F. Hopkins, *Political Roles in a New State, Tanzania's First Decade* (New Haven: Yale University Press, 1971), p. 29.

The poster held by Julius Nyerere leaves little doubt about the major goals and demands of TANU. Independence was achieved in 1961. UPI Photo.

Since great emphasis was placed on the need to involve the population in the transformation of Tanzanian society, the lack of participation presented a serious threat to the regime. The goal of the party was to eliminate opposition from outside the party, and at the same time to allow discussion and dissent within the ranks of the party. Participation was to be regularized at the local level, but participation in building the national, rather than subnational, system.

During this early independence period the decision was made to reorganize the party and to increase participation. Kivukoni College was created to train middle- and lower-level party workers in the goals and positions of the movement. In 1963 TANU opened its membership to Asian and European members. Members of other groups, like civil servants and soldiers, previously barred from joining were allowed and encouraged to become members. The admission of soldiers and civil servants to the party was in direct contradiction to British colonial policy of forbidding bureaucrats and soldiers from engaging in partisan politics. Party officials realized, however, that it is wise to have opposition or potential opposition within the party, rather than without. Following an attempted army mutiny in 1964 this point was driven home with special force.

Two other decisions during this period had an important effect on the pattern of participation. The first banned opposition political parties. Although they did not present a serious electoral threat to TANU, opposition parties did present a potential focus for organization outside the control of the party. The second major change was the creation of the cell system at the local level. In 1964 the party leadership grouped each 10 houses or 10 families into a party cell. These cells were to be the party base—a way of participating at the most local level. The goal was to build a pyramid organization to allow for communication between leaders and participants.

At the same time that the party was curbing opposition outside of TANU, it provided representation for various groups within the party structure. A TANU youth league and the women's organization were formed. Party membership is open to all Tanzanian citizens, but traditionally most of the important positions have been held by men. Politically active women tend to have either a special expertise or to come from the more modern sectors of Tanzanian society. The women's wing of the party exists mostly to receive input from the women.[24]

One of the recurrent dilemmas facing the TANU leadership is the potential conflict between mass participation and effective, efficient decision-making. On the one hand, mass participation is needed so that all Tanzanians understand and participate in the societal changes that are occurring. On the other hand, the party is partially responsible for making

---

[24] G. Andrew Maguire, *Toward 'Uhuru' in Tanzania* (Cambridge: University Press, 1969), p. 319.

and implementing political decisions. The emphasis on popular participation at the local level often has meant that the central organization has
had a difficult time controlling the party. This despite the fact that the
party is organized on a pyramid base. (See Chapter 5.)

The Arusha Declaration in 1967 signaled a shift from the goal of achieving as large a party membership as possible. Besides stressing that TANU
leaders be either peasants or workers, the declaration contained a new
philosophy concerning participation. It argued that during the independence struggle and the immediate postindependence period the emphasis
had been properly placed on mass membership in the party. The needs
and responsibilities of the party were different in 1967. Although the criteria for membership were not changed, the party leadership argued that
"if it is discovered that a man does not appear to accept the faith, the
objects, and the rules and regulations of the Party, then he should not
be accepted as a member."[25] The new aim was to create a more disciplined and dedicated party which "should put more emphasis on the
beliefs of our party and its policies of socialism."[26]

Although leadership attitudes toward who should belong to the party
have changed during the independence period, the party has not wavered
in its belief that citizens should be allowed to participate. One of the most
significant experiments to ensure popular participation began with the
1965 parliamentary elections. Although TANU was the only party allowed
to put forward candidates, there was competition for office within the
party. After the nominating procedure was complete, there were at least
two TANU candidates standing for each parliamentary seat. The electorate
took a much greater interest in this election than in the previous one; 50
percent of the electorate were registered, and about 75 percent of those
registered voted. During the campaign there were 3,500 political meetings
involving over 2 million people.[27]

The general attitude of Tanzanians appears to be that they do in fact
think they have an important role to play and that they have positive input
in the decision-making process. This supportive attitude toward participation has several component parts. A survey of legislators and administrators about the function of participation showed that many in this elite
group view participation as a mix between rights and duties. The most
often cited duties of the citizen were to "understand and participate in
the nation-building process," to show a loyalty to the nation, to obey the
law, and to help neighbors and, where necessary, sacrifice for others.
These values support the general values of building African socialism as

---

[25] Julius K. Nyerere, *Freedom and Socialism* (London: Oxford University Press, 1968),
   p. 248.
[26] Ibid.
[27] Christian P. Potholm, *Four African Political Systems* (Englewood Cliffs, N.J.: Prentice-
   Hall, Inc. 1970), p. 151.

defined by President Nyerere and the party. The rights of the citizen, according to the same group, were the right to government services such as education; the protection of the government and the just administration of justice; the protection of civil liberties; and the right to vote, criticize, and assemble. Here again the emphasis is on national unity, on joint participation, and on the duties of the people as a whole.[28]

The party is not without its critics and its opponents. Among the more common complaints according to one study were that there were still non-Africans holding positions of privilege, that taxes were too heavy and too frequently collected, that TANU officials often meddled in affairs that did not concern them, and that there was undue and unwanted pressure to join the party. Others complained that there was insufficient competition within the party, that qualified candidates were sometimes prevented from running for office, and that the party tended to dictate rather than discuss issues with the people.[29]

The loose structure of the party tends to place an emphasis on participation at the local level concerning local issues. The most direct link between individual participants and the party is the local or regional party representative. In recent years, in response to criticism, the party has attempted to recruit better qualified individuals for these positions, and to improve their training. The necessity of local representatives' being responsive to local needs is constantly stressed.

At the highest levels of the party there is an attempt to make sure that all groups are represented. The candidates who stood for election in the 1965 election provide an example of the diversity of groups represented. The most common occupations for those candidates who were successful in winning their seats were either Coop or National Union of Trade Association officials, local government officials (either political or civil service), civil servants, teachers, and farmers. Others were traders, businessmen, and lawyers.[30] The range of these occupations indicates that the party has been relatively successful in recruiting members from the different strata of Tanzanian society.

By its own admission, the party is not a highly institutionalized organization. It is a structure constantly changing. The experiment of institutionalizing competition within a one-party system is a new one. President Nyerere, stressing the importance of participation in the party, has compared the party to a road:

It is also necessary to have a strong political organization active in every village which acts like a toll way, all weather road, along which the purposes, plans and

---

[28] Hopkins, *Political Roles in a New State*, pp. 103–106.

[29] Maguire, *Toward 'Uhuru'*, pp. 367–368.

[30] Henry Bienen, *Tanzania: Party Transformation and Economic Development* (Princeton: Princeton University Press, 1970), p. 401.

problems of Government can travel to the people, at the same time as the ideas, desires and misunderstandings of the people can travel direct to the Government.[31]

It is impossible to separate participation from the party in Tanzanian politics. At all levels and in all forms, the party serves as a vehicle for participation. From the local village cell to the National Assembly the party structures and guides participation. What is unique about the Tanzanian system is the emphasis that party leaders place on the need for participation. One-party systems rarely encourage effective popular participation, fearing that it may endanger the authority and control of the state. Tanzanian leaders seek a balance between this danger and the positive effects of popular participation.

▪ CHILE ▪

The victory of the conservative presidential candidate in 1958, the moderate center candidate in 1964, and the more radical leftist candidate in 1970 exemplify the changes that have occurred in participation patterns in modern Chile. The twentieth century, to 1973, represents a period in which more and more Chileans participated in politics.

Early Patterns of Participation

The general trend in participation since independence has been for more and more Chileans to vote and participate in the political system. Although Chile was one of Latin America's oldest and most stable democratic systems, participation historically was limited both by law and tradition. The 1833 constitution that governed Chile until 1925 limited the franchise to males over 25 (21 if married), who could read and write, and who met certain property qualifications. The 1925 constitution established that in order to vote an individual had to be a citizen, over 21, male, and literate.

These restrictions limited the number of participants. As the restrictions were gradually removed, however, the number of Chilean voters dramatically increased. To cite only two twentieth-century examples: women were first allowed to vote in 1949, and illiterates and 18–21-year-olds were given the vote for the first (and as it turned out last) time in the 1973 congressional elections.

During the electoral period of 1925 to 1973 voting was viewed by the authorities as both a right and a duty. All eligible Chileans were required by law to register and to vote. Failure to do so was a punishable offense.

---

[31] Potholm, *Four African Political Systems,* p. 150.

President Salvadore Allende casts his ballot in the 1971 municipal elections. UPI Photo.

Registered voters' names were listed on registration lists with no more than 300 names on one list; and, since registration cards were necessary for conducting most banking, governmental, and financial business, registration was important.

Removing franchise restrictions swelled the voter rolls. In the 1938 presidential elections only about 10 percent of the population was registered to vote and the total number of votes cast was only 443,888 (out of a total population of 4,844,666). By 1964 the number of registered voters represented over 36 percent of the population, and over 2.5 million votes were cast.[32] In the hotly contested 1969 and 1973 congressional elections there were 3,250,000 and 4,500,000 registered eligible voters respectively.[33]

As more and more Chileans became eligible, the competition for their votes intensified. Political parties sought to create as broad political bases of support as possible by mobilizing the newly enfranchised. Often times

---

[32] *Chile Election Factbook, September 4, 1964* (Washington, D.C.: Institute for the Comparative Study of Political Systems, 1963), p. 15.

[33] The 1969 registration figures are from *Facts on File,* Vol. XXIX, No. 1480, pp. 136–137. Registration figures for 1970 are from *Facts on File,* Vol. XXX, No. 1558, p. 649.

the increases in registration were dramatic. In Santiago Province alone during a registration period of less than three months in 1964 over 110,000 women and over 45,000 men were registered.[34]

These new participants were important not only because of their numbers but also because of their political values. New participants challenged the domination of the traditionally powerful. Political power began to shift to those arguing for political and economic change. Socialist, Communist, and center parties began to appeal to middle- and lower-class groups by providing platforms for reform.

Political parties provide the crucial link between participation and power in Chile. As in most multi-party systems, the size and membership of a party is always much smaller than its support during elections. The Conservative party, for example, probably had an active membership of only about 5,000,[35] but with its electoral support often won congressional seats and, in coalition, even the presidency. The parties of the center and the left followed similar patterns.

Two Patterns of Participation—1964 and 1970 Presidential Elections

The crucial 1964 and 1970 presidential elections—victories for the center and the left—clearly gave notice that new participants were exercising political clout. Eighty-eight percent of those registered for the election voted in the 1964 election, which had become a contest between the candidate of the center and the right, Eduardo Frei, and the candidate of the left, Salvadore Allende. All candidates depended for the majority of their electoral support on urban areas; about 70 percent of each candidate's vote came from urban areas. The electoral area of *Cuidad Santiago* itself comprised about one-third of the total national vote. In this province Eduardo Frei, the Christian Democratic candidate, received about two-thirds of the vote, while his chief opponent, Salvadore Allende of the left, received about one-third. The power of the landed aristocracy, at least at the ballot box, was gone.

Female voters also emerged as an important force in the election. Female electoral support was crucial to Frei's victory and the Christian Democratic campaign appealed to both the female vote and the moderate, reformist Catholic vote. In terms of the electorate as a whole, men constituted about 54 percent of those registered. In terms of who actually voted, however, about 84 percent of the registered men voted, compared with over 90 percent of the women. Women, then, were more likely to

---

[34] Orville G. Cope, "The 1964 Presidential Election in Chile," in Richard Fenno and Wayne A. Cornelius, Jr., eds., *Political Power in Latin America: Seven Confrontations* (Englewood Cliffs, N.J.: Prentice-Hall, 1970), pp. 15–16.

[35] Russell Fitzgibbon, *Latin America* (New York: Appleton-Century-Crofts, 1971), p. 325.

cast their ballots than men.[36] They were also more likely to cast them for the moderate Frei. Frei received over 63 percent of the female vote, compared with 32 percent for Allende (and about 5 percent for the third-place finisher, Julio Duran). Men distributed their vote much more evenly—50 percent for Frei, 45 percent for Allende, and 5 percent for Duran.[37]

Just as the Christian Democrats and Frei capitalized on their middle-class, Catholic, and female support, Allende sought to mobilize the lower classes in both urban and rural areas. What is remarkable is that both men were appealing to many groups that only a short time earlier were not permitted to vote. The addition of illiterates and 18–21-year-olds in 1973 provided an even larger pool of potential participants.

In many respects the 1970 election appeared to be a repeat of the 1964 contest, with the important exception that the sitting president of Chile, Eduardo Frei, was not allowed to succeed himself. Candidates from the right, (Jorge Alessandri) the center, (Radomiro Tomic) and the left (Salvadore Allende) contested the election. The victory of Salvadore Allende and his Popular Unity coalition was due in part, as was Frei's 1964 victory, to his ability to mobilize those sectors of the population that provided him with the most support. Of those registered to vote, slightly more than 83 percent cast their ballots. Although Allende received only 36.4 percent of the popular vote, this gave him a plurality that the Congress in joint session recognized.

Allende's victory capped the change in participation patterns that began much earlier. The power of the elite, conservative, rural-dominated parties gave way to the power of the newer, more radical, urban-based parties of the Popular Unity coalition. The expansion of the franchise and electorate, the mobilization and politicization of the lower classes, and the platforms that called for both moderate and radical change indicated that political power in Chile had shifted to new groups.

The political attitudes of the Allende forces varied considerably. Different groups within the Allende coalition had different expectations about the benefits they hoped to receive from the election victory. Many copper workers in the North, for example, hoped for improvements in their life-styles and working conditions rather than radical social and economic transformations. Other groups shared a similar feeling that what was needed was improved individual welfare. As a result, they tended to emphasize the need for the new administration to make reformist changes and to perform efficiently.

Other groups, however, hoped for more radical or revolutionary change. Peasants and rural workers organized and demanded more sweeping land reform. Rural cooperatives and unions representing all shades

---

[36] Cope, pp. 15–29.

[37] *The Chilean Presidential Election of September 4, 1964, Part II* (Washington, D.C.: Institute for the Comparative Study of Political Systems, 1965), pp. 10–11.

of the political spectrum—conservative unions supported by the land-owners, moderate reformist movements supported by the Christian Democrats, and radical movements calling for the collectivization of the land—all began to actively participate. Of all the groups that voted for Allende, his rural supporters in many respects were the most radical and the most demanding of significant political and economic change.[38]

In short, the changing electoral laws and the changing social and economic environment in Chile changed participation patterns. As the society became more industrialized, urbanized, and complex, the new workers became more politicized. They participated in political parties, unions, and other groups willing to represent them and press for their demands. The power of the old elite gradually was transferred to a new elite; while it may not have held the economic power of the nation, this new elite did hold the power of the ballot box.

The Military Coup d'Etat—The End of Electoral Participation

Historically, the Chilean military has not intervened in politics as fre-quently as militaries have in other Latin American nations. When they did participate, it was often to control demonstrations, protect the interests of the military in the political system, or, as in 1924 and 1932, to establish military juntas as transitions between civilian governments. The tradition of military noninvolvement in politics was a strong one; officers were above politics. As the Allende presidency progressed, however, military noninvolvement gradually gave way to military involvement.

Since the 1950s the position of the military vis-à-vis other groups in society had deteriorated. Salaries for soldiers did not keep pace with the cost of living, and the quality of the military was deteriorating. By 1970 and the election of the radical Allende, many officers challenged the idea of military noninvolvement. More and more senior officers took political positions either supporting or opposing the president. In many respects the military came to represent not only themselves but also the larger interests of the middle class.

The strong electoral showing of the Allende forces in the 1973 con-gressional elections (winning 44 percent of the seats), coupled with the increasing number of military officers who served in Allende government, increased the possibility of military intervention and made it almost im-possible to unify the army and to assure their neutrality. Finally, in 1973, the conservative, anti-Allende wings of the armed forces intervened, violently ending the Allende government.

The end of civilian rule also changed who was allowed and encouraged

---

[38] James Petras, "Nationalization, Socioeconomic Change and Popular Participation," in Arturo Valenzuela and J. Samuel Valenzuela, eds., *Chile: Politics and Society* (New Brunswick, N.J.: Transaction Books, 1976), pp. 177–194.

to participate. The military junta leans toward the middle-class and conservative elements of society and has shown little inclination of quickly returning Chile to civilian rule. Many of the channels of participation in the previous system—like political parties and unions—have been banned or their activities curtailed. Participation has not ended in authoritarian Chile, but it has taken new directions and involved new participants.

CONCLUSION

Each nation has a cultural and historical tradition that influences how much importance leaders and citizens attach to political participation. Traditions of participation evolve as a response to changing political demands and to changing economic and social conditions.

The pattern of participation in any nation is a product of individual drives and societal opportunities. There are cultural forces that encourage certain forms of participation, and restraints that inhibit or prevent other political activities. Participation is largely symbolic in some nations; it is designed to provide individuals and groups with a sense of satisfaction and to provide legitimacy and support to the political leaders. This is the case in the Soviet Union. In other systems, like Tanzania, participation may be both symbolic and instrumental, and serve to recruit and train new political activists.

Established nations, with long-standing institutionalized patterns of participation, view participation as both a right and a civic duty. This is the case in the United Kingdom, where there are strong supports for participation. Traditions of pragmatism and gradual change have prevented widespread participation from severely dividing the citizenry. As more and more Britons entered the political arena and were allowed to participate, the political system was adapted to meet their new demands and desires.

Newer nations, with few traditions of participation, often experiment with different patterns of political activity and action. In Nigeria electoral activity from 1960 to 1966 led to sharp, violent political conflict. In Chile the gradual enfranchisement of more and more political participants during this century led to a shift from the right to the left and eventually to a military coup d'état that moved Chile back to the right.

Tanzania, the Soviet Union, West Germany, France, and Egypt likewise have experienced different patterns of participation. In each instance, different pools of participants were involved as political systems changed, either gradually or through revolutionary means. For example, Russia moved from very little participation during the tsarist period to widespread, symbolic participation during the Soviet period. Germany has alternated between periods of participation by many (Weimar and the

Federal Republic) and periods of authoritarian rule characterized by little effective participation (National Socialism).

Despite the wide variations in participatory patterns, all the nations have one important similarity: participation at the higher levels of government is restricted. Voting, the most common participatory act in almost all nations, is for many individuals their only political activity (and some do not even vote). Many do not belong to political parties. In each of the nation-states (whether single-party systems, two-party systems, or multi-party systems), parties always have a much smaller active membership than the number of votes they receive in an election. Participation at the higher levels of politics requires more time, more energy, and much greater motivation.

The urge to participate in politics at some level, then, is conditioned by historical and cultural factors and by the limitations and opportunities provided by the political system. An understanding of the patterns of participation is essential to understanding the role of political parties and elections in political systems. Chapters 5 and 6 explore the links between participation, parties, and elections.

CHAPTER 5
POLITICAL
PARTIES

What tasks do political parties perform in
modern nations?

Political parties, found in most political systems, are among the most important institutional features of twentieth-century politics regardless of their setting or context. Parties reflect the universal nature of politics emphasized in Chapter 1. They are institutional adaptions to the challenges familiar to most nations today—the need to control conflict, to respond to group demands, and to cope with political, economic, and social change.

Political parties are firmly grounded in the nation's cultural setting, reflecting and responding to its group life and societal divisions. Parties are sensitive to the most important values of a system's political culture—those relating to political conflict and competition versus unity and consensus. In systems with clear group differences in interests and demands, parties may represent the conflict between groups, while in deeply divided societies, a single party may try to enforce unity according to the values of the national culture or the leadership.

Cultural and historical differences produce different types of party systems. Party systems vary from country to country as to the number of parties, their goals and philosophies, their organizational strength, and their styles of action. These variations in how party systems have developed are critical in understanding and explaining differences in the performance of different political systems.

Types of Party Systems

The most basic feature of a party system is the number of parties in it. One-party systems seem to originate in two specific sets of circumstances. First, one-party systems may develop where there is no tradition of political opposition, as was the case with authoritarian Russia or in parts of ex-colonial Africa. Second, one-party systems may be the result of efforts of an elite political leadership to enforce unity on a divided society. Tanzania is a leading example of this sort of development, as again is Russia. Tanzania and Russia have over a hundred distinct languages or ethnic groups, all of whose specific demands could not be incorporated in a party system.

Two-party systems are associated with economically advanced nations in which group differences in life-style, education, and income are not deep. Britain and the United States are the outstanding examples. Since these societies are not deeply divided on the basis of religion, language, kinship, or region, parties can put together a broad following. They can focus on moderate questions that are less emotional and productive of violence.

West Germany represents an interesting transitional case to a two-party system. The dramatic postwar economic success of the German economy has, step by step, eliminated older issues that divided Germans. Rural/urban differences, for example, no longer have the impact they once did. As the issues disappeared, so did the specific parties representing them. West Germany is on the verge of becoming a two-party system partly because of the impact of economic change on society and politics.

In contrast, multi-party systems such as Fourth Republic France and pre-1966 Nigeria represent settings where a number of group differences are important in politics. Fundamental issues separating groups have not been resolved through political action or through social and economic change. France had over a dozen parties representing religious, regional, and class interests. Nigeria had over 80 political parties and movements. Religious, regional, and ethnic groups had their own specific organizations.

Parties also vary in their goals and appeals. Some appeal to a narrow section of society by promoting rigid ideologies or issue positions. In that way the party retains a following by appealing to the narrow interests of a well-defined group. In divided societies that permit competitive politics, such as France, this is a familiar pattern.

Other parties broaden their appeals to cross group lines in an attempt to gain a majority in their system. These parties are sometimes called "catch-all" parties because of their desire to "catch" as many voters as possible. In so doing, they cannot emphasize specific demands and issues but rather find general themes to which large numbers of people can respond. Their goal is to bring as many voters as possible under the broad party umbrella. Obviously, this type of style works best in a society where group differences are less important. British political parties and the current West German parties are of this type.

Finally, parties differ in party organization, that is, according to how centralized and hierarchical they are. The Communist party of the Soviet Union and, to a lesser extent, the Arab Socialist Union in Egypt are organized as hierarchical pyramids. Central authority at the top of the pyramid sends directives for action downward and outward through subordinate units. These types of organizations are designed for control, discipline, and concerted political action for achieving party goals. (See Figure 5–1.)

Most other parties have less organizational strength and coherence. Britain's Labour party, though somewhat centralized, does not have clear

FIGURE 5–1   Party Systems in Eight Nations

Number of Parties	Party Appeals and Goals	Party Organization
Multi-party systems France Nigeria (before 1966) Chile (before 1973)	High ideological content; narrow appeal to specific interests France Nigeria (before 1966) Chile (before 1973)	Decentralized, loosely organized France West Germany Nigeria (before 1966)
Two-party dominant systems United Kingdom West Germany	Low ideological content; broad appeal to all groups and interests United Kingdom West Germany	More highly centralized United Kingdom Chile (before 1973) Tanzania
Single-party systems Soviet Union Egypt Tanzania	High ideological content; appeal to all groups to join together under the party banner Soviet Union Egypt Tanzania	Highly centralized, hierarchical Soviet Union Egypt
No-party systems Nigeria (after 1966) Chile (after 1973)		

and simple authority patterns. The constituency and trade union components of the party are not simply subordinate bodies to carry out leadership directives but have their own independent role within the party framework. Many parties—such as those of the French center and right and many parties in developing countries—are very loose alliances of local leaders with no real national leadership.

The number of parties in a party system, the nature of their goals, and their manner of organization are often related. Rigid or ideological goals are associated with sectional or special-interest parties in multi-party systems. These kinds of goals also are associated with highly organized parties in one-party states such as TANU and with the Communist party of the Soviet Union. Two-party systems tend to be composed of moderate "catch-all" parties characterized by some degree of organizational decentralization.

Party Tasks and Functions

The carrying out of functions differs with each party system, but there are basic tasks that all party systems perform. These include recruiting individuals for elective, appointive, and voluntary political positions (Chapter 6); mobilizing the public for political action (Chapter 4); and providing governmental leadership teams (Chapter 7).

For all parties, recruitment is basic. In democratic systems parties select, train, and "package" persons as candidates for election. They bring in volunteers for campaign and program purposes. Party leaders also appoint persons to administrative and judicial positions. In noncompetitive systems the monopolistic party has total control over selection without concern for candidate appeal or the competition. In the Soviet Union, party loyalty or ideological orthodoxy are crucial in recruitment to powerful positions.

Varying patterns of recruitment affect what types of people occupy positions of responsibility. At one extreme, a one-party system makes party loyalty an unvarying criterion; only "party men" have influential positions. In competitive systems, parties select a wider variety of people, utilizing personal appeal and group connections.

Parties also move ordinary citizens to political action, which in democratic countries means facilitating the individual's role as a voter. Parties educate the electorate with regard to issues, party positions and records, and their choices. Putting together party programs, launching informational efforts, and campaigning at election time are the most obvious forms of political education in competitive systems.

In noncompetitive systems, parties also have a mobilizing role. They move people to symbolic participation, such as voting in uncontested elections. This is serious business in the Soviet Union, where, at considerable cost and effort, the Communist party consistently gets 99 percent turnout for elections. Monopolistic parties also move people to participate in carrying out plans and programs made by the party leadership.

Finally, parties man the offices of government. They provide national political leadership, make policy, and supervise the implementation of their policies. Parties operate within governmental institutions, like parliaments and executives, but differ in terms of the type and quality of the leadership they provide, the unity with which they govern, and the power they hold over the relatively nonpartisan governmental officials (the civil service, the judiciary, and the military).

Performance

Not all parties, of course, perform their basic tasks with equal efficiency. Party performance has a basic impact on political stability and the possibility of political change within a system. Party systems that perform well contribute to public support for institutions, leaders, and govern decisions made by leaders. Since leaders and their policies are products of partisan politics, it is often difficult for people to separate in their minds institutions from the parties that control them. Parties that consistently fail to provide leadership and programs are in the end equivalent to institutional failure. For example, it is difficult to separate the failure of German political parties in the 1920s or the Nigerian parties in the early 1960s from the failure of the German and Nigerian parliaments. Similarly, parties may be the objects of considerable loyalty and support in their own right. Individual affections for political parties and their leaders may benefit the institutions of government in trying times. The emotional attachment of Britons for their parties no doubt helps maintain general support for the system in prolonged periods of hard times.

Another key role of parties is the encouraging and channeling of political participation; hence, they may be judged according to whether participation is widespread. The Communist party in the Soviet Union, like parties in other systems, actively encourages symbolic participation. Other parties, such as the British Conservative party or the Christian Democrats of Germany, seemingly discourage widespread popular involvement in party affairs.

Party systems, as well as specific parties, influence whether participation is encouraged or discouraged in a nation. In democratic nations, with regularized elections, participation usually is stimulated when there are differences between two parties or between governmental and opposition coalitions. Likewise, sharp differences over policies or major issues encourages citizens to become politically active. Finally, some party systems help achieve an electoral outcome that determines who will lead the nation; that is, an electoral victory allows the majority party to control the government for a period. The British party system almost always leads to a decisive victory by a single party; victory by the Labour or Conservative party allows them to make decisions and form a government with relatively little interference from the "loyal opposition." In many multi-party systems there is often no clear-cut winner; then coalitions, based on election results and negotiations between party leaders, are necessary to form a government. Generally, decisive results lead to broader participation in competitive systems.

In one-party states, the extent and nature of participation is a direct result of party policy and organizational strength. Most monopoly parties value widespread participation in support of their goals. One-party systems are more likely to differ from country to country as to the organizational resources available to the leadership and their efficiency in employing them.

Studying the party systems in this chapter, we can see the results of different patterns of party organization. The Soviet Union, Egypt, and Tanzania are or have been one-party states. The United Kingdom is a leading example of a moderate two-party system, while West Germany exemplifies a two-party system in the making. Nigeria, Chile, and France give us insights into the nature of multi-party systems. Notable besides the variety in political structure are the differences between one-party politics in an economically advanced, modern setting and one-party politics in Africa. Similarly, multi-partyism in developed France contrasts to multi-partyism in Chile and Nigeria.

▪ THE UNITED KINGDOM ▪

The United Kingdom is usually described as a competitive two-party system characterized by a relatively low level of political conflict. In actuality there are several serious smaller parties including the Liberal party, the Scottish Nationalists, and the Plaid Cymru of Wales. Over 20 percent of the elected members of Parliament received less than one-half of the vote in the last election and therefore are survivors of at least three-way races. The British party system is considered a two-party system on the practical grounds that only the Conservatives or their Labour counter-parts have led a government since 1922; therefore, only these two are viewed as potential leadership teams.

The supposed moderation of the parties must be qualified as well. It is true that the style of the two parties reflects the British cultural affinity for pragmatism and compromise. However, the two parties represent working-class and middle-class elements of the population whose interests, attitudes, and life-styles are often sharply at odds with one another. Class conflict surfaces in periods of economic distress such as the 1930s or the current period of economic stagnation. Margaret Thatcher (who led the Conservative opposition from 1975 to 1979 and who became prime minister in 1979), for example, has challenged the welfare state after years of Conservative acquiescence on questions of social services and economic planning.

The Labour party for its part has always had a core of militants uncompromising on working-class issues. This left wing of Labour contributes to ideological polarization by an insistence on rigorous measures to produce economic equality, full employment, inexpensive housing, health care, and transportation services. The fact that the Labour party is directly affiliated with Britain's Trades Union Congress accentuates inter-party differences.

The Labour Party

The Labour party developed as an arm of the trade union movement in Britain in the early twentieth century. The original organization was called the Labour Representation Committee of the Trades Union Congress. The committee was the result of the combined efforts of the trade unions and Britain's leading socialist societies, notably the Fabian Society.

The origins of the Labour party are reflected in its political goals. Since the party was founded by groups outside the political establishment, Labour has emphasized the right and duty of rank-and-file members and its affiliated organizations to influence policy. The trade union aspect of the founding groups also is reflected in steady Labour support for legislation to improve working conditions, maintain full employment, and strengthen union bargaining capabilities. The Fabian socialist legacy may be found in Labour's dedication to a very sweeping interpretation of one democratic value—equality. The Labour leadership defines equality to include political equality, economic equality, and social equality. Rather than emphasize equality of opportunity, they stress government's responsibility to reduce the differences in income, power, status, and lifestyle that separate middle-class Britons from working-class Britons.

One way to create a more equal policy is to nationalize industries. The postwar Labour government under Clement Attlee (1945–1949) nationalized a number of basic industries such as the coal, iron and steel, and transport industries. Another round of nationalizations occurred with Harold Wilson's return to power in 1974. In each case the underlying notion was that government could use control of basic industry to further social goals. By becoming the owner of large industries, the government could tailor economic decisions to further equality and an equitable distribution of wealth. The efficacy of this approach was in question by the time that Labour left office in 1951. Even to Labour leaders, economic control and planning proved to be a difficult tool to use in promoting equality.

The Labour leadership turned to an alternative way to achieve its pri-

Leadership Profiles

The Prime Minister and the Leader of the Opposition, 1979

Leader	Background and Education
Margaret Thatcher Prime Minister (1979–present) and Leader of the Conservative Party	born: 1925 education: Somerville College, Oxford, M.A., B.S.
James Callaghan Prime Minister (1976–1979) and Leader of the Labour Party	born: 1912 education: Callaghan's father was in the navy and died when Callaghan was nine years old. The family received a pension through the in- tervention of a Labour MP. Callaghan left school at age 16.

mary goal—the "welfare state." The Labour party tends to favor broad health and welfare services with a flat rate of benefits or services available to all, regardless of individual means and without proof of need. Recently economics have forced Labour toward a two-tiered system in which those who can afford to pay can opt for better services. These issues have been very sensitive with regard to Britain's National Health Service. Because the Health Service is government controlled, insurance, hospitals, and medical staff are subject to the policy of the government of the day.

Early Occupations		Political Career	
1947–1951	Research chemist	1959– present	Conservative Member of Parliament from Finchley
1953	Barrister, Lincoln's Inn	1961–1964	Parliamentary Secretary, Ministry of Pensions and National Insurance
		1970–1974	Secretary of State for Education and Housing
		1975–1979	Leader of the Opposition (replaced Edward Heath)
		1979– present	Prime Minister
At age 24 Callaghan became a full-time salaried union official with a speciality in arbitration.		1945– present	Labour Member of Parliament for South Cardiff (Wales)
		1947	Junior post at the Transport Ministry
		1951	Junior post at the Admiralty
		1963	Challenged Harold Wilson for leadership of the Labour Party, but lost
		1964–1970	Chancellor of the Exchequer (Treasury) Home Secretary
		1974	Foreign Secretary
		1976–1979	Prime Minister (assumed office on the resignation of Harold Wilson)
		1979– present	Leader of the Opposition

Policies regarding special treatment or private patients alternate depending on whether Labour or the Conservatives are in charge.

A "membership party," Labour relies on a large number of dues-paying members for financial support and for a reservoir of political activists and voters. The Labour party has over 6 million members, 89 percent of whom are affiliated with the party through their trade union. The remainder, about 700,000 strong, are individual members affiliated through their local Labour party constituency organization.

Membership, though largely from the working class, also has a substantial proportion from the middle class. These middle-class members are drawn largely from the professions, primarily in the fields of education and law. They often are considered the intellectual core, who are attracted to the party because of its socialist traditions.

Labour *voters* are also predominantly working class. Over 70 percent of Britain's manual laborers vote Labour. The figure is closer to 80 percent if the individual's own perception of his class is used rather than occupation only. This fairly stable voting bloc provides Labour with steady support from election to election. The voters' loyalty is based on their emotional attachment to the party, their union affiliation, and their sense of the importance of class differences.

The Conservative Party

The goals of the Conservative party are not as easy to determine as those of the Labour party. The Conservatives seem to enjoy their role as the most practical and pragmatic party in pragmatic Britain. The Conservatives'

Edward Heath addresses the 1975 British Conservative party conference. Peter Marlow, Sygma.

positions are difficult to determine in part because they stress the party's role as a national party above particular interests and group attachments. They perceive themselves not to be a class party, although their leadership and a majority of their following are drawn from the middle and upper classes. Another source of confusion is that the Conservatives are not strictly the party of free enterprise and small government. They endorsed and helped implement a wide variety of social welfare programs and have not shied away from an activist, interventionist governmental style.

In the two decades following Attlee's Labour government, the Conservatives made no large-scale attempt to "roll back" the welfare state and the important nationalizations, focusing instead on reduced expenditure and rationalization of services. The Conservatives generally favor a more flexible welfare system allowing for a variety of options for individuals. They favor increased financial support from consumers while reducing or stabilizing taxes.

The Conservative shadow government under Margaret Thatcher (1975–1979), however, represented the strongest party adherents to the free-enterprise system. Thatcher's successful challenge to Edward Heath's leadership in early 1975 marked a departure from the party's acquiescence in welfare-state politics. In opposition she suggested that Britain needed a sharp turn back to a reliance on a market economy even if the market dictates that a number of Britain's inefficient businesses and industries go bankrupt. Thatcher also has suggested that the cost of the welfare program can no longer be borne and needs radical cutting—an outcome that she thinks will permit a beneficial return to individual initiative and self-reliance. Whether this is a lasting reorientation or a response to an immediate crisis is not clear.

Excerpts from Party Manifestos of September 1974

Party differences? The "me too" stand of the Conservatives was singled out as a cause for their defeat in October 1974. Edward Heath was later replaced as party leader by Margaret Thatcher for this reason.

Labour	Conservative	Liberal
"Britain faces its most dangerous crisis since the war. . . . The first priority must be a determined attack on inflation."	"The dangers facing Britain are greater than any we have seen since the last war. . . . For inflation . . . threatens . . . the survival of our free and democratic institutions."	". . . the greatest peace-time crisis we have known since the dark days of 1931. . . . The major single problem [is] that of inflation."

Excerpts from Party Manifestos of September 1974 *(Continued)*

Labour	Conservative	Liberal
"We want to be frank with you. . . . There will be no easy times and no easy pickings for anyone."	". . . there is no room for any early improvements in living standards."	"We must learn to live within our means. Strict economies in nonessential expenditure must now be made."
"[After the February election] we increased pensions . . . we restrained the rise in the cost of living by our subsidies. . . . [We] cut VAT from 10 percent to 8 percent. . . . We have given an extra £350 million for councils to build more new houses . . . given a £500 million loan to building societies to keep mortgage rates down. . . ."	". . . . But we will act now in three areas which have been particularly hard hit by inflation . . . pensions, housing and food production. . . . [We will] reduce the interest rate charged by building societies to home buyers to 9½ percent. . . . A Conservative government will . . . in-. crease retirement pensions . . . every six months. . . ."	"[We would] immediately introduce a statutory minimum earnings level [of £27 a week] . . . give an immediate commitment to tie the pension to a stated percentage of national earnings. . . . The total cost would be £1,400m . . . in the National Health Service . . . only a massive injection of capital can save it . . . and this will have to be done almost immediately. . . ."
"It is only with a sense of unity that we shall win through. . . . At the heart of this manifesto . . . lies the Social Contract between the Labour Government and the trade unions."	"[After the election I will immediately set out . . . to establish a government that can transcend party divisions. . . . The government of national unity would seek to put aside party bickering and concentrate on mobilizing the full resources of the nation."	"Liberals can become the catalyst to bind the country together. . . . The class war produces deep and irreconcilable differences between the Conservative and Labour parties. . . . Neither can achieve the necessary degree of unity."

Source: Michael Pinto-Duchinsky, "False Calm: Party Strategies in October 1974," in Howard R. Penniman, ed. *Britain at the Polls* (Washington, D.C.: American Enterprise Institute for Public Policy Research, 1974), p. 202. Reprinted by permission.

The Conservative party in trying to implement these goals relies much less on party membership than does Labour. Its activists and voters are found in the upper levels of Britain's class and occupational strata. (Almost 80 percent of the Britons in the top occupational categories support the Conservative party.) It does, however, rely on attracting a core of working-class individuals consistently from election to election. These "working-class Tories" enable the Conservatives to be competitive despite the fact that a majority of British voters are of the working class. The ability to draw these voters rests on the deferential attitudes of this element of British workers, who believe in the necessity of governments being handled by their social "betters."

The Liberal Party

The Liberal party, once a powerful political force, failed to adjust to the social and economic changes of this century and has been relegated to a minor political role. When its original issue—based on free trade and laissez-faire economics—declined in importance, the Liberals attempted to capture power based on a reform program. The reforms alienated their supporters in business and yet could not attract worker support in competition with Labour. To this day, the Liberal goals fall in between the goals of business and labor, offering in essence a vision of reformist capitalism that would reduce the role of government and promote individualism.

Liberal support is scattered among the middle-class occupations and professions. Liberal support comes from a core of party loyalists (who will have to hand down their attachment to their children if the party is to survive) and from major-party supporters who turn away from their own party but do not wish to vote for the major opposition. It also seems likely that an increasing portion of Liberal support comes from individuals fed up with the performance of both large parties—this may include a number of young Britons who disproportionately vote Liberal.

Party Organization

The parties in Britain are organized similarly. Each has a relatively centralized national political organization, with the local constituency organization as its basic unit. Each has a national executive and a national headquarters staff. In addition, each party has a yearly party conference at which representatives of the membership discuss party policy and pass policy resolutions.

The Labour party has always stressed the role of its extra-parliamentary organization. Nominally, the Labour Party Conference and the directing body it elects, the National Executive Committee, have the leading role in determining party goals and policy. In practice, though, it is the party organization in Parliament, referred to as the Parliamentary Labour party (PLP), that controls the direction of party policy. In dramatic cases of disagreement, such as the Conference resolution favoring unilateral disarmament in 1961, the PLP has overruled the Conference. Since, however, the Conference is largely made up of representatives of the nation's largest unions, the party leadership is anxious to avoid these sorts of confrontations and tries to respect Conference opinon.

The Conservative party feels much less of a commitment to intraparty democracy. The resolutions of their Conference have never been considered binding on the leadership. In practice the Conference has evolved into an organ for demonstrating party unity and rank-and-file support. In this spirit the Conservative Party Conference of 1976 served to heal the split between Edward Heath and Margaret Thatcher and to endorse Thatcher's policy preferences.

Party Performance

On the whole, the British party system has performed well for a long time. The disciplined two-party system performs admirably in publicizing clear choices for governmental action. It provides a continuing public debate between the government and its opposition, stimulating close competition and the alternation of the parties in office. Competition of this sort increases political interest and avoids abuse of power or political stagnation.

As far as leadership is concerned British parties receive mixed reviews. The parties subject promising young members to a long apprenticeship in the Commons and in junior posts in the ministries. The leadership that emerges seems cautious, overly patient, and not very innovative. During the trying period of the 1960s and nearly half of the 1970s, Britons saw electoral contests between the leadership teams of Harold Wilson (Labour) and Edward Heath (Conservative). The new leadership often seems very much the same as the old. When Wilson resigned Labour's leadership in 1976, he was replaced by James Callaghan, another Labour moderate with four decades of experience in the House and in the trade unions.

Basically, the British parties stimulate support for institutions and political participation. The emotional attachment that most Britons have for their parties seems to survive apparent failures of leadership, and their loyalty has been invaluable for the stability of the British political system.

■ THE FEDERAL REPUBLIC OF GERMANY ■

The West German party system today is a multi-party system consisting of two large evenly matched parties and one small party. The small party, the Free Democratic party (FDP), has tenuously survived as a junior partner of first one, then the other, of the large parties. The Social Democratic party (SPD) is a large moderate party on the left and is currently (1979) the major governing party in coalition with the FDP. The large conservative party is the Christian Democratic Union/Christian Socialist Union (CDU-CSU)—usually referred to simply as the Christian Democrats.

The party system has evolved into a very moderate low-conflict system, for the differences between parties are small. When a SPD leader was asked what would change when that party assumed power for the first time in 1969, he responded, "We will be in and they will be out." Both parties try to capture the support of a broad range of groups in their efforts to reach the elusive goal of becoming a majority party. Since they are concerned with winning power and broad support, they reject narrow or ideological appeals to the voters.

The party system appears to be approaching a competitive two-party system. The two big parties now are roughly even in their usual electoral shares—around 45 percent of the electorate. If the Free Democrats fail to receive 5 percent of the vote in the future, according to the West German Basic Law they will gain no seats in Parliament and therefore will effectively be eliminated as a national political party. In that likely event, the Federal Republic will have a moderate competitive two-party system on the order of Britain or the United States.

As the earlier discussion of German history suggests, the German party system has changed dramatically as it has moved toward a two-party system. During the Weimar Republic (1919–1933) over a dozen narrow, sectional, or ideological parties secured parliamentary seats. Almost as many parties attempted to establish themselves at the beginning of the Federal Republic in 1949. The party system has responded to economic, social, demographic, and international changes in the intervening years. These changes have contributed to a reduction in the number and severity of partisan divisions.

The Social Democratic Party of Germany (SPD)

The Social Democrats are the oldest political party in Germany and, in fact, one of the oldest workers' parties—dating from the 1870s. Few political parties have had as eventful and changeable history as has the SPD. They recently changed their ideology, philosophy, and goals in response to the contradictions between socialist theory and the nature of a German society dedicated to free enterprise. They were also forced to change tactics and alter their ambitions with the dramatic discontinuities and dislocations of twentieth-century German history.

Originally, the SPD was Karl Marx's own party, and his ideas provided the motivating force of the party. From the beginning, however, German socialism tended toward moderate reformist policies aimed more at improving the life conditions of workers than at playing a leading revolutionary role. The party platform in 1875, largely influenced by the reformist Ferdinand La Salle, was along these lines. The more militant revolutionary wing of the party won a policy victory at the 1891 party conference by getting party approval for the overthrow of the capitalist system as the major party objective.

The two wings of the party finally and irrevocably split under the pressure of World War I and the November revolution that set up the postwar

Weimar Republic. The moderate wing of the party acted as patriotic supporters of the war—a policy that the left wing of the party felt was inexcusable. Moderate SPD leaders such as the first president of the Weimar Republic, Friedrich Ebert, viewed the socialist left wing as an international revolutionary threat allied with Russian bolshevism in the 1919–1920 period. Their response was to ally with the old Imperial Army and to acquiesce in the liquidation of the revolutionary wing—then known as Spartacists. The political murders of Spartacist leader Karl Liebknecht and Rosa Luxemburg in 1919 forever sealed the split between the SPD and what became the German Communist party.

During the period of the Weimar Republic, the Social Democrats attempted to play a constructive role in building German democracy. As the largest and best-organized democratic party, they were in some ways the leading force; however, political inexperience and competition from Communists for worker loyalty led the SPD to fail in its responsibilities. At one point, for example, the SPD would not participate in a cabinet for four years (1924–1928) so that the Communists could not use their record as a government party against them in their appeal to workers.

At the beginning of the Federal Republic, the SPD—again viewed as an important democratic element in German politics—could boast of its record as the only political party that had resisted Hitler's seizure of power. Its last official act had been the heroic but futile vote cast in the German Parliament against the Enabling Act—the bill granting Hitler unlimited power in 1933. Of the 94 SPD members who voted against the Act, 24 were soon murdered and the rest jailed or forced into hiding. Unfortunately, the Social Democrats were also associated in some minds with the new European threat—Soviet communism. This fear of the SPD was based on its Marxist origins, on some Marxist goals retained by the party, and on the fact that a number of SPD leaders had fled to Moscow during the war to avoid Hitler's concentration camps.

During the 1950s the SPD was confined to its "working-class ghetto" in German politics. Its support stayed at around the 35 percent level, largely because its appeals drew worker support only. Its conservative opposition, the CDU/CSU, in the same period continued to grow—to the point that it received a majority in the 1957 election. The Social Democratic response was to scrap the last of the Marxist rhetoric from its program and to select as leader an attractive figure with well-known credentials in "free world" politics—Willy Brandt, the mayor of West Berlin. These actions were taken at the SPD party conference in 1959. In the 1960s under the leadership of Willy Brandt and the current chancellor, Helmut Schmidt, the Social Democrats became a competitive party viewed as a serious leadership alternative to the Christian Democrats.

Since the 1959 party conference the SPD has consistently followed a set of reformist goals geared toward social and economic equality. In domestic policy the party advocates equality in labor-management relations through larger worker participation in management decisions (an expansion of the established law, called codetermination). Social equality is promoted in the SPD program by its plans for educational reform, involving both student involvement in educational decisions and plans to broaden access to university education. The SPD advocates health policy reform but rejects nationalization of health services, preferring to provide low-cost insurance in cooperation with the private sector.

In international affairs the SPD endorses (and helped implement) a normalization of relations in Eastern Europe as well as with East Germany (the German Democratic Republic). Willy Brandt pioneered a policy, *Ostpolitik* (Eastern policy), which accepted the status quo in Eastern

---

Program of the Social Democratic Party for the Federal Election of October 3, 1976

Principles:
Socialists strive for a society in which each human being can develop his personality in freedom and function responsibly as a member of society contributing to the political, economic and cultural life of mankind. To working people, freedom means a greater measure of codetermination and more humane working conditions. To citizens in large cities and urban centers freedom means increased opportunity in education and training.

Economy:
The basis of the successful economic development of the Federal Republic was and is the market economy. It requires collective bargaining and free enterprise. The SPD wishes to strengthen and extend this system: this requires increased competition. The consumer, who has the weakest position in our economic system will also benefit from increased competition. . . .

A high level of employment is given highest priority by Social Democratic policy. As a second target, stable prices must be achieved at the same time. . . .

Social Democrats consider a just taxation policy as a means necessary for the attainment of a more equitable distribution of income. . . .

The long-standing demand for equal participation by capital and workers in the management of business is an important principle.

Foreign Policy:
The primary goal of Social Democratic policy remains the consolidation of the Federal Republic of Germany within the Western Alliance and further progress toward European integration within the framework of the European Community. . . .

The Social Democratic Party accords primary importance to utilizing the political and economic opportunities resulting from increased East-West cooperation.

Source: "Procedures, Programs and Profiles" published in Bonn-Bad Godesberg, West Germany, for *Inter Nationes,* 1976.

Leadership Profiles

The Chancellor and the Major Opposition Leader, 1978

Leader	Background and Education
Helmut Schmidt Chancellor (1974–present), Social Democratic Party	born: 1918 education: Studied political science and economics at Hamburg University. Graduate degree in economics
Helmut Kohl Leader of the Christian Democratic Union	born: 1930 education: Doctor of Philosophy in Jurisprudence, Heidelberg University

---

Europe including the loss of prewar German territory. In return, Brandt suggested that West Germans would benefit from increased trade, access rights to Berlin, and a general reduction in tensions and international threats. The issue remains important in politics despite the fact that Brandt accomplished many of its aims through treaties with the Soviet Union, East Germany, and other Communist nations. The Social Democrats have used these policies and the long-standing party image to put together a solid base of political support. The party retains its core of supporters who are urban, trade unionist, less prosperous, and less religious. The SPD's newer policies attract young people and white-collar workers. In addition, they are beginning to attract Catholic working-class supporters who had previously voted conservative because of their religion.

Early Occupations	Political Career	
Served in the Wehrmacht on both fronts during World War II. Achieved the rank of First Lieutenant (Reserve) and Battery Commander	1953–1961	Member of the Bundestag
	1961–1965	Minister of Interior for Hamburg State Government
Civil servant with Hamburg Authority for Economics	1965–present	Member of the Bundestag
	1968	Deputy Chairman of the SPD
	1969	Federal Minister of Defense
	1972	Federal Minister of Economics and Finance
	1972	Federal Minister of Finance
	1974	Elected Federal Chancellor
Departmental head of the Chemical Industry Association	1959	Elected to Parliament of the Rhineland-Palatinate State
	1966	Federal State Chairman of Rhineland-Palatinate CDU
	1969	Prime Minister of Rhineland-Palatinate
	1972	Elected Chairman of the Federal CDU
	1976	Candidate of the CDU for Chancellor, defeated

The Christian Democrats

The Christian Democrats (CDU and the Bavarian wing of CSU) make up a new party formed by postwar political forces. In a sense the CDU is an heir to the old Catholic party or *Zentrum* that existed during the empire and Weimar periods. However, the CDU/CSU represents a branch of the broader nonsectarian European Christian Democratic movement. As such, the party is not directly connected with the Catholic church and emphasizes its role as a modern political force.

From the beginning, the Christian Democrats established a pragmatic, broadly based party. In its early years it successfully absorbed political parties representing rural conservative and regional interests. One of its

Konrad   Adenauer speaking to a meeting of the West German Christian Democratic Union. Erich Lessing, Magnum Photos, Inc.

original triumphs involved the ability of its Bavarian affiliate to undercut regional parties in that southern province known for its distinct conservative culture.

The party provided the Federal Republic's first three chancellors: Konrad Adenauer (1949–1963), Ludwig Erhard (1963–1966), and Kurt Kiesinger (1966–1969). Because of its monopoly of power and the forceful personality of Adenauer, the party developed a firm image as the party of administrative leadership—the chancellor's party. Since the 1950s were insecure years in Central Europe, many Germans were afraid to change leadership and responded to the CDU slogan, "No Experiments!"

The party also became associated in the public mind with the German economic recovery or the "economic miracle." The German economy made a dramatic recovery in the mid–1950s under the leadership of Adenauer and his Economics Minister Ludwig Erhard. Although the recovery came about partly from an infusion of American funds and decisions made in international bodies, the CDU clearly benefited.

A last basic policy of the CDU years in power involved relations with

Program of the Christian Democratic Union/Christian Socialist Union for the Federal Election of October 3, 1976

Principles:
The objectives of CDU/CSU policy are freedom of the individual aware of his responsibility to the community, justice and equality of opportunity for everyone, and civic solidarity.

Economy:
The CDU wishes to continue the development of the social market economy in such a manner that personal initiative is strengthened, and an ever-increasing participation in social and economic progress is realized. The social market economy opposes privilege and every form of statism with its attendant planned economy. It opposes socialist restriction of liberal rights and the socialization of the means of production, as well as an uncontrolled economic system of liberalistic character.

Foreign Policy:
The political unity of a free Europe is a decisive contribution to European and World peace. . . .

The Foundation of this development is the European Community. It must be improved and strengthened. A common foreign policy and common defense policy must be developed. . . .

NATO must be strengthened and developed. . . .

The CDU/CSU policy toward the East will not be a one-way street for political and financial concessions by the Federal Republic of Germany.

Source: "Procedures, Programs and Profiles" published in Bonn-Bad Godesberg, West Germany, for *Inter Nationes,* 1976.

the United States and other NATO nations. Adenauer became the "Chancellor of the Allies" with a special place in American plans for the defense of Western Europe and its economic recovery. At the same time he refused to accept Germany's loss of territory and the Soviet occupation of East Germany. According to the Hallstein doctrine, the West German government was committed to breaking off relations with any government recognizing the German Democratic Republic.

Since this period, the CDU's image has suffered vis-à-vis the SPD. The German people have become used to SPD leadership and no longer view the CDU as the party that monopolizes executive talent. An economic recession during Erhard's chancellorship in the mid-1960s shook the CDU image as the party of economic prosperity. Today the Christian Democrats face the electorate with new leadership and modified goals.

The Christian Democrats still stress the political values of individualism and a "social market" economy (an economy entirely in private hands but allowing government a strong role in influencing economic decisions). The Christian Democrats suggest that government best plays its role by coordinating budgetary, financial, and monetary policies under vigorous leadership. Social problems such as health, welfare, and housing should be attacked in the same spirit, with executive leadership cooperating with private interests. This sort of government-group relation they describe as "creative co-responsibility [which] is a prerequisite for a society conceived as a partnership."[1]

In international relations, the current CDU leadership under Helmut Kohl still stresses defense of Western Europe and is highly critical of dealing with the East, a "one-way street for political and economic concessions." In their last party program the CDU called for a strengthening of the North Atlantic Treaty Organization and for greater coordination of Western European defense policies.

These generally conservative political themes and policies help consolidate support for the CDU among traditionally conservative elements. The CDU/CSU is stronger among older Germans, religious (and, particularly, Catholic) Germans, and among those living in towns and rural areas. Geographically, the CDU/CSU has done better in the more rural and conservative South.

Free Democrats

The Free Democrats are a small party dedicated in part to classical liberal principles—those of small government and individualism. Through 1966 it was usually associated with Christian Democrat governments, emphasizing traditions of economic freedom that coincided with the views of the more conservative CDU/CSU. Since then, the party has moved somewhat to the left and has emphasized social and economic reforms, even forming a governmental coalition with the SPD that has lasted since 1969. The major policy tension in that partnership involves the fact that Free Democrats do not approve of trade-union involvement in major economic decisions, as happens in the SPD.

Performance of the Party System

The party system in the Federal Republic has been most successful in reducing and controlling political conflict. In a very real sense, the party leadership in postwar Germany is responsible for the moderate level of political conflict. By avoiding ideological stands and broadening their appeals, the large parties have reduced their policy differences.

The system has been less successful in stimulating political participation.

---

[1] German Information Center, *Federal Republic of Germany: Elections, Parliament and Political Parties* (September 1976): 5–7.

The very cooling off of political tensions has probably lessened the desire of some people to participate in politics. The fact that governments are still based on coalitions makes the act of voting less satisfying for many. They know that much depends on bargains and agreements that have nothing to do with elections or public opinion.

Given the substantial changes that have already taken place in the German party system, it is not unreasonable to expect that a true two-party system will soon be established. In that event the current flaws in the German party system would largely be resolved. The only remaining problems would be the perennial problems of moderate two-party politics—an absence of real choice and an absence of party differences.

■ FRANCE ■

The French party system is a fluid multi-party system. In this century politics usually have been dominated by six or so political parties, often of relatively equal strength. The parties seem to be based on narrow ideological grounds, yet there is always room for political flexibility and opportunism. The opportunism of particular leaders contributes to the fluid nature of the system. Parties change names with regularity, and party leaders frequently change parties or preside over party realignments. The Gaullist party, for example has had four names, while the Socialist leader, François Mitterand, has been a member of at least five political parties. Adding to this confusion, parties are prone to form electoral alliances that may carry distinct names and separate programs from their component parties.

Despite its fluid nature, the party system has a basic continuity. Regardless of particular alignments, the notion of political left and right—which originated in France—still provides an anchoring point. Traditionally, the left parties were anti-clerical, and the right parties represented clerical opinion; but the clerical issue is less important now, and the left-right division follows a class division based on attitude toward social, economic, and political change. Whatever the criteria, the Communists, Socialists, and Radicals have long provided the core of the political left. The right now is dominated by the Gaullists and their conservative allies, the Independent Republicans. There is a small but important center section straddling the old clerical division. The center parties are postwar, nonsectarian, reformist groups who reject the older political classifications.

The French Communist Party (PCF)

For much of its history the French Communist party was considered a "hard-line" Communist party that followed Moscow's lead on most issues.

The party originated in 1920 as a wing of the Socialist party desirous of meeting Lenin's standards of organization, discipline, and ideological orthodoxy. In 1936 the party responded to Soviet policy by joining an anti-fascist coalition government of the left, the Popular Front. In 1939 the party endorsed the Soviet-German nonaggression pact and reversed its policy on German fascism. In June 1941, as the Germans invaded the Soviet Union, the PCF became an active force in the resistance movement against the occupying Nazi forces in France.

The often heroic role of Communists during the resistance period led to a postwar resurgence of the PCF. Despite this political lease on life, the Communist party of France played a negative role during the Fourth Republic and for a large portion of the Fifth. During the 1950s the party usually opposed the government of the day and generally made the task of governing difficult. The party resisted the return to power of Charles de Gaulle in 1958 and opposed his new constitution with its strong presidency.

The PCF seized the opportunity to become a more mainstream party in 1964, when its long-time leader, Maurice Thorez, died and the liberalizing de-Stalinization trend was well established in the Soviet Union. Not attempting to put forward its own candidate, the party in 1965 supported the presidential candidacy of the Socialist François Mitterand. In the parliamentary elections of 1967 the PCF worked hard to achieve an agreement with the main left-wing parties, then organized as the Federation of the Democratic and Socialist Left. Their agreement to support the strongest left-wing candidate in the parliamentary elections benefited both their Socialist partners and themselves.

Public opinion toward the PCF changed following the moderating policies of 1964–1967. Fully 60 percent of the public felt that the Communists had become more conciliatory in this period. Well over half of the electorate saw the possibility of Communist–Socialist cooperation. Finally, a larger proportion of voters viewed the PCF as a more independent force vis-à-vis Moscow.[2]

The Communist party's progress was checked by the two crippling events of 1968 and 1969. In May 1968 a general strike and a massive student protest brought widespread criticism of the PCF and other left-wing political forces. Although the party strenuously avoided a leading role in the "Events of May," it was largely blamed for the excesses of this period. More public criticism of the PCF came during the 1969 Soviet invasion of Alexander Dubcek's liberalized Czechoslovakia. The PCF itself was severely split by these events and found itself continually on the defensive.

The damage of 1968–1969 was largely forgotten by 1972 when Georges Marchais became secretary general of the party. In that year the PCF

---

[2] Stanley Rothman, Howard Scarrow, and Martin Schain, *European Society and Politics* (New York: West, 1976), pp. 186–187.

agreed on a "Common Program" with the Socialists. In the 1973 parliamentary elections the Communists entered into an electoral alliance with the Socialists based in part on the Common Program. In the 1974 presidential election, which occurred after Georges Pompidou's death, the PCF backed the left's candidate, the Socialist François Mitterand. In that election the newly united left of Communists and Socialists came within less than one percentage point of capturing France's most powerful office.

The goals of the PCF in this period of accommodation and democratic participation reflect a fundamental change in the party. The PCF has come to accept the current political regime with its strong presidency, although it is still pledged to increase the power of Parliament vis-à-vis the president. In foreign policy the party accepts the Gaullist emphasis on independence, but rejects any cooperation with the American-dominated NATO alliance. In domestic matters the PCF calls for limited nationalization of industry, substantial tax reform, and sharp increases in welfare programs. In all areas the Communist program is currently well within the bounds of the European tradition of democratic socialism.

The Socialists

The Socialist party was the major non-Communist left party of the Third, Fourth, and Fifth Republics. It began as the French Section of the Workers' International (SFIO); but, after the split with the Communists in 1920, it became a more moderate, reformist party. Like the Communists, the Socialists benefited from their great role in resisting German aggression from 1940 to 1944.

The party strove to play a constructive role in the Fourth Republic (1945–1958). Often the Socialists supported unpopular and weak governments. On several occasions in the 1950s the Socialists provided leadership in thankless situations, as when Pierre Mendès-France liquidated French involvement in Indochina and when Guy Mollet tried to cope with the Algerian crisis before assisting in De Gaulle's return to power in 1958.

During the Fifth Republic the party has tried to counter the government's center-right coalition by a variety of alliances of the left. It became greatly revitalized after the 1969 presidential election, when it changed both its leadership (from Guy Mollet to François Mitterand as secretary general) and its name (from SFIO to simply *Parti socialiste* or PS). Under François Mitterand the Socialist party has pursued its alliance with the Communists despite perpetual wrangling. The parliamentary elections of 1973 and presidential elections of 1974 have established the Communist-Socialist alliance as a potentially powerful force.

The Socialist program is basically unchanged from the Common Program established with the Communists in 1972. The Socialist following is largely white-collar, professional, and "intellectual." This complements the Communist following, which is 70 percent working-class. Together

Leadership Profiles

Leaders of the French Left

Leader	*Background and Education*	
François Mitterand Leader of the Socialists and left candidate for president (1974–present)	born: education:	1916 University of Paris
Georges Marchais Leader of the Communist Party (1972– present)	born: education:	1920 no higher education

these two left parties control the typical intellectual–working class following of Western European parties of the left.

The parliamentary election of March 1978 forced a partial split between the Socialists and Communists. Abandoning the Common Program, the two parties presented separate platforms. The Socialist platform remained fairly similar to the 1972 Common Program, while the Communists made more sweeping demands for nationalization of industry. Despite the split on programs, the parties for the most part supported the strongest left candidate in particular electoral districts.

Early Occupations and Political Career

Prisoner of war to Germans, 1940; escaped and became active in the resistance movement, 1940–1944

1946–1958	Member of Parliament
1962–present	(National Assembly)
1947–1948	Minister for Ex-servicemen
1948–1949	Secretary of State for Information
1950–1951	Minister for Overseas Territories
1951–1952	Chairman of the Union of the Democratic and Socialist Resistance (UDSR)
1954–1955	Minister of the Interior
1956–1957	Minister of State
1959–1962	Senator
1965, 1974	Candidate for President
1965–1968	President of the Federation of the Democratic and Socialist left
1971–present	First Secretary, Socialist Party

Metal worker and trade union activist

1947	Joined the Communist Party of France (PCF)
1956	Named to Central Committee of PCF
1959	Named to Political Bureau of PCF
1961	Secretary of the Central Committee of PCF
1972–present	Secretary General of the PCF
1973	Elected to Parliament (National Assembly)

Socialist successes under the alliance probably provoked the 1978 break in the alliance. Though the Socialist party was smaller and weaker than the PCF before the alliance, more Socialists than Communists were elected to parliamentary seats in both 1973 and 1978. Opinion polls showed that the supporters of the Socialist party rose from 10 percent of the electorate in 1972 to 30 percent of French voters in 1978. The popularity of the Communists remained stable at 20 percent over these years. The Communists in 1978 clearly felt that they needed to compete with the Socialists for the support of those Frenchmen attracted to the left alliance. They chose to emphasize their militant workin -class credentials and to attack the "latently bourgeois" Socialists.

The Radical Socialists

The Radical Socialists were the great power brokers of the Third and Fourth Republics. In reflecting the Jacobin anti-clericalism of France's small towns, they were considered a party of the left; however, the Radicals wore their pocketbooks on the right just as they wore their hearts on the left. This ambiguity between the party's view of the French Revolution (leftist) and its view of economics and political change (rightist) put it in a pivotal central position in the Parliaments of the Third and Fourth Republics.

Today's Radical Socialists have split. A left wing supports the Communist-Socialist alliance. A larger core has affiliated with a small center party associated with the center-right governmental group of parties that currently support the policies of President Giscard d'Estaing.

Center Parties

In the Fourth Republic the dominant center party was the Popular Republican Movement (MRP). This group emerged from World War II as the French representative of European Christian democracy. As such, the MRP favored social reform, economic reform, traditional French republicanism, *and* a Catholic or Christian outlook. This placed the social and economic aims of the party on the left and its religious orientation on the right. The MRP was unable to continue its difficult political balancing act after Charles de Gaulle and his supporters attacked their vulnerable position during the early period of the Fifth Republic.

During the Fifth Republic, MRP and center strength was sapped by de-

Leadership Profile

Leader	Background and Education	
Jacques Chirac Leader of the Gaullists (1976–present)	born: education:	1932 Ecole Nationale d'Administration (National School of Administration)

fections to the Gaullists, who had their own powerful credentials as modernizers with conservative religious ties. One section of the MRP drifted toward the new Reformer's Movement and the broader Federation of Reformers in 1974. Another section gravitated toward two centrist combinations—the Democratic Center (CD) and the Center for Democracy and Progress (CDP), which have been a part of the presidential majority in Parliament. Both segments of the old MRP were united into the Federation of Reformers in March of 1975.

The Gaullists

The Gaullist movement has been known under a variety of names, from the Rally of the French People in 1947 (RPF) to the Union of the Democrats for the New Republic (UDR). In 1977 Gaullist leader Jacques Chirac changed the name again to the Assembly for the Republic. The goals of the movement have always been vague, perhaps largely because of the mind and philosophy of its inspiring force, Charles de Gaulle. De Gaulle's philosophy was made up of two ingredients—the necessity for the *grandeur* of France and the special role of charismatic leadership. Both elements were tied to the particular personality of the leader.

Gaullism also straddled traditional conservative France and the modernizing forces of postwar France. De Gaulle was a modernizer who saw the need for economic planning and for reform of the traditional forces in French politics. At the same time, De Gaulle and his followers had an affinity for the nationalist political right and Catholic conservatism.

After De Gaulle's fall from power in 1969, two men tried to rejuvenate and shape the Gaullist movement. Georges Pompidou, De Gaulle's successor, stressed organizational reform. Before his death in 1974, he had strengthened Gaullist organization down to the parliamentary constituency level. The current Gaullist leader, Jacques Chirac, has tried to tie the

---

Early Occupations and Political Career

Civil servant

1962–1965	Head of Department, Private Office of Georges Pompidou
1967	Secretary of State for Employment Problems
1968	Secretary of State for Economy and Finance
1971	Minister for Parliamentary Relations
1972	Minister for Agriculture and Rural Development
1974	Minister of the Interior
1974–1976	Prime Minister
1976	Reformed Gaullists into Assembly of the Republic and was elected leader
1977	Elected Mayor of Paris

Gaullist organization to his personal leadership in a manner reminiscent of De Gaulle's personalist style.

Jacques Chirac has gambled heavily on duplicating De Gaulle's personal leadership style. He has changed the name and symbols of the party to emphasize his personal leadership. When Chirac changed the name of the Gaullist party to the Assembly for the Republic, he called a massive party conference. Chirac's leadership was confirmed by a mock intra-party election in which he was the only candidate and in a convention hall hung with his portraits. Finally, he modified the traditional symbol of Gaullism, De Gaulle's "cross of Lorraine." Chirac added a red bonnet—the symbol of his home and political base.

The support for the Gaullist party has been fairly broad-based and independent of particular social and economic groups. Gaullist voters come disproportionately from traditionally conservative demographic groups: the old, women, and the highly educated. Support is evenly distributed geographically but is greatest in the north of France. No other French party enjoys support among as many groups and geographical areas.

The Traditional Right

The French right wing has a lengthy record stemming from its defense of the old monarchy, the Catholic church, and traditional authority. The postwar era has seen two major groups on the traditional right—the Independent Republicans (RI) and the National Center of Independents and Peasants. The Independent Republicans have prospered from the fact that the current president, Valéry Giscard d'Estaing, comes from their ranks. This honor has also served to modernize the group's goals and methods.

Performance of the Party System

Parties do not play as active or effective a role in French elections as British parties do. The complexity of the party system means that parties often do not present clear alternative programs and leadership. The loose organization of most French parties, aside from the left parties, made them weak vehicles for developing programs and campaigning. Under the Fifth Republic, however, the parties have begun to broaden their appeals through the use of electoral alliances and agreements. In their desire to capture the strong presidential office and a supporting parliamentary majority, parties cooperate within broad aggregations of the left and of the right. In recent years the party alliances of the left and the government coalition of the right have started to resemble government and opposition groupings in a competitive party system.

The streamlining of the party system makes it easier for the French to participate in politics meaningfully. At election time voters can compare the Common Program of the left opposition with the record in office of the government coalition. Since roughly half of all voters support the left parties, close contests and alternation in office between these groupings seems possible. This should increase political interest and participation and permit a more rational use of the vote.

The optimistic observations on the changing role of the French party system must, however, be strongly qualified. The system never seems to stabilize or settle into an enduring pattern. Party support varies widely from election to election (as Gaullist politicians have learned to their dismay), and leaders still feel free to tinker with current alignments. Finally, most parties are so weak structurally that they can hardly be called political organizations. The French mistrust for groups and organizations may ultimately defeat any attempts to rationalize politics in France.

▪ THE SOVIET UNION ▪

The Soviet Union is dominated by a single monopolistic political party. The Communist party of the Soviet Union (CPSU), through its highly organized hierarchical structure, controls the state institutions, the national group life, and the economy. The party's control is based on its special place in Marxist-Leninist theory and the political power it can generate through its pyramidal structure. Both Marxist theory and practical politics combine to make the CPSU a model instrument of political control.

Lenin, the party's leader of the revolutionary period, developed a view of the role of the party that tailored Marx's philosophy to revolutionary circumstance. The chaos of revolutionary Russia required that the party be a sure and willing instrument of a small leadership group. With millions of workers on general strike, the economy in a shambles, a civil war on the horizon, and the intervention of foreign troops, Lenin emphasized the need for absolute obedience to an elite revolutionary leadership. The hard decisions required in consolidating power could not be left to continual debate and indifferent execution of decisions.

Lenin's view of the party as an organization was set out in his book *What Is to Be Done*. The key organizational principle was to be *democratic centralism*. Democratic accountability is secured by lower party bodies electing those above them and participating in policy discussion before a decision is reached. Centralism is assured by the requirement that the minority will always submit to the majority; more critically, the decisions of upper bodies are absolutely binding on lower bodies. In practice the centralizing aims of this principle predominate over the democratic. Democratic centralism is a simple description of policy-making in any authoritarian hierarchy.

A second Leninist principle is that the CPSU should not be a mass party aiming at universal membership. The party is an elite or vanguard party. Only those who meet the stringent standards are eligible for membership.

By the logic of Lenin's use of the word *vanguard,* the chief requirement for membership would be ideological reliability and orthodoxy. The vanguard should be made up only of those who understand the laws of history as revealed through Marx and the top party leadership. Only then can they play the directing or guiding role required of them.

The guiding role is exercised in pursuing economic and social change—to work toward the utopian ideal of a classless worker's society. The party basically achieves this task by directing the economy, forcing economic change that will alter social relationships.

Party Organization

The CPSU conforms closely to Lenin's organizational principles. The party is an enormous organizational pyramid with a base of over 370,000 primary party organizations. These basic units are organized at work places whether factory, farm, or office. Above this level the party is organized in 5,000 localities and 150 regions. Above this are the party organizations of the fourteen republics. At the union or national level the party is organized as the All-Union Party Congress and its executive committees and agencies.

At each level the party organizations elect their leadership, which thereafter supervises their activities. The leadership of each level is absolutely responsible to the party leadership at the next higher level. Only the fifteen or so officials at the very peak of the pyramid are not subject to the chain of command. These are the members of the Politburo of the Central Committee of the All-Union Party Congress.

The National Party Organization

In theory the All-Union Party Congress determines party policy. It currently meets every five years and consists of approximately 5,000 delegates. Party Congress delegates are selected by an indirect electoral process. Primary organizations elect delegates to local congresses, which send delegates to either regional or republic congresses. These party congresses finally make the selections for the All-Union Congress.

In the early years the All-Union Party Congress actually had a serious deliberative role, but soon its unwieldy size hampered its ability as a directing body. There was also the problem of determining the locus of authority between sessions, which occurred yearly in the 1920s. Under Stalin's drive to centralize power, the Congress ceased to be an important organization in itself—it did not meet between 1939 and 1952.

The Party Congress elects the Central Committee, a much more important organization. The Congress, in practice, uncritically elects those recommended by the top party leadership, the vote on the leadership slate has always been unanimous. There is no fixed size for the Central

Committee; recent membership has ranged between 200 and 300. The Central Committee formally supervises the Congress's business between sessions and therefore should be the effective party authority. In reality its power varies widely. Stalin, at the height of his power, virtually stripped the Central Committee of its functions; there were only three meetings between 1940 and 1952.

The Central Committee elects two very important bodies, the Politburo and the Secretariat. The Politburo, usually made up of about a dozen persons, is the ultimate policy-making body of the party and the locus of ultimate authority. The Politburo is a deliberative body that stresses discussion and solidarity. A unified Politburo has the final say in the Soviet system, and disagreement to its policies is equivalent to treason or "anti-party activity."

The Secretariat is the central bureaucracy of the party, keeping track of the implementation of party policies and decisions. It is at the top of a massive party command and reporting system that is staffed by over 100,000 members of the party "apparatus." By sifting and collating the reports of party professionals the Secretariat can make an estimate on the fulfillment of a large number of goals and targets and take necessary corrective action.

The Central Committee also formally elects the party's First Secretary, who usually becomes the dominant figure of Soviet politics. Stalin was unquestionably in charge of the key party organs. Subsequent leadership teams emphasized collegial or team leadership to a greater extent. General Secretary Leonid Brezhnev, and First Secretary Nikita Khrushchev were clearly preeminent.

In the post-Stalin period the relationships among the major organs of the party have changed considerably. First of all, the General Secretary has become more the first among equals in the Politburo. There were certainly occasions, for example, when Khrushchev was overruled by his Politburo colleagues. Another change has been the increased importance of the Central Committee, which Khrushchev used as a mechanism to announce major policy or leadership changes at Central Committee plenums. He also began the practice of publishing the discussions of policy that occurred in the plenums; this lasted until 1965. There finally is some evidence that the Central Committee may have some real power in those rare cases when the Politburo is profoundly divided. In this event the contending sides must seek support for their views in the Central Committee.

Party Membership

Today the CPSU has about 15 million members, or about 9 percent of the adult population. The membership is larger and more diverse in background than in its earliest years. The party in the 1920s was less than 1

Local Communist party officials meeting in a Soviet town. Henri Cartier-Bresson, Magnum Photos, Inc.

percent of the population and was largely young, male, and Russian in nationality. Today there is a greater proportion of white-collar workers, scientific and technical workers, women, and members of national groups other than the dominant Russian.

Fluctuations in the size and composition result from conscious party policy. For example, the CPSU almost doubled during World War II in an effort to promote support for the war effort. The greatest surge of recruitment occurred during the dark days of the seige of Stalingrad when over a half million members were added. In the postwar era the party changed membership rules to make an easier entry for white-collar members. The party has added members from the important occupational groups to build support for party policy and to extend control over these groups.

Techniques of Party Control

The ability to control all social, economic and governmental units requires the application of sophisticated management techniques. The party's most important technique is control of personnel in all economic and social sectors through party selection of supervisory personnel in government, industry, and labor unions. In an industrial plant, for example, the party names the plant management, the foremen, and the union representatives.

These people need not be party members, but their loyalty is assured by the honor that they have received and by the fact that they are carefully held accountable for their performance.

Another technique is interlocking leadership. Leaders of important organizations may be members of important CPSU organs simultaneously. Party control of governmental institutions is effective if leading administrators are party leaders as well.

Finally, the party uses more direct control by its network of monitoring bodies. The Secretariat research system is used in this way. The party Control Committee attached to the Central Committee has enforcement powers over party and governmental officials; they may single out officials for formal rebuke, expulsion, or loss of position. There are also volunteer Control Committees operating at all levels of party and governmental organization.

Performance

The Communist party of the Soviet Union is successful in a number of areas. First of all, it does a masterful job of both encouraging and controlling political participation. The party provides many ways in which people can participate and uses propaganda and incentives to encourage such activity, which, of course, it limits to tasks that help implement party policy.

The CPSU is an apparently efficient policy-making organization; that is, it makes basic decisions related to the very comprehensive system it controls with minimal conflict and with a certain devotion to rational decision-making criteria. Probably its major weakness in this area is the information base for these decisions. The hierarchical party system cannot get open and frank opinions from the people in the middle levels of the party who are needed to implement the decisions. They also cannot get full information on the views and assessments of governmental and economic experts. The leadership, in essence, hears what it wants to hear.

An obvious flaw regarding this "party system" is that it does not provide choice. The monopoly party is not checked or chastened by an alert opposition. Nor does the party system match the societal cleavages and group differences. As we have seen, the Soviet Union has a varied group structure that necessarily has varied interests and opinions. These interests are not represented in a formal and public way.

▪ NIGERIA ▪

From the beginning of organized nationalist politics in Nigeria in the late 1940s and early 1950s to the end of the parliamentary period in 1966, political parties in Nigeria provided the crucial link between the government and the electorate. Competition centered on the electoral contests between parties at both national and regional levels. Until 1966, when the military banned political activity, there were over 80 wide-ranging political parties and organizations with different values, goals, bases of support, and types of organizations.

The Nigerian party system, while complex, does have several general characteristics. The nationalist struggle in Nigeria during the 1950s and the Westminster parliamentary model that Great Britain left to Nigeria supported the formation of a multi-party system. Parliamentary seats at the national level were awarded on the basis of single-member districts; the number of seats that each region received in the federal Parliament was based on the population of that region. The mutual mistrust and suspicion with which each of the regions viewed one another made the counting of Nigerians in each region a thorny and controversial issue.

No political party either before or after independence won a nationally accepted absolute majority of the seats in the national Parliament or, more importantly, built a platform and organization appealing to all Nigerians regardless of ethnicity, religion, or region. Political parties came to be associated with specific regional interests rather than with general national interests. The major political parties in the three regions—the National People's Congress (NPC) in the Northern Region, the Action Group (AG) in the Western Region, and the National Council of Nigerian Citizens in the Eastern Region (NCNC)—were all accused, and rightly so, at one time or another of being parties concerned only with their respective regions.

The inability to build a national political party that would cut across the sharp cleavages in Nigeria was made more difficult by the ongoing controversy over what type of political system was most suited to Nigeria. The weak center–strong regions/strong center–weak regions issue was a constant, unresolvable issue dividing Nigerians. Whatever the outcome of this debate, it was clear that there would eventually be a federal Parliament and at least three regional parliaments. Politicians in the major parties placed a premium on ensuring that they held control of their regional parliament. This aim made them more parochial and less able to appeal to wider constituencies outside their region.

What evolved was a situation in which the NPC was dominant in the North, the Action Group in the West, and the NCNC in the East. When these parties did seek votes outside of their regions, they tended to appeal to dissatisfied minority groups in the other regions. This created tension among the major parties, and between the major parties and the minority parties.

In general, Nigerian political parties tended to be nonideological, and their most important political issues were local rather than national. Their major concerns were protecting their various interests and securing the spoils of office for their constituents and followers. The party that "produced the goods" was most often the best vote-getter in its region.

The inability of any one party to win a nationwide majority in Parliament resulted in a series of coalitions between various parties. The most important of these political coalitions—and certainly one of convenience rather than a similarity of goals or ideals—joined the NPC and the NCNC. Joining at the national level, these two parties (with the NPC the dominant partner) formed the first independence government in Nigeria. The Action Group became the opposition party.

Three crises in the 1960 to 1966 period testify to the complexity of party patterns in Nigeria. The first crisis occurred when the 1963 census results were announced. Since the census figures were to be used in apportioning the new National Assembly, the dramatic increases reported in the North's population raised fears in the East and West that they would become a permanent parliamentary minority. A second crisis occurred during and after the 1964 national elections. Questionable election returns and a threat by the defeated parties not to accept the results almost led to military intervention. Finally, the 1965 regional election in the West showed just how widespread the political corruption in Nigeria had become, and how difficult it was to conduct a fair and honest election.

The Northern People's Congress—The Northern Party

The Northern People's Congress first presented its party platform to Northerners in 1954, although its first annual convention was in 1949. In 1951 the NPC officially became a political party, claiming 65 branches throughout the North and a membership of about 6,000. As with most Nigerian parties, this figure included both those who were active members and those who were members in name only.

The NPC is pictured as the party of conservatism and tradition in the North. Its platform and policies called for the preservation of the traditional authorities and traditional practices in the largely Islamic region. The party's motto, "One North, One People, irrespective of Religion, Rank, or Tribe," belied the fact that the party drew most of its support and leadership from the traditionally important Hausa-Fulani groups in the North. Those who were powerful in the party often also held high traditional positions in the emirate system or religious spheres.

The NPC, both as a political/cultural organization and as an active political party, depended upon the widespread support given to traditional authority by the common man. The aims of the party were clear:

To inculcate in the minds of the Northerners a genuine love for the Northern Region and all that is northern, and a special reverence for Religion, Laws and Order, and the preservation of good customs and traditions, and the feeling that the sorrow of one Northerner shall be the sorrow of all and that the happiness of one is also the happiness of all.[3]

---

[3] As quoted in *Africa Yearbook and Who's Who 1977* (London: Africa Journal Limited, 1976), p. 663.

From a very early date, politics in the North, as practiced by the NPC, followed the axiom "United we stand, divided we fall."

One survey of the more militant members of the party indicated that almost 70 percent of the actives were either Native Authority officials, district or village heads, or traders (a high status position in the North). In a hierarchical social and political system like that of the North, position was based not so much on achievement as on one's family or hereditary position. In contrast, a study of one of the major opposition group to the NPC in the North, the Northern Elements Progressive Union (which split from the NPC because of its narrow northern focus), reveals that only 20 percent of its militant members came from the high-status positions; almost 80 percent were either small farmers, tailors, butchers, dyers, or tanners.[4]

There were few effective challenges to the dominance of the NPC leaders in the regional parliament of the North or to their representatives in the federal Parliament. The social and economic structure in the North, combined with the popularity of the party's leaders, ensured NPC dominance. The leader of the NPC in the North, the Sardauna of Sokoto, Sir Ahmadu Bello was respected both as a traditional authority (who traced his lineage to Usman dan Fodio, the founder of the emirate system) and as a respected religious leader. Sir Abubakar Tafawa Balewa, the leader of the party in the federal Parliament, was born into much more humble circumstances but enjoyed a widespread popularity throughout the North.

NPC power rested not only with its control of the regional Assembly but also in the fact that the North comprised about 50 percent of the total Nigerian population. This combination of factors ensured that the NPC would be able to exercise considerable control at the national level, as long as it controlled the North. Throughout the entire parliamentary period, the prime minister of Nigeria was Sir Abubakar Tafawa Balewa. The strength of the NPC made it a formidable opponent for the two major parties in the South.

The National Council of Nigeria and the Camerouns—The Eastern Party

The National Council of Nigeria and the Camerouns, later the National Council of Nigerian Citizens (NCNC), is the oldest political party in Nigeria. Formed in 1944 the NCNC was also one of the few Nigerian parties to at least attempt to build broad-based national support. The leader of the party, Dr. Nnamdi Azikiwe, hoped in the early nationalist period to mobilize all politically aware Nigerians to his party and his cause, but he could not gain large support outside of southern areas. In 1959 the NCNC had 142 branches in the East, 126 in the West, 37 in the North, and 1 in Lagos.[5]

---

[4] Billy Dudley, *Parties and Politics in Northern Nigeria* (London, Frank Cass, 1968), p. 118.

[5] K. W. J. Post, "The National Council of Nigeria and the Camerouns, The Decision of December 1959" in John P. Mackintosh, *Nigerian Government and Politics* (Evanston, Ill.: Northwestern University Press, 1966), p. 411.

The NCNC in its early period focused much more on Nigerian problems and questions than on eastern ones. Some of its aims were

to maintain and protect the unity and sovereignty of Nigeria, and to secure for Nigeria an enviable place in the community of Nations; to achieve socialism for Nigeria, and raise the standard of living of the people, and generally make Nigerians a contented and happy people.[6]

Although never completely successful, the "Zikists" (from the name of the leader) sought a national constituency, attempting to maintain the unity of Nigeria against those who favored strong regions and a weak center.

Much more so than the NPC in the North, the NCNC sought the support of newly educated and more politically aware segments of Nigerian society. The Ibo and the Yoruba tended to have a higher percentage of their populations who had received Western educations and who were more concerned with "modern" political issues. Although it often appealed to traditional issues and authorities for support, it also sought to develop a political platform less tied to these traditional aspects of society than did the NPC. For example, Dr. Azikiwe, the leader of the party, was a political scientist, author, journalist, educator, and public speaker. He studied in the United States at Howard and Lincoln universities before becoming politically active in Nigeria. In the first independence government he served as Governor General of Nigeria and in 1963 was appointed president of the Federal Republic of Nigeria. Likewise, many of the most active supporters of the party were those young men and women who had been more exposed to the nationalist thought and to missionary and Western education.

The problems faced by the NCNC were similar to those faced by other political parties in Nigeria. There was conflict within the party between the regional leadership and the national leadership, and at times the national organization was not well organized. Local issues tended to overshadow national issues, just as local officials often attempted to ignore directives from the national headquarters. Where the NCNC did exercise control, however, was in the East. The East—and primarily the Ibo populations—provided the NCNC with a consistent and strong core of support.

The Action Group—The Western Political Party

Many of the conflicts, dramas, and tensions of Nigerian party life are summed up in the political histories of the Western Region and the Action Group. The Action Group (AG), formed in 1951 by Chief Obafemi Awolowo, was closely associated with the Yoruba cultural revival and cultural movement. Just as the NPC and the NCNC depended respectively on Hausa-Fulani and Ibo support, the AG depended on the Yoruba for its power and influence.

---

[6] As quoted in *Africa Yearbook and Who's Who 1977*, p. 660.

Leadership Profiles

Founding Fathers of Nigeria's Major Political Parties

Leader	Background and Education
Sir Abubakar Tafawa Balewa Northern People's Congress (party of the Northern Region, founded 1951)	born: 1912 died: January 1966 education: Katsina College, Katsina, Nigeria London School of Economics ethnicity: Hausa
Chief Obafemi Awolowo Action Group (party of the Western Region, founded 1951)	born: 1909 education: Wesleyan School, Abeokuta, Nigeria Wesley College, Ibadan, Nigeria London University (external) ethnicity: Yoruba
Alhaji Sir Ahmadu Bello, **Sardauna of Sokoto** Northern People's Congress (party of the Northern Region)	born: 1910 died: January 1966 education: Sokoto Provincial School Katsina College, Katsina, Nigeria ethnicity: Fulani
Dr. Nnamdi Azikiwe, "Zik" National Council of Nigerian Citizens (party of the Eastern Region, founded 1944)	born: 1904 education: Hope Waddel Institute, Calabar, Nigeria Methodist Boy's High School, Lagos, Nigeria Storer College, West Virginia Howard University, Washington, D.C. Lincoln University, Pennsylvania ethnicity: Ibo

Early Occupations	Political Career
Schoolteacher	1952 Federal Minister of Works 1954 Federal Minister of Transport 1957–1966 Chief Minister and Prime Minister of the Federal Republic of Nigeria
Journalist, politician, lawyer, author	1954–1959 Premier of the Western Region 1960–1962 Leader of the Opposition, Federal Assembly of Nigeria 1967–1971 Federal Commissioner for Finance and Vice Chairman of the Federal Executive Council
Local government official	Northern Regional Minister of Works Northern Regional Minister of Local Government 1954–1966 Premier of the Northern Region of Nigeria
Political scientist, author, journalist, educator, politician	1954–1959 Premier of the Eastern Region 1960–1963 Governor General of Nigeria 1963–1966 President of the Federal Republic of Nigeria

The platforms and policies of the Action Group called for social change and Yoruba unity. The AG sought "to bring and organize within its fold all nationalists in the Western Region, so that they may work together as a united group, and submit themselves to party loyalty and discipline."[7] The AG, like the NPC, realized that its ability to influence politics rested in part on its ability to maintain control of its region.

Party goals were a mixture of socialism (applied to the African case and interpreted by Chief Awolowo) and traditional Yoruba ideals and practices. The AG was able to maintain control partly because of these values and partly because it had the power of appointment and the power to improve conditions. In short, the AG could provide tangible benefits that other parties in the West could not. Its power rested with the "chiefs, businessmen, and politicians."[8]

Chief Awolowo's background and career is one of the most interesting and significant in Nigeria. At one time or another he has been a lawyer, an author, a federal minister, a journalist, and (always) a politician. He studied at London University, began the newspaper *Nigerian Tribune,* served an extended prison term in the 1960s for treason, and most recently has been actively involved in the plans for the return to civilian rule.

As might be expected from a man with so diverse a background, he was not without his opponents and critics. In the West during the parliamentary period, the major opposition to Chief Awolowo came from another chief, Samuel Akintola. Awolowo represented the Action Group at the national level as the Leader of the Opposition, while Akintola represented the Action Group at the regional level as the premier of the Western Region. Eventually, because of personality as well as political conflicts, Akintola left the Action Group to form the rival party, the Nigerian National Democratic Party (NNDP), which sought to win seats from the Action Group in the region. In addition, the new party allied itself with the major opponent of the Action Group at the national level, the NPC.

The Action Group, "The Party of the Yoruba," continued to challenge the control of the NNDP at the regional level despite the fact that Chief Awolowo was sent to prison in 1963 for alleged treason against the federal government. The 1965 regional election, which saw the NNDP win a majority of the seats, is noted in Nigerian history as perhaps one of the most corrupt and scandal-ridden elections in Nigerian history and one that contributed directly to the collapse of the civilian regime in 1966.

Minority Parties—The Fourth Force

Although the three major parties were the dominant political forces during the parliamentary period, for several reasons minority parties

---

[7] Ibid., p. 663.
[8] Mackintosh, *Nigerian Government and Politics,* p. 439.

played important roles. First, none of the regions was ethnically or religiously homogeneous. Minority groups in each region often felt like second-class citizens; for example, the Tiv people in the North are not Muslim and have long resisted Hausa-Fulani domination. The Tiv response during this period was to form a political party to bargain for and protect their position, and perhaps even to carve out a new region of their own. The United Middle Belt Congress, under the leadership of Joseph Tarka, was able during this period to mobilize and capture most of the Tiv vote.

A second reason why minority groups and parties were important was because opposition parties often sought alliances with them. The Action Group and the NCNC at various times sought alliances with the anti-NPC Northern Elements Progressive Union led by Aminu Kano. NEPU could thus hope to gain the backing of a larger organization and hence more potential power while the southern parties could hope to dent the strength of the dominant NPC.

Party Performance

It is not surprising that a nation as complex and fractionalized as Nigeria has a party system equally as fractionalized and complex. In many respects Nigerian political parties were little more than patronage organizations mirroring the sharp divisions in society. In other cases, they attempted to form more viable organizations both to contest elections and to provide representation.

In general, though, the performance of Nigerian parties from 1960 to 1966 was poor. Conflicts within parties and between parties went beyond honest competition and petty chicanery to deep-seated political corruption. "Politician" in Nigeria became a dirty word,[9] associated in the public mind with ostentatious wealth, conspicuous consumption, bribery, and scandal. Certainly not all politicians fitted this mold, but enough did to create and preserve a powerful image.

The performance of political parties contributed to the downfall of multi-party politics in Nigeria and the parliamentary system itself. When the military ended party politics in January 1966 there was little public outcry; many, in fact, openly welcomed it. Now, as Nigeria prepares to return to civilian rule the question of the role of political parties has surfaced again. Many of the old-line political figures, like Azikiwe and Awolowo, have announced their candidacies for president. Nigeria's military leaders are attempting this time, however, to make sure that a return to party politics does not mean a return to party politics as practiced from 1960 to 1966. Whether parties can be built on national, rather

---

[9] Idea attributed to General Ironsi. Cited in Martin J. Dent, "The Military and Politics," *St. Anthony's Papers*, no. 21, *African Affairs*, no. 3, p. 129.

than regional or ethnic, bases is perhaps going to be the severest test facing the new post-1979 civilian government.

▪ EGYPT ▪

Unlike many nationalist movements, the 1952 revolution in Egypt was not led or directed by a political party but by a small group of military officers. These Free Officers, led by Colonel Nasser, were dissatisfied with the major political party of the period, the Wafd. Almost immediately on assuming power, they banned the Wafd and other parties and restricted open political activity.

As we have seen, Nasser sought to replace the traditional political parties with a single-party system with the ability to mobilize and direct the Egyptian population. Three successive parties were formed, each designed to provide direction and organization to the revolutionary movement. The Liberation Rally from 1953 to 1956 was designed to counter the more traditional Egyptian political parties. The National Union, from 1957 to 1961, was closely associated with the union between Egypt and Syria. With the dissolution of the union in 1961, the National Union was disbanded. The third attempt, the Arab Socialist Union (ASU), has been the most effective and the most long-lasting of Egyptian political parties. Created by President Nasser in 1963, it has undergone a series of transformations designed to adapt it to the changing Egyptian economic, political, and social climate.

The problems facing these three political parties are not dissimilar to those facing all single-party systems. In general, Egyptian leaders have difficulty institutionalizing and regularizing the party structure. The parties in Egypt have been the conscious creations of the political elite; in one sense they have been built from the top down, rather than from the bottom up. Because the parties are government creations, whenever the values of the leadership change the structure of the party also is likely to change. The Arab Socialist Union provides an example of an Egyptian political organization undergoing rapid change.

One particular area of dispute concerns the relationship between the party and the government. At various times government leaders accuse party leaders of encroaching on the responsibility and prerogatives of the government, while at other times party leaders accuse government leaders of downplaying the role of the party. There is a constant competition between party and government for political power.

The ASU traditionally suffers from the tendency to become over-bureaucratized. Maintaining the administration often becomes more important than carrying out the actual duties and responsibilities of the party. By the same token, the massive nature of the Egyptian bureaucracy makes it difficult for party activists to introduce changes in the government.

Finally, leaders of the ASU and earlier parties are torn between the desire and the need to create popular, mass-based political parties, and the desire and need to develop a small group of dedicated party activists who can perform the vanguard role required of a "revolutionary" political party. The changing membership rolls discussed in Chapter 4 are only one indication of this indecision.

The ASU, like its predecessors, was dominated by the thought, personality, and power of President Nasser. The ups and downs of the party vis-à-vis other political organizations like the cabinet and the National Assembly often were related to changes in the thinking of the president. Both Nasser and Sadat often played one organization off against another. Activists in the party, like Ali Sabri, have attempted to make the ASU into an important and powerful organization in the Egyptian political arena. Although they have not won every political battle, ASU leaders have proved flexible enough to change as the situation changes and to continue to play important political roles in Egyptian politics.

The Arab Socialist Union—A Party Created by the Government

Many commentators suggest that one of the major differences between the Communist party in the Soviet Union and the Arab Socialist Union in Egypt is that in the Soviet Union the party created the government, while in Egypt the government created the party. The ASU was created with several goals: it was to both represent and lead the masses, it was to be the major channel for participation in society, and it was to be the major institution for determining broad-range policy and policy directions. The party was formed to play a central role in the political education and socialization of the population. As the only legal political party from 1962 until 1975 the ASU also had the responsibility of representing the broad and differing interests in Egyptian society. Politically, the ASU has tended to be on the left of the Egyptian political spectrum—more radical than its potential rivals in the army, the bureaucracy and civil service, and the National Assembly.

The Charter of National Action, issued by President Nasser in 1962, spelled out the guiding principles of Egyptian democracy. In so doing the document also stated what the role of the party was to be. "Democracy of the people—the whole of the working people" occurs only when the following conditions are met:

First.   *Political democracy cannot be separated from social democracy....*
Second.   *Political democracy cannot exist under the domination of any one class....*
Third.   *It is the national unity created by the cooperation between those representative powers of the people which will be able to set up the Arab Socialist Union....*

Fourth.   *Popular organizations, especially cooperatives and trade unions, can play an effective and influential role in promoting sound democracy . . . .*

Fifth.   *Criticism and self-criticism are among the most important guarantees to freedom . . . .*

Sixth.   *The new revolutionary concepts of true democracy must impose themselves on the factors influencing the formation of the citizen—foremost among which are education and the administrative laws and regulations.*[10]

Given the goals enumerated in the Charter of National Action, it was clear that the role of the party was important. It was equally clear that the success of the party in implementing the democratic goals would depend on the organization of the party. Organizationally, the ASU is based on the hierarchical or pyramid principle common to authoritarian and totalitarian political parties (see Figure 5–2). At the most basic level are the village, factory, school, or city district units. At the founding of the party in 1962 there were some 7,000 of these basic units. Each unit elects a 20-man committee responsible for meeting twice monthly and conducting unit business.

At the *markaz* or district level, two members from each local unit represent their constituents. In turn, the district group elects a council that meets twice monthly. District units are then grouped at the governorate level. Two members from each district serve four-year terms at this level.

It is at the national level that political power is most heavily concentrated. The General National Congress of the ASU has 1,500 members from the governorates, members of the army and the police, and various ASU auxiliary groups. In the 1968 National Congress the over 1,600 members included 578 workers and 281 peasants.[11]

One of the responsibilities of the National Congress is the selection of a smaller Central Committee. The Central Committee meets twice yearly and carries out the administrative and policy-making roles of the National Congress when it is not in session. It is the main link between the National Congress and the smaller groups drawn from it. The 150 full members (and 50 alternate members) include workers, academics, peasants, party officials, and government ministers.

The highest body of the Arab Socialist Union is the Supreme Executive Committee, which implements the directives of the Central Committee and carries out the policies of the ASU. In 1968 20 candidates submitted their names for election to the Central Committee as nominees for the Executive Committee. Of these, 13 were civilians, and 7 were ex-military officers; 12 were either ministers in the government or ex-ministers. The Central Committee then voted to choose 10 members out of the 20. Only 8 received the necessary majority: 4 civilians and 4 ex-officers. The

---

[10] *The Charter* (Cairo: Information Administration, no date, c. 1962), pp. 54–60.

[11] R. Hrair Dekmejian, *Egypt Under Nasir* (Albany: State University of New York Press, 1971), p. 273.

FIGURE 5–2   The Arab Socialist Union, 1968

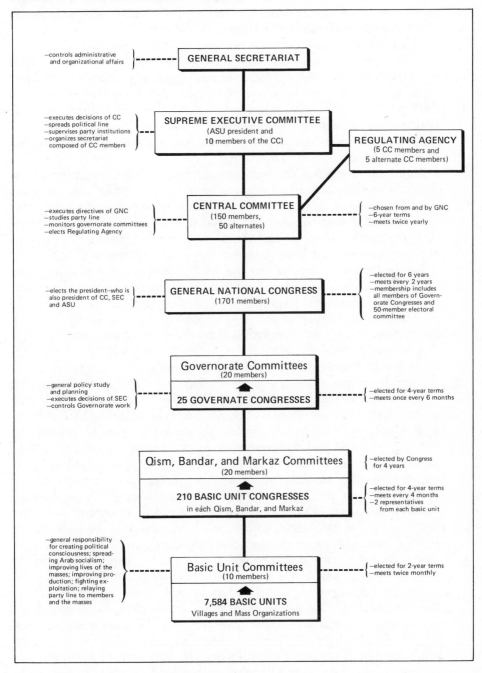

Source: Adapted from: R. Hrair Dekmejian, *Egypt Under Nasir* (Albany: State University of New York Press, 1971), pp. 274–275. Reprinted by permission.

Supreme Executive Committee organized itself into five permanent committees: political affairs, administration, internal affairs, economic development, and culture and information.

The inability of the Egyptian political elite to regularize and institutionalize the patterns of political participation and the role of the ASU in Egyptian political life resulted in several shifts in organization and party goals. One of the most serious of these occurred following the defeat of the Egyptian forces by Israel in the June 1967 war. The trauma and magnitude of the defeat led President Nasser to resign. The ASU, by mobilizing the Egyptian population, played a key role in coaxing President Nasser to rescind his announced retirement.

On reassuming office, the president announced that the Egyptian defeat forced a re-evaluation of all Egyptian political institutions and structures from the office of president on down. Included in this re-evaluation was the role of the Arab Socialist Union and its relationship to other government institutions. Two general views of the role of the ASU in Egyptian political life were put forward by the president's advisers and confidants.

The first position argued that the ASU should become a power base unto itself. It should serve as a revolutionary vanguard party; it not only would provide political legitimacy for Egyptian politicians but also would mobilize the population to achieve the goals of the revolution. The revolution, men like Ali Sabri argued, was the preserve of the party.

A second position argued that the party was not a vanguard-type party in the strictest sense of the word, but an "umbrella" organization representing the broad interests and viewpoints found in Egyptian society. It was not the sole source of political legitimacy and authority but one among many. In many respects this position was closest to that of President Nasser. In this view new attention should be paid to making the party accountable and representative. More emphasis should be placed on the election of officials to the party ranks rather than merely appointing them. Neither view was ever completely accepted or implemented.

The problems plaguing the ASU continued after President Nasser's death. Nasser, partly through his charisma, was able to control and guide the fortunes of the party, whose role and organization were of his shaping. When his views changed, the party changed. He saw the party as "the supreme popular authority, which assumed the leadership role in the people's name," and it was to exercise "popular political control on the governmental organism."[12] Sadat lacked the charisma and power of President Nasser when he assumed office. It was clear to the new president, however, that he would have to place his own stamp on the organization of the party, just as it was clear he would have to control other sources of political power. During the early part of his presidency the most important political questions centered on what organizations

---

[12] As quoted in Dekmejian, p. 284.

should exercise real political power. There were several possible sources—the military, the old Nasser elite, the ASU, the National Assembly, the cabinet, or the powerful entrenched bureaucracy. The ASU became one of the bastions that claimed to represent the beliefs of the late president, and therefore was anti-Sadat. An attempted coup against President Sadat in 1971 (in which many ASU leaders were implicated) led to a sharp curtailing of the influence and power of the party.

Since 1975 the role of the ASU has changed significantly. In 1975 the ASU established feminist and youth sections, and in March 1976 President Sadat announced that groups within the ASU were to be allowed to present political platforms. The three major groups were the Progressive Union Organization representing the left, the Arab Socialist Organization representing the center, and the Socialist-Liberal Organization representing the right. By the end of 1976 about 30 groups had asked to present platforms. Following the 1976 elections the president announced that new parties could exist alongside the Arab Socialist Union. Again, parties were to represent the left, the center, and the right of the political spectrum. The ASU was to continue in its role as the major representative body and the major channel for participation, but it was no longer the only avenue of participation.

Party Performance

The Arab Socialist Union has existed longer than any of the previous political parties in post-1952 Egypt. Although it resembles an authoritarian party in terms of organization, the ASU's level of control and degree of penetration of society is not so high or so deep as in other parties in single-party states. It exists as one political institution among many. The relationship of the ASU to the National Assembly, the chief legislative body, remains murky, and its relationship to the military varies according to the political climate in Egypt. During some periods the presence of ex-officers in the policy-making committees was more prevalent than in others. Finally, the domination of the party by President Nasser left a void at his death. It was difficult to separate the party from the president, for the ASU's evolutionary nature was often a reflection of changes in the president's thinking.

The party also is plagued by its inability to adequately define its own role. The question of whether it should be a small, elite party in the forefront of the revolution or a mass-based party representing interests of all Egyptians has never been resolved. Within the party this can result in a split between the left and the right. Often the leadership finds itself placed in the uncomfortable middle.

Where the ASU has shown success is in providing new avenues for participation and new forums for debate. Unlike many authoritarian parties, it has moved more toward the election of officials rather than their appointment. It also provides avenues of participation for those who previously had none. It is safe to assume that the nature of the ASU, both in terms of organization and its political role in Egyptian society, will continue to change as the Egyptian political situation changes.

■ TANZANIA ■

The Tanzanian African National Union (TANU) has dominated political life in Tanzania since well before independence. The party and its leader, President Julius Nyerere, have been instrumental in formulating the goals and values of the Tanzanian nation. TANU articulates the goals of the political elite, represents the Tanzanian population, and is the central forum for political debate and discussion.

The party was officially formed in 1954, seven years before independence. It grew from the Tanganyikan African Association (a voluntary organization seeking to represent the better-educated, urban African population) that in 1948 claimed to have 39 branches throughout Tanzania and over 1,700 members.[13] The aims of this new organization in 1954 were more specifically political. The party demanded increased participation by the Africans and eventual independence.

TANU quickly became the dominant political force in preindependence Tanzania. In elections to the newly formed legislature prior to independence, TANU and Nyerere won overwhelming majorities and clearly represented better than any other party the attitudes of the African population. In 1963, following independence, Tanzania officially became a one-party state when all other political parties were banned.

The Tanzanian African National Union is both similar to and different from other one-party systems. Like the Communist party in the Soviet Union and the Arab Socialist Union in Egypt, TANU is organized on the pyramid principle. This authoritarian organization, common to so many single-party systems, is designed to ensure two-way communication between local and national levels; it also provides the party with greater potential for control.

Unlike many other authoritarian or totalitarian parties, however, TANU has attempted to limit the coercive potential of the party and to introduce more democratic aspects into party life. In general, TANU is loosely organized. Local branches are largely autonomous and are of great importance to the party. They deal with the political and economic questions closest to the average Tanzanian. The party elite, since independence, has made a conscious decision to emphasize participation and responsiveness at this level.

TANU also differs from the typical authoritarian single-party system in

---

[13] Raymond F. Hopkins, *Political Roles in a New State, Tanzania's First Decade* (New Haven: Yale University Press, 1971), p. 19.

that it encourages relatively open competition for positions within the party. The competition for parliamentary seats is not between candidates representing different parties, but between different TANU members. Party leadership argues that since competition between different parties works against national unity, Tanzanians should choose between candidates *within* the party. Thus, Tanzanians can have effective political participation by choosing one candidate over another, new leaders can be recruited into the system, and those already in power will be closer to and less isolated from the citizenry that elected them.

TANU, then, has characteristics of both one-party and multi-party systems. The relationship between the party and other government institutions, such as the National Assembly, is close. The party also has become increasingly tied to the ruling party of Zanzibar. The head of the Afro-Shirazi party in Zanzibar, for example, serves as the first vice-president of Tanzania. Since 1978 the relationship between the Afro-Shirazi party of Zanzibar and TANU has become even closer. The parties have been merged officially to form a new party, *Chama Cha Mapinduzi* (the revolutionary party).

The Tanzanian African National Union—Goals and Organization

The Supremacy of the Party Act, issued in 1975, confirmed what had been apparent for a long time—the party was to be dominant over the government, not the reverse. Under the guidance of President Nyerere, the party is responsible for formulating the goals of African socialism and monitoring their implementation. Debate, discussion, and arguments over these policies are to be carried out at all levels of the party.

The functions of the party were made clear in the 1965 constitution.

To consolidate and maintain the independence of this country.

To ensure that this country shall be governed by a democratic socialist government of the people.

To see that the Government mobilizes all the resources of this country towards the elimination of poverty, ignorance and disease.

To see that wherever possible the Government itself directly participates in the economic development of the country.

To see that the Government eradicates all types of exploitation, intimidation, discrimination, bribery, and corruption.

To see that the Government exercises effective control over the principal means of production and pursues policies which facilitate the way to collective ownership of the resources of this country.[14]

These goals are constantly stressed and reinforced by the party and the media. Public political education focuses on the need for political and

---

[14] From the TANU constitution as reproduced in William Tordoff, *Government and Politics in Tanzania* (Nairobi, Kenya: East African Publishing House, 1967), pp. 236–237.

economic change. The achievement of these goals constitutes one reason for the existence of the party.

Party Organization

The party is organized to provide channels of communication between various levels and to implement party and government decisions once reached. At the most local level are the 1,500 party cells—the party's foundation—each consisting of 10 houses grouped together. Cells elect a leader to represent them at the next higher level of the party. At this branch level an elected branch executive committee is responsible for carrying out the decisions reached at the higher levels of the party. In addition, each branch sends delegates to the district level.

Branches are grouped into 60 different districts. At this level an annual district conference is held, a district executive committee is selected, and a district working committee is responsible for the day-to-day operations of the party. Districts also have the responsibility of considering names of candidates for the parliamentary and local government elections.

Districts operate within 17 regions. They, too, have a regional conference, regional executive committees, and regional working committees. Regions have the responsibility for coordinating and supervising policy at their level.

At the national level the supreme body of the party is the National Conference, which meets every two years. Of its membership of around 400, around 300 are voting members. Membership is drawn from representatives of the districts and the regions, members of Parliament, and national officials such as the president and vice president. The National Conference is responsible for discussing broad questions of policy and for linking the different levels of the party. In addition, the National Conference symbolizes national solidarity. It does not take an active role in the actual making or implementation of governmental or party policy.

Also at the national level is the National Executive Council, which meets four times a year. It considers candidates for parliamentary elections, some party finances, and party policy. Its membership includes the president and vice president, delegates elected by the National Conference, regional chairman and secretaries, and various other officials of the party and its affiliated organizations.

More active and powerful than either the National Executive Committee or the National Conference is the party's Central Committee, which normally meets weekly and is responsible for the day-to-day operations of the party. In addition to the president and the vice president, the Committee includes individuals appointed by the president. Since it meets much more frequently than other national party institutions and is smaller, it has been able to exercise greater influence in party affairs.

In terms of actual power and influence over the party, President Nyerere and his appointed advisers, along with the government cabinet ministers, exercise greatest influence and control over party affairs. These leaders determine the agenda of debate. In many cases they decide policy that is then ratified by other party organizations. While the debate concerning these policies is often lively and while it is not uncommon for opposition to government-party initiatives to develop, it remains true that most policy initiatives originate with the president and his most trusted advisers.

Although the organization of the party is hierarchical and has the potential to control political activity from the top, there has been relatively little central direction in party affairs. The party does not have the manpower or the finances to exert strong control over the various levels of the party; moreover, its belief in local participation gives the local branches a good deal of freedom. Party officials make sure that local levels have an input into the political discussion and debates concerning the future of Tanzania. Although not all Tanzanians are politically active, about 10 percent of the population belonged to TANU at independence, and it enjoys widespread political support.

By stressing open debate within the party, TANU officials seek to bring opposition groups into the party. The party has active youth, women's, and elders' sections that contribute at all levels. The party also directs and influences many of the other national institutions. Among the most important of these are the military (especially after a military mutiny in 1964), the bureaucracy and civil service, and the National Union of Tanganyikan Workers. The goal, once again, is to provide the opportunity for discussion within the party rather than among contending groups.

The Performance of TANU

Not a static political party, TANU has changed since its formation in 1954. These changes are the result of new situations (for example, moving from colonialism to independence), new development plans (the ujamaa village scheme), and new political goals (competition within the party). The party's flexibility, however, has created certain problems. For one, open debate within the party often limits the ability of the party to control the economy. Lack of central direction from party headquarters and the ambiguous relationship between party and government often mean that the party is not able to exercise much central direction (as, for example, the Communist party does in the Soviet Union).

The lack of skilled party activists and the generally poor state of party finances also detract from the potential power of the party in its relationship with the government and government ministers. This is most clearly seen in the increasing power of government ministers (all party members) who often have greater resources at their command than party officials do. A government minister can call on the financial and technical resources of his ministry whereas a party official often receives little help from the party organization. By the same token, the lack of well-trained party officials at the lower levels of the party often means that they do not work well with local residents. One of the most common complaints voiced against local party officials is that they are not sensitive and sympathetic to local concerns—a serious problem in a system that emphasizes the responsiveness of the party at the local level.

TANU is best characterized as a hybrid political party. It has the organization common to authoritarian parties and the potential to exercise greater control, but it has consciously sought to limit the use of authoritarian techniques within the party and the government. It seeks to create a society based on consensus, rather than relying solely on its coercive capabilities (which are relatively few). In attempting this, TANU stresses national unity and purpose; the party serves as a major channel for both representation and active participation in Tanzanian political life. As shown in future chapters, however, it is far from a perfect solution to a difficult problem.

■ CHILE ■

Political parties were the most important voices of the different interests of the Chilean electorate prior to the 1973 military takeover. Party opinions and values ranged from the conservative right to the radical left, with different shades of opinion in the center. The final presidential election— that of the leftist coalition led by Salvadore Allende—set the stage for the military intervention of 1973 with its prohibitions on party activity.

Chile was a multi-party political system. During the twentieth century new political parties represented the newly enfranchised; older, more established parties were forced to evolve to meet the changing economic and social conditions. In general, the more conservative and traditional parties lost ground to more radical parties arguing for rapid social change. By the time of the 1964 presidential election, the fortunes of the parties on the right were at such a low ebb that they were forced to support the Christian Democratic party of Eduardo Frei over the more radical Salvadore Allende. From the perspective of the right, Frei was the lesser of two evils.

Political parties in Chile also were characterized by their differing emphasis on the need for a party ideology. Many parties, especially those occupying the center positions on the political spectrum, were willing to sacrifice ideological purity in order to achieve some political power. The inability of a political party to achieve a stable majority would force it into both electoral and governmental coalitions. Coalitions, however, did not eliminate the differences and conflicts between the various coalition partners. It was not at all uncommon for parties to drop out of the coalition or for new parties to be added during the life of a government coalition.

Political parties and movements in Chile have tended to split and divide. Almost all political parties in Chile, whatever their political persuasion, have at one time or another been faced with the problem of splinter groups breaking away to form a new party. Personality disputes and questions of party policy and ideology were the most common causes of the splits.

Traditionally, political parties in Chile have been grouped according to their supporters and to their positions on the major issues of the day. Since the 1950s the dominant parties and coalitions have been those that represent the status quo–oriented conservatives, the reformist-oriented parties (represented mainly by the Christian Democratic movement), and the parties of the left that joined in coalitions arguing for more radical and revolutionary change.

The Conservative Parties—The Vanishing Majority

The earliest political parties in Chile represented the traditional, land-owning elites and the emerging commercial and business classes. In general they favored a strong, centralized government and a limited franchise. Their political power derived from their control of who could vote, from their economic power, and from their ability to control the rural masses. However, as more and more Chileans received the right to vote, and as the economic and social changes of the twentieth century began to influence the political system, the influence of these conservative parties decreased; by the mid-1960s much of their traditional electoral power had vanished. For example, in the March 1965 congressional elections, the Conservative party failed to elect any senators and elected only three deputies. In 1965 the two strongest parties on the right, the Liberals and the Conservatives, joined to form the *Partido Nacional* (National Party), making official a working coalition that they had practiced since the 1950s.

Formed in the 1820s, the Conservative party was Chile's oldest party. Even with much of its power lost by the early twentieth century, it still exerted a strong influence on Chilean politics. But in the 1930s serious splits depleted party ranks, especially when a group of young members left the party to form the *Falange National;* eventually this rump became the nucleus of the new center party, the Christian Democratic party.

In addition to representing the status quo and the tradition-oriented, the Conservatives had a close working relationship with the Catholic church. In 1947 a Catholic cleric indicated what he thought the relationship between party and church was:

The Church recognizes in the Conservative Party its better children, those who sacrifice themselves for the defense of its rights, those who confess in public their Christian faith without being ashamed of it, those who stand courageously before attacks of its adversaries, those who foot by foot defend the cause of God in the government of peoples. For this Party the Church has its affections of gratitude and its better blessings.[15]

Although the relationship between church and party became less intimate in the 1950s and 1960s, much of the Conservative platform drew heavily on church support.

The Liberal party, a second party of the right, allied with the Conservatives in the 1950s and 1960s. Their last electoral success at the presidential level was in 1958: Jorge Alessandri, the son of former President Arturo Alessandri, running as an independent but with rightist support, won the presidency. The 1964 presidential election coalition between the Liberals, the Conservatives, and the Radicals—the Democratic Front—collapsed before the election. Liberals and Conservatives then threw their support to the Christian Democratic candidate, Eduardo Frei.

The policies of the Liberal party in the modern electoral period were much like those of the Conservative party. Both parties had strong planks of support for private enterprise over state ownership, for strong government authority, and for the traditional powerholders in Chile.

The power of the parties on the right was diluted as more and more Chileans won the right to vote. Urbanization, education, and industrialization all changed the nature of the political game; a new electorate demanded new answers to new questions. Although the conservative parties continued to represent and protect the interests of the wealthy, their political power was declining well before the military intervention.

Parties of the Center—Shifting Alliances and the Need for Reform

Before the electoral victories of the Christian Democratic party in the late 1950s and early 1960s, the center of the Chilean political spectrum was dominated by the Radical party. The Radical party was formed in the 1860s by a group of dissatisfied Liberals. Although some were early Socialists, more were opposed to the interference of the church in politics and argued for the separation of church and state.

By the turn of the century the Radicals represented the Chilean middle class; from 1938, when they joined the Popular Front government, until 1952 they dominated the political scene. The Radicals suffered numerous splits and divisions; but, like many center parties, they were flexible and pragmatic, willing to ally themselves with parties of the left and right to gain political power. But by 1962 the party was no longer the largest party in Chile and in the 1971 municipal elections received only 8 percent of the total vote. One indication of the shifting nature of Chilean alliances,

---

[15] As quoted in Ben G. Burnett, *Political Groups in Chile* (Austin: University of Texas Press, 1970), p. 179.

FIGURE 5–3   The Changing Fortunes of Chile's Left, Center, and Right Factions: Presidential Elections, 1952–1970

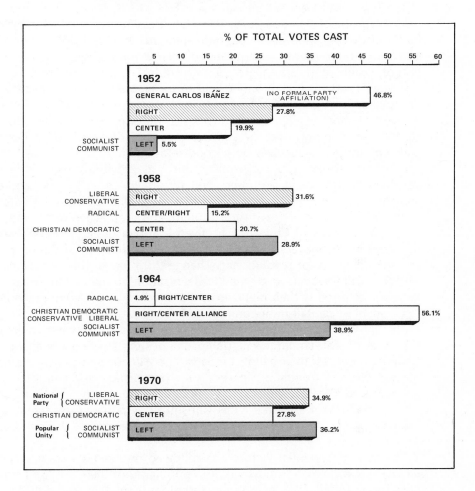

and the Radical party in particular, was the alliance of the Radicals with Conservatives and the Liberals on the right in the 1964 election. In 1969 a faction of the party agreed to join the *Unidad Popular* (Popular Unity) movement on the left, which included Communists, Socialists, and Christian Democrats. (See Figure 5–3.)

More recently dominating the center was the Christian Democratic party, formed in the 1930s by dissident members of the Conservative party. The percentage of the vote it received in various elections steadily increased between 1941 and 1964, when its presidential candidate, Eduardo Frei, won a large victory. From 1941 to 1953, for example, the party received 3 percent of the vote, climbing to 10 percent in 1957 and to 23 percent in 1963. Frei won the presidency with 55.6 percent of the vote. By

1971 the percentage of the vote received by the Christian Democrats dropped to 26 percent.[16]

The high watermark for the party was Frei's 1964 victory. The party ran on a platform of "revolution in liberty," stressing the need to maintain traditional democratic standards, but calling for extensive political, social, and economic reforms. Tax reforms to ensure a more equitable distribution of wealth, land reform, greater state control over the copper industry, a stronger executive, a reformed and more responsive civil service, and improvement of conditions in rural Chile were only a few of the most important Christian Democratic promises. Reform, however, was to be carried out within the democratic framework of Chile. Christian Democrats considered themselves both good leftists and good Catholics.[17]

The party sought support from groups that previously were little involved with politics. It proposed land reform to appeal to the landless and the rural poor, it appealed to women (who first received the vote in 1949 and tended to vote with the church), and it appealed to the rapidly increasing number of Chileans who lived in urban slums. The goal was a middle ground between the conservatism and capitalism of the far right and the demands for revolutionary change from the far left (for example, Christian Democrats favored the "Chileanization" of many industries and generally referred to their platform as the middle way of "communitarianism"—neither capitalism or communism).

The 1964 Christian Democratic campaign appealed to many voters on the basis of anti-communism. Campaign posters stressed the threat to Chile if voters cast their ballots for Salvadore Allende and the coalition of the Socialist and Communist parties. One poster pictured Santa Claus on one side and a Soviet soldier on the other with the caption, "Who do you want to knock on your door this Christmas?" Another used the soccer motif and suggested that the winners voted for Frei, "Chile 2 (Frei), USSR 1 (Allende)."[18]

The 1964 presidential victory was followed by the 1965 congressional victory. Soon thereafter, however, the popularity of the Christian Democrats began to fall. Like those in power before them, they found that solutions were more difficult to provide than campaign promises were to make. The inability of party leaders to control the rate of inflation cost them dearly in terms of political support. Divisions within the party over what reforms were needed and how fast they should be carried out further eroded support. These problems and others contributed to the Christian

---

[16] Robert J. Alexander, *Latin American Political Parties* (New York: Praeger, 1973), p. 322.

[17] Federico G. Gil and Charles Partish, *The Chilean Presidential Election of September 4, 1964, Part I* (Washington, D.C.: Institute for the Comparative Study of Political Systems, 1965), pp. 28–30.

[18] Ibid., p. 39.

Democrats' defeat in the 1970 presidential election, which passed power to the coalition of leftist forces led by Allende.

The Parties of the Left—The Call for Radical Change

Socialists and Communists have a long tradition of participation in Chilean politics. Socialists were first elected to the legislature in the nineteenth century, and since then have actively participated. The early Socialist party split in 1912 between those who were more and less militant concerning the position of workers in Chile. Increasing industrialization and the prosperity of the mines made the question of workers' rights an important one. One faction eventually formed the Communist party of Chile, while the other still committed itself to socialism though it suffered further splits. Competition between Socialists and Communists centered on the control of the trade union movement. Each party tried to mobilize the workers to its banner and to create unions loyal to its cause. This competition between the leftist parties, as well as from the parties of the center and, to a lesser extent, from the parties of the right, hindered the development of a unified trade union movement.

In 1938 Communists, Socialists, and Radicals joined to form the Popular Front (following the European example), with campaign slogans such as this: "Workers of the city, of the country, and of the mines, we are faced with a single and great enemy—reaction; let us form the only solid great union—the Popular Front."[19] Their early unity did not last. When the fragile coalition of the left fell apart, so did the Socialist party and the various trade unions. Again a major dividing point within the socialist movement was its ambiguous relationship to the Communist party—antagonism or cooperation.

Even though the socialist parties were split, Communists and Socialists —or at least factions of each party—were normally able to join together to compete in national elections. In 1952 the candidate of the left, for both Communists and Socialists, was the Socialist leader Salvadore Allende. He ran a poor third in this election, but in 1958 and 1964 came in second. Finally, in 1970, he was elected with only a plurality (not a majority) of votes; the Popular Unity coalition included Communists, Socialists, Radicals, and some Christian Democrats. It represented those demanding rapid, radical change.

The platform of the victorious Popular Unity coalition described the problems facing Chile as follows:

Chile is going through a grave crisis, manifested by social and economic stag-nation, widespread poverty and deprivation of all sorts suffered by workers,

---

[19] Quoted in Alexander, *Latin American Political Parties*, p. 128.

A poster for Salvadore Allende, topped by the red star and the hammer and sickle. Opposition to Allende stressed his Marxist and Communist ties. Wide World Photos, Inc.

peasants, and other exploited classes as well as in the growing difficulties which confront white-collar workers, professional people, small and medium businessmen, and in the very limited opportunities open to women and young people.[20]

And this was the cause:

What has failed in Chile is the system—a system which does not correspond to present-day requirements. Chile is a capitalist country, dependent on the imperialist nations and dominated by bourgeois groups who are structurally related to foreign capital and who cannot resolve the country's fundamental problems— problems which are clearly the result of a class privilege which will never be given up voluntarily.[21]

---

[20] Platform statements are from the "Popular Unity's Programme" as printed in J. Ann Zammit, ed., *The Chilean Road to Socialism* (Austin: University of Texas Press, 1973), p. 225.

[21] Ibid.

Christian Democrats, Socialists, and Communists agreed on many of the problems facing Chile, but they disagreed on the proper solutions. While the Christian Democrats stressed reform within traditional democratic institutions, the Popular Unity coalition called for sweeping changes in Chilean political, social, and economic life. They promised to respect "democratic rights" and to permit opposition that would not endanger the program.

The program of the Popular Unity coalition stated that the "central policy objective of the united popular forces will be the search for a replacement for the present economic structure."[22] This included the nationalization of much of Chilean industry (including the mining interests), a greater reliance on planning, and the expropriation of large agrarian landholdings. The masses were to be mobilized at the grass-roots level; participation was to be channeled through unions and through organizations representing the rural and urban poor. Education was to be made available to all, social services extended. Among the first 40 measures promised by the coalition were: an end to enormous salaries, social security for everyone, fixed rents, a new economy to put an end to inflation, and an end to class justice.[23]

The changes promised and implemented by the Popular Unity pleased many Chileans, frightened and alienated others, and provoked strong resistance among still others. Allende and the Popular Unity wanted to change not only policies of previous governments but also the system itself. Reaction against these changes caused the 1973 coup d'état.

The Performance of Chilean Political Parties

Political parties were an active and an important part of Chilean political life. In many respects the changes in parties and party activity mirror other changes that have occurred in Chile. The shift from the right to the left, the rapid industrialization and urbanization of Chile, the demands for land reform and better working conditions for rural workers, and an increasing Chilean nationalism concerning the economy are all reflected in the wide variety of Chilean parties.

Both at the presidential and the legislative levels, parties continuously competed for office. This competition involved temporary alliances and coalitions, and splits and reunions within parties. Parties were characterized by both their ideological content and their ability, gained from long experience, to play practical politics.

Parties also influenced other institutions and organizations within Chile. Parties of all persuasions, for example, were involved in the trade union movement and sought to mobilize the increasingly important and numer-

---

[22] Ibid., p. 266.
[23] Ibid., pp. 277–281.

ous workers. Likewise, parties attempted to gain supporters in the military; this was especially true in the 1970 to 1973 period. The officer corps fell prey to the splits and divisions that characterized party life—some supported the government of the day, others increasingly came to oppose it. Military officers, sometimes willingly and other times not, were involved in the critical political issues of the period. The culmination of this involvement was the military intervention in 1973. Military officers provided their solution to the problems of multi-party political life—ban the parties.

CONCLUSION

Parties and politics are so closely associated in many people's minds that they seem one and the same. Many people define their political values and beliefs by naming their party preference. "I'm Labour" or "I'm a Christian Democrat" often is as far as many can go in describing their political beliefs. This chapter showed, though, how complex and varied party patterns are in our eight nations. Parties develop in response to the needs of the leaders, the expectations of the citizens, the values of society, and the historical circumstances of the nation.

Patterns range from one-party states (Tanzania, Egypt, and the USSR), to basically two-party systems (United Kingdom and West Germany), to multi-party systems (Nigeria, France, and Chile), but there are significant differences between nations that have the same type of party system.

Political parties perform many tasks in the political system. They educate the citizenry, provide choices between different goals and ideologies, mobilize the population for the achievement of goals, provide representation for participants, and contest elections that determine who will govern. What varies between nations and between parties within a nation is the emphasis placed on these functions.

In single-party states the party leadership sets the goals, and the party organization mobilizes the population to approve these goals. The party organization acts as a vehicle for participation and representation and for two-way communication between leaders and citizens. Conflict between competing positions normally is resolved within the party rather than between parties. A single party may be able to govern efficiently, but it runs the dangerous risk of becoming static and bureaucratized from the lack of effective criticism.

A comparison of Egypt and Tanzania with the USSR reveals that there are important differences between one-party systems. In the USSR the Communist party encourages symbolic rather than effective participation, but Egypt and Tanzania, with varying degrees of success, have allowed effective participation within the party. Tanzania, especially, has tried to do so by holding competitive elections between party candidates.

The level of control and the coercive potential of the party in the Soviet Union also are much greater than in Tanzania and Egypt. While the strong Communist party in the Soviet Union dominates all other institutions and branches of government, in Egypt and Tanzania the official party often competes with other branches of government such as the bureaucracy, the military, or government ministries. Thus, while TANU and the ASU may be the only political parties in their respective nations, they are not the only effective, powerful political institutions.

Party goals and values also differ significantly in one-party states. TANU and the Arab Socialist Union allow much more inter-party discussion and debate than the Communist party does in the Soviet Union. This diversity within the ranks of the Egyptian and Tanzanian parties means that the party cannot act as a vanguard party and shape opinions. Discussion and debate detract from a singleness of purpose.

Multi-party systems, like one-party systems, exhibit different characteristics. Whatever the governmental changes in France, the multi-party system endures. Names change and party leaders may reinterpret their position within the system (as does the present-day Communist party), but parties remain the most important mobilizing and participatory institutions in the French political system.

The multi-party systems of Nigeria and Chile provide an interesting contrast to that of France. Chile's long tradition of multi-party politics and coalition formation appeared to be well institutionalized and relatively stable. The election of leftist Salvadore Allende in 1970, however, with considerably less than a majority of the vote, placed an intolerable strain on some segments of the society, most notably the military. By 1970 Chileans had stopped supporting the more conservative parties in favor of parties demanding either gradual or radical change. The refusal of the military and other groups to accept the choice of the electorate reveals the extent to which parties can polarize the population.

Sharp conflict also typifies the 1960–1966 Nigerian party experience. Party politics polarized an already divided population; the problems were compounded when many politicians refused to accept the rules of the game and electoral outcomes. Political parties magnified the linguistic, ethnic, and cultural cleavages described in Chapter 3. The dominance of the NPC in the North, the Action Group in the West, and the NCNC in the East made it impossible for one party to achieve a majority based on a national platform. As in Chile, the military finally intervened to end the "divisiveness of party politics."

Dominant two-party systems, like the United Kingdom's, often are pictured as the most stable of all types. In two-party situations it is easier for one party to win a majority (or almost a majority) and hence rule without having to form unstable coalitions. The experiences of Britain and West Germany indicate, however, that even these systems are not immune to problems. Voters complain that differences between the parties are insignificant and that voting has little real meaning. "Umbrella" or catch-all parties may represent so many factions that it is difficult to find a political platform on which all party members and activists agree. British Labour party leaders juggle so many interests and issues that presenting a coherent, consistent platform is difficult. Finally, two-party systems in parliamentary governments may find themselves with such a narrow majority in parliament that their ability to act and make decisions is restricted. Legislative stagnation and parliamentary stalemates result. The narrow Labour "majority" in the British House of Commons in the mid-1970s made it difficult for Wilson and Callaghan to initiate their programs.

The importance of political parties is attested to by the frequency with which they are outlawed. Military takeovers in Chile in 1973 and Nigeria in 1966 banned organized political activity. TANU in Tanzania forbade opposition political parties in 1963; the Communist party in the Soviet Union has outlawed opposition since the Revolution in 1917. Although the Egyptian leadership recently has allowed the formation of potential opposition parties to the ASU, the ASU remains the dominant political party. The well-established and institutionalized party systems of West Germany, France, and the United Kingdom provide examples of political systems (very recently in the West German case) that appear to have achieved that delicate balance between participation, representation, mobilization, and performance. Chapter 6 describes how leaders are chosen and exactly how delicate the balance is.

CHAPTER 6
LEADERSHIP
SELECTION

What role do elections play in choosing
the nation's leaders?

Leaders exercise power. Because they do, there is usually fierce competion for leadership positions. Every political system periodically needs to change its political leaders. New decision-makers are recruited to positions of power and influence while older leaders retire, gracefully or otherwise. Changes in leadership create potential crises for all political systems because they involve uncertainty. Those systems that handle the transition smoothly are better able to perform effectively and efficiently. For the others, changes in leadership present severe problems not only for leaders and participants, but also for the maintenance of the system itself.

This chapter discusses the two fundamental ways—institutionalized and noninstitutionalized—of selecting leaders. The selection is institutionalized if it proceeds according to regularized, predictable, and generally accepted procedures and rules. Elections are the most common form of institutionalized leader selection. The rules of competition, understood by the contestants and the public, are applied consistently to all contestants and from one period of selection to the next. "Decision rules" determine who wins and who loses. Ideally, these rules are not ambiguous. When the above conditions are met, most contenders readily accept the verdict of the selectors.

Noninstitutionalized selection is an extraordinary, unpredictable means of leadership change. Military coups, full-scale revolution, or struggles for power on the death of a leader are examples. It also may refer to the bureaucratic infighting among leaders competing in totalitarian systems. In situations such as these, it may take a long time for the dust to settle and a new leader to emerge.

Elections

The chief form of institutionalized selection is the election. Elections are scheduled at regular intervals, and the rules governing their conduct and outcome do not change greatly over time. All candidates know in advance the criteria of determining winners—the candidate or candidates with the majority of votes wins. The aim of these rules is to ensure decisive, unambiguous results.

There are two sets of rules for two relatively distinct contests in parliamentary systems: the rules to elect parliamentary representatives and the rules to select a leader and a government from within the parliament. The two-step nature of this contest makes it difficult at times—especially in multi-party parliaments—to "find" a government.

Rules and institutionalized procedures are sometimes controversial because they favor a candidate, group, or party, thus defeating one of the purposes of institutionalized selection. For example, in France electoral rules traditionally give the Communists many fewer parliamentary seats than their popularity might dictate, and electoral rules in Britain and West Germany frankly discriminate against small parties.

Besides formal rules and procedures, the informal patterns of electoral behavior set limits on the contest just as much as electoral laws do. Normally voters develop loyalties or habits that limit the number of possible outcomes. In this sense, their stable preferences become a part of the rules of the game. For example, the fact that in the past 90 percent of the British electorate were psychologically attached and loyal to the Labour or Conservative parties limited the possible outcomes to a majority for one or the other of these parties.

Partisan attachments differ from nation to nation. An overwhelming majority of Britons, for example, feel close emotional ties to one of the large parties. Germans are less likely to feel these attachments but do develop consistent preferences based on their view of party performances. French voters are the least party-oriented of any developed nation. Elections in Nigeria suggested that individuals cared less about specific parties than about the ethnic groups and regions the various parties represented.

Societies characterized by widespread strong partisan attachments tend to have more continuity in leadership and policy goals, and less sudden disruptive change. French politics are volatile largely because French voters are open to new political movements, leaders, and ideas, but often the price that they pay for flexibility is disorder. The pattern of partisan attachments in Nigeria contributed to political violence and conflict as well as to sudden political change. The regional distribution of attachments reinforced the explosive tribal cleavages and helped lead to civil war.

Though loyalties toward political parties are strong, party strengths can undergo gradual changes of real importance. Currently, some extremely important trends in European electoral behavior are appearing that may change the fundamental nature of politics in European parliamentary democracies. First, there is the growing strength of Communist parties with their desire to play a significant role in the leadership selection process. Second, West Germany and France are undergoing a change toward more simplified patterns of voting behavior which are consistent with a simple two-way contest between a government and a unified opposition. Finally, there are some small signs that the psychological ties between Britons and their two large parties are weakening. Each of these trends affects virtually every other important aspect of politics in these countries.

Noninstitutionalized Selection

Noninstitutionalized selection includes many types of political events and practices, the most familiar being the coup d'état. Sometimes coups are the result of the failure of electoral politics; for example, the Nigerian military took over in 1966 in part because they were one of the few truly national, rather than regional or ethnic, institutions. Because parties and politicians had played tribal politics, the military sought national leaders. Unfortunately, once in power, even the military was unable to avoid tribalism or the appearance of tribalism.

Sometimes the military acts as a quasi-interest group and intervenes when its own interests are threatened. Factions in the Chilean military became politically involved because of their political attitudes, interests, and alliances with other groups. In their system of values and loyalties, the election of a leftist president was unacceptable. Unlike other interest groups, the military has the ability to enforce its political will.

Single-party states offer another arena for noninstitutionalized leadership selection. Who holds the top leadership positions in nations such as Egypt, and the Soviet Union is decided in part by political infighting among the leading contenders for power. The deaths of Stalin and Nasser set off fierce struggles among potential future leaders. Below the highest level, attainment of political positions may be quite regularized and predictable, but the top positions usually are filled by those strong enough to take them.

Selection of the top leader in a one-party state is particularly sensitive. Leaders in one-party states generally consolidate their power, eliminate rivals, and avoid having a clear successor because of fear of competition. When a leader dies, it is usually not clear who should replace him. Since the position is so powerful, the rewards of the successful candidate are enormous, as are the penalties against losers. Competition under these circumstances may take any form from murder to lobbying among the systems' most powerful groups.

Institutionalized vs. Noninstitutionalized Selection

The two types of selection procedures discussed in this chapter are ideal types. Each electoral system has elements that appear just as arbitrary and unpredictable as so-called noninstitutionalized systems. Each noninstitutionalized selection involves elements that are ordered and predictable. The distinction, then, is not foolproof but is useful in understanding an important aspect of politics that differs from nation to nation.

Institutionalized selection promotes stability and reduces conflict. Conflict is reduced because everyone knows and agrees to the rules beforehand. Conflict is lessened because the verdict is open, public, and not subject to doubt. Noninstitutionalized selection invites relatively unrestrained conflict and the intensity that builds up over high stakes and a dangerous game.

The distinction employed in this chapter does not follow simply from the basic difference between developed and developing nations. While developed nations may tend to have more institutionalized leadership selection, they are also subject to conflict and instability. On the other hand, developing nations do not automatically suffer leadership selection crises. Our case studies include a developed nation whose top leadership selection is not institutionalized as well as several developing nations that have important traditions in electoral politics.

▪ THE UNITED KINGDOM ▪

The British have selected their national leadership in a regularized and predictable way for many years. The rules of selection have gradually evolved over Britain's long history and have remained essentially stable for at least the last century. The national leaders, or cabinet, are selected by the people's representatives in Parliament. The citizen's role in the process is played through participation in parliamentary elections. In fact, the only important vote cast by Britons is the single vote that they cast for their member of Parliament.

The informal features of the selection process have been just as stable and predictable as the formal rules; that is, British citizens have responded to particular parties, leaders, and issues in a consistent way for a long time. Most adult Britons have fixed ideas about the party they support, the important issues, and the kind of leader they admire. As a result, there are fewer real surprises in British elections than are found in elections elsewhere. The advantage of this predictability is political stability.

There are signs, however, of changing patterns of electoral behavior; for example, the two major parties, Labour and the Conservatives, are losing support to smaller parties. The smaller parties would like to change the electoral rules so that more parties could gain representation in Parliament. It is difficult to know whether these trends represent a basic change in British loyalties or a reaction to a currently faltering economy. A change to a permanent multi-party system would alter considerably the existing electoral pattern.

The Electoral System

Frankly designed to encourage a two-party system, the British electoral system works against any proliferation of parties. The electoral system makes it easier for one political party to win a majority of the seats in the House of Commons. In this way the electoral system contributes to maintaining Britain's "responsible party system" in which one party has the undivided responsibilities of office. The fact that smaller parties have been gaining representation in Parliament is all the more remarkable, given the rules under which they must compete with their larger opponents.

The British electoral system is a "first past the post system." In all the United Kingdom's 635 constituencies, the candidate who gets the largest number of votes (a plurality) is the winner. There is no need to attain an absolute majority of "50 percent plus one" to gain a seat.

It is clear that this system benefits the larger parties by rewarding their nationwide strength and organization. The system builds majorities in Parliament—where they are significant—even though the two main parties seldom get a majority of the parliamentary votes. In a three- or four-way contest the large parties are more likely to get the 30 to 40 percent needed for a plurality. Small nationwide parties such as the Liberals receive wasted votes in many constituencies where they come in second or third, getting no seats for votes received.

Examples of the result of the big party bias are not hard to find. Neither large party has received a majority of the votes since 1935 (a Conservative triumph), and yet only once has an election failed to produce a majority in Parliament for either Labour or the Conservatives. The 1974 Labour government under James Callaghan is a case in point. Labour received 39.2 percent of the votes cast and transformed that into 50.2 percent of the seats in Parliament (319 seats of 635.)[1]

---

[1] Richard M. Scammon, "The Election and the Future of British Electoral Reform," in Howard R. Penniman, ed., *Britain at the Polls* (Washington, D.C.: American Enterprise Institute for Public Policy Research, 1974), pp. 163–176.

James Callaghan, leader of the Labour party, served as prime minister from 1976 to 1979. Keystone Press.

Small-party success is possible, however, if support is concentrated in a specific region where it can compete with the big parties. A regional party's strength is not spread thinly over the United Kingdom; thus it can win on its own ground. This, of course, is what has happened in nationality areas, particularly in Scotland and its Scottish National party. The nationality issue has the potential of negating the majority-building features of the current system.

Voting Patterns

Britons are still guided in large part by considerations of class in their voting decisions. This has been the dominant political alignment in the United Kingdom for over 50 years and continues to influence voting patterns powerfully. The working class–middle class differences in voting behavior became ingrained with the rise of Britain's trade union movement in the early twentieth century. The powerful new labor movement and the political party it founded emphasized class differences and reduced the political importance of other group distinctions, notably religious differences. Today it is estimated that between 70 and 80 percent of Britain's middle class support the Conservative party, while approximately 65 or 70 percent of those who call themselves workers support the Labour party.[2]

The figures regarding class support of the parties make it clear that class is not an infallible way to predict or understand voting in Britain. A large number of people do not vote their class. The largest category of these are the so-called "working-class Tories"—members of the working class who consistently vote for the Conservative party. "Class deviants," then, form a substantial part of the electorate, enough to swing the election. These people do not feel that class issues are important for their lives. Regardless of occupation and income, they do not identify personally with a particular class. They may come from families that are either upwardly or downwardly mobile. Class deviants may also live in situations where they come into contact with people of other class backgrounds rather than in a more homogeneous working-class or middle-class area.

In historical and political terms the phenomena of working-class Tories is not difficult to understand. The leaders of the Conservative party long ago realized that their natural class following was in the minority. As a result, the Conservatives have aggressively sought working-class support since workers' votes became important in the late nineteenth century. They initiated some social reforms and cooperated in the creation of Britain's welfare system. The party has also benefited from the British value placed on respect for political authority. The Conservatives, an elite group in part descended from the great old families, like to play the part of the natural political class—born to rule.

The class basis of voting and the association of class interests with the two major parties builds strong bonds of loyalty between most Britons and one of the parties. In one survey, 80 percent of those interviewed claimed that they had always voted for the same party, while 90 percent consider themselves committed to one party or another in a general sense.[3] This characteristic attachment to party and its class origins means that British elections are usually close and that the party shares of the electorate do not vary greatly from election to election. In the 11 elections since World War II, Labour averaged 43.8 percent of the vote. For the same period the Conservatives averaged 43.6 percent. The average percentage difference between the two has been just over 3 percent.

Trends and Recent Elections

Recent electoral results suggest that the current balance of strength between the parties may soon be upset by basic economic and cultural

---

[2] Richard Rose, *Politics in England* (Boston: Little, Brown, 1974), p. 169, and David Butler and Donald Stokes, *Political Change in Britain* (New York: St. Martin's Press, 1971), p. 156.

[3] Butler and Stokes, *Political Change in Britain*, p. 27.

Leadership Profiles

Leaders of the Labour and Conservative Parties During the 1974 General Elections

Leader	Background and Education
Harold Wilson Labour Party	born: 1916 education: Jesus College, Oxford
Edward Heath Conservative Party	born: 1916 education: Balliol College, Oxford (Honors, Fellow in 1969)

developments. The most obvious trend is the strengthening of the nationalist movements; the other is the deterioration of support for both
major parties.

In 1974 there were two elections because the first—in February—was
indecisive, no party gaining a majority in the House of Commons. Harold
Wilson's Labour party formed a minority government based on their
301-seat plurality. In October new elections to establish a firm parliamentary majority gave Wilson's government a three-seat majority in
the House.

The elections demonstrated first of all that the nationalist parties were
a real threat to the established parties. The Scottish National party (SNP),

Early Occupations		Political Career	
1937–1945	Lecturer in Economics, New College, Oxford	1945–1950	Member of Parliament for Ormskirk
1943–1944	Director, Economics and Statistics, Office of the Department of Fuel and Power	1950–1976	Member of Parliament for Huyton
		1947–1951	President of the Board of Trade
		1959–1963	Chairman of the House of Commons, Public Accounts Committee
		1963–1964	Leader of the Opposition
		1964–1970, 1974–1976	Prime Minister
1940–1946	Army service, Lieutenant Colonel	1947	Candidate for Parliament from Bexley, defeated
		1950–present	Member of Parliament for Bexley
		1959–1960	Minister of Labour
		1960–1963	Lord Privy Seal
		1963–1964	President, Board of Trade
		1965–1970	Leader of the Opposition
		1970–1974	Prime Minister
		1974–1975	Leader of the Opposition
		1975	Removed as Leader of the Opposition by the Conservative Party

Plaid Cymru (Wales), and the Ulster Loyalists won 20 seats in the February election and increased that total to 25 in October. Particularly surprising was the performance of the SNP. In October the SNP won 11 seats in Scotland, averaging over 30 percent of the vote in all the 71 constituencies in which the party was entered.[4] For Scotland at least, the SNP was competitive with the large parties.

The gains made by nationalists are particularly damaging to the Labour party. Since Scotland and Wales are more economically backward, they

---

[4] Anthony King, "The Election That Someone Won—More or Less," in Penniman, ed., *Britain at the Polls,* p. 196.

TABLE 6–1   Recent British Election Results in Percentage of the Vote and
             Parliamentary Seats

	1964		1966	
	Percentage	Seats	Percentage	Seats
Labour	44.1	317	48.0	364
Conservative	43.4	304	41.9	253
Liberal	11.2	9	8.5	12
Nationalists	0.9	0	1.2	1
Others	0.4	0	0.4	0

Sources: Thomas J. Mackie and Richard Rose, The International Almanac of Electoral History (New York: The Free Press, 1974); and Facts on File.

have a higher proportion of poor and working-class inhabitants than England does. Labour traditionally has done well in both areas, and the party leaders believe that these seats are necessary in building Labour parliamentary majorities. Changes in loyalties in Northern Ireland have hurt the Conservatives as well. In the past they could count on the ideologically conservative Protestant parties of Ulster for support. Now, however, dissatisfaction with the British policy toward the Protestant-Catholic conflict in Northern Ireland has given these seats to Ulster Loyalists—a very independent and unpredictable group.

The second major departure in the 1974 elections is the erosion of support for the two major parties (see Table 6–1). The share of votes gained by each party is fairly low compared to their previous percentages. The vote for Conservatives was over 8 percent less than the postwar average while "victorious" Labour polled 5.2 percent below their expected level of support (October). The two parties taken together polled only 75.1 percent of the votes—the lowest share for the major parties since the unstable period of the 1920s.

Undoubtedly, long-term failure in the economic realm plagued both parties. The election of February 1974 was fought under crisis conditions, when all of Britain's 269,000 coal miners were on strike, industry was forced to cut back to a three-day work week, and many of Britain's cities were dark at night. This labor crisis aggravated the chronic economic problems that had already led to record levels of unemployment, work stoppages, and inflation. Since the Conservatives had been in power for four years (1970–1974) under Prime Minister Edward Heath, Labour should have had a great advantage. Normally voters punish the national executive leadership for economic difficulties and turn to the opposition regardless of particular policy differences. However, Labour's performance from

1970		Feb. 1974		Oct. 1974	
Percentage	Seats	Percentage	Seats	Percentage	Seats
43.1	288	37.3	301	39.2	319
46.4	330	38.1	296	35.9	276
7.5	6	19.3	14	18.3	13
2.4	3	} 5.3	20	} 6.6	25
0.7	2		4		2

1964 to 1970, when *they* made the economic decisions, evidently did not encourage the public. English voters turned to the small Liberal party, who got their largest postwar share of the vote (19.3 percent) and nearly quadrupled their percentage from the 1970 election. Outside England voters turned to the nationalists. Another election in October, with the miners' strike settled, reaffirmed these judgments—the Liberals held even and the nationalist parties improved their performance.

The Liberal party, whose fortunes depend largely on big-party problems, always benefits from a protest vote against one of the large parties. For example, when people are fed up with a Labour administration, it is natural that many normal Labour supporters vote Liberal. In this way, they can avoid going over to the other side while registering their complaint. It seems likely that in 1974 normal supporters of both big parties went Liberal in protest at the failure of both government and opposition to handle the economic crisis.

Even some of the nationalist vote may have been a protest vote. The Scottish National party has advocated independence from the United Kingdom. (The independence issue, along with SNP claims that "It's Scotland's North Sea oil" is all that the party stands for.) And yet, while the SNP's popularity continues to rise, the small proportion of Scots who want independence is on the decline—only 18 percent.[5] Many Scots, then, voted for SNP while disagreeing with the sum and substance of its program. The most likely reason for this kind of behavior is a rejection of the British political elite as personified by the two major parties.

The victory of the Conservative party in the May 1979 parliamentary election indicates that two-party government is still possible. The Tory

---

[5] The poll results were reported in the *Christian Science Monitor,* 10 February 1977.

Margaret Thatcher receives a standing ovation from the Conservative party faithful at the October 1978 party conference. She led the party to a 1979 parliamentary election victory. Keystone Press.

party of Margaret Thatcher won a clear majority of 339 seats to 269 seats for the Labour party of James Callaghan. The parliamentary strength of the Liberals and the various nationalist parties was halved from their 1974 highwater mark. (The Liberals won 11 seats; the Scottish Nationalist party and the Welsh Plaid Cymru each won 2 seats; and the various nationalist factions of Northern Ireland captured 11 seats). Once again, however, the majority party fell considerably short of winning 50 percent of the national popular vote.

To summarize, British voters have long supported a two-party system. In so doing, they have cooperated in creating a majority or government party in Parliament. They have given great power and latitude to the governing party and judged the opposition according to its performance. In this sense, patterns of voting in Britain fit well with traditional British political values and parliamentary institutions. Prolonged economic difficulties may undermine a key element in the old pattern of voting—the emotional attachment of most Britons to one or the other of the major parties. A large part of the drift away from Labour and the Tories is protest. To the extent that it is only protest, recent changes do not yet mean a basic shift of partisan loyalties. It is too soon to judge whether a long-term change in voters' loyalties is under way.

▪ THE FEDERAL REPUBLIC OF GERMANY ▪

Since the first election in 1949, voting patterns in West Germany have undergone a gradual change. The most obvious change has been that Germans have rejected narrowly ideological, regional, or special-interest parties in favor of the two large broadly based parties—the Christian Democrats (CDU/CSU) and the Social Democrats (SPD). The third party in the system, the Free Democratic Party (FDP), is now largely viewed as a partner of one of the large parties (currently the SPD) and therefore as an integral part of either the government or the opposition.

As the two major parties are now relatively equal in strength, elections are competitive. If the West Germans had an electoral system like the United Kingdom's, undoubtedly one of the large parties would consistently achieve a majority of seats in West Germany's Parliament (Bundestag). Since each party's followings are relatively stable, a British-style electoral system would probably lead to the alternation in office of the two large moderate parties. Of course, then, Germany's governing party would be a single, wholly "responsible" party on the traditional English model. As matters stand, however, the two major parties come just short of a parliamentary majority needed to form a government. Thus they must form a coalition with the Free Democrats—a fact of life to which the German elector has gradually adjusted.

The Electoral System

British and American occupation authorities helped to design the German electoral system. It is intended to combine the best features of a "winner take all" system (like Britain's) with the best features of a system of proportional representation (each party receiving the same proportion of seats in Parliament as its proportion of votes). The latter has the advantage of truly reflecting popular sentiment, while an advantage of Britain's system is that there is one person elected as a representative of a particular district and thus every citizen has a particular representative whom he/she may contact.

The complex German electoral law specifies that each voter mark his ballot twice in national elections. The voter selects a candidate in the first column and a party in the second. In each electoral district the candidate who attains a plurality wins the district's seat (like Britain's system). Candidates selected in this way, however, fill only half of the seats in the Bundestag; the others are filled by persons whose names are on party

TABLE 6–2 An Example of the German Voting System in a Mythical State

Party	Percentage of Party Votes Received	Number of Constituency Seats Won		Number of Candidates Drawn from Party Lists	Total Seats
SPD	50	1	+	4	5
CDU	40	4	+	0	4
FDP	10	0	+	1	1
	100				10

lists in each state. Names are drawn in such a way that for each state total party seats are proportional to the party's share in the second column (party votes). The overall effect is that of proportional representation, since the seats in the Bundestag are proportional to the party vote percentages. But, unlike a normal proportional representation system, each electoral district has a personal representative.[6]

A mythical example may help clarify the way the system works. In a state with ten parliamentary seats and five constituencies, suppose the SPD got 50 percent of the party votes, the CDU 40 percent, and FDP 10 percent. Further suppose that the CDU candidate wins in four districts, the SPD candidate in one district, and the Free Democratic candidate in none. According to the proportional principle, the CDU should get four total seats, the SPD five seats, and the Free Democrats one. Each party draws as many names off their party lists as they need to make up the difference between what they won in the candidate races and what they are due (see Table 6–2). The Christian Democrats draw no seats, while the SPD needs to draw four to fill its allotted or "fair share" of seats. The Free Democrats—who had no winning candidate—are awarded one seat for their 10 percent party vote showing.

The electoral law also provides that only parties receiving 5 percent of the party votes nationwide may have seats in the Bundestag. The intent is to make it difficult for small parties to survive. The "5 percent clause," important in the early years when there were many small parties, is still important because it may eliminate West Germany's last small party, the FDP. If the Free Democrats fail to secure 5 percent of the national vote, West Germany will have a two-party system.

The full provisions of this "personalized proportional representation" system have even greater importance than the 5 percent clause. First of all, the proportional nature of the system makes it impossible to develop

---

[6] Alfred Grosser, *Germany in Our Time* (New York: Praeger, 1971), pp. 140–142.

single-party majorities in the Bundestag. This makes the German government a coalition government with divided responsibility. Second, the system is so confusing that most Germans are only now beginning to use it properly and to their own advantage. The possible uses of the two votes are many. For example, an FDP voter may elect to vote for a SPD candidate in the first column and for his party, the FDP, in the second column. In this way he supports a member of the SPD-FDP national coalition rather than wasting his vote on the candidate of his small party. His second vote for the FDP helps secure seats for his party and helps ensure that it gets 5 percent of the vote for survival.

Voting Patterns

West Germans do not have the strong feelings of party attachments that the British do; thus one important element of voting stability is missing in the Federal Republic. As few as one in five Germans feels a close psychological identification with one of the parties. The reasons for the reluctance of West Germans to develop party identification is understandable. In the first place, West Germans are only now getting used to two of the three parties, the CDU/CSU and the FDP, which are post-World War II creations. Further, Germany's history, as discussed in Chapter 2, has not encouraged partisan activity or helped attach a positive value to the parties themselves. Finally, the current pattern of German politics, with its coalition governments, seems to reduce the importance of any particular party and its policies.

All this does not mean that West Germans do not have party preferences based on fairly stable party images. Throughout the 1950s, for example, the balance of party strength was fairly stable. The balance that favored the Christian Democrats was partly founded on its image as the "chancellor's party"—the party with the ablest leaders. The SPD was viewed as the defender of working-class interests with vague connections to the ideas of Karl Marx. These images finally yielded to time and experience in the 1960s; but, while they lasted, they added predictability and stability to German politics.

The balance of party support is also affected by ties between social and economic groups and the parties. Religion has always been an important influence: Catholics tend to favor the Christian Democrats; Protestants and the less religious, the SPD. Class is also important, with the natural working-class attachments to the Social Democrats. Finally, rural groups and individuals have tended to support the CDU, while the SPD relies more on urban support. Over the years the parties have captured consistent bases of support. Even groups with conflicting motivations, such as Catholic workers have begun to show a preference for one of the parties. Their religion suggests a CDU vote, while the conditions of their employment argue for the SPD. Recent SPD gains here have helped the SPD catch up with the dominant party of the 1950s.

Recent Elections and Trends

Three distinct electoral eras have occurred in the almost 30 years of the Federal Republic. First, there was the era of Konrad Adenauer and CDU dominance in the 1950s. Next, in the '60s, came a transition period toward competitive politics. Finally, the election of 1969, resulting in the election of the first Social Democratic chancellor, marked the beginning of the competitive era. Now close competition and frequent alternation in office will probably characterize the selection of future West German leaders.

Konrad Adenauer dominated the West Germany of the 1950s. When he resigned in 1963, he had been its only chancellor since 1949. In that sense many West Germans viewed him and his team as indispensable guides in an insecure world. Adenauer and the CDU, after all, firmly entrenched West Germany as a respected member of NATO and pre-sided over the remarkable economic growth of the 1950s. West Germany's newfound economic and military security seemed to depend on *Der Alte* (the Old One) and his advisers.

Adenauer skillfully played on these feelings in elections. The Christian Democrats' slogan "No experiments!" played on a fear of political change, while it emphasized the socialist and Marxist past of the SPD. This was a powerful tactic in a West Germany faced with the division of Germany,

Leadership Profile

Chancellor of the Federal Republic of Germany, 1949–1963

Leader	*Background and Education*
Konrad Adenauer	born: 1876 died: 1967 education: Studied law and economics at the Universities of Freiburg, Munich, and Berlin. Father was a civil servant in judicial service in Cologne.

the loss of land to Communist Poland, and Russian occupation of East Germany. The CDU emphasized its successful "social market" economy, which promised full private ownership of property, a strong governmental guiding role, and "capitalism with a conscience." But most of all they promised Konrad Adenauer.

The elections of the 1950s have been described as "chancellor plebescites,"[7] suggesting that the only real issue was whether Konrad Adenauer should continue in office with further evidence of public trust. The high-water mark of public trust for Adenauer was his third election in 1957, when his party polled over 50 percent of the votes—the only time in German history that a single party gained a majority.

It was clear by the election of 1961—Adenauer's fourth victory—that the Christian Democrats must soon face its opposition without Adenauer, who was now 85. When the issue of age split even his own party, Adenauer promised to retire early and to help the transition to his successor's government.

Politics of the 1960s showed that no CDU chancellor would be as skillful or lucky as Der Alte. Adenauer's immediate successor was Ludwig Erhard, a logical choice because he was widely respected as the economics minister who presided over the economic miracle. After winning the 1965 election in his own right, Erhard was brought down by West Ger-

---

[7] Arnold J. Heidenheimer, "The Chancellor Effect in the Federal Republic," in Donald Schoonmaker, ed., *German Politics* (Lexington, Mass.: D. C. Heath, 1971), pp. 100–108.

Early Occupations and Political Career

Solicitor

1906	Elected to the Cologne Municipal Assembly
1909	Deputy Mayor of Cologne
1916–1933	Mayor of Cologne
1920–1933	President of the Prussian State Council
1934	Arrested by National Socialists and briefly detained
1944	Arrested by Nazis in the aftermath of the Generals' plot against Hitler
1945	Appointed Mayor of Cologne at American insistence and "fired" from that position by the British
1948	President of the Parliamentary Council charged with advising the occupying powers on a new German constitution
1949–1963	Chancellor of the Federal Republic of Germany—elected to office 1949, 1953, 1957, 1961

TABLE 6–3 Recent West German Elections in Percentage of the Vote and Parliamentary Seats

	1961		1965	
	Percentage	Seats	Percentage	Seats
CDU/CSU	45.3	242	47.6	245
SPD	36.2	190	39.3	202
FDP	12.8	67	9.5	49
Others	5.7	0	3.6	0

Sources: Thomas J. Mackie and Richard Rose, The International Almanac of Electoral History (New York: The Free Press, 1974); and Facts on File.

many's first serious postwar economic downturn. He resigned in favor of another Christian Democrat, Kurt Kiesinger, who presided over an economic recovery but was forced to allow the Social Democrats a place in the government. For the first time Social Democrats had a place in the cabinet.

The CDU's problems were exploited by re-invigorated Social Democrats, who had started in 1959 to remedy their two weakest points—their Marxist past and their reputed absence of leadership. The first step was to remove from the party program all Marxist references to class warfare and ownership of the means of production.[8] The other was to promote their top national candidates as strong and competent leaders. In the past the SPD had followed the practice of many working-class parties in not emphasizing the personal qualities of their leaders. But now they selected an attractive, internationally known figure, Willy Brandt. Brandt as mayor of West Berlin was able to emphasize his close relations with the Americans—previously an Adenauer strength. His association with President Kennedy's visit to Berlin in 1961 likewise gave dramatic evidence of his anti-communism.

The party made steady progress in the 1961 and 1965 campaigns—in 1961 scoring over 4 percent above their previous high and in 1965 adding another 3 percent above that record level. In 1966, when the party entered the "Great Coalition" with the Christian Democrats, Brandt was named vice chancellor and foreign minister. For the first time the Social Democrats held positions of responsibility, and the old fears were finally dispelled; the SPD became a real alternative to CDU government (see Table 6–3).

In the key 1969 election Chancellor Kiesinger of the CDU ran against Vice Chancellor Brandt of the SPD. Despite the fact that Kiesinger was

---

[8] The Godesberg program of the SPD is discussed in Chapter 5.

1969		1972		1976	
Percentage	Seats	Percentage	Seats	Percentage	Seats
46.1	242	44.9	225	48.6	243
42.7	224	45.8	230	42.6	214
5.8	30	8.4	41	7.9	39
5.4	0	1.0	0	0.9	0

personally more popular, the Social Democrats marked their fourth straight increase, coming within 3 percentage points of the CDU. They had increased their share of the vote from 28.8 percent to 42.7 percent in the period from 1957 to 1969—a steady gain of approximately 15 percent. The reasons for this improvement shocked the CDU. The public came to view the Social Democrats as being more competent to handle the nation's affairs, including the economy. The old notion of a CDU monopoly of economic wisdom had finally died. The growing public confidence was reflected in the fact that the SPD made important gains in white-collar and professional circles. When the Free Democrats decided to support a Brandt government, Willy Brandt became the first postwar Social Democratic chancellor.

In 1972 Brandt used a complicated parliamentary procedure to call for an early election. He wanted a mandate for his policies, particularly his Eastern policy *(Ostpolitik),* a major policy departure signaling a final break with the Adenauer era. Under Ostpolitik, West Germany renounced its claims to the lost Eastern territories and began normalizing relations with the Soviet Union and Eastern Europe through a series of bilateral treaties. This implied a renunciation of the old dream of a reunified Germany. The outcome was all that the chancellor could have wished: his party for the first time drew more votes than the CDU, and the SPD-FDP coalition gained firm control of Parliament.

The election of 1976 probably was influenced by short-term factors rather than basic party loyalties. Willy Brandt resigned in 1974 after the incredibly embarrassing revelation that a close political adviser was an East German spy. The scandal affected public confidence in the party but seemingly did not affect feelings for the new chancellor—Brandt's colleague Helmut Schmidt—who was soon widely respected. Schmidt's firm and generally conservative handling of the economy gained much support, as did his assertive foreign-policy posture that earned him the nickname "Schmidt the Lip." In 1976 Schmidt's coalition maintained a thin majority although the SPD lost seats and the CDU gained.

Electoral politics in West Germany seems to be settling into a predictable, stable pattern. West German voters are now familiar with the complicated electoral system and know how to use it. They seem to cast their votes on the basis of the performance of the governing coalition and their assessment of the competence of the opposition. Since voters are more familiar with the parties, it seems likely that party attachments are developing. Adenauer's lasting legacy seems to be the importance given to the leadership abilities of the chancellor candidates. Just as in Adenauer's era, the incumbent has a tremendous advantage over any still unproven rival.

The long-range trend in electoral behavior suggests the inevitability of true moderate two-party politics in West Germany. Though the Germans have adjusted to coalition government and use their votes with a view toward supporting or opposing a coalition, over 90 percent of the electorate still prefers one of the two big parties; and they have increased their support as the parties have moderated their views. The Free Democrats have a tenuous future caught between the 5 percent clause and proposals for a British-style electoral system. Since the Free Democrats have been unable to win a single constituency contest in some time, a "first past the post system" would lead to a two-party system in West Germany.

▪ FRANCE ▪

Electoral politics in France are changeable and unpredictable. The French have been unable to fully institutionalize and order electoral behavior at either the formal or informal levels. The formal element of electoral politics, the electoral laws, have changed three times since 1945. In each case the changes were based on partisan consideration. The actions of French voters have been just as changeable. In large part the explanation for these fluid political patterns is cultural. The French culture undermines partisan institutions and personalizes politics. Because they value individuality (discussed in Chapter 3), the French focus on the most changeable elements of electoral politics—candidate personalities and issues—rather than on party or group ties.

The election results for parliamentary and presidential elections (since 1962) clearly show the traditional instability of voting patterns. In the first 10 postwar years the electorate moved from support for the political center-left (MRP, Socialist, Communist) to the center-extreme right in 1956 (including Poujadists). In the 20 years since, they have repeated the extreme fluctuations. Often, as in the emergence of the extreme right in 1956, these electoral tides have been sudden and inexplicable.

Young French Communists campaigning for their party's leader, Georges Marchais. Diégo Goldberg, Sygma.

Since the establishment of De Gaulle's Fifth Republic, there is the appearance of more stable, rational patterns of electoral behavior. This takes the form of turning both presidential and parliamentary elections into more orderly contests between the governing parties of the center-right and the left opposition. Support for particular parties and leaders, however, seems still volatile in comparison to West Germany and Britain.

The Electoral System

Since World War II the French have employed three complex electoral systems.[9] The purpose of the systems used during the Fourth Republic (1946–1958) was to reduce the number of Communists and Gaullists in Parliament. These parties were opposed to the regime and fought against the programs offered by most cabinets during this period.

The first two postwar elections used a proportional representation sys-

---

[9] Roy Pierce, *French Politics and Political Institutions* (New York: Harper & Row, 1973), pp. 202–209.

tem. Because of the way that seats are allocated under this system (which favors the large parties), the Socialists, Communists, and Popular Republicans gained representation beyond their shares of the vote. By the "cold war" 1951 election, the Communists with their ties to the Kremlin were viewed as a threat by most established parties, as was the new Gaullist party—the Rally of the French People (RPF). In order to isolate these groups, the government parties added a provision that parties could enter into alliances in selected districts and have their total votes added together for purposes of determining the allocation of seats. Since no party woud ally with the Communists and few would deal with the anti-regime RPF, only the parties of the center who formed the cabinets of the day benefited.

One electoral system has been used since the founding of the Fifth Republic in 1958. This system—the one that was used in Third Republic France—is a single-member district "winner take all" arrangement with runoffs. A candidate receiving a majority on the first round wins the seat. If, however, there is no outright winner, the election is repeated a week later, when a plurality is sufficient for victory. The system makes it easy for parties to create either formal or informal electoral alliances. All that is required is a stipulation that whichever party's candidate fares worst in the first round will withdraw and throw his support to the candidate of allied party for the second balloting. This has been the basis of the Socialist-Communist alliance of the last 10 years.

The Fifth Republic, unlike its predecessor, has direct national elections for the presidency. The presidential elections have rules very similar to those of the parliamentary elections. The major difference is that if a majority is lacking on the first ballot, only the top two vote-getters face each other in the runoff. This ensures that the president will always have a majority mandate whether a runoff is necessary or not.

The presidential rules also suggest the necessity of inter-party cooperation. Since the extremely powerful presidential office cannot be divided, the only remaining course is for several parties to back a "sympathetic" candidate—at least in the second round. In the 1974 presidential election, for example, the Communists and Socialists agreed on François Mitterand, the Socialist leader, as their candidate from the beginning. The government parties of the center and right had no agreed-on candidate. They used the first ballot to determine their most attractive leader—who turned out to be Valéry Giscard d'Estaing rather than the Gaullist, Jacques Chaban-Delmas.

Voting Patterns

In contrast to the Germans or British, the French are striking in their absence of party ties. Therein lies the major reason for the celebrated fickleness of the French voter. Several elections during the French Fifth

Republic were marked by very large numbers of voters switching their votes from the previous election. For example, over one-third of the voters in 1962 switched from their party choice of 1958.[10] Admittedly, this is an improvement over the Fourth Republic where approximately one-half of the voters switched in the last election of that regime from their previous loyalty.

There are two major reasons cited for the failure of the French to see the political world in partisan terms. The first is cultural and social. Frenchmen simply do not discuss politics in the home and do not instill a partisan loyalty in children. The idea of party work and loyalty conflicts with important feelings about individuality and prejudices toward outside groups. The behavior of political parties and their leaders is a second major reason for the absence of party attachments. Parties do not engage in those concrete activities that help voters to choose; their programs are sketchy and are not binding on candidates. Parties do very little real campaigning and publicity work—only going through the motions with the traditional local meeting and poster campaigns. The parties have even let the basic nomination task slip away from them. Parliamentary nomination is greatly influenced by localism and the national parties have little say in who is nominated. In presidential elections the candidates nominate themselves, create their own organizations, make up their own platforms, and invite the support of the parties. In this sense it is not surprising that voters do not look for party cues, since the parties do not give very many.

In the absence of party attachments, voters count on one or more traditional French political issues to help decide their vote. The oldest is the religious issue, which has traditionally divided the political left from the right. This is of little help as a guide to behavior in the first ballot of either parliamentary or presidential elections but may be decisive once the field is narrowed. Class loyalties may act as a guide for many Frenchmen, particularly when economic issues are particularly important. Still others may be moved according to their views about the nature of communism and the motives of the Communist party. Emotional debate about the Communist party and its threat/promise has existed long enough in France to move people in their voting decisions.

A last factor in French voting deserves special mention, that of attitudes toward political personalities. Always moved by striking political figures, the French are willing to alter their political behavior accordingly. In the Fourth Republic, diverse characters such as Premier Pierre Mendès-France or Pierre Poujade, the leader of a 1956 antitax movement, could catch the public's fancy and change the nature of politics for as long as they cast their spell. While they held the public's attention, these leaders could alter political alignments and attract the support of a cross-section of both professional politicians and voters.

---

[10] William Safran, *The French Polity* (New York: McKay, 1977), p. 103.

TABLE 6–4 Recent French Parliamentary Election Results in Percentage of the Vote and Parliamentary Seats

	1962		1967	
	Percentage	Seats	Percentage	Seats
Communist Party	21.8	41	22.5	72
Socialists and Allies	12.7	65	19.0	117
Radical Socialist	7.6	43	—	—
Popular Republicans	8.9	36	—	—
Gaullists	36.3	229	37.7	232
Democratic Center	—	—	16.3	45
Others	12.7	51	4.5	4

Sources: Thomas J. Mackie and Richard Rose, The International Almanac of Electoral History (New York: The Free Press, 1974); and Facts on File.

No personality, of course, dominated contemporary French politics more than did Charles de Gaulle. For all of the Fifth Republic and at times the Fourth, many votes were cast at all levels of government according to the voter's disposition toward De Gaulle. Few Frenchmen are neutral with regard to De Gaulle's personal attributes, his vision of France, and "De Gaulle's Republic." Attitudes toward De Gaulle were most important in referendum elections, since these responded to his request for public support of his personal policies. After losing a referendum on local government reform in 1969, De Gaulle resigned, for he viewed this election as a direct expression of public dissatisfaction with his leadership. People's feelings toward De Gaulle also influenced parliamentary elections. Although his party was never as popular as the General himself, the success of Gaullist candidates clearly depended on De Gaulle. The Gaullists received 43.7 percent of the vote (over half of the parliamentary seats) in 1968 while De Gaulle was still president. In 1973 they received only 23.9 percent of the vote. Attitudes toward De Gaulle still affect voting behavior since Gaullist policies are debated even now, and the Gaullist party remains important in the governing coalition. Other personalities have become more important, however, particularly the incumbent president (Giscard), his chief rival of the left (Mitterand), and the heir of the Gaullist legacy (Chirac).

Trends and Recent Elections

The elections of 1974 and 1978 have followed simple left-right class lines corresponding to the major government and opposition forces. Since 1967 parliamentary elections have turned on a coherent left opposition

1968		1973		1978	
Percentage	Seats	Percentage	Seats	Percentage	Seats
20.0	33	23.1	73	18.2	86
16.5	57	25.8	103	28.3	103
—	—	13.5	31	2.4	10
—	—	4.0	14	24.4*	137
46.1	349	7.5	54	26.1	148
12.2	31	26.0	184		
5.1	0				

* Includes parties pledged to support Giscard d'Estaing.

challenge to Gaullist-dominated governments, and since 1965 presidential elections have featured a similar alignment of political forces. In that year Mitterand was supported by Communist, Socialist, and left-center voters, while De Gaulle attracted the rest. The most recent elections show a continuation of the trend.

The outstanding feature of the March 1973 parliamentary election was the coordination of the opposition campaign (see Table 6–4). The Socialists and Communists referred to themselves as the "Union of the Left." As in previous elections, they agreed to run independently of each other on the first ballot but to support the leading left candidate on the second ballot. Unlike some previous elections, this agreement was honored in every district. The major innovation in this campaign was the parties' pledge to a joint program—the "Common Program of Government."

The Common Program of the Union of the Left criticized the governing coalition's policies and invited comparisons with the government's programs. It favored constitutional changes to weaken presidential powers vis-à-vis the Parliament and to introduce proportional representation. The Common Program called for an end to French participation in activities related to the defense of Western Europe. It also called for unilateral nuclear disarmament. Finally, the program called for tax reforms, extensive social services, and limited nationalization of selected industries. Although programs were not particularly important to voters (37 percent mentioned the programs as a reason for their intended vote, however), they had a broader left-right choice.[11]

---

[11] Roy C. Macridis, *French Politics in Transition* (Cambridge, Mass.: Winthrop, 1975), pp. 73–79.

Leadership Profile

President of France, 1974 to Present

Leader	*Background and Education*
Valéry Giscard d'Estaing	born: 1926
	education: National School of Admin-
	istration, Ecole Poly-
	technique

The results of the election suggest that the electorate did respond to the left-right nature of the contest. In popular votes the two sides were very competitive, the party balance reflecting the closeness of recent presidential elections. Voters responded to national issues set out in the program. There were fewer regional and local deviations from the national voting pattern. Finally, class was more important in the voting decision than it has been in the postwar era. The Union of the Left support was predominantly working-class, while the governing coalition had to rely more on middle-class voters. Perhaps, then, the apparent government-opposition polarization is based on class division. Older issues and divisions that have complicated French politics may be on the wane.

The presidential election of 1974 (necessary after the death of De Gaulle's successor, Georges Pompidou) confirms the new left-right basis of voting. Quickly agreeing on a candidate, François Mitterand, the left launched a campaign based upon the Common Program. The government coalition had more difficulty settling on a leader and on the proper campaign tactics. While Mitterand campaigned against the government, the government's candidates campaigned against each other.

The first ballot showed the consistency of the left-right alignment today. Mitterand led the divided opposition with 43.2 percent of the vote (see Table 6–5), very close to the 44.1 percent the opposition of the left gained in the 1973 parliamentary elections. The group and class base of the vote was also similar to the parliamentary elections. On the second ballot Giscard got a 50.8 percent vote compared to Mitterand's 49.2 percent. Again Mitterand drew heavily from the working class, gaining over 70

Early Occupations	Political Career	
Civil servant	1958–1974	Member of Parliament (National Assembly)
Inspector of Finance	1959	Secretary of State for Finance
	1960	Minister of Finance
	1962–1966, 1969–1972, 1972–1974	Minister of Finance and Economic Affairs
	1974– present	President of France

percent of the workers' votes. His support matched very closely with the left's areas of strength in 1973.

The parliamentary elections of March 1978 confirm some of the recent trends. The vote divided almost evenly on the first ballot. The left opposition drew 13,878,573 votes and the governing parties 13,276,296. The right benefited from the traditional move toward the government on the second ballot and gained a slight majority in popular votes. They retained their parliamentary majority with a new total of 290 seats as opposed to the left's 201 seats.

The erosion of Gaullist strength continued in these most recent elections. The Gaullists lost 20 more seats—largely to party formations allied with President Giscard. This is in line with the tendency for the French to vote for leaders rather than parties. The left parties gained 17 seats, proving that the "threat" from the left is real.

French politics seems to continually evolve and adapt to circumstances without settling on a fixed form. All of the recent signs point to a new left-right alignment that follows the current division of government and opposition. The trend will probably become established if party leaders continue to stress class issues. The new alignment also depends on the weakening of old cleavages, notably the clerical and Communist/anti-Communist cleavages. The new alignment promises close competitive elections based on relatively coherent political programs, with probable alternation of the left and the right in power. If the Union of the Left can occupy positions of responsibility without realizing the gravest fears of anti-Communists, the pattern may persist.

TABLE 6–5 **Recent French Presidential Elections (in percent)**

	1965			1969			1974	
	First Ballot	Second Ballot		First Ballot	Second Ballot		First Ballot	Second Ballot
De Gaulle (Gaullists)	43.7	54.5	Pompidou (Gaullists)	44.0	57.6	Giscard (Independent Republicans)	32.6	50.8
Mitterand (Socialist)	32.2	45.5	Defferre (Socialist)	5.1		Mitterand (Socialist)	43.2	49.2
Lecanuet (Popular Republican)	15.9		Poher (Radical Socialists/ Center Democrats)	23.4	42.4	Chaban-Delmas (Gaullist)	15.1	
Tixier-Vignancour (Conservative)	5.3		Duclos (Communist)	21.5				
Others	2.9		Others	6.1		Others	9.1	

Sources: Thomas J. Mackie and Richard Rose, *The International Almanac of Electoral History* (New York: The Free Press, 1974); and *Facts on File.*

▪ THE SOVIET UNION ▪

Top national leaders in the Soviet Union are not selected in an institutionalized way. There are no agreed-on procedures to guide the contest for the top party and governmental positions; there are no universally approved "decision rules" to decide the winners and losers. In Western Europe elaborate electoral laws and parliamentary procedures are used to decide a change in leadership. In the Soviet Union leadership changes occur in an atmosphere of uncertainty and risk.

There have been only three changes of top leadership—upon Lenin's death (1924), upon Stalin's death (1953), and as a result of a revolt against Khrushchev's leadership (1964). There have been other leadership shake-ups below the level of the dominant leader, such as those associated with the purges of the 1930s and the transition from collective leadership following Stalin's death. However, the major leadership changes exemplify the methods of leadership selection in the Soviet Union. These three succession crises show that patterns of leadership selection *are* changing in the Soviet Union—becoming more regularized, predictable, and institutionalized. The earlier leadership changes engendered intramural conflict, violence, and uncertainty, but the most recent succession crisis (October 1964) was handled smoothly within the appropriate party organs.

Stalin's Rise to Power

Lenin died in 1924 before many of the institutions and principles of Soviet communism were fully developed. One principle, though, was developed and unquestioned: the top leadership—and in particular the dominant leader—defined party policy, and opposition to that policy was treasonable. Lenin made it clear that no group, including heroes of the Bolshevik revolution, had opposition rights. As a result, a portion of the trade union leadership (the workers' opposition) and democratic reformers (the Democratic Centralists) were expelled from the party for policy errors and deviant views.

This principle of leadership infallibility meant that leaders would have to emerge from the Central Committee and its specialized organs. Groups outside the leadership were automatically eliminated from consideration. The principle also meant that the succession would be determined by the maneuvering of a handful of the previous leader's protegés. Since the contest could not be public or open, tactics and strategies were not limited by public opinion or formal legalities.

The major figures of the crisis period that began within the party before Lenin's death were Stalin, Lev Kamenev, Gregory Zinoviev, and Leon Trotsky. Trotsky, by far the most compelling figure of the period, had been very close to Lenin in the critical revolutionary days and had been the leader of the Red Army. Trotsky's brilliance and his diverse following made him the major target in Stalin's bid for power. Stalin formed a triumvirate with the other two rivals and used them to deliver blows against Trotsky, finally eliminating him from his various positions of power.

Stalin promoted his own power by gaining control of the party machinery, or apparatus, as he quickly realized its potential for control. He also began lining up allies against Kamenev and Zinoviev, among them the ill-fated Nikolai Bukharin. Stalin used his former collaborators' strident attacks on Trotsky as being evidence of "left deviation." As Stalin's strength became apparent, the old members of the triumvirate began to confess their errors publicly, and no longer figured in the game.

Once Stalin eliminated the "left deviationists," he began to commit himself to some of their pet projects—notably the collectivization of agriculture.[12] When Bukharin and other members of the Politburo ob-

---

[12] Samuel H. Beer, Adam B. Ulum, Suzanne Berger, and Guido Goldman, *Patterns of Government* (New York: Random House, 1974), pp. 699–705.

jected, they were promptly accused of "right deviation" and systematically removed. Thus Stalin used his party power base and his remarkable
skills at bureaucratic infighting to eliminate all major rivals.

Stalin's takeover was not a violent or bloody one. Most of the "deviant"
leaders simply lost their positions and their party membership. Once
Stalin consolidated his power, however, he systematically eliminated his
old rivals. In the 1930s Zinoviev, Kamenev, and Bukharin were sentenced
to death after public trials in which they confessed their crimes and
errors. Most of the immediate post-Lenin leadership met similar fates with
or without trial.

Stalin set several precedents for leaders. He concentrated on control of
the party apparatus—that portion of the party responsible mainly for recruitment and administrative supervision. Thus he could influence important personnel decisions, line up faithful supporters, and monitor party
and government actions. Stalin also mobilized mistrust and resentment
against rivals and played one group against another. He created subgroups
of the leadership for his own purposes and then denounced them as
treasonable factions.

Khrushchev's Consolidation of Power

Stalin died in 1953 in the midst of plans to rearrange the party leadership
and perhaps to launch a new major purge. The Nineteenth Party Congress
(the first since 1939) had met the year before to double the size of the
Politburo, renaming it the Presidium of the Central Committee. The en-
larged party organ was packed with younger leaders who presumably
would edge out their elders with Stalin's help. The pretext for a purge was
laid by the revelation of a "doctor's plot" in January 1953. (Some prominent doctors were charged with the attempted assassination of leading
party and army figures.)

The death of Stalin pre-empted the purge, and set off a struggle for the
top leadership positions. A leading candidate was Georgi Malenkov, who
had delivered the primary address at the Nineteenth Party Congress.
Malenkov was a member of the Politburo, the Secretariat, and the Council
of Ministers. He had been the second-ranking member of the important
wartime State Defense Committee. The second contender was Lavrenti
Beria, whose power rested on his control of Stalin's secret police. Stalin
had used Beria, by all accounts a truly sadistic person, to instill fear in the
party elite. Beria's strength and, ironically, his weakness derived from his
well-deserved reputation for bloodthirstiness. If the rival leaders feared
Beria, they also could easily agree to the necessity of eliminating him. The
third candidate, Nikita Khrushchev, was First Secretary of the Ukrainian
party organization until brought to Moscow by Stalin to counterbalance
Malenkov in 1949. His national role was established by his membership
in the Politburo dating from 1939. Khrushchev was also a member of the
Secretariat, a position he would use to great effect.

None of the three rivals could immediately consolidate power. The leadership described itself as "collective," and the prominent men divided up the key positions. Malenkov was named the new chairman of the Council of Ministers and therefore established himself as leader of the state institutions. Malenkov was forced to resign from the party's Secretariat on the grounds that holding key party and state positions violated the new collective principle. This left Khrushchev as the leading figure on the Secretariat, although officially there would be no "General Secretary" or "First Secretary" named.

Beria was soon eliminated from the contest. He clumsily attempted to fill key positions with his men in a way that threatened the collective leadership. Charged with an assortment of crimes that amounted to treason, Beria was tried and executed by the end of 1953.

Malenkov and Khrushchev began to compete by making policy statements touching on the interests of important social and economic groups. Khrushchev became associated with a call for sweeping agricultural reforms. He emphasized the development of wilderness or "virgin lands," fertilizer production, and increased farm technology. Malenkov became associated with a program to redirect investment from heavy industry to consumer and luxury goods. Khrushchev's policies were popular with the party apparatus (particularly the provincial apparatus where Khrushchev had his political roots) and the army. Malenkov appealed to middle-class groups, notably state bureaucrats.

By 1955 the issue was largely settled. A Politburo (then Presidium) majority forced Malenkov to resign from the chairmanship of the Council of Ministers because of the error of his consumer goods policy. A last challenge to Khrushchev's leadership was put down in 1957. In the midst of an economic crisis Malenkov put together a majority of the Politburo to oppose Khrushchev's industrial reorganization plans designed to deal with the crisis. This anti-Khrushchev majority tried to force his resignation, but Khrushchev saved himself by demanding a meeting of the Central Committee. Khrushchev's broad strength within the more representative Central Committee not only preserved his position but also removed the "anti-party group" led by Malenkov.

Khrushchev's consolidation of power was more institutionalized and less violent than Stalin's. Khrushchev referred the dispute to the Central Committee, which in effect acted as the party's representative body. Both sides abided by the decision, and no violence was necessary. The only political execution of the 1953–1957 period was that of the hated Beria.

Khrushchev's Removal

In the years following his consolidation of power, Khrushchev faced strong, if not public, criticism of his policies—which by 1964 had produced a series of prominent failures. His gamble on placing missiles in Cuba proved to be an undying embarrassment. The lack of agricultural

Leadership Profiles

The Top Soviet Leaders

Leader	Background and Education	
Leonid Brezhnev First Secretary of the Communist Party of the Soviet Union	born: education:	1906 Secondary School for Land Organization and Land Reclamation Dnieprodzerzhinsk Metallurgical Institute
Alexi Kosygin Chairman of the Soviet Council of Ministers	born: education:	1904 Leningrad Co-op Technical School Leningrad Textile Institute

---

progress also damaged his prestige; when the 1963 grain crop failed, the Soviet Union was forced to buy from the West. Apparently unaware of the depth of his political problems, Khrushchev tried to launch a new set of economic reforms, even touring extensively to promote his program. On October 2, 1964, he made a strong speech in favor of consumer goods production—his first public endorsement of this course of action.

In October 1964 Khrushchev was removed by a nearly unanimous vote of the Politburo. It was apparently a widely shared view that his leadership was bankrupt, and the Central Committee merely ratified the Politburo decision on October 14, 1964.

Khrushchev's successors were largely his protegés. The new chairman of the Council of Ministers, Alexei Kosygin, benefited from Khrushchev's interest in his career. The new First Secretary, Leonid Brezhnev, had been close to Khrushchev and shared his Ukrainian political roots. The aging Khrushchev went quietly (not even his reputation was unduly damaged) into retirement. Apparently the main grounds for his removal was the

Early Occupations and Political Career

Land surveyor, engineer

1941–1945	Political cadre in Army
1946–1947	First Secretary, regional area party
1950–1952	Central Committee, Communist Party of Moldavia
1952	Elected Member of the CPSU Central Committee
1952–1953	Secretary of CPSU Central Committee
1957–present	Member of Politburo
1964–present	First Secretary, Communist Party of the Soviet Union

Foreman and superintendent in textile mills

1938	Head of Department, Leningrad Regional Committee of CPSU
1940–1946	People's Commissar for Textile Industries
1946–1964	Deputy Chairman, Council of Ministers
1953	Minister of Light Industry and Food
1953–1954	Minister of Consumer Goods Industry
1957	First Deputy Chairman, State Planning Committee
1959–1960	Chairman, State Planning Committee
1964–present	Chairman, Council of Ministers

belief that the secondary leaders could perform the leadership functions more efficiently.

The selection of leadership in the Soviet Union remains uncertain and unpredictable. The timing and means of changing leaders is never known in advance. Powerful men conduct the process largely behind the scenes. It is difficult for even honest policy-related differences among the top leaders to be discussed and handled without raising the specter of a challenge to existing authorities.

Changes in selection procedures since Stalin's day, however, suggest the development of some informal "rules" that limit violence, uncertainty, and ambiguity. First of all, the Central Committee has the potential to settle disputes among factions in the Politburo. Khrushchev set the important precedents, particularly in 1957, that justify this Central Committee function. Further, if a First Secretary's failures are obvious and belief in the need for a change is widespread, the Politburo may remove him without the necessity of charging criminal conduct. The ability of the Politburo

Leonid Brezhnev, First Secretary of the Communist party of the Soviet Union, addresses the sixteenth Congress of Soviet Trade Unions. Novosti Press Agency (A.P.N.)

and the Central Committee to remove a leader implies the ultimate power of the important groups represented in these bodies. This precedent is essential if leadership selection in the Soviet Union is to become even more institutionalized in the future.

■ NIGERIA ■

Nigeria's brief experiment with electoral politics was stormy. Participants and politicians fought for political power in a series of hotly contested elections. National elections in 1959 and 1964 and the 1965 Western regional election sharply divided the nation and magnified the differences separating groups, regions, and political opinions. Politicians scrambled to ensure that their political party received its fair share of political power and the spoils of office.

In many ways elections symbolize the fractionalized nature of Nigerian politics from 1960 to 1966. The lack of established electoral traditions and the inability of politicians and voters to agree on a set of political rules of the game led to long periods of political instability. The end result, instead of the reform of the electoral system suggested by many, was the end of electoral politics altogether.

Since 1966 new ways of selecting leaders have emerged. Although many of the politicians and civil servants associated with the parliamentary period continue to exert influence on the military government, military officers are now the dominant political decision-makers. The projected return to civilian rule in 1979 will undoubtedly reintroduce "politics" into Nigerian political life, and create a central place of importance for elections. The ultimate question concerning this transition must be: Can leaders be chosen by elections without the divisiveness and bitterness that characterized the 1960–1966 period?

Nigerian Elections—1959–1966

As Nigerians approached independence, there was little doubt or disagreement among them that the outcome of elections would be crucial in determining the nation's political future. The "Westminster model" that established the National Assembly was based on political parties freely and honestly competing in elections. Members to the National Assembly were elected from 312 single-member districts throughout Nigeria. With the exception of the Northern Region, where women did not have the vote, all adults were entitled to vote.

Political power rested in the House of Assembly, modeled on the British House of Commons. The party that won the most seats was most likely the party that would name the prime minister and form the government. But political practices so well established and institutionalized in Britain were strange and untested in Nigeria. (Colonialism as an administrative system did not encourage political participation.)

The first real test of the new system was the parliamentary election held just before independence in 1959. This election—at a time of hope and apprehension—determined the government responsible for taking over from the British. In almost all respects the election results indicated the sharp divisions within Nigerian society; the distribution of the vote served as a warning for the future. As expected, the strong regional bases of the three major parties provided them with stable electoral support. In effect, there were three strong regional parties, each with intense but narrow bases of support, but no national parties that appealed to all Nigerians, regardless of region, ethnicity, or language.

The Northern People's Congress won 134 out of a possible 174 Northern Region seats. They won no seats outside of the North. The National Council of Nigerian Citizens (NCNC) won, with its affiliated parties, 89 seats most of which were either in the East (58 seats) or the West (21 seats).

TABLE 6–6 Distribution of Seats in the Nigerian House of Assembly, Based on the 1959 and 1964 Federal Election Results

	North	West	East	Mid-West	Lagos	Totals
Northern People's	134 (1959)a	—	—	b	—	134
Congress	162 (1964)	—	—	—	—	162
National Council of	8	21	58		2	89
Nigerian Citizens	—	5	64	14	1	84
Action Group	25	33	14		1	73
	—	15	4	—	2	21
Nigerian National Democratic Partyc	— (1964)	36	—	—	—	36
Others	7	8	1		—	16
	5	1	2	1	—	9

Sources: K. W. J. Post, *The Nigerian Federal Election of 1959* (London: Oxford University Press, 1963), p. 373; and K. W. J. Post and Michael Vickers, *Structure and Conflict in Nigeria,* 1960–1965 (Madison: University of Wisconsin Press, 1973), p 213.

a Top figure in each cell is the 1959 return; bottom figure is the 1964 return.

b The Mid-West Region was not created until 1963 and hence there are no 1959 election returns for the Region.

c The Nigerian National Democratic party was not created until 1962 and hence there are no 1959 election returns.

The party of the West, the Action Group (AG), won 73 seats; 33 were in the West and 25 in the North, mainly in minority group areas.[13] (See Table 6–6.)

The NPC won a clear plurality, but not a majority, of seats in the House of Assembly. After much discussion the NCNC, led by Dr. Nnamdi Azikiwe, and the NPC, led by the Sardauna of Sokoto and Sir Abubakar Tafawa Balewa, agreed to form a coalition. Balewa as the leader of the NPC parliamentary group became the first Nigerian prime minister, and Dr. Azikiwe became first the governor general of Nigeria and then, following independence, the first president of Nigeria. Chief Awolowo and his Action Group formed the first "loyal opposition."

Though the next national elections were scheduled for 1964, politics never stopped in Nigeria. The coalition between the NPC and the NCNC was one of convenience, not ideological affinity. Conflict occurred between the head of government, Balewa, and the head of state, Azikiwe.

[13] K. W. J. Post, *The Nigerian Federal Election of 1959* (London: Oxford University Press, 1963), p. 373.

Sharp disagreements arose over the executive powers of the president versus the power of the prime minister, over the power of the national government versus the regional governments, over the treatment of minorities, and over the creation of new regions. The arrest, trial, conviction, and imprisonment of Chief Awolowo in 1963 for plotting treason against the federal government further inflamed the situation. Finally, the 1963 census, which was to be used as the foundation for apportioning the 1964 Parliament, showed a marked increase in the population of the Northern Region. The new figures indicated that more than 50 percent of the population now lived in the North. Western and Eastern politicians feared becoming a permanent parliamentary minority.

These fears and problems were crystalized and sharpened by the 1964 election. Rather than resolving conflict, the election magnified the divisions within Nigeria. Two grand coalitions emerged to fight the election. The Nigerian National Alliance (NNA) was composed of the NPC and the newly formed Nigerian National Democratic party (NNDP) from the West. The NNDP was led by the premier of the Western Region and former AG member Chief Samuel Akintola. The United Progressive Grand Alliance (UPGA) consisted of the NCNC (the former coalition partner of the NPC), the Action Group (the former opposition party), and the Northern Elements Progressive Union (the opposition party in the North).

After a confusing, bitter campaign, part of the UPGA coalition decided to boycott the election, which necessitated holding a "little election" in certain districts in 1965. The final outcome of the election again showed how strong the NPC was in the North, where they won 162 out of 167 seats. The NNDP won 36 seats in the West, giving the Nigerian National Alliance 198 seats, 42 more than the 156 needed for a majority.[14] The divisiveness of the election threatened the entire system and brought on the threat of military intervention. After much discussion, Balewa and Azikiwe agreed to form a larger coalition by inviting certain members of the NCNC to join the government's coalition. The coalition proved fragile and unstable.

One final election sealed the fate of the parliamentary regime. The peace agreed to by Balewa and Azikiwe after the 1964 elections preserved some semblance of order at the national level. The 1965 regional election in the West, however, indicated just how far the corruption and electoral foul play in Nigeria had gone. The contest was between the Nigerian National Democratic party led by Akintola (the premier) and the Action Group (still loyal to the imprisoned Awolowo). The prize was control of the Western Region.

The election featured corruption and thuggery: individuals were pre-

---

[14] K. W. J. Post and Michael Vickers, *Structure and Conflict in Nigeria, 1960–1965* (Madison: University of Wisconsin Press, 1973), p. 213.

vented from standing for office, candidates and voters were beaten by rival gangs, and still other candidates were defeated by widespread vote fraud. The disputes between Chief Awolowo and Chief Akintola, and between the AG and the NNDP, were bitter. For example, a melee in the West's Assembly in 1962 came about as follows:

> ... after prayers, as Chief Odebiyi rose to move the first motion, Mr. E. O. Oke, a supporter of Chief Akintola, jumped on the table shouting "There is a fire on the mountain." He proceeded to fling chairs about the chamber. Mr. E. Ebubedike, also a supporter of Chief Akintola, seized the mace, attempted to club the Speaker with it but missed and broke the mace on the table. The supporters of Alhaji Adegbenro sat quiet as they had been instructed to do, with the exception of one member who was hit with a chair and retaliated. Mr. Akinyemi (NCNC) and Messrs. Adigun and Adeniya (pro-Akintola) continued to throw chairs, the opposition joined in and there was such disorder that the Nigerian Police released teargas and cleared the House.[15]

It is not surprising that the victory of the NNDP and Chief Akintola was accepted as legitimate by few other than the most ardent NNDP party stalwarts. One observer described the significance of the 1965 Western election:

> I had an uneasy and perhaps unwarranted premonition that here, among all Chief Awolowo's legal books, by flickering candlelight, was being enacted the funeral rites of the Westminster model as a practical proposition in African politics.[16]

New Avenues of Recruitment—The Military

The death of the parliamentary regime and the Westminster model was not long in coming. In January 1966 the military took over, banning political parties and all party activity. Most observers felt that the electoral period had degenerated into little more than a corrupt contest for the spoils of office. Both the legitimacy and the authority of the politicians and the political system itself were called into question. Although the new military leaders were not well known to the general public, many expressed the opinion that they could do no worse than the politicians.

Military government produced administrative and political changes; one of the most important changes was the fact that soldiers were now ultimately responsible for exercising political power. The early pronouncements of the officers indicated that they viewed their political role as a temporary one. They sought to restore order and honest government, hand

---

[15] John P. Mackintosh, *Nigerian Government and Politics* (Evanston, Ill.: Northwestern University Press, 1966), p. 448.
[16] As cited in Post and Vickers, *Structure and Conflict in Nigeria*, p. 229.

power to new civilian leaders, and then to return to the barracks. But, as is often the case, the military leaders found themselves more and more responsible for making decisions and less and less able to return power to civilian leaders. In a short period of time they moved from the periphery of politics to the center. The army provided order and controlled the administrative apparatus of the government. By their own admission, however, it was a job they were not trained for, since the life of the soldier was considerably different from that of the politician.

The Nigerian army, at the time of intervention, was not a political organization, it considered itself to be primarily a military organization. In 1960 it had only about 7,500 men and an officer corps that was three-quarters British; by 1966 it had grown to about 10,000 men with an officer corps that was entirely Nigerian. The army fought in the Congo crisis in the early 1960s and later helped to train the reconstituted Tanzanian armed forces. They had no experience, however, in running a government.

Most of the senior Nigerian officers during this period received their military training and much of their advanced education during the colonial period. Many went to the British military academy, Sandhurst, learning not only military tactics and strategy but also the political values associated with the British military—among them the importance of being "non-political" officers. The officer's duty was to defend and protect Nigeria, not to become involved in the political quarrels and issues of the day. The officer was a military man, not a politician.

These values were deeply ingrained in most Nigerian officers, who, from different regions and backgrounds, held in common the duty of serving in a national institution. They were "brother officers" rather than being Ibo, Hausa, or Yoruba officers. The crises and conflicts that characterized Nigeria from 1960 to 1966, however, made it difficult to maintain these beliefs. By the time that the military intervened in January 1966, it was clear to some that many of the divisions that separated civilian leaders now also separated officers.

Two related problems faced the newly powerful officers. The first was the lack of administrative expertise in the military. Since it was a military, not a political, organization the new leaders were forced to rely on the civilian civil service and many of the old political elite to provide the administrative know-how for the day-to-day operation of the government. This produced in Nigeria a mixed civilian-military government. The senior officers and their selected civilian advisers make the decisions, which are then carried out by a civil service and bureaucracy that is largely civilian. In many cases civilian politicians, like Chief Awolowo, were recalled from imprisonment to play important roles in the military government.

A second problem, and more serious, was the threatened collapse of the military and of Nigeria itself. The culmination of these crises was the civil war that split both the military and the nation. The army grew in size

Nigerian Heads of Government, 1960 to present

Leader	Background and Education		Early Occupations
Sir Abubakar Tafawa Balewa Prime Minister of the Federal Republic of Nigeria, 1960–1966	born: died: education: ethnicity:	1912 January 1966 Katsina College, Katsina, Nigeria London School of Economics Hausa	Politician; founding member of the Northern People's Congress; teacher
Major General Johnson Aguiyi-Ironsi Head of the Federal Military Government, January–July 1966	born: died: education: ethnicity:	c. 1925 July 1966 School of Infantry (England) Ibo	Soldier
General Yakubu Gowon Head of the Federal Military Government, August 1966–July 1975	born: education: ethnicity:	1934 Government College, Zaria, Nigeria Sandhurst Military Academy (England) Angas (Plateau cluster)	Soldier
General Murtala Mohammed Head of the Federal Military Government, July 1975–January 1976	born: died: education: ethnicity:	1937 1976 Government College, Zaria, Nigeria Sandhurst Military Academy (England) Royal School of Signals (England) Hausa-Fulani	Soldier
General Olusegun Obasanjo Head of the Federal Military Government, January 1976 to present	born: education: ethnicity:	1937 Baptist High School, Abeokuta, Nigeria Mons Officer Cadets School (England) Yoruba	Soldier, engineer

from 10,000 to over 250,000 men in less than two years. The officer corps grew rapidly to meet the wartime needs of the federal government. In turn, rapid growth made efficient, corruption-free administration difficult.

Leadership at the top in Nigeria has shifted several times since the first military coup. Contending factions within the officer corps have sought to gain control at the expense of their fellow officers. For example, the leaders of the first coup d'état were primarily Ibos, who selected as their leader another Ibo officer, Major General Johnson Aguiyi-Ironsi. Tragically, for Nigeria, many of those who were killed in this first coup were of northern origin. In addition to several senior officers from the North who were killed, the prime minister and premier of the Northern and Western Regions (Ahmadu Bello and Chief Akintola) also were killed. From the perspective of many in the North, the coup was an Ibo one carried against the North.

In July 1966 a counter-coup within the military resulted in the killing of General Ironsi and several other Ibo officers. The new leaders, primarily of northern origin, chose as their leader a relatively young and "neutral" officer, Colonel Yakubu Gowon. From the perspective of many Ibos this was a northern coup carried out against the East. As a compromise candidate Colonel (soon to be General) Gowon illustrates the complex "ethnic arithmetic" that characterizes Nigerian politics. General Gowon was from the North, but was not Hausa-Fulani, nor was he Muslim. He was a Christian member of a small minority group, the Angas. This tended to make him more acceptable to more groups; he was a compromise selection.

General Gowon held power from July 1966 until his overthrow in July 1975. In a nonviolent coup General Gowon was replaced by General Murtala Mohammed—a Muslim and a member of the Hausa-Fulani aristocracy. General Mohammed, like most of his predecessors, attempted to maintain the delicate balance between contending groups. His immediate staff included fellow officers and civilians from all of Nigeria's major ethnic groups.

In January 1976 a fourth coup was attempted. Although the coup failed, General Mohammed was killed. General Olusegun Obasanjo, second in command to General Mohammed, became the new head of state. General Obasanjo, the first Yoruba to lead Nigeria, has continued many of the policies initiated by General Mohammed. Among the most notable and important of these are the development of plans for the return to civilian rule and the establishment of new civilian political institutions and structures.

Leadership selection in Nigeria is closely related to Nigeria's complex ethnic picture. Whether military or civilian, all governments and regimes must face the importance of ethnicity in politics and leadership choice. Conflict was not resolved during the elections of the civilian period, but made more pronounced and severe. Elections magnified the importance of ethnicity as a factor in leadership selection.

Prior to their intervention military officers remained largely aloof from politics and viewed themselves as members of a national institution. Once in power, however, they too found themselves violently involved in playing ethnic politics. Especially since the end of the civil war in 1970 and the reunification of the nation, military leaders have been careful to maintain a balance between contending groups and to ensure that no one group becomes either too powerful or too weak.

Leadership selection is one of the most severe crises facing Nigerian political actors and participants. Several patterns of selection have developed since independence, but none has proved successful. Elections led to political disintegration, while the military period is characterized by numerous coups d'état within the army. In a political system as fragmented as Nigeria's, selecting political actors who will hold political power is an extremely sensitive issue.

▪ EGYPT ▪

Both soldiers and civilians have played important leadership roles in post–1952 Egypt. Whether military officers or civilian politicians are dominant tends to change as the economic, social, and political conditions in Egypt change, and as the goals of the top leadership—primarily Presidents Nasser and Sadat—evolve.

Traditionally Egyptian recruitment patterns have been based on a patron-client relationship. Individuals in lower positions attach themselves as clients to patrons in higher positions. As a result, a complex network of relationships is created, which, though not permanent or institutionalized, wields considerable political power. From 1954 until 1970 President Nasser's personal power was so great that the advance of an individual or group—whether civilian or military—depended on finding favor with the president.

A second characteristic of leadership selection is the ever-increasing need for administrative and technical experts to guide the industrialization and modernization of the Egyptian economy. Often civilian experts must implement and enforce the decisions made by military or former military officers. Not surprisingly, this situation provides the potential for conflict between decision-makers and decision-enforcers.

In the recent past key decision-makers have tended to be found in four groups: the military, the cabinet, the National Assembly, and the Arab Socialist Union. The military has been an important channel for recruiting people into the cabinet and other policy-making bodies. In addition, the military is a powerful institution in itself. The cabinet has been the most important institution for formulating and administering policy, while the

President Sadat and former Soviet President Nikolai Podgorny at President Nasser's grave. Camera Press, Ltd.

National Assembly has been the national legislative institution. The Arab Socialist Union (described in Chapter 5) has been the primary organization for directing and encouraging political participation. What emerges in Egypt is a balance between the need for military power and authority and the need for civilian participation and expertise. The following sections examine recruitment to the cabinet, the Arab Socialist Union, and the National Assembly, paying particular attention to the balance between civilians and soldiers.

The Cabinet—Key Decision-Makers

The core of political power in post-1952 Egypt is the original group of 11 Free Officers who carried out the coup against King Farouk and the old guard. All were born between 1917 and 1922. Nine were in the same class at the military academy and graduated together in 1938; another graduated in 1939, and the last in 1940. This gave them in the early years a unity of outlook and purpose. Joining the inner circle of Free Officers later were 11 more officers. These 22 men became Egypt's most important decision-

The Eleven Founders of the Free Officer Movement, 1949

Name	Born/Died	Rank in 1949	Year Grad from Milit Academ
Gamal Abdul Nasser	1915–1970	Lt. Colonel	1938
Anwar Sadat	1918	Lt. Colonel	1938
Abdul Hakim Amer	1919–1967	Major	1938
Zakariyya Muhieddin	1918	Lt. Colonel	1938
Hasan Ibrahim	1917	Sqd. Leader	1939
Khaled Muhieddin	1922	Major	1940
Salah Salem	1920–1962	Major	1938
Husein Safei	1918	Lt. Colonel	1938
Gamal Salem	1918	Wing Commander	1938
Abdel Latif al–Boghdadi	1917	Wing Commander	1938
Kamal al–Din Husein	1921	Major	1939

Source: Adapted from P. J. Vatikiotis, The Egyptian Army in Politics (Bloomington: Indiana University Press, 1961), pp. 48–49. Reprinted by permission.

makers and political leaders. Presidents Nasser and Sadat were members of this inner circle.[17]

Once the power of the military and the Free Officers was consolidated, their presence in the cabinet became regularized. Between 1952 and 1968 out of 131 individuals in various Egyptian cabinets, 44 were military officers. About 34 percent of the cabinet were either military men or military

[17] Shahrough Akhavi, "Egypt: Neo-Patrimonial Elite," in Frank Tachau, ed., Political Elites and Political Development in the Middle East (Cambridge, Mass.: Schenkman, 1975), pp. 87–88.

Major Government Positions Held

Deputy Prime Minister and Minister of Interior (1953–1954); Prime Minister (1954–1956); President of Egypt (1956–1970)

Minister of State (1954–1956); Secretary-General, National Union (1957–1961); Vice Chairman, National Assembly (1957–1964); Vice President of Egypt (1964–1966, 1969–1970); Chairman, National Assembly (1964–1969); President of Egypt (1970–   )

Commander-in-Chief, Armed Forces (1952–1967); Minister of War (1954); Vice President (1958)

Minister of Interior (1953–1964); Vice President, U.A.R. (1961); Deputy President (1964–1965); Prime Minister (1965–1966); Deputy Prime Minister (1967–1968)

Minister for Presidency and Production (1954–1956); President Economic Development Organization (1957–1959); Presidential Council (1962–1964): Vice President (1964–1966); Ambassador (1967)

Only Communist member of Free Officers; supported Neguib over Nasser; exiled to Switzerland; returned to become newspaper editor (1956–1959); elected to National Assembly (1964); opposition leader

Fell from grace during the 1950s

Minister of War and Marine (1954); Minister of Social Affairs (1958–1961); Presidential Council (1962–1964); Deputy Prime Minister (1967–1970); Vice President (1970–1974)

Fell from grace during the 1950s

Fell from grace during the 1950s

Fell from grace during the 1950s

men with specialized expertise.[18] The presence or absence of military men varied with specific situations. During periods of crisis such as the June 1967 defeat when the army was discredited, the percentage of military men decreased. During the 1961 crisis between Egypt and Syria over the United Arab Republic union, and just before the 1967 war, the percentage of military men in the cabinet increased.

The general characteristics of the cabinet members provide a clue to the

[18] R. Hrair Dekmejian, *Egypt Under Nasir* (Albany: State University of New York Press, 1971), p. 171.

type of individuals recruited to power in Egypt. They were fairly young men: the average age for entering the cabinet was 47; the average age for leaving it was 52. Military men tended to spend more time in the cabinet than did civilians. The average tenure in office for soldiers was about five years, while for civilians it was just over three years.[19]

The educational level of cabinet members, as would be expected, is much higher than that of the average Egyptian. What is startling, however, is just how high that educational level is. Among the same 131 cabinet members, 62, or about half, had either a medical degree or a Ph.D., 22 percent held a master's degree, and 29 percent held a bachelor's degree. In terms of occupation the most common professions were (in this order) the military, academia, engineering, law, the ministerial bureaucracy, and business/professional groups.[20]

Occupations of 1968–1972 cabinet members were both similar and different from earlier cabinet members'. Thirty-one percent were from the military, while 25 percent came from academia. The sharpest drop proportionately were the engineering and law professions. (The number of cabinet members with engineering backgrounds dropped from about 15 percent to 1 percent, and those in law from 13 percent to 6 percent.) Bureaucrats were more represented in the later cabinets than in the early ones.[21]

While the presence of the military was strongly felt at the highest cabinet level, civilians dominated the bureaucracy just beneath the top. Although as the military power became entrenched the number of officers with specialized skills rapidly increased, there were never enough officers to fill the huge bureaucracy and civil service.

The political power of the cabinet, both potential and actual, is great. Cabinets vary in size and have included as many as 44 members. The average size is usually 30. These men close to the president are well educated, well trained, and politically powerful. In a personalized system such as Egypt's, many of these actors increase their influence by developing client relations with individuals up and down the political and administrative ladders. Any discussion of the power elite must focus on the cabinet members both individually and as a group and with their relationships to the president.

The Arab Socialist Union—Political Avenues of Recruitment

While the power of the cabinet is great, it is only one of the centers of power in Egyptian politics. Another important one is the Arab Socialist Union. Although the party is no longer the sole political party in President Sadat's Egypt, its importance remains considerable. Many of the politicians

---

[19] Ibid., p. 179.
[20] Ibid., p. 200.
[21] Akhavi, "Egypt: Neo-Patrimonial Elite," p. 92.

that currently are forming new parties and platforms have risen through the ranks of the ASU.

The Arab Socialist Union is responsible for encouraging and guiding the political participation of the masses. As such it seeks to represent peasants and workers and provide them with a voice in the decision-making process. Party laws call for the representation of peasants and workers at all levels of the party—from local to national. From the mid-1960s to the mid-1970s the ASU also was responsible for providing candidates for the National Assembly and for providing a forum for debating the broad political issues of the day. President Nasser, for example, often used the ASU as a sounding board for new political ideas.

The composition of the most important political structures of the party varies. The 1968 National Congress of the ASU had 859 peasants (281) and workers (578) out of a total attendance of 1,648.[22] (By party law half of its Congress must be either workers or peasants.) Other delegates were academics, professionals, managers, lawyers, doctors, students, and property owners who met certain requirements. One aim of the Congress is to achieve as broad a cross-section of Egyptian groups as possible.

Perhaps more important than the party's Congress in terms of political power are its Central Committee, the General Secretariat, and the Supreme Executive of the ASU. At these levels individuals may have greater influence on decision-makers, and in some cases, may even take part in the decision-making process. The Central Committee, for example, has 150 full members and 50 alternate members. An analysis of the 1968 Central Committee reveals that workers and peasants again made up about 50 percent of the organization's membership. Workers and peasants of all types (including many who worked for worker syndicates and larger farm operations) comprised about 20 percent and 30 percent of the full members of the Central Committee respectively. Strongly represented on the committee were party regulars, deputies in the National Assembly, government ministers, and academics.[23]

At the higher levels of the party, the General Secretariat and the Supreme Executive Council, the presence of peasants and workers is much less noticeable. From 1962 to 1971 a total of 54 persons served in the General Secretariat of the party. Of these, 22, or roughly 41 percent, were military men. This figure is somewhat deceptive, however, when the military presence is studied year by year. In 1971, for example, military officers were ousted from the General Secretariat following an attempted coup d'état against President Sadat. Many of the officers were implicated in the plot. From 1962 to 1970 the military membership had varied from a low of 43 percent in 1970 to a high of 75 percent in 1962.[24] In the smaller Supreme

[22] Dekmejian, *Egypt Under Nasir,* p. 273.
[23] Ibid., p. 278.
[24] Akhavi, "Egypt: Neo-Patrimonial Elite," p. 89.

Executive Council, the eight members who were elected by a majority vote of the Central Committee in 1968 were divided evenly between military men and civilians. Of the 20 candidates who stood for office there were more civilians than officers; included were academics, political leaders, government ministers, and certain workers.[25]

As in all party bodies during this period the dominant actor was President Nasser. Besides possessing the most powerful personality, he had considerable powers of appointment and held the highest positions in most party councils. President Sadat has sought, in his own way, to maintain his personal power. This requires delicately balancing the power of the different institutions of government, as well as controlling those who occupy positions of influence.

Ali Sabri, one of Egypt's most durable, controversial politicians, has tried many times to use his ASU position to increase his power. He has had successes and failures, often falling from grace only to rise to power soon after. In 1971 he and several supporters challenged President Sadat's authority. The issue was the proposed merger of Egypt, Libya, and Syria; the arena of the challenge was the Supreme Executive Committee of the ASU, to which both Sabri and Sadat belonged. Sabri lost, was tried for subversion, and was imprisoned. President Sadat effectively outmaneuvered his opponents and protected his position.

The National Assembly—Selecting Legislative Actors

The National or People's Assembly is Egypt's national legislative body. In 1969 350 deputies were elected. Fully 73 percent of the new members had not served in the old Assembly. In this large turnover from the 1964 National Assembly, only 92 former members were returned to office. This change included those who decided not to run for office, those who ran but were defeated, and those who were prohibited from running because of new financial restrictions on members.[26]

The 1969 election results also indicated change in the composition of the National Assembly. Whereas in 1964 the number of peasant representatives outnumbered the number of worker representatives by 108 to 74, in 1969 the figures were reversed and workers outnumbered peasants by 119 to 64. Overall, peasants and workers comprised 53 percent of the new Assembly. This trend parallels trends in other institutions during the same period. Also, 23 members were elected to the Assembly as independents running without the backing of the ASU. These members provided a core of independent members.[27]

---

[25] Dekmejian, *Egypt Under Nasir,* p. 280.

[26] Ibid., pp. 284–285.

[27] Ibid.

Results of the 1976 elections are not strictly comparable with other elections. In this Assembly election candidates stood representing platforms, and not just under the ASU banner. What the results do indicate is that the center platform—fully 80 percent of the new members—overwhelmingly won over the platforms of the left and the right.

The paths to leadership positions in Egypt have been changing constantly since the 1952 coup. While certain paths to power appear more successful and longer lasting than others, none is permanent or guarantees success. The towering presence of President Nasser for 18 years deeply influenced the development of Egyptian institutions and attitudes. The bureaucracy, the National Assembly, the Arab Socialist Union, the cabinet, and the military have all been through periods of declining influence; at other times, however, each of these institutions has been on the ascendant with dramatically increased power. The institutions themselves endure, while their roles and importance change. Success today in Egyptian politics never guarantees success tomorrow, just as failure today does not necessarily mean permanent removal from the political game.

▪ TANZANIA ▪

Previous chapters documented the dominance of the Tanzanian African National Union in Tanzanian politics. Chapter 4 described how political participation is channeled through the party and how various interest groups are incorporated under the party umbrella. Chapter 5 described the organization of the party and outlined the goals of the party in a one-party state.

Not surprisingly, the party is also an important agent for recruiting Tanzanians to positions of political importance. Normally two-party or multi-party systems are associated with elections—competing parties offer opposing platforms and candidates for the voters' approval. Until 1963 Tanzania was considered a multi-party system, although TANU clearly was the electorate's overwhelming favorite. After 1963, Tanzania officially became a one-party state, creating a dilemma for the political leadership. Unlike the leaders of many one-party states, TANU leaders decided that competitive elections, in which voters were offered a choice of candidates, were important components of the party philosophy. President Nyerere stressed the role elections play in keeping the leadership responsive to the demands and needs of the electorate and in making sure that leadership positions are accessible to Tanzanians from all walks of life. How to give voters a choice in a system that recognized only one legal party presented a challenge. The solution has been to allow for competition within the party, with all candidates running under the TANU banner. This experiment in "one-party democracy" had its first test in the 1965 parliamentary elections.

The 1965 Election—The First Test

To understand this electoral experiment, we must study both the format and the results of the 1965 parliamentary elections. The Tanzanian Parliament of 1965 had a potential maximum size of 214 members: 107 directly elected from single-member districts and 97 appointed or nominated. Among the nominated and appointed members were regional commissioners, national members of the party, members appointed by the president, and members from Zanzibar's party, the Afro-Shirazi party. By 1966 the actual size of the Parliament was 183 members: 107 elected MPs, 37 ex-officio, and 24 nominated.

The key to the success of the 1965 election was the selection and election of the 107 MPs from the various districts throughout Tanzania. All who wished to stand for election had to be members of TANU, have the signatures of 25 registered voters, and appear before the TANU district conference, which made the initial selection of candidates.

The TANU district conference listened to and questioned the potential candidates and ranked them in terms of preference. Once this process was completed, the conferences forwarded their ranking of candidates to the National Executive Committee of TANU, which then determined the candidates for each district. In almost all cases there were more than two candidates sent forward to the party's National Executive for consideration, and usually the National Executive selected the top two ranked candidates. In six cases candidates were sent forward unopposed. In all, the district conferences received more than 800 potential candidates, or 7.5 candidates per district.[28]

The characteristics of the candidates elected present interesting case studies of who the new potential political leaders in Tanzania were. Candidates were predominantly male (only 16 women were nominated at the district level) and young. Of the 101 candidates who eventually won the contested seats, 59 were 35 or younger. The candidates also had a higher education than the average Tanzanian. Of the 101 winners, 72 had either a secondary or a college education, and only 7 had no schooling at all. Many types of occupation were represented. Ministers in the government, civil servants, local government officials, teachers, cooperative or trade union personnel and farmers were all represented by more than 10 winners in the election.[29]

---

[28] Lionel Cliffe, ed., *One Party Democracy, The 1965 Tanzanian General Elections* (Nairobi, Kenya: East African Publishing House, 1967), p. 254.

[29] Ibid., pp. 262–265.

Summary of Those Defeated in the 1965 Parliamentary Elections

2 ministers
6 junior ministers
3 present or former TANU regional chairmen
13 district chairmen
5 present or former area commissioners
the chairman of the Mwananchi Development Corporation
Deputy Commissioner of the Civil Service Commission
former editor of *Mwafrica*
9 backbenchers in former Parliament

In addition, 3 present or former junior ministers and 6 MPs did not receive the support of their districts.

27 backbenchers chose not to stand, many because of fear of losing.

In Summary, 22 of 31 TANU officeholders were unsuccessful
16 of 31 MPs lost

Source: Figures compiled from data in Henry Bienen, *Tanzania: Party Transformation and Economic Development,* expanded edition, (Princeton, N.J.: Princeton University Press, 1970), pp. 393–394.

An interesting, important aspect of the election was the fate of those sitting MPs and ministers in the government: 31 MPs chose not to stand, while 50 MPs and ministers sought nomination. Of the 50, 12 were not selected by the district conference, 17 were nominated and lost their seats in the election, 15 won the election in contested areas, and 6 MPs won their seats unopposed. These figures suggest that the nominating process at the district and national levels was relatively open, not simply a symbolic election to return those already in power. Voters indicated a willingness to "throw the rascals out." Of the 17 MPs who lost their seats, 2 were ministers in the government, and 9 were junior ministers. The nominating process also showed that it was not impossible for an unknown or a person with local, but not national, connections to run for office.

The election campaign is not designed to choose between two parties with different platforms but rather to choose those individuals in TANU who are most representative of the various districts. The election manifesto for the 1975 election made this clear:

In our country electing a Parliament does not imply a choice between different policies, such as is the case in countries which have multi-party political systems. In our country there is only one dominating policy, namely the policy of Socialism and Self-reliance adopted by Tanu and the Afro-Shirazi Party. Therefore in our circumstances, the act of electing a Parliament merely implies the choosing of suitable persons who are distinctly capable and committed, and who can be

President Nyerere, pictured addressing a Tanzanian crowd, has encouraged competition for office within the ranks of TANU. Marc Riboud, Magnum Photos, Inc.

relied upon to be in the forefront in implementing the accepted policies of our Parties, Tanu and ASP.[30]

In 1965, in order to assure this equality between candidates, the candidates were required to travel together, to share the same platform during campaign speeches, and to observe the same strict rules. The campaign was conducted in Swahili and monitored by three-man boards in each district.

Since many of the eligible voters were illiterate, each candidate was also given a symbol—a hoe or a house, distributed in such a way that no candidate or group could claim favoritism. Although both symbols were thought to be equal, election results show that 59 candidates with the hoe symbol won, while only 40 with the house were victorious. Some suggest that those candidates with the hoe symbol were better able to use their symbol to their advantage than were those with the house. Slogans such as "The hoe has never failed you; choose the hoe," "The hoe is traditional," and "All wealth comes from the hoe" were used by

[30] Colin Legum, ed., *Africa Contemporary Record, 1975–1976* (London: Rex Collings, 1976), p. B321.

some candidates. "Choose the house so that I can serve you. Do not choose the hoe whose owner does not even own a farm," and "Our homes are here" were two phrases used by those assigned the house.[31]

Candidates who most effectively capitalized on local issues and who had long, strong ties with the local community were most likely to win. Voters were concerned with electing candidates who could best represent them, not necessarily those who appeared to have power or position. (This probably accounts for the failure of those ministers, junior ministers, and MPs who either were not renominated or who lost their seats.) Appeals to ethnic loyalty or other divisive loyalties were forbidden, and election results suggest that, except in a few cases, these issues were not a factor. Finally, many MPs or others who were associated with government in a strong way and who were seeking seats from economically depressed or poor areas often found themselves losers because the voters felt they had not "produced" for their district.[32]

The presidential election was held at the same time as the parliamentary elections, but without opposition to President Nyerere. Voters were asked to give their approval or disapproval to a new term for the president. As expected, he received overwhelming support—96 percent of the vote.

The 1965 parliamentary election, a unique experiment, was by most standards an efficiently run, honest election. The party and the voters faced problems of poor communication, not enough ballot boxes (which forced the election to be held on two separate days), and a general lack of electoral experience. Despite these handicaps, and the added handicap of an electorate that included illiterates, there was a high turnout for these truly competitive races. Although it would have been possible to return defeated ministers and MPs to Parliament from the nominated or ex-officio seats, most were not. The new Parliament may have had members who were short on experience, but it did produce a much more vocal and questioning Parliament than in the past. While much of the effective political power continued to rest with the president, his cabinet, and his closest advisers, the new Parliament provided an open arena—a group willing to serve both the debating and watchdog functions of a Parliament.

The 1970 and 1975 Elections—Institutionalizing Competition Within the Party

Observers in and out of Tanzania considered the 1965 election successful. An important question raised by many, however, was whether future elections could maintain the standards achieved in 1965—removing the

---

[31] Henry Bienen, *Tanzania: Party Transformation and Economic Development,* expanded ed. (Princeton: Princeton University Press, 1970), p. 390.

[32] Cliffe, *One Party Democracy,* pp. 319–320.

Leadership Profiles

Selected Tanzanian Government and Political Leaders	
Leader	*Background and Education*
Julius K. Nyerere	born: 1922 education: Tabora Secondary School Makerere University, Uganda Edinburgh University (first Tanganyikan to attend a British university)
Rashidi Kawawa	born: 1929 education: Tabora Secondary School
Aboud M. Jumbe	born: 1920 education: Government School, Mnazimoja, Zanzibar Makerere University, Uganda
Edward M. Sokoine	born: 1938 education: Umbwe Secondary School Mzumbe Local Government Training School
Derek Bryceson	born: 1922 (in China; immigrated to East Africa in 1947) education: St. Paul's School, London Trinity College, Cambridge

Early Occupations	Political Career	
Teacher, author, politician	1959–1963	Chief Minister and Prime Minister
	1963–present	President of Tanganyika and Tanzania
Civil Servant, union organizer, member of the Tanganyikan African Association	1961–1962	Minister without Portfolio
	1962	Prime Minister
	1962–1964	First Vice President of Tanganyika
	1964–1977	Second Vice President of Tanzania
	1972–1977	Prime Minister
Teacher, political organizer	1960–1964	Party official in the Afro-Shirazi Party
	1964	Minister of State in the Office of the First Vice President
	1972–present	First Vice President of Tanzania (President of Zanzibar)
Government official	1965	Elected Member of Parliament
	1970–1977	Minister of State in the Vice President's Office
	1972–1977	Minister of Defense
	1977–present	Prime Minister
Farmer	1959	Minister for Mines and Commerce
	1960	Minister for Health and Labour
	1962	Minister for Agriculture
	1964	Minister for Health
	1965–1972	Minister for Agriculture

Leadership Profiles

Selected Tanzanian Government and Political Leaders (*Continued*)

Leader	Background and Education
Amir Jamal	born: 1922 (of Asian descent) education: Calcutta University, India

---

unpopular and replacing them with new political faces. Since 1965 there have been two tests of the new system. In both 1970 and 1975 President Nyerere was returned to office, unopposed, by overwhelming majorities. In 1975 the president gave strong hints that this election might well be the last he would participate in, and that it would be good for the nation if he were to step down from the presidency. In a perceptive statement on the dangers of remaining in power too long, he stated:

There have been some great and gifted leaders who have remained in office when they were past their prime. They have been re-elected not because of their continuing ability to serve, but because of the great service they have given in the past, and because people are afraid to change. . . . There is an old saying "Better the devil you know. . . ."[33]

The president did not make it clear if he did step down, whether he would also resign his party post.

The results of the 1970 and 1975 parliamentary elections were not as startling as the 1965 returns; fewer sitting MPs and ministers were rejected. In 1970 three members of the government who chose to run again were defeated. All ministers who chose to run again, and who won their seats, were reappointed to the government but not necessarily with their same portfolio. Two of the most surprising victors were Derek Bryceson, a white running in a largely African district, and Amir Jamal, a leading member of the Asian community; Bryceson won with the largest majority of any candidate. One of the major changes from the 1965 campaign was that potential candidates at the lowest level were selected at the district level. This gave the party candidates a somewhat wider base of support.[34]

---

[33] *Africa Contemporary Record, 1975–1976*, p. B314.
[34] Colin Legum, ed., *Africa Contemporary Record, 1970–1971* (London: Rex Collings, 1971), pp. B167–168.

Early Occupations	Political Career	
Businessman	1959	Minister for Urban Local Government
	1960	Minister for Communications, Power and Works
	1964	Minister of State in President's Office
	1965	Minister of Finance
	1972	Minister of Commerce and Industry

In the 1975 election 958 potential candidates forwarded their names to contest 92 seats. Four ministers in the government announced that they would not stand this election, and three others were returned unopposed. As in the past elections the National Executive Committee of the party selected the two candidates from each district who would stand for election. In the final election 184 candidates contested the 92 available seats. In addition to these district seats, there were contests for the regional seats, the nominated seats, and the seats that represented the East African Legislative Assembly (a grouping that included members from Kenya and Uganda).

The membership of the 1975 Parliament was chosen in a different way than the membership of earlier Parliaments. The number of MPs elected from districts was changed from 107 to 96. In addition there were 15 MPs from the national institutions of the party (youth league, women's branch, and the like), 20 national members from the 20 mainland regions, 20 regional commissioners, 10 members nominated by the president, and finally a combined total of 57 members from the Zanzibar regional and national districts and the Zanzibar Revolutionary Council.[35]

The results again showed that the voters were not afraid to turn out sitting members of Parliament. Of the 184 individuals contesting the 92 seats, 86 were former members of Parliament. Of the 86, only 43 were re-elected. Two cabinet ministers were defeated, one junior minister lost, while twelve ministers were re-elected. Four members of the army were elected, and three women (out of eleven running) were victorious. Again, the only white candidate, Derek Bryceson, and the popular Asian candidate, Amir Jamal, won their seats.[36]

---

[35] *Africa Contemporary Record, 1975–1976*, pp. B322–323.
[36] Ibid.

It is difficult to evaluate the success of the Tanzanian experiment, which is a unique electoral framework devised to meet the needs of the political system at a specific time. Clearly, the electoral plan devised by TANU seeks to provide for participation, to ensure accountability, and to provide a new avenue for the recruitment of those who might not normally become political leaders. How effective and how open that avenue of recruitment has been may be questioned. The party argues that openness, responsiveness, and participation are central both to the goals of the party and the development of the Tanzanian political system, but that competitive party politics would tear the nation apart. The delicate balance is clearly between the need for participation and for selection of new political actors, and the need for national unity to achieve the goals of the party and the national leaders.

▪ CHILE ▪

From the establishment of the constitutional regime in 1925 to the military intervention of 1973, political leaders in Chile were chosen through a well-established electoral system. Candidates representing different political parties and different shades of political opinion contested for both presidential and congressional offices. Elections provided a regularized channel for recruiting new leaders and for giving them authority to govern. Since 1973 the recruitment patterns have changed and new means of selecting leaders have been established.

Presidential Elections

Presidential candidates, during the constitutional period, had to be Chilean citizens 30 years of age or older; they were required to register to stand for office at least 45 days before the election and to have the signatures of 20,000 registered voters. Presidential hopefuls who won a majority of the popular votes cast in the election were confirmed in office by a joint session of Congress. If no candidate won a majority—as in the 1958 and 1970 elections—a joint session of Congress chose the new president. In every case (since 1925) the Congress chose the man with the most popular votes.

The results of the 1958, 1964, and 1970 presidential elections indicate the dramatic shift to the left among the Chilean electorate described in Chapters 4 and 5. In each election candidates represented the three major points on the ideological spectrum. The coalition of the right included Conservatives, Liberals, and sometimes Radicals. The center was represented by the Christian Democrats; the left, by Socialists and Communists.

The 1958 election, in which 1.7 million Chileans voted, did not produce a clear winner. Jorge Alessandri, representing the conservative right, received most votes, although far short of a majority. Salvadore Allende, the leader of the socialist movement and the left coalition, finished a strong second and trailed Alessandri by only two percentage points. Finishing third with 20 percent of the vote was Eduardo Frei of the Christian Democrats. Despite the victory of the conservative candidate, the election results clearly indicated a change in voter preference. Almost 50 percent of the electorate voted for candidates who were calling for economic and social change—Frei and Allende.

The number of voters demanding political reform and change grew steadily between 1958 and 1964. The conservatives found it difficult to solve Chile's severe economic problems. They were not alone in this respect. Most parties, once in power, found that practical solutions to Chile's problems were considerably different from the campaign solutions offered at election time. In 1964 it was the turn of the incumbent conservative parties to answer to the electorate. The collapse of the Conservative/Radical/Liberal alliance shortly before the election prevented the parties of the right from agreeing on one candidate. The Radicals nominated their own candidate, and the Conservatives and Liberals, fearing an Allende victory, threw their support to Eduardo Frei. Though not agreeing with many of Frei's policies, they saw an Allende victory as a greater threat.

The Christian Democrats and the coalition of left parties won a combined total of almost 95 percent of the popular vote in the 1964 election. Frei received the largest majority ever given a Chilean president, 56.1 percent of the vote. Allende, once again, finished second but with a larger percentage of the vote than in 1958 (38.9 percent compared to 28.9 percent in 1958). Julio Duran, the Radical candidate, finished a poor third (see Table 6–7).

The striking victory of Frei and the Christian Democrats in 1964 did not guarantee future success. Despite their majority in the presidential election and later congressional victory, the national leaders could not maintain support and popularity. Large portions of the electorate became dissatisfied with the Christian Democrats' failure to solve severe problems.

The 1970 election, like past presidential elections, was a three-man race. Salvadore Allende represented the left, which called for radical economic, political, and social change. Ex-President Alessandri represented the right-oriented nationalist coalition, and Radomiro Tomic stood for the Christian Democrats, as Chilean electoral law forbade a sitting president to run for a second term.

After so many near misses, Salvadore Allende and his Popular Unity coalition won the election with a plurality of votes. (Allende received 36.3 percent of the vote to 34.9 percent for Alessandri and 27.8 percent for Tomic; 16 percent of the electorate abstained.) Since no candidate won a majority, a joint session of Congress was called to select the new president. Congress, after much debate, ratified Allende's election by a vote of 153 for Allende, 35 for Alessandri.

TABLE 6–7   Trends in Chilean Presidential Elections

	1958		1964		1970	
	Candi-date	% of Vote	Candi-date	% of Vote	Candi-date	% of Vote
Conservative/ Right Coalition	Jorge Alessandri	31.6	*		Jorge Alessandri	34.9
Center/Christian Democratic	Eduardo Frei	20.7	Eduardo Frei	56.1	Radomiro Tomic	27.8
Left Coalition	Salvadore Allende	28.9	Salvadore Allende	38.9	Salvadore Allende	36.3
Radical Party Candidate	Luis Bossay	15.6	Julio Duran	5.0		
Other/ Independent	Antonio Zamorano	3.3				

Sources: The New York Times, Facts on File, and Federico G. Gil, The Political System of Chile (Boston: Houghton Mifflin, 1966), p. 233.

 * The coalition between the Conservative party, the Liberal party, and the Radical party collapsed before the election. The Radicals nominated their own candidate, Julio Duran, while the Conservatives and Liberals gave their support to Eduardo Frei, the Christian Democratic candidate.

In one sense the 1970 election capped a trend developing for years in Chilean politics. In three successive elections candidates of the right, the center, and the left won victories; clearly more Chileans wanted change. In another sense the 1970 election indicated just how divided the Chilean society had become. Although Allende won, he did not receive a majority. His 36.3 percent of the vote made it difficult for him to govern since many Chileans feared and opposed him. The fact that there were sharp differences within the Popular Unity coalition as to what policies the new government should follow added to Allende's problems. As with Alessandri and Frei before him, the severity of the economic, political, and social problems facing the government made it difficult to maintain popular support. In the case of Alessandri and Frei, the electorate voted in new leaders; in the case of Allende, the military made the decisions concerning who should lead Chile.

Congressional Elections—A Balance to Presidential Elections

Congressional elections during the 1960s and 1970s greatly influenced Chilean politics; presidents were not all-powerful. Congress, especially when controlled by parties opposed to the president, had the power to block presidential actions. As Frei and Allende introduced more and more reforms, the more conservative elements in Congress used this power, maintaining a strong voice and presence during the 1950s and 1960s. In the 1970s, following the election of Allende, the conservative right and center Christian Democrats joined together to strongly oppose the president from their positions in the Congress.

Candidates to the Chamber of Deputies were elected from districts based on a formula of one deputy per every 30,000 persons. The entire Chamber of 150 was required to stand for re-election every four years. Election involved a complicated system based on proportional representation. In essence, candidates stood under a party label and seats were proportioned according to the number of votes a party received. Candidates had to be at least 21, have 2,000 signatures of registered voters, and have been a member of their party for at least 180 days prior to the election. Election reforms in the 1950s and 1960s limited the number of minority parties contesting elections.

Senatorial candidates needed 5,000 signatures on their petitions, and had to be at least 35. Initially, five senators were elected from nine districts. Later the number of senators was raised from 45 to 50. About half of the members stood for re-election every four years.

Senate and Deputy campaigns were held in March of election years, and the campaigns were supposed to last no longer than two months (although they often did). Congressional candidates registered their intention to run at least 120 days prior to the election. Campaign activities and ballot counting were supervised by a nonpartisan election registry.[37]

Congressional election results between 1961 and 1973 vary considerably. The trend in congressional elections, like presidential ones, was for candidates demanding change to gain the upper hand. The pattern is not, however, so clear as in the 1958, 1964, and 1970 presidential elections. For example, those classified as leftists controlled 40 seats in the Chamber of Deputies and 13 in the Senate in 1961, while those in the coalition of the right controlled 84 in the Chamber of Deputies and 26 in the Senate. Not surprisingly, the Conservative, Liberal, and Radical legislators of the right coalition tended to support President Alessandri's policies.

Christian Democrats, following their sweeping 1964 presidential victory, were the big winners in the 1965 congressional elections (see Table 6–8). With 82 deputies and 13 senators, they had a majority in the Chamber of Deputies and a strong core of support in the Senate.

The 1969 elections were indecisive; no one party was able to win convincing majorities. The National party (Conservatives and Liberals) won 35 seats in the Chamber of Deputies and 5 in the Senate; they received just over 20 percent of the total popular vote. The Christian Democrats

---

[37] Federico G. Gil, *The Political System of Chile* (Boston: Houghton Mifflin, 1966), pp. 208, 219–220.

Leadership Profiles

Chilean Presidents, 1958 to present

Leader	*Background and Education*
Jorge Alessandri Rodriguez President of Chile, 1958–1964, Independent candidate of the Right	born: 1896, son of Arturo Alessandri education: University of Chile, engineering
Eduardo Frei Montalva President of Chile, 1964–1970, Christian Democratic Party	born: 1911 education: Catholic University of Chile
Salvadore Allende Gossens President of Chile, 1970–1973, Socialist Party and candidate of the Left	born: 1908 died: 1973 education: University of Chile, medicine
General Augusto Pinochet Ugarte President of Chile, 1973 to Present, General in the Army	born: 1915 education: National Defence Academy

---

won only 55 Chamber seats and 23 Senate seats, while the Communists won 22 in the Chamber of Deputies and 6 in the Senate. The Socialists won 15 Chamber seats and 4 Senate seats. Clearly, the big losers were the Christian Democrats, who could not repeat their strong 1965 showing. Five years of Christian Democratic rule, like five years of conservative rule before, could not resolve the economic crises facing Chile. The dissatis-

Early Occupations	*Political Career*	
Businessman and financier	1925	Elected to Chamber of Deputies
	1931	Paving Commissioner for Santiago
	1932–1938	President of the Mortgage Credit Bank
	1947–1950	Minister of Finance
	1957	Elected to the Senate
	1958–1964	President of Chile
Lawyer, professor		Founder, organizer, and president of the National Falange (forerunner of the Christian Democratic movement)
	1949, 1957	Elected to the Senate
	1964–1970	President of Chile
Medical doctor	1939–1942	Minister of Public Health
	1945, 1953	Elected to the Senate
	1970–1973	President of Chile
	1937	Elected to Chamber of Deputies
General of the Army, professor	1953	Assumed rank of Major
	1961	Assumed rank of Lieutenant Colonel
	1972	Chief of Army GHQ
	1973	General and Commander-in-Chief of Army
	1973–present	President of Chile

faction of the voters was made clear at the polls; the Christian Democrats lost 27 seats in the Chamber of Deputies.

The 1973 congressional elections were held during Allende's presidency, just six months before the coup d'état that ended all elections. The contest was between a center and right coalition called the Democratic Confederation (CODE) and the leftist coalition, Popular Unity (UP). Popular

TABLE 6–8 Distribution of Seats in the Chilean Congress for the Major Political Coalitions

| | 1961 | | 1965 | | 1969 | | 1973 | |
	Depu-ties	Sen-ate	Depu-ties	Sen-ate	Depu-ties	Sen-ate	Depu-ties	Sen-ate
Right Coalition: Conservative Party Liberal Party Radical Party	84	26	29	17	58	14	87[a]	30
Center Coalition: Christian Democratic Party	23	6	82	13	55	23		
Left Coalition: Socialist Party Communist Party Other Left Parties	40	13	36	15	37	13	63[b]	20
Totals	147	45	147	45	150	50	150	50

Sources: Federico G. Gil, *The Political System of Chile* (Boston: Houghton Mifflin, 1966); *Latin American Digest;* and John Paxton, ed., *Statesman's Yearbook, 1976–1977* (New York: St. Martin's Press, 1977).

[a] Democratic Confederation (CODE) = right and center parties
[b] Popular Unity = leftist parties

Unity supported Allende, while the Democratic Confederation opposed Allende's policies. CODE included the Conservative party and the Christian Democratic party, among others, while UP was made up of the Socialist and Communist parties as well as other sympathetic leftist parties. For the first time, 18–20-year-olds and illiterates were allowed to vote. CODE won 87 seats in the Chamber of Deputies compared with 63 for the Popular Unity coalition. After the balloting CODE also held 30 Senate seats to 20 for the UP. The significance of the election was unclear. Before the election each side had hoped for a big win—the UP so that they could move ahead with their policies, CODE so that they could block the proposed radical changes. Although both sides claimed victory, it was not clear that either side could claim a convincing victory.

The results of the congressional elections are not so clear and sharp as those of the presidential elections. Congressional elections were held two years after the presidential election and often reflected a dissatisfaction with the party in power. (For example, the congressional strength of the Christian Democrats began to wane considerably before the end of the Frei term and the beginning of the Allende period.) As in other political systems with an independent president and Congress, the two branches in Chile were often at loggerheads. As the problems facing Chile became more pressing and as the threat of military intervention increased, the tension grew between parties, coalitions, and individuals.

The Military Period—New Avenues of Recruitment

The military junta that took power in 1973 dramatically and violently changed the pattern of leadership selection: new players and new rules were established. The military first turned its attention to the previous powerholders—leftist parties and politicians. Many politicians, including President Allende, were killed; others were imprisoned or exiled for life. Universities and other institutions that supported Allende were purged.

The early cabinets of the military regime replaced civilian leaders with army, air force, navy, and national police officers. The first cabinet, for example, included 10 military men, 3 members of the national police and 2 civilians. The Christian Democrats and the Nationalists on the right gave early but tentative support to the military junta, and several agreed to serve the new leaders.

Since this first cabinet, more and more civilians have been brought into the cabinet. In June of 1974 General Pinochet lessened the power of the navy, the air force, and the national police representatives by assuming full executive powers. He shuffled his cabinet, replacing 8 ministers and creating 2 new portfolios. The new cabinet included 14 military men (5 army and 3 each from the police, navy, and air force), and 3 civilians in important economic positions.

A 1975 cabinet reorganization further changed the complexion of the cabinet and the civilian/military balance. The April 1975 cabinet included 5 army officers, 2 ministers each from the navy, air force, and police, and 5 civilian ministers. One civilian minister, Jorge Cavas, became a super-minister with control over several economic departments. And by 1976 the new cabinet included 8 civilians and 6 military men. Not unlike the situation in Nigeria, Chilean officers found that they were forced to rely on the civil service for a good bit of the expertise needed to run a modern and complex government.

On seizing power the military junta promised an early return to civilian rule. (The same announcement was made by the military in Nigeria and in fact is made by most military officers when they seize power.) It is not clear when the civilians will once again assume power or what the new rules of the game will be. The current mood of the junta favors restricting leftist political parties and leaders. The electoral tradition in Chile was strong and politically important, both for regulating recruitment into the system and for indicating shifting opinion in the electorate. The military junta has attempted to develop new means of recruitment without resorting to elections. Whether these new patterns will become as institutionalized and as regularized as the long electoral tradition in Chile remains to be seen.

CONCLUSION

Leadership selection poses a potential threat to the stability of all political systems. Established rules and institutions for choosing new leaders are often fragile, subject to either gradual or radical change. Leadership selection involves recruiting people to positions of power, the power to make decisions and to control the political game. The competition and conflict arising over choosing new actors who will exercise political power is a common reason for the collapse of political systems.

Because the issues involved in leadership selection are so important and the stakes so high, it is difficult for powerholders and participants to agree on the rules of the game. Some losers in the leadership-selection process try to achieve power by changing the rules of the game rather than waiting for the next election. Seizing power by force is a relatively common political occurrence in many nations; in other systems the losers are content to wait until the next election to try their luck at the polls again. Our case studies indicate that there are many different ways that leaders are chosen and many different types of elections.

Despite their differences in traditions, practices, party issues, and electoral laws, important similarities are found in the United Kingdom, West Germany, and France. First, the elections are regularly held, and both winners and losers can plan on future elections. Thus, a defeated party will have another chance at power. Second, all participants accept election results, and they do not expect serious disruptions following the elections. Winners will take office, and losers will form a responsible opposition. Third, in each case the contest for office revolves around the competition between political parties. The number of parties competing for office varies from nation to nation and from election to election, but the parties remain the central organizing force for elections.

The Tanzanian case differs considerably from familiar electoral patterns. Its system is designed to provide effective means of participation for the electorate by providing competing candidates for office. (In this sense it is similar to the United Kingdom, France, and West Germany.) The choice, however, is not between different candidates offering different platforms, but between different candidates subscribing to the same TANU platform. Tanzanians seek the best of both worlds—open competition for office and national unity.

Egypt, Nigeria, and Chile have undergone changing patterns of leadership selection. Long-standing electoral patterns in Chile and less well developed patterns in Nigeria were ended by military coups d'état. In each case the military was unwilling to accept the electoral outcomes or to tolerate the severe conflict created by elections. Military officers who assumed command positions call, where necessary, on civilian personnel and expertise.

Both soldiers and civilians hold powerful political positions in Egypt.

President Nasser's power prevented the development of institutionalized patterns of selection. Success or failure heavily depended on a person's relationship with the president. The ratio of military men to civilians in important positions varies, depending on specific events. More than other nations in the study, Egypt represents a mixed (civilian and military), non-institutionalized pattern of leadership selection.

Finally, there have been so few top leadership changes in the Soviet Union that it is difficult to describe a pattern. Control of the party and government apparatus depends upon the ability of the key players to mobilize party support, the number of participants competing for office, and the influence of auxiliary institutions such as the secret police. In the first two cases of succession—following the deaths of Lenin and Stalin—there were periods of uncertainty while Stalin and Khrushchev sought to consolidate their power. In 1964 the removal of Khrushchev was carried out in a shorter period of time and with more confidence. It is as yet unclear how the transition from the Brezhnev period will be conducted.

Succession breeds uncertainty and is one of the most difficult functions for governments to institutionalize. In political systems with highly personalized leadership, such as the Soviet Union under Stalin or Egypt under Nasser, the question of succession remains unresolved until the last moment—the death of the leader. In Chile and Nigeria the conflicts created by elections were so strong and bitter that they eventually resulted in the end of all elections. Though Tanzania, the United Kingdom, France, and West Germany have all developed fairly regularized patterns for selecting new political leaders, none is completely immune from the succession problems that have faced Egypt, Chile, Nigeria, and the Soviet Union.

CHAPTER 7
POLICY-MAKING INSTITUTIONS

Where are decisions made and by whom?

Every nation must develop institutional arrangements for making public policy. Normally, the political executive arrives at policy decisions. Executives differ, however, in the specific arrangement of offices and rules that accompany this central function. Nation-states differ, too, in the extent to which policy-making within them is institutionalized.

Policy-making is the process of making society's most fundamental decisions: regulating behavior, allocating resources, and distributing resources. Regulating behavior includes decisions that set rules for political competition. These may be considered constitutional issues. Resource allocation decisions are those that determine which sectors of society will be favored by governmental action. Finally, government decisions to change the existing pattern of resource allocation—to shift resources from one sector of the economy to another—involve the distribution, or redistribution, of resources.

These basic decisions are the essential "stuff" of politics. They determine winners and losers in the political game and set the rules of competition. Policies are shaped in a nation's center of political power—the executive. Some of these executives, as in the Soviet Politburo, have the power to make policy without consulting or getting approval from other political groups or institutions. Others, as in the British cabinet, must consult with other actors, touch base with interest groups, and, in the final step, get the approval of Parliament.

Even powerful, self-contained executives, however, must be concerned with the views and actions of other actors. President Nasser of Egypt was forced to consider the views of civil service experts, the military, certain politicians, and important economic interests. The members of the Politburo are aware of the opinions of the military, government experts, economic managers, and other relevant actors. Formal consultation does not occur in all nations. Though parliamentary systems tend to have more regular channels of group consultation, one-party and military states are less predictable in the way that they solicit the opinions of important groups.

A nation's policy-making is institutionalized if it is stable, predictable, and rule-bound. Predictability means that most policy decisions are reached by the same, certain process. The same actors will be involved, and they will operate according to the same set of understood rules. One-man policy-making systems, such as that of Stalin's Russia, might at first glance meet this definition, for the same leader makes all of the decisions. But dictators use different advisers (or, if they see fit, no advisers), and they change the criteria they use for making decisions from case to case. For example, they may make a decision because of some personal criteria, or they may invoke the "national interest." Thus, they do not meet the requirement of stability in our definition of institutionalized decision-making.

The eight countries of our study present an interesting variety of policy-making arrangements. The locus of policy-making varies from the office of the Egyptian president, to the collective leadership of the British cabinet, to a council of military leaders in Nigeria and Chile. The political executives vary considerably as to decision rules they employ, groups they consult, and need for outside approval for their actions. Most fundamentally, they vary in the degree to which their policy-making process is institutionalized. Britain, France, and West Germany have highly institutionalized styles of decision-making. Chile and Nigeria recently have undergone dramatic changes in their patterns of decision-making. The Soviet Union, Tanzania, and Egypt represent more intermediate cases, where some elements are predictable while others seem arbitrary.

▪ THE UNITED KINGDOM ▪

Policy-making in the United Kingdom is the work of the cabinet, whose chairman is the prime minister. He/she is named by the monarch and approved by a majority of the House of Commons. The cabinet, as the monarch's official advisory body, has inherited the power and responsibility of the Crown, and its decisions are subject only to the approval of the House of Commons. In the modern era of disciplined parties and majority party dominance, the cabinet can make most decisions with complete confidence that they will be upheld.

Before reaching a decision, the cabinet consults with civil servants in the executive departments of "Whitehall" and with important interest groups. Finally, the cabinet considers the wishes of ordinary members of Parliament.

Power relationships within the cabinet are important as well, as some positions traditionally carry greater influence. The most influential is, of course, the prime minister; he is much more than the oft-quoted *primus inter pares* or "first among equals." His powers are substantial, as is his potential for influence on every policy question. The chancellor of the exchequer (Treasury) also carries special weight in the decision process, as do other experts with information at their disposal.

The outcome for any given policy decision depends on the nature of the issue and the skill and resources of the actors. In a matter of foreign policy, for example, the leading actors are likely to be the prime minister, the foreign secretary, and the secretary of state for defense. Affected interest groups and civil servants provide much of the informational raw material for the decision.

Composition of the Cabinet

As the monarch's primary adviser, the prime minister is responsible for naming the members of Her Majesty's Government. In all, he names over a hundred individuals to senior and junior posts in the ministries (executive departments). The prime minister selects his government from the House of Commons and the House of Lords; normally, most positions go to members of his party in the House of Commons. Of those selected for ministerial positions, 15 or 20 are named to the cabinet and therefore participate in the "final determination of policy to be submitted to Parliament."[1]

The prime minister does not have a free hand in building his cabinet. Practical politics dictate which offices and individuals must be included in his cabinet. The positions of chancellor of the exchequer, foreign secretary, and home secretary must be included because of the importance of their responsibilities. Similarly, some members of Parliament are too important to exclude because of the strength of their personalities and weight of their party following. Prime ministers are often forced to include enemies and rivals in order to bind them to the fate of the government. (Prime Minister Attlee [1945–1951] tried to control the troublesome Aneurin Bevan by appointing him minister of health.) Prime ministers

---

[1] R. M. Punnett, *British Government and Politics* (New York: Norton, 1971), p. 171.

The British Cabinet, 1979

Name	Position
Margaret Thatcher	Prime Minister
Lord Hailsham	Lord Chancellor
Sir Geoffrey Howe	Chancellor of the Exchequer
Lord Carrington	Secretary of State for Foreign and Commonwealth Affairs
Norman St. John-Stevas	Chancellor of the Duchy of Lancaster and leader of the House of Commons
William Whitelaw	Secretary of State for the Home Department
Mark Carlisle	Secretary of State for Education and Science
David Howell	Secretary of State for Energy
Sir Keith Joseph	Secretary of State for Industry
Michael Heseltine	Secretary of State for the Environment
Humphrey Atkins	Secretary of State for Northern Ireland
George Younger	Secretary of State for Scotland
Nicholas Edwards	Secretary of State for Wales
Francis Pym	Secretary of State for Defense
James Prior	Secretary of State for Employment
Patrick Jenkin	Secretary of State for Social Services
John Nott	Secretary of State for Trade
Sir Ian Gilmour	Lord Privy Seal and foreign affairs spokesman in the House of Commons
John Biffen	Chief Secretary at the Treasury
Angus Maude	Paymaster General
Michael Jopling	Chief Whip
Norman Fowler	Secretary of State for Transportation
Lord Soames	Lord President of the Council and leader of the House of Lords
Peter Walker	Minister of Agriculture, Fisheries and Food

usually try to balance different party wings or factions as well. (Wilson put "moderate" James Callaghan and "radical" Michael Foot in important positions.)

Obviously, the prime minister still retains a good bit of leeway in building his cabinet. Several cabinet-level offices are largely ceremonial and may be filled with able men free to take on special tasks. The lord privy seal, the chancellor of the duchy of Lancaster, and the lord president of the council are sometimes used in this way. The prime minister also has leeway in determining which men get which posts. He may give to rivals difficult or impossible tasks; for example, responsibility for Northern Ireland.

Powers of the Prime Minister

Besides his appointive powers, the prime minister has many other formal powers, the greatest of which is the power of dissolution. The prime minister alone consults with the monarch regarding the appropriate time to dissolve Parliament and to hold new elections. He need not wait the statutory five years for a mandatory election date but may prefer to pick a politically expeditious time for a new election. Thus, Harold Wilson chose to stage a new election in 1966 only 17 months after taking office on the correct assumption that he could increase his support in Parliament.

The power of dissolution which gives a prime minister an advantage in political timing, also gives him leverage over his party and his government team. If a prime minister dissolves Parliament, he forces all its members to stand for election again. He also forces members of his party to resign from executive positions in the government. By giving over one-third of his party's MPs executive jobs, the prime minister gives them a powerful reason to please him on policy matters.

The prime minister has important patronage at his disposal, most notably the ministerial positions critical to the career advancement of his junior party colleagues. Every junior person knows what type of position he needs next and the person he needs to please.

The prime minister's influence is also enhanced by the fact that his job does not involve substantive ministerial responsibilities. Free to supervise and coordinate the policy-making process, he is supported in this role by the cabinet's administrative personnel at his disposal.

A British policeman guards the prime minister's residence. The British Tourist Authority.

The fact that a prime minister chairs cabinet meetings lends a subtle but important source of influence, and he has a good deal of freedom in setting the agenda. He guides the discussion of the pros and cons of a particular policy choice. Normally, there are no votes in a cabinet meeting; the prime minister summarizes the "sense of the meeting" and votes the course of action suggested by the discussion. Often cabinet members have been surprised to learn what they have "approved."

Since the prime minister directs the work of the cabinet, he can set up special task groups, formal or informal, to develop policy. These groups can work independently on the prime minister's pet projects and overcome the scattered opposition of individual cabinet members. Former Labour cabinet member Richard Crossman observed, for example:

Here we see another interesting constitutional development, the setting up of these inner groups . . . . There are small groups of Ministers close to Harold [Wilson], groups that are not even given names. It is "the Ministers most closely affected have been meeting." There are four of these: a little group who meet about the economic situation, certainly an inner defense group . . . , the informal group on Rhodesia, which is now never discussed, . . . but is dealt with by the P.M. and his closest friends and then presented as a fait accompli *to Cabinet, and now this inner group on the constitution.*[2]

By carefully selecting ministers for these study groups, the prime minister puts added weight behind his proposals. Often these special task groups meet secretly, further confounding potential opponents.

Specialized Cabinet Structures

Several organizations aid the cabinet in its work. The cabinet secretariat, a twentieth-century addition, is composed of civil servants led by a senior civil servant who is secretary of the cabinet. The secretariat prepares the agenda for cabinet meetings, along with supporting documents relevant to the policy discussions. The secretariat also prepares the minutes of the meeting; each "minute" represents a decision and has the effect of an order for relevant officials in the executive departments. Finally, the secretariat has the responsibility of checking on the implementations of cabinet decisions.

The cabinet is also assisted by specialized cabinet committees, a system dating back to 1902 and the creation of the Committee of Imperial Defense. Since 1902 others have been added such as those for Economic Policy, Social Services, and Home Affairs. The purpose of the committees is to help coordinate the actions of a number of ministries in a similar policy area. Their work is relatively informal in that they report only to the cabinet and they work in private. As cabinets come to rely more heav-

[2] Richard Crossman, *The Diaries of a Cabinet Minister,* Vol. 3 (London: Hamish Hamilton and Jonathan Cape, 1977), p. 243.

ily on these committees, their decisions carry independent weight; that is, committee decisions are binding orders on members of the executive unless the decision is appealed to the cabinet and reversed.[3]

Styles of Decision-Making

The principles of decision-making within the cabinet are *cabinet solidarity* and *cabinet confidentiality*. Cabinet solidarity means that a decision of the cabinet as revealed in the cabinet minutes is binding on all members of the government, including ministers not of cabinet rank. Government members are expected to refrain from public criticism of the collective decision. The only appropriate public expression of disagreement is resignation from the government.

This principle tends to promote a solid front and enhances the power of the prime minister and his closest colleagues. Less influential members of the government must go along or lose a valued position and risk developing a dangerous reputation for unreliability. The principle also enhances the power of the cabinet as a group vis-à-vis Parliament as a whole and major interest groups. Disagreement only plays into the hands of opposed interests outside the cabinet.

Cabinet solidarity appears to be less evenly applied in recent governments. On a number of occasions prime ministers have "taken the muzzle off" critical cabinet members. This reflects the weakness and marginal majorities of recent governments more than disenchantment with the established principle. The fact that Wilson permitted cabinet members to publicly disagree with the full cabinet's Common Market recommendation (pro-entry) in 1975 is largely due to his very tenuous control over Parliament.

Cabinet confidentiality, the principle that cabinet deliberations are secret, has also been eroded recently. In several celebrated cases descriptions of cabinet meetings were published. Richard Crossman, an ex-Labour minister, and his heirs successfully challenged the prohibition of the sale and distribution of his political diary, which contained descriptions of cabinet meetings during the 1960s. More recently, an unknown insider leaked the cabinet deliberations on the 1976 Child Benefits bill. When a news weekly printed the account, the government was embarrassed over the frankly political considerations that went into the decision as well as by the prime minister's dominance in the proceedings. Despite recent departures from the principles of cabinet solidarity and cabinet confidentiality, cabinet and committee proceedings are still essentially secret and binding. Both principles are probably necessary if the cabinet is to remain dominant in policy-making.

The cabinet's style of decision-making has not changed greatly since the

---

[3] Punnett, *British Government and Politics,* pp. 207–208.

great policy battles over the creation of the "welfare state." These post-war confrontations between Labour and the Tories are typical of the basic pattern of cabinet dominance that has held since that time. No issue has been more important that the 1946 decision to go forward with a full-fledged National Health Service. Subsequent policy decisions have largely followed the decision-making pattern of 1946.

The first stage in most British policy decisions is usually the electoral contest. Since party and program appeals are relatively direct, few Britons are surprised by postelection policy initiatives. In the case of 1946 Britain, it was clear that a victorious Labour government would institute a far-reaching National Health Service. The only question was how it would be operated.

The origin of the basic Health Service operation can be found in the civil service of several British governments. The wartime coalition government led by Winston Churchill developed a number of department-based proposals for such a comprehensive health care service. The White Paper of 1944 developed by the Ministry of Health included all of the essential provisions of Labour's later health service package.[4]

The Labour government elected in 1945 adopted these coalition proposals as their own. The new minister of health, Aneurin Bevan, immediately began consultations intended to clarify the principles behind Labour's specific health care program. Bevan took nine months after the election to consult with representatives of the British Medical Association and with the specialist groups associated with that umbrella organization. At no time did the young minister reveal the cabinet's "point of view," but he did leak enough details to calm the doctors' worst fears.[5]

The Labour cabinet agreed to the series of compromises agreed to by its minister of health and the representatives of the medical profession. For the government's part, public hospitals, free beds and standardized service were included as essential to the purpose of the new health system. At the same time the cabinet agreed to allowing a specified number of "private beds" in public hospitals and to the principle that doctors should not be solely salaried employees of the new service.

In essence, the cabinet agreed to support the best and most reasonable deal that its health experts could make with the health professions. Once this principle was established in cabinet session, the full weight of the government came down in favor of the National Health Service Bill of 1946. The solid majority held by Labour was sufficient to guarantee parliamentary passage without incident. The rank and file of Parliament could not resist the cumulative power of the government and the consulted interest groups.

---

[4] James B. Christoph, "The Birth of the National Health Service," in James B. Christoph and Bernard Brown, eds., *Cases in Comparative Politics* (Boston: Little, Brown, 1976), pp. 50–51.

[5] Ibid., pp. 56–57.

The basic decision-making principles followed in 1946 apply today in most "normal" circumstances. The cabinet keeps its deliberations to itself, consults major interest groups, and puts its full weight behind the resultant policy package. Exceptions tend to occur only when weak (minority or near-minority) cabinets must make policy initiatives, in which case no strong policy initiative is possible. If future British governments tend to be weak one-party governments or multi-party coalitions, a new pattern of decision-making must be found.

▪ THE FEDERAL REPUBLIC OF GERMANY ▪

Policy-making in West Germany is the preserve of the chancellor and his civil service staff. The chancellor is the executive figure of the government and is elected by the Parliament, as is his counterpart in Britain, the prime minister. The principle of collegiality that evolved in Britain has never been important in Germany. The provisions of the Basic Law clearly place the chancellor in a preeminent position. This dominance by the chancellor was expanded by the precedents set during Konrad Adenauer's 14-year tenure as West Germany's first chancellor.

The cabinet tends to be manned by experts and specialists without a background in politics. The cabinet's role is more in the spirit of the American cabinet than is its British counterpart. The chancellor himself can control much of the broad direction of policy-making without help from his "governmental team."

One qualification must be added to this picture of "chancellor democracy." Since no party has been able to gain a majority in the Bundestag, coalitions must be formed. A vice chancellor is included in the cabinet because of his role as leader of the smaller of the two coalition parties. Policy, in part, involves interparty negotiation. The perennial junior coalition party, the Free Democrats (FDP), for example, has exacted a wide variety of promises from its larger partners. In 1961 it demanded the midterm resignation of the 87-year-old Konrad Adenauer as a condition of its support. Later the FDP enforced its preferences for a continuation of proportional representation on the parties.

The Chancellor's Powers

The Basic Law expressly designates the chancellor as having the sole responsibility for the formation of public policy; it does not mention the cabinet as a collective policy-making body. The chancellor's position is enhanced by the fact that only he is responsible to the Bundestag for his actions, and in parliamentary governments responsibility essentially is equivalent to power. Chancellors insist that they must have control over the decisions since it is they who are solely accountable to the Bundestag.

The Cabinet of the Federal Republic of Germany, 1977

Name	Position
Helmut Schmidt (SPD)	Chancellor
Manfred Schüler (SPD)	Head of the Chancellor's Office
Hans-Dietrich Genscher (FDP)	Vice Chancellor and Minister of Foreign Affairs
Werner Maihofer (FDP)	Federal Minister of the Interior
Hans Apel (SPD)	Federal Minister of Finance
Hans Friderichs (FDP)	Federal Minister of Economics
Georg Leber (SPD)	Federal Minister of Defense
Hans-Jochen Vogel (SPD)	Federal Minister of Justice
Katherina Focke (SPD)	Federal Minister of Youth, Family and Health
Karl Ravens (SPD)	Federal Minister of Regional Planning, Housing and City Planning
Helmut Rohde (SPD)	Federal Minister of Education and Science
Josef Ertl (FDP)	Federal Minister of Food, Agriculture and Forestry
Herbert Ehrenburg	Federal Minister of Labour and Social Affairs
Hans Matthöfer (SPD)	Minister for Research and Technology
Kurt Gscheidle (SPD)	Federal Minister for Transport, Posts and Telecommunications
Egon Bahr (SPD)	Federal Minister for Economic Cooperation
Egon Franke (SPD)	Federal Minister for Inner-German Relations
Klaus Bölling	Head of Federal Press Office

Source: The International Year Book and Statesman's Who's Who (Bath, England: Pitman Press, 1977), p. 151.

His unique position also stems from the fact that it is exceedingly difficult to remove a chancellor from office. Opponents in the Bundestag can attempt to bring a vote of "no confidence" against an incumbent chancellor, but, unlike other parliamentary systems, they must at the same time elect someone to take his place. This "constructive vote of no confidence" stems from a German wariness of the more negative aspects of parliamentary opposition. In the Weimar Republic, governments were brought down by coalitions of antigovernment actors who did not have enough in common to provide an alternative leadership team. The difficulty of simultaneously bringing down a government and electing a new one has given West German chancellors considerable job security.

To line up support for a controversial issue or in a crisis, the chancellor may call for a vote of confidence himself. The idea is to demonstrate to the public and to other political actors that the chancellor is very much in control. He does, however, have no obligation to call for a vote of confidence and does not have to resign if he loses the vote.

The chancellor's power is enhanced by the fact that he names all federal ministers, who are responsible only to him. Thus, the cabinet is much more likely to be composed of "chancellor's men" than is the case in Britain. They need not come from the Bundestag, although a good number of the 15 to 20 cabinet ministers usually are members of Parliament. There is less need to name powerful, experienced politicians since most party leaders prefer the action in the Bundestag to the secondary role of the cabinet. A German tradition of respect for civil service expertise also minimizes the political makeup of the cabinet; most German cabinet members have some technical expertise related to their office. The distinction betwen the "political" minister and the "expert" civil servant is blurred in Germany.

The formal power of a German chancellor has one notable gap: he cannot dissolve Parliament and call for new elections on his own initiative. Thus, because Parliament members are not threatened with the prospect of facing the voters before the normal four-year term of Parliament is up, a stalemate may result. An unpopular or weak chancellor may limp along for several years without firm control of Parliament.

There is a provision for legislative emergencies—but it is limited and only a temporary expedient. If the chancellor feels that the Bundestag is holding up legislation vital to his program, he may petition the president of the Federal Republic to declare a state of legislative emergency. The lower house (Bundestag) is then given a second chance to pass the legislation. If it refuses, the bill becomes a law if the upper house of Parliament (Bundesrat) agrees.

Another way for the chancellor to break a deadlock is to set up a situation in which he may ask the president to call for new elections. The chancellor may ask for a vote of confidence, which he deliberately loses. In this situation he is permitted to request a new election based on his supposed inability to get his program through the Bundestag. Willy Brandt used this strategy in 1972 to get new elections to pad his narrow Bundestag majority. The plan worked but not without a good bit of confusion and charges of illegality; clearly, this procedure cannot be used very often.

Adenauer's Legacy

The first incumbent of a political office inevitably sets many precedents that define the office. Chief executives from George Washington to Charles de Gaulle shaped new institutions to their personalities, personal needs, and philosophies. Undoubtedly, Konrad Adenauer did much in his tenure as the first chancellor of the Federal Republic of Germany to establish the dominance of the chancellor in the policy process.

First of all, Adenauer made it clear that he did not see the cabinet as a policy-making body. He would submit his actions to the cabinet after the fact to get formal approval and to enter them into the record. The style

Konrad Adenauer addresses the West German Parliament in 1960. Courtesy, German Information Center.

was established early. Gustav Heinemann, for example, resigned from the government in 1950 because Adenauer submitted an executive decision to the cabinet for approval two days after it had been sent out to the governmental ministries as an executive order.[6]

Adenauer carried out his conception of the chancellor's role by centralizing the policy-making machinery around his office. To monopolize the research and informational resources of the government, he created policy research committees that reported only to the chancellor. Adenauer shared the information with his cabinet as he saw fit, usually to justify a decision that he had reached. The ministers, of course, had their own sources of information from their ministries but lacked the full range of information available to the chancellor.

Adenauer was very skillful at promoting the political opportunities available to the chancellor. He tailored his role to the political attitudes and values prevalent in the German political culture. Downplaying his functions as party leader, he cultivated his role as chancellor, especially in

---

[6] Elmer Plischke, *Contemporary Governments in Germany* (Boston: Houghton Mifflin, 1969), p. 107.

foreign relations. In the context of the 1950s Adenauer appeared to be Germany's spokesman and protecter in a hostile and dangerous world.

As Adenauer emphasized his personal leadership skills, Germans focused their attention on the center of action—their political executive. By placing himself "above party," he built a following that was not totally based on partisan attachments; Adenauer and his abilities, compared to his rivals, became the important issue in political campaigns. The stunning 1957 electoral triumph was largely a personal victory. Many members of Parliament felt they owed their election to Der Alte. Few would claim that Adenauer owed his dominant position to the party organization or the public's feeling about his party.

Subsequent chancellors lacked Adenauer's peculiar skills and forceful personality—particularly his two CDU successors, Ludwig Erhard (1963–1966) and Kurt Georg Kiesinger (1966–1969)—but all later chancellors benefited by the centralization of the policy process around the chancellor's office. On some occasions it seems that the SPD chancellors, Willy Brandt (1969–1974) and Helmut Schmidt (1974–   ), learned lessons from Adenauer's political style. In particular, Schmidt has used foreign policy and a strong leadership style to build a following reminiscent of Adenauer's. In the 1974 election Schmidt held on to his job despite the fact that his party was a great deal less popular than the CDU. As in the 1950s, the issue was leadership and a great number of SPD and FDP members of Parliament realize that they owe a great deal to the chancellor.

The Chancellery

The chief organizational instrument of the chancellor's influence is the federal chancellery. Its work is directed by the chancellor through a permanent civil servant, with the title of state secretary. The chancellery, like the cabinet secretariat of Britain, is responsible for gathering the research and information necessary for major policy decisions. Beyond this, it has emerged as a body that coordinates the efforts of the several ministries and parliamentary committees concerned with any given policy matter. In essence, the chancellery aides the chancellor in supervising the development of policy from primary ministerial studies through final legislative action.

The chancellery was designed by Adenauer to fit his needs. It was most powerful during his tenure. In fact, Adenauer's state secretary, Hans Globke, was widely considered the second most powerful man in the Federal Republic as well as the most knowledgeable in the details of government. Under Chancellor Brandt, the chancellery became a full-fledged ministry and its state secretary became a cabinet-level minister. This particular experiment did not last; however, it suggests that chancellors of both parties have tried to strengthen the chancellery and are very comfortable with its essentially bureaucratic or "rational" approach to policy-making.

Styles of Decision-Making

Although the chancellor and the chancellery dominate the policy initiation process, this prelegislative stage also involves other powerful actors: interest groups, representatives of individual ministries, and junior coalition leaders. Specific bills and the plans for policy initiatives normally originate in several related ministries. As the chancellor and the cabinet begin discussions regarding a particular policy, interest groups become active in pressing their views on the participants. Since West German cabinets are coalitions, the leadership of both parties must be consulted as well. The chancellor's role is to act as coordinator and mediator among these actors. If he is skillful, the outcome may be closer to his personal conception than to that of the interested party.

The 1976 bill on "codetermination" in corporate management provides an example of the process.[7] Codetermination is the practice of permitting labor representation on the boards of directors of German companies. It has been in effect in West Germany since 1951; but the major German trade union organization, the German Federation of Trade Unions (DGB), had been pressing for an expansion and reform of the law for some time prior to 1976.

The DGB pressure was sufficient for the Social Democrats to include codetermination reform in their election program for 1969. The principal demand of the trade unions was for exact parity between management and labor on the boards. The labor representatives, in the view of the DGB, should include both local plant workers and DGB trade unionists. A second demand was to increase the DGB representation within the labor contingent on the boards of directors.

The principal difficulty in devising a specific plan for a revised codetermination bill was the opposition of the Free Democratic (FDP) coalition partners. Originally, the Free Democrats were opposed to any expansion of codetermination because they have traditionally opposed the large unions. Instead they offered to accept another DGB proposal—an extensive profit-sharing scheme. FDP opposition resulted in a delay beyond the 1972 election and was a factor in Brandt's resignation in 1974. The issue was not resolved until after Helmut Schmidt assumed the chancellorship in 1974. Both Brandt and Schmidt, committed to some sort of bill that would satisfy the DGB, were caught between their most powerful and loyal political allies in the trade unions and their indispensable

---

[7] For a detailed account of the passage of the Codetermination Bill of 1976 see Gerhard Braunthal, "Codetermination in West Germany," in Christoph and Brown, eds., *Cases in Comparative Politics*, pp. 215–247.

coalition partners. The chancellor's role, then, was to mediate a compromise solution.

Brandt and Schmidt laid the groundwork for the compromise patiently and carefully. They began by authorizing two cabinet ministers to develop alternative bills. The Ministry of Labor, under trade unionist Walter Arendt (SPD), developed a bill after close consultation with the DGB, while the minister of special affairs, Werner Maihofer (FDP), drafted a plan in consultation with the Free Democratic leadership. The chancellor and his office assisted in coming up with a compromise bill that was completed in 1974. By the time it had official cabinet endorsement, the main lines of the bill had been established. The final bill gave greater labor representation than had been the case previously but stopped short of the "parity" position endorsed by the DGB.

The chancellors in question, Willy Brandt and Helmut Schmidt, followed the principles that had guided earlier chancellors in similar situations. After deciding that a policy initiative was necessary, they decided which actors should be brought into the decision-making process. The chancellors then presided over the consultations, leading to a compromise decision that in the end was acceptable to the chancellor's office.

■ FRANCE ■

The French president and his civil service assistants are the most influential persons in making public policy in France. The president has a wide array of constitutional powers that guarantee his leading role in policy-making. Theoretically, the premier should play a major part in day-to-day decisions, but in practice French presidents have not let premiers play a strong role in the process.

The presidential office is the personal creation of Charles de Gaulle—its powers, prerogatives, and trappings are all tailored to fit the Gaullist philosophy of government. The outlines of the office are clear in his famous 1946 Bayeux speech that sets out his preferred form of French postwar government. His conception of the presidency is also outlined in his memoirs written during his temporary retirement from politics between 1946 and 1958.[8]

De Gaulle's view of the presidency is shaped by the Bonapartist tradition of French political culture. The president is to be above politics, an arbiter above special interests and political parties. His role is to step in when it is necessary to defend the national interest, which may be lost

---

[8] Charles de Gaulle, *War Memoirs I: The Call to Honour* (New York: Simon and Schuster, 1959); Charles de Gaulle, *War Memoirs II: Unity* (New York: Simon and Schuster, 1959); and Charles de Gaulle, *War Memoirs III: Salvation* (New York: Simon and Schuster, 1960).

amid partisan bickering. His authority is based on his special relationship with the people, to whom he appeals directly, not through intermediaries.

This conception is based on De Gaulle's belief that France was dying because of a lack of leadership. France's situation in the postwar world required action that a Parliament full of politicians could not take. The national interest required action—and "action is the work of one alone" in De Gaulle's view. "Assemblies beneath their fine speeches," he wrote, "are ruled by the fear of action."[9] The president's role was to determine the national interest and to act on it in behalf of the people and his vision of France.

Powers of the President

De Gaulle's view of leadership is not compatible with constitutional provisions that seem to give a secondary role to the president in the policy process. The president was given sufficient powers to control policy initiatives—through the provisions of the 1958 constitution. The president's powers, true to the Gaullist philosophy, are based on his standing with the people. They are in the nature of appeals to the people over the heads of the parliamentary actors. If the people desert the president, he may become almost totally ineffective.

The president's first link to the people is that (since the constitutional amendment of 1962) he is directly elected—an unusual feature for a parliamentary system. In De Gaulle's view it is essential for the president's authority that he can claim to speak for all the people rather than for particular interests. In the original formulation the president was elected by an electoral college dominated by rural conservative interests. De Gaulle felt that this type of election would tie the president to a narrow and ideological section of the French public.

The president's independence is guaranteed by the fact that he is elected for a seven-year term, with no limit on the number of terms he may serve. The president is not responsible to Parliament and cannot be removed from office through normal parliamentary means. De Gaulle resigned from office in 1969 in the middle of his term after having lost a public referendum on local government reform. The resignation might have set a precedent for resignation in the face of a referendum defeat or in the case of parliamentary elections favoring the president's political opposition, but there is no constitutional requirement that a president resign in these or similar circumstances.

An unusual power of the president is his ability to call for a referendum for approval of a constitutional revision or on a matter that relates to "the organization of public powers." Technically, he must consult with the

---

[9] Stanley Hoffman, *France: Decline or Renewal* (New York: Viking Press, 1974), pp. 194–195.

premier and the presiding officers of both parliamentary houses before bringing a matter before the public. Feeling that referendum politics were his personal preserve, De Gaulle used referenda to ratify his Algerian settlement and to establish the direct election of the president. He was defeated in the referendum of April 27, 1969, when 53 percent of the voters rejected his sweeping reorganization of local government. The referendum, in addition to creating regional local government assemblies, would have changed the nature of the upper house of Parliament—the Senate.

De Gaulle's style in each referendum was to turn the vote into a plebiscite on his leadership. "If you have confidence in me, you will vote *Oui*" was the appeal in each case. De Gaulle always made it clear that he would resign if the people showed they had lost confidence in him. In his last referendum, the strategy of campaigning on the theme "me or the void" finally failed. De Gaulle's successor, Georges Pompidou, used the referendum power once. He staged a vote on Britain's entry into the Common Market (April 1972), certain that his pro-entry view would carry the day. Although he won, a low turnout and a surprising show of opposition disillusioned Pompidou with regard to his tool of presidential power.

Another extraordinary presidential power is the so-called "emergency powers" of Article 16. According to this provision, "When the institutions of the Republic, the independence of the nation, the integrity of its territory are threatened in a grave and immediate manner and the regular functioning of the constitutional governmental authorities is interrupted, the President of the Republic shall take measures required by these circumstances." The president must consult with the premier, the presidents of the houses of Parliament, and the Constitutional Council. The president is also required to "inform the nation" as to his actions, and he may not dissolve Parliament during an emergency. Article 16 seems to be a sweeping yet vague measure that would permit presidential abuse of power; but, in the tradition of Continental politics, it has not yet been unduly abused. De Gaulle used it once with regard to the Algerian insurrection of 1961.

The president's power vis-à-vis the premier is partially based on the fact that the president designates the premier subject to National Assembly approval. Since France is a multi-party system, the power of nomination is particularly important. He may choose from a number of leaders of the coalition parties. The premier has been the "president's man" throughout the Fifth Republic. Prominent premiers—like Pompidou under De Gaulle and Jacques Chirac under Giscard's presidency—have been dismissed or squeezed out once they achieved popularity in their own right.

One further presidential power deserves special mention: the power to dissolve Parliament and call for new elections. Article 12 of the 1958 constitution states that the president may dissolve Parliament after consulting with the premier and the presidents of the two houses of Parliament. The only restrictions are that a president may not dissolve Parliament within a year of the last election, and he may not dissolve the legislative chambers while emergency powers are in effect. (The premier may request a dissolution, but the president can refuse the request.) This fairly broad power of dissolution gives the president a tool comparable to the British prime minister's. The president may take advantage of particular political circumstances to enhance his position, and he may hold the threat of dissolution over the heads of reluctant legislators. The potential of this power was shown in the election of June 1968 that De Gaulle called before the constitutional term of Parliament expired. De Gaulle took advantage of a widespread student and worker revolt, by calling the election at a time when people were longing for political order—a value associated with the political right and De Gaulle's government.

It should be clear at this point that the presidential powers are sweeping, but they do rest on the popularity of the president. The use of referenda clearly requires popular support as does the threat of dissolution. The referendum can ruin an unpopular president, as it finally ruined De Gaulle. An unpopular president will most likely not call for early elections for fear of the return of a hostile Parliament. Since many presidential powers require the agreement of others, notably the premier's, an unpopular president could be successfully defied by a strong premier.

The Premier and the Cabinet

The cabinet is led by the premier, who is nominated by the president and elected by the National Assembly. The premier selects approximately 30 ministers to his cabinet. The president plays a role in the selection of the cabinet as well, since he formally appoints its members on the recommendation of the premier. In practice, the cabinet reflects presidential preferences as well as those of the premier.

The premiers of the Fifth Republic typically come from civil service, business, and other nonpolitical fields. Pompidou, for example, was a banker and academic. Couve de Murville, Pierre Messmer, and Jacques Chirac were all primarily prominent administrators and civil servants. The pattern established under the Fifth Republic is that the cabinet should be composed of technical experts, often professors and civil servants. These people are not politicians and owe their new status to their personal relationships with the president.

The cabinet as a whole tends to be drawn from the civil service or the private sector of the economy. This partly is due to the provision of the constitution forbidding cabinet members from simultaneously serving in Parliament. This "incompatibility rule" means that in France, unlike Britain, the memberships of the cabinet and the Parliament are totally separate and distinct. When a member of Parliament is asked to join the government, he has 30 days to resign his seat. This fact in itself tends to discourage professional politicians from becoming cabinet members, since

The French Cabinet, 1977

Name	Position
Raymond Barre	Prime Minister, Minister of Economy and Finance
Louis de Guiringaud	Minister of Foreign Affairs
Michel Poniatowski	Minister of Interior
Olivier Guichard	Minister of Justice
Jean Lecanuet	Minister of Planning and Development
Michel Durafour	Minister Delegate to Economy and Finance Minister
Yvon Bourges	Minister of Defense
René Haby	Minister of Education
Robert Galley	Minister of Cooperation
Jean-Pierre Fourcade	Minister of Supply
Robert Boulin	Minister of Parliamentary Relations
Christian Bonnet	Minister of Agriculture
André Rossi	Minister of Foreign Trade
Christian Beullac	Minister of Labour
Simone Veil	Minister of Health
Michel d'Ornano	Minister of Industry and Research
Vincent Ansquer	Minister of Quality of Life
Pierre Brousse	Minister of Trade and Crafts
Norbert Segard	Minister of Posts and Telecommunications
Andre Bord	Secretary of State for War Veterans
Françoise Giroud	Secretary of State for Culture

Source: The International Year Book and Statesman's Who's Who (Bath, England: Pitman Press, 1977), p. 138.

they may be losing their political base in return for a temporary executive appointment.

The incompatibility rule was included in the constitution to discourage the practice of Parliament members' voting against a government solely on the hope of gaining a ministry after a cabinet reshuffling. This game of "musical portfolios" characterized much of Fourth Republic parliamentary action, but the Gaullist philosophy rejected the idea that partisan and political considerations should govern the composition of the cabinet. The cabinet, in their view, should be made up of like-minded individuals who were experts in their respective fields.

Styles of Decision-Making

The cabinet may be chaired by either the president or the premier. It is called the council of the cabinet when the premier presides, the council of ministers when the president presides. The president has used the council of ministers as a sounding board, but it has met relatively infrequently and often is effectively bypassed in many policy matters. Presidents prefer to use smaller, interministerial committees shaped to specific tasks to generate the information needed for policy decisions.

Cabinet members, regardless of the presiding officer, tend to follow the principle of collective responsibility, and view themselves as a governmental team with the same goals, commitments, and loyalties. Ministers do not criticize the government publicly even though the cabinet is drawn from the several parties of the governmental coalition.

The essential features of French policy-making are exemplified in the case of the French university reform of 1968.[10] The reform was made necessary by the student-led riots of May 1968. The radical students, unhappy with their educations and with French society at large, sparked a nationwide general strike that eventually involved 7 million workers. De Gaulle skillfully turned the rioting to his advantage. General De Gaulle, speaking of the threat of "totalitarian communism," dissolved the National Assembly and called for new elections. The result was an incredible triumph as the Gaullists won 358 of 485 seats in Parliament.

De Gaulle next determined that educational reform would be a major priority. As he prepared to reshuffle the cabinet after the election, De Gaulle was concerned with choosing a team that could carry off university reform in a hostile situation. He signaled his intention to preside over the reform himself by changing premiers. In July 1968 he dropped Pompidou for the more pliable Maurice Couve de Murville. Soon thereafter he took a personal role in selecting the new minister of education, Edgar Faure. Faure's account of the period leaves no doubt that his interview with De Gaulle two days after Pompidou's departure led to his appointment.

Faure, confident that De Gaulle approved his basic conception of the reform, set out to draft the legislation. After De Gaulle, Couve de Murville, and Faure agreed to the basic lines of the legislation, Faure presented his views to the National Assembly in order to inform that friendly audience of the government's intentions. Faure then proceeded to hold discussions with all interested parties—most importantly the various teachers' and students' unions. The details were worked out within Faure's ministry and among his personal advisers. Questions affecting other ministries were handled either through direct negotiation or through interministerial committee work. Before the *"Loi Faure"* reached the Parliament for formal consideration, De Gaulle gave it his blessing and an implied promise of support. The resulting legislation promised a democraticization of the educational system, an upgrading of scientific and technical education, and promotion of interdisciplinary cooperation. With the president's support the bill had little difficulty in the Gaullist-dominated National Assembly.

---

[10] Bernard E. Brown, "The Decision to Reform the Universities," in Christoph and Brown, eds., *Cases in Comparative Politics*, pp. 121–166.

The drafting of the Loi Faure demonstrates the role of the Gaullist presidency in policy-making. Personally deciding on the reform as a legislative priority, De Gaulle developed his own general view of the proper way to approach reform and handpicked Faure to carry out the draft stage. Thereafter, the presidential role was to monitor progress and lend support as necessary. The role of the premier was to act as a liaison between the president and the ministry of education. Later he was important in the legislative stage. In terms of the familiar prerogative of the executive to initiate and promote policy programs, the president held a monopoly position.

▪ THE SOVIET UNION ▪

Policy-making in the Soviet Union today is directed by the Politburo of the Central Committee of the Communist party of the Soviet Union. Other bodies such as the party Secretariat and the governmental Council of Ministers are involved in policy decisions, but only the Politburo brings together the top men of government and party in one decision-making unit. A leading role within the Politburo is given to the General Secretary of the party, currently Leonid Brezhnev.

During the Stalinist period the Politburo played a much weaker part in making public policy decisions. Stalin gathered all power and the official positions of authority unto himself; the Politburo acted as a board of his lieutenants. At times the Politburo met infrequently, and during the war it gave way to the State Defense Committee. However, since Stalin's death the full membership of the Politburo has been involved in the policy-making process. Although public diagreement is exceedingly rare, a real political give-and-take has characterized the proceedings of the Politburo in the Khrushchev and Brezhnev periods.

The Position of General Secretary

The General Secretary of the party has always had a leading position within the Politburo. His power derives from his directorship of the party Secretariat and, through that body, of the party apparatus. He is not a chairman or presiding officer of the Politburo. The General Secretary is "first among equals" in the sense that his power resources are superior to his colleagues at the highest level of the party. His apparent preeminence is consistent with party protocol, which places him in the first position at any gathering.

The General Secretary's practical power is based on his control over an immense central apparatus—the administrative, supervisory, and personnel-related business of the Communist party. Ideology and indoctrination, the assessment of job performance, and political recruitment are included in his responsibilities. The General Secretary is in a position to advance or short-circuit the careers of thousands of ambitious party bureaucrats. He is able to direct their widespread activities, which include control and supervision of government and economic institutions. The General Secretary's threats and promises simply carry more weight than those of any other official.

Stalin initially built the power of the position when he was appointed by Lenin in 1922. He took advantage of the fact that his rivals, notably Leon Trotsky, viewed administrative work as dull and routine. It was this position that made him dominant in the party because he supervised the work of that large corps of professional party workers which is the backbone of the Communist party. Stalin did not really control the Politburo until at least 1930. He attacked his enemies from his base in the Secretariat.

On Stalin's death the job fell to Khrushchev. Malenkov, gambling that the Council of Ministers would be the future center of power, resigned from the Secretariat, while Khrushchev correctly followed Stalin's example and emphasized his Secretariat position. Khrushchev was aware that he must go slowly in claiming to be Stalin's heir as head of the apparatus. He did not call himself General Secretary but settled for the title First Secretary. Initially, he even cautiously demurred from suggestions that the title should be capitalized and modestly accepted the title "first secretary" in the spirit of collegiality.

Khrushchev's position gradually wore down opposition claims, and eventually he was acknowledged as the top party leader. He never achieved the dominance of the Politburo, however, that characterized Stalin's latter days. In 1957 he was outvoted seven to four in what amounted to a "vote of no confidence" in his leadership. Khrushchev had to resort to calling a special meeting of the Central Committee to back down his rivals—a risky and extraordinary procedure. Even after Khrushchev put down the "anti-party" group, his position was not undisputed, and conflict over policy matters was fairly sharp. Evidence of conflict is found in the fact that of nine new Politburo members selected in 1957, five were demoted before 1961.[11] The victims of Politburo disagreements included several of Khrushchev's valued protégés.

Brezhnev's tenure as General Secretary suggests that he is quite comfortable with the principle of collective leadership. Brezhnev has gone slowly in identifying himself with program initiatives and has been careful to emphasize the unity of the top leadership. Conflict seems to be rather subdued, limited to the confines of private Politburo meetings. If Brezhnev has not been challenged as Khrushchev was, it is partly because he has been even more cautious in playing the role of leader.

---

[11] Darrell P. Hammer, *USSR: The Politics of Oligarchy* (Hinsdale, Ill.: The Dryden Press, 1974), p. 303.

Politburo of the Communist Party of the Soviet Union, 1977

Name	Position

Full Members

Leonid Ilyich Brezhnev	General Secretary, Central Committee, CPSU
Yuri Vladimirovich Andropov	Minister of State Security (KGB)
Viktor Vasilyevich Grishin	1st Secretary, Moscow City Party Organization
Andrei Andreyevich Gromyko	Foreign Minister
Andrei Pavlovich Kirilenko	Secretary, CC, CPSU
Aleksei Nikolayevich Kosygin	Premier
Fyodor Davydovich Kulakov	Secretary, CC, CPSU
Dinmukhamed Akhmedovich Kunaev	1st Secretary, Kazakh Communist Party
Kirill Trofimovich Mazurov	1st Deputy Premier
Arvid Yanovich Pelshe	Chairman, Party Control Commission
Grigorii Vasilyevich Romanov	1st Secretary, Leningrad Oblast Party Organization
Mihail Andreyevich Suslov	Secretary, CC, CPSU
Dmitrii Fyodorovich Ustinov	Defense Minister
Vladimir Vasilyevich Shcherbitskii	1st Secretary, Ukrainian Communist Party

Candidate Members

Geidar Ali Aliev	1st Secretary, Azerbaidjan Communist Party
Pyotr Nilovich Demichev	Minister of Culture
Pyotr Mironovich Masherov	1st Secretary, Belorussian Communist Party
Boris Nikolayevich Ponomaryov	Secretary, CC, CPSU
Sharaf Rashidovich Rashidov	1st Secretary, Uzbek Communist Party
Mihail Sergeyevich Solomentsev	Chairman, RSFSR Council of Ministers

Source: John L. Scherer, ed., *USSR: Facts & Figures Annual,* Vol. I (1977) (Gulf Breeze, Fla.: Academic International Press, 1977), p. 45.

The Politburo

The Politburo, as a decision-making body, resembles the cabinet in a parliamentary system. It is a collegial body made up of prominent men with independent political bases. Like the British cabinet, it is a deliberative body that works out policy decisions on a consensus basis. The most striking similarity is the emphasis placed on group solidarity—public criticism of the group's action is forbidden to members. In the case of the Politburo, the act of opposition to the group decision is by definition a high crime. The most important departure from the cabinet analogy lies in the fact that members of the Politburo do not have departmental responsibilities. At times Stalin tried to enforce a division of responsibilities by policy area, but this was abandoned. The Politburo has no defined individual responsibilities and, strictly speaking, no chairman.

Members of the Politburo are often veterans of the party apparatus, usually with experience as the top party leaders at the level of republic or region. Others reach prominence through important governmental careers, especially the management of the Soviet economy.

The Politburo normally includes the General Secretary, the chairman of the Council of Ministers (premier), and the chairman of the Presidium of the Supreme Soviet (president). This is almost always true because the incumbents of these positions use Politburo status to achieve their office, not the reverse. In essence, the Politburo is the small elite body that, after deliberations and inner struggles, fills the top party and government jobs from its own ranks. The incumbents of these positions stay in the Politburo, which remains the locus of their policy-making activities.

Beyond the top three leaders, the Politburo usually includes the first secretaries of large party organizations. The first secretaries of the Ukrainian organization and of the Moscow party apparatus are usually included. Influential government ministers such as the ministers of defense or of foreign affairs may well be included. Finally, the chairman of the secret police (KGB) may find his way to the Politburo. In all, only 10 to 15 prominent leaders will comprise the Politburo. A small number of candidate members will stand just below the top leadership.

The actual operation of the Politburo is not known outside the inner circles of the party. Currently, it meets frequently, perhaps as often as twice a week, and is therefore an ongoing decision-making body, unlike the larger Central Committee which meets only a few times a year for short sessions. It is clear that all policy matters are discussed here and that the Politburo sets policy for both party and government. It is doubtful whether actual votes are taken. Rather a "sense of the meeting" consensus is sought.

The Politburo is a self-contained decision-making unit in that it is not dependent on any nonparty sources of information or expertise. The Secretariat channels all of the necessary information from its control, surveillance, and research units. The fact that roughly one-fourth of the Politburo members are also secretaries of the Communist party suggests the importance of the information-generating organ. The method of obtaining the raw material for policy decisions means that all background material is filtered through the same party source. The Politburo does not consult with affected interests and actors but relies on the assessments of its own party professionals.

Styles of Decision-Making

Soviet decision-making in normal times appears fairly smooth and free of conflict. At all times, however, there is a subtle struggle within the Politburo. Each man in the elite has allies who represent concrete interests. A military representative has views on foreign policy and priorities of production reflecting his power base. A representative of the state bureaucracy or manager of the economy will have views on détente and consumer production reflecting his career experience and the views of those who have supported his personal career. In short, policy decisions are made by a small group of men with divergent interest-based opinions.

If individuals become associated with particular views or programs that arouse conflict, a simple policy decision may threaten their political careers. Since Lenin's day the party leadership has lived in fear of the development of party factions—even looking warily at a group of Politburo members who advocate a particular policy. Politburo members try to avoid splits; their policy-making reflects this conservative concern. Splits would likely lead to a leadership reshuffling with major policy implications.

Examples of Politburo decision-making style show a good deal of continuity from the Khrushchev to the Brezhnev period. Khrushchev defeated his rivals in part on the basis of policy appeals to important interests. Ironically, he discredited Malenkov by criticizing his emphasis on consumer goods production, a policy he later adopted. Khrushchev became associated with an improvement in the Soviet citizen's standard of living. This position, opposed by the Soviet military and party ideologues, implied a shift from heavy industrial production. Khrushchev's domestic policy also included an emphasis on agriculture, focusing on chemical fertilizer production and the development of virgin land. He said that he intended to improve the quality and quantity of foodstuffs available to Soviet citizens.

Internationally, Khrushchev associated himself with the notion of peaceful coexistence. He emphasized that competition between the United States and the Soviet Union should be economic only; other nations, he said, would copy the system with the strongest economy. (This basic policy preference did not prevent the First Secretary from military adventures and threats, but his basic position was unmistakable.) While Khrushchev was in power, he was able to carry the broad lines of his policies. However, he had occasional setbacks. After the American spy plane, the U-2, was shot down over the Soviet Union in 1960, his conservative opponents forced him to react sharply;[12] moreover, he had to scuttle his own pet project—the Paris summit conference. Khrushchev also was unable to push for his consumer production program. The opposition to his ideas influenced him to take a cautious approach. He finally made a public speech on October 2, 1964, at an unusual joint meeting of the Politburo and the Council of Ministers. Khrushchev was forced out of office 12 days later by a firm coalition of Politburo members and their allies who repudiated both Khrushchev and his policies.

The new leadership under Brezhnev quickly restored the traditional

---

[12] Ibid., p. 311.

heavy industry priority. They also increased the size of the Soviet military as a signal of their intention to be firm in international affairs. The conflict about basic policy had been resolved by the bureaucratic contest between leadership rivals and their interest-based allies.

To summarize, policy-making in the post-Stalin era has followed the pattern revealed in the transition from Khrushchev to Brezhnev. Conflict among powerful interests are settled within the Politburo, whose membership reflects some of those interests. Consensus and mutual accommodation are the operating principles of normal politics. Basic changes in policy direction eventually require the ritual sacrifice of a leader or a portion of the leadership.

▪ NIGERIA ▪

Nigeria's civilian parliamentary government was founded on the principles of the British Westminster model. From 1960 to 1966 the prime minister was Sir Abubakar Tafawa Balewa, national leader of the largest political party in the National Assembly, the Northern People's Congress. His cabinet was drawn from parliamentary MPs of his party, or those parties in coalition with the NPC (primarily the National Council of Nigerian Citizens). The head of state during this period was Dr. Nnamdi Azikiwe, who held the office of president. Key decision-making authority rested with the prime minister.

Nigeria was a federal system with specific powers granted to the federal government and others to the regional governments. The Western, Eastern, Northern, and later the Mid-Western Regions, along with the federal territory of Lagos, jealously guarded their prerogatives and powers. Throughout the civilian period those who favored a strong central government and weak regions conflicted with those who favored strong regions and a weak center.

The military officers who took control of Nigeria in January 1966 suspended Parliament, dismissed the governors of the various regions, and eliminated the offices of president and prime minister. Civilian, parliamentary institutions were replaced with a new set of structures dominated by the military. Since 1966 the military has been the most important institution for making policy and political decisions.

Executive Decision-Making During the Military Period

Decree No. 1 issued by the new military government on January 17, 1966, made clear where political power rested. According to the Suspension and Modification of the Constitution Decree, the "Federal Military Government shall have power to make laws for the peace, order and good government of Nigeria or any party thereof with respect to any matter whatsoever."[13] The new government made laws and policy by issuing decrees signed by the head of the military government, while regional policy was made by newly installed military governors who issued edicts. Executive authority at the national level was "vested in the Head of the Federal Military Government and may be exercised by him either directly or through persons or authorities subordinate to him."[14]

Since the issuance of Decree No. 1, Nigeria has had four military heads of state. Major General Johnson Aguiyi-Ironsi held office from January to July 1966, when he was killed in a coup d'état. Then General Yakubu Gowon held office until removed from power in a nonviolent coup d'état in July 1975. The leader of this coup, General Murtala Mohammed, served as head of the military government until January 1976, when he was killed in an abortive coup d'état. The most recent head of the federal military government is General Olusegun Obasanjo, who was General Mohammed's second in command and chief of staff at Supreme Headquarters.

Following the January 1966 coup, two new institutions were created at the national level to make and enforce policy and law. The Supreme Military Council (SMC) is the most important in regard to policy-making. Its membership includes the head of the federal military government (who serves as president of the Supreme Military Council); the heads of the army, navy, and air force; the chief of staff of the armed forces, the chief of staff of the Nigerian army, the attorney-general, and the military governors of the various regions or states. The SMC has the power to delegate its power and responsibility where it sees fit.

The second new political institution that was created was the Federal Executive Council (FEC). In practice, the FEC functions as the cabinet. The number of people in the cabinet varies, but it usually includes from 15 to 25 members. In some cases high-ranking military men in the Supreme Military Council also hold posts in the Federal Executive Council. Decree No. 8, issued in 1967 by the new Head of Military Government General Gowon, clarified the relationship between the SMC and the Federal Executive Council by giving both executive and legislative authority to the Supreme Military Council. As a result of this decision, the powers of the FEC are those delegated to it by the SMC.

The composition of the Federal Executive Council has changed since its establishment. The 1968 cabinet, which remained relatively stable until 1971, included General Gowon (who served as chairman and held the portfolios of Defense and External Affairs) and Chief Obafemi Awolowo, who acted as vice chairman and also finance chairman. Several other

---

[13] Decree No. 1, 1966. Constitution (Suspension and Modification) Decree 1966, Section 3.1. Cited in A. H. M. Kirk-Greene, *Crisis and Conflict in Nigeria: A Documentary Sourcebook*, Vol. 1 (London: Oxford University Press, 1971), p. 131.

[14] Ibid., p. 132.

positions were held by civilians, many of whom were old-line politicians, or men with specialized expertise. The 1968 cabinet included representatives from all Nigerian states and was in many respects a wartime cabinet, since from 1967 to 1970 the federal government was engaged in dealing with the secessionist Eastern Region (Biafra).

Cabinet composition changed in 1971 when General Gowon announced that commissioners in the government were to serve only three-year terms. This policy was designed to prevent any commissioner from becoming entrenched in office and to allow civilian politicians to resign from the cabinet and prepare for the return to civilian rule. (General Gowon initially scheduled 1974 as the date for the return to civilian rule, but later postponed the date). New members were appointed to the cabinet, General Gowon relinquished the post of External Affairs, and a new finance minister was appointed to replace Chief Awolowo who resigned his posts in June 1971.

The Federal Executive Council plays an important role in policy formation. Its membership includes "political" appointees as well as individuals with specialized expertise. Nigeria's new oil wealth, for example, has made necessary the creation of new ministries, staffed by experts, to deal with oil production, sale, and revenues. With their control over vast bureaucracies, commissioners often influence the policy determination as well as its interpretation and implementation.

Changes in executive leadership have produced changes in the composition and structure of the cabinet. When General Mohammed replaced General Gowon in July 1975, there were important changes in the FEC. The new cabinet totaled 25 members—14 military ministers and 11 civilians. New portfolios were created for Aviation; Petroleum and Energy; Co-operatives and Supply; Youth and Sports; Water; and Works. Only four members from the January 1974 cabinet were reappointed to the August 1975 cabinet.

Changes in the Federal Executive Council were not the only changes following the 1975 coup. In addition to General Gowon (the head of state and commander-in-chief of the armed forces), the chief of staff, the deputy chief of staff, and the chiefs of staff of the army, navy, and air force were retired. All officers holding the rank of major general and above were retired, as were all military and civilian state governors. Finally, the inspector-general of police and his deputy were removed from office. The 1975 shift is notable for the magnitude of change. A new set of political leaders and decision-makers assumed office with the intentions of reversing what they felt were the dangerous trends developing in the Gowon period and of producing new policy directions.

The abortive coup against the government of General Mohammed did not produce the dramatic cabinet changes that followed the 1975 coup. The transition to General Obasanjo's rule appeared to be handled smoothly and with little open conflict. Early in his rule General Obasanjo

Policy-Making Institutions in Nigeria—

The Supreme Military Council and the Federal Executive Council, 1976

Position	Name
Supreme Military Council	
Head of the Federal Military Government, Commander-in-Chief of the Armed Forces	Lt.-General Olusegun Obasanjo
Chief of Staff, Supreme Headquarters	Brigadier Shehu M. Yar'Adua
Chief of Army Staff	Lt.-General T. Y. Danjuma
Chief of Naval Staff	Rear Admiral Michael A. Adelanwa
Chief of Air Staff	Air Commander John Yisa-Doko
Inspector-General of Police	Alhaji M. W. Yusufu
Federal Executive Council	
Ministers of:	
Agriculture	B. O. W. Mafeni
Aviation	Shuaibu Kazaure
Communications	S. O. Williams
Co-operatives and Supply	U. A. Mutallab
Defense	
Economic Development	Dr. M. T. O. Akobo
Education	Colonel (Dr.) A. A. Ali
Establishments	Major-General J. J. Oluleye
External Affairs	Brigadier J. N. Garba
Finance	A. E. Ekukinam
Health	Commissioner of Police Mr. K. Tinubu
Housing, Urban Development, and Environment	Lt.-Colonel M. Mohammed
Industries	Dr. R. A. Adeleye
Information	Major-General I. B. M. Haruna
Internal Affairs	U. Shinkafi
Justice	Justice Dan Ibekwe
Labour	Major-General H. E. O. Adefope
Mines and Power	Effiom Otu Ekong
Petroleum and Energy	Colonel M. Buhari
Social Development, Youth, and Sports	Major-General O. Olutoye
Trade	Major-General M. Shuwa
Transport	Lt.-Colonel M. Magoro
Water Resources	Dr. I. U. William-Osisiogu
Works	Major-General O. E. Obada
Special Duties (Black Arts Festival)	Commander O. P. Fingesi
Special Duties Capital Development Authority	M. Ajose-Adeogun

Source: Colin Legum, ed., *Africa Contemporary Record, 1975–1976,* (London: Rex Collings, 1976), pp. B796–797.

General Olusegun Obasanjo (right) is Nigeria's fourth general to lead Nigeria since 1966. The military has scheduled a return to civilian rule in 1979. Camera Press, Ltd.

directed much of his attention toward dealing with those responsible for the attempted coup. The highest-ranking officer executed for his role in the plot was the former minister of defense, Major General I. D. Bisalla. Altogether, 39 military men were reported executed, 3 persons (including 2 civilians) were sentenced to life in prison, and 7 soldiers were sentenced to 15-year terms.

It is clear that the head of the military government and his chief military aides are the key decision-makers. Their power, however, is not unlimited. They must consult and rely on both civilian and military advisers. These advisers are selected on the basis of their technical expertise, rank, and often, ethnic or regional origin. Since the civil war all governments have attempted to ensure that no region or group is either over- or under-represented in positions of power. The constraints on the power of the military leaders are very real; these constraints are clearly evident when analyzing the decision-making styles of the military governments.

Styles of Decision-Making

The military leaders created an authoritarian decision-making structure but were the first to admit in 1966 that they were unprepared to exercise political power. Nigerian officers viewed themselves, rightly so, as well-trained, professional, nonpolitical soldiers used to hierarchical authority. A leader of the first coup in January 1966 described the enemies of the soldiers and of most Nigerians as follows:

Our enemies are the political profiteers, the swindlers, the men in high and low places that seek bribes and demand 10 per cent; those that seek to keep the country divided permanently so that they can remain in office as ministers or VIPs at least; the tribalists, the nepotists, those that have corrupted our society and put the Nigerian political calendar back by their words and deeds.[15]

The military, then, had no detailed blueprint for governing Nigeria. They had no specific ideology and no set of specific goals for development. Their initial pronouncements clearly stressed restoration of order and an end to corruption; but they were not so clear as to how they hoped to change Nigerian politics. In February 1966 General Ironsi indicated that the new government had yet to find an answer:

On the question of the political future of the country, the experiences and mistakes of the previous governments in the Federation have clearly indicated that far-reaching constitutional reforms are badly needed for peaceful and orderly progress. . . . No doubt, the country would welcome a clean break with the deficiencies of the system of government to which the country has been subjected in the recent past. A solution suitable to our national needs must be found.[16]

Despite the implied desire in the above statement to quickly return to civilian government, the military has exercised political power for over 10 years. The military leaders realized, that, like it or not, they were involved in politics, and that in order to govern they needed the advice and support of others. Civilians, many of them ex-politicians, had technical and administrative know-how that the soldiers lacked. What began to emerge was a pattern in which the SMC would make the decisions, but only after consultation with others. These decisions were then implemented by the civil service and the bureaucracy. The civilian permanent secretaries in the ministries became increasingly important both because they could advise and because they "knew how to get things done."

Of the several important issues facing these leaders, a crucial one is the relationship between the national government and local regional or state governments. The twin issues of how many regions or states there should be and what power they should exercise have never been satisfactorily resolved. During the colonial period the British created three regions—North, West, and East—plus the federal territory of Lagos. In 1963 the civilian parliamentary government created the Mid-West Region, between the East and the West. General Ironsi's controversial Decree No. 34 in

---

[15] S. K. Panter-Brick, ed., *Nigerian Politics and Military Rule: Prelude to the Civil War* (London: Athlone Press, University of London, 1970), p. 185.

[16] Ibid., p. 189.

1966 (which played an important part in his downfall) abolished the regions and created a strong unitary government. Later in 1966 General Gowon reversed this decision and created 12 new states: the Northern Region was divided into 6 new states, the West into 3, and the East into 3. The aim was to prevent any region from dominating the others and to prevent the Eastern Region from carrying out its threat to secede. The creation of the 12 states, however, was too late to prevent the attempted secession of the Eastern Region. The 12 states became 19 in February 1976, when General Mohammed announced the creation of 7 new states and the site of a new, centrally located capital city (see maps in Chapter 2).

In each case the decision-makers were attempting to find a solution to a pressing problem. How could the central government maintain its authority while meeting the demands of the three major groups and countless minority groups for some regional autonomy? This question produced a series of answers, some more successful than others. The aim of the 1976 decision creating 19 states was to satisfy certain minority groups who claimed that they deserved a state of their own and to settle the question of "how many states" once and for all. Despite the statement by General Mohammed that no new states would be created in the future, many groups continue to demand the establishment of their state or, at least, significant boundary changes in the current system. As we shall see, this problem and others like it defy easy solution and are often passed unresolved from regime to regime.

New leaders, on taking office, often attempt to resolve problems by taking dramatic action early in their administrations. On the one hand, this hampers continuity and consistency from regime to regime. Periods of activity are followed by long periods of inactivity. On the other hand, these bursts of activity are important precisely because they produce change. One reason stated for the removal of General Gowon—at the time a personally popular political figure—was that his advisers had become corrupt and entrenched in office and that the government failed to make necessary decisions. These criticisms are reminiscent of those that the new military leaders of January 1966 leveled against *civilian* leaders.

General Mohammed and his supporters, on assuming office in 1975, promised dynamism, change, and a general housecleaning. Soon General Mohammed created new states, announced the site of the new capital in the nation's center, planned the demobilization of part of the army, and began ending the notorious congestion at the Lagos port (see Chapter 11). In addition, he retired 10,000 civil servants and officials, and pushed Nigeria into a more active role in foreign affairs. General Obasanjo has continued many of the policies and changes initiated by General Mohammed (although perhaps not with his dynamic style); but, like leaders in systems with more regularized systems of succession, new Nigerian leaders find that resolving to make changes is considerably easier than actually making them.

Nigerian decision-makers face a dilemma. The military leaders have promised a return to civilian rule in 1979. To accomplish this, Nigerians must agree on a decision-making structure that is stable and regularized and that will not tear Nigeria apart. Some argue for a presidential system with a strong, national president (similar to the executive in the United States), while others argue for a return to a modified, parliamentary regime in which political parties would not be allowed to appeal to narrow sectional interests. Still others argue that realistically the military, despite its faults, should remain in power. At this writing, the consensus appears to favor a strong executive, nationally chosen.

If the military does return power to civilians in 1979 as promised, it will end 13 years of decision-making by senior military officers with the support and assistance of the civilian sector. In a system like Nigeria that is not fully institutionalized, administrators and bureaucrats may exercise de facto power by the way in which they interpret and carry out policy. They act as a check on the decision-makers' power.

The tendency in Nigeria has been that the longer a group holds office, the more corrupt it becomes. Leaders become more concerned with holding power than with governing. While new leaders begin with the best of intentions, the problems facing them, the range of available solutions, and the already existing political structures limit their power to take dramatic action. Soldiers as decision-makers face many of the same problems as civilians as decision-makers.

■ EGYPT ■

Executive authority in Egypt is vested in the office of the president. According to the 1971 constitution, the government, which includes the president and his ministers, is the "supreme executive and administrative organ of the state." The actual and potential power of the presidency is tremendous. Both Presidents Nasser and Sadat have been able to dominate and control the decision-making process in modern-day Egypt.

Presidential Power

By law the Egyptian president must be at least 40 years old. He serves a six-year term and can be re-elected to serve another. The selection process requires that the president be nominated by at least one-third of the members of the People's Assembly (known as the National Assembly during the Nasser presidency), approved by at least two-thirds of the membership, and then elected by a popular referendum. The selection process was most recently used following the death of President Nasser. Vice President Sadat was confirmed in office by the Higher Executive Com-

President Nasser toasts then Soviet leader Nikita Khrushchev. Erich Lessing, Magnum Photos, Inc.

mittee of the Arab Socialist Union and the National Assembly in October 1970. Shortly thereafter, he received his popular mandate through a nationwide referendum.

The Egyptian president has wide-ranging powers of appointment. He appoints the vice presidents, the prime minister, the deputy prime ministers, and the various government ministers. As Egypt's bureaucracy is powerful, this appointive power is significant. The July 1975 Council of Ministers contained a prime minister, 3 deputy prime ministers, and 31 ministers. The president also has the power to appoint up to 10 members of the People's Assembly, and, at various times, has had the power to appoint individuals to important party posts in the Arab Socialist Union.

Ministers ultimately are responsible to the president. The Assembly can express a vote of no confidence or censure a minister—in which case the minister must resign—but a more likely occurrence is that the president himself will remove controversial or politically troublesome ministers. When the Assembly votes no confidence in the prime minister, there is a popular referendum on the prime minister. If the referendum goes against the prime minister, he must resign; if it favors the prime minister and hence the president, the Assembly is dissolved and new elections are held.

It is difficult to separate the presidency from President Nasser. Nasser's presence was so overwhelming that he was able to define the roles and powers of the presidency. His power and popularity were such that he could weather crises that would have forced out many other chief executives. For example, after Egypt's disasterous defeat in the June 1967 war with Israel, Nasser resigned but was soon recalled to office by popular and governmental demand. His reputation was tarnished, but his power remained largely intact. Much like De Gaulle in the early period of France's Fifth Republic, Nasser was able to place his personal stamp on the office.

Executive Power During the Early Sadat Presidency

The sudden death of President Nasser in September 1970 created a potential political vacuum and crisis for the Egyptian political elite. As long as President Nasser remained leader, he was able, with varying degrees of success, to manage the various interests or "centers of power" in Egypt. The military, the Arab Socialist Union, the National Assembly, and the bureaucracy all held different perspectives on governing Egypt and all sought influence with the president. With Nasser's death, however, the thread that held the various groups together was broken.

When President Nasser selected Anwar Sadat to be his vice president in 1969, Sadat seemed to be a compromise candidate who would not alienate the various powerful interests within Egyptian government. On assuming the presidency, Sadat needed, first of all, to establish his own authority and to show potential rivals that he did not consider himself merely a caretaker president. Second, he needed to establish a policy toward Israel, the Soviet Union, and the United States. Egypt's heavy dependence on the Soviet Union for both military and general economic aid during most of the 1960s had several important policy implications. Third, the president needed to develop a comprehensive economic policy to begin tackling some of Egypt's more serious economic problems. The population explosion, rapid urbanization, housing and transportation problems, and the need to strengthen the industrial sector required comprehensive, decisive planning. Finally, the new president faced the unenviable task of succeeeding a charismatic political leader. A favorite speculation in Egypt was how long the new president could maintain his power and control.

The president first turned his attention to the makeup of his cabinet. President Sadat, as a compromise president himself, tried to form a cabinet representative of the diverse interests vying for power and influence. The new prime minister appointed in October 1970 was a career diplomat, a civilian, and considerably older than most other ministers. In turn, Dr. Mahmud Fawzy reappointed the ministers who had served in the 1968 cabinet of President Nasser. Continuity in the immediate post-Nasser period was important. Shortly after these appointments were announced, the cabinet itself was reorganized.

The reorganization divided the cabinet into three departments. The

Policy-Making Institutions in Egypt—

The Presidency and the Council of Ministers, June 1976

Position	Name
The Presidency	
President	Colonel Muhammad Anwar Sadat
Vice President	Lt.-General Muhammad Hosni Mubarak

Council of Ministers	
Prime Minister, and in charge of Economic Affairs Ministries	General Mamdouh Muhammad Salem
Deputy Premier and Minister of Foreign Affairs	Muhammad Ismail Fahmi
Deputy Premier and Minister for War and War Production	General Muhammad Abdul Ghani al-Gamassi
Deputy Premier for Production and Minister of Energy	Ahmad Sultan
Deputy Premier for Social Development and Head of Local Government Ministerial Committee	Muhammad Hafez Ghanem
Economic Affairs Ministries	
Economy and Economic Co-operation	Muhammad Zaki Shafei
Finance	Ahmad Abu-Ismail
Trade and Supply	Zakariya Taufiq Abdel-Fattah
Planning	Muhammad Mahmoud Imam
Production Ministries	
Industry and Mineral Resources	Issa Shahin
Oil	Ahmad Izzedin Hilal
Agriculture and Irrigation	Abdel-Azim Abdul-Ata
Transport and Communications	Abdel-Fattah Abdulla
Maritime Transport	Mahmoud Gahmi
Tourism and Aviation	Ibrahim Nagib
Minister of State for War Production	Gamal Sidqi
Minister of State for Agriculture and Sudanese Affairs	Abdel-Aziz Husain
Social Development and Services	
Interior	Sayed Husain Fahmi
Housing and Reconstruction	Osman Ahmed Osman
Education	Mustafa Kamal Hilmi
Health	Dr. Ahmad Fuad Muhieddin
Justice and Chairman of Legislative Com.	Ahmed Samih Talaat

The Presidency and the Council of Ministers, June 1976 (*Continued*)

Position	Name
Labour and Vocational Training	Abdel-Latif Bultiya
Social Affairs and Insurance	Aisha Rateb
Information and Culture	Gamal Otaifi
Waqfs and Al-Azhar Affairs	Muhammad Husain Dahabi
Minister of State for Housing and Reconstruction	Muhammad Bahjat Hasanain
General Ministries	
Minister of State for National Assembly Affairs	Albert Barsoum Salama
Minister of State for Local Government, Popular and Political Organizations	Muhammad Hamid Mahmoud
Minister of State for Scientific Research and Atomic Energy	Ahmad Abdel-Maaboud Jubaili
Minister of State for Foreign Affairs	Muhammad Riyad
Minister of State for Cabinet Affairs and Administrative Development	Fuad Sharif

Source: The Middle East and North Africa, 1976–1977 Edition (London: Europa Publications Limited, 1976), p. 309.

ministries of War, Foreign Affairs, Information, Planning and Presidential Affairs were joined as a department concerned with the sovereignty of the state. Agriculture, Industry, Labor, Marketing and Distribution of Commodities, and Scientific Research were grouped under the heading of production and trade. Health, Education, and Cultural and Social Services were viewed as ministries that provided services but did not raise revenues. The aim was to consolidate and, by so doing, to make planning more efficient and rational.[17] At the same time that the reorganization was carried out, Prime Minister Fawzy announced several cabinet changes.

President Sadat faced several challenges to his power in his early presidency. One of the most severe came from political opponents with strong bases of power, who challenged the president's authority. By 1971 the conflict was fairly visible as men such as Ali Sabri (a power within the ASU), General Sadek (a power in the military), and Shawarri Gomma (a power in the Ministry of Interior) openly challenged the president. Through skillful maneuvering President Sadat outflanked his opponents,

---

[17] Colin Legum, ed., *Africa Contemporary Record, 1970–1971* (London: Rex Collings, 1971), pp. B72–73.

defused the crisis, and removed his most serious opponents from office, replacing them with people loyal to him (see Chapter 10).

The president's popularity has fluctuated during his tenure in office. He proclaimed 1971 a "year of decision" and promised decisive action against Israel. The goal was to regain control of the Sinai Peninsula and the Suez Canal, both lost during the 1967 war with Israel. When no action was forthcoming, the president's standing dropped precipitously. The "year of decision" was followed by a year of "no peace, no war." The economy slumped, and Egypt's relations with the Soviet Union deteriorated. In March 1973 President Sadat began wearing three hats: he became prime minister and military governor as well as remaining president. A sweeping cabinet change brought in economic ministers who advocated a new economic policy—a policy that would have a significant impact on Egypt's foreign relations as well.

Cabinet changes signaled a shift away from the Soviet Union toward a more pro-Western policy. The aim was to change the direction of the economy and to create a situation favorable to United States and Western investment. This "new opening" involved "more capitalistic" rather than "more socialistic" approaches to economic problem-solving. Not surprisingly, this change provoked a debate within the Egyptian government, but the president and his supporters ultimately triumphed.

The war of October 1973, in which the Egyptian army crossed the Suez Canal and pushed Israeli troops away from the east bank of the canal, dramatically raised the prestige of the president. Although Egypt's showing was far from a decisive or clear-cut military victory, President Sadat's power, authority, and prestige increased. To many Egyptians he became the "Hero of the Crossing."

When President Sadat assumed office, he clearly lacked the power and prestige of his predecessor. Although many viewed him only as a caretaker who would occupy the office until a more permanent successor took charge, President Sadat consolidated and strengthened his claim to the office. He did this partly through the appointments he made to the cabinet, and partly through his ability to manipulate the various centers of power surrounding the office of president. By 1973 most positions in the government (at least at the higher levels) were staffed by individuals loyal and responsible to the new president.

President Sadat also has made skillful use of his power to formulate legislation. While attempting to maintain the spirit of the 1952 revolution the Sadat presidency places its own stamp on and interpretation of what the revolution means. The opening to the West and the lessening of dependence on the Soviet Union for military and economic aid were designed in part to separate the Sadat presidency from the Nasser presidency. Likewise, the "liberalization" that permitted more open political discussion was an attempt to place a distinctive Sadat stamp on Egyptian politics.

There is little question that executive authority is firmly entrenched in the office of president. With his ministerial advisers, he originates and administers policy from this branch of Egyptian government. Changes in ministerial posts often indicate changes in policy. The power of the president stems from his broad powers stated in the constitution and from his ability to control and manipulate the centers of power in Egypt. The military, bureaucracy, Arab Socialist Union, and People's Assembly all present potential challenges to the office of the president. The power of the president is great, but to hold that power the president must be a skillful politician. He must have access to information, understand people, and carefully balance and weigh conflicting interests and positions. The magnitude of the problems facing the Egyptian president severely tests his political skill.

▪ TANZANIA ▪

Julius Nyerere has been the chief decision-maker and dominant political figure in Tanzania since before independence. When Tanganyika became a republic in 1962, Prime Minister Nyerere became President Nyerere; in 1964, when Tanganyika joined with Zanzibar, Nyerere became president of the United Republic of Tanzania. He has been confirmed in office by uncontested popular referenda in 1965, 1970, and most recently in 1975. Following his renomination in 1975, Nyerere reflected on whether

it would not be a service to my country if I stood down from national leadership while still in full possession of my senses and strength, in order that I, together with my fellow citizens, could set an example of support and loyalty to my successor.[18]

As Nyerere is head of state, head of government, and head of the only legal political party in Tanzania, the style of executive authority in Tanzania is shaped by his philosophy and values. These values emphasize the creation of a socialist state, the importance of politicians' and administrators' remaining responsive to the demands of the populace, and the necessity of popular participation in decision-making at the local level.

In a developing political system where the political institutions are not well established, decision-making can be risky. Among the more common problems plaguing decision-makers are coordinating the various ministries concerned with political, economic, and social development; the delegation of power and authority from national institutions to local govern-

---

[18] Colin Legum, ed., *Africa Contemporary Record, 1975–1976* (London: Rex Collings, 1976), p. B315.

ments; the general lack of technical experts; and conflicts between political actors and administrative planners.

Executive Power in Tanzania

The 1965 Tanzanian constitution vests executive authority in the president and states that "the President shall act in his own discretion and shall not be obliged to follow advice tendered by any other person."[19] A constitutional amendment in 1975 affirms the supremacy of the Tanzanian African National Union over the government and all other institutions in Tanzania. In practice, the top leadership of the party and the key actors in the government are often the same persons. While the party may establish general policy orientations and guidelines, the president and his government formulate and carry out specific policy.

The chief executive officer is the president. His term is five years, and the candidate must be nominated by TANU and elected by the national electorate. In case of the death, resignation, or removal of the president, the first vice president of the United Republic succeeds, followed by the second vice president. The two appointed vice presidents represent mainland Tanganyika and the island of Zanzibar and are also high officials in TANU and the Afro-Shirazi party in Zanzibar. If the president dismisses the National Assembly and calls for a new election, the president himself must also stand for re-election.

The powers of the president are wide-ranging. One of his most important prerogatives is the power of appointment. He appoints the two vice presidents, his cabinet ministers (he can also discipline and dismiss his ministers), and regional commissioners throughout Tanganyika. Ten members of the National Assembly are nominated by the president. He serves as commander-in-chief of the armed forces, controls the civil service, and has the power of pardon.

The size, influence, and structure of the principal advisory body, the cabinet, varies. All ministers in the cabinet, except the president, must be members of the National Assembly and hence of TANU. Though Tanganyika became a presidential republic rather than a parliamentary system in 1962, this parliamentary characteristic was retained. A second parliamentary trait retained was the powerful Treasury. Although after 1962 the Treasury no longer controlled the civil service, establishments, or regional administration, it continued to exercise control over the budget process and the collection of revenue.

The cabinet membership in 1965 included the president, his vice presidents, and 21 cabinet ministers. The Ministry of State for Union Affairs

---

[19] "The Interim Constitution of Tanzania, 1965," (Dar es Salaam, Tanzania: Government Printer, 1965), Chapter II, Section 6, Sub-section (2).

and the Ministry of Foreign Affairs were in the president's office; Central Establishment was in the first vice president's office; and Defense, Justice, and National Service were in the second vice president's office. Defense was upgraded in importance and transferred to the second vice president's office in 1964 following an army mutiny.

Other ministries were grouped in three categories—administrative, social, and economic ministries. The administrative category included such ministries as Home Affairs, Economic Affairs and Development Planning, Regional Administration, and Finance. Among the more important social ministries were Education, Health, Housing, Community Development, and Labour. Finally, economic ministries included, among others, Agriculture, Land Settlement and Water, Mineral Resources and Power, and Commerce and Cooperatives. The Exchequer and Audit Department, the Local Government Service Commission, the Speaker's Office of the National Assembly and the Civil Service Commission were classed as extra ministerial departments and rounded out the central government.[20]

By 1975 both cabinet structure and personnel had changed; new ministries were created while others were reorganized. For example, the Finance and Planning Ministries were joined, while the Commerce and Industry Ministry was split. One of the most important offices, Economic Affairs, was incorporated under the president's office. The occupants of the first and second vice presidencies continued to serve, respectively, as the president of Zanzibar and the prime minister (both cabinet positions).[21]

In terms of cabinet membership two new members were added at the ministerial level and four at the junior minister level. Women, for the first time, were appointed to ministerial positions, in Justice, and in Lands, Housing and Urban Development. Cabinet members appeared to receive their postings for one of two typical reasons—either they had a specialized technical expertise or they performed important political tasks.[22]

According to the constitution, the cabinet is an advisory body to the president, but the law does not require the president to accept the advice of his cabinet. In practice, though, the cabinet plays an important role in policy-making. Like the party, it is a forum for debating and discussing ideas and policies and how best decisions can be implemented. President Nyerere is a strong leader, with wide-ranging powers, but he has kept his lines of communication open and has accepted advice and comment from people representing diverse views. His leadership style has been characterized as one of "strength, independence, and legality."[23] There is little

---

[20] Henry Bienen, *Tanzania, Party Transformation and Economic Development,* expanded ed. (Princeton: Princeton University Press, 1971), p. 283.

[21] *African Contemporary Record, 1975–1976,* p. B323.

[22] Ibid.

[23] Raymond F. Hopkins, *Political Roles in a New State, Tanzania's First Decade* (New Haven: Yale University Press, 1971), p. 207.

Policy-Making Institutions in Tanzania—

The Tanzanian Government, February 1977

Position	Name
President	Julius Nyerere
First Vice President	Aboud Jumbe
Second Vice President	Vacant
Prime Minister	Edward Moringe Sokoine
Ministers of State in the President's Office	Abdallah Natepe, Hussein Shekilango
Minister of State in the First Vice President's Office	Ali Mzee
Minister of State in the Prime Minister's Office	Jackson Makweta

Ministers of:

Position	Name
Defense	Rashidi Kawawa
Works	Alfred Tandau
Labour and Social Welfare	Crispin Tungaraza
Lands, Housing and Urban Development	Tabitha Siwale
Information and Broadcasting	Isaac Sepetu
Capital Development	Hasnu Makame
National Culture and Youth	Mirisho Sarakikya
Health	Leader Stirling
Education	Nicholas Kuhanga
Manpower Development	Abel Mwanga
Water, Energy and Minerals	Al-Noor Kassum
Justice	Julie Manning
Commerce	Alphose Rulegura
Industries	Cleopa Msuya
Agriculture	John Malecela
Communications and Transport	Amir Jamal
Home Affairs	Nassor Moyo
Foreign Affairs	Benjamin Mkapa
Finance and Planning	Edwin Mtei
Natural Resources and Tourism	Solomon Ole Saibull
East African Community Affairs	Wilbert Chagula
Junior Minister in the Prime Minister's Office	Robert Ng'itu
Junior Ministers in the Defense Ministry	Colonel Seif Bakari Colonal Moses Nnauye

Source: Africa Research Bulletin, Vol. 14, No. 2 (March 15, 1977), p. 4317.

question who is the ultimate decision-maker and on whom ultimate responsibility rests—President Nyerere.

Styles of Decision-Making

An evaluation of the successes and failures of Tanzania's sweeping political, economic, and social programs is made in Chapter 11. The way in which the various five year plans were developed, however, presents an interesting case study of how decisions are made in Tanzania. Of particular interest is the relationship between the president and his cabinet. The first Five Year Plan, and the two succeeding plans, are designed to develop and coordinate the diverse sectors of the economy and to provide the blueprints for future development.

The institutional framework for decision-making in Tanzania changes constantly, as is typical of most developing nations. As the goals of the political system change and as problems arise, new leaders are recruited to fill new positions; the lines of authority and responsibility change. In the Tanzanian case, the decision to develop a Five Year Plan in 1963/1964 required new ministries and new departments as well as the recruiting of new planners and administrators.

The broad aims of the first Five Year Plan were to increase the average income of Tanzanians, to raise life expectancy, and to reduce the participation of foreigners in the Tanzanian economy. There were three phases in the development of the Five Year Plan: the first phase determined the long-range goals, the second established the goals to be achieved during the plan period, and the third stage established the detailed plan itself.[24]

A Ministry of Development and Planning was created in 1963 to "formulate and direct a Five Year Plan." Foreign experts were called in; a Frenchman became the first director of planning. Initially the ministry was responsible for providing new ideas; consulting with the appropriate ministries; developing national, regional, and local projects; coordinating the various governmental and nongovernmental branches involved in the plan; and keeping the president informed of both the progress and the problems of the plan.[25]

A year after this ministry was established, it was abolished and replaced by a Directorate of Development and Planning operating out of the president's office. Three ministers of state were responsible for running the program's three sectors: manpower, economics and statistics, and program and control. At the same time that the Directorate was moved to the president's office, the Central Statistical Office was transferred from Treasury to the Directorate. The hope was that grouping many of the

---

[24] Bienen, *Tanzania*, pp. 294–295.
[25] Ibid., pp. 285–286.

departments in one directorate would facilitate planning and coordination. The Directorate was responsible for receiving ideas and input from other national institutions such as the National Assembly and TANU, from extra-governmental bodies in the private sector, and from local and regional organizations. With this information and with the general guidelines provided by the president, the expert planners could translate plans into policies.

The development of new ministries, directorates, agencies, and committees does not resolve all of the problems associated with long-term planning. Tanzania is still critically short of trained manpower; many of the specialized positions must be staffed by foreign experts. Although more and more Tanzanians are acquiring the necessary skills, the education process takes time.

The constantly changing institutional framework for making decisions also can adversely affect effective decision-making. Lines of authority and responsibility become blurred, and the government as described in organization charts differs considerably from the government in practice. One obvious problem (discussed in Chapter 8) is that decisions made in this situation are difficult to carry out efficiently.

What is clear in the Tanzanian system is that President Nyerere is the dominant figure and the key decision-maker. President Nyerere himself has wondered aloud what this fact implies for the future. A political system dependent on one individual must worry about a future without that person. France after De Gaulle and Egypt after Nasser both went through periods of adjustment. Tanzania, which has yet to develop a stable, regularized pattern of decision-making, may face a similar period of adjustment after Nyerere.

■ CHILE ■

Two distinct styles of executive leadership characterize Chile's recent past. From 1925 until 1973 executive authority was vested in the office of the president, who in all but a few cases was a popularly elected civilian. Since 1973 the military has controlled all aspects of Chilean politics and has introduced new, more authoritarian, decision-making structures. The tumultuous events of the Allende presidency and the resulting coup d'état altered both the style and the structure of decision-making in Chile.

Executive Decision-Making During the Civilian Period

The 1925 Chilean constitution established a strong, centralized executive authority. The president was elected for a six-year term and could not succeed himself immediately. There was no popularly elected vice president, but traditionally the minister of the interior occupied the office and succeeded to the presidency until new elections could be held. The president had broad stated powers and often was able to expand these powers by interpreting the constitution in his favor. The practical effect of this situation was to give a president more power than the legislative Congress had.

The president had extensive powers of appointment: ambassadors (with Senate approval), military officers below a certain rank, some judges, and, most importantly, his cabinet. Cabinet ministers were hired and fired by the president and were responsible to him; they could not be removed by a vote of no confidence or censure in the Congress but could be impeached (as many were). The size of the cabinet varied during the civilian period but usually included between 11 and 15 ministers. In addition to the ministers of state, there were junior ministers and secretaries.

The president and his cabinet were responsible for formulating legislation and administering law and policy. Ministers, although not members of Congress, defended executive policy before the legislative bodies and were subject to question by legislators. Each minister also was responsible for helping to determine policy and for issuing regulations for his specific ministry. Perhaps most important in the cabinet was the minister of the interior, who not only took over in the absence of the president but also supervised elections, the police, and many communications channels throughout the nation.

The president's legislative powers made it easier for him to shepherd his legislation through the Congress, in some cases bypassing it altogether. Besides introducing legislation for consideration by Congress, he could issue decrees. During the civilian period there were two types of legislative decrees. The first, often of questionable legality, were *decretos-leyes* (decree laws), issued by the president without congressional approval, usually when constitutional institutions were not functioning properly. The second type, *decretos confuezza de ley* (decrees having the force of law), were issued by the president with congressional approval.

In addition to these powers, the president could categorize legislation according to its urgency; in effect, he had the power to limit debate. Bills classified by the president as urgent required Senate action in 20 days and Chamber of Deputies action in 15 days; very urgent legislation forced the Senate to act within 10 days and the Deputies within 5; extremely urgent legislation required both houses to act within 3 days. Although bills did not automatically become law if not acted on, the president had considerable power to structure and guide congressional debate.

One of the president's greatest powers was his authority to interpret existing legislation and to issue decrees implementing certain general legislation. There were three different types of administrative decrees. A simple decree (*decreto*) issued by the president implemented a specific action, such as an appointment. These decrees clearly fell within the power and authority of his office. More wide-ranging were the *regla-mentos,* which established the specific implementation of general laws and normally involved a series of administrative plans. Reglamentos often had a wider scope and more impact, since they allowed greater interpretation. The president also had the power to issue *instruccións* dealing with application of laws.[26] The power of decree was one of the most significant and important to the president because it allowed him to "make policy" without "making laws." By interpreting existing legislation in different ways, the president often had no need to go to the Congress with his programs.

Despite these considerable powers, the president was not all-powerful. Congress could override presidential vetoes, had the power to approve certain appointments, and served as a watchdog on executive authority. One of the most important and powerful checks on the president was the *Contraloría General.* Created in 1927, the Comptroller General's office was responsible for monitoring, supervising, and ultimately being responsible for the expenditure of Chile's money. Although the president appointed and the Senate approved the comptroller, he and his office were independent of both branches. By most accounts, the creation of this separate agency with ultimate jurisdiction over finances was a success and performed efficiently and honestly.

The powers of the president under the 1925 constitution were considerable. As commander-in-chief of the military, and as the chief executive officer with administrative, legislative, and appointive powers, a president proposed, enacted, and issued much policy. He was, however, ultimately responsible to the constitution and the electorate. The election of Salvadore Allende as a representative of those calling for drastic change proved to be one of the severest tests for the pattern of decision-making established in 1925 and institutionalized through almost 50 years of practice.

Executive Decision-Making During the Military Period

The radical changes proposed and carried out by the Allende government polarized the Chilean population and eventually led the military to intervene. The violent coup d'état of 1973 dramatically changed the pattern of decision-making in Chile by changing both leaders and institutions. Among the first acts of the new military leaders were the ending of elections, the recessing (indefinitely) of Congress, and the banning of the political parties of the left and suspending of those of the center and right. The constitutional system, in short, was dismantled. In its place the military established an authoritarian structure without the checks and balances of the previous system. The military junta, composed of the heads of the army, the air force, the navy, and the national police, centralized power. Led by General Pinochet of the army, these men hold the key decision-

---

[26] Federico G. Gil, *The Political System of Chile* (Boston: Houghton Mifflin, 1966), p. 93.

Policy-Making Institutions in Chile—

The Government Junta and the Cabinet, 1976

Position	Name
President	General Augusto Pinochet
Government Junta	General Augusto Pinochet
	Admiral José Toribio Merino
	Air Marshal Gustavo Leigh
	General (Carabineros) Cesar Mendoza

Cabinet

Ministers of:

Home Affairs	General Cesar Benavides
Foreign Affairs	Vice-Admiral Patricio Carvajal
Finance	Jorge Cauas
The Economy	Sergio de Castro
Justice	Miguel Schwitzer
Agriculture	General of Carabineers Tucapel Vallejos
Labour	Air Brigade General Nicanor Dias
Health	Air Brigade General Francisco Herrera
Public Works	Hugo Leon
Land	General of Carabineers Mario Mackay
Education	Admiral Arturo Trancoso
Housing	Carlos Granifo
Transport	General Enrique Garin
Economic Co-ordination	Raul Saez
Secretary General	General Hernan Bejares

Source: The International Year Book and Statesman's Who's Who (Bath, England: Pitman Press, 1977), p. 90.

making positions. Over time, the tendency has been for more and more power to be vested in General Pinochet himself rather than the collegial junta.

The executive cabinet formed to advise the new leaders was mostly military but with civilian input in important economic posts. Not surprisingly, civilian advisers were selected from the political right and from the more conservative political parties. Since 1973 more and more civilians have been brought into the government, often with the hope that they can solve the pressing economic problems.

The authority of Chile's military leaders is not constitutionally defined, as was the authority of the president. Military leaders are not all-powerful, but they clearly have more unrestricted freedom to act than did their civilian predecessors. They must consult with outside groups and in many cases rely on civilian expertise, but it is clear who is responsible for making the decisions. Power is concentrated in the hands of a very few and, more particularly, in the hands of General Pinochet.

Styles of Decision-Making

The decision-making styles of Salvadore Allende, the last popularly elected president, and General Pinochet, the first military leader, provide stark contrasts and interesting comparisons. The violent change of 1973 proved how important presidential decisions were and how decision-making creates conflicts.

Salvadore Allende came to the presidency in 1970 after campaigning on a platform calling for radical, but constitutional, change. His appeal and popularity were based partly on the belief that, once he was in office, fundamental political and economic changes would improve the lives of the poor rural and urban Chileans, his constituency. The "Chilean road to socialism," he argued, was unique. He was, however, a minority president (elected with only 36 percent of the total vote). Allende faced opposition from many groups and institutions, not the least important of which was the Congress, dominated by the Christian Democratic party of the center and the National party of the right.

Allende also faced opposition and challenges from within the Unidad Popular (Popular Unity) coalition. The UP was made up of Communists, Socialists of all persuasions, and Radicals; it also included Marxists and non-Marxists, and those both willing and unwilling to cooperate and be conciliatory toward opponents of change. Only a skillful politician could juggle the various diverse interests of the coalition. Allende's first cabinet reflected the difficult balancing act.

All points of view on the political spectrum of the UP were represented. The important posts of minister of interior and foreign minister went to Socialists and close advisers of the president. Radicals (and non-Marxists) held the offices of defense, education, and mining. Communists were appointed to the Ministries of Labor, Finance, and Public Works and Transport, while members of the smaller coalition parties occupied the Ministries of Agriculture, Health, Land and Settlement, and Justice. The chief economic post, certainly one of the most important if not the most important cabinet position, went to a former Communist who considered himself an independent Marxist.[27] Of 15 posts in the first Allende cabinet, Socialists held 4, Communists 3, and Radicals 3.[28]

---

[27] Thomas G. Sanders, "Allende's First Months," *American Universities Field Staff Reports,* West Coast South America Series, Vol. XVIII, No. 2 (January 1971), p. 3.

[28] Ian Roxborough, Philip O'Brien, and Jackie Roddick, *Chile: The State and Revolution* (New York: Holmes & Meier, 1977), p. 82.

Allende's goal was to exercise strong leadership and to prevent any one political party or faction from dominating the cabinet or a specific ministry. To this end, for example, he might appoint a Communist to head a ministry, a Socialist to be second in command, and a Radical to hold the third position. So long as there was general agreement on the program, cabinet unity could be preserved.[29]

The platform on which the Popular Unity coalition ran, however, demanded change, and with change came controversy. No area of Chilean life was to be left untouched. The new president called for the nationalization of the copper and mining interests, the control of private banks by the state, agrarian reform, the creation of a new legislative body, and the closing of the gap between the rich and poor through a redistribution of the wealth.

Such sweeping proposals required much new legislation and policy initiative. The relationship between the executive and legislative branches became a tense one, characterized by sharp and constant conflict. The Allende government, rather than introduce new legislation sure to be defeated by the Congress, sought to use already existing legislation and to interpret it in new ways. For example, much of the nationalization of industry was carried out under a law enacted, but never repealed, in 1932. The use of such tactics provoked bitter responses from the Congress and raised complex legal questions.

The Congress responded to the Allende policies by seeking, where possible, to destabilize the Allende government, to defeat the government's legislative initiatives, or to hinder the implementation of executive decisions. Although it was not always successful, Congress made political and economic life difficult for the Allende government.

One tactic that Congress resorted to with increasing frequency was the impeachment of cabinet ministers. From early 1972 until the end of the Allende presidency in 1973, Congress frequently impeached (by a simple majority vote) the president's appointed ministers. Impeachment and the threat of impeachment made forming stable, efficient cabinets difficult. In turn, this hampered the formulating and implementing of policy.[30]

The government unity of 1970–1971 weakened in 1972–1973. The political climate became more fractionalized, bitter, and unstable. Splits appeared within the Popular Unity coalition over the degree of change needed and the proper pace for bringing about changes. Communists advocated a gradual approach, while more radical Socialists and revolutionaries argued that drastic political and economic activity was needed. In 1972 the military, against the will and better judgment of many officers, joined the Allende government. Three cabinet posts were held by officers.

---

[29] Sanders, "Allende's First Months," p. 4.
[30] Roxborough, O'Brien, and Roddick, *Chile: The State and Revolution*, pp. 110–111.

Chile's General Augusto Pinochet assumed power in September 1973. Wide World Photos, Inc.

General Carlos Prats, the commander-in-chief of the army, became minister of the interior and the de facto vice president.

Throughout the latter part of 1972 and early 1973, Allende sought an effective balance between the contending forces in his cabinet. His inability to create a stable, effective cabinet meant that decision-making lacked continuity and direction, and the rapidly deteriorating economic situation inflamed the problem. In August 1973 President Allende announced another "new" cabinet, which again included several military officers. This cabinet, really Allende's last chance, was a cabinet of "national security" and desperately sought to restore order. When it failed in late August, military members of the cabinet resigned. Under the direction of General Pinochet, military and police opponents of the government intervened on September 11, 1973, ending the political chaos of the previous two years.

The economic chaos was not ended as easily as the political chaos. Although new men took control of the decision-making process, the economic problems plaguing Chile remained the same. The new military leaders first sought to solidify their political control, to halt and reverse the policies of the Allende government, and to return Chile to a more conservative fiscal policy. Foreign investment was encouraged to return and re-invest in Chile, and nationalization of industries was ended. Many industries were returned to the private sector (see Chapter 11).

The cabinets that formulated and carried out these policies were mixed military/civilian cabinets. The power and authority of the new leaders has not been significantly challenged by outside opposition forces. Interest groups, political parties, the Congress, and the courts no longer act as independent checks on the executive decision-makers. The decision-makers' control is firm and their power extensive.

Chile during the 1970s has been witness to political and economic upheavals. The patterns of decision-making established in 1925 gave way to new patterns. Large segments of the Chilean population in 1973 were unwilling to accept the decisions made by the Allende government and, most importantly, were unwilling to wait until the next election to express their dissatisfaction. The institutionalization of military rule after the turbulence of 1970–1973 demonstrates both the importance of policy-making and the fragile nature of even the most institutionalized decision-making structures.

CONCLUSION

Decision-making requires political power. The key political figures in any political system are those who have the resources to make and enforce political decisions. One of the most difficult problems facing all political systems is the development of a regularized, stable pattern of decision-making. The description of decision-making in our eight nations presents us with similarities and differences both between and within nations.

There are two general models of decision-making in the eight nations. The first model is characterized by the domination of the process by one individual: men such as Nasser, De Gaulle, Adenauer, and Nyerere were able to shape their offices to meet their needs. In all four cases these men were the first to hold their respective offices under new political systems. Their drive, their personalities, and their ability to manipulate and control the institutional arrangement gave them tremendous power in making political decisions. Although they had advisers, they normally reached the important decisions.

A second model is characterized by more collegial decision-making. The British and pre-coup Chilean cabinets, the Politburo in the Soviet Union, and the Supreme Military Council in Nigeria are all examples. Although one man within each of these bodies may be dominant or the first among equals, there is greater reliance on collective decision-making and responsibility.

As we have seen, political systems are constantly changing, and patterns of policy-making do not remain stable. For example, while the British pattern is among the most stable, it recently has undergone changes that have weakened the central concepts of cabinet collective responsibility and cabinet confidentiality. Post-Adenauer Germany, post-Nasser Egypt, post-De Gaulle France, and the post-Stalin Soviet Union have all undergone changes in their patterns of decision-making. The successors to these leaders found it difficult to marshal the power and resources of their predecessors. As a result, they have had to change their style of leadership to accommodate new circumstances and new political realities.

Two political systems, Nigeria and Chile, have experienced complete changes in their decision-making processes. In both cases civilian regimes —in which decisions were made by either a president or prime minister and his cabinet—were replaced by military regimes. Although the new military leaders often rely on civilian administrators, bureaucrats, experts, and politicians for advice, military officers are now making and enforcing the political decisions.

Whether decision-making is carried out by civilian or soldier, by individual or collective, all actors seek political power. The resources of power available to the various groups and individuals making decisions are wide-ranging. One of the most important is the power of appointment. This power allows the executive authority to surround himself with advisers who are loyal and responsible to him. Cabinet ministers will always be subordinate to a head of state or head of government who appoints, disciplines, and dismisses them.

Most executives are vested with some form of constitutional power and authority. The chief executive is not only granted the power to make decisions but also is ultimately responsible for their outcome. For many chief executives this centralization of power has proved as much a curse as a benefit, for leaders of violent coups d'état (Chile in 1973 and Nigeria in 1966) specifically hold them responsible for the ills of the nation.

Other powers are related to an individual's personality and his role in the nation. Konrad Adenauer represented a mixture of qualities prized by Germans as well as presiding over the rebirth of postwar Germany. Gamal Abdul Nasser represented the Egyptian revolution of 1952 and the hope of a new, prosperous Egypt; following the 1973 war with Israel, Anwar Sadat, the "Hero of the Crossing," came to represent a militarily stronger and more powerful Egypt. Julius Nyerere is both a political philosopher and the leader of the nationalist struggle in Tanzania. In each case, the individual shaped the office, expanding its given or constitutional powers.

Finally, those individuals or groups that control the nation's coercive apparatus have a very potent political power. The military in Egypt, Nigeria, and Chile used this power to take political control. Once in power they made the major political decisions, usually with the help of the civilian bureaucracy. Senior military officers often find themselves facing problems similar to those that plagued their civilian predecessors. For example, in Chile and Nigeria the soldiers have had to deal with various interest and pressure groups.

This chapter is the first of four that examine political institutions. In some of our nations the patterns of decision-making are easily definable and identifiable; they have existed for a long time and are well institutionalized. Decisions are made by leaders following regularized patterns of behavior. Britain, West Germany, and France, although different in terms of style, have developed relatively stable patterns of decision-making. Other political systems are characterized by patterns of decision-making that are constantly evolving. Tanzania, Egypt, and the Soviet Union follow regularized patterns in certain areas but not in others. For example, some policy decisions in the Soviet Union are reached by well-established procedures; but others, such as succession, are not. Finally, Nigeria and Chile represent political systems that have undergone sharp discontinuities in their decision-making process. New actors introduced new frameworks for arriving at decisions. In Chile an institutionalized pattern of civilian decision-making was ended by a violent military coup d'état; in Nigeria a less developed pattern was ended. Both Nigeria and Chile have faced problems of continuity in decision-making. The difficulty of institution-building is attested to by the number of political systems that are constantly changing their ways of arriving at important political decisions. As with the problem of succession, where the distribution of political power is involved, the political stakes are high and the conflicts are intense.

CHAPTER 8
POLICY IMPLEMENTATION INSTITUTIONS

Once made, who enforces the decisions?

Policy-makers expect that, once they have settled on a policy, their decisions will be efficiently and effectively carried out; in most political systems this is the job of the bureaucracy. Bureaucracies in different nations can be compared in terms of the functions they perform, their structural makeup, the attitudes and values of the bureaucrats or civil servants, and the effectiveness with which civil servants perform their duties. In assessing the performance of political systems, we must examine the link between policy-making and implementation.

The primary function of most bureaucracies is to carry out the decisions made by the political actors. Civil servants are responsible or accountable to the current elected or appointed political leaders. In this traditional view they do not make or question policy. For example, in the United Kingdom the highly trained, professional civil service serves both Labour and Conservative governments with the same degree of loyalty. The political preferences of civil servants are secondary to their job of non-partisan administration.

The distinction between politicians and administrators is not as clearly drawn in other political systems. In addition to implementing policy, bureaucrats often become involved in the policy-making process itself. Because of their expertise and their access to information, their advice is solicited before the decision is made. For example, in pre-coup Chile the bureaucracy had a dual role: it acted as one interest group among many in the policy-making process; then, once a decision was made, the civil servants carried it out. In independent Tanzania the government has made a conscious decision to involve civil servants actively in the decision-making process, rather than having them follow the more nonpartisan British model.

Whatever the relationship between the political actors and the administrators, the goal of all concerned is to establish a stable structure for the efficient implementation of policy. Individuals in the civil service must be sure of their roles and responsibilities and of their relationship with those responsible for making decisions. The development of these roles is helped in more developed nations by the fact that the civil service has evolved over a long period of time. Deeply ingrained civil service traditions and practices are accepted by civil servant and public alike. In many developing nations the civil service, like other political institutions, is new and has yet to develop stable role patterns and traditions. Bureaucracies in colonial times were staffed by foreigners who controlled, as well as served, the population. Their first loyalty was to the mother country. Independence required that the new political leaders re-evaluate the role of the civil service and begin the process of replacing foreign with national civil servants.

There are several ways to develop professional administrative roles and behavior. Most nations have specific schools of public administration. In France these schools have been very effective not only in training civil servants but also in socializing them to the French civil service pattern of behavior. Civil servants may also be drawn from a specific class of the population. If the public views the civil service as a high-status occupation, civil servants may come from the upper class, as they traditionally do in Britain. Where there is a sharp distinction between those with an education and those without, as in developing nations, the small educated class may staff the bureaucracy. Once recruited, class or educational solidarity may be reinforced by occupational solidarity. A civil service class begins to emerge based on a similarity of background, training, and attitude.

The civil service and bureaucracy differ from other political institutions. They help to create an institution that is characterized by the specific jobs it carries out and by the attitudes of its members. In political systems with weak civil service traditions, problems may occur. The bureaucracy may be unable to coordinate the various policies of the government; or, once decisions are made, they may not be efficiently carried out. Also, there may be corruption within the bureaucracy. All these problems plague most bureaucracies but are especially common in developing or rapidly changing systems.

The bureaucracy has at its command several resources that give it tremendous potential or actual political power. One is the power of expertise. Civil servants often are the only individuals in a society who have the knowledge necessary to implement technical policies. Technical experts, rather than specialists (or "generalists") in administration, increasingly staff bureaucracies as the business of government becomes more complex. Developing nations, already short on technical expertise, face especially severe problems. Often they must rely on foreign assistance until they can train their own nationals.

A second significant power, to interpret policy, is greater in some nation-states than in others. Where the political authorities have clear control, bureaucrats have limited freedom of action and interpretation. However, where the lines of authority and responsibility are not clearly drawn, bureaucrats may be able to exercise wide latitude in administering policy. They may either frustrate or support political actors. A frequent complaint of decision-makers in this situation is that they have little control over the decision that they have made.

The degree of control exercised by other political institutions and actors over the bureaucracy varies from nation to nation. In some, there is strict accountability, and political leaders closely monitor the actions of the bureaucracy. Political ministers are selected in part for their ability to control complex and large ministries. This tradition of accountability is so well established in some nations that little monitoring is necessary. The public and politicians expect administrators to be efficient and honest, and the bureaucrats gladly comply. Other political systems have few checks, if any, against bureaucracies, which then become powerful. Bureaucrats may directly influence policy by involving themselves in the policy-making process, or they may do so indirectly by the way in which they implement policy. The bureaucracy has grown so large in some nations that it is almost a physical impossibility for a few ministers to control or monitor thousands of bureaucrats.

Bureaucracies are among the most maligned political institutions in any nation. It is a rare nation indeed where the bureaucracy is not accused of either being unresponsive to demands, of not being innovative, or of not being accountable to elected political leaders. In those rare nations where the bureaucracy is viewed positively by the public and political leaders, the civil service is considered a partner in government. Popular opinion that the bureaucracy frustrates efficient government is, however, more common.

Bureaucrats are important not only because of their relationship with the political decision-makers but also because they are often the political figures closest to the people. Citizens deal most often with administrators who tell them what they can and cannot do. Among their more unpopular jobs, administrators collect taxes and issue regulations. When the bureaucracy is held in low public esteem or when the bureaucrats carry out their jobs unevenly or unfairly, all of the political actors suffer the consequences.

Our eight nations present a wide variety of bureaucratic patterns. They vary from the highly professional, well-trained civil services of the United Kingdom, France, and West Germany to the developing bureaucracies of Tanzania and Nigeria. While developed bureaucracies are concerned with problems of accountability and responsiveness, developing bureaucracies are often more concerned with discovering their particular role. New leaders, whether they are elected or whether they seize power, attempt to shape the bureaucracy to meet their needs. What is clear in all nations, however, is that the bureaucracy plays a central role in the political process.

▪ THE UNITED KINGDOM ▪

Policy implementation in the United Kingdom is largely in the hands of the British civil service, which has traditionally been given wide discretion. This reflects the trust that the public and elected politicians have in the professional bureaucrat. When governments change, only about a hundred political appointees are brought in to the ministries to supervise the administration of government. Both political parties rely on professional civil servants to carry out their policies. They have rarely been greatly disappointed.

The term "civil service" in Britain refers to the approximately 700,000 individuals in national administrative positions. It excludes other public employees such as the armed forces, police, and those who work for the nationalized industries and local governments. Civil servants are formally defined as "servants of the Crown, other than holders of political and judicial offices, who are employed in a civil capacity, and whose remuneration is paid wholly and directly out of monies voted by parliament."[1]

The civil service of the United Kingdom is particularly efficient and capable by comparative standards. Among the impressive resources it brings to bear in performing its task is the tradition of the British civil service itself. The long history of Britain's administrative corps has given it a reputation that makes its job easier and ensures that talented people will continually aspire to civil service careers. The quality of recruits is reflected in their education and backgrounds. This results in a service that can marshal substantial expertise.

The tradition and resources of the civil service contribute to bureaucrats' considerable power in the United Kingdom, but public accountability is promoted by balancing factors that prevent widespread misuse of bureaucratic power. Chief among these are the norms of the service,

---

[1] Douglas Verney, *British Government and Politics* (New York: Harper & Row, 1976) p. 84.

Whitehall, the home of the British civil service. Courtesy, Central Office of Information, London.

which emphasize the civil servant's role as the neutral instrument of the political authorities.

Traditions of the Civil Service

The outlines of the modern civil service can be traced to the Middle Ages. The Treasury began operating as a department of state in 1572. Other ministries and the civil service as a whole began to take its modern shape during the eighteenth and nineteenth centuries, when the pressures of administrating a worldwide empire encouraged the standardization of recruitment and other procedures.

The basis for the organization of the modern civil service in Britain is found in the Report on the Organization of the Permanent Civil Service of 1854 (the Northcote-Trevelyan Report) recommending that the civil service recruit on the basis of open examination. It further recommended the creation of a Civil Service Commission to supervise the examinations and questions of promotion. The full report was gradually implemented from 1855 to 1870, with open examinations meeting the greatest resistance from opponents of reform.[2]

---

[2] R. M. Punnett, *British Government and Politics* (New York: Norton, 1971), pp. 306–309.

The Northcote-Trevelyan reforms represented an advance on the previous practices, notably patronage appointments. The elite of the old civil service had been recruited on the basis of family connections. The new service retained the hierarchy and elite status of top administrators but with the additional credentials of academic excellence. In nineteenth-century England, as today, this meant an "Oxbridge" education. Britain's civil service was led by a small group from exclusive public schools and a university degree from Oxford or Cambridge. Class was still a factor in recruitment, since this sort of education was reserved for the privileged. The difference was that talent guided the selection from the pool of those with the proper credentials.

Oxford and Cambridge students learned by reading the classics and studying Latin and Greek. This sort of general education did not produce experts in important policy fields, nor was it intended to do so. The classical education was designed to produce gentlemen who could think— who could work through general or abstract problems based on the experience of the past.

The classical education fit well with the philosophy that shaped the civil service. An elite civil servant was expected to be able to suggest a logical course of action given any set of facts or circumstances. It was in this sense that the British civil service began to glorify the "amateur"—the public official who could bring sound judgment to bear on a problem without the benefit of a specialist's knowledge. The civil service regulations until recently have insisted on top personnel rotating among several departments for this very reason. It was feared that administrators would get too close to their subject matter.

It would be a mistake to suggest that top-level civil servants were without expertise. They were expert at exercising political judgment. The administrative class operated with thorough professionalism. Their amateur style enabled them to work under any set of conditions without preconceived notions. This accounts for the ability of the British administrative elite to throw themselves into the task of implementing conflicting partisan programs. The civil service had no difficulty, for example, in adjusting to the socialist and welfare-oriented programs of the Labour government in 1946. They presided over the nationalization of major sectors of the economy and the introduction of expensive welfare services. There is no doubt that these measures ran counter to the political values and beliefs of most senior civil servants.

The Organizational Reform of the Service

The traditional ordering of the civil service was based on class divisions. The heart of the service was made up of the professionals who made up the general or Treasury classes. (They were termed Treasury classes because their employment was supervised by the Treasury Department.) The

Treasury classes were subdivided into the administrative, the executive, and the clerical classes, each referring to a subdivision of the professional civil service hierarchy. The administrative class consisted of the 2,500 senior civil servants who had great influence over policy matters. This elite consisted of the permanent secretaries, deputy secretaries, and under secretaries of the ministries who worked directly under the political appointees and provided the continuity in ministerial operations. The administrative class was filled by those promoted from the executive class and by recent university graduates with prestigious honours degrees (mostly Oxford and Cambridge).

The executive class consisted of 70,000 or so individuals charged with the implementation of policy under the supervision of the administrative class. These positions have been subject to open examinations. The recruits to the executive class came from those who left school at 18 as well as some university graduates. Most in the executive class continued their educations in hopes that they would be promoted to the administrative class.

The old class system reflected the underlying social structure of England—particularly during the period of the British Empire. The administrative class was a key part of a larger political or ruling class that governed on the basis of birth, privilege, and academic merit. The norms of the civil service matched those of other groups in the political class, notably elected politicians who often had similar backgrounds. The system worked well so long as government played a passive regulative role; it showed some strains as post-World War II Britain embarked on the redistributive and egalitarian policies originally sponsored by the Labour party.

Reforms came shortly after the 1968 publication of the Fulton Report, which aimed at removing the overtly class-based organization of the civil service. The three classes were replaced by a single administrative class that incorporated all of the positions from clerical to policy-related jobs. Placement in this single hierarchy was to be based on written examinations and interviews regardless of prior credentials.[3] The Fulton reforms also led to the creation of a Civil Service Department that took over the duties of the old Civil Service Commission. The Civil Service Department was given responsibility for supervising and setting standards for civil servants. This had been the job of the Treasury Department before the reforms.

Criticizing the traditional amateur style of civil servants, the Fulton Report encouraged the recruitment of specialists for some clearly defined positions. A new civil service college opened in 1970 to teach the latest managerial and organizational techniques. The trend in recruitment is

---

[3] Ibid., pp. 313–314.

only now beginning to favor managerial specialists over classically educated generalists for some positions.

The Fulton reforms have not totally undone the leading traditions of the service or its class basis. There are still approximately 2,500 to 3,000 top administrative positions; 86 percent of their occupants are Oxford or Cambridge graduates,[4] and 90 percent come from middle-class or affluent backgrounds.[5] An elite education is still a great advantage. Time will tell if the character of the service or its most prominent members will change greatly from the old service.

The Fulton reforms have not changed the basic structure of the key departments and ministries. The top figures are the political appointees. In addition to the minister, there normally are several other political appointees who carry the titles minister of state, under secretary, and parliamentary secretary. As a member of the government, the minister normally has heavy outside commitments on his time; he may have cabinet responsibilities, and he certainly has responsibilities in Parliament. The other political appointees can help with the minister's responsibilities. The civil service staff of a department or ministry is led by a handful of experienced, elite administrators, including the permanent secretary and deputy secretaries. These men have the advantage of long experience and are usually relied on heavily by their hard-pressed ministers.

The Treasury

The Treasury has long acted as the master department of state. Until 1971, when the new Civil Service Department took over, the Treasury directly controlled and supervised civil service employees. Its permanent secretary of the Treasury was the head of the civil service, and the Treasury set guidelines and rules that held for civil servants in all departments. Although the Treasury has lost this function, it retains its preeminent place.

The Treasury is a small, elite, coordinating department led by the chancellor of the exchequer (although the prime minister retains the title of first lord of the Treasury). The Treasury supervises the drawing up of budget estimates for each department and is responsible for accounting for the spending of each. The Treasury also raises the funds to meet budgetary allotments. This obviously has policy implications, since Treasury is influential in determining what programs can be afforded and how far existing programs can be supported. In addition to this day-to-day budgeting and financial role, the Treasury is largely responsible for national

---

[4] Alex N. Dragnich and Jorgen Rasmussen, *Major European Governments* (Homewood, Ill.: The Dorsey Press, 1974), p. 127.

[5] This was reported by Lord Fulton's committee on the civil service (Command Paper 3638, Vol. 1, 1968).

economic planning. All departments, as well as the nationalized industries, must coordinate their long-range plans through the Treasury.

The chancellor of the exchequer occupies a central role in cabinet politics as a result of the powers of his department. He is involved in all policy decisions and is influential in the supervision of ongoing programs. In matters of finance and taxation as well as economic planning the chancellor is virtually independent of the cabinet; he consults only the prime minister.

The chancellor's power is based on the coordinating and supervisory tasks performed by the Treasury's civil servants. This highly trained elite corps maintains constant liaison with the ministries and departments. They make the reports and recommendations on which the important decisions are made. They monitor the efficiency with which the executive departments carry out funded programs. They enforce planning guidelines and standards. In short, they supervise the way that policy is implemented in the United Kingdom.

The civil service has streamlined its practices and procedures without seriously affecting its values and traditions. It is still a high-status group with high standards of professionalism; the top administrators are still a self-conscious, well-educated elite, and the Treasury elite still sets the tone for the rest of the civil service.

Reforms have affected some older values, notably the tradition of the amateur administrator. Recent emphasis has been on developing managerial and substantive expertise within the service, but this does not mean that there is no longer a role for a generalist—the educational background of the current top administrators attest to this fact. The movement to specialization reflects both the increasing complexity of governmental problems and the British government's increasing responsibility for managing the economy.

The current civil service continues to balance expertise and public accountability in an acceptable way. The political appointees, who are normally powerful party politicians, have the strength to enforce their political control over the bureaucrats. The civil servants are given sufficient leeway to operate with efficiency.

■ THE FEDERAL REPUBLIC OF GERMANY ■

The civil service of the Federal Republic of Germany is a modern, efficient service with substantial resources. It has a distinguished tradition dating from seventeenth-century Prussia. Supported by the nearly universal admiration of the German public, the civil service has standards and status so high that there is relatively little political supervision of its operation.

Despite these social and organizational resources, the postwar West German bureaucracy has faced serious problems. First, it had to go through the agony of de-Nazification. Since the new Bonn regime could not do without the administrative skills of the civil service, many bureaucrats who had served Hitler stayed on. All of these people underwent at least a superficial investigation and some embarrassment. Of the 53,000 bureaucrats removed by the Allied occupation authorities, almost 52,000 were eventually reinstated.[6] This process did not enhance the esprit de corps that normally characterized the German civil service.

A second adjustment involved the federal nature of the 1949 Basic Law. No group was more affected by the introduction of the federal arrangement than the bureaucracy. West German federalism has split the bureaucracy into federal and state divisions. The federal civil service deals more with policy initiation and development, while the state bureaucracies deal almost entirely with policy implementation. This unusual brand of federalism has introduced the predictable problems of coordination.

Civil Service Traditions

The German civil service traces its origins to the reign of Frederick William of Prussia (1640–1688). Its form took firm shape under Frederick the Great (1740–1786). Prussian state power was built on the twin pillars of the army and the bureaucracy. From the beginning, both the military and civil service were viewed as elite institutions that exemplified the best in German culture, notably orderliness and efficiency. The early Prussian monarchs deliberately held up the civil service as an example of the way that society should be ordered—as a disciplined hierarchy.

Introducing professional standards early, the Prussian civil service was an elite body that demanded rigorous academic—particularly legal—training. All top administrators had the legal education that was thought to prepare an individual to handle any specific administrative problem.

From the beginning of Bismarck's Second Reich (1871), the civil service (largely dispersed at the state level, as it is today) played a dominant role. The state civil services copied the Prussian bureaucratic model and implemented national laws under the supervision of the Bundesrat which, as now, was an assembly of delegates from the states.

Since the legislative arm of government was virtually powerless under the empire, the civil service at the national and state levels performed many political functions, making decisions that would be made by a deliberative body in a democratic system. Accustomed to power, they developed a contempt for elected politicians who were, by and large, their social as well as political inferiors.

---

[6] Arnold J. Heidenheimer, *The Governments of Germany* (New York: Crowell, 1971), p. 211.

The federal government complex in Bonn, West Germany. Courtesy, German Information Center.

This pattern carried over into the first German democratic regime, the Weimar Republic following World War I. The inexperienced politicians, harassed with political violence and economic disorder stemming from the German defeat, were unable to provide stable democratic government. The civil service, which the public esteemed more than they did the party politicians, played a greater role than its constitutional mandate intended.

Civil servants virtually ran the economy in crisis periods when the elected president declared a state of emergency.[7] Top civil servants were brought into cabinets to prop up the popularity of weak governments. In difficult periods presidents appointed a "cabinet of experts," the kind preferred by the public. Highly educated and reputedly incorruptible civil servants were preferable to demagogic politicians.

German history has created a powerful tradition enhancing the authority accorded the *Beamte* (civil servant), a term that carries great status, prestige, and respect. Germans have treated their civil servants well in terms of financial reward, titles, and privileges. The middle classes have been care-

---

[7] Hans Boldt, "Article 48 of the Weimar Constitution: Its Historical and Political Implications," in Anthony Nicholls, ed. *German Democracy and the Triumph of Hitler* (New York: Allen & Unwin, 1971), pp. 79–97.

fully attuned to distinctions of rank among civil service employees, for these carry important social distinctions. German businessmen, for example, have vied for honorary titles, which in a social sense make them honorary Beamte.

Germans trust their civil servants and expect them to use careful, impartial reasoning in their decisions. Rather than contact a legislator to right an injustice, many Germans prefer to take their chances with an administrator. When the Allies introduced personal representation in Parliament after World War II, they expected Germans to use their constituency representative as a sounding board for grievances; but German reliance on the bureaucratic system prevailed.

Another tradition of the civil service is the emphasis on legal training for civil servants. This stems in part from Germany's Roman law tradition. Rather than depending on case law and its precedents the German legal system has relied on detailed codification, which means that legalities have to be spelled out in ordinary legislation. A legal training has been required to deal with the drafting and implementation of these kinds of detailed laws. Outsiders, such as the American occupation authorities, have been struck by the seemingly excessive legalism that has resulted.

All of the traditions of the German civil service are undergoing gradual modification. Though Beamte status is probably not as high as it once was and legal training is no longer all-important, the weight of these traditions is still considerable.

Organization of the Civil Service in the Federal Republic

Public employees in the Federal Republic are divided into three categories. Civil servants make up slightly less than half of the total, while the other categories are termed salaried employees and wage-earning laborers. The civil servants are distinguished from other public personnel by their constitutionally defined role. The Basic Law specified that among public employees only civil servants may engage in activities that exercise public authority; in practice, however, civil servants are sometimes indistinguishable from salaried employees, since they often handle similar jobs and since salaried employees enjoy similar rights after a period of apprenticeship.

The civil service itself is divided vertically into the lower, medium, intermediate, and higher civil service. Traditionally, the higher civil service, which includes only 8,000 officials, has played a role similar to the British administrative class. Promotion from one class to another is fairly difficult. Only 10 percent of civil servants have achieved it.[8]

Horizontally, the service is divided by many technical specialties, such as health, finance, and education. The category of "general administration"

---

[8] Renate Mayntz and Fritz W. Scharpf, *Policy-Making in the German Federal Bureaucracy* (Amsterdam: Elsevier, 1975), p. 52.

occupies a special supervisory place. Horizontal groups are self-contained in that personnel virtually cannot move from one category to another. Promotion occurs within the distinct specialty groupings.

Background and Training of Civil Servants

For most civil servants—those of the middle and intermediate service—training proceeds on an in-service basis. After individuals with the required aptitude and educational credentials are recruited, they are trained by special institutes within the civil service. Training is geared to the category of service to which the individual is recruited (that is, general administration, health, education, and so on).

The higher civil service requires special university training prior to recruitment. These elite recruits are given further training on the job, but in-service education is more theoretical than is the case for the lower grades. The persistence of the value placed on legal training is apparent in the academic backgrounds of the higher civil service, where fully 60 percent have advanced legal degrees when they are hired.[9]

The distinctive backgrounds of the top civil servants have led them to develop distinctive attitudes. The attitudes of West German civil servants are not totally narrow and legalistic as might be supposed. They see themselves as playing a partly political role that requires adjustments based on the views of important actors. They feel that they have a right to private political opinions if these do not interfere with their work, and they are very sensitive to the interests of those whom their actions affect, though emphasizing impartiality and independence from specific interest groups. The legal orientation of top civil servants is still strong—top civil servants see the application of the law as a major element in their role.[10]

The Impact of Federalism

The civil service is deeply affected by West Germany's federal structure. The federal government has wide-ranging powers in policy-making and legislation, while, in practice, the state governments make policy only in the area of cultural affairs (including education and religious policy). Through the upper house of Parliament (the Bundesrat), comprised of delegates of state governments, states have a considerable role in the federal legislative process.

The powers of the states are in the area of policy implementation; 90 percent of the civil servants and other public employees work at the state level. Officials on the state level often have broad leeway in how laws will be implemented in particular states. The Bundesrat has the key super-

---

[9] Ibid., p. 53.
[10] Ibid., p. 60.

visory role in the system, as it must approve the standards and procedures that apply to the state bureaucracies.

The result of this division of labor is that "policy-making" bureaucrats are separated from "policy-implementing" bureaucrats. Policy-implementing bureaucrats are divided into the distinct corps of the 11 states. In a sense, this enforces an artificial distinction on civil servants. Policy-makers are isolated and may have no feel for the problems of administration. On the other hand, those responsible for policy implementation may not fully understand the purpose behind a particular law. In practice, the two functions are impossible to separate totally.

At the federal level the ministries are small and thinly manned. The 16 ministries range in size from 300 to 1,800 employees. Typically the top civil servants have political and policy roles: senior civil servants must often act as political aides since there are few political appointees in the ministries. It has not been uncommon for ministers to send their civil servants to represent them before Parliament. Civil servants have frequently taken what amounts to leaves of absence to serve in Parliament for a period of time, returning to their ministry after their parliamentary career. In the present Bundestag 112 members list their profession as civil servant. The effect has been that at the level of the federal government there is little distinction drawn between civil servant and politician.

At the state level the civil servants perform the more classical bureaucratic functions of applying and implementing laws. They are supposed to apply them with an eye to local conditions, but the standardization of their operation is enforced from the federal level—from the Bundesrat and the federal civil service.

Accountability of the Bureaucracy

The West German civil service does not receive a great deal of supervision from elected public officials. Until 1967 the minister was the only elected official in any ministry. Today there are still only a handful more elected officials serving in an administrative capacity. Ministers are not directly responsible to Parliament in any case—only to the chancellor. In this sense there are no accountable politicians in the ministries.

The only check against the abuse of bureaucratic power is exercised by a system of administrative courts. These courts are charged with ruling on charges related to specific bureaucratic improprieties. There is a federal administrative court that can take appeals from the lower administrative courts. The courts may only judge whether a rule was correctly applied by the civil servants in question and do not deal with more political questions such as whether the rule itself should be changed.

With or without the familiar political checks on bureaucratic performance, the record of the post-World War II West German bureaucracy is good. The civil service certainly deserves partial credit for West Germany's highly successful economic and social policies. In the process of achieving this enviable record, the new German civil service has largely policed itself by relying on its own high standards.

▪ FRANCE ▪

France has civil service traditions more similar to Germany's than to those of the United Kingdom. The French civil service originated long before democratic institutions were established. As in Germany, the civil servant is a high-status officer of the state. These similarities with Germany come from the similar histories and problems shared by Continental countries. In particular, France shares West Germany's problem of making sure civil servants are accountable to the elected representatives of the people.

French Civil Service Traditions

France was one of the first nations to develop a powerful bureaucratic arm of the state. French monarchs were relentless centralizers who sought to extend state control over all of the regions of France. By the time of Louis XIV (1643–1715), the king's agents went everywhere on errands involving taxation, regulation, and the administration of justice. The Ancient Regime's civil servants were the privileged favorites of influential members of the court. Civil servants were selected on the basis of family connections or the buying of offices.

The French Revolution and the Napoleonic era brought reform and reorganization. Elaborate regulations spelled out the duties and functions of bureaucrats. Administration was streamlined and rationalized. One notable innovation was the creation of geographical administrative units, called departments, which would be ruled by *prefects* appointed in Paris. Recruitment standards changed to emphasize academic training. Merit standards stressing advanced scientific training were introduced. The early great national schools (*grandes écoles*) produced the Napoleonic civil servants.

The political flux of the mid-nineteenth century produced five very different political regimes and threw public administration into chaos. Turnover of personnel was high, as were standards of recruitment. The basic features of the Napoleonic system, however, remained in force.

Reforms instituted in the Third Republic (1875–1940) specified educational and other requirements for civil service employment. Ministries did their own hiring and selected people in part according to their own criteria. The chief requirement was unquestioned loyalty to the ministry. Civil servants were not encouraged to think of themselves as a part of a larger corps of public servants. Recruitment in the Third Republic favored the "great families" for positions of particular distinction. Otherwise civil servants were largely drawn from middle- and upper middle-class families who could afford the requisite educations for their children. Civil servants were staunchly conservative, and Parliament often deferred to them. Parliamentary government was unstable, while the civil service provided strength and continuity. Third Republic politicians in any event were not very change-oriented themselves and had no objection to letting the civil service dominate.

The French civil service was not fully modernized and reformed until 1945, when a Civil Service Commission was established, charged with standardizing procedures and wresting supervision of the civil service from the individual ministries. French history has, nevertheless, left its mark on the modern civil service. First of all, history has dictated that the civil service will play an extremely important role. Political instability in France has put great pressure on civil service. As a result, it has often appeared that "France is not governed. It is administrated."[11] French civil servants and agents of the government have often taken important decisions into their own hands without reference to politicians. On-the-spot administrative decisions in the Fourth Republic, for example, included the decision to try to recapture Indochina by force.[12] A second tradition of the French civil service is its reliance on the grandes écoles for recruits. An elite education in one of several specialized national schools has become an important criterion for success; thus, recruitment to the French civil service is rather narrow by modern standards. Moreover, it tends to breed a self-conscious civil service elite who have similar backgrounds and who know each other socially.

Organization of the Civil Service

The French civil service, comprised of 1.25 million individuals, is divided into four major groups. At the top is the administrative category (*fonctionnaire de conception*); next is the executive category (*fonctionnaire d'application*), while the lowest categories are clerical and custodial. Each category is broken down according to the type of service performed; for example, an executive category civil servant may be in the prefectoral corps (responsible for local administration). Very elaborate distinctions are also made within each category regarding rank and salary.

Civil servants are recruited on the basis of academic credentials and examinations. Clerical employees are expected to have an elementary school education, executive employees must have earned a secondary school degree, and the administrative category draws from those appli-

---

[11] William Safran, *The French Polity* (New York: David McKay, 1977), p. 11.
[12] Philip M. Williams, *French Politicians and Elections* (Cambridge: Cambridge University Press, 1970), p. 7.

A student at the French National School of Administration (Ecole Nationale d'Administration). Bruno Barbey, Magnum Photos, Inc.

cants with a university education. Traditionally, a legal education has been important. An essential for the top administrative personnel is advanced training at one of the grandes écoles, the most famous of which is Ecole Polytechnique. Other national schools prepare individuals for more specialized tasks such as tax administration; some schools are run by the ministries themselves.

A major post-World War II reform was the creation of the National School of Administration (Ecole Nationale d'Administration, ENA), designed in particular to help break down class-based recruitment and recruitment from the law faculties of the universities. The ENA has emphasized "modern" academic subjects such as economics, statistics, and public administration. Encouraging in-service training, the school admits experienced civil servants as well as students direct from the universities. Since training at the ENA dramatically increases the chances of promotions, bureaucrats have a powerful incentive to further education.

The ENA reform has not had a democratizing influence on the civil service. Though the ENA gives scholarships and competitive entrance examinations, these measures have not broadened the civil service. Paris is favored over the provinces, and graduates of the ENA are typically the sons and daughters of other civil servants or professionals. Finally, virtually all ENA graduates come from middle-class and upper-class backgrounds; working-class graduates are hard to find.[13]

The background of France's top bureaucrats leads to a conservative orientation. There is a good bit of evidence that bureaucrats are highly motivated by material considerations, since many jump to lucrative business careers. While they are in the service, however, they do meet high professional standards that include impartiality and resistance to interest-group pressure.

At the national level, senior civil servants have had powerful roles to play in the ministries. As in Germany, the minister has little assistance in dealing with an entrenched bureaucratic elite. This problem of control has been aggravated by the traditional instability of French cabinets. In the period when ministers came and went almost monthly, some top administrators ran their ministries with little reference to its political head. Ministers were forced to develop their own corps of advisers, called ministerial cabinets, to act as a counter to the power of the senior civil servants. The tradition of weak political supervision has persisted into the Fifth Republic.

Local Government

As France is a unitary system, local government units are controlled from Paris, a pattern that began under the later Bourbon monarchs. The centralized system of local government instituted by Napoleon in 1799 has persisted to this day. Since the localities have no political functions, French local government is simply a vast administrative system that applies the central government's laws and regulations in the provinces.

The local administrative units are the department, the district (*arrondissement*), the *canton*, and the *commune*, each existing for a particular administrative purpose. The department is presided over by the chief agent of the central government, the prefect. The district, or arrondissement, serves as the electoral unit for parliamentary elections. Each canton contains an office of the national police force. The commune permits some citizen involvement and participation in community affairs.

A prefect—the dominant figure in this local government system—presides over each of France's 95 departments as an appointed civil servant of the central government. He is responsible to the minister of interior, who supervises the system of local government. A large part of the prefect's job is to supervise local services. A civil service assistant and a group of service specialists work under his direction. The specialists preside over

---

[13] Safran, *The French Polity,* pp. 209–210.

the specific service sectors, such as water, public health, and housing. The prefect contacts the relevant national ministries to make sure the activities of his specialists meet national policies and regulations.

Another major task of the prefect is to act as a liaison between the national government and local communities. He consults frequently with locally elected officials of both the commune and the department. Thus, local communities can air grievances, and the prefect can promote national policies. The public relations aspect of the job is considerable, given the small number of outlets that individual Frenchmen have to influence local government and given the resistance to change that characterizes many French localities.

The other important unit of local administration is the commune, each with a council elected for a six-year term. As there are 37,000 communes in France and the number of councillors ranges from 9 to 90 depending on the size of the commune, France has several hundred thousand municipal councillors at any given time. The main job of the council is to elect one of their number to be mayor, who becomes the executive official of the commune and is subject to central government direction. The mayor is the arm of the national government in the localities and is responsible for implementing national law and for supervising the finances of the commune.

The subnational administrative system of France has many critics, mainly because of the sheer number of administrative units. The units are too small to reflect modern service delivery systems. Many of the communes are virtually unpopulated since these basic units are derived from the traditional Napoleonic system. The sheer number and variety of local government divisions has led to the creation of a massive, unwieldy local government bureaucracy.

Some reformers suggest regionalization[14]—creating larger administrative units. Usually regionalization implies the creation of administrative or planning regions that follow the lines of France's historic regions, for example Brittany and Burgundy. This would permit a more efficient delivery of services, recognition of cultural distinctions, and more meaningful popular participation in local government. No serious suggestions have been made regarding a true federal arrangement. The larger units would have a relationship to the central government similar to that of today's departments.

Reforms have been tried out. Laws have been passed that allow the merger of communes and the development of cooperative communal associations that may share services. The most serious reform is the creation of regions for the purposes of economic planning. Since 1964 each planning region has had a "superprefect," who acts as a coordinator of the

---

[14] William G. Andrews, "The Politics of Regionalization in France," in Martin O. Heisler, ed., *Politics in Europe* (New York: David McKay, 1974), pp. 293–322.

prefects in his region for economic planning and development purposes. Each region also has a Regional Economic Development Commission (*Commissions de Développement Economique Régional,* or CODER), which advises the superprefect concerning the region's economic needs. Since 1972 the regions have also elected advisory councils. The region is still not an official governmental unit, and it cannot enforce recommendations for economic planning. Regionalization has been thwarted by those who currently have political power bases in the older governmental units.

Control of the Civil Service

The French political system relies on administrative law and its administrative courts to control the civil service. French administrative law sets out the rights and prerogatives of the citizen vis-à-vis the national administration. It also defines the rights and duties of the civil servant. Breaches of the law governing public administration are handled in a national system of administrative courts.

As in West Germany, civil servants must adhere to the fine print of a specified administrative code. As a result, officious, unbending bureaucrats often make the simplest administrative task complicated. This obviously affects the efficiency and adaptability of the civil service. Finally, the civil service is not supervised in its more political tasks and functions. The only supervision here comes from the harried political heads of the national ministries.

▪ THE SOVIET UNION ▪

In the Soviet Union, policy is implemented by the state bureaucracy under the close supervision of the party apparatus. The administrative part of the Soviet polity has been aptly described as a party-state bureaucracy. "In these systems it is the party, and more particularly its leadership which plays the transcendent role. The state bureaucracy . . . is penetrated, controlled and dominated by the party bureaucracy."[15]

Despite party dominance, the state bureaucracy does the bulk of the work of policy implementation. The administrative center of the government is the Council of Ministers, whose job is to regulate and coordinate the activities of the massive state machine. The job is made difficult by the immense scope of governmental activities in the Soviet Union.

Much of the administrative arm of the government is involved in the

---

[15] Merle Fainsod, "Bureaucracy and Modernization: The Russian and Soviet Case," in Joseph LaPalombara, ed., *Bureaucracy and Political Development* (Princeton: Princeton University Press, 1967), p. 235.

supervision of the state-directed Soviet economy. It is also involved in economic planning, and the development of the Five Year Plans.

Scope and Size of the Bureaucracy

The most basic features of the Soviet bureaucracy are its size and the scope of its activities. The size of the bureaucracy is difficult to determine because of conflicting official figures. Truly administrative and executive personnel probably exceed 2 million. If one counts all government employees, the figure would be between 10 and 15 million, not including the party apparatus or military and police officials. The actual size dwarfs the size of any other European civil service.

A massive administrative corps is necessary because of the scope of the activities for which the state bureaucracy is responsible. One Soviet official listed the states functions in this way:

On the basis of and in the execution of laws, Soviet state organs organize the defense of the USSR, strengthen its power and independence, exercise leadership over the building of the armed forces, conduct foreign trade by means of a state monopoly, protect state security, assure public order, strengthen and develop socialist property, protect the life, health, rights and lawful interests of citizens, organize to satisfy their social and cultural needs, and take measures looking toward the constant elevation of the material prosperity of the Soviet people.[16]

In more prosaic terms the state is responsible for regulating and guiding all aspects of social and economic life. This all-embracing field of action includes a myriad of functions untouched by Western liberal democracies with their emphasis on limited government.

The size of this complex bureaucracy is necessitated also by the sheer size of the nation-state it administers, in terms both of territory and of population. The nation-state also includes a number of distinct nationality groups, some of whom require separate administrative treatment. Below the all-union level are 15 union republics that are divided into regions (*oblasti*) approximately the size of American states. The 100 oblasti are divided into cities or rural districts (*raiony*), and large cities have further administrative subdivisions. The all-union or national ministries are responsible for implementating the law throughout this complicated structure.

The Ministries and the Council of Ministers

The state bureaucracy is basically organized within three kinds of ministries. The all-union ministries have authority throughout the Soviet Union. They may have local branches depending on the nature of their function. Union republic ministries located in each of the 15 union republics,

---

[16] Frederick C. Barghoorn, *Politics in the U.S.S.R.* (Boston: Little, Brown, 1972), p. 250.

The head of the Soviet State Planning Committee (Gosplan) addresses the Supreme Soviet. UPI Photo.

are coordinated by a central ministry in Moscow. Republic ministries operate solely at the republic level and are responsible to the republic governments.

The total number of national ministries varies widely depending on reorganization and decisions regarding the optimal size of ministries. Since Stalin's death the number of ministries has ranged from 25 to 100. The large numbers of ministries reflect the variety of governmental tasks and the fact that the state bureaucracy runs the economy in its entirety. The central ministries include familiar departments such as finance, interior, and foreign affairs; others have included ministries for heavy industry, the automobile industry, and other sectors of the economy. In addition, a number of "committees" have ministerial status. The most important of these include the Committee to Plan the National Economy *(Gosplan)* and the Committee for State Security.

The Council of Ministries is the top of the state bureaucracy pyramid. As it is the chief executive and administrative body, its executive decrees are binding on the state hierarchy. Its important decisions are made in a smaller body (approximately 10) called the presidium of the Council of Ministers: the premier, his chief deputies, and the chairman of Gosplan are normally included. Their work, most of which is management of the Soviet economy, is subject only to the policy decisions of the party Politburo.

The full Council of Ministers is too large and unwieldy to act as an executive body. It is led by a chairman, who is referred to as the premier, assisted by deputy premiers who are included on the council. Usually there are over 50 ministers represented as well as the heads of Gosplan, the state bank, and other agencies. In addition, the 15 premiers of the union republics have a seat on the Council of Ministers.

The economic basis of the Council of Ministers' functions make Gosplan quite important in all deliberations. Gosplan, or the State Planning Committee, was created in 1921 and later was given responsibility for preparing the Five Year Plans. Gosplan actually coordinates the activities of a number of planning bodies responsible for estimating economic needs and production targets at all levels of Soviet public administration. The head of Gosplan is a deputy premier and has a seat in the presidium of the Council of Ministers.

Party Control of the State Bureaucracy

It is a well-established principle that the party sets policy guidelines while the state is responsible for administration; nevertheless, the party does engage in a great deal of administrative activity. The party's administrative role is largely of a coordinating, enforcing, and supervisory nature. The party apparatus carefully monitors the implementation of party policy decisions.

One major party involvement in administration is in the recruitment of state personnel. The party can monitor and control the recruitment and promotion of state bureaucrats. At the highest level it controls the careers of the people in the Council of Ministers and those people who run Soviet economic enterprises. At lower levels the party can control the type of person recruited for particular job categories by shifting educational and ideological requirements for employment.

The second way in which the party is involved in administration is through direct surveillance of bureaucratic agencies. State control agencies have operated since the earliest days of the Soviet system; they are concerned primarily with malfeasance and violation of regulations affecting the economy (such as black-market activities or attempts to falsify production totals to "meet the plan"). During Khrushchev's regime the First Secretary boasted that he had over 7 million "activists and volunteers" overseeing the activities of the state bureaucracy.

Backgrounds and Attitudes of State Bureaucrats

The views of the top figures in the state administrative hierarchy reflect both their backgrounds as economic specialists and their dependence on the party for career advancement. Most of the men in Council of Ministers arrived at their positions through the state hierarchy. This holds true for premiers as well. Nikolai Bulganin (1955–1958) and the current premier,

Alexei Kosygin, had almost identical backgrounds. Both had served as mayor of a large city, premier of the Russian republic (RSFSR), minister with financial responsibilities (minister of finance or head of the state bank), and finally deputy premier.

The careers of Bulganin and Kosygin suggest that a career in the state hierarchy can lead to power and a position in the party Politburo, though neither man attained the top leadership position. The usual pattern is for career state bureaucrats to be somewhat removed from the center of party power. They seem to be content with a secondary party role. Most end up in the party's Central Committee but not in the Politburo.

The relatively restrained ambitions of career civil servants and ministers provides them with a good deal of security; it is not unusual for specialist ministers to retain their positions for 20 years. They do not get caught in the dangerous leadership realignments that cut short the careers of many a professional party man. As a result, most state bureaucrats are cautious and conservative in performing their jobs and in their dealings with political leaders. They work within the party's policy guidelines and refrain from dramatic departures from accepted procedures.

Bureaucratic Performance and the Command Economy

Since the state bureaucracy emphasizes its role as manager of the economy, bureaucratic performance is often gauged by national economic performance. Economic performance is measured according to the targets set by the Five Year Plan. State bureaucrats, of course, may be only as good as the party policy they implement. Party leaders often intervene to press for their pet projects or to enforce reorganization schemes on the state administrators, but bureaucratic power is strong enough so that state officials are often able to resist outside encroachment. As in other political systems, bureaucratic power is often the power to resist change in existing patterns and procedures of administration.[17]

No leader was more anxious to reorganize the administration of the economy than was Nikita Khrushchev. In agriculture Khrushchev virtually cut off the Ministry of Agriculture from farmers and farm operations. The ministry had controlled the practical aspects of farming through its field service located in machine tractor stations (MTS). Through the MTS system the ministry could implement policy with regard to machinery, fertilizer, seeds, and other aspects of planting and harvesting. In 1958 Khrushchev dissolved the MTS units, dispersing its machinery and supplies to the collective farms. From 1958 until Khrushchev's fall in 1964, local

---

[17] Gertrude E. Schroeder, "Soviet Economic Reform at an Impasse," in Henry S. Albinski and Lawrence K. Pettit, eds., *European Political Processes* (Boston: Allyn and Bacon, 1974), pp. 523–538.

party organizations controlled the farms. The Ministry of Agriculture was reduced to a role as the central research organization.

The Ministry of Agriculture reclaimed its position in 1964. The agricultural failures of Khrushchev repudiated his reorganization plans as well as his agricultural policies. Today, the collective and state farms are considered branches of the ministry. The state employees of the ministry are charged with seeing that their economic branches meet their quotas. They do this by coordinating the activities of the agricultural production units and providing technical assistance. Party organizations on the farms monitor efficiency and effectiveness.

Khrushchev introduced sweeping reforms of the management of the industrial economy as well. Feeling that the centralized system presided over by the Council of Ministers was rigid and inflexible, he began in 1957 a reorganization of the economic decision-making process. The idea was to let officals in territorial subunits determine their own needs and productive capacity. He created a council of the national economy, or *sovnarkhoz,* for each oblast. When this system led to uneven performance because of provincial special interests, Khrushchev experimented with different sizes of administrative units and different party supervisory methods.

This experiment of Khrushchev's was also repudiated. It was resisted by state bureaucrats because it was inefficient and reduced ministerial power. Khrushchev's political enemies had been from the state bureaucracy (and some of his plans were clearly aimed at reducing the state's influence), while his allies were in the territorial party apparatus. Both sets of reforms introduced under Khrushchev benefited party officials in the provinces.

Khrushchev's successors have been less interested in reorganization or altering the traditional role of the state bureaucracy. In 1965 and 1973 Brezhnev and Kosygin introduced some reforms that gave plant managers greater discretion in running their operations. Managers were rewarded if they could turn a "profit" with their new independence. This obviously reduced the scope of government operations and was another scheme for decentralization. But the experiment was never allowed to reach its implied goal—greater use of market mechanisms to promote efficiency. Prices continue to be set by the state, and talk of profit incentives is somewhat misleading. The only freedoms that the plant manager has retained from the reform are his ability to shop around for raw materials and some control over labor supply. Again, the state bureaucracy has resisted change and virtually reintroduced the old system. Today plant managers are under a ministry in Moscow with one administrative layer in between. Interference from the ministry is frequent, and close supervision is the normal state of affairs. Direct orders are often given plant managers by the minister responsible for his production quota.

To summarize, the state bureaucracy in the Soviet Union is effective in preserving its role as manager of the command economy. The traditional bureaucratic weapons of red tape and inertia beat off attempts to change the state's manner of operation. It is a rival to the party apparatus, which performs similar functions and which has been called on to replace "inefficient" state bureaucrats. The political interlopers seldom fare any better in terms of efficiency. Change and innovation are perhaps unrealistic political goals in a massive, highly bureaucratized polity.

▪ NIGERIA ▪

The Nigerian civil service is one of the largest and best trained in Africa. At the senior levels it is not uncommon for Nigerian civil servants to be seconded to other developing nations to help in administration. The role played by the civil servant has evolved in response to new economic, social, and political conditions. As intimated in Chapter 7, the modern civil service in Nigeria is now an active partner with the military in governing the nation.

Despite its strengths, the civil service is not without problems. Critics point to inefficiency, corruption, and general poor performance. For the individual Nigerian, dealing with the bureaucracy can be one of his or her most frustrating tasks. One Nigerian pundit defined bureaucracy as practiced in Nigeria as "the art of officialdom by officials for the sake of officialdom."[18]

Initially, the civil service in colonial Nigeria established law and order while allowing the consolidation of British control. The service was staffed at the senior levels by British civil servants, and at the lower levels by Nigerians. Prior to World War II, few Nigerians were promoted to the senior ranks; but afterward more and more Nigerians entered the higher ranks of the civil service and assumed increased responsibility.

"Nigerianization" and "Regionalization" of the Civil Service

Two issues dominated the discussion of the civil service during the nationalist period (1950s). The first was the need to increase the number of Nigerians at the senior levels; the second was the delicate question of whether there should be a unitary national civil service or a federal civil service along with regional services.

In 1938 there were only 26 Nigerians in senior civil service posts. By

---

[18] Peter Enahoro, *How to Be a Nigerian* (Lagos, Nigeria: The Daily Times of Nigeria Limited, 1966), p. 47.

1948 the number had increased to 172 out of a total of 2,207. British civil servants, however, continued to dominate the senior civil service throughout the early and middle 1950s. For example, as late as 1954 only 824 out of 5,137 senior posts were held by Nigerians.[19]

Several factors worked against the rapid "Nigerianization" of the civil service. First, few Nigerians were qualified for the most senior posts. Educational and training programs designed to increase the number of qualified Nigerians were more effective in the long run than in the short run. Second, there was a commonly held fear (mainly among the British) that rapid Nigerianization would lead to a mass exodus of senior British civil servants. The British thought that this would leave Nigeria dangerously short on technical expertise. Finally, there was a fear in the Northern Region that rapid Nigerianization was synonymous with the domination of the civil service by the South. The educational imbalance between North and South meant that there were more qualified Southerners than Northerners to fill civil service positions.

Nigerian politics, as we have seen in earlier chapters, often centered on ethnic arithmetic and (during the pre-1966 period) on the ability of regional parties to protect regional interests. Parties were expected to provide their respective regions with the region's fair share of the economic and political spoils. Since fewer Northerners had Western educations, the Northern People's Congress wanted British or expatriate officials to remain in their positions until enough Northerners were qualified to fill the many government positions. This policy, along with other related policies, was referred to as "Northernization." Northerners stressed the need to train Northerners and to ensure that as civil service vacancies opened, there would be qualified Northerners on hand to fill them.

Nigerianization, despite the above-mentioned problems, was a success. By independence in 1960 Nigerians staffed two-thirds of the senior posts in the federal civil service; when Nigeria became a republic in 1963, they held 87 percent of the higher posts.[20] Nigerianization was equally successful at the regional level, where Nigerians occupied almost all senior posts by the early 1960s.

A second major change that characterized the civil service during this period was the regionalization of the service. Between 1914 and 1954 the civil service had been a unitary, centralized institution; administrators were responsible to the national colonial administration. But in 1954 four regional civil services were added. The regional civil services became responsible to their respective regional governments; the much smaller federal civil service remained responsible for national matters.

---

[19] A. H. M. Kirk-Greene, "The Higher Public Service," in L. Franklin Blitz, ed., *The Politics and Administration of Nigerian Government* (New York: Praeger, 1965), pp. 219–220.

[20] Ibid., p. 225.

Regionalization was necessary because of the fears and antagonisms between regions. The 1954 constitution, creating a federal system, meant that specific powers were to be granted to the regions. In turn, this required each region to establish public services to implement regional decisions. Northernization, for example, was designed to protect the interests of the North—Northerners, not Southerners, should staff civil service positions in the North. Regionalization and Northernization became closely related policies.

Despite these changes, the British administrative values of an efficient, politically neutral civil service remained intact. A handbook for officers planning service in the Western Region had this reminder:

Your [civil servant] loyalty is to the Minister of the day. If and when a different party comes into power, your new Minister may require radical changes in the policy of your Ministry. Your duty is to carry out new policy with the same loyalty as you gave the old.[21]

The Civil Service During the Independence Period

The role of the civil servant in independent Nigeria has gone considerably beyond simply implementing policy. Senior civil servants are responsible not only for administering policies but also for providing ministers, both civilian and military, with information and policy alternatives. The permanent secretary in the civil service hierarchy serves as a link between the civil service and his respective minister in the Federal Executive Council. The power of the civil service is great, for development plans depend on bureaucrats' ability and willingness to administer them efficiently. Following the coups d'état in 1966, many civilian "political" ministers were replaced by civilian "civil servant" ministers. More and more, the military came to rely on senior civil servants for both administrative assistance and technical expertise.

The civil service has become much more specialized as a result of this expanded responsibility. During the colonial period many were generalists in the British tradition—experts in administration rather than in specific substantive areas. Nigeria today, however, needs specialists. Its vast oil wealth and detailed development plans require engineers, geologists, environmentalists, finance and monetary experts, and others who understand the complexities of the petroleum industry and the effects of rapid development on the society.

The postindependence civil service also is much larger than the pre-1960 service was. The creation of 12 states in 1967 and 19 in 1976 means that each new state becomes responsible for its state civil service. The growing involvement of the government in providing social services such

---

[21] Ibid., p. 217.

as education, health care, and social security, as well as direct government intervention in the economy, contributes to the swelling of the civil service. Rapid expansion has produced severe manpower shortages at both state and federal levels. In 1975 there were 100,000 civil servants in the national civil service, and some 700,000 in public services of all types.[22]

The government is seeking solutions to these problems. A 1975 government White Paper based on a commissioned study—the Udoji Report— of the civil service clearly analyzes both the problems and prospects of the civil service. Besides recommending that the salaries of civil servants be increased, the commission pointed to several problems facing the Nigerian civil service. One serious problem is that the civil service appears to lack direction and purpose. The rapid growth in the number of government agencies often means that there is little coordination or cooperation among branches. The report pointed out that as government becomes more complex and technical, cooperation between administrators and professionals is essential. The civil service should provide managers as well as regulators. These problem-solvers and planners will increase the efficiency of government and make the development plans more realistic.

The commission's report also attacked seniority. The number of years of service, rather than performance, tends to be the major criterion in explaining promotion (according to the report). This makes it difficult for an individual to move from lower to higher levels in the service. Outside experts also find it difficult to enter the civil service at high rank. The report stressed the necessity of recruiting these outside experts, especially for positions that remain vacant for long periods.

Corruption, nepotism, and elitism in education received detailed attention. The report confirmed what many already suspected. Appointment to positions is often based on ethnic or regional favoritism. A member of one group, for example, often will appoint others from his or her group to civil service positions, rather than making appointments on the basis of merit. With regard to corruption, the commission realized that it is impossible to completely eliminate, but they argued that it can be diminished by closer supervision and auditing. Obvious corruption has seriously compromised the image of the civil service in the public's eye.

Finally, manpower and manpower training were cited as problems. Public service has to be made attractive enough, both financially and in terms of working conditions, so that it can effectively compete with the private sector for qualified employees. Many states, for example, suffer from severe manpower shortages. In one state, shortly after its creation, there were no engineers in the water supply section, the five most important jobs in the Forestry Department were unoccupied, and most of the key jobs in the Highway Department were unfilled. At the same time,

---

[22] *West Africa*, 3050 (December 8, 1975), p. 1473.

10 percent of the state budget was directed to increasing the water supply and 20 percent to improving and building roads.[23]

The military government that took power in July 1975 acted on the Udoji Report. The previous Gowon government had doubled the minimum wage for civil servants. Now the new Mohammed government "retired" some 10,000 public employees for reasons of age, health, inefficiency, and/or malpractices. Among those dismissed were the chairman of the federal Public Service Commission and three board members. The commission itself was disbanded. Others who lost their jobs were senior servants in most states, permanent secretaries, and several ministers. The aim of the action was both to increase efficiency and to cut down on corruption.

The problems facing the civil service in Nigeria are not unique. The roles and the expectations of civil servants changed with independence and again with military rule. Its expertise and tremendous manpower resources make the civil service a partner in Nigerian government. Its rapid growth creates problems of efficiency, performance, responsiveness, and corruption at the same time that the bureaucracy has become one of the most powerful institutions in Nigeria.

▪ EGYPT ▪

Bureaucratic participation in the political life of Egypt is an established tradition. The government is the largest employer of manpower, and since 1952 the maintenance of the bureaucracy has required a greater and greater percentage of the government's revenue. Among the most common complaints raised in modern Egypt are that the bureaucracy is too large, inefficient, corrupt, and not responsive enough to public demands and interests.

The modern Egyptian bureaucracy dates from the rule of Muhammad Ali in the early nineteenth century. The modernization and industrialization of Egypt required an educated, well-trained elite. Since Egypt lacked this trained cadre, Muhammad Ali from 1813 to 1848 sent over 300 students overseas—mainly to France and England—for technical and general training. In 1829 he also established a school in Egypt for the training of bureaucrats and civil servants.[24]

The bureaucracy grew rapidly during this period. Many of the successors of Muhammad Ali lost control of the growing institution, and it became unclear at times who was governing whom. The British systematized and standardized the bureaucracy during their period of rule. Top civil

---

[23] *West Africa*, 3095 (October 25, 1976), p. 1569.

[24] Morroe Berger, *Bureaucracy and Society in Egypt: A Study of the Higher Civil Service* (Princeton, N.J.: Princeton University Press, 1957), p. 22.

service posts were held not by Egyptians, but by Englishmen or other foreigners. Turks, Armenians, Jews, and Egyptian Copts, as well as Englishmen, staffed most important positions. Egyptians held the lower-ranking, lower-paying positions; by 1920 they held just over 50 percent of civil service positions, but only one-quarter of the senior posts (Englishmen held a majority of these).[25]

One of the strongest demands made by Egyptians during the British period was for the "Egyptianization" of the bureaucracy. Not unlike the situations in Nigeria and Tanzania, Egyptians demanded to be allowed to participate not only in politics but also in administration. Limited self-government in the 1920s had the positive effect of increasing the number of Egyptian civil servants, but the negative effect of involving the civil service in politics. Besides developing a reputation for corruption and inefficiency, the bureaucracy was viewed by many as a reflection of the attitudes of the monarchy or the government of the day.

The Bureaucracy and Policy Implementation

The relationship between education and employment is a strong one in the Egyptian bureaucracy. One of the most common patterns followed by Egyptian students is to move directly into government service after completing their education. During the British period, it became almost a right for students to be given positions in government service; since 1962 the unofficial policy has been official. University graduates are guaranteed a government position on their graduation. As the number of Egyptians who receive a university education increases, the bureaucracy also is likely to increase. The problem is compounded since there are relatively few opportunities open to graduates in the private sector.

Another reason for the swelling bureaucracy is the government's increased role in economic management. The massive nationalizations carried out by President Nasser in 1961 and 1962 required the creation of agencies to manage, regulate, and supervise the new government acquisitions. Banks, industries, and manufacturing concerns were placed under direct government management.

One indicator of the growing bureaucracy is the rising cost of maintaining it. In the immediate postrevolutionary period of 1952–1953 the government payroll was about 55 million Egyptian pounds, and the total government expenditure was about 108 million Egyptian pounds. In 1961–1962 the payroll had risen to just over 100 million Egyptian pounds, while the government spent 191 million Egyptian pounds. After the massive nationalization period, the government spent 318 million pounds (1965–1966) and had a government payroll of 234 million pounds.[26]

---

[25] Ibid., p. 32.

[26] R. Hrair Dekmejian, *Egypt Under Nasir* (Albany: State University of New York Press, 1971), p. 230.

Egypt's Public Sector—The Case of the Alexandria Shipbuilding Company

---

A common complaint leveled against the public sector in Egypt is that it is inefficient. A 1973 Egyptian government study seemed to confirm this charge, at least against one company. The case of the Alexandria Shipbuilding Company highlights many of the problems facing Egyptian industry.

The report found that:

—although the company was started in 1955 with Soviet assistance, it did not complete its first ship until 1969;

—5,100 workers were employed in a company that needed no more than 3,000 full-time workers;

—2,500 "trainees, drafted workers, and foreign experts" also were employed;

—the payroll of the company was estimated to be six times larger than the level of production warranted.

Source: Case cited and reported in John Waterbury, "Public versus Private in the Egyptian Economy," American Universities Field Staff Reports, Northeast Africa Series, Vol. XXI, No. 5 (April 1976), p. 21.

This rapid growth creates severe problems for the bureaucracy. Co-ordination between the different branches of government tends to be poor. This makes the development of middle- and long-range plans difficult (despite the fact that the government was initially divided into sectors to deal with specific policy areas). The size of the bureaucracy, coupled with its important role in Egyptian politics, works against those who would like to streamline it and make it more efficient.

Like most bureaucracies, the Egyptian bureaucracy is not an innovative or particularly responsive force in Egyptian life. It tends to be conservative and to resist radical change. This creates tension in a political system committed by its leaders to economic, political, and social changes that require bureaucratic implementation. Operating in a bureaucratic setting individuals and groups often find that it is much easier and safer to maintain the status quo than to attempt to introduce changes.

The bureaucracy is not, however, without its strengths. It is staffed by well-trained and well-educated Egyptians; increasingly many of these people also have a technical, rather than general, training. This has allowed the bureaucracy to carry out several large-scale projects that have had a significant impact on Egyptian life. Despite the doubts raised by many, for example, the Egyptians efficiently operated the Suez Canal when Egypt took control of it from the British. The Aswan Dam, the largest undertaking yet carried out in Egypt, is another example of a project requiring Egyptian bureaucratic expertise. Finally, many projects, although they may not be efficiently carried out, would not even have been possible without the bureaucracy.[27] Land reform, increased social benefits, and nationalization are good examples.

Bureaucratic Values in Egypt

Traditionally, high status accompanies bureaucratic appointment in Egypt. Bureaucrats are better educated and better salaried than the average Egyptian. They realize that they form an elite, but they have serious doubts about their role and their status. One study of civil servant values conducted after the revolution found that most joined the service because it provided job security, because opportunities were limited in other areas, and because it provided economic benefits.[28] Most, however, indicated that they would leave the service if they received a better opportunity. Civil servants also expressed certain dislikes concerning the civil service. The most common complaints centered on the dullness or the routine of their job, the favoritism that characterizes the system and makes advancement on merit difficult, and the ineffective use of personnel.[29]

To summarize, the bureaucratic framework in Egypt mixes both modern and traditional patterns. There is an emphasis on technical expertise and the need for rational, coordinated planning. At the same time, favoritism and the existence of small groups within the service often work against planning and coordination. Personal relations are often the determining factor in promotion. A patron-client relationship exists throughout the different levels. A person in authority will protect those beneath him, while those in the lower levels will repay protection with loyalty to the senior official.

In Egypt, as elsewhere, the political actors promise to control the bureaucracy and to make it more responsive and efficient. But decision-makers in Egypt are often at the mercy of the bureaucrats responsible for implementing their policies. The bureaucrats' reluctance to act often results in confusion as well as in poorly implemented decisions.

▪ TANZANIA ▪

The Tanzanian civil service has changed dramatically since its creation in the colonial period. Prior to independence, the British district officer or

---

[27] Malcolm Kerr, "The United Arab Republic: The Domestic, Political and Economic Background of Foreign Policy," in Paul Hammond and Sidney Alexander, eds., *Political Dynamics in the Middle East* (New York: American Elsevier, 1972), pp. 213–214.

[28] Berger, *Bureaucracy and Society in Egypt*, p. 71.

[29] Ibid., p. 85.

commissioner often was responsible for both policy-making and policy implementation. Poor communications and a lack of resources forced him to be both a political and administrative official with wide discretionary powers. The senior ranks of the civil service were staffed primarily with British colonial officers. Few Africans rose to positions of importance.

Independence and the development plans and goals established by TANU altered the role and composition of the civil service. Although foreign technical help is still recruited for many development projects, administration is now largely in the hands of Tanzanian citizens (of all races). Civil servants are expected to be politically conscious and aware of the development goals established by the party. An integral component of the nation-building process, the civil service in many cases initiates and interprets policy as well as administers it. As both an administrative and political institution, it faces many problems. Among the more serious are the responsiveness of the civil service to the demands and expectations of citizens and leaders, and the efficient performance of the bureaucracy in implementing political and economic decisions.

The Africanization of the Civil Service

The British developed a civil service patterned on their own experiences. The primary role of the civil servant was to administer policy made by political decision-makers, not to become involved in the decision-making process itself or to interpret decisions once made. African civil servants, for example, were forbidden to join political parties during the nationalist period in the 1950s and early 1960s. Although many Africans in the middle and lower ranks of the civil service did join the party and actively participated in politics, their activity was unlawful and certainly unprofessional (in the British view).

The most striking characteristic of the civil service during the colonial period was the lack of African representation at the senior levels. In September 1960 they held only 453 out of 3,000 senior posts in the civil service.[30] An insistent demand made by Africans when self-government was granted Tanganyika was that the civil service quickly be Africanized.

Prime Minister Nyerere's position on Africanization was ambivalent. He realized that the demand for greater participation in the civil service was important and politically volatile, yet he also knew that it would be difficult to replace expatriate civil servants with Tanganyikans quickly. The effective performance of the government required individuals with specific skills and expertise. In 1961 he announced that by the end of the year he hoped at least one-half of all district commissioner posts, important administrative positions, would be held by Africans. (At the time, Africans held only 5 of 58.)

---

[30] William Tordoff, *Government and Politics in Tanzania* (Nairobi, Kenya: East African Publishing House, 1967), p. 194.

The major problem with Africanization during this period was that the colonial administration had not trained enough Africans to qualify for senior posts. Recruiting agencies were established and manpower units created to speed the process, but it could not be done overnight. By the end of 1965 about two-thirds of the senior and middle-grade positions were occupied by Tanzanian citizens (of all races).[31] Perhaps more importantly, Tanzanians now controlled the most sensitive posts, such as the commissioner of police and the chairman of the Public Service Commission.

Civil Servants and Politicians

The Africanization of the civil service was only one of the issues facing Tanganyikan leaders at independence. In the early 1960s the commonly held opinion in Tanganyika was that political leaders should make decisions and that civil servants should faithfully execute them. There was no attempt immediately following independence to politicize the civil service. This position was in line with the British conception of a neutral, "professional" civil service.

By 1964 this attitude had changed; in fact, it was dramatically reversed. For the fiirst time civil servants were allowed to join the party officially. Second Vice President Kawawa announced: "We want civil servants to join TANU so that they can help us in our struggle against poverty, disease, and ignorance. Civil servants are the most educated people in our country."[32] Most civil servants took the opportunity to join the party. Many moved into important party posts.

This new policy of allowing civil servants to become party members represented a fundamental shift in Tanzanian politics. Political leaders argued that the party's ability to exercise control over civil servants was limited, while they remained outside of the party. The party provided direction and guidance; hence, all groups should be included within its ranks. (Military men, for much the same reason, also were allowed to join the party during this period.)

The civil service's role in administering government policy expanded as the government took on more responsibility for providing goods and services and for controlling the economy. Civil servants also assumed responsibility for helping to develop the plans for modernization. This is certainly a much more active role than envisioned by the British administrators. The head of the civil service in 1966 made the new role quite clear: "Here the civil servant is expected to be committed to development for the masses."[33] A study of a sample of senior administrators suggests

---

[31] Ibid., p. 202.

[32] Henry Bienen, *Tanzania: Party Transformation and Economic Development* (Princeton, N.J.: Princeton University Press, 1970), p. 148.

[33] Raymond F. Hopkins, *Political Roles in a New State, Tanzania's First Decade* (New Haven, Conn.: Yale University Press, 1971), p. 116.

that the above idea has been fairly effectively ingrained in new civil servants. For example, 65 percent of the sample thought it important that citizens understand and participate in the nation-building process. Other often-mentioned duties of citizens were the need to show loyalty to the nation, to make sacrifices for the nation and neighbors, and to obey the laws.[34]

Civil Service Values

Establishing and maintaining a strong civil service tradition is difficult in a society undergoing rapid, radical change. This is the case in Tanzania. The British civil service tradition evolved over a long period; in Tanzania, where the civil service initially was based on the British model, the service's role and composition has changed dramatically in less than 25 years, moving from a civil service based on political neutrality to a system in which administrators are expected to be politically active.

It is difficult to describe the values of the "average" Tanzanian civil servant. The dramatic changes described above have produced a wide variety of attitudes among bureaucrats. Many, especially those who entered the service when it was still controlled by Britain, stress their roles as policy implementers. Younger members of the service often emphasize their roles as politically active participants as well as administrators. Technocrats tend to view themselves as administrators responsible for carrying out, not making, policy.

In the study shown in Table 8–1, the civil servants came from diverse backgrounds, but a majority were from rural environments (not surprising in a largely rural nation), and most were from families that did not have a high traditional status. Many senior administrators went to a local or missionary school, followed by a secondary boarding school, and then, for the most fortunate, an overseas university. Their most common occupations prior to assuming their positions were that of student, teacher, or lower-level civil servant. Fathers of civil servants also tended either to be teachers or civil servants.[35]

The civil servants form an elite that is better educated and often more politically aware than the average Tanzanian. Again quoting the former head of the civil service:

The good Tanzanian civil servant thus recognizes two things; firstly that the Ministers and other political officers are responsible for policy, and secondly that his role is to help the politician to achieve the national objectives by full use of his brains, training and experience.[36]

---

[34] Ibid., p. 194.
[35] Ibid., pp. 71–75.
[36] Ibid., p. 117.

TABLE 8–1   Characteristics of Tanzanian Administrators,[1] by Percentage

	Veterans[2]	Technocrats[3]	Moderns[4]
Age			
35 or under	9	25	71
36–40	27	25	23
41–45	41	37.5	0
46 or over	23	12.5	6
Religion			
Protestant	64	50	59
Catholic	18	37.5	29
Muslim	14	0	12
Traditional Status of Family			
High	54.5	25	6
Low	45.5	75	94

[1] The 47 administrators interviewed in this study "are responsible for the government's operation. They supervise the work of the bureaucracy and implement policy decisions."
[2] Veterans are "those with low education and long service"; 22 were interviewed.
[3] Technocrats are "those with high education and long tenure"; 8 were interviewed.
[4] Moderns are "those with high education and short government service"; 17 were interviewed.

Source: Data in table and description of categories are from Raymond F. Hopkins, *Political Roles in a New State* (New Haven: Yale University Press, 1971), pp. 108, 110. Reprinted by permission.

As an elite in a developing society, the civil service has tremendous potential power. And they also face many problems. Complaints are frequently lodged that bureaucrats and administrators at all levels have illegally used their offices to achieve personal financial gain. They are also charged with being unresponsive to the needs of the people and of having established themselves as a power outside party control. Abuse of power (real or perceived) is a common charge. President Nyerere summarized the difficult relationship between the civil servant and the people. The people's point of view he sees as this:

It is a civil servant who tells a householder that he may, or may not, build at a particular place. It is the civil servant—again, up to a point—who notifies a parent that his child has, or has not, gained admission to a particular school or college. . . . The extent to which these civil servants are merely implementing the law, or carrying out the instructions of the Minister, is not obvious to ordinary people. The civil servants appear to be all-powerful, and it is sometimes assumed they are.[37]

---

[37] Julius K. Nyerere, *Freedom and Socialism* (London: Oxford University Press, 1968), p. 225.

On the other hand, the civil servant is often unsure of his position and responsibility.

And the civil servant himself, who knows the extent to which he is governed by the law, by political instructions, or by the sheer bureaucracy of Government, is not always able to explain the limitations of his own position. Indeed—being human—he often does not want to! After all, we all like to have our importance acknowledged by other people, and there are few men or women who are not flattered by being told that they are very powerful.[38]

To summarize, the Tanzanian bureaucracy has grown rapidly as the government has become more active. The civil service has become so large in some sectors that its ability to perform has become impaired. In 1976 the government dismissed fully 10 percent of the public service and attempted to crack down on corruption. The size of the bureaucracy makes it difficult to coordinate policy between different branches of government. Because the lines of authority and responsibility are not precisely defined, long-term, broad development plans may be hampered. Finally, the civil service in Tanzania has yet to develop a consistent, mutually accepted set of traditions and role patterns to govern its behavior. As with all institutions in developing nations, the process of institutionalizing values and actions is a difficult one.

▪ CHILE ▪

The bureaucracy is a powerful force in policy implementation in Chile. Prior to the polarization of the electorate during the Allende presidency, the bureaucracy often acted as a stabilizing, moderating force in Chilean politics. The political values of many civil servants were those of Chile's broad middle class. These values stressed gradual, not radical, change. Thus, whatever the beliefs of the decision-maker, in the final analysis it was the civil servant who implemented the policy.

The bureaucracy is one of the major employers in the nation. From 1940 to 1955 the bureaucracy grew by almost 60 percent; the number of employees increased from about 72,000 to over 116,000. This was due in part to the rapidly expanding role of the government in the administration and control of the economy and in part to the inability of the private sector to create enough new jobs.[39]

During the civilian period the executive branch of government was responsible for the civil service. The president could, with congressional

---

[38] Ibid.
[39] Federico G. Gil, *The Political System of Chile* (Boston: Houghton Mifflin, 1966), pp. 183–184.

Chile's ruling military junta governs from this well-protected building in Santiago. Raymond Darolle, Sygma.

approval, initiate new public services. Since the president could not remove civil servants from office, a common presidential practice was to create new agencies for administering new policies rather than to work through established structures. Adding to the president's control of the service was his power to raise the pay of civil servants.

Rapid growth of the bureaucracy often negatively affected coordination between the executive branch and the bureaucracy, and between various bureaucracies. Although the executive branch had considerable power vis-à-vis the bureaucracy, the executive was not always able to control the bureaucrat. Semi-autonomous agencies developed and, once established, were apt to act independently. The president and government ministers found it difficult to monitor these agencies, and it was not always clear who was responsible to whom.

These agencies play an important role in Chilean politics. Some are so independent that they could do their own hiring, firing, and, in some cases, set their own budgets. One estimate suggests that about 40 percent of all public employees work for the 50 or so semi-autonomous agencies in the Chilean bureaucracy. Included are workers in such diverse fields as agriculture, social security, and economic development.[40] One of the most important agencies, CORFO—the Chilean Development Corporation—is described below.

The lack of a uniform codified set of administrative rules governing bureaucratic behavior adds to the difficulty of executive control over the bureaucracy. Agencies are governed by broad sets of administrative statutes (known as *Estatuto Administrativo*) that evolve as new problems and agencies arise. Centralized control and coordination are difficult since there tend to be different rules for different agencies.

These problems make the Chilean bureaucracy liable to criticisms similar to those leveled against almost all bureaucracies. It is accused of being too large to be efficient, responsive, or innovative. Bureaucrats tend to be more legalistically, than performance, oriented. Poor coordination between various branches of the bureaucracy prevents the development of consistent, long-range plans. And, with thousands of workers employed by the government in nonproductive positions, an economic strain (and drain) is added to the already strained Chilean economy.

Despite these serious problems, the bureaucracy does exercise a strong influence on the policy process in Chile. As the government rapidly increased its control and involvement in the economy through the creation of public agencies, civil servants influenced policy by their interpretation of executive and legislative laws and decrees. Since they were semi-autonomous and protected from removal from office by law, agencies and individuals often acted independently of the government of the day. During the tumultuous days of the Allende presidency, this became an important political variable. Like the other institutions of government during this period, the civil service was embroiled in political controversy.

CORFO—An Example of a Public Agency in Chile

The Chilean Development Corporation (CORFO), one of the strongest semi-autonomous agencies in the Chilean government, was created in 1939 by the Popular Front government to coordinate economic development. Though technically under the Ministry of Economics, it is, for most practical purposes, a strong, independent agency. The government participates by appointing government representatives to CORFO's board of directors. Over the years CORFO has been one of the most important agencies for manging, owning, and providing expertise to Chilean businesses.

---

[40] Arturo Valenzuela, "Political Constraints to the Establishment of Socialism in Chile," in Arturo Valenzuela and J. Samuel Valenzuela, eds., *Chile: Politics and Society* (New Brunswick, N.J.: Transaction Books, 1976), pp. 18–19.

Initially, the corporation organized many of the state industries and publicly owned corporations in Chile (for example, the electricity company (ENDESA) was established in 1944–1945, the steel company (CAP) in 1946, and the petroleum company (ENAP) in 1950). CORFO also was instrumental in establishing such diverse concerns as a hotel consortium, a beet sugar industry, refrigerating plants, and a telecommunications industry.[41]

The semi-autonomous agencies created by CORFO are governed by boards of directors, normally consisting of one-third government representatives, one-third private representatives, and one-third technical experts. CORFO provides much of the technical expertise, as well as guaranteeing much of the financing for projects. At the height of its power (before the coup), CORFO held stock (often a majority of shares) in such wide-ranging fields as agriculture, communications, fishing, coal, films, television, energy, petroleum, steel and metallurgy, electronics, and tourism.[42] CORFO coordinates activities of these various agencies by annually contributing to the budgets of the various concerns, by granting benefits and providing guarantees for loans, and by discussing policy at the executive staff level.

Two examples show the scope of CORFO influence in policy implementation and formation. CORFO owns 97 percent of shares in ENDESA, the electricity company that produces two-thirds of Chile's electric needs. The rest of the electricity needs are produced by a private company in which the government bought 51 percent of the shares in 1970. A second example is ENAP, the petroleum company of the Chilean government—a complete state monopoly. In 1968 ENAP produced 55 percent of the crude oil refined in Chile. CORFO developed both industries. These semi-autonomous agencies within the Chilean government have characteristics both of public ownership and private enterprise.

During the 1950s and 1960s the public share of industry increased; as a result, more bureaucrats and civil servants became involved in policy administration. The Allende presidency aimed at considerably increasing public holdings at the expense of private enterprise, but faced the opposition of the bureaucrats. They favored changes but not the types proposed by Allende—radical change, a strongly collectivist solution, and the rapid nationalization of many industries. As indicated, since many of these agencies were semi-autonomous, Allende found it difficult to implement many of his proposed reforms.

The military government, which is trying to reverse the trend of increasing public ownership, emphasizes private enterprise and encourages

---

[41] "Public Enterprises: Their Present Significance and Their Potential in Development," *Economic Bulletin for Latin America*, Vol. XVI, 1971, first half (New York: United Nations, 1971), p. 3.

[42] Ibid., p. 21.

foreign, private investment. At the time of the coup in 1973, the government, mainly through CORFO, controlled 95 percent of the banking and financial institutions, 90 percent of mining, 40 percent of manufacturing, and 60 percent of the distributive industries.[43] Some of these had been purchased by organizations such as CORFO, others were privately owned but managed by the state, and some were seized by workers during the Allende period.

Some 500 companies seized by workers were returned to former owners after the coup. With regard to CORFO, the military took steps to decrease the holdings of the corporation. In 1974 the military head of CORFO announced that those firms taken over after June 1973 had been returned to private owners and that action was being taken on some 304 firms in the "social property" sector of the economy. Of these, 188 were returned to former owners, 21 were being returned, 17 had been sold by CORFO to the private sector, 31 were in the process of being sold, 111 would be sold, 33 were in limbo since it was not clear if the former owners wished them back, and 14 were to be kept by CORFO. Plans were also announced to follow similar procedures in other sectors of the economy such as agriculture and banking.[44] It is not surprising that institutions like CORFO would have been affected by military intervention. Their importance in policy-making and implementation made it essential for the new military government to gain control over them.

Bureaucratic Values

Another way of studying the bureaucracy's influence on politics is to analyze the characteristics and values of its personnel. The value patterns of many bureaucrats are like those of many others in the changing Chilean society—a mix of the traditional and the modern. On the one hand, for example, they seek to protect and improve their position within the bureaucracy; on the other, they recognize that change and reform are necessary.

In pre-coup Chile, where policy was made by different groups bargaining among themselves, bureaucrats often acted as one of these groups in order to maximize their influence and input. Yet, while they may have acted as an interest group in influencing policy-making, they also ultimately had the responsibility for carrying out the policies, once decided. This often resulted in ambivalence in both the thought and action of Chilean bureaucratic officials.

In some respects a profile of the bureaucracy is a profile of middle-class Chile. One study[45] of a sample of the Chilean civil service, at all

---

[43] Philip O'Brien, *Allende's Chile* (New York: Praeger, 1976), p. 279.

[44] Ibid., p. 280.

[45] James Petras, *Politics and Social Forces in Chilean Development* (Berkeley: University of California Press, 1969), pp. 288–337.

TABLE 8–2   Characteristics of a Sample of the Chilean Bureaucracy, by Percentage

	Administrative Elite	Technicians & Professionals	Skilled & Semi-Professional	General Office Workers	Technical Assistant	Service, Unskilled
Sex						
Male	76	47.5	50	35.2	45	65.1
Female	24	52.5	50	64.8	55	34.9
Age						
51 years	32.6	13.2	13.8	4.7	10.8	28.5
41–50	28.2	25.0	15.3	20.0	17.1	11.1
31–40	26.0	36.7	25.1	36.2	34.2	33.3
30 and under	13.2	22.9	40.2	35.2	35.1	23.8
no data	0	2.2	5.6	3.9	2.8	3.3
Religion						
Catholic	72	62	76	87	92	92
Protestant or other	2	5	3	2	2	0
Atheist or no religion	22	28	15	8	5	5
Secondary Education						
Attended public secondary school	52	84	76	66	59	24
Attended private secondary school	46	15	18	27	20	13
Did not attend secondary school	1	1	4	7	21	60

Source: The percentages in this profile are based on interviews with 573 bureaucrats in all ranks of the Chilean bureaucracy. The data are from tables in James Petras, *Politics and Social Forces in Chilean Development* (Berkeley: University of California Press, 1969), pp. 301, 302, 305, 306. Reprinted by permission.

levels, provides a detailed description of the demographic, social, and economic characteristics of civil servants (see Table 8–2). Women were well represented in the middle ranks of the civil service, but men predominated at the higher administrative and technical levels. The survey suggested little apparent discrimination based on religion in this largely Catholic nation (many of the highest-ranking bureaucrats considered themselves nonpracticing Catholics). Those bureaucrats with long tenure in office tended to be well socialized in bureaucratic politics and manners; many had known each other since school days and formed an "old boy" network within the organization. Bureaucrats exhibited a strong sense of professionalism, but at the same time were convinced that the road to advancement was through favoritism rather than efficient performance. While a bureaucrat's position in the system may be based on education and training, many of his/her political values are based on social class.[46]

These values reinforce the middle-class profile drawn above. Almost 75 percent of the top administrative and technical elites thought of themselves as belonging to the large middle class. They felt that this class, despite its large size, had the least influence on the government and that the upper class, entrepreneurs, and political parties exerted much more influence.[47]

The general findings that emerge from this survey are of a group recognizing the need for change, but also strongly attached to the maintenance of the system and the status quo.[48] Although many civil servants do not favor free enterprise, most are not in favor of a strictly collectivist solution either. All groups in the bureaucracy favored a mixed economy. Again, in a mixed economy such as Chile's, the power of the bureaucracy to control and administer can be great.[49] Given these values, it is little wonder that large segments of the bureaucracy were hostile to the radical changes proposed by the Allende government, which, in turn, accused many bureaucrats of failing to execute faithfully the decisions of the government of the day.

To summarize, the political and administrative role of the bureaucracy has changed since the advent of military rule. The new leaders, at least in principle, stress a return to private enterprise and less reliance on government control of the economy. Centralized bureaucratic systems, however, are powerful and not easily dismantled. Although the rules of the political game have changed, the bureaucracy still provides some stability and continuity. The rulers and the rules are different, but the need for bureaucrats with the administrative and technical expertise to implement the rules remains.

---

[46] Ibid., p. 290.
[47] Ibid., pp. 317–319.
[48] Ibid., pp. 324–326.
[49] Ibid., p. 331.

CONCLUSION

The bureaucracies of the eight nations vary considerably with regard to their traditions, resources, and social composition. These differences help explain variations in their performance. On the one hand, performance can be measured in terms of efficiency and effectiveness in implementing policy goals. On the other hand, performance may be judged in terms of the accountability of civil servants to public officials and to the public.

The differences among the nations in the strength and nature of bureaucratic traditions are striking. The traditions of the British, French, and German civil service are the result of at least 300 years of political history. In each nation the civil service is widely respected by the public. The German civil service, for example, is credited with helping unify Germany over the period from Frederick William to Bismarck (1640–1871). It also is credited with helping to hold Germany together in the turbulent century since unification. Germans have clear expectations about civil servants and their job performance. In turn, German civil servants have strong feelings about their own role, which is largely compatible with the public's expectations. Because of their previous colonial status, Egypt, Nigeria, and Tanzania do not have as clear guidelines for their civil servants. Lack of tradition may lead to corruption and inefficient performance based on "careerism." It is not uncommon in developing nations for civil servants to be uncertain about their political and bureaucratic roles.

Nations also vary in the competencies that their civil servants bring to the task of policy implementation. Civil servants in all eight countries are highly educated when compared to the general populations of their respective countries, but the quality and appropriateness of the training varies. Developing nations suffer from severe shortages of skilled manpower in technical fields. Large-scale development projects often require the importing of foreign technical assistance. Some developed nations, such as Britain, have had problems because of the value they traditionally have placed on "generalist" civil servants, rather than on "specialist" civil servants.

The composition of the bureaucratic elite also differs from nation to nation. Britain and France have developed a highly elite service in terms of education and social status. In France, for example, a few families have dominated parts of the service. Most developing nations have not had time to develop a true elite of this kind. Coupled with the lack of traditions in the civil service, this can often produce performance problems.

We also have seen how the political attitudes of bureaucrats can vary. The British, for example, seek to suppress partisan activity among bureaucrats while Tanzania encourages its civil servants to be party members and to be actively engaged in nation-building. The Soviet Union's state bureaucrats may or may not belong to the party, but they are not isolated from partisan influences.

Finally, some bureaucratic establishments are accountable to political authorities or the public, while others are not. Nations such as Britain with strong traditions of accountability do not need elaborate mechanisms to ensure that bureaucrats are responsive to the wishes of elected politicians. France and Germany, with traditions of elite political bureaucracies, are more difficult to control and require complex systems of administrative law and courts. The Soviet Union, which has an ideology supporting one-party rule, requires direct party oversight of the civil service. In developing nations, however, leaders often find it difficult to control the civil service. In these cases the bureaucracy may operate almost independently of its executive overseers.

The above-mentioned differences help us to judge the effectiveness and efficiency of bureaucracies in achieving policy goals. Largely because of their professional standards and highly institutionalized nature, the established civil services of Western Europe rate highly in terms of effectiveness and efficiency. The state bureaucracy of the Soviet Union is also highly effective in implementing the decisions of the party apparatus. These bureaucratic systems have at their command tremendous resources. Among developing nations the performance of the bureaucracy is more problematic. Although they may not rank as highly as Western European nations in terms of efficiency, our studies indicate that they nevertheless play an important role in the policy process. In fact, in many cases the civil servant of a developing nation is expected to perform more roles and to take a more active political stance than is his/her European or Soviet counterpart.

CHAPTER 9
SYMBOLIC
AND REPRESENTATIVE
INSTITUTIONS

What role does pomp and circumstance
play in politics?

In the recent past all the nations in our study have experienced problems of legitimacy. Many people in each nation have not recognized the authority of institutions or leaders to make and enforce political decisions. The problems of generating feelings of legitimacy and of building public support are difficult ones. This chapter describes some of the institutional arrangements that countries develop to build support through the use of national symbols, ceremony, and ritual.

Ways of solidifying legitimacy and support differ from nation to nation. The legitimacy crises of postwar France and Germany stem from the sudden war-related changes of regime that resulted in creating new, unfamiliar rules and institutions. West Germany, in particular, can claim to be a "new nation"; the institutions, boundaries, and population of postwar Germany are very different from those of prewar Germany. In both Fifth Republic France and postwar West Germany, new institutions have been designed specifically to evoke national symbols and build support for unfamiliar regimes.

The United Kingdom's legitimacy problems do not stem from political discontinuities, but from repeated failures in the realm of economics and world politics. Even highly valued institutions such as Britain's are not immune from loss of support in the face of persistent public disappointment in the national political leadership.

Developing nations such as Nigeria and Tanzania that recently have undergone colonial experiences face special problems because their own national traditions and institutions are weak. In Nigeria, for example, where subnational or regional symbols are stronger than those of the nation, problems of national integration center in part on the need to build strong national loyalties.

Symbolic Activity and Symbolic Institutions

Symbolic political activity—the pomp, ritual, and ceremony of politics—often appears trivial. This is not the case. Symbolic activity can be defined as noninstrumental political activity that elicits emotional responses from the public. By this definition, symbolic activity is valuable if it has meaning for the national group. The historical connotations associated with ceremony and ritual provide them with strong emotional impact for most citizens. In turn, political leaders seek to translate this emotional impact into political support.

Symbolic activity helps then to build supportive feelings within a nation's mass public; in particular, it helps develop diffuse support (see Chapter 1). Diffuse support is critically important because it does not depend on the day-to-day performance of the government. A stable reservoir of public affection and goodwill for government institutions and authorities, it lends legitimacy to the decisions made by leaders.

Some institutions are designed specifically to perform symbolic functions. The Supreme Soviet of the Soviet Union comes close to this case, as does the West German presidency. These institutions handle the important ceremonial duties and build support for the more effective political institutions; rarely do they have any important instrumental functions. The Supreme Soviet ratifies and legitimizes decisions made elsewhere solely for the purpose of increasing public acceptance. The West German president handles all of the ceremonial duties of the executive, leaving the chancellor free to do the real work of government.

Some primarily symbolic institutions were once instrumental institutions. The British monarchy and House of Lords are the best examples of this type of institution that exercised real power in the recent past. Both evolved into symbolic institutions during the period of democratization. These institutions have special emotional holds on the public because of their long history and because they are living symbols of the national past.

Political institutions often perform both instrumental and symbolic functions. Parliaments, for example, play both legislative and symbolic roles. The parliaments of Western Europe, the Tanzanian National Assembly, and the People's (National) Assembly of Egypt are examples of legislative branches that play this dual role. Parliaments, over time, usually place increasing emphasis on ceremony. They build support by engaging in ritualized debate, by representing or mirroring the national community, and by the customs and traditions they themselves develop.

Executive leaders also frequently combine instrumental and ceremonial duties. The presidents of France, Tanzania, and Egypt engage in much ceremonial and support-building activity. President Nyerere of Tanzania, for example, is referred to as the "Father of the Nation" and "Teacher." Although these titles do not carry with them specific powers, the fact that he is thought of as the father of his nation and a wise teacher legitimizes his authority and helps win support for government programs and policies.

A leader's power is often based on his personal magnetism or charisma. Charisma, of course, does not necessarily come with the office of president, but in some cases those individuals fortunate enough to possess this personal grace can use it to expand their powers. President Nasser, for example, was able to use his personal popularity to help consolidate his powerful hold on the reins of Egyptian government. Successors to charismatic leaders find it difficult to assert their own authority and to separate their governments and policies from their predecessors'. Charles de Gaulle's charisma was not transferable to Presidents Pompidou or Giscard d'Estaing, nor did President Sadat inherit President Nasser's emotional appeal.

There are other ways of building support. An ideology or a national language program may unify a nation and help develop its symbols. (Swahili in Tanzania serves the important function of binding together diverse language groups.) Another symbol develops when leaders make constant reference to specific historical events. Many nationalist movements in ex-colonial areas (Nigeria, Tanzania, and Egypt) remain symbols long after the instrumental goal—achieving independence—is reached.

The effectiveness of leaders and institutions in creating symbols and carrying out the symbolic functions varies. Certain circumstances appear to increase their effectiveness and performance. Noncontroversial leaders and institutions not identified with particular groups lessen the possibility of group antagonisms developing. Institutions characterized by stability in personnel, activities, and public image also tend to be more effective, as do institutions that represent historical continuity. They become national symbols in themselves. Newer institutions can build support by drawing on the myths and symbols of the national past.

The nations in our study represent a wide variety of institutional forms. The developed nations of democratic Western Europe tend to rely on ceremonial heads of state in conjunction with their parliaments to provide the ceremony and ritual of politics. The Soviet Union borrowed a Western institution, the popular assembly, to help party leaders create and ensure support. Developing nations often find that they lack support-building institutions. In many cases they must rely on the office and person of the national leader to hold the nation together. In other cases they may appeal to their histories or attempt to adapt other institutions, like parliaments, in order to build support. Whatever the pattern, symbols and symbolic institutions are important in understanding national politics.

▪ THE UNITED KINGDOM ▪

The United Kingdom is blessed with a variety of institutions capable of generating public support. Chief among these are the "dignified" institutions—the monarchy and the House of Lords. Even the House of Commons spends the greater portion of its time on symbolic activity, as we shall see. The political support generated by these ancient institutions has undoubtedly helped Britain through its recent problems.

The British are fortunate in having preserved ancient and seemingly archaic institutions. The institutions of the monarchy and the Lords represent a direct link to almost a thousand years of English history (Queen Elizabeth II can trace her ancestral line back to the ninth century). The queen and the peers of the realm are living symbols of England's ancient ruling elite who are associated with all of England's great triumphs and moments of crisis. Since the monarchy and the House of Lords are not currently primarily instrumental or working institutions, it is easy for most Britons to form bonds of affection with these "harmless" but compelling ancient institutions and their specific incumbents.

The Monarchy

The Crown is the supreme legal power in Britain. The power of the Crown "rests in the Queen but in general its functions are exercised by Ministers responsible to Parliament. The Queen reigns but does not rule. The United Kingdom is governed by Her Majesty's Government in the name of the Queen."[1] The Crown power is exercised directly by the queen only in the few matters that are still her personal prerogative. The rest of the Crown powers have been taken over by the cabinet through centuries of usage and precedent.

The formal powers of the Crown include the power of dissolving Parliament, the approval or disapproval (veto) of all bills, pardons, the granting of honors, approval of cabinet appointments, and the power to make treaties and declare war. Of these formal or Crown powers, the queen

---

[1] Douglas Verney, *British Government and Politics* (New York: Harper & Row, 1976), p. 138.

Queen Elizabeth II presides over the opening of Parliament. The queen and Prince Philip are seated on their thrones in the chamber of the House of Lords. Courtesy, Central Office of Information, London.

personally exercises only the power to confer honors on deserving subjects. The rest have been passed on to her advisers.

The monarch does retain some influence with regard to some important Crown powers. In particular, the monarch can influence the selection of the prime minister and other cabinet members. The queen must, of course, select the leader of the majority party after an election; however, there are occasions when there is no clear leader or when there is no majority party. This likelihood is greatest when a prime minister resigns between elections. The resignations of Anthony Eden in 1957 and Harold Macmillan in 1963 led to controversial selections (Macmillan in 1957 and Sir Alec Douglas-Home in 1963). The likelihood of there being no majority party is greatest when the party system is undergoing realignment, as it may be doing today.

There is little chance that the monarch will regain any significant powers. The queen must earn her keep by performing ceremonial functions: acting as head of state, greeting and entertaining foreign dignitaries, and presiding over endless ceremonies such as the opening of the North Sea oil pipeline. She also opens Parliament and delivers the queen's speech regarding the state of the realm (written for her by the prime minister).

The queen's keep comes high, and many think that she does not come close to earning it. The royal family draws several million pounds from the Treasury for allowances, upkeep on forty castles and palaces, the expenses of the royal yacht *Britannia,* and the maintenance of the queen's airplanes. She has a large personal staff that includes such exotic figures as the mistress of the robes, lord black rod, and the keeper of the royal swans. Privileges include immunity from civil suit and criminal action.

The queen perhaps does most to earn her way by building support for the other British political institutions, notably the cabinet and Parliament. The affection and trust that most Britons feel for the queen is later transferred to the "efficient" institutions of government. There is little doubt that the stable, enduring, noncontroversial monarch is an ideal support-building figure.[2] Feelings of affection are obvious in the replies of young Britons to questions about their queen. For example:

Interviewer: Who is the Queen?
Susan (age 12): The Queen is a member of the royal family that *looks after* the country and her problems. [Italics added]
Interviewer: What sort of things does she do?
Susan: Well, she lives in Buckingham Palace, which is in the middle of London. And she rules over England.[3]

Susan's answers show that she feels the queen to be a benevolent authority figure—The queen "looks after the country." Susan's feelings have

[2] Fred I. Greenstein and Sidney Tarrow, *The Political Orientations of Children* (Beverly Hills, Calif.: Sage Publications, 1970).
[3] Ibid., p. 485.

special force because she believes that the queen actually "rules over England."

The House of Lords

The House of Lords is now virtually powerless as a legislative institution. The Parliament Act of 1911 broke the power of the Lords, which at that time was composed entirely of nonelected hereditary peers. The upper house had rejected the 1909 Finance Bill and therefore raised the question of the Lords' modern powers over financial as well as ordinary legislation. Before this crisis period the Lords had acquiesced to the House of Commons on financial bills and had generally deferred to the democratic house on legislative matters in general. Liberal Prime Minister Herbert Asquith dissolved Parliament and called for an election in January 1910. The Liberal victory that followed sealed the fate of the Lords.

The Liberal government produced the 1911 Parliament Act to reform the Lords, despite the fact that the upper house had dutifully accepted the 1910 Finance Bill. The Parliament Act stipulated that a finance bill would become law with or without the approval of the House of Lords one month after being sent to that chamber. It also stipulated that any bill passing the House of Commons in three successive sessions was to become law without regard to the wishes of the House of Lords, providing that two years elapsed in the course of these deliberations.

Two more recent bills have further reduced the practical importance of the House of Lords. The Parliament Bill of 1949 limited the time in which the Lords could delay passage of a bill. The bill permitted the House of Commons to overcome Lords' objections by passing a bill in each of two successive sessions providing that a year lapses in the process. The Life Peerages Act of 1958 also affected the independent powers of the Lords. This act, creating the new nonhereditary titles *life peer* and *life peeress,* was meant to change the character of the house by adding more politically and professionally oriented peers.

Today there are over a thousand members of the upper house. Over 800 are hereditary peers, as, for example, the marquis of Salisbury, representing a great old family of the realm. Almost half of the peerages, however, have been recently created for outstanding services (often distinctly political) to the nation. The other peers are life peers who fall into several separate categories. First of all, there are the approximately 150 ordinary life peers created since 1958. In addition, there are 26 lords spiritual: the 2 archbishops and 24 bishops of the Church of England. There are also 9 law lords who comprise the highest British court.[4]

The active members of the House of Lords number no more than 200.

---

[4] Janet P. Morgan, *The House of Lords and the Labour Government, 1964–1970* (Oxford: The Clarendon Press, 1975), pp. 11–27.

The absenteeism of the lords has led to the establishment of a £8.50 per diem expense allowance for the lords to pay for their food and transportation while in town. This provision has been credited with increasing attendance since it was introduced in 1958.

The partisan balance of the full house greatly favors the Conservatives, but the balance is much more even for those who are regular attenders. The life peers, particularly Wilson's post-1964 group, have evened things considerably. One recent estimate suggests that there are 125 Conservatives and 95 Labourites in the House of Lords, with a substantial number of independent or "Crossbench" members among the more active peers.[5]

The House of Lords engages in some practical or instrumental activity. It introduces amendments intended to strengthen House of Commons bills, most of which the Commons accepts. It sometimes initiates bills and considers them at length to help relieve the time pressure normally gripping the lower house. The House of Lords regularly questions the government on its conduct and publicizes any indiscretions uncovered. In all these activities, the House of Lords acts as a cooperative supplementary body that accepts the dominance of the Commons.

The members of the House of Lords are particularly proud of the quality of debate that occurs in their chamber. They would agree with the fictional peer who said:

> While the Commons must bray like an ass every day
> To appease the electoral hordes
> We don't say a thing till we've something to say
> There's a lot to be said for the Lords.[6]

The quality of discussion is stimulated by the presence of elder statesmen who have been "kicked upstairs" from the House of Commons. The peers' excellent academic training can be put to use in debate; 90 percent are graduates of Oxford, Cambridge, or Sandhurst (the military college).[7] At its best the Lords can project the image of an elite, if largely powerless, deliberative assembly comprised of the nation's finest citizens. The fact that many of the lords carry great historical names gives added emotional weight to the lords' thoughtful discussions.

The House of Commons

If one excludes the executive committee of the House of Commons—the cabinet—much of the work of the full house can be characterized as symbolic. In particular, the daily debate between government and opposi-

---

[5] Ibid., p. 23.
[6] The Viscount Massereene and Ferrard, *The Lords* (London: Leslie Frewin, 1973), p. 154.
[7] Ibid., p. 152.

tion has the flavor of stylized ritual; since the house is comprised of highly disciplined party members, the outcome on all votes is known in advance. The House of Commons has virtually no independent sources of information or expertise; it is dependent on the government or the national parties. As the majority party and cabinet have almost unlimited power, opposition and criticism are largely for the record and for an audience outside Westminster. Debates in Commons are symbolic conflict between the important groups (in this instance, classes) in society. They have an important emotional impact on the public.

The fact that the modern House of Commons is not a real decision-making or policy-making body is not contested by either scholars or practical politicians. Walter Bagehot, in his classic book *The English Constitution* (1867), emphasized its "lyrical functions" that focus on debate. Bagehot maintained that the Commons did not govern or make laws—occupations for which the House was "radically unfit"—but rather taught, informed, and expressed popular feelings in debate. This is perhaps more true today than in Bagehot's day.

Geared to debate, the House of Commons spends more time in activities involving the whole house than does any other major parliamentary body. Its central action is the debate of government-sponsored bills. Debate occurs at the second reading (the first reading is a formality introducing the bill). The debate on the second reading focuses on the principles of the bill and occurs before the bill has been through its committee stage. The government and shadow cabinet marshal speakers to favor and oppose the bill. The debate is controlled by the scrupulously nonpartisan speaker of the house (who virtually gives up his political career to demonstrate fairness). In the end the government always wins (at least since 1895 on government bills). The Labour government of James Callaghan ended one long-standing pattern when it lost (311–310) a vote of confidence in 1979. The Conservatives won the election that Callaghan was forced to call following the party's parliamentary defeat.

The physical structure of the house itself has symbolic importance that lends emotional impact to the debates. The chamber can trace its main features to St. Stephen's Chapel of the Palace of Westminster, which was first used in 1527. New chambers reflecting the early model were built after the fire of 1834 and the bombing of World War II. The government and opposition contingents face each other from their benches or pews. The benches seat only 437 of the current 630 members, for the chamber is deliberately undersized to give a sense of urgency to important debates. Members almost literally hang from the rafters on these occasions. The speaker's platform in between the benches raises the presiding officer high above the partisan conflict. Lines are drawn on the floor to keep speakers separated during heated exchanges.

Voting after debates may require a division if a voice vote is not clear. Divisions involve members filing into either the "Aye lobby" or the "Nay lobby" where they are counted by tellers. The chamber is arranged so that if a member does not vote with his party he must "cross the floor" to join the opposition conspicuously.

The house does engage in instrumental work of a kind in addition to ritualized debate. After the ritual debate, bills are referred to standing committees for detailed scrutiny. These standing committees are not specialized, however; they are merely labeled A, B, C, D, E, and F. There are no experts to go over the bill—no calling in of outsiders to "testify" or aid them in their deliberations. Experience shows at any rate that few changes will be tolerated at the report stage.

Another supposedly instrumental task involves controlling the executive through written and oral questions. Question hour occurs Monday through Friday from 2:45 to 3:30 P.M. Oral questions are presented to a minister, and a follow-up is permitted. The first question is known in advance; the second is not. Even this "instrumental" task is more dramatic than practical. Ministers may be embarrassed as they stand at the government dispatch box on the floor without help from solicitous aides. The public at times enjoys the show and feels better for it, but the practical implications of the procedure are slight. Like the debates, the question hour educates the public and builds support for the institutions of government.

Few nations can compete with the United Kingdom in the quantity and quality of symbolic institutions. The power of these institutions stems from their historical origins. The monarchy and the Lords survived because particular monarchs and peers in the past were willing to adapt themselves to modern democratic politics. There was no need to abolish these institutions whose members willingly made themselves useful. They have been very useful in making the British public supportive of the institutions and norms of British politics and the actions of political authorities.

■ THE FEDERAL REPUBLIC OF GERMANY ■

The Federal Republic of Germany is in many ways a new nation. Many of the ties with the old Germany were irrevocably broken during the period of Hitler's regime and World War II. The Federal Republic, founded in 1949, was supported by only a minority of democratically oriented Germans. The new institutions, the rules supporting the institutions, and the new political officeholders did not appear legitimate to many Germans.

The occupying powers of the Western zones of Germany tried to design institutions capable of generating diffuse support for democratic institutions. Their hopes rested on the office of federal president, an office they viewed as a nonpartisan ceremonial position. The occupiers tried to emulate some of the key features of the British monarchy in their conception of West Germany's federal presidency. The subsequent years have shown that the West German presidency has not been as effective in its symbolic function as was originally hoped. The West Germans themselves began to experiment with other institutions in the hope that they could help create supportive feelings among the general public. The lower house of Parliament, the Bundestag, has been partially reformed to increase its share of symbolic functions. The West Germans have looked to the British for inspiration for their parliamentary reforms, just as the occupying authorities had done previously.

The Problem of Legitimation

It is difficult to exaggerate the crisis of legitimacy in the early Federal Republic. The German public had no part in drafting or approving the West German constitution, or Basic Law. Germans did not vote for the members of the assembly that was consulted in the drafting of the Basic Law. They had no part in ratifying the document once it was produced. Germans were well aware that British, French, and American occupiers dictated the major outlines of the constitutional document; thus, the Basic Law was widely viewed as an alien document imposed by the Western victors of World War II.

West Germany was not a fully sovereign nation upon its creation. The federal government did not have a foreign office until 1951. The Occupation Statute, under which the occupying authorities governed West Germany, did not formally lapse until 1955. Even after 1955, the "Three Powers" have retained rights with regard to a full peace settlement, Berlin, and matters regarding the reunification of East and West Germany. At the beginning West Germany was viewed by Germans and occupying powers alike as a temporary entity that fell short of full legal statehood. For this reason Germans resisted calling their constitution a constitution, preferring the more transitory title, Basic Law.[8]

The new Federal Republic did not resemble the old Germany in territory and population. Territory was lost to the Communists in the eastern zone of occupation, while the new Poland gained a large part of the old Germany beyond the Oder-Neisse. Berlin was isolated from the western zone and could not be used or claimed as an integral part of West Germany. For this reason a new capital, Bonn, had to be chosen.

In sum, the Federal Republic had overwhelming problems in establishing its legitimacy. Its legal basis was questioned. Its connections with the old Germany were severed. The basics of geography and population worked against the new regime's claims of legitimacy.

The Allied occupying authorities and their German advisers faced conflicting symbols in German history. They wanted the Federal Republic

---

[8] Alfred Grosser, Germany in Our Time (New York: Praeger, 1971), pp. 78–79.

to represent German traditions, but the political instability of Germany had created several distinct traditions (monarchy, republicanism, totalitarianism). The appropriate tradition, German republicanism, was not necessarily the one to which most of Germany felt emotionally attached.

The founders of the Federal Republic wasted no opportunity to sponsor the symbols of German republicanism. They selected the black, red, and gold flag of Weimar and of the liberals of 1848. They selected Bonn—the home of Goethe, Schiller, and German liberal humanism—as the capital of the Federal Republic. In the early years, as even the founders were aware, these ties to liberalism were not popular; for example, twice as many Germans preferred the black, white, and red flag of the German monarchy to the flag of German liberalism.[9]

The Presidency

The founders of the Federal Republic expected that support for the new regime could be built by a presidential office designed like the British monarchy. They observed that the British monarchy had a number of features that tied the public's emotions to the institutions of government. The monarch was nonpartisan and therefore not a controversial figure. The monarch was a stable fixture with a long tenure. The British "ruler" gave the appearance of ruling and therefore did not appear trivial in the eyes of subjects.

The federal presidency is modeled along these lines. Nonpartisanship is encouraged by the way in which the president is selected, not directly elected. He is chosen by a body called the Federal Assembly *(Bundesversammlung)*, composed of all of the members of the Bundestag and an equal number of delegates from the state legislatures, with each party being represented in proportion to its strength. The Bundestag president presides as the Federal Assembly casts a maximum of three ballots. If no one has attained a majority by that time, the person with the most votes is elected.

The manner of election reduces the political activities of candidates for the presidency, for there is no national political campaign. The matter is almost known in advance by the relative strengths of the parties. Each party has its own candidate, and party members follow the party recommendations. The election of the president is further insulated from partisan politics by its timing. Since presidential elections do not coincide with parliamentary elections, presidential candidates avoid the issues and public debate surrounding the elections for the Bundestag. The election of the

---

[9] G. R. Boynton and Gerhard Loewenberg, "The Decay of Support for Monarchy and Dictatorship in Postwar Germany," paper presented at the 1973 Annual Meeting of the American Political Science Association, New Orleans, September 4, 1973.

current president, Walter Scheel (FDP), occurred in 1974, between the 1972 and 1976 parliamentary elections.

The founders intended the president to be an elder statesman—a "favorite uncle" or grandfatherly type. The Basic Law prescribes that the president must be 40 years of age or older. Age is respected by Germans, who have demonstrated their affection for such octogenarians as President Paul von Hindenburg (1925–1934) and Chancellor Konrad Adenauer (1949–1963).

The president has a five-year term and may be re-elected once; thus, a popular president can hold office for ten years. The founders felt that ten years was sufficient to establish the desired relationship with the public. They feared that a longer tenure would tempt a popular president to overstep his powers. The term of five years is longer than Parliament's four-year term.

Like the queen of England, the president of the Federal Republic is a head of state who appears to rule without actually ruling. He represents the Federal Republic for all purposes of international law and presides over the ceremonies marking treaty agreements with foreign states. The president receives and accredits foreign envoys; he grants pardons and appoints judges and other federal officials on the advice of the more political element of the executive—the chancellor.

The president nominates a candidate for chancellor to the Bundestag following elections. The Bundestag may reject his nominee and select their own without referring the matter back to the president. Given the nature of parliamentary majorities in recent times, the president has very little leeway in submitting names to the Bundestag for approval. There has been an obvious candidate in almost every case representing the choice of the majority coalition. The president's nominee has always been accepted, with 1949 being the closest call—Adenauer won by one vote in that more divided Parliament.

Before laws go into effect, they must be signed by the president and countersigned by the chancellor and appropriate minister. What was intended as a formality has sometimes blocked or delayed legislation when presidents have withheld their signatures. President Theodor Heuss (1949–1959) refused to sign a treaty committing West German defense forces to the European Defense Community in 1952 because he doubted the constitutionality of the treaty. Heuss also blocked a tax law revision on the same grounds. Normally, though, the president bestows his approval on all bills that receive parliamentary approval.

The president lacks the powers that have made other parliamentary system presidents powerful. He is not commander-in-chief of the military, nor does he have emergency powers, as does the French president and as did the German president in Weimar. The president can dissolve Parliament only in clearly delimited cases of deadlock—the conditions have been met only once (1972) and then not at the initiative of the president. The president does not preside over cabinet meetings (as does the French president). His powers are only formal and are mainly illusory.

The styles of the four federal presidents have varied considerably. The first, Theodor Heuss (FDP), was ideally suited for a symbolic presidency. He was 65 upon his election in 1949. With superb academic and intellectual credentials, Heuss was a teacher by style and temperament, patiently striving in his carefully constructed speeches to cultivate a liberal democratic spirit in his audiences. Heuss was so successful at his nonpartisan tasks that he was re-elected without opposition in 1954. Many wanted to introduce a constitutional amendment to permit Heuss to have a third term in 1959. Characteristically, Heuss declined by saying: "I want you to see the handing over of the presidency as an educative process for the benefit of ordinary citizens. . . . Democracy is leadership with a time limit."[10]

Subsequent presidents have not been as successful or as well cut out for a symbolic role. Heinrich Lübke (CDU, 1959–1969) became embroiled in political machinations regarding his pet project—the creation of a grand coalition between the Christian Democrats and the Social Democrats. He also had an unfortunate political style that invited ridicule and innuendo regarding his integrity. The last two presidents, Gustav Heinemann (1969–1974, SPD) and Walter Scheel (1974–present, FDP), have been interested in upgrading the political importance of the office. Both were distinguished politicians before becoming president (Scheel as the leader of the FDP, Heinemann as an SPD minister of justice), and both felt the need to remain influential in office.

The Bundestag's Symbolic Role

The failure of the presidency in its symbolic role has led to efforts to use other institutions for building diffuse support for the new regime. The Bundestag, or lower house of Parliament, has tended to be the focus of these reforms.

The Bundestag is more specialized and complexly organized than the British House of Commons. Specialized standing committees do a large part of the house's business. Each committee (there are 19 currently) reflects the partisan balance of the whole house. The house also contains a complex party-related structure. Each party meets as a *Fraktionen* (party group) that contains its own specialized party committees paralleling the house standing committees. The business of the Bundestag is run by presiding officers and a council of elders, both made up of the party leaders of the house.

This complex organization makes the Bundestag more important in

---

[10] Grosser, *Germany in Our Time*, p. 106.

policy-making and less important in symbolic activities than the British House of Commons. Much of the Bundestag's work is done in party or house committees; very little time is spent in general debate on the floor. The quality of debate has been so poor and lacking in spontaneity that Bundestag leaders had to introduce a rule forbidding the reading of speeches (a rule that is generally disregarded).

Reforms have increased the time devoted to debate. Reforms have also increased the role of oral questions in the Bundestag. Originally oral questions were permitted only once a month (compared to four times a week in Britain); now "urgent questions" may be raised more frequently, and follow-up and supplementary questions are allowed.

The upper house of Parliament, the Bundesrat, is not as effective in building supportive attitudes as the House of Lords. Comprised of delegates of the states (*Lander*), it currently has 41 members. The Land governments may choose five, four or three delegates to the Bundesrat depending on their population. The role of the upper house is to protect states' rights and privileges under the Basic Law; it has an absolute veto on legislation affecting the states (administration, taxes, boundaries), and it must approve amendments to the Basic Law. On ordinary pieces of legislation, it may be overridden by an equivalent majority of the Bundestag.

The Bundesrat, given its composition and legislative roles, does not engage in much ceremony or ritual. It is not an ordinary democratic representative assembly and lacks the public nature that characterizes those bodies. The Bundesrat does, however, have the weight of tradition behind it, tracing its origins to the empire period (1871–1918). To this extent, the Bundesrat may attract popular support by its position as one of the more stable and continuous German institutions.

The efforts of the framers of the Basic Law to develop symbolic institutions seems to have been largely a failure. The federal presidency has become increasingly partisan and its incumbents more controversial. The Bundestag is an unusually bureaucratic parliament that neglects its public relations, while the Bundesrat is not a deliberative or debating body and cannot be made into one. The institutions of the Federal Republic rely on performance, not style or ceremony, to build support. It remains to be seen what prolonged economic or political failure would do to the support that they currently enjoy.

▪ FRANCE ▪

The president of the Republic as head of state has major responsibility for symbolic and support-building functions—an aspect of the presidency that Charles de Gaulle took very seriously. De Gaulle, however, relied on his own presence or charisma; he did not design the office itself for this task of building support. Rather, he insisted that the president be the leading policy-maker and politician of the nation; in practice, though, the role of policy-maker conflicts with that of symbolic leader.

The Parliament of the Fifth Republic is capable of performing symbolic functions. Since the Parliament lost many of its powers in the transition to the new republic, it is logical that it should now increase its support-building work. Still adjusting to the new system, Parliament remains uncertain about the proper balance of functions.

The Fifth Republic faces a crisis of legitimacy as severe as that of the German Federal Republic; therefore symbolic functions are important. In this century the French have operated under four sets of political institutions, none of which has been fully accepted. World War II and 15 years of colonial warfare that followed placed a great strain on the system. The French are only now recovering from that 20-year period of national trauma.

The Presidency

De Gaulle's original conception of the presidency emphasized the importance of symbolic functions and activities. He described the office as being above politics—a moral instrument that could intervene and influence the institutions of government when the national good required it. His view suggested that the president would avoid day-to-day decision-making and ordinary political issues.

The original Gaullist conception permitted the president to emphasize his symbolic duties: representing the state and the people of France. He could act as a representative of the people in the ordinary sense of international law. The president could also stand for the people in a moral sense, guarding them against the intrigues of politicians, both foreign and domestic.

These themes are evident in De Gaulle's famous Bayeux speech, (June 16, 1946) whose purpose was to convince the people and the constitutional assembly to favor a presidential system for the Fourth Republic. De Gaulle described the idea in this way: "It is then the chief of State—placed above political parties, elected by an electoral college that includes Parliament but which is much broader . . . who should hold executive power."[11] De Gaulle went on to describe the president as "arbiter above political contingencies." The president should have "the duty of reconciling the national interest with the general orientation of Parliament" and "the obligation to act as the guarantor of national independence and of the treaties that bind France."[12]

---

[11] John S. Ambler, *The Government and Politics of France* (Boston: Houghton Mifflin, 1971), p. 123.
[12] Ibid.

General Charles de Gaulle, former president of the Fifth Republic. H. Roger Viollet.

The Bayeux speech was interpreted by some as advocating a presidency that would be symbolic and ceremonial in its day-to-day routine. The president was to intervene periodically on the great issues or in time of crisis but was clearly to be above ordinary politics and politicians. The indirect election of the president was meant to make the office less political.

Michel Debré, the Gaullist lieutenant who actually drafted the constitution of the Fifth Republic, believed in this original conception of an "arbiter" president. For Debré, the president's role was as a "higher judge of the national interest," his power mainly that of moral influence. Debré suggested that "the President of the Republic . . . has no other power than that of appealing to another power: he appeals to Parliament, he appeals to the Constitutional Council, he appeals to the electorate. But this power to appeal is fundamental."[13] Debré did not see the president as either a day-to-day decision-maker or the nation's top policy-maker. The president's role was viewed as an intermittent one.

Despite the conception of the president as arbiter, in practice De Gaulle

---

[13] Ibid., p. 127.

(1958–1969) gathered the powers of policy-making to the president's office and had a hand in all major decisions. Dominating his premiers, De Gaulle even ousted most loyal ally Debré when their views of presidential power began to diverge. He dismissed Georges Pompidou as premier immediately after Pompidou had engineered the great Gaullist parliamentary election victory of 1968. The general would not permit a strong independent premier to handle the business of government.

A clear signal that De Gaulle would not be satisfied with an intermittent role came with the referendum on the direct election of the president in September of 1962. Instead of asking the advice of the premier or cabinet, as his own constitution proposed, De Gaulle informed them of his decision to hold a referendum on this constitutional issue. The direct election of the president made the head of state a preeminently political figure.

A Charismatic President

De Gaulle felt that the job of being top policy-maker was not incompatible with a ceremonial role. His war memories, written between 1946 and 1958, reflect his self-consciousness about developing himself as a charismatic figure. De Gaulle defined charisma as "communicated self-confidence." A charismatic leader had a vision that he could communicate to the people and make them believe—in this case the *grandeur,* or greatness, of France.[14]

This power to touch the public's emotions was, in De Gaulle's view, personal. Leadership and personal greatness were proven by decisive reaction to perilous events (his extraordinary efforts as a savior of the nation during World War II and in the crisis of 1958). The general maintained that "in economy, as in politics or strategy, there exists, I believe, no absolute truth. There are only the circumstances."[15] From this point of view, charisma—the ability to create a bond with the public—could not be written into a constitution or built into an office. De Gaulle maintained that charisma lost its power when it was "routinized."

Some evidence suggests that the presidential office has not been an effective support-building and symbolic institution comparable to the British monarchy. A study of British, American, and French children conducted in the spring of 1969 (during De Gaulle's presidency) made this point dramatically. The study found that French children had a less trusting and affectionate view of their head of state than did American and British children. They did not see the French president as a benign, protective authority figure but as a politician who gave orders and punished those who did not obey.

The children's answers make the point clearer than any general descrip-

---

[14] Stanley Hoffman, *France: Decline or Renewal* (New York: The Viking Press, 1974), p. 234.
[15] Ibid., p. 189.

tion could. Asked what the president does, one 12-year-old child responded: "The President of the Republic is the one who rules. Everyone must obey him." Asked if De Gaulle carried out his duties well, the same child said: "He *must* carry them out . . . If he does not, he is nevertheless kept on, because he is President and everyone must respect him . . . even if certain people conclude that he has done some stupid things—even so they must obey him." There is an understanding of authority relations in these answers but not the warmth and affection that characterize the description of American children of their president and the description of the monarch given by British youngsters.[16]

The Parliament as a Symbolic Institution

The Parliament of France was the dominant political institution of Third and Fourth Republic France (1875–1958), while the presidency was a weak symbolic office. The constitution of the Fifth Republic reversed the positions of the two institutions: the president became the leading policy-making actor with some ceremonial duties; Parliament was left to search for a new role.

The new Parliament looks very much like its predecessors. There is a lower house, the National Assembly, composed of 490 members elected to five-year terms by universal suffrage. The upper house, or Senate, is comprised of 283 members elected for nine-year terms by an electoral college made up of the National Assembly and members of local government bodies. A speaker for each house is elected by the full membership of the house. A steering committee of party leaders helps these presiding officers with the legislative business of each house.

Parliament's legislative and political tasks, however, have been reduced by a number of constitutional provisions. Parliament can act only on policy matters that are specifically mentioned in the constitution. Matters outside this jurisdiction must be handled by legislative framework laws (which provide only general policy guidelines) or governmental decrees. The cabinet controls the legislative timetable. The number of specialized committees has been greatly reduced, as has the time which they have to meet. All of these measures are designed to "streamline" or "rationalize" the legislative process. They also reduce the power of Parliament vis-à-vis the executive.

The real policy-making executive, the president, is not responsible to Parliament, but the cabinet and premier are. A newly nominated premier submits his program to the Parliament for approval before the cabinet can be "invested." The National Assembly may introduce a motion of censure against the cabinet on the signature of one-tenth of the Assembly. A vote on the motion is held 48 hours after the petition is submitted, with absen-

[16] Greenstein and Tarrow, *The Political Orientations of Children,* p. 489.

tions counting in the government's favor. They must resign if the motion carries. If it fails, those who brought the motion cannot initiate another censure motion in the same session. Finally, the premier himself may make the vote on any bill a matter of confidence. If he does so, the bill becomes law without a vote unless there is a successful motion of censure carried in the next 24 hours—an unlikely prospect. The cabinet has been fairly secure against opposition challenges under these arrangements. The president has nothing to fear from parliamentary opposition.

The cabinet also has a number of options in the legislative process that give it the upper hand. If there is a disagreement between the Assembly and the Senate (the two are nearly equal in the process), the cabinet may request a shuttle (sending the bill back and forth until there is agreement), they may submit the bill to conference committee, they may reintroduce the original bill in both houses and start over, or they may ask the Assembly alone to determine the final version. Thus, the cabinet can use one house against the other: the Senate can kill Assembly-sponsored legislation; the Assembly can be used to sidestep the Senate. In addition, the Fifth Republic constitution has added time limits for the Parliament's acceptance of finance bills and the budget. If the Parliament cannot or will not act on these matters, they become law by decree.

The dominance of the executive leaves the French Parliament with the option of accepting a role more like the British House of Commons or becoming increasingly irrelevant. The Parliament has rejected the Commons model because it is weak by French parliamentary standards. The government has made it difficult for Parliament to play this symbolic role by its control of the agenda and its disdain for such procedures as "question hour." Debate is designed to "streamline" the passage of legislation, not to permit opposition criticism. Question time, which meets once a week, suffers from the hostility of the ministers who are often not parliamentarians and who have little sympathy for the institution.

The French Fifth Republic suffers from the performance of symbolic institutions. The presidency is too powerful and political to act as a support-building head of state. The Parliament is not yet accustomed to a secondary role in the political system. This partially explains why Frenchmen seem to show more support and loyalty for individual leaders than for their political institutions. Frenchmen tend to focus on the great men who get things done despite the inertia and corruption of the formal political system.

▪ THE SOVIET UNION ▪

The symbolic institutions of the Soviet Union are the elective assemblies, or Soviets. This system of popular assemblies is headed at the national level by the Supreme Soviet. Elections for the Soviets have symbolic importance by providing the democratic basis for Soviet government, but the Supreme Soviet and the lower assemblies have only a ceremonial role. The Soviets are controlled by the party through the executive organs of the assemblies; they have no say in policy-making or practical politics. The party uses the Soviets to legitimate their policy decisions, to educate the public, and to gain public affirmation for their actions.

Traditions of the Soviets

Effective symbolic institutions usually have a history that attaches special emotional importance to them. The British monarchy is a very effective symbolic institution partly because of the history and events with which it is associated. When institutions come to stand for important elements of national history and culture, they themselves become symbols capable of moving people emotionally.

The Soviets are symbolic institutions largely because of their historical origins. The forerunner of the Soviets were ad hoc workers councils that first appeared to help coordinate and direct the general strike that touched off the revolutionary activity of 1905. The first Soviets were the spontaneous creations of the workers themselves, independent of political groups including the Bolsheviks.

Leonid Brezhnev and other Communist party leaders review troops from a stand in front of the Lenin Mausoleum in Moscow. Novosti Press Agency (A.P.N.)

Lenin approved of these groups since they rose from the proletariat and were geared for revolutionary action. They were not like Western "bourgeois talk shops" or parliaments. The Soviets came back to life in 1917. This time the Bolsheviks were successful in penetrating the major Soviets of the large cities, using them as a power base against the provisional government led by the Duma (tsarist representative assembly). Becoming an important symbol of the new regime, the Soviets provided legitimacy for the Bolshevik leadership in the critical period in which power was consolidated. Though current Soviets are unlike the original model in a number of ways (for example, districts rather than factories are represented), they still bear the name and tradition of the early revolutionary bodies.

The Supreme Soviet

The Supreme Soviet is the national legislative body in the USSR. According to the 1936 constitution,[17] the Supreme Soviet is "the highest organ of state power" (article 30), meaning—in theory—that the Supreme Soviet is the locus of governmental sovereignty, the ultimate authority. The constitution states that "the legislative power of the USSR is exercised exclusively by the Supreme Soviet of the USSR" (article 32). In practice, of course, the authority of the Supreme Soviet is exercised by its executive body. This small executive organ of the Supreme Soviet, the Presidium of the Supreme Soviet, is controlled by the party. Party control is exercised by the familiar means discussed previously, such as interlocking leadership and party control of recruitment.

The Supreme Soviet legally controls its own executive, the Presidium, and the administrative executive, the Council of Ministers. The Supreme Soviet elects the members of these two executive bodies; but, since the Supreme Soviet meets only twice a year for two to three days, there is no pretense of real control. The Presidium handles the Supreme Soviet's business between sessions and structures its activities during the brief legislative sessions. The Council of Ministers, as described earlier, operates independently of the Supreme Soviet, subject only to party supervision.

The Supreme Soviet is a bicameral body, thus differing from the lower Soviets, which are all unicameral. The Soviet of the Union is the chamber providing basic representation for all Soviet citizens. Its members are elected from single-member constituencies on the basis of one representative for each 300,000 persons. The Soviet of Nationalities is viewed as

---

[17] As of this writing, the 1936 constitution is still in force. A new constitution will go into effect in late 1977. The provisions of this constitution, as revealed in published discussion drafts, do not conflict with the basic principles of the 1936 constitution as they are discussed here. The draft constitution was printed in *Pravda* and *Isvestia,* June 4, 1977, and translated in *The Current Digest of the Soviet Press,* Vol. XXIX, No. 22 (June 29, 1977), pp. 1–12.

providing representation for national groups. Its members are elected at large from the nationality territories (the union and autonomous republics).

The Supreme Soviet is re-elected every four years, and turnover among its membership is high; usually about two-thirds are new after each election. This reflects the leadership's desire to see that as many people as possible have experience as political representatives. It also reflects the fact that members have other occupational concerns while serving. There is no need to develop an experienced legislature in any case, since no special skills are required to serve in the Supreme Soviet.

Both houses are large—over 700 members in each. The members represent a cross-section of the full population as far as social and economic criteria are concerned. Approximately half of the current Supreme Soviet is comprised of workers and peasants. Almost one-third are women.[18]

The Supreme Soviet membership does not reflect the composition of the populace in one important respect. Three-fourths of the Supreme Soviet members are members of the party, in contrast to approximately 5 percent for the full citizenry of the Soviet Union. The overrepresentation of party members in the Supreme Soviet demonstrates the concern of the party leadership with control of state institutions. Since the party controls nomination for the Supreme Soviet, members are selected for their reliability and often to reward party service.

The Supreme Soviet is a very "streamlined" legislative institution, with procedures designed to expedite the passage of party-approved legislation. Sessions are characterized by set speeches rather than debate, and items for consideration are often approved in a block. The houses do have provisions for standing committees that screen legislation before it is presented, but their discussions and operations are closely managed by party observers. Many items of legislation are never submitted to the Supreme Soviet for approval, but simply issued as decrees of the Presidium of the Supreme Soviet. The Presidium, comprised of 30–40 members, acts as a "collective executive" or, more properly, a "collective head of state." This group actually handles the legislative business of the Supreme Soviet and carefully manages the brief semi-annual sessions.

The chairman of the Presidium of the Supreme Soviet acts as a ceremonial head of state and is sometimes referred to as president of the USSR. Like any other head of state, he represents the Soviet Union for the purposes of international law. He is the equal of other heads of state in protocol and engages in ceremonial activities. The actual power of the chairman of the Presidium of the Supreme Soviet has been slight. Along with the secretary he has been the only person engaged in Presidium business on a full-time basis. Normally he presides over the issuing of executive decrees that are forwarded to the Presidium from party organs. This is in addition,

---

[18] Darrell P. Hammer, *USSR: The Politics of Oligarchy* (Hinsdale, Ill.: The Dryden Press, 1974), pp. 258–260.

of course, to ceremonial duties. In 1977 Leonid Brezhnev was named president, replacing Nikolai Podgorny. Brezhnev is primarily interested in the position's protocol status, enabling him to meet foreign heads of state on an equal footing. The work of the Presidium is being carried out by his assistants.

Nominations and Elections

The Supreme Soviet provides the Soviet system with the offices for which national elections are held. Elections are viewed as valuable in emphasizing public support and as propaganda for foreign audiences, but the main purpose seems to be to permit widespread participation in formally democratic elections.

The first thing that strikes Westerners about Soviet elections is that there is almost always only one candidate for each position. Ideologically, this is explained by the identity of interests and needs of people in a socialist society. Multi-party systems of the West reflect class-based antagonisms that supposedly do not exist in the Soviet Union. An oft-quoted speech of M. I. Kalinin captures the idea: "This is a hallmark of socialism, a sign that there is no, and cannot be any, discord among our labouring masses, the kind of discord which exists in a bourgeois society."[19] Candidates are selected by district commissions appointed by party-dominated republic and regional governments. The Central Committee and other party organs have the right to suggest names to the district commissions. Though there is no restriction against nominating more than one candidate, that rarely happens.

Many times districts nominate important party leaders; then these leaders pick one of the several districts that have nominated them and allow themselves to be selected. Somewhere between one-third and one-half of the Supreme Soviet seats are filled this way. The rest are filled with ordinary people, the ones who usually have one term. The party leaders evidently serve over and over again, taking this as a matter or status or as an honorary title.

Elections are predetermined, but no expense or effort is spared to get the normal 99 percent turnout. The nominated candidate usually receives almost 99 percent as well. The other votes consist of write-ins or spoiled ballots. Each voter has the right to mark his ballot privately, but he may vote for the listed candidates without marking his ballot. The only reason to ask for a private booth is to write in a candidate's name. This obviously does not happen often.

To summarize, the Supreme Soviet and the system of subnational assemblies are specialized symbolic institutions, performing no efficient or

---

[19] John A. Armstrong, *Ideology, Politics and Government in the Soviet Union* (New York: Praeger, 1974), p. 159.

practical function. They are designed solely to legitimate policy made elsewhere and to build support for the policies, the men who made them, and the Soviet system. The effectiveness of the Soviets is enhanced by the history of the revolutionary Soviets. The system of elections permits widespread participation according to the party's understanding of democracy. There is no doubt that the party leadership considers this a useful enterprise and not a charade.

▪ NIGERIA ▪

The national motto of Nigeria is "Unity and Faith" (the white in the green and white national flag represents unity and peace), but the most difficult task facing leaders is maintaining that unity and peace among Nigeria's diverse groups. One of the most striking characteristics of Nigerian politics is the depth and political significance of the cleavages among groups. The forces separating Nigerians often are more politically important and stronger than those factors uniting them.

Both civilian and military leaders at the national level have tried to

An Eastern Region Nigerian poster calling for the different ethnic groups in the East to unite against a common enemy—the North. Note the distinctive traditional dress of the Northerner and the more modern dress of the Easterners. Courtesy, Eastern Ministry of Information.

create national symbols that would appeal to all groups. How difficult this is is indicated by the relatively few national symbols Nigeria possesses almost 20 years after independence. Powerful traditional and local symbols continue to influence politics, sharpening group differences and working against national unity.

The most severe challenge to national unity occurred from 1967 to 1970 when the former Eastern Region attempted to secede from the Federal Republic and establish the independent nation of Biafra. The leader of the secession attempt, General Ojukwu, made clear his position concerning a united Nigeria: "Nigeria never was and can never be a united country."[20] The reuniting of the Eastern Region to Nigeria in 1970 resolved one crisis but did not solve the underlying dilemma of Nigerian nationhood—how to build a sense of national unity and purpose.

Factors Working Against National Unity

Several factors work against the development of national values and institutions. First of all, Nigeria in many respects is an artificial creation. The British acquired the various territories of Nigeria in a piecemeal fashion; only in 1914 did they amalgamate under a central administration the Northern and Southern Protectorates of Nigeria. Even then, British colonial authorities administered the regions differently and did little to encourage interaction and interdependence. A colonial policy of divide and rule stressed differences, rather than similarities, among groups. This made colonial control easier but did little to help create a sense of Nigerian nationhood.

The severity of ethnic, linguistic, and religious differences separating Nigerians also worked against the development of a national consciousness. Competition among the three dominant groups began well before independence: relations between Hausa-Fulani, Yoruba, and Ibo often were characterized by mistrust and conflict. Within regions, minority groups felt culturally persecuted, economically disadvantaged, and politically underrepresented by the dominant regional groups. The colonial authority and power held the territory together, but few territory-wide institutions encouraged cooperation or gave Nigerians the experience of working together.

The nationalist movement reflected this situation. Unlike the Tanzanian situation, no one political party emerged as a national symbol capable of mobilizing the entire nation. Political parties such as the Northern People's Congress (NPC), the Action Group (AG), and the National Council of Nigerian Citizens (NCNC) represented specific groups and interests. Only the National Council of Nigerian Citizens (see Chapter 5) made an early attempt to develop a national following; ultimately it failed.

---

[20] C. Odumegwu Ojukwu, *Biafra* (New York: Harper & Row, 1969), p. 1.

As the nationalist struggle quickened during the 1950s, conflicts between political parties in Nigeria were as significant as differences between Nigerians and the British. As we have seen, the North feared southern domination, and the NPC was willing to delay independence until the North could "catch up" with the South. On the other hand, the South pictured the North as backward and traditional, and too much under British control. The different nationalist groups found it difficult to agree on when independence should be granted and on what form the new government should take.

Just as parties became symbols of regions, individuals also became symbols of specific regions or groups. Dr. Nnamdi Azikiwe, leader of the NCNC, came to represent the East. Chief Obafemi Awolowo became an important symbol of Yoruba nationhood and the Yoruba cultural revival. In the North, the traditional leader, the Sardauna of Sokoto, Sir Ahmadu Bello, built a widespread following based in part on his powerful traditional position.

At independence the national political institutions lacked the strength to overcome these powerful subnational symbols. No one leader could claim a truly national following, and the national Parliament became an arena for conflict between regional parties and interests. President Azikiwe (head of state) and Prime Minister Tafawa Balewa (head of government), although both strong supporters of a united Nigeria, often found themselves at political odds. No specific set of characteristics defined what it meant to be a Nigerian.

The conflict peaked from 1967 to 1970. The hope in 1966 that the military could act as a national institution and unify the nation disappeared by 1967. The officer corps of the military, as long as it remained an organization above politics, was a truly national institution; however, once officers became politically involved and were forced to operate the government on a day-to-day basis, they fell prey to divisions and conflicts similar to those that plagued the civilian government. Very quickly the January and July 1966 coups came to be viewed by many as ethnic plots.

The claims and counterclaims made following both coups fanned the fires of division within the military. In the January coup, those killed were primarily from the Northern or Western Regions, while the plotters were primarily of Eastern Region origin. The prime minister, governors of the Western and Northern Regions, and four of five senior military officers of northern origin were killed. The one northern senior officer to survive, Lieutenant Colonel Yakubu Gowon, did so only through luck. None of the seven senior officers (rank of lieutenant colonel or above) of eastern origin were killed.[21]

In the countercoup of July 1966, 27 Ibo officers were killed, along with

---

[21] Robin Luckham, *The Nigerian Military* (Cambridge: Cambridge University Press, 1971), p. 43.

12 others from the Western, Mid-Western, and Eastern Regions. No northern officers were killed.[22] The fact that there were factors other than ethnicity involved in each coup was overshadowed by the above figures. The violent nature of each event sharpened divisions in Nigeria as a whole, began the fragmentation of the army, and made compromise much more difficult. Each side began to fear that, if out of power, their political position and physical safety would be endangered.

As ethnic violence spread to the population as a whole, the military proved unable to rally all groups under its national banner. Ibos living in the Northern Region began to fear for their personal safety. In Kano, the largest city in the old Northern Region, hundreds of Ibos were massacred on two separate occasions. Ibos began to return to the Eastern Region. Northerners living in the Eastern Region also were mistreated and began leaving the East to return to the North. In May 1967 the final attempts to mediate the conflict failed; and the Eastern Region, led by its military commander, Colonel Odemegwu Ojukwu, attempted to secede from the federation. Biafra, as the former region called itself, fought Nigeria from May 1967 until its defeat and surrender in January 1970.

Each side during the civil war manipulated political symbols in an attempt to gain both domestic and foreign support. Biafrans characterized the federal government as a "modern Dracula" and accused General Gowon of wishing to become a dictator.[23] The federal government's slogan during the war was "To keep Nigeria one is a task that must be done."[24] General Ojukwu was pictured as a pied piper leading unknowing Easterners to destruction. General Gowon (who assumed power following the July 1966 coup) became the symbol of Nigerian unity and victory. Even his name took on political significance: G-O-W-O-N—Go On With One Nigeria.

The war cost Nigeria and all Nigerians dearly. Biafrans accused the federal government of waging a war of "genocide" against the Ibo peoples. News accounts of starving children gained for Biafra much international sympathy and some official recognition. On the other hand, the federal government accused General Ojukuwu of carrying on a war that Biafra could never win and of forcing many non-Ibo Easterners to fight an Ibo war. Whatever the merits of either side, the civil war ripped the nation apart. Many outside commentators predicted that retribution against the defeated would follow the victory of the federal government; General Gowon, however, initiated a policy of reconciliation. The goal was to create a climate ensuring that another tragic civil war could not occur and

---

[22] Ibid., p. 76.

[23] A. H. M Kirk-Greene, *Crisis and Conflict in Nigeria, A Documentary Sourcebook*, Vol. 1, January 1966–July 1967 (London: Oxford University Press, 1971), pp. 101–102.

[24] Ibid., p. 100.

A Nigerian federal government poster picturing General Gowon and expressing the sentiments of the federal government during the civil war (1967–1970). Courtesy, Federal Ministry of Information.

TO KEEP NIGERIA ONE IS A TASK THAT MUST BE DONE

to reintegrate the Ibos back into Nigerian society. This involved not only political reintegration but also social and economic advancement. General Ojukwu went into exile in the African nation of the Ivory Coast, but many other officers in the Biafran army were retired without benefits, retired with benefits, or, in a few cases, reintegrated into the Nigerian army. Others, mainly at the most senior levels, were tried for their part in the civil war. Not surprisingly, bitter memories exist on both sides long after the fighting has stopped.

Potential Sources of National Unity

The postwar Gowon, Mohammed, and Obasanjo administrations have introduced a number of policies designed to prevent another civil war and to begin the process of creating a sense of national unity. National values, however, are not developed quickly or without some rationale. It is difficult to persuade individuals and groups who have strong traditional loyalties and ties simply to give them up; reasons must be given, and new policies instituted. In the Nigerian case, the central government has approached the problems associated with building national unity on several fronts.

One of the most important steps taken by government leaders has been the creation of new states. The number of states has grown from 4 regions before 1966 to 12 states in 1967 to 19 states in 1976. In 1976 the government also decided to move the nation's capital from Lagos (in the extreme southwest of Nigeria) to a more central location (near Abuja). The decisions to create more states were taken in part to lessen the possibility of one state or group of states from ever joining together to attempt secession.

At the same time that new states were being created, the central government was also assuming many of the powers once exercised by states. The collection and distribution of Nigeria's oil revenues, for example, is now the responsibility of the national government. State governments must depend on the central government for much of their operating revenue. It is hoped that greater economic interdependence among the various states and the national government will foster integration. In order for national institutions to become effective symbols, however, they must be able to perform efficiently. Citizens come to expect and demand that the central government provide them with goods and services. If the government does not, or cannot, meet these needs, public support decreases.

The central government is also taking a more active role in sponsoring and controlling education. At the university level the national government now controls Nigeria's major universities. By so doing, the government hopes to lessen the possibility that centers of learning will foster regional or sectional political discord. The goal is to create national rather than regional universities. Students from one area of the nation are encouraged to attend universities outside their areas, and it is not uncommon for the chancellor of a university in one area to be from another area. The chancellor of a major university in one of the eastern states, for example, is often a prominent citizen from one of the northern states. The government also has created a national youth corps that requires college graduates to devote two years to national service.

Universal primary education, introduced as a policy in 1975, seeks to ensure that all Nigerian children of primary school age receive an education. This will not only help to solve Nigeria's skilled manpower shortage but will also help children to develop a national rather than a parochial perspective. Emphasis is placed on national values and symbols. A further benefit of this scheme may be that more and more Nigerians will speak English. Although English is not an indigenous language, the growing number of Nigerians who speak and understand it may help to build common experiences and expectations.

Nigerian military leaders have made a firm commitment to return to civilian rule. Much of the constitutional debate (1976–1979) on Nigeria's new civilian government focused on the need to maintain national unity.

The questions are important ones: Should there be a strong executive president independent of the legislative branch, or should Nigeria return to another parliamentary system? What relationship should exist between the 19 states and the federal government? How can political parties and politicians be prevented from appealing to narrow sectional or ethnic loyalties? Finding the answers to these questions is made more difficult because of the lack of national symbols and values. The symbols that separated groups must be replaced by those that join groups. One Nigerian began a book entitled *How to Be a Nigerian* with a short verse from the national anthem:

> *Though tribe and tongue may differ*
> *In brotherhood we stand,*
> *Nigerians all.*

In discussing what a Nigerian was, the same author stated: "The search for the Nigerian is in progress. Optimists say that before this century is out, the experiment begun in the 19th century will produce such a people."[25]

▪ EGYPT ▪

Gamal Abdul Nasser was the most important political figure in Egypt and the Arab world from 1954 until his death in 1970. His political values and actions influenced the development of the new Egyptian political system. Like President De Gaulle, President Nasser was able to create a political system tailored to his vision of politics and government. For many, Nasser became not only a leader and spokesman for Egypt, but also a living symbol of the modern Arab renaissance. No political leader matched his popularity or appeal. His influence was so great that even after his death people still vie to represent him and to call themselves "Nasserists."

At the same time that he represented and expressed popular political ideas in Egypt and the Arab world, he also created new political institutions in Egypt. It was not enough to end the old order, ban political parties like the Wafd, and abolish the monarchy. The young Free Officers needed to create political institutions capable of building political support and carrying out their new ideas. Symbolic institutions played an important part in this process.

The Development of Charismatic Authority

As we have seen, the small group of middle-ranking officers who seized power in 1952 had little idea of the type of society or government they

---

[25] Peter Enahoro, *How to Be a Nigerian* (Lagos, Nigeria: The Daily Times of Nigeria Limited, 1966), p. 1.

wanted. They opposed palace and Wafd corruption and the British presence in Egypt, but they had little practical experience in government. They were soldiers, not politicians.

From 1952 until 1954 two power struggles occurred. The first was between the Free Officers and potential rival sources of power and authority. The Muslim Brotherhood, the Communist party of Egypt, old-line Wafd politicians, and those loyal to the palace posed possible threats. Although many in the former elite fell from grace, lost their positions, were imprisoned, or sent into exile, the new leaders did not govern unchallenged. The most serious threat to the young regime came from the Muslim Brotherhood; but in 1954, following an attempted assassination of Nasser, their major leaders were imprisoned. By 1954 most serious domestic threats had been removed or were at least manageable.

A second power struggle occurred within the revolutionary movement itself. The young officers (see Chapter 6), to increase their popular appeal and authority, enlisted the support of General Muhammad Neguib. Neguib was a respected, popular, fatherlike figure who gave the movement the appearance of stability and direction. In short, he served as a symbol of stability during a time of uncertainty and instability. Not content, however, with being merely a figurehead, Neguib tried to become a real power rather than simply a symbolic one. By 1954 Nasser had successfully outmaneuvered Neguib and was firmly in control. General Neguib was retired from politics.

Although he held power, Nasser lacked widespread popular support and visibility in this early period. (Neguib had been the far better known.) But all this changed in the middle and late 1950s. The new president negotiated an arms deal with Czechoslovakia and the Soviet Union in 1955, arguing forcibly that Arab nations should not be taken for granted as allies of the Western powers (specifically the United Kingdom and the United States). In 1956, in a swiftly moving scenario, Nasser turned to the Soviet Union for aid to build the Aswan Dam, nationalized the Suez Canal, and found himself at war with Israel, Britain, and France. While Nasser and Egypt did not win the war, the international pressure that forced the Israeli, British, and French forces to withdraw from Egypt dramatically increased Nasser's prestige in the Arab world and Egypt.

Nasser quickly became a symbol of the changing role and status of Egypt and the Arab world—representing independence rather than dependence. The colonial period officially ended with the withdrawing of troops from Egypt and with Egyptian control of the canal. Nasser expressed the desire of Arabs for pan-Arab unity and for increasingly close relations between Egypt and other Arab states.

Nasser's political power in this early period was based in part on his growing charismatic appeal and on his ability to manipulate the symbols of his early victories. Coupled with the increasing coercive power, the authority of the new regime increased. Popular support and popularity were not enough, however, to carry out the revolution. With power assured, Nasser now turned his attention to developing political structures to carry out the revolution and institutionalize his charisma. The new government made several experiments in political institution-building to fill the vacuum created after the old order collapsed. The National Liberation Rally—designed to represent the new powers, to provide an avenue for participation, and to symbolize the revolution—was characterized by poor organization and vague goals. The National Union, developed in 1958 to symbolize the unity between Syria and Egypt, collapsed when the union itself ended in 1961.

The need to develop symbolic institutions became all the more important as the economic, political, and social goals of the regime became clearer. The 1961 nationalization of many industries and firms and the issuance of the National Charter in 1962 required the development of institutions to represent both the aims of the revolutionary leaders and the new political participants. The Arab Socialist Union and the People's Assembly (previously known as the National Assembly) were created to perform many of the symbolic functions.

The Arab Socialist Union and the National Assembly as Symbolic Institutions

The Arab Socialist Union (ASU) is the successor organization to the National Liberation Rally and the National Union (see Chapter 5). Formed in 1962, the ASU was the only legal political party in Egypt until President Sadat's liberalization in 1976–1977. The ASU was designed to allow for political participation by all Egyptians (especially those previously not allowed to participate), to represent the various interests and interest groups in Egypt, and to mobilize and educate the population. In short, it was made to build support for the political leaders and their goals.

The People's (or National) Assembly is the legislative branch of Egyptian government and provides support for the decisions of political leaders. Its 350 elected members serve five-year terms; by law, half of the membership must be either farmers or workers. In addition, the president has the power to appoint 10 members.

The constitution grants the People's Assembly several powers; these powers, however, do not severely limit the strong powers of the executive president described in Chapter 7. The Assembly must approve the general policy of the government, as well as the budget. Also, by a two-thirds vote, it can give the president the power to rule by decree during periods of emergency.

In addition, the Assembly can vote no confidence in the government's ministers, deputy prime ministers, and the prime minister himself. A minister must resign following a vote of no confidence (provided three days' notice is given before the vote). The prime minister's position is more secure, but the People's Assembly can question his actions and policies. In case of serious disagreement or dispute, it can limit the authority of the prime minister and appeal directly to the president. If the president and the Assembly disagree over the conduct of the prime minister, a referendum is held. If the president and prime minister are upheld, the Assembly is dissolved and new elections called; but if the Assembly position is upheld, the president must abide by the decision. The president retains the power to dissolve the assembly and call for new elections within 60 days.

Although its decision-making role is restricted, the Assembly does perform several important functions. Like the ASU, it allows diverse groups to have representation in the central government. Deputies have the right, and vocally use it, to question government ministers. Question hour in the Assembly provides a platform for deputies to air their thoughts and opinions to the government. The People's Assembly also serves as a national forum for the president and government. Important policy addresses and changes often are first announced in its chamber; for example, many of President Sadat's initiatives toward Irsael in 1976–1977 were first voiced publicly there.

Deputies express concern over a wide range of issues. Among the more common issues are higher education, foreign policy, the budget, housing, and problems concerning the cost of living and wages.[26] Opinions expressed during debate are by no means unanimously supportive of the government, although the degree of dissent allowed varies. The executive and legislative branches of government are not co-equal in Egypt, but the legislature generally serves an important role as a support-building institution for the government. In addition, it serves as a valuable forum for debating and discussing government policy.

President Sadat—The Difficulty of Following a Symbol

President Sadat, early in his term, faced the twin tasks of exerting his authority over the political system and affirming his right to hold office. It was no easy job following the charismatic Nasser. The new president needed, at the same time, to de-emphasize Nasser and Nasser's rule, and to build his own credibility and stature. "De-Nasserfication" involved in part revealing to the public some of the less positive aspects of the Nasser period. For example, Nasser's imprisonment of political dissidents and prominent figures received wide publicity in Egypt. At the same time, the role of President Sadat was magnified. His political stock rapidly rose following the 1973 war when he became known as the "Hero of the Crossing." His popularity soared again after his 1976–1977 peace initiatives

---

[26] R. Hrair Dekmejian, *Egypt Under Nasir* (Albany: State University of New York Press, 1971), pp. 156–166.

President Nasser's funeral in 1970 brought millions of mourning Egyptians into the streets. Bruno Barbey, Magnum Photos, Inc.

toward Israel were carried out. His political stock declines when the perpetual economic crises (rising prices coupled with shortages) worsen or when the difficult negotiations with Israel appear to stall.

Political symbols and symbolic institutions are important in Egyptian politics. The 1952 revolution enjoyed widespread initial support, for Egyptians were disillusioned with the old regime and hoped for better. The job of the new leaders was to transform this early popularity into more stable political support. This was accomplished partly by capitalizing on President Nasser's growing charismatic appeal and partly by building political institutions to involve Egyptians in politics. The ASU and the People's Assembly played, and continue to play, important roles in popularizing the government's platforms and policies. Widespread support allowed Egyptian leaders to begin the economic and social transformation outlined in public statements.

The close relationships among charisma, institutions, and support were clearest following the defeat of Egypt and the Arab nations by Israel in 1967. President Nasser resigned his office, but almost immediately the ASU began mobilizing popular support for his return. The party and other political institutions were able to tap the already strong and deep-seated sentiment favoring the president's return. Few political leaders have been recalled to office following such a crushing defeat.

Succeeding such a strong leader presents President Sadat with some of his most difficult moments. He has sought to carve out his own policies (such as the economic "new opening" to the Western nations), to establish his own credentials as an Egyptian leader (through such means as his initiatives toward Israel), and to end the "cult of the personality" surrounding the late president. This requires establishing symbols of the Sadat presidency, just as Nasser established symbols of the Nasser presidency.

Egyptian leaders have been fairly effective in establishing support-building institutions. While the structure of the party and the People's Assembly may change, they continue to perform the valuable and important tasks of marshaling public support for the government, mobilizing popular public opinion, educating the citizenry, and providing a political forum. Without these supports, the economic and military problems facing Egypt might overwhelm whoever holds political office and power.

▪ TANZANIA ▪

Two main themes characterize most political discussions in Tanzania. Political leaders stress the need to create an independent nation based on the principles of African socialism. To realize these goals, national unity and purpose must be achieved. Most party and government pronounce-ments echo these themes and cite them to justify the authority exercised by national political leaders.

Symbolic and legislative institutions play an important role in the na-tion-building process in Tanzania, but long-standing traditions that tie people together are lacking. Unlike Britain, with its centuries of political heritage to call upon, Tanzania must build on a short but rich history. The creation of political symbols and institutions that perform both real and symbolic functions is a real need in the national integration process. One indication of Tanzania's success in creating these symbols of national unity in a fairly short time is the relative stability of its political system. A distinc-tive Tanzanian "perspective" on politics has begun to emerge.

National Symbols—Processes and Institutions

The German and British colonialists who first carved Tanganyika out of East Africa did not concern themselves with the problems that a new in-dependent nation might face. Little was done to unite the diverse peoples of the new territory; though different ethnic, language and religious groups found themselves under the same foreign authority, they had little else in common.

The earliest nationalist leaders after World War II had to convince the various groups in the colony that they should unite to achieve a common goal—independence. Subnational loyalty was a much more powerful force during this period than vague promises of independence and better lives to come. The problem was made all the more difficult in Tanganyika because the population was so widely scattered throughout the nation. Communication between groups was hampered.

The initial spark and later direction of the nationalist movement came from the small educated elite, who sought symbols and organizations that could transcend narrow ethnic, religious, or linguistic loyalties. By focusing on the common opponents—colonialism and racialism—the new politi-cians were able to bridge many of the gaps. Among the most important symbols during this period were the Swahili language and the nationalist movement itself. These symbols became even more powerful and effective as independence approached.

The emerging leadership developed early on a national organization to demand that its political aspirations be recognized. The small educated elite of the Tanganyikan African Association (see Chapters 2 and 5) trans-formed their interest group into the first Tanganyikan political party in 1954. The Tanganyikan African National Union (TANU) assumed responsi-bility for representing the majority of the African population and negoti-ating with the British colonial authorities. They rallied the African population to political action. TANU also became a symbolic organization

representing the growing sense of Tanganyikan nationalism. Not dominated by one tribal group, its leadership and its membership were drawn
from groups throughout the entire nation. The party platform argued that
all groups, despite differences, were united by their desire to achieve
independence from the colonial power.

Tanganyikan political leaders were fortunate that this desire could be
expressed in an African language, Swahili. Swahili performed two very
important roles in Tanganyikan political life during this period. First, it
served as a common language for groups that otherwise would not have
been able to communicate. Although most of the Western-educated political leadership spoke English, the great mass of Tanganyikans did not.
Swahili allowed the political leaders to address the increasingly politically
active population in an African language.

Second, Swahili, like TANU, became a symbol of the nation. A national
language policy emerged. Political leaders argued that, wherever possible,
Swahili be used rather than English, especially in education, literature, and
the mass media. Since the language was not associated with any one group
or section of the nation, no group need fear that its language and traditions were being sacrificed for those of another. Swahili became a symbol
of African and Tanganyikan culture; well before independence a national
culture, expressed through the medium of Swahili, began to emerge.

The language situation in Tanzania offers a contrast to that in Nigeria.
Both are linguistically heterogeneous nations in which English was the
dominant foreign/colonial language, but Nigeria has no African language
that can play the role Swahili plays in Tanzania. To have chosen Hausa,
Yoruba, or Ibo as the language of the nationalist movement in Nigeria
would have provoked resistance from groups whose language was not
chosen. In Nigeria this resulted in the nationalist movement being divided
rather than unified. The educated nationalist elite spoke English; to appeal
to the masses, however, they had to resort to indigenous African languages. Thus, political parties like the NCNC, Action Group, and NPC
were forced to narrow their audiences.

By the time of independence, the nationalist movement itself in Tanganyika had become a powerful political symbol. Representing a strong
united effort by most Tanganyikans, the long-term movement against
colonialism minimized group differences in pursuit of a common goal.
National leaders became more visible and politically important than traditional leaders. Political power and legitimacy shifted from the subnational level to the national.

The importance of these political symbols continued after independence. Pre-independence symbols were strengthened and re-inforced.
TANU is now the only legal political party, and is, by law, the supreme
political organization in the nation; government is responsible to TANU.
The use of Swahili has been expanded in government, social, and cultural

The Role and Duties of the Tanzanian Member of Parliament

Excerpted from President Nyerere's opening address to the National Assembly, October 1965

Keeping in contact with the people is, in fact, one of the most important functions of a Member of Parliament. If a Member really works hard in the constituency, he will be able to act as a bridge between people and Government for the transmission of ideas; both from the people and to the people. He will be able to explain to the people what Government is trying to achieve, and how they can use the machinery which has been set up to help in the development of the country and the betterment of the people's lives. He will also be able to explain to Government how new measures are working, and how best the people can be helped to help themselves, or what is worrying them.

The job of the Members of Parliament is, in fact, three-fold. They have to act as a bridge; they have jointly to deliberate on new legislation; and they have to keep the Government actively devoted to the people's interest by their intelligent criticism.

Source: Julius K. Nyerere, *Freedom and Socialism* (London: Oxford University Press, 1968), p. 93. Reprinted by permission of the author.

life. Fully 90 percent of the population probably now speak and understand Swahili. In addition, new symbols and institutions have been developed since independence. Two of the most important are TANU's ideology and the National Assembly. Each has proved to be a strong unifying factor in Tanzanian politics.

The ideology of ujamaa or "familyhood" (more fully described in Chapters 2 and 11) is a blend of different political and cultural values. President Nyerere argues that it is drawn from the general African traditions that existed before colonialism and from more modern values of humanistic socialism. As such, ujamaa does not represent the values of a specific African group but the values of African groups in general, regardless of other differences they might normally exhibit. Traditional values emphasizing group life, responsiblity to the community, and communal work are applied to the nation rather than the tribe. While some groups resist attempts to implement the various development plans, the ideology nonetheless remains a powerful unifying force.

The National Assembly acts as a national legislative body representing all groups within society. Although all MPs are members of TANU (by law), differences of opinion on policy and its implementation exist and are debated. One of the most important roles of the legislator is to act as a link between the government and his/her constituency. The member of Parliament is viewed as a representative of the national government. "The people, the National Assembly, the National Executive Committee (of TANU), and the government are all partners in the political field," according to the president.[27]

The President as a Political Symbol

The strongest national political symbol in Tanzania is the president himself. President Nyerere has held office continuously (with one brief exception in 1962, when he voluntarily stepped down from office) since Tanganyika became independent. His political impact spans the nationalist and independence periods.

It is difficult to overestimate the importance and the power of the president as a political symbol and as an effective political leader. He is known as *Baba Ya Taifa* (Father of the Nation), and *Mwalimu* (Teacher). Even though he sometimes tries to lessen the importance attached to him as an individual leader, he clearly is the dominant national political figure. In the 1965, 1970, and 1975 presidential elections, running unopposed, he received 92, 95, and 93 percent of the vote respectively. No political figure in Tanzania significantly challenges his popularity or commands as wide a following.

Nyerere was born into a large family in 1922. He is a member of a small ethnic group, the Zanaki; his father was a traditional chief. Nyerere was one of the few Tanganyikans of his day fortunate enough to receive an education. Following his primary and secondary education at government schools, he was the first Tanganyikan to travel abroad for higher education, attending Makerere College in Kampala, Uganda, then Edinburgh University in Scotland. On his return from Scotland he became a teacher and almost immediately involved himself in politics.

In 1954 he was instrumental in transforming the Tanganyikan African Association into TANU. He became the first president of the newly formed party and remains to this writing its only president. From 1954 until 1960 and self-government, he acted as the major spokesman for the Africans demanding independence and an end to racialism. From 1960 to 1962 he served as prime minister and from 1963 to the present as the president of Tanganyika, (after 1964, Tanzania).

Nyerere's importance as a political leader goes beyond his offices. African socialism, as practiced in Tanzania, is primarily the thought and philosophy of the president. His writings and speeches provide the most important and comprehensive source for understanding the goals of the political leadership in Tanzania. While he encourages discussion and debate within limits, his role is the central one. Ideas attributable mainly to the president are the need for the development of competition within

---

[27] Julius K. Nyerere, *Freedom and Socialism* (London: Oxford University Press, 1968), p. 94.

President Nyerere, the "father of his country" and "teacher," photographs Tanzanian schoolchildren. Camera Press, Ltd.

the party, the need to maintain a responsive party, and the stress on local development. He also speaks widely on international issues of concern to Tanzania and Africa—particularly the racial issues and conflicts in Zimbabwe and South Africa.

Tanzania can be judged successful in creating national symbols that emphasize national unity and are accepted by large numbers of Tanzanians. The need for national unity is reinforced constantly by referring to these symbols. TANU, Swahili, the independence movement, the national ideology, and the National Assembly all have become important symbols of politics as practiced in Tanzania. In addition, the National Assembly and TANU perform valuable, effective political functions. Uniting all of these factors is the towering presence of President Nyerere himself; his philosophy of government and his leadership help unite the nation and allow the national government to exercise authority.

Although Tanzania has been successful in creating a national culture, the process is not complete. Serious differences between groups remain. Not all Tanzanians accept the leadership or the general development of ideas expressed by the party. Perhaps the greatest threat to national unity, however, also is one of the greatest supports encouraging unity. President

Nyerere dominates and influences all aspects of the political system and political life. The question must be raised: Who will, or can, succeed him? Once he no longer holds office, the conflicts between those factors that unify the nation and those that divide it may become more intense. The problem is not unique to Tanzania; it faced France after De Gaulle and Egypt after Nasser. The successors to these men discovered that it is extremely difficult to transfer personal authority and legitimacy from one political leader to another.

▪ CHILE ▪

Before the military intervened in 1973, the strong executive power of the Chilean president was balanced by a stable legislative branch. Congress was one of the most effective, powerful, and independent legislatures in Latin America as it played the important legislative, symbolic and political roles given to it by the constitution.

Since 1973 almost all of the political institutions of the civilian period have been abolished, dismissed, or radically curtailed. The military leaders have relied on a strong coercive apparatus to ensure acquiescence from hostile elements of Chilean society. The middle class and other interest groups that supported the military intervention are favored by the new regime and provide the major bases of support for military government. New political symbols and symbolic institutions have replaced those of the civilian period.

The Chilean Congress—Symbolic and Instrumental Functions

The enactment of the 1925 constitution officially ended Chile's experiment with parliamentary government and passed executive authority to the president, who was given broad powers to initiate legislation and control the administration of government (see Chapter 7). The balance of power between the legislative and executive branches was weighted in favor of the president. Cabinet ministers no longer served in Congress, but they retained the right to participate in congressional debates and discussions (but not to vote). By declaring certain bills vital, the president could limit Congress's allotted time for considering his proposals and also manage the legislative agenda. Added to this were the presidential powers to change political and administrative boundaries and to create new agencies.

Not stripped completely of its powers, however, Congress played a vital role in the legislative process and in influencing the direction of Chilean politics from 1925 until 1973. Legislators generally were well qualified and the quality of legislative debate high. Modern presidents, such as Eduardo Frei and Salvadore Allende, first served terms in the Senate. Frei, after his presidential term ended, returned to the Senate, where he acted as a rallying point for congressional opposition to the Allende presidency.

The Chilean Congress was divided into two houses. The Senate, or upper house, was composed of 50 members elected from 10 province groupings. Senators served eight-year terms, and about half of the Senate was elected every four years. The Senate chose its own president and vice presidents to serve as presiding officers. The normal legislative session from May to September could be extended by special sessions called to deal with specific issues.

Senate sessions normally were divided into two parts. The "first hour" concerned legislative matters and focused on the consideration of government policies; the "second hour" allowed senators more freedom to bring up matters of concern to them and personal legislation.[28] Much of the work of the Senate was done in committee. Party affiliation and the strength of the various parties determined in large measure who received the important committee assignments. Parties also played an important part in organizing the Senate and directing debate.

Among the Senate's most important powers was its exclusive right to try impeachment cases. Charges against the president or his ministers were initiated in the Chamber of Deputies but tried in the Senate. A two-thirds vote was required for the impeachment of the president, a simple majority for that of cabinet ministers. During the Allende period this impeachment tool became an important political weapon in the hands of the Senate. For example, in 1972, Allende's minister of the interior, José Tohá, was impeached by the center/right opposition in the Senate. One goal of the opposition in the 1973 congressional election was to win enough seats to impeach President Allende; however, the strong showing (44 percent of the popular vote) of the Allende coalition prevented any legal impeachment attempt. The impeachment of cabinet ministers, however, remained a common practice during the 1972–1973 period.

The constitution also granted the Senate the power to approve or reject certain presidential appointments and to draft laws on amnesties and general pardons. In addition to these exclusive powers, the Senate, with the Chamber of Deputies, had to pass on presidential legislation.

The Chamber of Deputies, or lower house, had 150 members—one representative for approximately every 30,000 Chileans. Deputies served four-year terms, and all members were required to stand for election at the same time. Chamber sessions, like Senate sessions, were divided into two parts. The "second hour" in the lower house allowed many members

---

[28] Federico G. Gil, *The Political System of Chile* (Boston: Houghton Mifflin, 1966), p. 112.

to make speeches and to discuss questions of general public interest.[29] Committees and political parties played important roles in the Chamber of Deputies, especially in the election of presiding officers.

The Chamber of Deputies reserved the exclusive power to make charges against the president and other government officials, thus initiating the impeachment procedure that eventually was concluded in the Senate. They also had the sole power to introduce bills concerning the budget and taxation.

On certain occasions the two houses met in joint session, the most important of which was to select the president when no presidential candidate won a majority of the popular vote. The long-standing congressional tradition was to select the candidate who had received the most votes. Perhaps as an omen of trouble to come, much confusion and debate occurred when the joint session met in 1970. Finally, Salvadore Allende, after making certain concessions, was elected president and installed in office.

In many respects the Congress of Chile resembled the Congress of the United States. It had the power to supervise and monitor the actions of the executive, and each house had some exclusive powers. While the chief executive was the strongest actor in the Chilean civilian political system, Congress often was able to block the president's initiatives and to make his political life difficult—especially when the president and the majority of Congress were from different political parties.

The Allende Presidency—A Case Study of the Relationship Between the Congress and the Executive

The election of Salvadore Allende and his difficult relations with Congress exemplify the conflicts that could occur between the executive and legislative branches. When elected president in 1970, Allende was a minority president. Opposition center and right political parties controlled the Congress and generally were unsympathetic to Allende's platform. As the split between the leftist Allende and the centrist/rightist Congress intensified, the president's freedom of action drastically decreased. From 1970 until 1973 the performance of the political system faltered; confronted with a hostile Congress, the president found it increasingly difficult to enforce his political decisions.

From the perspective of center and right congressmen, Allende threatened the economic and political foundations of the nation. Some congressional leaders feared that the programs espoused by Allende would end in a dictatorship of the left and an economic system in which the middle and upper classes would suffer. Even more importantly, some feared the end of the constitutional, democratic political system. These

---

[29] Ibid.

fears led the Congress to attempt to limit the power of the president and to force from him guarantees that he would not fundamentally change the political system.

The congressional opposition to Allende employed various tactics. Shortly after the Allende election and before congressional ratification of his victory, some senators and deputies wanted to choose another candidate for president. Some favored Jorge Alessandri (an ex-president and the second-highest vote-getter in the election). Alessandri, once chosen, would resign, forcing a new election. Then Eduardo Frei, not allowed to succeed himself directly, would have been eligible to stand for election. This plan ran against the Chilean tradition of choosing the man with the most votes, even if less than a majority. But the proposal never received enough backing, and Allende was confirmed in office.

A second and more successful tactic centered on the complex relationship between the president and Congress. Congress and other political institutions not under the control of Allende and the Popular Unity coalition sought to frustrate and block the government's legislative initiatives. This required the active cooperation of the anti-Allende forces in Congress. As the crisis worsened in 1972 and 1973, the Christian Democrats and the National party members in Congress worked in closer and closer harmony to curb and limit Allende's ability to make and enforce policy. The Hamilton-Funtealba bill, for example, limited Allende's ability to nationalize much of Chile's industry. The constant threat of congressional impeachment of cabinet ministers further limited Allende's freedom of action.

Finally, a third option—direct military intervention—appealed to more and more legislators. Although there had been some suggestion of direct military intervention immediately after the 1970 election, it was not until 1972 and 1973 that this option became more likely. Certainly the most drastic of the three tactics, it resulted in the end not only of the Allende presidency but also of the civilian constitutional system itself.

All three options focused on the fragile relationships between the military and the president, and the president and Congress. By 1973 the battle lines were drawn; there was little room for compromise. The Congress and the military viewed themselves as spokesmen for the middle- and upper-class elements in society and as defenders of Chilean democracy. Their support came from groups that traditionally exercised political power in Chile; by 1972–1973 these groups were no longer willing to support the Allende government.[30]

The confrontation between the presidency and the Congress from 1970 to 1973 proved that, despite the 1925 constitution, Congress was still able

---

[30] For a discussion of the three alternatives open to the opposition, see Ian Roxborough, "Reversing the Revolution: The Chilean Opposition to Allende," in Philip O'Brien, ed., *Allende's Chile* (New York: Praeger, 1976), pp. 192–216.

to exercise strong political powers. The Congress that traditionally deferred to the president and the executive refused to do so in this case, becoming instead a symbol and rallying point for the strong opposition to Allende. The Congress came to represent, support, and in some ways mobilize those sections of the population most hostile to the government.

Support Building During the Military Period

On assuming power, the new military leaders relied heavily on coercion to ensure support. Dissident politicians and those who threatened the new regime were arrested, imprisoned, and in some cases executed. Others were forcibly exiled. The secret police concentrated their efforts among groups sympathetic to the Allende government: labor union leaders, liberal Catholic clergy, university faculty and students, and leaders and activists in the Popular Unity coalition (see Chapter 10).

Chile's institutional framework changed dramatically. Traditional checks and balances operating in Chilean politics no longer work. Congress, a traditional support-building institution and check on the power of the chief executive, has been recessed permanently. The constitution has been suspended, and the unchecked power of the military junta increased.

All regimes, however powerful, need support, and the military regime in Chile is no exception. As their support comes largely from those groups and interests who felt most threatened by the Allende regime, the military leaders aim at restoring the confidence and influence of these groups. Many in business, in professional occupations and, in general, in the middle and upper classes supported the intervention as a temporary necessity. They are hoping that the military will restore political and economic order and return power to those who have traditionally been active in Chilean politics.

To date, no decisions on the return to civilian rule have been made. The support for the military is based in part on their ability to meet the expectations of their primary constituencies, and in part on the ability of the police and coercive institutions to control dissidents. The longer the military remains in power, the more necessary it will become for them to turn their attention to creating support-building institutions. Clearly, however, the military leaders are unwilling to return to the traditional support-building institutions that served Chile from 1925 to 1973.

CONCLUSION

This chapter suggests that political leaders not only must make and enforce decisions but must also justify them. Symbolic institutions are important in the process of legitimating authority. Without political legitimacy, political leaders increasingly are forced to rely on coercion to enforce their decisions.

Several patterns emerge from our study of eight nations. The United Kingdom stands almost alone as a nation possessing well-developed, long-standing symbolic institutions. The monarchy and the House of Lords evolved over centuries to the present point of performing largely symbolic functions. They relieve the prime minister of some of the more ceremonial tasks of politics and provide a stable setting for the effective political leaders to make and enforce their decisions.

A second group of nations have had more difficulty in developing symbolic institutions. They have experienced many different types of political systems and hence many different types of symbolic institutions. Unlike the evolutionary British system, the changes in the type of government often have been sharp and even revolutionary. In these nations symbolic institutions and political symbols may separate, rather than unite, the population. France, West Germany, the Soviet Union, Egypt, and recently Chile fall into this classification.

The inability of the French to agree on the type of political system that they want makes it difficult to develop symbolic, support-building institutions. For example, the change from the parliamentary-dominated Third and Fourth Republics to the executive-dominated Fifth Republic required a change in political symbols as well as changes in the institutional framework.

The sharp discontinuities in German politics provide another example of how difficult it is to develop nonpartisan symbolic institutions. After World War II the Germans faced the unenviable task of building support for a political system that they did not create. Although the political system has proved itself efficient and capable of high performance, West Germany has yet to develop political symbols that rival those of the United Kingdom.

Chile and Egypt have experienced radical changes in their political orders. From 1925 until 1973 Chile was a relatively stable constitutional system in which the executive exerted strong central authority, checked by Congress and other institutions. The polarization of the political system during the 1960s and early 1970s, however, placed too great a strain on the political leaders and participants. Many military leaders no longer were willing to accept the instrumental and symbolic institutions of the civilian regime. The danger presented by the Allende government (from their perspective) was greater than their attachment to constitutional rule. In short, the challenges to the system were greater than the ability of the support-building institutions to manage and mediate them.

In Egypt the Free Officers enjoyed widespread initial support after assuming power in 1952, for the old, corrupt regime was in public disrepute. The new leaders—and especially Gamal Abdul Nasser—needed, however, to institutionalize the popularity and support of both regime and leader.

Nasser effectively institutionalized his charisma, which in turn, added significantly to his political power.

More than any other nation in our study, the Soviet Union has created a purely symbolic institution to legitimize decisions made by the party and government leaderships. The Supreme Soviet ratifies decisions almost always by unanimous vote. Though purely symbolic, this institution is important. It allows for participation in the political system and provides the party leaders with justifications for their decisions.

Finally, a third pattern can be identified. In Nigeria and Tanzania the fragmented political systems hinder the development of institutions and symbols that transcend sharp group differences. Although Tanzania may be judged more successful than Nigeria in creating national symbols, serious problems face both nations. Tanzania is fortunate in having one language, Swahili, that most all Tanzanians can speak and support, and in having the historical tradition of a nationalist movement directed by TANU, a truly national political party. In addition, the personal popularity of, and respect accorded to, President Nyerere and his ideology reinforce the supremacy of national, over subnational, loyalties.

Nigeria, the most divided of the eight nations, provides an example of how difficult it is to develop unifying political symbols. Nigeria began its independence with so few national symbols that the nation's disintegration became a very real possibility. Subnational groups, who share little in common, sometimes feel that there is little to be gained by developing peaceful relations with other groups. Conflict, not cooperation, becomes the norm. Neither civilian nor military regimes have been able completely to resolve the dilemma of subnational versus national loyalties.

Political symbols and symbolic institutions are not really as trivial as they appear to be. They perform the important jobs of instilling loyalty in participants and providing political leaders with legitimacy and authority. Without this legitimacy leaders must enforce their decisions by using other means—often coercive means. When political participants no longer have a sense of belonging to the political system, a political crisis may be in the making. The crises and conflicts facing the nation, and ways in which they can be managed, are the subjects of Chapter 10.

CHAPTER 10
CONFLICT-MANAGING INSTITUTIONS

When people disagree, who decides who is right?

Conflict occurs in all political systems. Political disputes involve the allocation of economic benefits and rewards or the distribution of political power. Individuals and groups disagree, sometimes violently, over "who gets what, when, and how."[1] To assess conflict in the nation-state, we need to analyze the severity of the conflicts and the manner in which conflicts are managed.

The severity and political importance of political conflict varies from nation to nation. In many nations the areas of dispute between groups or political factions are relatively narrow. Although individuals, groups, and political parties differ on specific policies, they are united in their acceptance of the legitimacy and authority of the political system. An agreement on the rules of the political game binds together political participants.

In other nations the conflicts are much more severe, divisive, and potentially disruptive. Governments face groups or factions who refuse to accept the authority of the system or its leaders. Dissidents question the actors' decisions and policies and the manner in which they are made. Such conflicts have the potential for political violence.

---

[1] Harold Lasswell, *Politics: Who Gets What, When, How* (Cleveland and New York: Meridian Books, 1958).

Political powerholders have two ways of handling opposition and dissent. The first way is *conflict resolution*, which involves making and enforcing decisions between competing groups or positions. Political officials are responsible for making judgments between disputants based on the presented evidence. Conflict management focuses not on deciding in favor of one of the sides but on managing the conflict and keeping it within acceptable limits. Parties to a dispute may "agree to disagree" and to keep their conflicts within certain boundaries. The specific institutions that resolve and manage conflict are political parties, legislatures, and the judiciary.

Coercion, the second way to control conflict, is the means taken by the government (or groups within it) to eliminate opposition completely and to prevent the development of dissent. Physical coercion includes such tactics as preventive detention, forced exiling of political opponents, torture during detention, or execution of political prisoners. In some cases, even the threat of such tactics is enough to ensure compliance. Coercion, then, also has a psychological component, that of instilling fear in the population. Arbitrary arrests or constant surveillance can convince individuals and groups that opposition is useless. The regime seeks to make group dissent dangerous and difficult by creating a climate of fear and mistrust. Individuals begin to believe that there is no one they can trust; everyone becomes a potential spy or informer.

The institutions most responsible for coercion are the military and the police. In nations with a highly developed frequently used coercive apparatus, the police are divided between a regular police force, responsible for maintaining law and order in everyday life, and a state security force, charged with investigating and interrogating "political criminals."

Whether a government responds to conflicts by using coercion or whether it relies on conflict-managing institutions depends on several factors. Regimes with strong ideologies and those beset by severe domestic crises often feel compelled to use whatever means necessary to prevent opposition and open criticism. More well-established, stable political structures, not plagued by severe or sharp political divisions, may be able to channel and control political conflict through conflict-managing institutions. Governments also vary in the types and amounts of opposition allowed. For example, strikes, nonviolent demonstrations, or partisan political criticism and activity may be permissible in some systems but expressly forbidden in others. What is clear is that no system encourages or can long tolerate violent political opposition. Some systems, however, are obviously more effective than others in dealing with and preventing violent opposition to their authority.

Conflict Resolution Through Judicial Institutions

Institutional arrangements for resolving conflict exist in all nation-states. The performance of these institutions is a measure of the effectiveness in the political system. In the modern nation the most common institution for resolving conflict is the judiciary. Judges are expected to make decisions based on their interpretation of a systematic body of law, which derives from many different sources. Here the most common source is the statutory law made by the political decision-makers.

To evaluate the performance and effectiveness of the judicial structure, we must study several related factors. One of the most important is the degree to which judges and others in the judicial system are independent of outside political pressure. Although the principle of an independent judiciary, free from political interference, is embodied in most national constitutions, the actual independence of judiciaries varies considerably.

Measures of judicial independence include the method of appointing judges, their freedom of action once appointed, the way in which they may be removed from the bench, and the professional standards expected from them. For example, judges who are appointed by political leaders for political reasons—and who can be easily removed from the bench—may have less independence than those judges who must meet rigid professional standards and who cannot be removed except by following stringent, unchanging procedures. Judges in the first instance are wary of making decisions that offend the government, while those in the second feel relatively secure in their positions regardless of their decisions. The power of others outside the judiciary to overrule court decisions is another factor influencing judicial independence. If judicial decisions consistently are overturned or altered, the impact of the judiciary is lessened.

The scope of cases considered by the judiciary is a second indicator of their role in the political life of the nation. Though most judiciaries have the power to hear both civil and criminal cases, some cases may fall outside their sphere. Political parties or legislatures, for example, may be responsible for resolving partisan political conflicts, not the judiciary. Political leaders also may severely limit the power of the court to decide controversial and complex constitutional issues. Finally, in some nations special political courts are convened to try political crimes. It is not uncommon, for example, for military tribunals to try military men and others accused of political offenses.

The eight nations in our study have marked differences in their judicial structure. Several have highly institutionalized legal frameworks and well-established legal traditions. These judicial systems prove fairly successful in resolving a wide range of potentially disruptive conflicts. Judges, lawyers, and others in the systems have high professional standards; and, barring misbehavior or the inability to carry out their duties, their positions are secure. The judicial systems are characterized by the effectiveness of their structures, their accountability, and their responsiveness. Coercion is rarely needed. It must be pointed out, however, that even in these systems the government retains its coercive potential and, if the conflicts become severe enough, may even be forced to use it.

The independence and role of the judiciary are not so clear or precise in other nations. Judges are influenced more by political considerations than in the first pattern, since political actors expect judges to take positions supporting the leadership and government. If they do not, they face removal from the bench. Political motives dominate legal and judicial concerns.

Still a third pattern is found in those nations that rely primarily on coercion to maintain political control. In these nations the judiciary's role is severely circumscribed, and the power of the police or military greatly expanded. Military regimes, for example, shortly after taking power may seek to crush all active and potential dissent. In the short run, coercion may be much more effective and efficient than the judicial remedy.

To understand a political system, then, we must know how its leaders and citizens define dissent, what limits are placed on the right to dissent, and what means are used to resolve conflict. In those countries with highly institutionalized and effective means of resolving conflict, the emphasis in this chapter is on describing the judicial system and its performance. In nations beset by severe political, economic, and social crises, the emphasis is on the nature of the conflicts and on how political actors have attempted to solve their problems. As the problems facing political leaders and citizens change, the means of resolving conflict also change. One way of comparing nations is to study the manner in which leaders and participants respond to conflict. Another method is to study the conflicts themselves.

▪ THE UNITED KINGDOM ▪

The resolution of civil and political conflict in the United Kingdom is the main task of the British judicial system.[2] The judicial system developed over a long period of time in response to the practical needs of rulers and the ruled. The system that resulted appears rather haphazard and disorganized to outsiders, but it is an effective instrument with substantial strengths and resources.

Development of the Legal System

The present court system was set out in the Judicature Acts of 1873–1875 and the Courts Act of 1971. Its essential shape was the product of centuries of development; some features can be traced to Anglo-Saxon and Norman times.

The court system and the legal principles supporting it are in a sense

---

[2] It should be noted that Scotland maintains a somewhat distinct legal system that is heavily influenced by Roman law traditions. Law and legal reasoning is distinct from the rest of the United Kingdom.

the product of a 700–800-year-old struggle between the king's courts and rival tribunals. In Norman times the king's court was only one of a number of courts with no special status or claim to primacy. Others were the surviving Anglo-Saxon courts, county courts, and courts of the hundred (a subdivision of the county). Feudal courts were run by any feudal overlords who cared to establish them. The right to establish a court and to pocket legal fees was in the nature of the right to private property—comparable to establishing a ferry or a toll road. Justice, or more properly the settlement of a dispute, was a service to be bought, and individuals could in some sense shop for the best service.[3]

The king's court gradually established itself as the best vehicle for solving disputes. Rivals were slowly eliminated as people came to prefer the king's justice. Traveling royal commissioners became itinerant judges who presided over cases of a serious criminal nature. Civil disputes, though, were heard only at Westminster, and parties to a case had to endure considerable inconvenience to enjoy the benefits of the king's justice. Then a compromise evolved whereby so-called justices of the assize courts traveled to the counties to hear civil cases. The facts of the cases were still considered at Westminster once they were collected.

During the reign of Henry II (1133–1189) the main features of the national legal system were systematized and perfected. Henry rationalized and clearly established the system of itinerant judges: all crime was a breach of the king's peace and therefore a wrong against the state. Henry also introduced reforms leading to the introduction of trial by jury. Finally, and most importantly, he began to perfect common law procedure.[4]

The Common Law System

The king's itinerant justices were charged with administering the law and with ruling on the basis of the "general immemorial custom of the realm." Divergent local customs were pulled together into a single national customary law. Gradually, judge-made law was developed by drawing on the customs, habits, and innate wisdom of the people. Custom and previous court decisions that represented the application of legal reasoning to specific cases became the core of the national legal system. The principle of stare decisis, or the "obligation to subsume new decisions under the principles of previous ones," became the master principle of the system.

The use of custom and precedent proved to be a powerful tool in gaining the consent and compliance of the citizenry; thus, the king's courts were able to supersede local rivals. Only the growing central authority of

---

[3] R. M. Jackson, *The Machinery of Justice in England* (Cambridge: Cambridge University Press, 1972), pp. 2–9.

[4] Ibid.

the state could standardize and enforce a body of laws that reflected the evolving national culture. The legitimacy of law and the legal profession was established by its connection with that culture.

The reliance on precedent also proved valuable in establishing the independence and power of the judiciary. Judges could resist the arbitrary actions of the monarch (and later the parliamentary-based executive) by relying on custom and previously decided cases. In this way judges enhanced their power and prestige by appearing to champion the people's rights against the arbitrary actions of the nation's political leaders.

From the beginning weaknesses in the common law system have been apparent. Reports of previous cases, initially used as evidence that a law or principle existed, now became a binding rule for subsequent cases. Judges had to go through a cumbersome, haphazard process of discovering and applying the appropriate precedent. Gradually, they came to rely on the commentaries of noted jurists who collected precedents on given subjects and for similar sets of facts. A more serious problem with common law was its conservative or backward-looking bias. New situations often were not covered by the established law. Since it is a principle of common law that one may lawfully do anything not expressly forbidden by law, considerable injustice has been lawfully done, particularly in times of social and political change. The legal system must find and apply laws appropriate to new circumstances—a slow and uncertain business at best.

The British system addressed this problem by establishing a set of rules called equity. When a subject felt that the existing law worked a special hardship or was unjust, an appeal could be made to the king for a ruling by his chief legal officer, the lord chancellor. These cases gradually developed a system of principles to protect individuals from the rigid and conservative nature of the system.[5]

Parliament has increased its role in creating statutes applicable to court cases. Parliamentary action has been greatest in areas not covered by common law precedents, particularly in new situations created by social and political change. By and large, Parliament intervenes reluctantly, preferring to rely on established common law.

The Modern Courts

The British court system was streamlined and reorganized by Parliament in 1971. The traditional distinction between civil and criminal courts that has existed since the Norman period was retained. Separate civil and criminal court hierarchies are joined only at the highest level—in the House of Lords.

The head of the legal system is the lord chancellor, who is a member

---

[5] Alex N. Dragnich and Jorgen Rasmussen, *Major European Governments* (Homewood, Ill.: The Dorsey Press, 1974), p. 146.

Members of Britain's highest court, the "Law Lords." Courtesy, Central Office of Information, London.

of the House of Lords and the cabinet. He and ten "lords of appeal in ordinary" (or, more popularly, law lords) act as the nation's highest court. The lord chancellor has no set term of office and is always removed with a change in government, while the law lords are professional judges who have been given life peerages to serve as the nation's leading jurists.

The House of Lords takes appeals from civil and criminal cases involving a point of law that they consider to be of general public importance. Theoretically, all members of the upper house may participate in these appeals cases, but a firm custom has been established that they should not. A lay lord who once tried to participate in an appeals proceeding was simply ignored. In practice, the law lords are a distinct entity from the larger house with regard to their legal duties.

Below the House of Lords are two appeals courts, the Court of Appeal for civil cases and the Court of Criminal Appeal. The next lower level of courts are the High Court of Justice (civil) and the crown courts (criminal). The lowest civil courts are the county courts for cases involving damages less than £5,000. The lowest criminal courts are magistrates' courts, courts of petty sessions, and juvenile courts.[6] (See Figure 10–1.)

---

6 Jackson, *The Machinery of Justice*, pp. 87, 153.

FIGURE 10–1 The British Court System

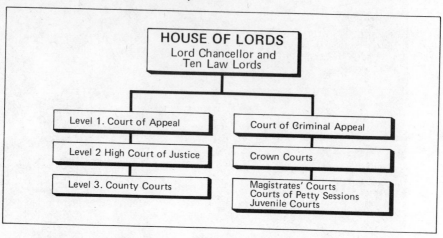

The court reorganization did much to simplify the system, although it kept a bewildering assortment of traditional court names. The lowest courts (level 3 in Figure 10–1) handle minor matters involving small civil judgments and less serious crimes. The next higher courts—the crown courts and the High Court of Justice—handle major original criminal and civil cases. Cases from these courts may be appealed to the two appeals courts. The House of Lords becomes involved only in a major principle of law that has important consequences for the public welfare.

The legal profession in Britain has been the preserve of a relatively small privileged elite. The British make a distinction between barristers (who try cases in court) and solicitors (who deal with clients and prepare cases but do not appear in court). The barristers—who until 1972 provided all of England's judges—are products of exclusive public school educations and the intense socialization that comes from one of the lawyers' guilds, the so-called Inns of Court. These associations of lawyers are important in introducing young lawyers to the traditional judicial norms, such as judicial independence. Since 1972 solicitors may also become judges, but this has not had a democratizing effect on the legal profession nor was such an effect necessarily intended. Most judges still have independent incomes and distinguished social connections. There are really no political appointments of judges in Britain except for the lord chancellor. He and the prime minister appoint judges on the basis of legal qualifications and on the recommendations of the leading professional associations.

Effectiveness and Accountability

The British legal system consists of a substantial body of law that adequately protects most Britons and an independent judiciary of high professional competence. The effectiveness of the legal system is jeopardized only by the peculiar weaknesses of the common law. New social situations and rapid social change are particularly difficult for the British court system.

The influx of nonwhite immigrants from the West Indies and Pakistan in the early 1960s created a situation that was difficult to resolve by the existing legal system. As there were insufficient precedents regarding cases of minority group discrimination, the courts could not act on many cases of obvious injustice. As a result, the House of Commons had to develop the appropriate statutes, thus politicizing the issue. Parliament's immediate reaction was to restrict immigration—hardly a solution designed to resolve the existing conflict.

The legal system has also failed in coping with conflict arising from feelings of Irish or Scottish nationalism. The conflict in Northern Ireland between Catholics identifying themselves as Irish and Protestants who consider themselves English has caused severe strains on British legal institutions. The government has been forced to enact emergency legislation that in effect suspends the rights of political suspects and permits detention or the interning of subjects without normal criminal process.[7]

British troops on duty in Belfast, Northern Ireland, in 1969. Alan Band Associates.

---

[7] Internment without trial for terrorists in Northern Ireland was ordered by the Northern Ireland government in August 1971. After the British suspended the government of Northern Ireland in 1972, the British government introduced a similar system of "detention" in November 1972. The British Special Branch was authorized to take similar actions throughout the United Kingdom under the Prevention of Terrorism Act of 1974.

TABLE 10–1   The Effectiveness of Internship Measured by Incidents of Political Violence

	January–July 1971 (7 months)	August 1971 INTERNSHIP BEGINS	August–December 1971 (5 months)
Army Deaths	10		38
Police Deaths	2		9
Civilian Deaths	15		99
Total Deaths	27		146
Shooting Incidents	319		1437
Bombings	685		1007

Source: Tom Hadden, "The Debacle of Ulster Internment," *New Society,* Vol. 43, February 6, 1975. Reprinted by permission of *New Society,* London, the weekly review of the social sciences.

The emergency laws were justified by the reasoning that the Irish Republican Army (IRA) is an underground terrorist organization dedicated to ending British rule in Northern Ireland. The suspension of rights and normal judicial process is an admission that the normal judicial remedies were ineffective. The emergency legislation, however, has been even more ineffective (see Table 10–1). It appears to have increased violence and has failed in controlling the real revolutionaries as opposed to marginal, easily identifiable suspects. The majority of those detained have been declared relatively harmless when released by authorities of the detention system. Finally, the presence of detention camps is incompatible with the legal principles that have evolved into the British common law and no doubt weakens the legal basis of the system.[8]

In sum, the British legal system has been effective, independent, and responsive to popular needs. Recent trends toward group conflict based on race and nationality have placed strains on the system and exposed its weaknesses. This sort of conflict, difficult for any system to resolve or control, is particularly difficult for Britain's common law system.

■ THE FEDERAL REPUBLIC OF GERMANY ■

No country has placed more hope and reliance on the rule of law than Germany has. Despite the reverence placed on law and legality, no other nation has known the extensive violation of individual and group rights

---

[8] Tom Hadden, "The Debacle of Ulster Internment," *New Society,* Vol. 43, February 6, 1975.

that has characterized recent German history. Law has often served as the inflexible tool of the status quo and of political order in Germany. The Allied and German founders of the Federal Republic (1949) attempted to preserve the traditional respect for law and at the same time encourage a new respect for individual and group rights.

Development of the System

The German legal tradition is of the Romano-Germanic variety. The Roman basis of German law derives from the legal codification of a sixth-century Roman emperor, Justinian, who supervised the first major compilations of laws. The codes of Justinian relied on rational principles but gave wide latitude to the trained legal experts who would apply them. The universities in Romanic and German countries kept the underlying principles alive and adapted them to modern circumstances. Modern codifiers of this tradition, notably the French Emperor Napoleon, could rely on a well-established set of principles as well as a pragmatic tradition that invited modification to changed circumstances.[9]

The Napoleonic code was updated by important modifications early in the twentieth century: the German empire code of 1900 and the Swiss code of 1907. Particularly helpful in elaborating the relatively new field of private law, code law was copied in many new nations and spread to a large number of disparate cultural settings. Unlike the English common law, the new code law was not the unique product of a particular culture or nationality; it could be easily "packaged" and exported. Despite the culture-free nature of Romano-Germanic law, the code law was the object of particular German pride. Advances in codified law were associated with German jurists, and this type of law seemed well attuned to German culture. Germans became attached to the notion of the German *Rechtstaat* (the German state based on the rule of law). Unfortunately, the rule of law was identified with the preservation of political order rather than with the protection of individual and group rights.

Hitler's regime exposed the major weaknesses of the Romano-Germanic legal tradition. Relying on a widespread respect for law to buttress his power, Hitler used German judges to ensure compliance with the orders of his totalitarian regime. Hitler kept on many judges of the pre-fascist era and gave guarantees of their independence. At the same time, he gave clear guidelines as to the ways in which German law must bend to changing circumstances. In particular, the "will of the Führer" became a positive source of law as did the "sound feelings of the people."[10] The pragmatic, flexible element of Romano-Germanic law enabled Hitler to shift the basis

---

[9] Henry W. Ehrmann, *Comparative Legal Cultures* (Englewood Cliffs, N.J.: Prentice-Hall, 1976), pp. 13–14.

[10] Ibid., p. 117.

of the legal system. The fixed tradition of the Rechtstaat ensured that the German legal system would support the authority of Hitler's regime. It also helped make the German public ready to comply with the orders and laws of the National Socialist order.

The founders of the German Federal Republic—the Allied powers and their German consultants—felt that a major modification must be made in the German legal system. They, like the public, rightly admired much of the German legal tradition, but they saw the need for additional protections in the realm of individual and group rights. To meet that end, they settled on a compromise: they retained the bulk of the Romano-Germanic apparatus for ordinary civil and criminal cases but also introduced a constitutional court (along the lines of the United States Supreme Court) to deal with constitutional issues, in particular those involving violation of the rights of German citizens.

The Court System

Ordinary courts in West Germany apply law in the traditional German manner. They recognize the absolute principles of justice associated with the term *Recht,* along with the more particular and relative principles of the law, *Gesetz.*[11] Judges have wide latitude in applying the established legal principles; they may, in particular, use discretion in application based on social values or cultural norms. The judges usually are unencumbered by juries. Panels of judges determine cases by secret ballot.

Ordinary courts handling both civil and criminal cases exist at the district and state levels, where virtually all cases originate. District courts, state courts, and superior state courts form the base of the system. At the top of the ordinary court system is the Federal Court of Justice, the chief appellate court for both civil and criminal cases. It can rule only on the uniform application of rules and procedures to each case; thus, it does not have an active, independent role.

As in most Romano-Germanic systems, the Federal Republic of Germany has an extensive administrative court system charged with protecting individuals from arbitrary actions by officials of the state. The administrative court system is headed at the federal level by the Federal Administrative Court. The decisions in administrative courts also turn on whether rules and procedures are properly and uniformly applied. Government agencies may appeal cases to the Federal Administrative Court to establish the propriety of their actions.

The major innovation in the German court system since World War II is the constitutional courts—both state and federal—charged especially with the protection of individual rights, the maintenance of the proper

---

[11] Dragnich and Rasmussen, *Major European Governments,* pp. 350–351.

The Constitutional Court of the Federal Republic of Germany. Courtesy, German Information Center.

balance of institutional powers, and the settlement of political disputes. The Federal Constitutional Court consists of 16 judges in two chambers. The two houses of Parliament alternate in naming members to the court, making their selections from a comprehensive list compiled by the Ministry of Justice. Justices serve a 12-year term. They are charged with enforcing the first 20 articles of the Basic Law. The first articles set out in elaborate detail the rights of German citizens. The eighteenth article provides that "whoever abuses freedom of expression of opinion, in particular freedom of the press, freedom of teaching, freedom of assembly, freedom of association, the secrecy of mail, posts and communications, the right of property, or the right of asylum, in order to attack the free democratic basic order, forfeits these basic rights."

The Constitutional Court is aided in its task by having a broad jurisdiction. It may consider actual cases involving constitutional issues, as does the United States Supreme Court, or it may rule on a constitutional question when there is no actual case before it. Often the state or federal governments use this procedure to get a ruling on a proposed or contemplated law. Finally, the court may consider a constitutional complaint; any person or group may challenge a particular law if they feel that it infringes on their rights. This procedure may be used without costs and lawyers. The last two types of jurisdiction, (rulings on constitutional questions and constitutional complaints) do not exist for the United States Supreme Court and represent "improvements" on the model that the Germans emulated.

The Legal Profession

Lawyers, judges, and jurists have always been highly respected in Germany. Modern West Germany has retained an elite and highly qualified set of legal practitioners, graduates from the law faculties of leading universities. These law faculties have been described as the "functional equivalent of British public schools."[12] The members of the legal profession go to school with other members of the German elite who desire a prestigious legal education. Many of their law faculty classmates become important figures in business and politics.

German judges still tend to be the sons and daughters of judges, lawyers, and civil servants; they are a self-conscious elite. Although the judicial and legal corps is inbred and restricted in background, it is also highly independent and professional. Its self-image is very close to that of the highly respected German civil service.

Accountability and Performance

The German judicial system has been effective in reducing political conflict in West Germany; in particular, the decisions of the Constitutional Court have been respected and obeyed. This court has stayed close to the spirit of the Basic Law and its concern for individual political rights; it has never avoided controversial political issues. In the 1950s the Constitutional Court used its authority to outlaw two political parties on the grounds that they were fundamentally opposed to the democratic order. In October 1952 it declared the Socialist Reich's party (*Sozialistische Reichspartei,* SRP) to be illegal. This right-wing party was judged to be undemocratic in its political principles and internal organization. In August 1956 the court ruled the Communist party to be illegal according to the same criteria. In so doing, the court took controversial actions: the rights of some Germans to political participation were withdrawn because they advocated philosophies considered incompatible with the rights of all Germans.

The Constitutional Court, by using all its powers, has promoted the rights of individuals, clarified constitutional principles, and decided controversies among governmental bodies. Together with the ordinary civil and criminal court hierarchies, the Constitutional Court has been professional

---

[12] Ehrmann, *Comparative Legal Cultures,* p. 68.

and competent in resolving conflict. Even its most controversial judgments, such as those regarding political parties and participation, have
been understood and accepted by the general public.

▪ FRANCE ▪

France has developed a complex system of civil, criminal, and specialized
courts to deal with social and political conflict. The judicial system,
directed and staffed by a highly trained, highly competent elite, has effectively handled some sorts of political conflict, notably those having to do
with governmental maladministration. It has been less successful in protecting individual and group rights and in settling constitutional disputes.
Problems of human rights and constitutional law stem from the nature of
the system and the French conception of law. Since the French view law
as a legitimate power resource of the government and of the dominant
social and economic classes, the protection of individual rights is difficult.
The problems in constitutional law stem from the nature of the French legal
system, which is of the Romano-Germanic code law variety.

Development of the Legal System

The French legal system is based on extensive legal codes. Emperor
Napoleon Bonaparte directed a massive systemization of the French legal
code that still forms the basis of French law. Revisions of the so-called
Napoleonic code have been made periodically, most recently early in the
Fifth Republic (1959). A code law system permits a judge to directly rely
on legal statutes for every case instead of having to search for the law in
previous cases. The common law principle of stare decisis is not accepted.

The fact that French law is *administrative law* is an extremely important
element in the French legal system, influencing all the legal specialties and
the legal profession generally. Judges are trained and treated as civil
servants or administrators rather than as lawyers.

The great strength of French code law has been its uniformity. The law
is applied similarly in a wide variety of cases, with little leeway for judicial
interpretation. Uniform application means that all French citizens are
treated relatively equally at the formal level. It also means that disputes
and criminal cases face a less ambiguous process than in, for example, the
Anglo-Saxon countries.

The weaknesses of the code system are its rigidity and its tendency to
become outdated. Law in the Romano-Germanic countries is resistant to
social, economic, and political change. Jurists and judges do not feel free
to make adjustments to changed circumstances or to make adjustments

based on the peculiar features of particular cases. Justice sometimes is not well served by the mechanical application of code law.

The Courts

Courts in France are organized into civil and criminal hierarchies. The basic units of the civil hierarchy are the local courts of first instance (*tribunaux d'instance*). These are organized in 455 districts (*arrondissements*), as are their criminal court counterparts—the local police courts (*tribunaux de police*). Above these are the major courts of first instance (which handle more important civil cases and some appeals) and the higher police courts (for the criminal courts). These are organized in each of 172 departments. There are 27 courts of appeal handling appeals from the lower civil and criminal courts.

The highest court in the judicial hierarchy is the Court of Cassation, which is subdivided into the criminal chamber, the civil chamber, and the chamber of requests. Each chamber consists of 15 judges and the president of the chamber. Criminal appeals go directly to the criminal chamber, while civil cases have to go through the court of requests before they can be considered by the civil chamber. The chamber of requests is charged with screening civil cases in order to forward only those cases with strong grounds for reversal. Any case successfully appealed will be sent back to the appropriate lower court for retrial.[13]

There are specialized courts—some dating from before the French Revolution—in addition to the more familiar civil and criminal courts just described. These include rent tribunals, labor courts, social security courts, and commercial courts. They have been recently (1970) integrated with the ordinary court system at the appeal level. Cases from the specialized courts may be appealed to the 27 courts of appeal that also handle civil and criminal cases.

The administrative court system deserves special attention, because the French may use administrative courts to contest the legality of bureaucratic regulations or actions. The top of the administrative court system is the Council of State, part of the French national civil service and, in that sense, not independent or "judicial." It handles such specifically executive or civil service issues as advising the government on the language of bills and on the legality of regulations. More importantly, over half of the 186 councillors and civil servants who make up the council are engaged in the judicial section, which rules on petitions for redress of administrative grievances. The Council of State, nominally headed by the minister of justice, is actually directed by the vice president of the council, chosen

---

[13] William Safran, *The French Polity* (New York: David McKay, 1977), p. 236.

from among the other councillors. The members of the council are appointed by the cabinet and are subject to removal by that body.

Disputes of a constitutional nature are handled by a Constitutional Council that is separate from the major judicial hierarchies. The Constitutional Council is made up of nine officials appointed for nine-year terms. Three members are selected by the president of the Republic, three by the president of the National Assembly, and three by the president of the Senate. Former presidents of the Republic are also members.

The Constitutional Council was established at the beginning of the Fifth Republic to determine whether laws passed by Parliament are within the legislative competence of Parliament as spelled out in the Fifth Republic constitution. That document limited the power of Parliament in a number of ways, one of which was to spell out limited areas in which Parliament could legislate. It gave a wide competence to the executive to issue decrees in areas outside the legislative competence. If the Constitutional Council rules that Parliament acted improperly in passing a law outside its defined sphere, the government is allowed to modify the law by decree.

The Constitutional Council may also rule on the constitutionality of a law during a 15-day period between passage and promulgation, but only if a ruling is requested by the prime minister, the president of the Republic, or the president of either house of Parliament. The ruling is made strictly in an abstract or theoretical way and does not deal with specific cases regarding the actual application of the law.

The Legal Profession

The highly specialized legal profession includes judges and at least six kinds of legal professionals engaged in what Americans would consider the work of a lawyer. There are people trained to plead in trial courts (*avocats*), people who prepare legal briefs (*avoués*), people who appear before commercial tribunals (*agrées*), specialists in wills and contracts (*notaires*), specialists in tax problems (*fiduciaires*), and persons who give general legal advice (*conseillers juridiques*).

Judges are distinguished from other members of the legal profession by the nature of their professional training. After having completed a course of study at a faculty of law, prospective judges must enter the National Center of Judicial Studies (*Centre National d'Etudes Judiciares, CNEJ*). Modeled on the National School of Administration (ENA), this school emphasizes administrative or civil service traditions. On completion of this three-year program, judges are considered higher civil servants and enjoy the status and social connections connoted by that label in France.

Other members of the legal profession enjoy considerable prestige with their law degrees. The established law faculties in France are so highly regarded that many of the political and administrative elite collect legal degrees with no intention of working with the legal profession. Legal professionals benefit from these connections.

Effectiveness and Accountability

The French legal system has two marked deficiencies in resolving political and social conflict. First, the French system has been weak in protecting individual and group rights when conflict and potential violence appear to threaten the government. Second, the French Fifth Republic judicial system has not demonstrated its ability to settle disputes between the institutions of government, that is, conflict over constitutional issues.

The difficulty in protecting individuals is related to the nature of French criminal procedure. France has an "inquisitional" trial procedure, as opposed to the "adversary" system of Anglo-Saxon countries. The judge in the French system takes an active part in all aspects of the case as he interrogates the accused, all the witnesses, and the lawyers in order to arrive at the "truth" of the case. Most lower courts consist of a panel of judges with no jury. Appeals courts may consist of panels of nine jurists and three judges who decide cases by a two-thirds vote.

The rights of the accused are not so carefully protected as they are in adversary systems. Normally, the accused spends a long time in pretrial detention while a case is developed, for there is no writ of habeas corpus to force the authorities to state their charges and begin the judicial process promptly. There is a constitutional principle (Article 66) that "no person shall be detained arbitrarily," but this has not proven to be a practical limit on the actions of the authorities.

Violations of individuals' rights seem to occur disproportionately against working-class persons. The way that the judicial system operates seems to aggravate rather than resolve class-based conflict. Judges treat defendants quite differently according to their class. Middle-class defendants are uniformly addressed as *monsieur,* while working-class prisoners are addressed curtly by their last name. Celebrated miscarriages of justice are cited by leftists as a sign of the class basis of French law.

Important political rights such as freedom of the press and freedom of speech have not been adequately guaranteed in France. Political opposition groups have been met with severe governmental sanctions in sensitive periods, such as the 1960–1962 Algerian crisis period. In this period suspected Algerian plotters were denied their normal rights and were tried by military tribunal. Critical newspapers were shut down as well. In 1963 a state security court was created for trials of subversives; this extraordinary court has since handled over 200 cases. Moreover, governments of the Fifth Republic have passed laws to give them special powers during periods of political unrest.

Governmental leaders often use the government-owned radio and television systems for political purposes. Until recently, all broadcasting was centralized and directly subservient to the government. President De Gaulle used the system to great effect in campaign periods. All the opposition parties had to divide up an opposition time share, based on the Gaullist party share. News reporting was biased under De Gaulle, and television news lost much credibility in its reporting of the riots of May 1968. This coverage of the "events of May" led to a parliamentary act in 1972 that decentralizd the broadcast system and created a watch-dog advisory board including consumers and press delegates.

Though constitutional issues are settled by the Constitutional Council, only the president of the Republic, the premier, and the presidents of the two houses of Parliament can appeal to that body for a ruling. This law has eliminated access by opposition groups. It also allowed Charles de Gaulle to violate his own constitution, as he did in insisting on the 1962 referendum on the direct election of the president without the constitutional preliminaries. The Constitutional Council was designed to support the president and the cabinet in disputes with Parliament—and, by and large, that is what it has done.[14]

France clearly represents a case where legal traditions and the structure of the legal profession have supported the political authorities against opposition groups. This is not surprising in a political system that has never developed fully legitimate institutions. Political opposition groups in France often are desirous of overthrowing the government and the regime as well. Unfortunately, in this environment, the governmental authorities sometimes feel obliged to act harshly against more legitimate opposition groups.

▪ THE SOVIET UNION ▪

To control political conflict and opposition, the Soviet authorities rely to a great extent on coercion by security police. This emphasis on coercion reflects the inherited legal tradition, principles of Marxism-Leninism, and the revolutionary origins of the system. In particular, reliance on force is a natural corollary to the still necessary "dictatorship of the proletariat."

At the same time, there is a tradition of "socialist legality" that imposes uniform principles on all participants in the system. Clear, unambiguous guidelines spell out what are considered unacceptable actions in the economic, social, and political realm. These rules reflect the necessity for public order and for stable, predictable (that is, institutionalized) behavior.

For much of its 60-year existence, the Soviet Union has been a "dual state—a regime of dictatorial arbitrariness coexisting with a regime of law

---

[14] Ibid., p. 238.

and order."[15] The balance between the two traditions has altered over the years. During Stalin's regime dictatorial arbitrariness dominated, while Khrushchev emphasized the "reintroduction of socialist legality" in his anti-Stalinist campaign. Both traditions have always existed side by side, and there have always been cases that the leadership felt required arbitrary police action.

The Development of the Legal System

After their experiences with the tsar's prisons and secret police, the revolutionary leaders of 1917 were strongly committed to a total break with the tsarist legal system. The tsar's system was of the Continental "prosecutorial" variety; as the case of France illustrates, this type of system can be harsh on political opposition groups. Suspects can be detained and interrogated at length, hearsay is admitted, and suspects have little protection against self-incrimination. Undoubtedly, the Bolsheviks sincerely felt that this system supported a class-based system of exploitation.

The rejection of previous standards of legality was also supported by the Marxist tenet that "bourgeois" law is a weapon of the capitalist class. The owners of property control their workers through the law, the court system, and the agents of law enforcement. From this point of view, crime originates with the despair of the exploited class. When workers are hungry and abused, crime is their only means of resistance or relief. Thus, crime is a result of class differences and will disappear when classes cease to exist.

The early Soviet period reflected the utopian ideal. At a single stroke, all the old courts and laws were voided by decree. "People's courts" were established, often made up of ordinary citizens. Detailed procedures and rules were scorned, and "simple justice" based on common sense was encouraged. The official party position was that all courts, judges, and prisons should be eliminated as soon as possible.

At the same time, the civil war that threatened the new state had to be put down with force. In this period internal opposition was very real and very dangerous. Six weeks after the revolution the "extraordinary commission," or *Cheka*, was set up to deal with the counterrevolutionary threat. The so-called Red Terror decree of 1918 explained that "it is necessary to protect the Soviet Republic from class enemies by means of isolating them in concentration camps; that all persons involved in White Guard organizations, conspiracies, and uprisings are subject to shooting; that it is necessary to publish the names of all those who have been shot, as well as the basis on which the measure was applied to them."[16] This was, in essence, the job of the Cheka. Both the court system and security

---

[15] Darrell P. Hammer, *U.S.S.R.: The Politics of Oligarchy* (Hinsdale, Ill.: The Dryden Press, 1974), p. 334.
[16] Ibid., p. 336.

police system that developed afterward were marked by this critical period. The legal system has developed far beyond its utopian origins but still reflects the Marxist ideal. The security police system clearly reflects its Chekist origins.

The Courts

Law became much more complex than it was in the early utopian period. Criminal law codes now resemble Western systems although the terminology has been superficially altered (for example, prisoners are sentenced to ten years' "deprivation of liberty"). Unusual categories of Soviet crime include economic crimes: carelessness, incompetence, or profiteering at the expense of the Soviet economy. An unusual provision permits prosecutors to bring a case even if no specific law is broken. If the law did not exist, the defendant could be tried for a "similar crime" (this has been technically prohibited since 1958).

The court system has become more complex as well, though the base of the system is still called the people's courts. Existing in every district in the Soviet Union, they consist of an elected professional judge and two "people's assessors," not professionally trained, who act as people's representatives. All decisions are by majority vote. Above the people's courts are two appeals courts—regional courts and the supreme courts of the republics. These consist of panels of professional judges. Each has a civil and criminal division.

The Supreme Court of the USSR, standing at the top of the judicial hierarchy, does not take cases on appeal but does review lower court cases if an important point of law is involved. The Supreme Court has the ability to draft decrees binding on lower courts. Not in any sense independent, the Supreme Court is directly subservient to the Supreme Soviet and is, of course, influenced by the party in manifold ways.

In addition to the courts, the prosecutor's office, or procuracy, carries out important legal functions. The office is responsible for criminal prosecution and for supervising the judicial and administrative application of Soviet law. It reviews all court cases and may demand review by a higher court.

The legal profession consists of judges, advocates, and procurators. Most of today's judges have advanced legal training. The tradition of the amateur or people's judge has almost totally died out (in 1936 over half of Soviet judges had no legal training of any kind). Most judges are members of the Communist party of the Soviet Union.

Advocates are trial lawyers. They tend not to have as much training and prestige as other members of the legal establishment, although they seem to manage higher incomes. Slightly over half of the advocates are party members, and their professional organizations are closely controlled by the party.

Procurators, the elite of the legal profession, have a great deal of supervisory responsibility and more power than other legal professionals. Power is also inherent in their role of initiating investigations and authorizing arrests. The training and status of the procurators reflect the dominance of the state in criminal proceedings.[17]

The Security Police

The security police have special responsibility for political crime and political opposition. They have been organized as the "Committee for State Security" (KGB) since March 1954 (previous organizations were known as the Cheka, the OGPU, and the MGP). The KGB is a complex organization that is, for all practical purposes, a government ministry.

Its most important function is in investigating state crimes: treason, sabotage, "anti-Soviet agitation and propaganda," and "anti-Soviet organization." Particularly important is what they define as "agitation and propaganda which is conducted for the purpose of subverting or weakening Soviet authority" and as the "distribution . . . of slanderous fabrications which discredit the Soviet political or social system." These laws give the KGB wide discretion in seeking out political opposition groups. The KGB operates in the area that the leadership defines as unacceptable political dissent or opposition. It has been very sensitive to party views regarding the seriousness of threats based on social, cultural, or political differences.

Effectiveness of the System

The system of law and courts has been effective in that great body of civil and criminal cases that are not "political." The legal system effectively and uniformly regulates a wide range of social and economic behavior. In political cases the courts are subject to intervention by the party, which also closely supervises the legal profession.

The courts are totally ineffective in handling "constitutional" disputes—those between institutions of government and between the government and Soviet citizens. They provide no control over the actions of the political leaders. The law does regulate day-to-day administrative behavior but not more basic political disputes.

The arbitrary or dictatorial tradition is still strong in cases involving political dissent or opposition. The anti-Stalinist return to "socialist legality", however, has made even the KGB cautious in its approach to dissent, particularly when it occurs in the large cities among well-known members of the intelligentsia. Realizing this, some of the human rights dissidents of the 1960s and 1970s dared to organize a publication called the *Chronicle of Current Events* that first appeared in 1968. The *Chronicle*, distributed in an extensive underground network by a secret editorial group, gave information on persecution outside the judicial-legal system, conditions

---

[17] Peter H. Juviler, *Revolutionary Law and Order* (New York: The Free Press, 1976), pp. 116–117.

in the prison camps and mental hospitals that held dissenters, and reactions from the outside world. Interestingly, the *Chronicle* felt it worthwhile to advise its readers on their legal rights and the procedures of the legal system. The *Chronicle* insisted that the authorities apply the laws as written and in a uniform manner.

The KGB was slow to close in on the editors of the *Chronicle* but in 1972 was evidently given directions to crack down on these dissenters. In that year they induced two dissenters, Pyotr Yakir and Victor Krusin, to cooperate after several months of interrogation. The *Chronicle* network was essentially shut down in 1973, and its job was taken over by famous visible figures, notably Alexander Solzhenitsyn and Andrei Sakharov. The *Chronicle* case suggests that political opposition groups are still controlled by force and that the security police still have a great role in the Soviet system. It also suggests that there are at least potential legal and political constraints against police action.[18]

▪ NIGERIA ▪

Previous chapters have described Nigeria as a nation beset by conflict; often this conflict has been violent. Nonviolent means of resolving conflict have given way during periods of crisis to civil war and many coups d'état. This violence has not been limited to the political elite but has involved the general population as well. The divisions within Nigerian society hinder the development of conflict-managing institutions that are acceptable to all.

The Nigerian judicial system that evolved during the colonial period has served as one important avenue for resolving certain types of conflict. The change from civilian to military government did not appreciably change the judiciary and the judicial system. Judges continued to take an active role; in many cases they were selected by military leaders to investigate particularly difficult problems or to serve on special government commissions. The court system, however, is not responsible for resolving the fundamental political problems of Nigeria. Since 1966 the military has been the final arbiter of disputes and the supreme political power in the nation—especially in political conflicts between different branches of government, different levels of government, and different groups. The role played by the judiciary is limited but important.

The Nigerian Legal System

Nigerian law is derived from many sources. One old, important source is customary law. Groups have different traditional and customary laws that

---

[18] Peter Reddaway, "The Development of Dissent and Opposition," in Archie Brown and Michael Kaser, eds., *The Soviet Union Since the Fall of Khrushchev* (New York: The Free Press, 1975), pp. 124–135.

govern and regulate social, economic, political, and religious aspects of their lives. Traditional law plays an important role in deciding such complex and controversial issues as land tenure, inheritance, marriage contracts, divorce, and the protection of minorities.[19]

During the colonial period the British did not attempt to supplant traditional law completely. Administrators allowed traditional laws to stand as long as they did not directly conflict with specific British laws or moral standards. For example, in northern Nigeria the well-developed, highly codified Islamic religious system (Sharia courts) continued to regulate most matters of direct concern to Muslims within the community. As long as both parties in the dispute were Nigerian, and agreed to the jurisdiction of the customary court, local laws generally took precedence if there was no direct conflict with statute law.

Disputes between non-Nigerians and Nigerians, cases where customary law was not applicable, and a growing number of other specific situations were regulated by new legal prescriptions during the colonial period. English common law and statutory law became the most important sources of law in Nigeria. Since independence the legal code has taken on a much more Nigerian, rather than British, character.

The diverse sources of Nigerian law made it difficult to develop a standardized legal system applicable and acceptable to all groups in the nation. Regional fears and prejudices led groups to guard their legal prerogatives, legal traditions, and legal systems. Regions feared giving too much power to the central government to make decisions concerning them. The legal system during the independence period reflects these regional and ethnic apprehensions as well as the colonial experience. As in the British system, Parliament ultimately remained supreme over all other branches of government, but achieving a regional balance in all political structures became the paramount political goal. The Supreme Court of the Federation of Nigeria was made up of the chief justice and eight justices appointed by the president. The president did not have an entirely free hand in making his judicial appointments. Four of the justices were appointed by the president after consultation with the four regional premiers so that each region would have at least one member on the Supreme Court bench. The other four justices and the chief justice were appointed by the president with the advice of the prime minister.

Each of the four regions was served by a High Court of Justice, with unlimited jurisdiction except for cases reserved for the Supreme Court. Justices to the High Courts were appointed by regional premiers (later by state governors). At the next level were magistrate courts with jurisdiction

---

[19] S. S. Richardson, "The Courts and the Legal System," in L. Franklin Blitz, ed., *The Politics and Administration of Nigerian Government* (New York: Praeger, 1965), pp. 171–172.

in both civil and criminal matters. Finally, customary courts of varying degrees of importance and power applied traditional law where applicable.

While judicial appointments were often based on regional considerations, the competence of the judiciary was (and is) high. The constitution sought to ensure the independence of the judiciary from direct political influence. Judges were paid from a Consolidated Fund outside of the direct control of politicians. They could be removed from office only after either the national or regional parliaments concurred with a two-thirds vote. The only stated causes for removal were misbehavior or inability to carry out the duties of office.

The modification of the constitution decrees (1966) declared that all laws of the parliamentary period were to remain in effect except for those explicitly changed by the military government and those of a constitutional nature. The new leaders created an Advisory Judicial Committee composed of the chief justice, the chief justices of the high courts in the four regions, the grand kadi of the Sharia Court of Appeal, and the attorney general of the Federation of Nigeria. The power of judicial appointment passed from the president to the newly formed Supreme Military Council (SMC) in consultation with the Advisory Judicial Committee. The SMC also assumed the power to remove judges.

The Political Role of the Courts

As stated above, the resolution of Nigeria's severe political conflicts has not been the responsibility of the judicial system. Neither the parliamentary government nor the military government of the day were able to halt Nigeria's slide toward civil war. It is doubtful that the judiciary could have significantly altered the political situation. The divisions among groups, regions, and interests were too severe for a judicial remedy. Conflicts over the distribution of resources and the allocation of government positions (especially at the national level), besides long-standing animosities, led to the attempted secession of the Eastern Region. These were political, not judicial, questions.

The court and the justices are not, however, without a political role. Individual justices can perform political services and make decisions that have political impact. One example was the role played by Mr. Justice Udo Udoma, a Supreme Court justice, as chairman of the meetings of the Constitutent Assembly charged with drafting Nigeria's new (1979) constitution. The different opinions and positions expressed in the Assembly meetings (held in 1977–1978) required a man with a judicial mind and temperament.

Mr. Justice Udoma was well suited for this difficult task and represents the highest traditions of the Nigerian judiciary. Born in 1917 in the present-day Cross Rivers State, he received his early education in Methodist schools in Nigeria. Later he studied law at Trinity College in Dublin and then received a doctorate of law from Oxford in England. After being admitted to the bar, he returned to Nigeria as the first member of his ethnic group (Ibibio) to become a lawyer and the first Nigerian to have both a law degree and a doctorate. His education in the United Kingdom and Ireland was supported in part by the Ibibio State Union, and throughout his career Justice Udoma has continued to support and encourage this cultural organization (See Chapter 2 for a description of the importance of these organizations to Nigerian society.)

Justice Udoma's career includes political, public, and legal roles. Running as an independent, he was elected to the Eastern House of Assembly in 1951 and later joined the National Council of Nigerian Citizens. He left the party in 1953. He was defeated in the 1959 parliamentary elections (held just before independence). His public life includes service on the Eastern Regional Production Development Board, the Oil Palm Produce Marketing Board, and the chairmanship of the *Eastern State Express*. He was appointed a federal justice in 1961 after practicing law and active service in the Nigerian Bar Association.[20]

The Constituent Assembly, chaired by Justice Udoma, dealt with many issues, some of them legal. One of the most vexing concerned the relationship between secular courts and religious courts. The conflict centered on whether there should be a Federal Sharia Court of Appeal. If established, this court (at the national level) would serve as the final court of appeal for Islamic religious matters, basing its decisions on Islamic law derived from the Quran and religious traditions. One draft of the constitution called for the Sharia Court of Appeal to include the grand mufti (a person trained in Sharia law), the deputy grand mufti, and at least three other muftis chosen by a method determined by the National Assembly. An alternative draft called for appeals from the Sharia state courts of appeal to go to the Federal Court of Appeal. In these cases (where religious issues were the concern), the Federal Appeals Court would consist of "three justices of appeal who are versed in Islamic Law."[21] The questions then are: Should there be a separate Islamic court, and, if so, Who should serve, and How should they be selected?

Whatever the resolution of the case, it points to the disputes that often face Nigerian decision-makers. Many Nigerian Muslims persuasively argue that in a nation where over half of the population are Muslims, Islamic legal traditions should be respected, protected, and institutionalized. Many non-Muslim Nigerians argue, just as persuasively, that one religion should not be singled out for special attention and consideration. The issue has

---

[20] Biographical data on Mr. Justice Udo Udoma from *West Africa*, 3142 (September 26, 1977), pp. 1969–1970.

[21] *West Africa*, 3170 (April 17, 1978), p. 737.

proved to be one of the most difficult for Constituent Assembly members to decide.

The Return to Civilian Rule

The military government's announced plans to return to civilian rule in 1979 include debates on how best to resolve conflicts in a democratic society. The constitutional discussion brings into focus the importance of developing nonviolent, effective means of managing conflicts that are accepted by all members of the society.

Staffed with well-trained justices, the Nigerian court system has a long and respected tradition of judicial independence. It is not, however, an institution suited to resolve many of the political conflicts facing Nigerians. Conflict in Nigeria centers on the relationship between various groups and their competition for offices and resources. The difficulty of achieving a national consensus and a national set of values means that many individuals and groups view politics as competition between groups. If one group wins, the others must, by definition, lose. This rule governs politics at the national, state, and local levels, and it is difficult to alter the common view of politics as the struggle between hostile groups. These issues and problems that faced civilian leaders governing through parliamentary institutions now face military leaders ruling by decree. The same issues and problems are sure to face new civilian leaders.

▪ EGYPT ▪

The most recent Egyptian constitution, approved by popular referendum in 1971, states the general legal principles governing Egypt. Like most constitutions, the Egyptian constitution establishes an independent judiciary, guarantees the individual's right of access to the courts, protects the defendant while in custody, and assures the right of all defendants to an attorney. Reflected in the constitution are some of the changes that have occurred in Egypt since the death of President Nasser and the consolidation of power by President Sadat.

The role of the courts in resolving political conflict is ambiguous. The principles of judicial immunity from political influence and control are stated but not always applied in practice. Judges have been removed from the bench for political reasons, and certain sensitive political cases are tried in security or military courts rather than in regular courts. The courts resolve both civil and criminal conflicts but are not the most important institutions for resolving political conflicts. The relationship of the courts to other political institutions is sensitive and fragile and has yet to be fully regularized and institutionalized.

The Legal System of Egypt

Secular law has replaced Islamic religious law as the foundation for the Egyptian legal system. Although religious scholars may provide counsel and present interpretations in certain situations, the legal system itself is secular. There are four levels in the court system. Decisions at each level may be appealed to the next higher level, with the Supreme Court as the final court of appeal.

The Supreme Court, or the Court of Cassation, sits in Cairo. Membership includes the chief justice, 4 deputy justices, and 36 justices. It hears both civil and criminal cases and plays a role in interpreting the constitution. At the second level are the six courts of appeal located in the governates of Cairo, Alexandria, Asyut, Mansura, Tanta, and Beni Suef. In addition to the courts of appeal, there are several primary tribunals located in the governates. Each chamber consists of a three-judge panel. The fourth level includes summary tribunals composed of one-judge chambers. The appeals, primary tribunal, and summary tribunal courts hear civil and criminal cases.

The Supreme Constitutional Court in Cairo has the power to decide the constitutionality of laws and regulations. Its members cannot be removed for political reasons, and the court itself ultimately is responsible for disciplining its own members. There is also a Supreme Judicial Council with responsibility for ensuring the independence of the judiciary and for regulating the promotion and disciplining of judges. Presided over by the president of the Republic, the Council includes the chief justice, two deputy justices, the under secretary of state for the Ministry of Justice, the attorney general, the president of the court of appeal in Cairo, and the president of the primary tribunal in Cairo.

The constitution also allows for the creation of courts of state security. The actions and jurisdiction of these courts are determined by law, and they operate outside the regular judicial system. Military courts can be convened to discipline and try military men accused of political crimes. The creation of special courts lessens the importance of regular courts in deciding and resolving political conflicts and questions.

Conflict During the Nasser and Sadat Presidencies

President Nasser used a variety of means to resolve conflict during his presidency. Methods varied according to the type of threat and those involved. Early in their tenure, the Free Officers banned political parties and curbed dissent from opposition groups on both the left and the right. The 1954 assassination attempt against Nasser by members of the Muslim Brotherhood resulted in the arrest, imprisonment and, in some cases, execution of many Brotherhood leaders. On the left, the Egyptian Communist party was, at various times, banned or proscribed. When allowed to openly exist, the party's activities were closely watched. This was the case even after Egypt closely allied itself with the Soviet Union.

In other areas, opposition groups were incorporated into the political party of the day. As the political ideology of the regime moved to the left or to the right, the groups favoring these positions would find themselves either in or out of favor. The Arab Socialist Union, for example, included various groups and factions during the 1960s and 1970s. Important political figures like Ali Sabri (former minister for presidential affairs and former head of the ASU), Sami Sharraf (former minister for presidential affairs), and Sha'arawi Goma'a (former minister of the interior) represented the leftist, more radical Nasserist positions in the ASU. Others represented center or right positions. What united most of them was their personal loyalty to President Nasser. After 1970 they often found themselves in conflict with one another or, more likely, with President Sadat.

The aim of incorporating opposition and potentially dissident groups under the umbrella of a mass political party is to prevent the development of alternative "centers of power." These centers have at least the potential of challenging the established order. Following the 1967 military victory of Israel, for example, it was announced that a "center of power" led by Field Marshal Abdul Hakim Amer (a close friend and confidant of the president) had been discovered in the military. Following the public announcement of the discovery of the center of power, Field Marshal Amer reportedly committed suicide.

President Nasser also often encouraged disputes and rivalries between various groups. This helped to prevent any one group or individual from ever becoming too powerful or too threatening. In this case by controlling information the president could control individuals and groups. To help in investigating political matters and gathering domestic intelligence, the president created a Republican Guard in 1967.

Other more obvious means of controlling dissent included imprisonment and dismissal from office. In August 1965, for example, 27,000 Egyptians were arrested and many tried in special security courts. (Many were suspected of being involved with the outlawed Muslim Brotherhood). In 1969, 4,000 judges were suspended from their judicial offices during a reorganization of the judiciary. Following the reorganization, 100 judges and judicial officials were dismissed, and 40 shifted to other positions.[22]

On assuming power in 1970 President Sadat's stated policy was not to end the revolution begun by President Nasser or to abandon his general policies but to introduce a "corrective revolution" to make changes where necessary. The actions of security and police forces, the treatment of prisoners while in detention, and the tampering with the judiciary were

---

[22] John Waterbury, "The Opening, Part III: De-Nasserization?" *American Universities Field Staff Reports*, Northeast Africa Series, Vol. XX, No. 4 (June 1975), pp. 6–7.

widely reported and discussed. President Sadat quickly realized that he both had to separate his presidency from Nasser's and establish his own distinctive style.

One change allowed individuals and groups (including the media) greater freedom to voice opinions and opposition. The National Assembly, renamed the People's Assembly, became a more open forum for debating different positions. Many political opponents of the regime arrested and imprisoned during the 1960s were released and in some cases given back their former positions. The corrective revolution called for the gradual reintroduction of parliamentary politics and procedure and a liberalization of Egyptian political activity.

There were limits, however, to this liberalization. Since assuming power, President Sadat has faced several serious crises. Each challenged his authority and forced him to deal with the question of how to respond to dissent and opposition. The first crisis, in 1971, involved Ali Sabri, Sami Sharraf, and Sha'arawi Goma'a (see the second paragraph in this section). These three men and their associates were accused of creating a "center of power" that threatened to grab political power. Civilian leaders were tried before a special three-man revolutionary court headed by Hafez Badawy (then chairman of the People's Assembly). General Fawzy, chief of staff of the Egyptian army, was implicated and tried before a special military tribunal. The leaders of the movement were given death sentences, which the president later commuted to life imprisonment.

A second challenge to the president occurred in January 1977. After a government announcement that prices on certain basic foods would be increased, widespread public rioting broke out throughout Egypt. President Sadat responded by banning premeditated strikes, demonstrations, sit-ins that might lead to disturbance of the peace, and actions that impeded the administration of the government. The three political parties or factions created to represent the right, the center, and the left in 1975 were declared the only organizations that could conduct political activity. Membership in other unauthorized organizations was forbidden.

During the two days of rioting, 1,250 individuals were arrested. Many were tried before state security courts for subversion, rioting, looting, and in some cases murder. The president accused the Progressive Union party (PUP) and Communists (representing the leftist position) of supporting and fomenting much of the trouble. Some PUP members were arrested.

Seeking approval for these actions, the president held a public referendum in February 1977. Government sources reported overwhelming public support for the president. Over 96 percent of those eligible voted, and of those, over 99 percent approved of the president's actions. Major opposition to the referendum and the government's position came from the left and certain student groups.

President Sadat used the referendum again in 1978 to justify a further crackdown on opposition from the left and right. Accusing both the fac-

The 1977 announcement that the prices of bread, tea, and other essentials were to be raised led to rioting throughout all of Egypt. Shown here is a street scene in Cairo. Wide World Photos, Inc.

tions of the left (again the PUP) and the right (a conservative new Wafd group) of creating dissension, spreading rumors, and preventing the effective running of government, the president asked voters for permission to prevent some people from participating in politics and holding government positions and to restrict the freedom of the press.

Again the government reported massive support for the president and his position; 85 percent of the 11 million eligible voters voted. Over 98 percent voted in favor of the president. The mandate allowed the government to exclude Communists and pro-Soviet persons from government service. In addition, the government can exclude those who held positions of political power before 1952—an exclusion directed at members of the new Wafd party.[23]

The crises of 1977 and 1978 point to the dilemmas facing Egyptian leaders. Although the intent of the liberalization begun in 1971 was to open Egyptian political life to freer political discussion, it is clear that leaders are willing to place limits on the role and freedom of opposition groups. The boundaries of dissent and opposition are flexible. Many of

---

[23] *New York Times,* May 23, 1978, p. 3.

the excesses of the Nasser period apparently have been eliminated, but current leaders have shown a willingness to use force to curb dissent where necessary.

▪ TANZANIA ▪

Tanzania, unlike many other developing nations, has witnessed little domestic political violence. With the exception of a short-lived army mutiny in 1964, the Tanzanian military has not intervened in politics, as have the Chilean, Egyptian, and Nigerian militaries. The widespread legitimacy that President Nyerere and TANU enjoy allows the political leadership to manage most political, economic, and social conflicts without resorting to massive coercion. When necessary, however, President Nyerere has shown a willingness to use force to curb dissent.

Despite Tanzania's political stability, its leaders face serious problems and potentially severe political conflicts. As one of the poorest nations in the world, Tanzania faces staggering economic problems. Conflicts also occur among different political institutions. While TANU is clearly the dominant organization in political life, its expanding role in political life may take power from other institutions such as the military, civil service, courts, and National Assembly. A third conflict revolves around how to weigh two political values: the need to preserve national unity and the desire to permit individual freedom. This problem involves the implementation of such policies as the Arusha Declaration, the creation of the ujamaa villages, and the use of preventive detention to curb dissidents. Finally, a potentially serious succession crisis faces Tanzania when President Nyerere, with his personal, charismatic power, no longer holds office.

The Tanzanian Legal System

The sources of Tanzanian law are diverse. The trend, since independence, has been for statutory law to take precedence over British common law and customary law traditions. Traditional leaders, for example, no longer perform judicial functions, and the title of chief has been eliminated. The 1965 constitution details the judicial structure of Tanzania, but the role of the judiciary in national development is stated and discussed more clearly in the writings and the speeches of President Nyerere.

The High Court, which sits in the capital, Dar es Salaam, is the highest court of appeal in Tanzania. This court consists of the chief justice and at least eight justices, all appointed by the president. In appointing the justices, the president consults with the chief justice. Justices on the High Court, once appointed, can be removed only because of inability to perform the duties of their office or for misbehavior. If there are questions concerning a justice's ability or performance, the president can appoint a tribunal with at least three members to make recommendations to him.

Lesser courts in Tanzania include the district courts, presided over by district magistrates, and primary courts, presided over by primary court magistrates. Decisions in these courts can be appealed to the higher courts. The power of traditional chiefs to rule in traditional courts was ended in 1969. This ruling is in line with the general practice of radically limiting the role of traditional authority in Tanzania.

The constitution establishes a Judicial Service Commission chaired by the chief justice. Other members of this Commission are a justice of the High Court (appointed by the president in consultation with the chief justice) and another member (also appointed by the president). While the president maintains the power of appointment, the Commission has the power to discipline, terminate, and remove from office certain judges.

Another monitoring institution with power to investigate other government agencies is the Permanent Commission of Enquiry consisting of three members appointed by the president for two-year terms. Members can be removed from office only for misbehavior or inability to perform their duties. The Commission is responsible for inquiring into the conduct of government agencies, the party, local governments, and public bodies and corporations.

The role of the judiciary has changed since its establishment during the colonial period. The principle of judicial independence remains, but President Nyerere argues that judges cannot isolate themselves from the problems facing Tanzania. They are allowed to become members of TANU, and there is a party cell in the High Court. Like all other individuals and groups, they are expected to become involved in the nation-building process. While judges are not to become involved in "internal party power conflicts" or "compete for party or national political office," the president asked: "Why should they not join with other members in nation-building activities when these take place at a time outside their hours of work?"[24] Justice and the law itself in Tanzania are tied closely to the goals and policies formulated by the political leadership.

Conflict in Tanzania

The supremacy of TANU in political life evolved gradually after the creation of the one-party state. Groups and institutions that were once distinct came under party control. The party provides ideological and organizational direction in the political system. One result of this change is that conflict, when it becomes open and public, occurs within the party, rather than between the party and other political institutions.

The relationship between the military and the party provides a good example. The army in 1964 was a small force of only about 2,000 men; a majority of the officer corps were British officers. Shortly after the Zanzibar

---

[24] Julius K. Nyerere, *Freedom and Socialism* (London: Oxford University Press, 1968), p. 113.

coup in 1964, the army in Tanganyika mutinied. The mutineers, concentrated in the capital city, demanded higher pay and the Africanization of the officer corps; their aim was not to take political power but to achieve better conditions within the service.

President Nyerere's popular support remained high during the mutiny, even though he was forced to go into hiding and even after he was forced to call on British troops to restore order. After the mutiny ended, British troops were replaced with Nigerian troops, and the president and party leadership began a re-evaluation of the political role of the army. The first step was the disbanding of the army and the creation of a new military force.

Soldiers in the new army, navy, and air force were required to be literate in Swahili and, for certain ranks, to have reached specific levels of schooling. More importantly, soldiers were expected to be politically loyal; they were encouraged to join TANU. The military (like the civil service and the judiciary) was no longer separated from the party. Members of the TANU Youth League (TYL) provided a nucleus for the new force. A National Reserve that included TYL members, the national service, the police force, and the prisons staff was also created.[25]

The size of the military has grown significantly since 1964 partly because of internal security needs and partly because of Tanzania's deteriorating relationship with neighboring Uganda. (The war of words between Tanzania and Uganda turned to a full-scale border war in late 1978 and early 1979.) In 1975 the army, air force, and navy consisted of 13,000, 1,000, and 600 men respectively. Tanzania's foreign policy of nonalignment also extends to the military. The People's Republic of China, West Germany, Canada, and Israel are all involved with training various units of the police and the military.

As of this writing, the integration of the military, the judiciary, and the civil service into the party framework has been a relatively effective form of conflict management in Tanzania. Party dominance, however, has not eliminated conflict and dissent. The problem of how to deal with individuals and groups who do not agree with the goals and policies of the leadership is serious. The party and government have at their disposal several methods to control actual and potential dissent.

Where there has been conflict between party policy and the stated law, party policy has usually won out. Two examples are the conflict over land allocation and the rights of those whose land is incorporated into ujamaa villages. Party leaders fear that a rigorously independent judiciary might frustrate national development plans. As a result, the courts usually bend where there is a sharp discrepancy between policy and law. Certain sensitive political areas also fall outside the court's jurisdiction.[26]

---

[25] Henry Bienen, *Tanzania: Party Transformation and Economic Development,* expanded ed. (Princeton, N. J.: Princeton University Press, 1970), pp. 363–381.

[26] James W. Rude, "Implementing the Arusha Declaration—The Role of the Legal System," *African Review,* Vol. 3 (June 1973), pp. 179–208.

The president has been given sweeping powers to control and curb dissent. By his own admission, he has "sufficient powers under the constitution to be a dictator."[27] The president can detain individuals without court approval; also, he can appoint or remove most officials in the government and the party. In practice, there are few effective curbs on his power to make policy, to appoint officials, or to control opposition.

Although the president has used these powers sparingly, he has shown a willingness to use them in what he determines a necessity. One estimate suggests that as many as 3,000 individuals may be under detention for political reasons.[28] Students who protested plans for a national service in 1966 were expelled by the president and returned to their homes to consider their actions. Again in 1977–1978 student protests led to widespread expulsions. Those students who changed their opinions were allowed to return to school, but not to continue their opposition openly. Active dissent within the party ranks often is resolved by removing the dissenters from the party. If newspapers and the media in general fail to support and generally to follow party and government policies, they may be censored. The media in Tanzania are nationalized and subject to government control.

Previous chapters described Tanzania as a society whose constantly changing conditions hamper the establishment of stable political institutions and roles. The strong sense of national unity and purpose established by the Tanzanian leadership lessens, but does not eliminate, the threat of severe, even violent, political conflict. The popularity of President Nyerere and the strength of TANU allow leaders to emphasize conciliation and resolution rather than coercion. As the response to student protests indicates, however, there are limits to the freedom of dissent. The emphasis on national unity and nation-building often is viewed as outweighing the right to oppose the government actively. The balance between coercion and conflict management changes as political situations and circumstances change.

▪ CHILE ▪

Chapter 9 described the traditional support-building institutions in Chile. Before 1973 institutions such as the Congress, political parties, and the presidency also played important roles in managing political conflict in Chile. Political competition occurred in a well-defined and regularized

---

[27] Raymond F. Hopkins, "Political Opposition in Tanzania: Containment v. Coercion," in Barbara McLennan, ed., *Political Opposition and Dissent* (New York: Dunellen, 1973), p. 277.

[28] Michael T. Kaufman, "Supporters Question the Success of Tanzania's Decade of Socialism," *New York Times,* February 17, 1977, p. 3.

political arena—the constitutional system. The rules for resolving political conflicts, known and accepted by most players, changed, however, after military intervention. Former politicians and leaders were arrested, tried, and imprisoned, exiled, or executed. Institutions were banned, recessed, or suspended.

The Chilean court system remained relatively intact but with limited power and independence of action. The constitutional safeguards concerning individual rights and the right to dissent have been suspended during the emergency. Early in the military period, attention focused on controlling opposition to the regime; the major responsibility was assumed by the secret police. The military leaders, unchecked by other political institutions, reinforce and strengthen their power through the effective and selective use of coercion. The military, under the leadership of General Pinochet, vigilantly monitors and controls how much political opposition is allowed to exist. Today all political and governmental institutions are subordinate to the military leadership. In the future President Pinochet has called for the creation of an "authoritarian democracy."

The Judicial System in Chile and Conflicts During the Allende Presidency

The chaotic and divisive politics of the parliamentary period (1891–1925) resulted in a highly politicized judiciary. Judges' decisions sometimes suggested that they had been appointed for political reasons rather than for their legal skills. The 1925 constitution, seeking to rectify this situation, established a system to ensure the impartiality and independence of the judiciary. A Supreme Court with 13 justices was created. The Court's president, chosen by the Court, served a three-year term. Justices were appointed by the president of Chile from a list of five names submitted by the Supreme Court itself and included the two most senior judges from the appeals courts. Justices were required to have a legal training and to have practiced law.

Once appointed, justices had life tenure and could be removed from office only for misbehavior or because they were unable to perform the duties of their office. Only the Court itself could remove a justice, and this required a two-thirds vote. Appointment based on merit, life tenure, and a restricted removal process were designed to keep the Supreme Court independent of the partisan fluctuations of Chilean politics.

Among several other important powers, the Supreme Court could declare legislative and executive acts to be unconstitutional. This power was interpreted narrowly since the Court could not create a general constitutional principle from a specific case. The Court's attempt to avoid controversial, divisive political issues helped to preserve judicial independence and impartiality.

The Supreme Court served as the final court of appeal from the lower courts. Decisions from the lower courts could, under certain circumstances, go directly to the Supreme Court, bypassing intermediate courts. In addition, the Supreme Court had the responsibility for supervising the budgets of many lower courts, for making recommendations to the president for lesser court judicial appointments, and for overseeing the general operation of lesser courts.

Like most other governmental institutions in pre-coup Chile, the court system was highly centralized. Nine appellate courts operated throughout the provinces. Appellate judges were appointed by the president from three-person lists, including senior judges from the next lower level, drawn up by the Supreme Court. Promotion in the lower courts was often on the basis of seniority. At the next level were courts presided over by "scholastic" judges, whose training fluctuated much more widely than the training of judges in higher courts. Special courts were also created in Chile to deal with specific issues such as electoral questions, Indian affairs, and juvenile problems.[29]

The courts in Chile had a reputation for nonpartisanship and slow, but equitable justice. The intense conflicts during the Allende presidency were, however, political rather than judicial. The resolution of these conflicts was outside the scope and jurisdiction of the courts. Despite this fact it is not surprising that the court system was drawn into the conflicts and tribulations of the 1970–1973 period. No institutions were immune.

The sweeping changes and reforms promulgated by President Allende often ended up for resolution in the courts. Supporters of the government claimed that the courts represented the traditional powerholders and that it was difficult for the urban and rural poor to obtain justice. Opponents of Allende, on the other hand, argued that the court system was in danger of becoming a politicized body, rather than a judicial/legal institution. The debate ended in September 1973.

One institution that clearly did not remain neutral during this period was the military. The general tradition of military noninvolvement in partisan politics gave way to direct military participation. Officers were recruited to cabinet positions to provide a balance to the more radical leftist members of Allende's faction. Others were recruited to forestall direct military takeover. The hope was that if military officers participated they would be less likely to carry out a coup d'état. As the army became more politicized the divisions that characterized politics in the civilian political arena began to appear within the miltary. One group of officers favored swift intervention to end the Allende presidency; another group supported the constitutionally elected president (if not his policies). The military, with its near monopoly on the state's coercive power, became an important factor in the conflict between contending political factors. Both

---

[29] Harry Kantor, *Patterns of Politics and Political Systems in Latin America* (Chicago: Rand McNally, 1969), p. 566.

The Allende government ended violently when the Chilean military seized power on September 11, 1973. S. Julienne, Sygma.

President Allende and his opponents sought to strengthen their support in the army.

The more conservative military forces took action in 1973. The victory of General Pinochet and other members of the military junta introduced different ways to manage political conflicts. Emphasis shifted from resolving conflict and potential conflict to eliminating the causes of the conflict. The emphasis was on control.

Control During the Military Period

The military and the police forces quickly strengthened their monopoly on the coercive apparatus. Coercion became the most important and effective weapon for ensuring compliance and loyalty. Various para-military organizations developed during the Allende presidency were disbanded and their leaders harshly dealt with. Labor union leaders, Roman Catholic church officials, and members of the leftist political parties were suspect. Legal safeguards for many of the arrested were suspended. For example, habeas corpus petitions were denied many in detention, and special courts to try prisoners were created. Some estimates suggest that between 1973 and 1975 as many as 18,000 to 30,000 people were killed.[30] By mid-1975

---

[30] Salvatore Bizzarro, "Chile Under the Jackboot," *Current History*, Vol. 28 (February 1977), p. 59.

as many as 50 to 100 persons were still being detained weekly in Santiago.[31]

The organization most responsible for security in the new regime is the *Dirección de Inteligencia Nacional* (DINA). DINA is a consolidation of the security forces from the various branches of the military and police; it has been reported to have 2,000 full-time military staff members, 2,000 civilian members, and perhaps as many as 30,000 paid informants.[32] The military director of DINA reports directly to General Pinochet. During the early period of consolidation of power, there were no effective checks on the power of DINA.

The military leaders, with the support of DINA, have been successful in controlling, if not eliminating, opposition to their regime. Much of the opposition to military rule in Chile now comes from those living outside of Chile. From 1973 to 1976 the military consolidated their power and broke the power of any organized opposition. While there are some indications that the number of political prisoners has decreased since 1977 and that DINA is no longer making arrests on a mass scale, the security forces continue to be accused of using torture during their interrogations.[33]

The military officers who assumed power in 1973 had little experience in government. Their goals were to reverse the economic trends and policies of the Allende government, to end what they viewed as a Marxist, Communist threat to the political system, and to re-establish the traditional order in Chile. In order to achieve these goals, they have governed in a state of siege. Coercion, censorship, preventive detention, the banning of the right of assembly, and the suspension of certain legal rights are their techniques for preventing dissent. One of the stated aims of the military leaders is to make sure that a situation like the one in Chile from 1970 to 1973 can never happen again.

CONCLUSION

The nations in this study face a wide range of political and social conflicts. Some nations, such as Nigeria, experience conflict based on ethnic and linguistic cleavages. The Soviet Union, France, and Chile, at various times, have felt threatened by groups that are fundamentally opposed to the very existence of the regime. The conflict between Protestant and Catholic in Northern Ireland plagues both Conservative and Labour gov-

---

[31] Thomas G. Sanders, "Military Government in Chile, Part II: The New Regime," *American Universities Field Staff Reports*, West Coast South American Series, Vol. XXII, No. 2 (September 1973), p. 29.

[32] Everett G. Martin, "Reshaping Chile, Franco Style," *Wall Street Journal*, April 20, 1976, p. 22.

[33] Jonathan Kandell, "Chile's Army Rulers Buoyed by Economic Gains and Flagging Criticism," *New York Times*, May 3, 1977, p. 16.

ernments. All eight nations contain less important dissident minorities. In addition, each nation, of course, must deal with "normal" conflict over the distribution of resources and other interest-based conflict.

Judicial systems provide one institutionalized means of conflict resolution. If all parties accept the legitimacy of the system and understand its principles and organization, contending groups trust the judgment of the courts. The legitimacy of the courts, as we have seen, is enhanced by their independence. This legitimacy, however, is not easy to achieve. In France the working class feels discriminated against in the courts because of the bourgeois character of the legal profession. Dissidents in the Soviet Union feel compelled to lecture the authorities on how their legal system is supposed to work in political cases.

The effectiveness of a nation's judicial system is tied to the nature and origins of the system. Common law England is weak in resolving conflict relating to ethnic minorities where there is not adequate precedent. Continental legal systems with a prosecutorial tradition are weak in the protection of the accused and in the protection of human rights. Former British colonies such as Nigeria and Tanzania are left with some common law elements, developed in another cultural setting, that become mixed with indigenous or code law traditions.

Nations are sometimes forced to rely on coercion to deal with conflict, particularly where the legal system is weak and not widely perceived as legitimate, or where social conflict is so severe that ordinary judicial remedies do not suffice. Even nations with well-established legal traditions, such as France and Britain, have had to resort to extraordinary non-judicial means of settling conflict (Northern Ireland for Britain; Algerian plots for France). The Soviet Union and Tanzania blend the judicial and police remedies in handling conflict as well. Military regimes such as Chile's seem to represent the final expression of the reliance on coercion. Political conflict in Chile was so severe that the agents of coercion felt compelled to install a regime dedicated to the forceful imposition of order.

CHAPTER 11
POLITICAL
PERFORMANCE

How does economic performance
affect political performance?

As we have seen, nations differ in many ways: in their histories and cultures, in the way that they conduct politics, and in the nature and form of their political institutions. Obviously, these differences affect the performance of political systems. The institutional arrangements of one nation, for example, may be better suited for achieving their political and economic goals than the institutional arrangements of another nation. One way of evaluating political practices and institutions is to assess how well they perform in meeting society's political and economic expectations, demands, and goals.

Defining Political Performance

Political performance is not easily defined. First, performance involves achieving national political and economic goals. It is often difficult, however, to determine what society's goals are and which goals are most important. One answer is to hold political elites accountable for the goals they articulate in important public speeches, in party programs, and in campaigns for political action. This is perhaps the best criterion for determining goals in centralized political systems where general public opinion is not important. Another method of establishing the most important goals is to base the selection on public expectations or demands for governmental action. This method can be especially useful when studying democratic political systems.

Performance itself may be judged by several standards.[1] Effectiveness in reaching goals might be the first criterion. Effectiveness involves the sheer ability of the government to reach goals and satisfy public expectations without regard to the way in which the goals are pursued. The criterion of efficiency introduces the notion of cost. Performance is efficient when the maximum achievement is attained with the minimum cost in money, labor, and time.

Assessing performance, however, involves more than evaluating effectiveness. Governmental performance involves an important change dimension. We are concerned not so much with absolute accomplishments as we are with the ability of the leaders and institutions to bring about change. Economic performance, for example, must be judged in terms of industrial growth, growth in agricultural production, and development of systems of communication and transportation. The absolute size of an economy does not in itself tell much about the effectiveness and efficiency of institutions and leaders.

Leaders also must be able to respond to changes in public expectations and demands. Meeting expectations is not easy to do simply because the expectations often change. For example, since Nigeria and the United Kingdom have benefited from the discovery of large oil deposits, citizens of these countries have greater expectations about their future standards of living. Limited economic success often can be self-defeating, raising public expectations more than it does the ability to satisfy demands.

One final consideration is important in evaluating performance. There are always many goals to which leaders are at least nominally committed. As a result, policy-makers and planners are always, implicitly or explicitly, setting priorities. We should consider the priorities because they involve a hidden cost of goal achievement—the opportunity cost. Part of the cost of achieving one goal is not achieving or only partially meeting other goals. For example, a nation that places almost total emphasis on economic growth may pay for that growth in terms of environmental safety. Unrestrained economic growth damages the air and water environment and affects public health. Sometimes the selection of one goal implies forsaking another goal; more often, compromises are made between conflicting goals: we put up with some environmental pollution for the jobs and standards of living that we expect.

Expectations

Citizens in most all nations share certain expectations regarding governmental performance. Everywhere, for example, citizens expect the govern-

---

[1] Karl W. Deutsch, *Politics and Government* (Boston: Houghton Mifflin, 1974), pp. 230–232.

ment to provide physical and economic security. Nation-states are in the business to protect the lives and property of their citizens, and increasingly, to ensure such needs as food, housing, and health care.

There also are, however, significant differences in the expectations of various peoples. In developing nations citizens and leaders focus on modernization and industrialization. The purpose of economic modernization is usually to raise standards of living and to promote equality of wealth and income. These goals are somewhat in conflict, since the gap between rich and poor actually increases in the early stages of economic expansion.

Western European nations pursue similar goals although they differ in their priorities. Economic growth and higher living standards are stressed in all these nations, but extensive welfare services, economic stability, and economic equality are important goals as well. As in the developing nations, leaders face apparently contradictory goals—such as the goals of growth and of equality.

Aside from economic goals, many Western European nations place greater emphasis on the goal of protecting citizens from political violence and terrorism. West Germany is struggling with the problem of political kidnapping and murder, while the United Kingdom has been faced with political violence in Northern Ireland for 10 years. Provision of personal security is so basic that few governments can tolerate failure in this area.

Resources

Nations vary considerably in the resources available to meet their goals. First of all, they vary greatly in terms of wealth and the size of their economies. Nations such as the Soviet Union and West Germany—economic giants by any standards—can commit massive resources in terms of money, skilled manpower, and natural resources to highly valued goals. This is obviously not the case for developing nations—even oil-rich Nigeria. In judging the performance of developing nations we must consider their low level of economic resources and their special economic problems.

Nations also differ in their organizational resources. Even nations with a modest economic base can improve performance by emphasizing efficiency. Organizational innovations may yield added results at a low cost. Planning organizations, in particular, may increase productivity (without using much money and manpower themselves) by finding the most efficient "mix" of investment, labor, and resources. Nations that do not emphasize planning, such as West Germany, may introduce organizational innovations in labor relations. In each case, organizational innovations are meant to promote the wise use of resources.

In judging performance according to all the criteria just discussed, we must particularly note how priorities are set and pursued. The setting of priorities in itself can have decisive results over a period of years. It is also important to evaluate how well leaders organize their efforts—seeking efficiency through organizational techniques.

■ THE UNITED KINGDOM ■

British subjects, like citizens in other developed nations, have developed firm expectations that their leaders should provide them with economic and physical security. Events of the past 10 years suggest apparent failure on the part of British leadership judged by the public's expectations. Two specific areas of governmental action seem particularly important—the government's handling of the economic crisis of the 1970s and its handling of the political crisis in Northern Ireland.

Economic Expectations

The economic expectations of today's Britons started to take shape in the 1950s and 1960s. A leading observer of British politics, Samuel Beer, labeled this set of expectations the "collectivist consensus."[2] The collectivist consensus willingly permitted extensive governmental intervention in the social and economic realms to achieve the collective good. The government was seen as having a responsibility to promote the economic equality of its citizens, to provide a wide range of social services, and to protect all Britons from want and fear based on economic insecurity.

The Labour party began to build the welfare state in its postwar government under Clement Attlee (1946–1951). Besides the familiar guarantees to the unemployed, the sick, and the elderly, the welfare state delved into the areas of public housing and education. The most important element in Labour's welfare system was its pledge to maintain full employment. In postwar Britain, employment was viewed as a basic right.

The Conservative party never totally opposed the welfare state or the pattern of group politics it bred. In 1947 the Conservative Party Conference emphasized the party's concern for social problems and underlined the fact that the Conservatives were never a "small government" party pledged to nonintervention in the economic realm—that was the basic policy of the Liberal party. Anthony Eden, hand-picked by Churchill to be his successor, explained: "We are not the party of unbridled capitalism and never have been. . . . We are not the political children of the laissez-faire school. We opposed them decade after decade."[3]

The Conservative governments expanded social services while in power

---

[2] Samuel H. Beer, *The British Political System* (New York: Random House, 1974), pp. 175–178.

[3] Ibid., p. 174.

from 1950 to 1959. In terms of absolute expenditures, welfare payments went from £1,537 in 1950 to £3,171 in 1959. The increase was from 13.9 percent of personal income to 16.1 percent of personal income in 1959.[4] These expenditures were made across the full spectrum of social services: national insurance benefits; retirement payments; allowances to widows and their dependents; death grants; and grants for sickness, disability, unemployment, and maternity. The Conservatives greatly expanded housing subsidies, which in effect were an income subsidy for hundreds of thousands of workers. The National Health Service was expanded in terms of facilities, staff, and services.

The issue of public ownership of industries at times laid outside the collectivist consensus. Between 1945 and 1951 Labour nationalized industries that had special importance for the public interest, that were in need of modernization, and that had not prospered under private management. Coal, air and rail transport utilities, and the Bank of England were made public for combinations of these reasons. The nationalization of the iron and steel industries, however, became a partisan issue, and in 1951 the Conservatives took most of the iron and steel industry out of the public sphere. During the 1950s, though, there was a consensus among both major parties and most Britons that the rest of Labour's nationalizations would remain in force.

The commitment of Conservatives to the new collectivist politics took welfare issues out of politics and shaped the public's expectations. The Conservative prime minister Harold Macmillan, for example, was called a "Tory Social Democrat" who could rhapsodize about the benefit and the "good life" his government was bringing to the workers. He wondered why "workers should spend their week-ends in the back-streets." He noted with approval that larger numbers of workers could afford a motor car and he "looked forward to the time, not far away, when these cars will be a little larger, a little more comfortable and when all of them will be carrying on their roofs boats which they may enjoy at the sea-side."[5]

With both parties committed to the welfare state, a system of group politics evolved; it still dominates British politics. Interest groups representing the productive element of the economy play a dominant role in national politics. Accustomed now to group politics, people approve of the new pattern of politics in which cabinets deal directly with the major economic interest groups in making economic decisions—often making Parliament a secondary stage of action.

Although the 1970s have disillusioned many Britons, the goals of the collectivist consensus form an important part of the public's expectations. Economic equality, extensive social services, a centrally managed economy, and full employment are still highly valued. There is still the ex-

[4] Ibid., p. 176.
[5] Stephen Haseler, The Death of British Democracy (London: Elek Books, 1976), p. 59.

pectation that these goals should be reached by the interaction of government leaders and planners and representatives of labor and industry.

Economic Performance

The British economy has not performed well for a number of years. The British have had the most serious "stagflation" of any of the developed countries. Economic productivity and growth has been weak, unemployment has been high, and yet Britain has had the highest sustained inflation of any developed country since 1973 (see Table 11–1). The balance-of-payment figures indicate that the British consistently sell less abroad than they must import for their own needs—a serious problem for a nation dependent on trade. A sign of the overall economic malaise is the fact that British currency lost 30 percent of its value from 1971 to 1975.

The "structural" explanations for Britain's economic problems suggest that the problems are built into the nature of Britain's and the world's economies. Much is made over the age of Britain's capital stock, which puts Britain at a disadvantage against the more modern German and Japanese plants. The shift from Commonwealth to Common Market trading patterns also may explain the economic difficulties. These explanations do not, however, seem as persuasive as the explanation that economic troubles came about from a political failure; specifically, the relationship between labor unions and governments of both parties. The trade unions, operating on the assumptions that full employment and increased living standards are accepted goals, have become more militant and intransigent in their demands. Inflationary wage demands and union militancy have hurt British productivity. In 1972, the worst economic year of the decade, Britain lost 23,909,000 work days (the number of men on strike multiplied by the duration of the strike) from labor disputes.

Political leaders have difficulty in controlling the unions. The union movement is large, centralized, and well organized. The Trade Unions Congress (TUC) is directly affiliated with one of the two major parties—the Labour party. Finally, the style of politics that has evolved under the welfare state and in the public enterprise system has strengthened the role of the large economic interest groups.

In the 1970s the leadership of both parties struggled with the problem of how to control wage demands without creating unprecedented labor unrest. Trying a new, tough approach to labor relations, the Conservative administration of Edward Heath (1970–1974) refused the inflationary demands of coal miners (who are government employees) and suffered through the crippling strikes of 1972 and 1974. The second strike forced an early election and Heath's subsequent electoral loss in October 1974.

Heath tried to institutionalize labor relations through his Industrial Relations Act, which forced arbitration procedures on unions and management. The act led to a number of tense confrontations, including at

TABLE 11–1   Selected Economic Indicators in the United Kingdom, 1970–1977

	1970	1971	1972	1973	1974	1975	1976	1977
Gross National Product (in millions of British pounds at market prices)	46,900	56,944	63,095	72,089	81,859	103,286	—	—
Balance of Trade (in millions of British pounds)	−964	−638	−1,384	−3,347	−6,634	−4,234	−6,700 (millions $U.S.)	−3,100 (millions $U.S.)
Unemployment (percent)	2.6	3.5	3.8	2.7	2.6	4.2	5.7	6.0
Rate of Inflation (Base=100 in 1970)	100.0	109.4	117.2	128.0	148.4	184.4	213.4	—

Sources: *Europa Yearbook: 1977 World Survey,* Vol. 1; "Key Indicators: Major Economies," *The Economist; Yearbook of Labour Statistics; United Nations Monthly Bulletin of Statistics.*
Note: Approximate 1978 exchange rate: U.S.$ 1 = .53 British pound sterling.

least one instance of a union having its headquarters and property sequestered for noncompliance with the act's compulsory arbitration procedures. Heath suffered greatly in opinion polls for increasing class antagonism without achieving the desired results.

Labour's policy has been to solicit voluntary cooperation with the unions. Harold Wilson's "social contract" of 1974 was made in this spirit. In return for wage restraint, Wilson promised social and tax programs demanded by the unions and a repeal of the Industrial Relations Act. The public's preference for this approach accounted for Wilson's victory in the parliamentary elections of October 1974. The social contract itself was a failure when judged against wage demands and the inflation rate for 1975. Massive strikes in 1979 by workers demanding pay increases of up to 20 percent forced the Labour government of James Callaghan to revise the social contract.

Both parties have been slow to come to grips with the labor problem and have clung to the full employment pledge longer than was realistic. Leaders of the two parties tried to fund the social welfare system at levels that the economy would not support long after it became apparent that a reduction in government expenditures was essential. In a sense, they are victims of powerful public expectations that they helped create and can no longer satisfy.

Political Expectations

The most basic expectation in any political system is that citizens will be protected from physical harm resulting from political disorder and violence. The British are no exception to this fundamental rule. The most immediate threat to their physical security is the political violence that has plagued Northern Ireland since 1969. The most severe threat, of course, has been to the lives and property of those living in Northern Ireland; but, as the 1972 Irish Republican Army (IRA) letter-bomb campaign showed, British subjects in London could be just as vulnerable as residents of Belfast.

The expectation of physical security is so basic that failure of performance at this level can have severe implications for a political system. Support for leaders and institutions may be quickly withdrawn. Eventually, the legitimacy of the political regime may be widely denied if it is incapable of protecting its own citizens.

Political Performance in Northern Ireland

The British have been exercising "direct rule" in Northern Ireland since 1972. From 1921 to 1972 this six-county area of Northeastern Ireland was ruled by a semi-autonomous government of Northern Ireland at Stormont (the 26 southern counties formed the independent state of Eire, or the

Republic of Ireland, at the beginning of that period). The parliamentary government of Northern Ireland had a wide range of "transferred powers" that included most governmental powers except those "reserved" to the Westminster government, involving defense, treaties, and taxation. The British were forced to suspend that government in 1972 and take direct responsibility after a violent confrontation between the majority Protestants and the minority Catholics.

Since 1972 the British have been committed to ending the conflict by both military and political means. The preferred solution and goal of successive British governments has been to draft a constitution for Northern Ireland that will be acceptable to both Catholics and Protestants. Successive cabinets brought pressure to bear on both sides to accept a political solution that involves "power sharing" or the inclusion of Catholics in any new government of Northern Ireland.

The patterns of politics in Northern Ireland has always turned on religion rather than class, although many Catholics feel themselves to be members of a disadvantaged economic group because of their religion. The religious division is reinforced by feelings of national and cultural difference. Catholics in Northern Ireland identify themselves as Irish, while Protestants generally feel themselves to be English or "Ulstermen." Differences in culture follow a traditional-modern pattern. Catholics tend toward traditional attitudes and beliefs, while the Protestants feel themselves to be the modern products of industrial society.

During the Stormont regime Protestants, under the political banner of Unionism (derived from the desire for permanent union with Britain) held a permanent majority. Catholics were discriminated against in terms of legal-political measures such as the gerrymandering of election districts to reduce Catholic representation. They were also discriminated against economically. Government jobs disproportionately went to Protestants, and Protestant leaders openly encouraged similar practices in large industries in the private sector—particularly during eras of high unemployment.

These conditions led to the development of a civil rights movement made up largely of Catholics. In the 1967–1969 period its leaders borrowed the peaceful tactics of the American civil rights movement in order to dramatize their grievances. The suppression of the civil rights activities by unofficial Protestant para-military groups and the Protestant-dominated Royal Ulster Constabulary (Ulster's police force) led to a resurgence of the Irish Republican Army (IRA). The provisional wing of the IRA (or Provos) began a campaign of violence and terrorism against the Protestant groups and ultimately against the British Army in Northern Ireland. The IRA's resurgence came under the guise of protecting Catholics and in response to the Protestant taunt "IRA—I RAN AWAY."

The British have made two separate initiatives to come up with a political solution to the crisis. Two separate elected assemblies of Ulster Protestants and Catholics have been charged with a power-sharing constitution. The first ended when Protestant extremists staged a general strike that forced the British to abandon the plan. The second was dominated by a Protestant majority unwilling to include Catholics in future cabinets of a Northern Ireland government.

The cost to Britain includes daily expenditures that run into millions of pounds and the fact that 14,000 British soldiers are required to maintain the peace in this tiny province. Economically ailing Britain cannot afford this cost; more seriously, the situation in Northern Ireland further erodes the political prestige and credibility that political leaders started to lose during the economic difficulties.

■ THE FEDERAL REPUBLIC OF GERMANY ■

The performance of the German economy has been unexcelled in postwar Europe. Partly because of this economic success, political stability has not been a problem. The widespread concern for economic security among citizens of West Germany is not lost on political leaders. There is little difference in economic policies and performance between Social Democratic and Christian Democratic governments.

Economic Expectations

West Germans are agreed on the proper economic goals and methods of achieving these goals. This consensus is shared by most party politicians and a large part of the general public. The West Germans favor a free market economy with as little government intervention as possible. They emphasize stable economic growth, controlled inflation, and full employment. The goal of economic equality has not been given high priority as it has in Britain.

The public does expect the government to be active and efficient in a wide assortment of indirect ways. The government is expected to encourage investment and productivity through its tax and monetary policies and to regulate industrial relations in a way that reduces labor-based conflict. West Germans also expect a wide assortment of social welfare benefits.

These economic expectations have special force because of the great importance that Germans attach to economic stability. Commercial pollsters have noted that Germans name the need for increased living standards and controlled inflation as their greatest political concerns year after year, even when it seems they have nothing to fear. The leaders of the Federal Republic have faced a difficult task in meeting the uncompromising demands and expectations of the West German electorate.

The extreme significance of economic performance is related to the severe dislocations of recent German history. After each lost war of this

Workers in West Germany's Krupp steel works. Courtesy, German Information Center.

century, the German currency totally collapsed. The "great inflation" of 1921–1923 was touched off by the strain of reparations payments to the victorious Allies. Stories of spending billions for bread or candy have been passed down from generation to generation. Heinrich Böll, the Nobel Prize-winning novelist, recalls:

My father used to slip me a banknote with which I was allowed to buy a handful of candies or a candy stick at the shop across the street. I recall that there were a great many noughts on the banknote, and was later told that they had represented a billion or even a trillion. . . . That was in the years 1921–1922 when on some mornings, for a minute or two, I was a billionaire or a millionaire.[6]

Income did not increase by the necessary proportion during the inflation; for example, a teacher's monthly salary could buy an umbrella.

During the great inflation people got by on barter—trading possessions for food and necessities—and on theft and begging. The meaning of property was totally distorted as long-standing possessions were traded for cigarettes, food, and coal or firewood.[7]

[6] Heinrich Böll, "The Inflation," *New York Times Magazine,* May 2, 1976, p. 17.
[7] Ibid.

The aftermath of World War II brought on a second currency collapse. From 1945 to 1948 an average worker's salary was 325 marks a month; in the same period, a pound of coffee or butter cost 600 marks. The lesson of the 1920s was reinforced in 1945. Böll observed: "In the 1920's they baled banknotes into wastepaper. In 1945, the currency collapsed again. The heritage is fear—unreasoning fear." The heritage is also the deep-felt value placed on the sanctity of private property in West Germany.

The German "economic miracle" of the 1950s greatly shaped orthodox economic thought in West Germany. Dr. Ludwig Erhard, minister of economic affairs between 1949 and 1966, was most influential in developing the West German economic philosophy. Erhard called his economy the "social market economy." Social welfare concerns were blended with a system designed to maximize competition and private ownership. Intervention by the state was limited to monetary and fiscal policy and measures designed to promote investment.

There is no doubt of the success of these policies. German productivity soared. The Gross National Product of the Federal Republic rose by 61 percent between 1953 and 1960 (see Table 11–2).[8] This is double the European average and triple the increase posted by the United Kingdom. The Federal Republic's living standards, as measured by categories of private consumption, outdistanced European rivals by similar ratios.

There is some controversy over the extent to which the miracle was due to Erhard's policies and "the honest efforts of the German people," as he was fond of saying. Clearly $3.5 billion from the United States and Marshall Plan loans helped, as did the liberal American policy on reparations. West Germans did not have to bear the heavy costs of defense that plagued other nations because of the controversy regarding German rearmament. West Germany was also blessed with an overabundance of skilled labor, including 12 million refugees from the East, as well as a pent-up demand for all types of products. Finally, the German economy was not quite as ravaged as it looked in 1945; West Germany had greater industrial capacity in 1946 than it did in 1936.

Whatever the reasons for the economic miracle, no chancellor of either party has repudiated the policies associated with Erhard's social market approach. West Germany's finance, welfare, and industrial relations policies have been mostly consistent. With the exception of the brief "recession" of 1966, these policies have continued to be successful.

Performance: Taxation, Spending, and Industrial Relations

The West German philosophy of taxation is shaped by its economic goals and public expectations of performance. West German leaders emphasize

---

[8] David Childs, *Germany Since 1918* (New York: Harper & Row, 1971), p. 136.

TABLE 11–2   Selected Economic Indicators in the Federal Republic of Germany, 1970–1977

	1970	1971	1972	1973	1974	1975	1976	1977
Gross National Product (in thousand million Deutschemarks)	610.8	676.8	833.9	927.5	997.0	1,043.6	—	—
Balance of Trade (million DM)	+16,014	+16,282	+20,769	+33,719	+52,101	+38,685	+13,800 (millions $U.S.)	+15,700 (millions $U.S.)
Unemployment (percent)	0.7	0.8	1.1	1.2	2.6	4.7	4.0	4.6
Rate of Inflation (Base=100 in 1970)	100.0	105.3	111.1	118.8	127.1	134.7	141.5	—

Sources: Europa Yearbook: 1977 World Survey, Vol. 1; *United Nations Monthly Bulletin of Statistics; "Key Indicators: Major Economies," The Economist; Yearbook of Labour Statistics.*
Note: Approximate 1978 exchange rate: U.S.$ 1 = 2.023 German Deutschemarks.

the use of taxation to influence investment, production, and consumption. Taxation policies are used to stimulate investment and growth. Unlike the British, the Germans have made little effort to use taxation to equalize income.

The West German tax structure promotes investment. Corporate taxes are lower than in any other developed nation of the West. Only 7.4 percent of the West German tax income comes from this source as compared with approximately 11 percent in France, 10 percent in Britain, and over 14 percent in the United States.[9] This policy assumes that low corporate taxation promotes reinvestment, which increases the individual's standard of living. Growth of this kind increases the state's take from individual income and indirect taxes and permits a high level of spending on social welfare services.

The taxes that individuals pay virtually do nothing to redistribute income. West Germany gets well over half of its tax income from indirect taxes paid by individual consumers on a wide variety of goods and services. The poorest taxpayers end up paying more in taxes than they would under any income tax scheme, as they pay the same tax on basic consumer items that wealthier consumers do. This form of taxation is not graduated in any sense. Indirect taxes do, however, give the government the power to influence patterns of consumption and demand by affecting prices.

Governmental spending, like tax policies, reflects West German economic goals. First of all, much governmental spending is in the form of subsidies to social, economic, and educational organizations in the private sector. This indirect role reflects the government's commitment to volunteerism and private institutions, while maintaining a policy stand in these important areas.

West German governments provide a high level of social welfare services for their citizens, a tradition that dates from Bismarck. In particular, West Germans benefit from a very extensive system of social insurance that includes health, disability, maternity, disablement, survivors, and retirement insurance. They pay much of the cost of these programs from their paychecks, but government contributions are substantial and the services are excellent. When one includes welfare, unemployment compensation, and other benefits, the federal government devotes slightly over a third of its budget to social benefits.[10] This proportion has remained relatively constant in the postwar period, but the overall growth in the federal budget means there has been a considerable expansion of services and benefits.

The West German economic philosophy also is seen in governmental regulation of business enterprises. Governments of both parties have

---

[9] Lewis J. Edinger, *Politics in West Germany* (Boston: Little, Brown, 1977), p. 319.
[10] Ibid., p. 328.

demonstrated their belief in the importance of business and, in particular, big business; they are reluctant to hold in check the private enterprises that have accounted for West Germany's phenomenal growth. Despite the existence of laws against certain forms of large economic concentrations and cartels, the trend in each important economic sector has been toward consolidation and dominance by large firms. For example, 1 percent of German industrial firms account for 40 percent of West German industrial production.[11]

Among the most successful West German economic policies are those involving industrial relations. Postwar industrial relations have been guided by a desire to make management and labor "social partners." The principle assumes that both groups are integral parts of industrial enterprise. Both benefit from growth and productivity; both suffer from labor unrest and work stoppages.

Two innovations have helped bring about the industrial democracy promised in the concept of social partnership. First, West German employees now elect works councils for each basic work unit in large enterprises. The councils represent the workers on issues relating to work conditions—such as shift schedules, vacation policy, safety, and rest breaks. Works councils essentially have a veto over projected changes in working conditions; they also play a "watchdog" role with regard to management's observance of labor contracts (although they do not play a role in contract negotiation). The second innovation is codetermination, or worker representation on the policy boards of major German corporations. (West Germany's two-tiered corporate board system has both general policy boards and more active management boards.) Worker representatives participate in the policy boards' activities of discussing corporate policy and selecting members of the management board.

Under the Codetermination Act of 1976, employees have equal representation on the policy boards of coal, iron, and steel companies. A neutral chairman presides over these boards. For all other companies with more than 2,000 employees, labor selects half of the board members, but one of their representatives must be selected by the salaried management-level staff. In effect, one of the labor representatives is selected by top management. Before 1976, employees selected one-third of the board members under provisions of the 1951 Codetermination Act. Even under those limited provisions, labor has supported the principle of economic democracy and demonstrated restraint in their demands.

West German economic policies are well coordinated and conceived for the particular context in which they operate. Consensus on these policies permits continuity in the economic realm, and the emphasis on economic growth with stability has been rewarded. The wide variety of

---

[11] Ibid., p. 333.

social benefits provided by the system suggests that the "social market" economy does indeed mean free enterprise with a conscience.

▪ FRANCE ▪

The greatest challenges to postwar French political systems are economic growth and modernization. World War II exposed French economic and social weaknesses, a result of the stagnation of the Third Republic. The leading political figures of the "new France," many of them veterans of the resistance movements, were determined to stimulate the economy through the use of modern, rational-scientific methods.

The modernizers realized that economic change was dependent on social and political change. French society was still very traditional by contemporary European standards in 1945; thus, old attitudes and values, such as those associated with subsistence farming, had to be altered. Most put their faith in technocratic planning machinery, but some felt that strong political leadership was needed. The planning machinery that developed under the Fourth Republic (1945–1958) was put at the disposal of the strong Fifth Republic presidency after 1958.

Expectations: The Traditional Legacy

Economic attitudes and expectations in France are still in a state of transition from the attitudes characteristic of the Third Republic (1875–1940). The traditional, conservative attitudes of that "stagnant society" still place limits on economic progress. The economic performance of French governments must be judged in part in terms of their success in modifying the old views.

The France of the Third Republic (1875–1940) had the lowest growth rate of all developed nations, while neighbors such as Germany, were experiencing rapid growth. The yearly growth rate averaged only 1.1 percent during the Third Republic, and a total lack of confidence in the future seemed to permeate the society. Also symptomatic of the French malaise was the declining birth rate after 1850; eventually reproduction fell behind the level necessary to replace the dying. The situation, of course, became worse in World War I. It is estimated that the net loss from the war in dead and from a more steeply declining birth rate was on the order of 3,000,000—over 7 percent of the population.[12] Over this period the French population was becoming older and less productive.

Another problem was the importance attached to the small French farm. In 1930 approximately 35 percent of the adult French population

---

[12] Henry W. Ehrmann, *Politics in France* (Boston: Little, Brown, 1976), pp. 20–21.

were farmers, and almost 50 percent of the population lived in communities with populations less than 2,000.[13] Most farms were small, existing to meet family food needs; this was not, of course, an efficient use of labor. The life of the small farm sustained a conservative culture that resisted every innovation.

French business also was based on small family enterprises. In 1930 80 percent of French firms employed fewer than 20 workers.[14] Retail trade was similarly dominated by family shops that were small by necessity and design.

Both agricultural and industrial-commercial France were influenced by a similar psychological syndrome. Individuals who owned land or a small firm felt that it was a temporary trust of the vital family inheritance; they avoided risk in order to pass the inheritance on intact. The family basis of enterprises bred fear of outsiders, including those interested in investing their money in the family operation. Business skills were mistrusted and not socially valued. It was enough to run the firm as it had always been run—in the family.

A political stagnation paralleled this social and economic stagnation. Parliament ruled in the Third Republic in the French republican tradition. Parliamentary government was small government that was not active or interventionist. The dominant party was that of small-town France, the Radicals. The party passionately believed in the individualism that supported the family-centered social and economic system; it was incapable of sparking needed changes and reforms.

The French collapse in 1940 seemed to expose all of the faults and weaknesses of the system. When the German army broke the very large French army in a week, the contrast between vigorous and modern Germany and backward France was at last obvious to virtually all Frenchmen of any influence. The defeat and humiliation would serve to clear the way for the new France.

Expectations: Postwar France

France's postwar leaders, particularly those of the 1944–1947 period before the Cold War, were united on a set of economic goals. Reconstruction was the first priority in the wake of war's destruction. The reconstruction plans were to be tailored to the needs for industrial growth after recovery. A second goal was to catch up with other nations in social and welfare services. French social policy had lagged far behind that of every other major European nation. There was a consensus on the need to reduce inequalities of wealth and income, particularly for the first few years after the war.

---

[13] John E. Talbott, ed., *France Since 1930* (New York: Quadrangle Books, 1972), p. 4.
[14] Ibid., p. 5.

The methods to meet these goals were also generally accepted. First of all, the major political actors of the period endorsed the nationalization of critical industries; this would permit an element of control for governmental planners and leaders. By following consistent policies on prices, production, and labor in the public sector, the planners could influence these elements in the private economy.

The second tool was a planning system. The planning machinery, supposed to use expertise on the technical problems of economic change, was also expected to bring in those who would have to implement the plans; thus the theoreticians would meet practitioners and exchange ideas.

The general public responded positively to this approach. In the early postwar period, there was solid support for the public enterprises and planning bodies. The necessity for government intervention in the economy was not a source of controversy, for there was no other choice. Later, the apparent success of the system encouraged French citizens to place their hopes and trust in the new economic system.

Performance

A remarkable success by most standards of performance, the new French economic system has accomplished most in the areas of economic growth and productivity. Currently, the French gross national product per capita rivals that of West Germany's and is among the highest in the world (see Table 11–3). Since the mid-1960s the French growth rate (percentage growth in GNP) has been greater than any other nation except Japan's. French industrial production rose 37 percent from 1969 to 1974.[15]

French governments have been much less successful in reducing inequalities of wealth and income. The gap between the income of the wealthiest 10 percent of the French public and the poorest 10 percent is wide and growing. This discrepancy is much greater than the economic disparities found in West Germany, the United Kingdom, or the United States. As President De Gaulle once remarked, "This egalitarian country is one in which the inequalities are greatest. And the category that fares worst at the common table are the workers."[16]

Figures on real wages suggest that workers have not benefited from the economic growth as much as it is sometimes supposed. Unskilled laborers, agricultural workers, and workers in the public enterprises, for example, have not had increases in real income (income adjusted for the cost of living) in the recent period of dramatic growth. Skilled labor, white-collar workers, and workers in private enterprises fared much better but not as well as their West German counterparts. This uneven pattern of performance is due partly to established patterns of politics. French work-

---

[15] Ehrmann, *Politics in France*, p. 20.
[16] Ibid., p. 48.

TABLE 11-3   Selected Economic Indicators in France, 1970–1977

	1970	1971	1972	1973	1974	1975	1976	1977
Gross National Product (in millions of French francs at market prices)	702,200	898,582	1,007,122	1,143,961	1,324,792	1,275,900	—	—
Balance of Trade (millions of francs)	−6,820	−4,034	−4,109	−6,409	−34,438	−7,907	−3,400 (million $U.S.)	−200 (million $U.S.)
Unemployment (in thousands)	262.1	338.2	383.5	393.9	497.7	839.7	813.0	1027.0
Rate of Inflation (Base = 100 in 1970)	100.0	105.5	112.0	120.2	136.7	152.8	165.6	—

Sources: Europa Yearbook: 1977 World Survey, Vol. 1; United Nations Monthly Bulletin of Statistics: "Key Indicators: Major Economies," The Economist; Yearbook of Labour Statistics.

Note: Approximate 1978 exchange rate: U.S.$ 1 = 4.58 French francs.

ers have always been at a disadvantage because of the dominance of center and right parties. The representatives of the working classes, including the Communists and militant unionists, have not been in government. The governments of the center and right often feel that they owe nothing to workers who, after all, do not support them.

The pattern of French economic performance also reflects the nature of the planning machinery and of the postwar public sector of the economy. The planning machinery is headed by the General Commission on Planning (*Commissariat Général au Plan*, or CGP), which is attached to the office of the French premier and is staffed by experts in the realms of economics, statistics, and other relevant specialities. The CGP develops alternative economic plans that include specific recommendations for the allocation of resources. It operates on the basis of the government objectives provided by the premier's office and statistical projections from governmental agencies.

The CGP submits its tentative plans to functional planning units and agencies for consultation. The opinions of labor, trade unions, business associations, agricultural groups, and representatives of regions and localities are solicited in this manner. Economic "modernization" commissions are among functional units consulted. They consist of approximately 50 representatives of government and private interests in a given economic sector. Modifications in the plan are made after this initial round of consultations, and the new package is submitted to the Social and Economic Council, a national board of interest group representatives. Finally, a finished plan is submitted to the cabinet for approval.

Traditionally, the planning machinery has been dominated by the established business community and the major industrialists. The postwar politicians were very sensitive to business fears of a socialist or collectivist system. The first chief planner was Jean Monnet, a respected businessman who persuaded major businessmen that planning was necessary to save the remaining private sector of the French economy. The plans themselves (four-year plans in the early period and more recently five-year plans) have emphasized growth and productivity to the exclusion of other goals, a reflection of continual business influence.

The plans' impact is largely felt through the impact of the public or nationalized sector of the economy. The government owns and operates transport, all energy production, 60 percent of bank deposits, one-third of the automobile industry, and one-third of the housing industry as well as less important enterprises. This public sector employs 27 percent of all adult French workers and pays them one-third of all the wages paid to French employees.[17] The policies of this massive public sector influence all private concerns and has a particular impact on prices, patterns of consumption, and resource allocation. In general, the managers of the public

---

[17] Ibid., p. 37.

sector are comfortable with the planners' emphasis on economic growth; they have not concerned themselves with the social and political impacts of the plans.

Governmental actions in the fiscal and monetary realm have followed the biases revealed in the French planning. In particular, the French tax laws seem dedicated to increasing disparities in wealth and income. France has the highest commitment to indirect taxation of any developed country: almost 70 percent of French tax revenues come from taxes on goods and services. Government officials explain that tax evasion is so widespread in France that they cannot rely on returns from any sort of standard graduated income tax; instead, they must tax essential goods and services so that no one can avoid payment. Under this system, lower income people often pay a higher proportion of their income in taxes than their more fortunate countrymen. Even the graduated personal income taxes are ineffective in redistributing wealth because of the wide variety of loopholes.

In sum, French governments have used innovations in planning and economic management to improve their industrial productivity greatly. White-collar and skilled employees have benefited in terms of better living standards, but many less-skilled workers have not. There has been no attempt to alleviate France's extreme disparities in income; in fact, France's inequitable tax system seems to have the reverse effect.

■ THE SOVIET UNION ■

As the Soviet leadership has consistently maintained that political and social goals are reached through reforms of the economy, their performance may be judged by their attainments in the economic realm. The Soviet party elite has held industrial growth as its primary goal from the beginning of the regime. Industrial growth and economic modernization are necessary to achieve social goals such as the classless society and political goals such as "building communism."

Goals and Expectations

The leadership of the Communist party has set goals that have greatly influenced the expectations of Soviet citizens. Since the era of Lenin, forced economic modernization has been a top political priority, necessitating the development of a heavy industrial sector. Agriculture and consumer goods have suffered from the lower priorities attached to them by party leaders.

Throughout the history of the regime the leadership has consistently supported individual economic equality as a political value—the right and duty of all Soviet citizens to work. Workers are guaranteed economic security or freedom from want; eventually, in the stage of mature communism, distinctions of income and living standards are to disappear. At present, the leadership recognizes the necessity of retaining material incentives to reward special contributions and talent.

Although inequalities persist, the leadership is committed to providing social benefits and subsidies that are meant to equalize the living standards of Soviet citizens. Health care, housing, education, and many other social items are viewed as legitimate areas of government action.

Finally, the party elite has placed a great deal of emphasis on economic stability. Soviet leaders are critical of capitalist economies for their tendency to alternate between "boom" and "bust" phases. One purpose of governmental management of the economy is to prevent such dislocations. Since government policy regulates prices, labor relations, and production targets, the Soviet system can avoid the Western symptoms of economic distress—inflation, unemployment, and work stoppages.

Organizational Resources

The Soviet system has developed elaborate organizational machinery to carry out economic planning and supervise the implementation of the plan. The intent of this organizational engineering is to promote efficiency; that is, to maximize production in priority areas by putting together the optimal mix of resources, labor, and investment.

The top planning organization is the State Planning Committee (Gosplan), which determines what goods will be produced and at what rate. Its experts estimate first the quantities of raw materials, parts, and equipment that will be required to meet the production targets. They then estimate the time that will be required to achieve stated production goals. These calculations have formed the basis of the Soviet Five Year Plans which have guided the Soviet economy.

The planning mechanism has been viewed as inadequate by many leaders since the mid-1950s. One problem has been the overcentralization of the planning organization. Many feel that the planning bodies have not understood local needs, problems, and conditions. Periodically, decentralization schemes have been initiated to correct this problem—the most ambitious of which was Khrushchev's *sovnarkhoz* reform (1957). Councils were set up in every region to decentralize economic decision-making, but it soon became apparent that these localized bodies were incapable of acting in a coordinated or national manner. Other experiments have had similar results.

A few reforms have been borrowed from market economies. One way to favor an efficient sector or enterprise over less successful rivals would be to analyze their "profits." Since the state sets prices, this has been difficult to gauge, as has the cost of production. As a result, decisions about which enterprises to favor with investment have been based on sheer output—number of units produced. The state controls demand by setting prices and levels of consumer protection. If the state wants to limit demand for a "luxury" item, it raises the price astronomically. The manufacturer makes an enormous, but artificial, profit that the state takes away through a turnover tax.[18] Much of this elaborate system is meant to retain incentives for efficient production in the absence of a real market situation where supply follows demand.

Supervision of production is handled through the state bureaucracy under the direction of the Council of Ministers. Ministries closely supervise enterprise managers, either directly or through an intervening management apparatus. Enterprise managers must always worry about their ability to "produce up to plan." Failure may have serious consequences. To avoid this problem, managers often become involved in deceptions and falsifications; for example, they try to underestimate their productive capacity to get a low production goal; they stockpile unaccounted finished goods to help with the next plan period; and they may divert supplies from other enterprises through theft or bribery. Efficiency is hardly promoted in these instances.

Performance

Performance in industrial growth has been remarkable in the Soviet Union. The Gross National Product, which was $62 billion in 1913, is currently over $600 billion. The growth rate has been phenomenal as well. The Soviet economy began to grow at a rapid rate with the first Five Year Plan of 1928. For the next 30 years the yearly growth rate fluctuated between 8.6 percent and 11.7 percent. In comparative terms this is unexcelled by any other industrial nation in a similar stage of development.[19]

Since this period of expansion, the growth rate has dropped considerably, hovering around the 5 percent mark—with occasional disastrous periods such as 1968–1969, when industrial growth was barely over 2 percent. One explanation of this tapering off is that the Soviet economy had developed to the point beyond which sheer effort and investment would not produce great gains. Another explanation suggests that Soviet planning and economic management were not efficient enough to sustain growth. Soviet leaders clearly believe that this is the case, as can be seen by the fact that they have been trying a variety of reforms and reorganizations to break down the rigid overcentralization of the system.

Lagging far behind the record set in industrialization is Soviet agricul-

---

[18] John A. Armstrong, *Ideology, Politics and Government in the Soviet Union* (New York: Praeger, 1974), p. 140.

[19] David F. Roth and Frank L. Wilson, *The Comparative Study of Politics* (Boston: Houghton Mifflin, 1976), p. 414.

Workers on a Soviet collective farm. Henri Cartier-Bresson, Magnum Photos, Inc.

tural production, its yield in the mid-1950s virtually the same as for 1913.[20] Since this period of stagnation, the policies of Khrushchev and Brezhnev have led to episodic bursts of growth but not the sort of steady expansion hoped for. The collapse of Khrushchev's ambitious farm programs in 1963–1964 helped bring on his early retirement in 1964.

There are many possible reasons for the poor performance of Soviet agriculture. First of all, the rural areas always resisted the social and economic changes associated with Communist economic plans. For the peasants, the revolution of 1917 was in fact for "peace, bread, and land," as the revolutionary leadership put it. Most peasants wanted the land denied them under the tsarist land tenure system. Farm tenants or subsistence farmers had great expectations about dividing the old aristocratic estates into sizable private farms.

Through the 1920s the land hunger of peasants was fueled by party promises about private plots and guaranteed land-holding. Stalin's collectivization drive, which began in 1929, forced the issue. Stalin saw no alternative but to break the rural population of their demands for private property. The more established peasants, or kulaks, were forceably driven from the land. The collectivization campaign, which was completed by 1936, claimed an estimated 5 million lives through state violence and

---

[20] Armstrong, *Ideology, Politics and Government in the Soviet Union,* p. 145.

engineered starvation. The Soviet Union's livestock herds were virtually decimated in this period by the starving population and were not replaced to 1930 levels until nearly 1960.

Another reason for agricultural failure is found in Soviet investment priorities. The Soviets "starved the farms" to help subsidize heavy industrial growth and the interests of the reliable urban population. Investment in farm machinery, chemical fertilizers, and genetics research was low, and the agricultural sector remained much more labor-intensive as the industrial sector modernized. Rather than make farm methods more efficient, the planners counted on a massive rural work force. Even now, the Soviet farm population (40 percent) is proportionally larger than that of other developed nations.

A last major reason for agricultural failure may be the geographical conditions. The Soviet Union has limited arable land in terms of fertility and general quality. What good land exists is not always easily accessible to population centers. Weather and climatic conditions are not favorable; much of the land is located in areas with short growing seasons and extreme weather conditions.

The Soviets organize most farm land into either *kolkhozes* or *sovkozes*. Kolkhozes are collective farms that are viewed by the state as farm cooperatives rather than state enterprises. Cultivation and livestock-tending is done on common lands and in collective herds. The collective farmers divide the proceeds from the sale of crops and livestock after the state extracts its predetermined share. Kolkhoz farmers are permitted a small plot (typically an acre) for their private use. These plots have been very productive. In 1971, for example, two-thirds of Soviet milk and meat production came from private plots.[21] The sovkozes are farms directly owned and operated by the state, which also directly employs farm laborers who may hold no private land. Approximately 40 percent of Soviet farmers work on sovkozes.

Since the 1950s, the governments of Khrushchev and Brezhnev have increased investment and incentives to productivity. Khrushchev's downfall seemed to stem from a mania for reorganization that resulted in crossed lines of authority and to a lack of coordination. The Brezhnev regime's cautious approach has been generally more satisfactory. Investment has increased greatly. Tractor production in 1972 was double that of 1960, and chemical fertilizer production increased five times in the same period. Today 25 percent of Soviet investment funds go to the agricultural sector (compared to 4 percent in the United States), and that percentage is growing. Brezhnev has also increased production incentives, such as a 50 percent bonus for overplan deliveries of agricultural production.[22]

---

[21] Ibid., p. 150.
[22] Alec Nove, "Agriculture," in Archie Brown and Michael Kaser, eds., *The Soviet Union Since the Fall of Khrushchev* (New York: The Free Press, 1975), pp. 1–15.

The overall record of the Soviet leadership in meeting public economic expectations and goals has been mixed. Generally, industrial growth has been excellent, as has been the provision of social benefits such as health care and education. The agricultural problem, far from solved, remains the persistent weak spot in the Soviet economic picture. The cost in economic failure is high in the inefficient use of labor and in terms of the massive investment required to achieve marginal gains.

▪ NIGERIA ▪

The relationship between the performance of the Nigerian political system and the economic development of Nigeria is an important one. Government leaders are attempting to modernize the economy and to narrow the wide gap betwen the very rich and the very poor. Increasing agricultural productivity, expanding and controlling the industrial capacity of the nation, and providing more extensive social welfare services to the population are all important parts of the development process. Success in achieving these goals, however, is hampered by poorly developed communication and transportation systems within the nation and by a severe shortage of skilled manpower.

Although the development goals of Nigeria resemble those of most developing nations, the Nigerian case differs in one very important respect. The discovery and production of oil allows Nigeria to formulate and carry out many development schemes that other nations can only hope for. Today resource-rich Nigeria is one of the world's top ten oil-producing nations; however, it remains a developing nation. Oil wealth has proved to be a mixed economic blessing. While providing needed revenue for development, it creates severe economic and political problems. National leaders must attempt to achieve a balance between the rapidly rising expectations of Nigerian citizens and the need for balanced economic growth and development. Rapid economic growth has resulted in corruption, rapid industrialization and urbanization, and uneven economic development between different groups and areas. Political leaders have the serious task of managing, directing, and controlling this growth.

Economic Development—Rising Expectations and Demands

The discovery and production of oil raised economic expectations by making feasible broad, sweeping economic development plans. Nigerians increasingly hope for and demand greater economic progress and prosperity. National economic goals, summarized in a series of five-year development plans, allocate government and private sector funds based

Although Nigeria's oil wealth has dramatically modernized the economy, traditional markets continue to perform important economic functions. Marilyn Silverstone, Magnum Photos, Inc.

on overall development plans. The plan initiated in 1975 outlines both in general and specific terms the economic direction that Nigeria will take in the five-year period 1975–1980. Like the two previous plans, the Third National Development Plan seeks "economic growth and development, price stability, and social equity."[23] To achieve these goals, the plan establishes seven short-term objectives: an increase in per capita income, a more even distribution of income, a reduction in unemployment, an increase in manpower, a diversification of the economy, balanced development, and Nigerian (rather than foreign) control over the economy.[24]

Several specific areas are singled out for special attention. Among the most important are the need to improve the social welfare benefits pro-

[23] Central Planning Office, Federal Ministry of Economic Development, Nigeria, *Third National Development Plan 1975–1980* (Lagos, Nigeria: 1975), p. 33.
[24] Ibid., p. 29.

vided Nigerian citizens. Housing, health care, and, most importantly, education are allocated large shares of both the development budget and the annual budgets. The proposed changes in the Nigerian educational system exemplify the scope of development plans. In 1975 General Gowon's government announced plans to achieve Universal Primary Education (UPE) in Nigeria—all Nigerian children would have access to a primary school. Enrollment in primary schools is expected to rise from about 4.5 million in 1975 to over 11 million in 1980. This rapid expansion requires building new schools and classrooms, and an estimated 280,000 new teachers will be needed between 1976 and 1982.[25] To achieve these goals, the government has allocated about 10 percent of the funds of the Third National Development Plan to education.

A second area receiving a large share of development funds is agriculture. Although Nigeria has the potential to produce most of its domestic food needs, it has yet to do so. Inefficient farming methods, poor distribution systems, and the effects of drought conditions in the 1970s forced Nigeria to increase the amount of imported foodstuffs, the cost of which increased dramatically by 800 percent between 1970 and 1975.

To improve agricultural productivity, the government encourages the use of more mechanized farming techniques, the greater use of fertilizers, and more large-scale farming. Tax credits are awarded those who use domestic raw materials, and much of the imported farm machinery is duty-free. The development plans for agriculture involve spending about 11 percent of the plan's revenue on improving productivity. "Operation Feed the Nation" was launched in the mid-1970s with the aim of meeting all of Nigeria's domestic food needs.

A third area receiving intensive study and attention is the industrial sector. Traditionally, the industrial sector of the economy has been controlled by foreign-owned concerns. In an attempt to reverse this situation, the government has begun the process of indigenizing the economy. The first phase of the indigenization program was announced in 1972 and completed in 1974; the second phase was announced in 1977. These decrees specify certain companies and industries that must be 100 percent Nigerian-owned. Others must have at least 60 percent Nigerian ownership, while a third group must have at least 40 percent Nigerian ownership.

The Nigerian Enterprises Promotion Decree of 1977 specified that, among others, the following concerns had to be 100 percent Nigerian owned: advertising and public relations firms, cinemas, bread- and cake-making establishments, garment manufacturers, laundry and dry-cleaners, municipal bus and taxi services, radio and TV broadcasting stations, travel agencies, and poultry farms. Concerns that had to be at least 60 percent Nigerian owned included banks, beer breweries, construction industries,

---

[25] *West Africa,* 3103 (December 20, 1976), p. 1987.

insurance companies, mines and quarries, restaurants, and a wide range of manufacturing and distributions concerns.[26] Firms that fail to abide by the new rules or that attempt to circumvent them are subject to direct government action.

Nigerian leaders have chosen this approach rather than outright government nationalization in the hope of achieving a balance between the need for foreign investment and the need for Nigerians to control the Nigerian economy. In a nation critically short of trained technical manpower, foreign investment and expertise are essential components of economic development. The goals of the indigenization program are to ensure that Nigerians are represented in the industrial sector as owners and managers and, at the same time, to maintain a favorable climate for investment.

Economic Development—Resources and Expenditures

Development goals must be weighed against economic resources and expenditures. Although oil revenues provide Nigeria with new resources and development funds, they are not a panacea for all economic problems. Nigeria has yet to develop a balanced, productive economy. A disproportionate number of the work force (64 percent in 1975) were employed in the agricultural sector compared with the productivity of that sector, while only about 17 and 12 percent respectively were engaged in manufacturing/processing and distribution concerns. The mining industry, which produces most of Nigeria's revenue, employed only .4 percent of the work force.[27]

Oil is the driving force of the Nigerian economy. It provides over 90 percent of Nigeria's exports and in 1975, along with agriculture, accounted for 72 percent of all national income.[28] The amount of revenue available yearly to the government depends on the world demand and price for oil. When the world demand and price for oil was high between 1972 and 1974, Nigeria's revenues soared; when the price and demand fell in 1975, so did Nigeria's revenues.

In 1976–1977 the situation became even more complex and difficult. Not only did the production of oil decrease as a result of the lack of demand on the world market, but also the value of oil produced declined as a result in the decline in value of the U.S. dollar. Since oil purchases are made in U.S. dollars and since the United States is the largest buyer of Nigerian oil, Nigeria was especially hard-hit. Production declined from 2,300,000 barrels of oil a day in December 1976 to 1,780,000 barrels a day in December 1977.[29] At the same time that production was declining, the

---

26 *West Africa*, 3108 (January 31, 1977), p. 200.
27 Guy Arnold, *Modern Nigeria* (London: Longman, 1977), p. 72.
28 *West Africa*, 3011 (March 10, 1975), p. 275.
29 *West Africa*, 3165 (March 13, 1978), p. 491.

U.S. dollar was losing value. Estimates suggest that during the first part of 1978 Nigeria was losing approximately $300,000 per day on oil revenues due to the decline in the value of the dollar. The year before, when production was higher, Nigeria lost approximately $390,000 per day. In yearly terms this amounted to a loss of about $142 million in 1977 and $109.5 million in 1978.[30]

Besides dealing with fluctuating prices and demand, government planners must also prepare for the time when Nigeria's oil resources are depleted. Some estimates indicate that the oil reserves may last until the late 1980s, after which Nigeria can no longer depend on oil for most of its revenues. Government officials recognize their dilemma. Oil provides revenues needed for economic and social change, but the revenues are not unlimited. The 1978–1979 budget, one of the last budgets prepared under military rule, made this clear. General Obasanjo stated: "No country has yet developed in history without sacrifice either of its people or of others. . . . Development has never been a painless process."[31] At the same time, the government needed to follow a "path of fairness, justice, humaneness and service," strive for self-reliance, and "curb our expensive tastes."[32]

The strains on the Nigerian budget are great. Over 25 percent of the amount allocated in the 1977/1978 recurrent expenditure budget went to support and maintain the military establishment. These funds to the Ministry of Defense paid soldiers' salaries, built new barracks, and generally supported the military's needs. General Obasanjo made clear in his 1978–1979 budget statement that it was imperative to demobilize some of the 250,000-man military, but not until these men could be fully reintegrated into the civilian economy. In 1977 only about 12,000 men were demobilized.[33]

Given the high cost of recurrent expenditures (see Table 11–4), what the government can accomplish from year to year is limited. The economic problems described in the 1978–1979 budget were relatively clear:

shortage of essential commodities, inflation, a substantial rise in government expenditure occasioned by a determined development drive, inequitable income distribution, unsatisfactory growth in agricultural and industrial output, inordinate craving for imported luxury items, over-dependence on the oil sector from which there has lately been a declining contribution resulting in a widening disparity between government resources and commitments, and balance of payments pressure.[34]

[30] Ibid., p. 499.

[31] *West Africa,* 3169 (April 10, 1978), p. 695.

[32] Ibid., p. 696.

[33] Ibid.

[34] *West Africa,* 3170 (April 17, 1978), p. 741.

To combat this impressive catalogue of economic ills, the government hoped to accomplish the following: re-order priorities so as to make better use of limited resources, reduce government spending, diversify to lessen dependence on oil, fight inflation, re-distribute income, work

TABLE 11–4 Where the Money Goes: Allocations in the 1978–1979 Nigerian Federal Budget

Recurrent Budget Expenditures		Capital Budget Expenditures	
Education	27.8% of total	Defense	13.6% of total
Defense	21.3	Land Transport Systems	12.3
Consolidate Revenue	16.2	Mining and Quarrying	10.5
Fund Charges		Power	9.7
Nonstatutory	6.2	Manufacturing and Craft	9.4
Appropriations		General Administration	6.7
Police	4.6	Education	5.8
Works	3.3	Posts and Telecom-	5.6
Health	2.9	munications	
Information	2.2	Water Resources	4.7
Finance	1.9	Water Transport Systems	4.6
Labour	1.7	External Financial	3.9
Internal Affairs	1.6	Obligations	
Cabinet Office	1.4	Air Transport Systems	2.9
External Affairs	1.1	Town and Country	2.5
National Science and	1.0	Planning	
Technology Develop-		Housing	2.3
ment Agency			
Contingencies	1.0	Other	5.5
Economic Development	.9		100.0%
and Reconstruction			
Agriculture and Rural	.7		
Development			
Aviation	.7		
Establishments and	.6		
Service Matters			
Others (each department	2.9		
less than .5% of total			
budget)			
	100.0%		

Total Recurrent Budget Expenditures	*Total Capital Budget Allocation*
2,800,000,000 naira	5,200,000,000 naira

Source: Data from *West Africa,* 3170 (April 17, 1978), p. 743, and *West Africa,* 3169 (April 10, 1978), p. 693.
Note: Approximate 1978 exchange rate: U.S.$ 1 = .62 Nigerian naira.

toward agricultural self-sufficiency, protect local industrial production, and change the trade patterns with other nations.[35]

Economic Development and Political Performance

The achievement of the economic development plans and policies described above is influenced strongly by the performance of the political system. The political instability that has plagued Nigeria since independence works against gradual, planned, sustained economic development. Compounding this problem is the inability of leaders and participants to agree on what type of political system is best for Nigeria, as well as on what type of system will most support economic development.

Like peoples in other developing nations, Nigerians must build not only new economic and political systems but also an infrastructure to support both systems. Roads, railroads, and telephone and telegraph links connecting all parts of Nigeria are desperately needed. For example, Nigeria found itself in 1975–1976 in the unenviable position of suffering severe oil and petroleum shortages domestically, while being one of the largest oil-producing nations in the world. The major reasons were poor refining and distribution facilities within the nation. The telephone system is another example of the need for, and the current lack of, communications links in the nation. At the beginning of the period for the Third Five Year Development Plan (1975), there were only about 52,000 telephone lines in Nigeria. The plan called for 700,000 by the end of the plan period; the 1978–1979 budget scaled down the estimate and projected an increase of some 190,000 lines.[36]

As might be expected in a system where the political structures are not regularized, corruption has plagued both civilian and military regimes. Leaders of most coups and attempted coups in Nigeria justify their actions in part on the corruption of the old regime and the need to establish honesty in government. An extreme case of corruption came to light in 1975 shortly after the dismissal of General Gowon. The new government discovered that various government agencies had placed orders with foreign concerns for the delivery of 20 million tons of cement over a one-year period. Nigeria's cement needs in 1974 were 3 million tons (2 million of which were imported). At one point in October 1975 there were 350 ships loaded with cement either in or expected soon in Lagos harbor, but only four berths capable of unloading cement.[37] Among the most difficult tasks facing the Mohammed government were clearing the existing port congestion, investigating who had become rich as a result of the cement orders, and attempting to ensure that it did not happen again.

The political system in Nigeria is under severe pressure. Corruption is

---

[35] Ibid.

[36] Ibid.

[37] Colin Legum, ed., *Africa Contemporary Record, 1975–1976* (London: Rex Collings, 1976), pp. B802–803.

in some respects a symptom of this pressure. Expectations and demands of the citizenry are increasing, but the capability and resources available to political leaders to meet these needs and expectations are limited. The size of the government at both the national and state levels has increased, but overall government efficiency often remains low. A shortage of trained manpower to fill important economic, technical, and management positions compounds the problem.

Nigeria's economy is young and rapidly changing. Political leaders, whether civilian or military, face a difficult economic task. Although it may seem a contradiction, Nigeria's oil wealth has not made the task simpler. In many respects, it intensifies political conflicts and raises sharp questions about who should get what. Some leaders have referred to this situation as "want amidst plenty." One certain indicator of the future political stability will be how effectively leaders meet the challenges of economic development.

▪ EGYPT ▪

Egypt faces such staggering economic problems that it is difficult to grasp their magnitude or to envision possible solutions. The Egyptian economy is characterized by a massive foreign debt, a large defense budget, an inefficient and unproductive industrial sector, and an agricultural sector that cannot feed the nation. The rapidly growing population consumes much of the nation's economic investment. To maintain current standards of living for all Egyptians, Egypt constantly must increase production.

Compounding these problems are the rising expectations and demands of Egyptian citizens. Post-1952 leaders have sought to improve the quality of life for the average Egyptian by increasing per capita income, widening employment opportunities, providing better and more extensive social welfare benefits, and subsidizing certain consumer goods. Egyptians have come to expect and demand more from their government, but the ability of the government to satisfy these desires has not always kept pace.

Political performance in the economic arena has not been encouraging. One of the greatest threats to the stability of the political system is the inability of the leadership to resolve or manage Egypt's economic dilemma. Despite the improvements made since 1952, many commentators hold a pessimistic view of Egypt's economic future. To evaluate the political performance of the leadership in the economic sphere, we should carefully balance the significant economic gains achieved with the problems facing decision-makers.

Egypt's Economy—An Insoluble Problem?

Egypt's economic problems stem in part from the relationship between the land and the people. Simply put, the population is too large and growing too rapidly for the amount of land available to support it. At the turn of the century the population of Egypt was about 10 million; by 1972 it had grown to 35 million and by mid-1978 to 38 million. The annual rate of growth of the population during the 1960s was about 2.5 percent per year, which, if maintained, means that the population will double itself about every 25 years.

Habitable land to support and feed this population is severely limited. Only 6 percent of the land is available for cultivation, and most of it is dependent on the Nile for water. Egyptian agriculture is not unproductive—much of the land is fertile, irrigated, and highly fertilized, providing high crop yields—but the limited land must support too many people. Rural population densities vary from an average of 700 persons per kilometer to as high as 1,200 persons per kilometer.[38]

Increasing population density in rural areas, along with other factors, stimulates rapid urbanization. Egyptians are leaving their traditional, rural homes for the city at an increasing rate. Some leave in hopes of bettering their positions, others because there is little hope of advancement in their villages, and still others because the land simply cannot support them and their families. During the 1960s the urban population grew by an average of 4.6 percent a year; in 1970 about 43 percent of Egypt's population lived in urban areas.[39] Some suggest that by the year 2000 the population of Cairo, Egypt's largest city, may be between 12 and 16 million persons.[40] Many of those arriving in the cities have little education and few skills. The rapid growth in size of urban areas strains the already overtaxed public service agencies. Cairo, for example, suffers from severe housing shortages (which drive rents up) and from outmoded transportation systems. Overcrowding and a high rate of unemployment produce tensions that have important political and social consequences. The nationwide rioting in 1977 over the cost of basic foodstuffs (discussed below and in Chapter 10) was only one example of the volatile political situation.

The population explosion, rapid urbanization, and high population densities are not the only problems facing Egyptian leaders. Problems in the public sector of the economy are equally severe. Between 1973 and 1974 the number of individuals employed in the government sector grew by 10 percent, and the wages they received by 20 percent. The productivity of the public sector, however, increased by only 5 percent. One estimate suggests that fully 25 percent of the public sector work force is redundant.[41] The government policy of assuring all college graduates a

---

[38] Peter Beaumont, Gerald Blake, and J. Malcolm Wagstaff, *The Middle East: A Geographical Study* (New York: John Wiley, 1976), p. 475.

[39] Ibid., p. 474.

[40] John Waterbury, "Cairo: Third World Metropolis, Part III: Housing and Shelter," *American Universities Field Staff Reports*, Northeast Africa Series, Vol. XVIII, No. 8 (November 1973), p. 1.

[41] John Waterbury, "Public versus Private in the Egyptian Economy," *American Universities Field Staff Reports*, Northeast Africa Series, Vol. XXI, No. 5 (April 1976), p. 17.

job in this sector swells the bureaucracy but adds little to governmental efficiency.

The money allocated to support the military further siphons needed funds from development projects. To maintain the 325,000-man force requires a tremendous allocation.[42] In 1974 the military budget required 25 percent of the nation's income; in 1977 fully 40 percent of the $12 billion budget was allocated for the support and maintenance of the military. Three wars with Israel (1956, 1967, and 1973) have taken their toll on the Egyptian economy and severely hampered attempts to deal with economic problems.

Another drain on the budget comes from the need to import foodstuffs. Almost half of the Egyptian work force is employed in the agricultural sector, but this sector produces only about 25 percent of the Egyptian Gross Domestic Product. Despite the productivity of the agricultural sector, farmers cannot produce enough to meet national needs; many of the agricultural workers could be employed more profitably in other areas of the economy (see Table 11–5).

This imbalance between the work force and productivity means that Egypt must import foodstuffs. For example, in 1973 Egypt imported £E68.2 million worth of cereals and milling products. (The approximate 1978 exchange rate betwen the U.S. dollar and the Egyptian pound was $1 = £E .39.) Also imported were mineral products, machinery, electrical equipment, chemical products, and transport equipment. In return, Egypt exported such items as raw cotton, rice, mineral oils, and cotton products such as yarn and fabrics. Always, however, Egypt must import more than it exports. (For example, in 1974 Egypt imported £E325.9 million more worth of goods than its exported.)[43]

Egyptian leaders must not only import foodstuffs but also must stabilize and subsidize the cost of basic necessities of life. This is done to preserve a certain standard of living for the average Egyptian and to lessen the impact of inflation. Over $1 billion a year is spent to maintain a stable price for such staples as bread and cooking oil. Although this expenditure is socially and politically necessary, it diverts revenues from other development projects.

The Egyptian economy then is caught in a vicious cycle. Modest increases in production are quickly consumed by the ever-increasing population. Leaders call for economic modernization and social change, but the resources available to implement these changes are limited. A sluggish bureaucracy and a relatively unproductive industrial sector add to the burden.

To meet economic needs, Egypt relies heavily on foreign aid. Egypt's foreign debt is huge. Estimates suggest that in 1977 Egypt owed the Soviet Union between $11 and $12 billion (U.S. dollars). Egypt in 1975 also owed

---

[42] *Africa Contemporary Record, 1975–1976,* p. B31.
[43] Ibid., pp. B53–54.

TABLE 11–5   Distribution of the Egyptian Work Force, by Sectors and Sex, 1967–1968

	Male	Female	TOTAL
Technical and Professional Personnel	247,500	80,700	328,200
	(3.4%)	(12.5%)	(4.2%)
Directors and Managers	137,800	7,100	144,900
	(1.9%)	(1.1%)	(1.8%)
Clerks	376,500	49,200	425,700
	(5.2%)	(7.6%)	(5.4%)
Sales and Commerce	454,700	49,600	504,300
	(6.3%)	(7.7%)	(6.4%)
Agriculture	3,757,800	245,700	4,003,500
	(52.1%)	(38.1%)	(50.1%)
Mining, Quarrying	9,000	—	9,000
	(.1%)	—	(.1%)
Transport and Communications	266,600	1,800	268,400
	(3.7%)	(.2%)	(3.4%)
Industrial Labor	1,350,700	71,000	1,421,700
	(18.7%)	(11.0%)	(18.1%)
Services	510,400	121,800	632,200
	(7.0%)	(18.9%)	(8.1%)
Other	89,300	15,400	104,700
	(1.2%)	(2.4%)	(1.3%)
Indeterminate	6,600	3,300	9,900
	(.1%)	(.5%)	(.1%)
Totals	7,206,900	645,600	7,852,500
	(99.7%)	(100.0%)	(99.0%)

Source: John Waterbury, "Manpower and Population Planning in the Arab Republic of Egypt; Part III: The Burden of Dependency," *American Universities Field Staff Reports,* Northeast Africa Series, Vol. XVII, No. 3 (March 1972), p. 3. Waterbury's source is Central Agency for Public Mobilization and Statistics, *Sample Survey of the Work Force in the UAR; Results of the May 1968 Round,* Reference No. 1–222, October 1970 (in Arabic). Percentages do not appear in the original table, but they are calculated from the data. Reprinted by permission.

the United States about $456 million and West Germany $405 million.[44] This massive foreign debt, and the constant need for more aid, often forces Egypt to borrow money at higher short-term interest rates, further increasing the total debt. The president of the Nasser Bank reported: "Every 24 hours we spend £E2m. repaying accumulated loans, and the interest on them, for every £E3m. we spend on importing the basic needs of our people and our factories."[45] After several years of trouble with the Soviet Union and after the "new opening" to the West, President Sadat

---

[44] Ibid., pp. B43–44.
[45] *Africa Research Bulletin,* Vol. 14, No. 1 (February 28, 1977), p. 4161.

announced in 1977 a 10-year moratorium on Egypt's debt payments to the Soviet Union.

Significant changes have occurred in the Egyptian economy despite the rather ominous description above. The picture is not entirely bleak. Land reclamation schemes increase the amount of land available for agriculture. Advances in irrigation techniques, better use of fertilizers, and modern farming techniques also increase the yield on existing cultivable land. In the social sector Egyptians are provided with more social services than ever before. Once-common diseases are now under control, and more Egyptians have access to education and other government-provided services. In fact, one reason for the rapidly increasing population is not so much an increase in the birth rate as a sharp decline in the death rate. The life expectancy for the average Egyptian is much higher today than ever before.

Despite these significant improvements, it appears that at a time when demands are increasing, the capability of Egyptian leaders to respond to demands is not keeping pace. As a result of the 1967 war with Israel, Egypt lost two of its major sources of revenue. The Suez Canal was closed to ship passage from 1967 to 1975 with an estimated revenue loss to Egypt of at least £E4 billion and £E2 billion were lost from the Israeli-occupied oil fields located in the Sinai peninsula.[46] Although aid from the Soviet Union and other Arab states increased following the 1967 war, these contributions and loans did not approach the amount of revenue lost.

The approaches of Nasser and Sadat to Egypt's economic problems are different. President Nasser during the 1960s nationalized much of the economy, centralized economic planning and control, and turned to the Soviet Union for military and nonmilitary assistance. The stated goal was the creation of a socialist state. The first Ten Year Plan (1960–1970) aimed at raising the per capita income, building a strong and productive industrial sector, and increasing agricultural efficiency (while implementing land reform programs).

The second Ten Year Development Plan was begun in 1973. The goals were similar to those of the first plan, but leaders emphasize different means of achieving them. President Sadat turned from the Soviet Union to the United States and other Western and Arab nations in 1973. This economic and political "opening" is designed to encourage Western and Arab investment in Egypt and to lessen the dependence of Egypt on the Soviet Union. As Sayyid Marei, the president of the People's Assembly in 1975, put it: "Arab Capital + Western technology + Egyptian labor and markets — the population explosion = economic growth."[47] Potential

---

[46] John Waterbury, "The Opening, Part I: Egypt's Economic New Look," *American Universities Field Staff Reports,* Northeast Africa Series, Vol. XX, No. 2 (February 1975), p. 3.

[47] Cited in John Waterbury, "The Opening, Part II: Luring Foreign Capital," *American Universities Field Staff Reports,* Northeast Africa Series, Vol. XX, No. 3 (June 1975), p. 1.

investors are awarded tax incentives and given assurances that their invest-ments will be safe from nationalization. The emphasis is less on state con-trol and direction and more on private sector investment in development projects.

The Egyptian Economy and Political Performance

The magnitude of the economic problems and the limited number of op-tions open to Egyptian leaders were made clear in January 1977. Since 1952 the Egyptian government has subsidized certain basic foodstuffs that form the core of the average Egyptian's diet. Subsidies maintain the price to the consumer of goods such as bread, cigarettes, and tea at artificially low, stable prices. Potential overseas donors in 1977 made their assistance to Egypt contingent on the removal of these subsidies. This would have resulted in a sharp increase to the consumer, but, at the same time, a sharp decrease in government spending.

When the government announced the decision to cut subsidies by half—raising the price of some commodities by as much as 50 percent—Egyptians responded with the worst rioting in over 25 years. To restore order, President Sadat rescinded the decree but retained the basic 10 per-cent increase in wages announced at the same time that the subsidy deci-sion was announced. (This further fired inflation.) Popular discontent in this case clearly influenced government policy and limited the freedom of action of government leaders.

Governmental performance also is affected by bureaucratic perfor-mance. The Egyptian bureaucracy (described in Chapter 8) has grown to such a size that it is often impossible for political leaders to exercise con-trol over it. The bureaucracy (to echo complaints heard in most nations) takes on an independent life. Lines of authority and responsibility are not defined clearly; and, once policies are made, the overstaffed bureaucracy has difficulty carrying the decision out efficiently. Competition between various branches of government makes detailed, long-term planning a difficult task.

Corruption often grows out of this type of situation. While the "open door" investment policy of President Sadat has increased private invest-ment in Egypt, a common complaint heard is that the new investment turns a quick profit for the investor but does little for the Egyptian. Many of the less profitable, and hence less attractive, areas necessary for economic development are slighted. The fact that many of these concerns, such as the steel industry, are unproductive and inefficient makes investment even less attractive.

There are no easy solutions to Egypt's economic problems. The Egyptian economy does not have the ability to produce enough income to meet the needs of the population. It must import both foodstuffs and the tech-nology needed for industrial growth. Better and more widely distributed health care will continue to drive the death rate down and the population up. One answer obviously is to establish effective means of lowering the rate of population growth. Recent indications are that the birth rate is in fact declining, but a truly effective program must be a long-term one. This requires in part a massive program to educate Egyptians on the merits of smaller families. The results of these programs, while important and significant, are not likely to be dramatic in the short run.

Foreign assistance, although important, is not a solution to the economic dilemma. The 1977 riots indicate that popular public opinion in Egypt can have a significant effect on decision-makers. What may make good economic sense may be politically impossible. Domestic political constraints severely limit economic freedom of action.

The inefficiency of the bureaucracy and the drain on the budget by the need to maintain a large military force also hamper Egyptian decision-makers in their attempts to transform the economy. Much of Egypt's budget allocations go to support sectors of the economy that consume but do not produce revenue. President Sadat's peace overtures to Israel partially stem from the hope that without war Egypt can divert funds from the military to more productive development projects.

The standard of living of the Egyptian citizen has increased in significant ways since 1952. Economic development, however, requires balanced growth. Leaders must make hard decisions concerning how the limited resources are allocated. The sluggish performance of the bureaucracy, the debilitating impact of corruption, increasing citizen demands and expectations, and the rapid population growth present Egyptian leaders with their most serious challenges and threats.

▪ TANZANIA ▪

According to United Nations' criteria, Tanzania is one of the 25 poorest nations in the world. Unlike oil-rich Nigeria, Tanzania is resource-poor. Although Tanzanian leaders emphasize the need for self-reliance, to meet many of its needs Tanzania must seek foreign aid. The rapidly rising world prices of the foodstuffs, heavy machinery, and oil that Tanzania must import place an added burden on Tanzanian leaders.

These and other conditions limit the options open to TANU and government leaders in their attempts to improve the economic situation. Since the mid-1960s Tanzanians have sought to maximize their limited resources and to minimize their dependence on other nations. Government and party policies stress the importance of agricultural development before beginning the industrialization process. President Nyerere states that the land and the people are Tanzania's greatest resources. These assests can be put to best use first in the agricultural sector. Although much of the financing and expertise necessary for economic development is provided by foreign aid, Tanzanian leaders attempt to steer a nonaligned course by accepting aid from many different nations with differing political perspectives.

Tanzania's important experiment in economic development has its severe critics and its enthusiastic supporters. Many commentators suggest that the Tanzanian experience can serve as a model for other resource-poor, developing nations. Because of this, we should make a careful assessment of the goals of the political leadership in the economic arena and of their performance in achieving their goals.

Tanzania's Economy—Resources and Goals

Tanzanian economic goals and plans are determined in part by the nation's resources or, more correctly, lack of resources. Tanzania is largely a rural nation; only about 10 percent of the population live in urban areas. The capital city Dar es Salaam, is small by most capital city standards, having a population of only about 300,000.

Prior to the 1960s, the rural population was widely scattered on the borders of the nation. Families and small groups lived in compounds rather than in rural towns and villages. Patterns of rural settlement worked against the development of a productive agricultural sector and the use of more modern farming techniques. Periods of climatic uncertainty, like the 1972–1974 rains, further aggravated agricultural problems.

The weak agricultural sector is not balanced by a strong industrial sector. There are few heavy industries in Tanzania, and little investment capital is available for expansion. Many of the smaller industries are poorly managed, unable to compete with larger foreign concerns. Lack of investment capital and of skilled manpower makes industrial development difficult.

In meeting economic needs, Tanzania finds itself in the unenviable position of having to import goods whose world market value is dramatically increasing while exporting goods whose value is declining. Foodstuffs, livestock, petroleum and other energy fuels, and many raw materials must be imported. In return, Tanzania exports coffee (whose world market value has been high in the late 1970s), cotton, cashew nuts, and sisal (a natural fiber used in making rope).

The Third Five Year Development Plan initiated in 1976 outlines the government's economic hopes. It seeks to raise the national income by about 6 percent annually by increasing agricultural and industrial productivity. Increased national income will be expended to raise the per capita income and standard of living of all Tanzanians, and to augment the social services that the government provides.

Allocations under the plan indicate the emphasis that party leaders place on agriculture and industry. About 27 percent of the total allocation is to be spent on industrial development; 15 percent to developing agriculture. Other areas given priority attention are the expansion of water and energy supplies, the improvement of transportation and communications systems within the nation, and the development of a more efficient administration.[48]

A central concern of decision-makers in Tanzania, besides the improvement of agricultural productivity, is the creation of an industrial sector that supports and complements an efficient agricultural economy. At present, agriculture produces about 40 percent of the Gross Domestic Product and about 80 percent of Tanzania's exports.[49]

The Arusha Declaration issued in 1967 is the keystone document in recent Tanzanian political and economic history. It clearly states the goals of the party and government: "TANU is involved in a war against poverty and oppression in our country; this struggle is aimed at moving the people of Tanzania . . . from a state of poverty to a state of prosperity."[50] Socialism, adapted to and influenced by African traditions and modified to fit the rural environment, is the method. Eventually, ujamaa ("familyhood") villages should be self-sufficient and self-governing, with local leaders making decisions on local issues with a minimum of interference from the national government.

New rural villages, limited in size to several hundred families, consolidate rural settlements. Agriculturally, the ujamaa village schemes are designed to increase productivity by increasing the size of farm plots. Members of the village are expected to provide three days of work on the large communal plots belonging to the village. In addition, they are provided small individual plots of two or three acres for their own use. The locally elected village council makes the decisions on what village crops are grown; decisions about what is grown on individual plots are made by each family.

Politically and socially, ujamaa villages are designed to allow for local control and improved social benefits. Leaders argue that only through consolidation can greater benefits be conferred on more Tanzanians. Wider access to educational facilities, better health care, and greater access to pure running water are economically feasible only in rural villages.

Since the mid-1970s industrial development and investment have received more government attention. The ujamaa village plan has not been abandoned, but decision-makers now stress the need to achieve a better balance between agricultural and industrial growth. The dramatic rise in the cost of certain imports, such as heavy machinery and oil, means that Tanzania cannot afford to rely solely on imports for its industrial needs.

Financing for development plans and the annual budget is achieved from domestic sources and foreign assistance. Tanzania receives about

---

[48] *Africa Research Bulletin,* Vol. 14, No. 4 (May 30, 1977), p. 4272.
[49] Ibid.
[50] Julius Nyerere, *Freedom and Socialism* (London: Oxford University Press, 1968), p. 235.

President Julius Nyerere breaks ground at a new ujamaa village. Keystone Press.

$300 million a year in foreign aid and loans. This sum accounts for approximately 80 percent of the general development budget.[51] Such diverse nations as the United States, the Soviet Union, Sweden, Cuba, Norway, West and East Germany, Israel, and the People's Republic of China, as well as the World Bank, provide assistance to Tanzania.

Political Performance—The Critical Variable

From 1963 to 1966 the government supported a voluntary "villagization" scheme. Rural families were encouraged to move to rural towns and change their traditional patterns of farming. By all accounts, the voluntary plan failed. The scheme was poorly planned and inefficiently executed, and many rural Tanzanians were unclear about the advantages of moving to the villages. Some expected too much too soon, while others felt their traditional way of life threatened. The government, by its own admission, provided little encouragement or explanation.

Following the Arusha Declaration, the party and government moved from voluntary to compulsory villagization. Since 1973 rural families have

---

[51] *Wall Street Journal,* August 5, 1977, p. 30.

been required to move to new cooperative villages. TANU and government officials attempt to politicize the rural population by stressing the economic, social, and political benefits of the program. Government planning and execution also has been much more comprehensive in the compulsory period. In one district, 340,000 Tanzanians were moved into 149 villages in a one-month period in 1974.[52] District leaders claimed that no individuals were moved farther than five miles from their previous home. By 1977, there were some 9,000 planned villages in Tanzania, with a total population of about 9 million.

Chamwino, a model ujamaa village and one of the most developed and productive, has a population of 664 families. Political power in the village rests with a 25-member council that makes decisions concerning what crops are grown and how they will be disposed of. The village has a school, a clinic, electricity, and a church. Cash crops are grown in the communal fields, and many of the families use their small (two or three acres) personal plots to grow food for their own use or for sale.[53]

Not all villages are as fortunate or well provided for as the model village of Chamwino. The villagization program has both its successes and failures. On the success side, over 4 million adult Tanzanians were enrolled in adult education classes in 1975. Other benefits of rural village life include purer drinking water and more readily accessible health care services. The average number of visits to a clinic by rural Tanzanians, to cite only one example, increased to three per year in 1975.[54]

Perhaps most disappointing is the fact that agricultural production has not increased as much as initially hoped for. Although the use of fertilizers, irrigation, and crop management techniques have increased productivity, overall productivity remains low. Also, many Tanzanians have resisted their move to cooperative villages. Some attempt to return to their more isolated, scattered settlements while others move to the city. Although the government forcibly removes large numbers of those who flock to urban areas, many quickly find ways to return.

The effectiveness of the villagization schemes is influenced by certain values held by the political leaders. Their emphasis on the need for villages to run themselves with a minimum of central government interference makes national coordination and planning difficult. There often is a tension between local village leaders and the representatives of the government and party. Local leaders accuse national and regional officials of interference and of not understanding the problems of the local area, while national and regional officials argue that local control often means inefficient implementation of national objectives.

In the industrial sector, the government recently has focused on the need to improve both the diversity and productivity of Tanzanian industry.

---

[52] Juma Mwapachu, "Operation Planned Villages in Rural Tanzania: A Revolutionary Strategy for Development," *African Review*, Vol. 6, No. 1 (1976), pp. 1–16.

[53] *New York Times*, January 27, 1977, p. 2.

[54] *Africa Contemporary Record, 1975–1976*, pp. B336–37.

Economic leaders stress the need to increase imports of industrial goods and raw materials to provide support for agricultural growth. At the same time, they seek to increase the size of the industrial sector to lessen reliance on imports. Limited foreign investment is encouraged as long as the government maintains at least majority control. Improving the efficiency and quality of management personnel is crucial to the Third Five Year Plan.

Any evaluation of the Tanzanian economic experiment must include both its successes and its failures. The development of ujamaa villages provides more Tanzanians with better and more extensive welfare services. More and more Tanzanian adults and children receive educations and have access to medical care. The application of modern farming techniques in these villages increases cotton, tobacco, and cashew nut production. On the minus side, agricultural production has not increased as rapidly as hoped, and Tanzania continues to rely on imports. Both industry and agriculture are plagued by poor management and inefficiency, while coordination between government policy and government action is often uneven. Tanzania, like most developing nations, suffers a shortage of trained manpower that forces the nation to depend on foreign expertise.

To sum up, Tanzanian leaders are attempting to change not only the economic structure of the nation but also the economic and political values of the population. Their success or failure is difficult to judge in so short a period of time. The relationship between agriculture and industry is fluid. The recent encouragement of foreign investment indicates a new emphasis on industry, but agriculture remains the number one priority. A unique characteristic of the Tanzanian experiment is that leaders—from the president to local village heads—are willing to admit to mistakes. Economic development in Tanzania remains a process of trial and error.

▪ CHILE ▪

All Chilean political leaders must face a bewildering array of economic problems. No political leader, party, or faction has been able to provide a long-term solution to Chile's economic woes. In the past, popularly elected governments watched their popularity decline as economic problems mounted.

The range of political solutions to economic problems has narrowed considerably since 1970, when two mutually hostile camps struggled for power. From 1970 to 1973 the supporters and followers of President Salvadore Allende implemented a series of sweeping economic and political reforms designed to transform Chile into a socialist state. As the first elected Marxist president of a Latin American nation, Salvadore Allende proposed a "Chilean road to socialism," but this ended in violence. Since 1973 the military junta has reversed and revoked almost all of the policies and laws of the three-year Allende presidency. They have restored many of the pre-1970 economic conditions and policies.

Although attempted solutions to Chile's economic problems vary, the problems themselves remain remarkably constant. The chronically high rate of inflation influences all political decisions. Inflation rates that would bring down many governments in Europe, for example, are considered normal and manageable in Chile. Achieving an annual rate of inflation in Chile of 80 percent in the late 1970s was considered by many to be a hopeful sign of economic recovery!

A second economic problem is Chile's dependence on copper for much of its foreign earnings. Almost 80 percent of Chile's total export trade comes from copper. Foreign exchange and foreign currency reserves in Chile, as well as the balance of trade, are dependent on the export of copper. A sharp decline in the world price of copper, such as occurred in 1972, may produce dramatic political and economic changes.

Chile's agricultural sector is a third problem. As in other developing nations, agriculture in Chile tends to be inefficient and unproductive. Paying for necessary imported foodstuffs depletes Chile's foreign reserves and diverts revenue from needed development projects to nonproductive expenditures. The inability to resolve the issues surrounding land reform further aggravates the agricultural problem.

These problems, and others, faced the Allende government and now face Pinochet's military government; the responses of the two governments to these economic problems differ. The economic and political transformation of Chile prior to 1970 set the stage for the conflict. Urbanization, industrialization, increasing educational opportunities, and growing revenues from the copper industry created a modern, complex economy. In the political sphere, power shifted from the upper to the middle to the lower classes. Political parties represented different groups with vastly different economic and political interests and expectations. Reform, not revolution, was the goal of most parties.

By the late 1960s and 1970s, however, the situation was more volatile. The changes begun in 1970 and ended in 1973 were revolutionary, and the responses of the military to these changes were equally sharp and dramatic. In the first case, government intervention in the economy increased, and plans were laid for the redistribution of wealth. In the second case, the government, representing those disenchanted with the Allende government, sought to end government's economic control and to restore the status quo. In perhaps no other nation in our study is the relationship between political performance and economic conditions clearer than in Chile from 1970 to the present.

Economic Policy and Political Performance During the Allende Presidency

The election of Salvadore Allende signaled a dramatic change in Chilean economic policy. Unlike past presidents, who wanted merely to reform the Chilean economy, President Allende and his supporters in the Popular Unity coalition wanted to revolutionize it. The opening statement of the Popular Unity manifesto was clear and unequivocal:

The central objective of the united popular forces is to replace the current economic structure ending the power of national and foreign monopoly capitalists and large landowners, in order to initiate the construction of socialism.[55]

Central to success in achieving these goals was the redistribution of wealth and political power—from the traditional holders, the upper and middle classes, to the lower, working classes. These were the rural and urban groups that gave Allende his electoral victory and whose expectations and demands the president needed to meet.

Sweeping changes were proposed and introduced almost immediately after President Allende assumed office. With congressional approval, the American-owned copper industries were nationalized. Over 90 other firms were scheduled for quick nationalization. In rural areas, a broad agrarian reform policy was initiated. The large landed estates were marked for breaking up and redistribution to those who previously did not own land. The government also assumed the major responsibility for planning, directing, and controlling the economy.

In addition, the wages of Chileans were increased at the same time that price controls on many consumer goods were introduced. This stimulated a demand for goods and increased production, as well as a decrease in unemployment. During 1971 more Chileans had more money to buy more goods whose prices were controlled; it appeared that Chile was undergoing a rapid economic boom.

Despite the apparent short-term success of the government's economic policy, there was serious opposition to Allende's programs. The Christian Democratic party and the National party controlled Congress, which they used as a focal point for the growing opposition. For example, although the nationalization of the copper industry was popularly received in Congress, many legislators were unwilling to support the wholesale nationalization of other industries. Congress, in general, supported and represented the political center and right, those groups who had the most to fear and to lose from rapid change. The increasingly sharp tension between the legislative and executive branches led Allende to use extra-legislative means to initiate and implement his policies.

Small-business owners and professional groups also opposed the Allende government. Periodic strikes during 1972 and 1973 by shopkeepers and small businessmen adversely effected the economy. Groups such as the independent truck owners feared government takeover or

---

[55] Barbara Stallings and Andy Zimbalist, "The Political Economy of the Unidad Popular," *Latin American Perspectives*, Vol. II, No. 1 (Spring 1975), p. 70.

massive government intervention in their concerns. A strike by truck owners and drivers was crippling to a nation dependent on trucks for the internal movement and distribution of goods.

As shortages of basic consumer goods became more severe and the lines grew longer, many middle and upper class women began to protest actively. A "march of the empty pots" in 1971, focusing attention on the deteriorating economic situation and the dissatisfaction of many groups with Allende, provoked some street violence.[56]

Foreign governments were a third source of opposition to the government. The United States opposed the new regime for several reasons. First, the U.S. government opposed the nationalization, without mutually agreed upon compensation, of the American-owned copper industries. Second, there was strong pressure on U.S. officials to protect the Chilean interests of powerful multinational corporations such as International Telephone and Telegraph. Third, there was a fear among many in the United States that a close relationship between socialist Chile and Fidel Castro's Cuba would endanger Latin American security. Some argued that the "Chilean road to socialism" might serve as a model for other Latin American nations. United States opposition to the Allende government took both economic and political forms. In the economic sphere, international and bilateral economic and investment aid was withheld. Politically, the U.S. government covertly supported and encouraged opposition groups to the Allende government.

The economic boom of 1971 soured in 1972, becoming a disaster in 1973 (see Table 11–6). The price of copper fell from $66 per ton in 1969 to about $48 per ton in 1972, reducing Chile's foreign earnings and depleting Chile's foreign reserves. Currency reserves dropped from $370 million in 1970 to $32 million in 1971. At the same time, the cost of importing food rose from $178 million in 1970 to $444 million in 1972. (All figures are in U.S. dollars.)

The most dramatic indicator of the economic crisis was the astronomical rate of inflation. Annual inflation rates varied between 300 and 400 percent during 1972 and 1973, and in some periods rose at an equivalent rate of 1,000 percent per year! A flourishing black market developed as the value of the Chilean *escudo* dropped and shortages of consumer goods increased.

The economic crisis created a political crisis that, in turn, exacerbated the economic crisis. Factions within the Popular Unity coalition were unable to agree on specific solutions to the economic problems, while the opposition forces increasingly agreed among themselves that extra-constitutional actions against the Allende government were necessary. The general strike (begun by independent truck owners and supported

---

[56] Ian Roxborough, Philip O'Brien, and Jackie Roddick, *Chile: The State and Revolution* (New York: Holmes & Meier, 1977), p. 115.

TABLE 11–6   Chile's Deteriorating Economic Condition, 1970–1973: Selected Economic Indicators

	1970	1971	1972	1973
Cost of Living Index in Santiago (Base = 100 in December 1969)	—	164.8	434.1	1271.1 (Sept.) 2640.0 (Dec.)
Percent Change in Cost of Living Index (from previous year)	—	22.1	163.4	192.8 (Sept.) 508.1 (Dec.)
Balance of Trade (in millions of U.S. dollars)	138.7	−110.4	−497.8	−318.7
Balance of Payment (in millions of U.S. dollars)	91.1	−303.5	−318.9	−253.2
International Reserves (in millions of U.S. dollars)	322.2	34.3	−293.6	n.a.

Source: Data from Ian Roxborough, Philip O'Brien, and Jackie Roddick, *Chile: The State and Revolution* (New York: Holmes & Meier, 1977), pp. 147, 156, 157.
Note: Approximate 1978 exchange rate: U.S. $1 = 30.22 Chilean escudos.

by large numbers of professional and merchant groups) in October 1972 ended only after the military agreed to enter the government and act as a moderating force. Chile was polarized between ardent supporters of the government and those who were just as ardently opposed to it. By the end of 1972 there was no middle position and little room for compromise.

The indecisive congressional elections of 1973 did not clarify the situation. The Christian Democratic party and the National party hoped for a victory that would give them the necessary two-thirds votes to impeach President Allende. The Popular Unity coalition hoped for a victory that would increase their congressional support and lessen the power of the opposition to frustrate their proposed policies. Although the Popular Unity coalition did improve their election showing, no faction could claim a large victory (see Chapter 6). What resulted was a deadlock and unbreachable division between the executive and the legislative branches. In September 1973 the military resolved the dilemma.

Economic Policy and Political Performance During the Military Junta

Military leaders have attempted to restore many aspects of the old economic order that existed prior to 1970. Much of the legislation passed during the Allende period has been repealed, and new economic criteria are used in establishing policy. Among the first steps taken by the new

The Chilean government depends on revenues produced by the sale of copper. These open pit copper mines are located in northern Chile. Foto du Monde, The Picture Cube.

regime were the denationalization of most firms and companies that were nationalized between 1970 and 1973. (The important copper industries, however, remained under government control and direction.) High import taxes have been lowered to encourage foreign imports, and foreign companies and multinational corporations are encouraged to invest or reinvest in Chile. Much of the land reform initiated between 1970 and 1973 has been reversed. General Pinochet stated that the goal of the regime was "not to make Chile a nation of proletarians, but a nation of entrepreneurs."[57] To this end, the military junta has lessened government control and intervention in economic affairs.

Chile's chronically high rate of inflation is one of the most pressing problems facing the military government. Early in its rule, the new government created a recessionary situation by lowering demand: government spending was cut drastically, price controls on most goods were lifted, and wage increases were limited. As a result, the purchasing power of the average Chilean decreased.

Despite these measures, inflation continued at a high rate following the coup. The annual rate of inflation in 1975 was 340 percent. In April

---

[57] Michael Moffitt, "Chicago Economics in Chile," *Challenge*, Vol. 20, No. 4 (S/O 1977), p. 35.

1975 the government took more drastic action to change the direction of the economy. A series of measures collectively known as the "shock treatment" were introduced. Government spending was cut by 20 percent, and government capital spending reduced by more than 50 percent. The Gross Domestic Product and industrial production decreased, while unemployment increased. For example, cement sales decreased by 40 percent following the April decisions, and general auto production in Chile decreased from a yearly output of 23,000 autos to 6,000. One auto manufacturer reported that it sold only 14 cars out of 1,200 produced in one month.[58] Unemployment in urban areas like Santiago rose to over 20 percent.

These measures most affected Chile's lower and middle classes, who had less money to purchase goods, which cost more. Many small businesses, never very efficient, were unable to compete with imported goods and went bankrupt. General Pinochet argued that while these policies did create a hardship, a short-term hardship was better than a long-term one. According to military leaders, the nature of the economic crisis and the necessity for decisive action left no other options.

Allende and the Junta—A Comparison of Political Performance

Any comparison of the political performance of the two regimes must take into consideration several factors. President Allende began his term in office as a minority president faced with strong congressional opposition. He also began with a clear, but general, set of economic and political goals for transforming Chile into a socialist state. But, even within his governing Popular Unity coalition, factions disagreed on specific priorities and on how fast the changes should be implemented.

Allende was never able to control, moderate, or eliminate those who opposed him. He operated within constitutional restraints that limited his freedom of action. As the economic situation began to deteriorate in 1972, so did the political situation. Strong opposition came from Congress, business and professional groups, and the United States. The economic crisis bred a political crisis that made economic solutions more difficult. President Allende lacked authority to quell the opposition or to solve the problems.

The military junta has created a vastly different political system. General Pinochet and his supporters control the coercive apparatus of the nation. Opposition political parties and leaders (as well as opposition ideas) are put down. Under fewer political constraints, the government has a freer hand in initiating and enforcing economic decisions.

Chile's experiments with different economic systems during the 1970s have been traumatic. From 1970 to 1973 Salvadore Allende attempted to

---

[58] *Wall Street Journal,* November 4, 1975, p. 1.

create an economic system based on socialism; since 1973 the military leaders have attempted to restore the pre-1970 economic system and erase all traces of Allende's experiments. Neither faction or position can claim to have found the certain answer to Chile's economic problems. One frustrated Chilean commented shortly after losing his job:

Why are we always a laboratory? We are a country for rent, complete with people, so that academics and fanatics from all over the world can come to try out their theories on us. The trouble is nothing ever works.[59]

The close relationship between economic and political performance is certainly one of the reasons that "theories" never appear to "work."

CONCLUSION

A central theme throughout the entire text has been the distinction between the developed and the developing nations of the world. Nowhere is the distinction quite so clear and important as in the comparison of the economic goals, expectations, policies, and performance of our eight nations. In fact, when most people distinguish between the developed and the developing nations, they are concerned primarily with economic considerations. One of the most crucial tests that faces all political leaders is their performance in the economic arena.

The nations in our study vary on three major dimensions—expectations and demands, resources, and performance. Not all nations face the same economic problems and dilemmas, nor is one solution necessarily applicable to all cases. As the case studies indicate, the relationship between expectations, resources, and performance often determines the fate of political leaders and, in some cases, the political system itself.

France, West Germany, and the United Kingdom have developed a consensus concerning what they expect. In each of these nations, for example, there is a relatively stable, comprehensive set of social welfare services that citizens expect to receive. While political leaders and parties may disagree on how best to meet these expectations, there is general agreement throughout society on the need for the services themselves. The governments of these three nations have been relatively successful in their attempts to satisfy their citizens' demands.

The case of the Soviet Union is considerably different. The consensus concerning demands and expectations is forced to the extent that the government and the party determine priorities with little input from the citizenry. This allows the Soviet leadership to emphasize industrialization

---

[59] Ibid.

at the expense of increased consumer goods production. Both expectations and demands are carefully controlled in the Soviet Union.

A much more common pattern throughout the world centers on constantly rising expectations. Individuals in changing societies expect and demand that their government produce more goods, provide more services, and raise the standard of living for the average citizen. In some nations the government leaders support increased expectations by promising their people more. Nigeria, Egypt, Tanzania, and Chile all can be characterized as nations in which the expectations of the citizenry have increased in the recent past.

Governments must react to these expectations and demands. In the European nations the governments have been fairly effective in satisfying their populations. In the Soviet Union the government and party leaders attempt to satisfy some demands and to control others. In developing nations, leaders try to satisfy increasing expectations. What often makes the difference between satisfying demands and not satisfying demands are the resources available to political leaders.

Britain, West Germany, France, the Soviet Union, and, to a lesser extent, Nigeria have the capability to meet many of the needs of their populations. European economies developed over time. Thus, although Germany was totally defeated in World War II, and although the French and British industrial sectors are antiquated, these nations do have a base on which to build. The Soviet Union also has transformed its largely agricultural economy into an industrial giant; in this case, the rapid transformation was accomplished at great expense to individual rights.

Nigeria and Chile provide still another resource pattern. Both are resource-rich, underdeveloped nations. Oil in Nigeria and copper in Chile provide the potential for economic growth but have not yet solved all of the problems of economic growth and development. These nations suffer from shortages of skilled manpower, unproductive agricultural sectors, inefficient industrial capabilities, and poorly developed communication and transportation systems.

Tanzania and Egypt are in much more precarious situations. In comparison to the other nations, these nations are resource-poor. They must attempt economic modernization and development without mineral wealth and without the economic bases of the European nations. Tanzania and Egypt are attempting to transform their economic and social systems in an uncertain political climate. Both nations are forced to rely on foreign assistance and imports to meet many of the needs of their people.

Finally, political systems differ in their overall performance. Relatively stable goals and manageable expectations, coupled with regularized political institutions, make efficient performance more likely, but not assured. The British, for example, face severe problems and challenges to government authority in Northern Ireland. The Soviet leadership, despite their political power, do not always manage to control and plan their economy in the most effective and productive way.

Performance problems most bedevil developing political systems. Economic and political change often produce conflicts that the political system is unable to respond to. Political instability is usually the result, which, in turn, makes economic development more difficult. The 1973 coup in Chile, the 1977 riots in Egypt, and the numerous attempted coups in Nigeria are examples of the relationship between economic performance and political stability. Tanzania, partly because of the widespread legitimacy of President Nyerere, has been fortunate to remain relatively free of political instability since independence.

This chapter, and the economic data provided in the appendixes, provide a strong data base for comparing different political systems. Each nation in the study has special problems that it must try to solve. Understanding the relationship between economic problems and possible political and economic solutions is crucial to understanding the complex operation of political systems. Leaders operate within limits; rarely is their power to influence economic situations or crises unlimited. What is clear is that no nation, whatever the stage of economic or political development, is immune from problems associated with political performance.

CHAPTER 12
ACHIEVEMENTS, GOALS, AND PROBLEMS

Can we predict the future by
understanding today's problems?

The previous eleven chapters point out the similarities and the differences among eight nations. Four of these nations—the United Kingdom, West Germany, France, and the Soviet Union—are considered developed nations. Four others—Nigeria, Egypt, Tanzania, and Chile—are considered developing nations.

Chapters 2 through 6 describe each nation's historical and cultural traditions and how they affect political life. Chapters 7 through 10 describe the political structures responsible for making, implementing, and enforcing decisions, and the institutions that resolve or moderate conflict. Finally, in Chapter 11, the performance of the political actors and political systems is analyzed.

In summary, we return to those factors and forces that most influence the politics in each of the eight nations. Political actors must allocate and distribute goods and services, provide public order, resolve conflicts between different groups and interests, and meet and/or control the expectations and demands of the citizenry. What differs is the manner in which these tasks are performed and the emphasis that political actors place on these various tasks. Whatever the emphasis, no nation is immune from challenges, problems, and potential crises.

Nations have historical and cultural traditions that establish the setting in which the game of politics is played. These traditions help establish the outer limits of what is acceptable political behavior. The United Kingdom, with its long and tradition-laden history, is a good example of a nation in which history influences modern-day politics. The highly institutionalized rules of the game are accepted by a large percentage of both political leaders and citizens. Other nations, like West Germany, have had to develop new traditions and practices. Since the end of World War II, Germans have sought to develop political mechanisms to support the maintenance of a democratic polity.

Another important factor that helps to explain politics is the nation's pattern of group life. The cleavages dividing and separating the population may be political, religious, linguistic, ethnic, economic, or regional. How important these cleavages are to politics varies over time and from situation to situation. Economic and class distinctions in Chile, for example, became increasingly important during the 1960s and 1970s. Ethnic and religious differences in Nigeria, perhaps the most cleavage-ridden nation in our study, helped to cause a civil war.

The political structures in each nation are designed to respond to the problems that face all nations and to meet the unique problems of the specific nation. In developing nations, leaders often place an emphasis on mobilizing the population to achieve economic development and political modernization. The political institutions of developing nations reflect these goals. In Tanzania, one political party is responsible for preserving national unity and mobilizing the population. In Egypt, President Nasser created a highly personalized system that had both civilian and military participation. Nigeria and Chile, both governed by soldiers, enlist civilian support from the bureaucracy to help implement their decisions.

The Soviet Union is, in many respects, a case unto itself. The domination of the Communist party in almost all aspects of life—and the degree of control that the party and government exercise—is unrivaled in any of the other nations in our study. The goal of the party and state is the creation of a new order based on the principles of Marx and Lenin. Accomplishing this requires, according to Soviet policy, the combined efforts of all Soviet citizens and the concentration of political power in the hands of a relatively small party elite.

The United Kingdom, France, and West Germany represent nations with different democratic traditions. Although each may be classed as a democratic system, their political structures differ according to their historical traditions, cultures, and political values. In France the political crises of the parliamentary Fourth Republic led to the creation of the more presidential Fifth Republic. The dominance of the House of Commons and the powerful rule of the prime minister and his cabinet in the British parliamentary system evolved over several hundred years. The West German political system was designed, in part, to ensure that the totalitarianism of Hitler could never occur again.

Political actors do not operate in a vacuum. They must take account of the cultural and historical traditions of the nation, the interests and demands of various groups, the limits and checks on their power, their ability to enforce decisions once made, and the implications of those decisions. Economic, social, and cultural changes produce new demands and interests that require political actors to make decisions; in turn, political decisions produce economic, social, and cultural changes. To understand the politics and political life of any nation requires that we look not only at the political structure of the nation but also at the arena in which the game of politics is played.

▪ THE UNITED KINGDOM ▪

The British political system has performed very well through most of the modern era—serving as a model for other nation-states. This exemplary record stems from a "fortunate" pattern of political development. The historical development of the United Kingdom permitted widespread consensus with regard to political attitudes and values; it also helped to build strong, flexible institutions that are considered legitimate by most Britons.

Despite Britain's "happy history," the current British political leaders and institutions face difficult problems. The nationality problem represents a flaw in British political development. In addition, the current economic difficulties threaten to erode the public support typically enjoyed by British political institutions.

History and Political Culture

Britain's historical development followed an almost ideal pattern. Major stages or crises of modernization and development were passed through over a 900-year period. Major issues and controversies were settled one at a time, and considerable time elapsed between the crisis periods. At the critical periods of change, group conflict was minimal.

The period of nation-building—or the development of a sense of nationality—occurred early for the English national group. William I (1066–1087) introduced a homogeneous social and economic system based on the Continental European pattern. William's social system reduced group differences with regard to language, customs, and life experiences. The English began to see themselves as a distinct people, unique and set apart from other inhabitants of the British Isles.

Later monarchs concentrated on building strong, efficient national institutions. Monarchs came to rely on Parliament to proclaim and publicize their laws, to declare new taxes, and to gain political support for other actions of the Crown. The development of courts followed a similar pattern. Monarchs initially used courts to raise revenue by collecting fees for the dispensing of Crown justice. Later, the courts and the legal system developed as an independent authority.

The pressure of modern governmental business eventually forced the development of more specialized governmental institutions. By the end of the Tudor period (1485–1603), the British monarchs were relying on simple bureaucratic administrative institutions. Each unit was assigned a specific task or function so that specialized expertise could be brought to bear on each type of governmental business.

In the 500 or 600 years after William I, the English had established a firm sense of national feeling and had evolved political institutions that could act in the name of the new nation. Constitutional issues involving the relative power of institutions and the proper relationship between rulers and the ruled were finally settled at the end of the turbulent seventeenth century with the victory of Parliament and its supporters over supporters of an absolutist monarchy. The victory of Parliament was associated with the formal recognition of the rights of English citizens.

Parliament's victory prepared the political system for adapting to demands for wider participation in the nineteenth century. The franchise was extended to the propertied classes, then to the working classes. Parliament also changed its procedures to reflect the realities of party and electoral politics. The majority party in Parliament and its executive committee, the cabinet, came to exercise power based on electoral mandate.

The group life of the United Kingdom reflects this gradual evolutionary development. Since the major issues of politics have been settled decisively over long periods of time, there is not a strong heritage of group violence and conflict. The most important political cleavage, that based on class, brought on the most recent major political crisis—the granting of the vote to workers. The class cleavage provides the basis for Britain's two-party political system and in that sense brings coherence and meaning to politics.

The nationality divisions are recent phenomena that may or may not prove of lasting importance in politics. In a sense, this source of cleavage is the result of incomplete nation-building. Nation-building occurred for the English nationality group several hundred years before the first national area (Wales) was added to the kingdom in the sixteenth century and long before the addition of Scotland (1707) and Ireland (1801). However, the English permitted the survival of traditional customs and institutions in these areas—particularly in Scotland and Ireland. Feelings of national distinctiveness were never fully eroded and became politically important in the era of the United Kingdom's economic decline.

Institutional Resources

The ability of the United Kingdom to meet the demands generated by its group structure is enhanced by the quality of its political institutions. These are highly valued by the public because they are products of a thousand years of shared national experience. The institutions also meet the requirements of efficiency and the need to bring expertise to the solution of governmental problems.

A highly centralized and powerful policy-making body, the British cabinet, through its committees and other channels of consultation, is at the very heart of British government. The cabinet interacts with interest groups, governmental departments, and the political parties. The information received—both political and technical—forms the basis of cabinet policy decisions. The cabinet has the advantage of having the undivided power necessary for the development of coherent programs and broadly conceived governmental planning.

The implementation of policy is in the hands of the British civil service, which is highly regarded and with good reason. Civil servants are well educated and tend to come from high-status backgrounds. The service itself has very high standards, based on traditions of independence, nonpartisanship, and honesty.

The work of these more "efficient" institutions is facilitated by the political support generated by Britain's symbolic institutions. The British monarch acts as a living symbol of the nation and performs necessary ceremonial tasks. The House of Lords is currently made up of representatives of Britain's great families and life peers who have been named for service to the nation. The pageantry of the upper house and the quality of its members have helped build ties of affection between citizens and their leaders and institutions. Finally, the stylized debate of the House of Commons helps to promote important values such as the rights of political opposition to criticize government.

The strength of the British legal system rests on the powerful tradition of its common law. British law developed along with feelings of national distinctiveness and, indeed, helped develop those feelings. Based on custom and precedent, the law closely reflects national political values.

Weaknesses of the common law, such as its difficulty in coping with new developments, have periodically caused serious problems, such as those associated with recent conflicts regarding ethnic minorities. But, by and large, the courts of the United Kingdom have been effective in resolving conflict and in protecting individual rights.

Problems

One of the United Kingdom's most serious problems—the nation's prolonged economic crisis—is partly beyond the control of British leaders. Although the newly discovered North Sea oil helps greatly, the British do not have adequate natural resources. The British industrial plant is outmoded and needs massive investment to modernize. International economic and political forces have forced a redirection of trade from the old colonies to the countries of the European Common Market.

Part of the economic crisis stems, however, from governmental policy and decisions. The British were late to realize that their future lay with the European Economic Community, or Common Market. They artificially inflated the value of their currency, seemingly for the sake of national pride, and therefore made their goods too expensive for foreign competition. British governments of both parties became committed to welfare programs that proved to be beyond their means. Policies to encourage investment were low-priority items for a time.

Whatever the cause of a crisis, prolonged failure leads to a withdrawal of public support for leaders, institutions, and even the regime itself. In this case, the erosion of public confidence is already apparent: the two major parties have lost a great deal of support. This implied rejection of the two-party system, which has been dominant in Britain since the democratization of politics, also implies a rejection of government regardless of party. The nationality problem can be seen in the same way. It is no longer an advantage for some in Scotland and Wales to be associated with a political system that is not economically sound and whose leadership is increasingly viewed as incompetent.

The second major problem is the nationality problem. At one extreme, the problem could result in the disintegration of the United Kingdom into independent or loosely federated political entities. The Labour government of James Callaghan proposed a devolution scheme that would create Scottish and Welsh parliaments responsible for educational and cultural affairs. These parliaments would have no powers over taxation or expenditure. The Labour government hoped that this measure would undercut the demands for independence that have been promoted by the Scottish Nationalist party (SNP). Prime Minister Callaghan also hoped that it would finish the SNP as a political force by eliminating its only reason for existence. The devolution plan, of course, would not necessarily preclude the continuation of more extreme demands.

The implications of failure for the devolution strategy stems from its impact on responsible majority party government. The proliferation of small nationalist parties reduces the likelihood that any British party can gain a majority. British politics now assumes the existence of a single governing party opposed by a single major alternative party and its "shadow government."

The situation in Northern Ireland is somewhat different. Northern Ireland is a small (six Irish counties) and costly element in the United Kingdom. Logically, it is a good deal more trouble and expense than it is worth. The money spent and English lives lost or disrupted in Northern Ireland have weakened English interest in maintaining exclusive responsibility for the province. Solutions are hard to come by, though. A unilateral withdrawal from Northern Ireland would damage British prestige, particularly since many observers predict that this action would lead to a bloodbath. The Catholics and Protestants in Northern Ireland might become involved in a bloody civil war as soon as the British left. The alternative is to return substantial autonomy to a Northern Ireland government within the United Kingdom. The persistent problem involves drafting of a constitution acceptable to both Protestants and Catholics. The current policy of both major British parties is to pursue the latter course of action.

The United Kingdom represents a political system with substantial resources in terms of tradition, public support for political institutions, and governmental capabilities. Each of these advantages is sorely needed in coping with current difficulties. The major danger is that some of the resources will be used up in the process—notably public support and affection for institutions and leaders.

▪ THE FEDERAL REPUBLIC OF GERMANY ▪

Germany's political history left twentieth-century Germany with problems and group antagonisms that were virtually insoluble. The result was the explosive and violent period of change associated with Hitler's Germany and World War II. The Federal Republic, comprising the western portion of the prewar state of Germany, has established itself as a stable and effective regime. The success of the regime may be said to have occurred despite the German historical experience. On the other hand, its success follows from the fact that Hitler's regime ruthlessly destroyed Germany's traditional group structure and, in so doing, left a much less divided society in its wake.

The institutions of the Federal Republic are a blend of traditionally German forms and imported forms imposed by the occupying powers. The German civil service and legal system follow from German predecessors. The occupying powers added a Constitutional Court, encouraged true federalism and tinkered with the electoral system—experiments that proved to be successful.

History and Political Culture

German history left a legacy of group conflict and unresolved political issues that had to be dealt with in the twentieth century. The critical events of German history are the Protestant Reformation and the religious wars that followed. The current pattern of cultural and political differences between the Catholic South and the Protestant North stems from this period.

A second consequence of the Reformation was the terrible loss of life that followed, leaving Germany weak and divided. The Reformation set off a German social revolution. Peasants equated religious, political, and economic freedom and refused to settle for religious liberty alone. Peasant uprisings became a regular feature of German life. Bloodshed also followed from the invasion of foreign armies that intervened in Germany on the pretense of religion. The Thirty Years' War (1618–1648) was extremely bloody by the standards of the time. At the end of the seventeenth century there were over 300 German states populated by roughly half the number of people that had resided in that territory in 1600.

Political fragmentation persisted into the nineteenth century. The religious differences in German-speaking Europe prevented consolidation and encouraged foreign interference. German national feelings were frustrated by continued political division. Frustration led to extreme forms of nationalism that exalted German character and culture and railed against the world of Germany's enemies. The difficulties in achieving German unification meant that unification could proceed only by force. This fact promoted the leading role of Prussia, the militaristic "power state" that eventually accomplished unification in 1871. During the empire (1871–1918) the traditional conservatism of Prussia was imposed on the entire Reich. After unification the Prussia-led state had to struggle against the influence of the groups that now were included in the empire —notably Catholics and the socialist working class.

The legacies of Germany's history are sharp political cleavages and explosive group conflict. The Reformation and its aftermath left religious and regional differences. Late unification meant a late, condensed period of industrialization and the rapid growth of a new working class. Group conflict accounted for the failure of German democracy in the 1920s and the rise of Hitler who skillfully played group against group.

The current West German political culture reflects some of the old divisions—notably religion, class, and region—but Hitler's regime destroyed much of German's old group life. Group-based organizations were either destroyed or co-opted within the Nazi system. The war and the excesses of Hitler's regime have made most Germans anxious to forget the prewar antagonisms; the result is a much less sharply divided society.

Institutional Resources

West Germany's institutions were born under unusual circumstances. The occupying powers supervised the writing of the 1949 constitution and in a sense imposed it on the German people. Although retaining some traditional German political forms and practices, the occupiers included some foreign innovations. Each of the innovations was borrowed from British or American traditions, and each was designed to correct problems associated with Germany's past regimes.

The Basic Law of the Federal Republic created a strong relatively independent office of the chancellor. The chancellor's office has become the center for West German policy-making activity. Fearing that Germany would have an unstable parliamentary system based on multi-party politics, the occupying powers provided for stability by making it difficult for Parliament to remove the chancellor or to hold him accountable for his actions. The Germans themselves approved of this arrangement, since the chancellor's office was compatible with German traditions of strong administrative leadership.

The occupying powers also strove to make Parliament an effective representative body that would be capable of playing a role in decision-making, carrying out public debate on the issues of the day, and overseeing the executive. The more specialized Parliament that resulted could carry out its role in decision-making better than its predecessors could. It also has endeavored to improve the quality of its public proceedings, such as public debate and the questioning of cabinet members. Finally, the occupying powers introduced an electoral law ensuring that each German would have a representative of his locality or district in Parliament. The electoral law was intended to improve the representational basis of the legislature. Most proportional representation systems do not provide direct constituency representation of this kind.

The Allies introduced a federal system to break up or decentralize the administrative agencies of government. The German states are basically responsible for policy implementation, and the federal government is largely responsible for policy-making. Most of Germany's bureaucratic and administrative offices and personnel are dispersed in the state capitals. State interests are protected at the national level in the Bundesrat, which gives the states some role in national policy-making as well.

The occupiers introduced one major innovation in the German court system. They created a Constitutional Court that has a special role in protecting individual and group rights. Based on the example of the American Supreme Court, this court has the power of judicial review; but, besides hearing cases on appeal, it can also hear petitions and new cases. The court has an explicitly political role, as can be seen in its power to declare political parties illegal based on their departure from democratic principles.

If there has been a failure in the occupiers' institutional engineering, it lies in the area of symbolic institutions. A federal presidency was created, a ceremonial office capable of building public support for democratic institutions. The presidency has not fulfilled these hopes, perhaps because this indirectly elected office has no tradition behind it. Or it may be that the office is too weak in terms of formal powers for Germans to notice it or its incumbent.

Problems

By all accounts, the new West German institutions have performed very well. In this stable, democratic system, individual rights are well protected. The economy has expanded and provided excellent progress in terms of living standards.

The West German successes have had some unintentional ill effects, however. German expectations regarding economic performance are unrealistically high. West Germany is not immune to the international pressures that have produced the syndrome of slow growth with inflation (or "stagflation") in many industrialized countries. While the West German record has been excellent by comparative standards during the period of the recent European economic malaise, Germans expect more. This accounts for Helmut Schmidt's 1976 election strategy of "running against Europe." Schmidt spent a good deal of his campaign time emphasizing that things were worse elsewhere.

Another West German success has had unfortunate results. West German leaders have greatly reduced the level of partisan and group conflict. In this mild political atmosphere, there is little difference between the parties and little conflict between interest groups. The West German unions work very quietly and cooperatively with their management and government counterparts. The result is that politics take place behind closed doors among a relatively small group of political and economic leaders.

The noncompetitive, bland nature of West German politics is a major point of criticism with dissatisfied and disaffected Germans. The government, they say, has created and now reflects a fat, uncritical society. This kind of dissatisfaction accounts for the style and intensity of West German's militant radicals such as the Baader-Meinhof gang. These groups desire, among other things, to shock Germans out of their complacency.

▪ FRANCE ▪

France, more than any other nation, has suffered from too much history. France's history has left behind a fragmented political culture that seemingly cannot support or tolerate any political regime for long. Political instability is France's greatest tradition of government.

The current regime is now 20 years old. The new institutions were designed explicitly as a vehicle for the leadership of Charles de Gaulle. In the years since De Gaulle's resignation in 1969, the system has operated as intended. There are signs, however, that political developments, such as political incompatibility between the president and Parliament, may transform the system in fundamental ways.

Despite severe political cleavages and political instability, the French political system has performed rather well. The French economy has grown remarkably since World War II, and the government has greatly increased its capacity to provide important services and social benefits to the populace. Weaknesses in performance have involved political failures —international setbacks, political instability, and occasional violations of political rights.

History and Political Culture

French political development was marked by early establishment of national feelings and the early growth of state power. In this sense, France was one of the first truly modern political systems. French monarchs were modernizing rulers who pioneered techniques of administration and created a centralized bureaucratic state.

The power of the French Crown choked off rival political institutions, in particular, parliamentary institutions. The French monarchs could extract taxes and resources from the general populace without recourse to a representative institution. Moreover, they publicized and enforced their laws without parliamentary assistance; there was no rival or alternative to Crown power. The monarchy allied itself with the church and the landed aristocracy. Social stratification was rigid, and the claims of new political groups were resisted. As demands for more widespread participation grew, the rigid social and political structure of the Ancient Regime produced a revolutionary situation.

The French Revolution of 1789 marked the beginning of a crisis period that left lasting scars. The Revolution was an abrupt break, rejecting the traditions of the Ancient Regime, and its widespread violence gave the lessons of the period lasting force. Violence against the aristocracy and the clergy heightened class and religious hostility.

After the Revolution, there were two major alternatives to monarchy in France—republicanism and Bonapartism. Republicanism, the political preference of anti-clerical, small-town France, meant government by a representative assembly and a weak executive. This sort of weak government would not interfere with independent and individualistic citizens. Bonapartism involved a preference for a strong leader—a people's emperor. Revolving around a single great man, the system would nevertheless be democratic because of the leader's special relationship with the people. The special bond could be affirmed by periodic plebiscitory elections.

In approximately 200 years the French experienced 13 regimes that followed a monarchical, republican, or Bonapartist pattern. The changes of regime continually reinforced the great issues that divided Frenchmen— those involving their constitutional preferences and religion. Religion, in particular, became involved with alternations between monarchical and republican forms of government in the nineteenth century. The republicans attacked the church, and the monarchists attempted to re-establish the special position accorded the church under the Ancient Regime. The political culture of France reflects this difficult history as religion remains a major divisive element in French politics. Frenchmen still define their political preferences according to whether they are clerical (political right) or anti-clerical (political left). Frenchmen are also divided according to whether they reside in rural or urban areas. Rural Frenchmen remain more traditional, conservative, and anti-government than their urban counterparts.

Economic modernization has added a third major cleavage—class. Because France remained predominantly rural and agrarian later than her European counterparts, industrialization created particularly difficult problems. Working-class participation was resisted by both traditional conservatives and the republicans of small-town France. The major workers' party, the French Communist party (PCF), was isolated and remained outside of the system. Sharp class antagonisms added another explosive division to French politics.

Politically, the three great political cleavages were important because of their impact on the French party system. For the last 50 years there have been 6 major party groupings in France (although party names and leadership have often changed). These roughly represent the way that the three major French political cleavages cut French society and separate one citizen from another. The great cleavages have prevented the French

*Leaders of the French left, Georges Marchais, François Mitterand, and Robert Fabre.
Jean Gaumy, Magnum Photos, Inc.*

people from cooperating in broadly based groups and have reduced the importance of group political participation.

Institutions

The current system seems to be a blend of the republican and Bonapartist forms. In form, it is still a parliamentary government for the purposes of day-to-day decision-making; however, the nationally elected president has such sweeping powers that he often appears to make Parliament, premier, and cabinet superfluous. A strong president, like Charles de Gaulle, made the system look decidedly Bonapartist.

The president is directly elected for a seven-year term with no restriction on re-election. He nominates the premier and consults on the composition of the cabinet. He may dissolve Parliament and call for new elections in case of political deadlock. The president has sweeping emergency powers in case of foreign threat or domestic disorder. He may call for a referendum on important issues, thereby bypassing Parliament. With even a moderately popular president, these powers are decisive and assure dominance in policy-making and even more routine decision-making.

Weakened by a number of provisions in the 1958 constitution, Parliament may act only in areas specifically enumerated in the constitution.

All other matters may be handled by executive order. The number of legislative areas, and by inference the expertise, of Parliament have been reduced. Parliament must deal with a powerful executive figure, the president, whom it cannot remove.

The institutions responsible for conflict resolution are weak. The courts have no real powers of judicial review; thus, individuals or groups have difficulty settling questions involving political rights. Courts have the capability only of settling constitutional disputes among governmental units—in particular, that of refereeing contests between president and Parliament.

There are also weaknesses in France's symbolic institutions. The president is supposedly the ceremonial executive, but his effectiveness in this role is greatly reduced by the obvious fact that he is a highly political figure. There is a good deal of evidence that French presidents are not viewed as positively and affectionately as British monarchs or even American presidents. The symbolic role of Parliament has been undercut by the abrupt change in parliamentary functions that occurred in 1958. The logic of De Gaulle's constitution dictates that Parliament should increase its ceremonial functions; however, French parliamentarians are used to a more active role.

Problems

Some serious problems came about from contradictions in the 1958 constitution. The greatest tension is between the president and Parliament or, more precisely, between the president and the premier. The premier is nominally in charge of day-to-day decision-making, with the president supposedly having an intermittent role—intervening in crises or periodically suggesting broad policy directions. The substantial powers of the presidency have partially tipped the balance in the president's direction. Political realities have also favored the president's dominant role. Fifth Republic presidents have had solid parliamentary majorities since 1958.

A major crisis will occur if a president faces a hostile parliamentary majority. In the 1978 French parliamentary elections there was a possibility that the rightist president (Valéry Giscard d'Estaing) would face a parliamentary majority of the left and a Socialist premier. This possibility will no doubt occur again. It is clear that the presidential government would come to a standstill under this sort of divided control of the key institutions of government.

Communist participation in government is another problem. The French Communist party (PCF) has followed a parliamentary strategy in the last 10 years, trying—through its electoral alliance with the Socialists— to gain cabinet level participation in the French government. At the time of this writing, the alliance has lapsed because of ideological and practical differences between the major left parties, but the potential of a leftist government is still alive. Such a government would be controversial and, to many Frenchmen, dangerous; it certainly would set off a constitutional crisis of some sort.

■ THE SOVIET UNION ■

The history of the Soviet Union is in some ways similar to that of France, but its political culture is very different. Like France, Russia was ruled by an absolutist monarchy. The rigid social and political system made it necessary for change to be sudden and revolutionary. Like France, industrialization occurred late and resulted in working-class militancy. The Soviet case differs, however, in the fact that a revolutionary elite representing the working class seized power in Russia. This elite was dedicated to state-directed social, economic, and political change. The current Soviet political culture and dominant patterns of politics are the product of centrally directed, forced change. Much of Russian history has been suppressed in the process.

History and Political Culture

Tsarist Russia evolved into a rigid autocracy over the centuries. The tsar's power was not held to be divisible or conditional. All Russians, including the nobility, were considered his subjects. Strong tsars, such as Peter the Great, deliberately used stern measures against the landowning nobility to demonstrate this supreme power. Totally reshuffling the ranks of the nobility, Peter based his new aristocracy on personal service to the tsar. Subsequent tsars used this weapon effectively to retain total power.

Since the tsar's power was indivisible, there was no question of parliamentary bodies exercising independent authority. Ancient local councils, called zemstvos, periodically petitioned the tsar for action but had no ongoing role. In the prerevolutionary period a national popular assembly, the Duma, was established with some real powers of legislation. This brief experiment was ineffective because of the political inexperience of both parliamentarians and the public. The important political institutions in the prerevolutionary period were the bureaucratic elements of government. The central ministries of the tsarist government worked under the supervision of the tsar and his closest advisers. The problems of local coordination and application of policy were considerable, and the bureaucratic machine was something less than smoothly efficient.

Tsarist authority crumbled in the 1905–1918 period, an era punctuated by two unsuccessful wars and serious economic dislocations. Widespread public disorder forced the tsar to accept the creation of the Duma. When failure in the Russo-Japanese War and the economic disruption caused by the war set off a wave of rioting, demonstrations, and political violence, the tsar was compelled to take steps toward becoming a constitutional monarch.

The disastrous management of World War I eroded the remaining authority of the tsarist regime. Nicholas II made the mistake of personally taking command of the Russian army in the field. Military reverses could be blamed only on the incompetence of the tsar and his generals, a number of whom were members of the royal family. The tsar's absence from the capital increased the influence of his wife Alexandra and her unsavory personal adviser, Gregory Rasputin. The German-born tsarina and the dissolute monk stirred bitter resentment.

The tsarist government simply collapsed in March 1917. Government orders were not obeyed, with the final collapse coming when the army and police mutinied—going over to revolutionary groups or disbanding. In the months after March 1917 a provisional government attempted to restore order. This government was made up of a strange assortment of liberal democratic politicians, revolutionary groups and workers, and soldiers' councils called Soviets. It faced monumental problems: settlement of a lost war, economic collapse, breakdown of public order, and foreign military intervention.

The most organized and ruthless revolutionary element, Lenin's Bolsheviks, had a decided advantage in this period. Lenin employed coercion, revolutionary discipline, and firm centralized leadership to consolidate his power. Only a vanguard elite, conscious of the laws of history, could apply their knowledge to the task of transforming society and the economy, according to Lenin.

The Soviet political culture directly reflects the necessities of the revolutionary period. The ideological value placed on the creation of a classless society was emphasized. Elite control of the economy gave leaders the means of changing class structure. Political violence against class enemies and control over education provided other means to build the new Soviet man.

Officially, there are now only two cooperative classes remaining in the Soviet Union—workers and peasants. In reality, Soviet society is divided on the basis of education, occupation, and standards of living. Some important political divisions are based on profession: scientists, economic managers, civil servants, the military, and other groups have distinctive attitudes based on professional background and interests.

Institutions

Policy-making in the Soviet Union is the preserve of the highest party organ, the Politburo. The dozen or so party leaders in the Politburo make all major policy decisions for the Soviet polity. They use information supplied by the party Secretariat and the state ministries and come to their decisions in the spirit of collegiality. The General Secretary of the party, currently Leonid Brezhnev, has a leading but not a totally dominant role in all discussions.

Policy is implemented by two massive bureaucracies: the state bureaucracy and the nationwide party organization. The state ministries are particularly important in managing the economy and in economic planning. Major sectors of the economy are run by a governmental ministry. The national civil servants in the economic ministries are responsible for management decisions down to the plant level. The state's planning role is centralized in an organ known as Gosplan, which gathers and processes the information necessary for the Soviet Five Year Plans. The party bureaucracy is a network of party units playing a supervisory and investigatory role. Party units are assigned to monitor the workings of the state organizations; they have a similar role with regard to the economy and the implementation of the state economic plan.

The Soviet Union has an elaborate set of symbolic institutions. The most important outlets for symbolic participation are the popularly elected assemblies, the Soviets, at every level of government. Voters participate in selecting representatives to the Soviets, although their role is strictly that of affirming the party's choice. The Soviets also provide symbolic participation for those citizens who are elected to an assembly. Since there are a large number of assemblies, each with almost total membership turnover, many can serve in this way.

The Supreme Soviet as the national-level assembly has several important symbolic roles. First, it is a bicameral body that includes a house for representatives of Soviet nationality groups. This provides important group representation. The Supreme Soviet's second symbolic feature is providing a national ceremonial leader for the system. The chairman of the Presidium of the Supreme Soviet acts as the Soviet Union's representative for the purpose of ritual and in international relations.

Problems

Despite the highly organized, advanced nature of Soviet politics, there are several persistent problems. Some stem from the very nature of the system; for example, since the Communist party controls the flow of information, leadership has a problem getting much of the information to make sound decisions.

A more specific problem involves the proper way to handle political dissent. In the Soviet Union, disagreement with the party Politburo is considered treason; thus, political dissenters are considered a criminal element. Publicity surrounding well-known dissidents such as Alexander Solzhenitsyn and Andrei Sakharov makes it difficult, however, to bring harsh action. With all forms of dissent, the problem has been to achieve the proper level of coercion. Large-scale crackdowns and harsh penalties tend to arouse sympathy in informed circles at home and abroad.

Another problem is that of nationality differences, which have survived tsarist and Communist attempts at assimilation. The problem is particularly difficult with regard to nonterritorial nationalities such as Poles, Germans, and Jews. These nationality or cultural groups suffer according to the na-

Soviet dissident Leonid Plyusch speaks to the press at a news conference in Paris in 1976. Jean-Paul Paireault, Magnum Photos, Inc.

ture of Soviet relations with the foreign nation-states that are thought to compete for their loyalty. The most obvious current case is the case of Soviet Jews who desire emigration to Israel.

A last problem is economic. Centralized planning has often proven inflexible and wasteful, but decentralization schemes, notably Khrushchev's, have been failures. The problem seems to involve the balance between creating incentives to produce and exercising strict control of the economy, especially in the agricultural sector—long neglected because of the leadership's emphasis on the development of heavy industry.

▪ NIGERIA ▪

Nigeria is a "new" nation composed of many different groups. Before the establishment of the British protectorate on January 1, 1900, the concept of a unified "Nigerian nation" did not exist. There were no Nigerians, only inhabitants of the Nigerian protectorates, which grouped together diverse peoples with little in common. None of the characteristics most commonly associated with a nation—one language, one set of national traditions, or clearly defined boundaries—existed. British authority and administration bound together the Northern and Southern Protectorates and the Crown Colony of Lagos.

The colonial period from 1900 to 1960 began, but did not complete, the nation-building process. The different groups in Nigeria had radically different perspectives, goals, ambitions, and interests. There was little consensus among competing regions, political parties, or ethnic groups. Unlike Tanzania, Nigeria did not have a national political party to unify different groups under the twin banners of anti-colonialism and national-ism. At independence, political leaders faced the unenviable task of gov-erning the young nation through an untested set of political structures. Although there was great hope for the independent "giant" of Africa, the rules of the game, and certainly the game's outcome, were uncertain in 1960.

Nigerian Government and Politics—Two Experiments

The parliamentary period (1960–1966) was characterized by mistrust, fear, rumor, and corruption as well as divisive parliamentary politics. Adapting the Westminster model to the Nigerian case proved difficult. The major political parties—the Northern People's Congress, the Action Group, and the National Council of Nigerian Citizens—drew their strength and sup-port from their respective regional strongholds. No political party could capture and hold a truly national constituency. "Ethnic arithmetic" was the order of the day; advancement, power, and position were dependent on an individual's ethnicity rather than on ability. As elections became more corrupt, their results were more frequently challenged.

The swift and violent end of parliamentary government in January 1966 began the second experiment in Nigerian institution-building—military rule. Military intervention ended parliamentary politics but did not re-solve the crises between different groups and regions; new military leaders discovered that there were no easy solutions acceptable to all. The conflict reached its peak in 1967 with the attempted secession of the Eastern Region (Biafra) from the federation. The civil war from 1967 to 1970 preserved the federation but at tremendous cost.

Postwar governments have focused their attention on a wide range of political, economic, and social problems facing Nigeria. The difficult issues of what type of political system is most suited for Nigeria, how best to allocate increased oil revenues, and how social, economic, and political modernization can proceed in a politically stable setting are in the forefront of political debate.

The Politics of Diversity and the Search for Consensus

The causes of the instability that plagues Nigerian politics are varied. Nigerian leaders, with differing degrees of success, seek to create national

---

Nigeria's Competition for a New National Anthem

In his 1976 independence-day speech, the head of state, Lieutenant General Obasanjo, announced an open competition among Nigerians to write a new national anthem. Nigerian citizens were encouraged to submit entries that stressed "strong patriotism, national determination and objective, dynamism, simplicity, brevity and good lyrical form." Below are excerpts from four of five published entries in the competition.

From Entry No. 179

Nigeria, dear fatherland,
We thy children, proud of thee
Sincerely pledge to stand,
Now ever loyal to thee,
For the glory of our land,
Great one Nigeria.

From Entry No. 394

Dear fatherland we rise in love,
One people, one purpose, one destiny,
To serve thee with all our hearts and
     might,
As did our heroes who gave up their lives,
All we have we owe to offer,
To protect and defend your honour,
To maintain with pride our heritage.

From Entry No. 807

May the challenges of our past
Give us understanding of our present
And strength to build a greater Nigeria
Grant each one a sense of devotion
As our leaders uphold our principles
Let us learn to cherish honour and truth
And the God of all abide with us.

From Entry No. 617

Nigeria, our motherland,
Our sun at last has risen,
Above a blood-stained horizon,
A new dawn for us has begun,
And there's much work still to be done,
On this strong and firm foundation,
Of mutual trust and selflessness,
God help us build a strong nation.

Source: As reported in a notice in *West Africa,* 3149 (November 14, 1977), p. 2324.

---

political symbols to unify Nigeria's many peoples under one banner. At the same time, they must create a political system with the legitimacy and authority necessary to make and enforce political decisions. The Nigerian historical experience and the divisive cleavages that characterize Nigerian society make these difficult tasks.

The "weight of history" has worked against the development of a common set of shared experiences and traditions. The long-standing traditions and cultures of groups such as the Hausa-Fulani, Yoruba, and Ibo often are not compatible with a new, larger loyalty to the nation. Colonial administration reinforced differences between regions and groups. The Northern and Southern, and later Northern, Eastern, and Western Regions, jealously guarded their power and position in the colonial union. Each region sponsored and supported its own political parties, politicians, and interests. The constitutional experiments carried

These Nigerian students are in a teacher training program. There is an increased demand for teachers so that the goal of universal primary education can be attained. Courtesy, United Nations.

out in the post-World War II period under the umbrella of the colonial administration failed to achieve a satisfactory working arrangement among groups.

Achieving a consensus is made even more difficult by the intensity and the sharpness of the cleavages. Each of the three major ethnic groups, and many numerically smaller groups, have distinct, powerful traditions that hold them together. To cite only one example, the Hausa differ from the Ibo in terms of religion, language, myth of common origin, and political and social traditions. Given the political and economic environments during the colonial period, little was to be gained by cooperation between groups. Following independence, these antagonisms often led to violence.

National integration in part is the attempt to build national symbols, traditions, and institutions that transcend these subnational loyalties. It involves creating such national symbols as a flag and new national anthem and, more importantly, creating shared political values and experiences. Education plays a vital role both in developing the values themselves and in passing them from one generation to the next. One of the most important aims of the Universal Primary Education program is to educate a generation of *Nigerian* children in *Nigerian* traditions and history.

Values and attitudes must be supported and reinforced by the governmental framework. Nigerians have experimented with federal and unitary systems, and with parliamentary and military regimes. During some periods the central government was strong, with weak regions and states; in other periods the states and regions were strong, with a weak central government. The number of states has grown from 3 regions at independence to 12 states in 1967 to 19 states in 1976. At this writing military leaders have refused to create more states and appear to have decided in favor of a strong central government.

The military government has announced its intention to return political power to civilian hands in October 1979. The new constitution calls for the creation of a presidential/executive system (patterned in some respects on the U.S. model) rather than a return to the prime minister/parliamentary system. Safeguards to prevent the election of a "regional" or "ethnic" president are stated clearly and precisely. Candidates must win nationwide support to be elected, and political parties must not appeal to narrow ethnic or regional issues.

The relationship among various groups and the national government is only one of the factors that complicates the search for a workable and efficient institutional framework. Economic and social cleavages also influence modern-day politics. Nigeria's rapid growth has produced many problems and created the potential for increased social and economic tension and conflict. Oil revenues have allowed Nigerians to formulate development plans calling for the creation of a modern economy, increased agricultural productivity, and an active and diversified industrial sector. Implementing plans, however, is much more difficult than formulating them. Questions of the allocation of vast resources are more difficult to resolve than questions of the allocation of scarce resources. In many cases rapid economic growth has widened the gap between rich and poor. The resolution of conflicts produced by "want in the midst of plenty" are among the most serious challenges to Nigeria's leaders.

Nigeria is a nation of social contrasts. The modern exists side by side with the traditional. Modern urban areas like Lagos, Kano, and Ibadan grow rapidly, while in other areas traditional farming practices and rural life-styles continue relatively unaffected by modernization. Rapid urbanization creates problems of unemployment and underemployment, crime, housing shortages, health care delivery, and transportation. Rural areas suffer from a scarcity of social services and poor agricultural productivity. A wide gap still exists between the educated and the uneducated, between the literate and the illiterate. Programs for the education of all Nigerian children and for the training of skilled manpower essential to a modern economy require time and vast expenditures of money. New teachers must be trained and new schools constructed. In some areas, traditional resistance and mistrust of "modern" education must also be overcome.

One author has grouped the problems and issues facing Nigerians into three categories. The first category includes those issues that are "perennial" and have dominated Nigerian politics since independence—

"centralization or separation," "government administration," and "nationalism." The second set stem from the civil war and military rule—the "size and cost of [the] army," "reconstruction and reconciliation," and the "status of properties abandoned during the war." Finally, oil wealth creates a third set—"inflation," "port congestion," and "complications caused by major new commitments."[1]

This is an impressive list of issues and problems for any nation to face. The modernization and development of Nigeria has not, and probably will not, follow a smooth path. The nation-building process is complex, difficult, and frustrating. New interests, demands, and expectations are emerging continuously. Growth and development produce calls for more growth and development. The challenges posed by the above issues will continue to face Nigerian citizens and leaders for the foreseeable future. But, at the same time, the benefits of development also will continue.

▪ EGYPT ▪

Few other nations face so bewildering and complex economic problems as does Egypt. The relationship between economics and politics is especially close. The leadership's freedom to act and make political decisions is limited by environmental, economic, and social factors as well as political ones.

The political game in Egypt is played against the backdrop of a rapidly increasing population with constantly changing characteristics. A limited amount of cultivable land must support this population. As more and more Egyptians leave rural areas for large urban centers such as Cairo and Alexandria, there is an even greater strain on the economy. Urbanized and industrialized Egyptians with new expectations make new demands: better health care and housing, higher wages, stable prices, and better education and work opportunities. The ability of the government to meet these and other demands is, however, constrained by a lack of resources. The dilemma is acute.

The Nasser Presidency—Establishment of a New Political System

It is difficult to separate the history of modern Egypt and the description of the post-1952 political system from the history of Gamal Abdul Nasser, a truly charismatic political figure. Nasser guided and controlled Egypt from 1954 until his death in 1970. During certain periods his power, authority, and legitimacy were unquestioned. The political system of modern-day Egypt reflects his interests, ambitions, visions, and prejudices.

---

[1] Nelson Kasfir, "Soldiers as Policymakers in Nigeria" *American Universities Field Staff Reports,* West Africa Series, Vol. XVII, No. 3 (January 1977), p. 2.

Following his consolidation of power in 1954, the political game revolved around Nasser for 16 years.

Nasser's popularity allowed him to make and enforce decisions that weaker leaders could not have made. Economic and military defeats were turned to his advantage. The June 1967 war with Israel may have tarnished his image but did not topple him from power. Few national leaders in any nation could have withstood such a defeat. Because he was the most important political figure in Egypt, the government, party, and bureaucracy revolved around him. The rise and fall of individuals in power depended in part on their relationship to the president. Likewise, changes in structure in the government or the Arab Socialist Union were most likely the result of changes in the president's thinking.

National economic goals reflected the president's goals. Throughout the 1960s, government intervention in the economy increased. Nationalizations of banks, industries, and certain agricultural concerns were designed to facilitate economic development, planning, and government control. The bureaucracy needed for administering and monitoring new government operations grew at a tremendous rate. The efficiency and performance of the bureaucracy, however, did not keep pace with the growth in its size.

In foreign affairs President Nasser played the role of Egyptian, Arab, and Third World leader. In his confrontations with Israel and the former colonial powers, he articulated what he defined as an Arab, anti-colonial position. One result of his international role was the rapid buildup of the military. The military was engaged not only against Israel but also, at times, against other Arab states (such as Yemen in the mid-1960s). Nasser turned increasingly to the Soviet Union to supply and train the Egyptian army.

The sudden death of President Nasser in 1970 created a political and structural vacuum. Although Vice President Sadat assumed the presidency, as ordered by the constitution, his authority and power were questioned by many. The legacy of President Nasser lived on, and many claimed to represent him best. This legacy, both its triumphs and its failures, made succession for any leader difficult.

The Sadat Presidency—The "Corrective Revolution"

The goals of the Sadat and Nasser presidencies are similar in many respects. The 1952 revolution (in which both Sadat and Nasser participated) was aimed at the social and economic transformation of Egypt and the establishment of territorial independence. Land reform, a higher standard of living for the common man, and a more equitable distribution of economic and political power were in the early platforms of the new leaders. Their means for achieving these ends do, however, differ.

The Nasser presidency in many ways represented an authoritarian re-

President Sadat greets Israeli Prime Minister Menachem Begin during President Sadat's historic visit to Israel in 1977. Karel, Sygma.

gime that restricted rights to oppose and criticize. In seeking to mobilize the population for the achievement of political and economic progress, Nasser emphasized the common good, not individual rights. President Sadat maintained the basic political structure inherited from President Nasser but has put his own stamp on it. He and his supporters refer to this as the "corrective revolution." Modified political parties or factions representing the left, center, and right are permitted to present and discuss different opinions. The media present a more diversified range of views than during the Nasser period. In the economic sphere, nationalization of industry has been curtailed and private enterprise given more encouragement. In foreign affairs President Sadat turned from the Soviet Union to the West, more specifically the United States. His "opening" to the West is an attempt to increase aid and assistance from Western nations and Egypt's more conservative, oil-rich, Arab neighbors.

President Sadat also has established his own leadership style. New advisers, loyal to Sadat and sharing his perspectives, have been appointed. Many of the "centers of power" that supported President Nasser, and hence were potentially threatening to President Sadat, have been broken. In an attempt to increase and diversify public political debate the president has allowed the People's Assembly to become a more important and vocal forum for political discussion than was the National Assembly during the Nasser period.

Despite these significant changes, the power of the presidency and its occupant remain formidable. President Sadat is the preeminent political figure in the nation. His powers of appointment and persuasion, along with his control of the governmental machinery make any challenge to his authority difficult. As indicated by his response to the riots of early 1977, the president is willing to use his coercive power to maintain order. There are limits to the liberalization and to the right of the opposition to challenge the president. If need be, many of the authoritarian aspects that characterized certain periods of the Nasser presidency can be reintroduced.

The Uncertain Future

Solutions may differ, but the problems facing Egypt remain remarkably constant. The bureaucracy continues to be too large, inefficient, and unresponsive. Development plans often are delayed because of the inability of the government and administrative apparatuses to implement them. Unemployment and underemployment compound problems of low industrial productivity.

The drain on the budget by military expenditure also presents a severe problem, acting as a brake on economic development. Egypt's central role in the Arab confrontation with Israel has required the building, equipping, and maintaining of a large military force. While this expenditure may be viewed as necessary for the maintenance of security, it diverts funds from development programs.

Much of Egypt's financial resources also must go to maintain the present standard of living. Population growth consumes much of what might otherwise be invested in long-term economic development. Subsidies to maintain stable consumer prices on staples like bread and cooking oil divert development funds.

Rapid industrialization and urbanization magnify many of the demands made on political leaders; for example, more widely distributed education requires new jobs for school graduates. In turn, the demands of this growing educated middle-class sector for more goods and better services increase. But, as the dilemma comes full circle, the capability of the leaders to meet these demands remains limited.

Egypt has relied on foreign assistance to meet many of its needs. However, whether the aid is from the Soviet Union, Western nations like the United States, or other Arab nations, foreign assistance does not resolve the basic conflicts in Egyptian political and economic life.

Solutions to Egypt's economic problems are not simple. A lower birth rate, increased agricultural and industrial productivity, and more efficient use of the Egyptian manpower pool are partial solutions, but they are not easily implemented. Political solutions must balance complex internal and external forces; domestic politics must take into account Egypt's foreign policy. Each decision made by Egyptian political actors influences all areas of Egyptian political life. The challenges facing leaders and participants alike are difficult and frustrating. Despite this, decisions must be made.

▪ TANZANIA ▪

Like most developing nations, Tanzania has goals for the economic transformation and political modernization of the nation; however, changes in Tanzania, unlike those of many developing nations, have occurred in a relatively stable political setting. Political stability, the emphasis on increasing agricultural production, the development of ujamaa villages, and the encouragement of participation within the one-party framework make Tanzania both a unique and interesting case study.

A poor nation, Tanzania lacks vast mineral wealth (like Nigeria's and Chile's) and it lacks a large pool of skilled manpower (like Egypt's). The colonial experience in Tanganyika did not result in the creation of an efficient, modern, balanced, and diversified economy. Agricultural production, both for export and internal use, remained unproductive, as farm settlements tended to be small and scattered throughout the nation. In the industrial sector, the infrastructure necessary for industrialization did not exist. The roads and communications links were poorly developed, and few internal markets for manufactured goods existed.

The political situation at independence was a bit more encouraging. Under the leadership of Julius Nyerere, the Tanganyikan (later Tanzanian) African National Union (TANU) developed a broad-based following. TANU membership cut across ethnic, religious, and linguistic divisions. Julius Nyerere, prime minister and then president, was able to mobilize the population during the nationalist period under the banners of "independence" and "African rule." The lack of a numerically dominant ethnic group and the existence of Swahili as a common language among many groups helped to strengthen the effectiveness of the party.

The Role of the Leader and Ideology in Tanzanian Politics

The roles that leadership and ideology play in nation-building are important to understanding Tanzanian politics. President Nyerere's long tenure in office is testimony to his political acumen; since independence, he has maintained control of both the party and the government. Change in both party and government organizations normally reflect changes in Nyerere's thinking. The president provides the government, the party, and the citizenry with their political cues and directions. There is little question that President Nyerere (*Mwalimu,* "the teacher") is both the ideological and executive leader of the nation. His leadership style stresses these roles.

Implementation of the goals expressed by the president and the party leadership are the responsibility of the party and government. TANU's organization seeks to be the directing agent of development while remaining open to criticism and input from all Tanzanians. Party history involves shifts in emphasis between the need to remain open to different shades of opinion and the need to mobilize the population to achieve national goals.

The government structure is subservient to the party. (In a one-party state, the party usually is supreme.) All members of the National Assembly must belong to it, and most officials of the government and administrative services are also party members. Colonial prohibitions against judges, civil servants, and soldiers belonging to a party have been lifted.

The hybrid political system of Tanzania combines characteristics of both democratic and authoritarian regimes. On the one hand, the party encourages competition within its ranks. The 1965 and subsequent elections indicated that election to office did not carry a lifetime guarantee. The 1967 Arusha Declaration spelled out who could and could not hold party positions, and what party leaders could and could not own. Peasants and workers were to be the backbone and leaders of the party. Participation is encouraged at all levels of the party and administrative apparatuses. Where possible, local officials make decisions concerning local matters.

On the other hand, the system has authoritarian characteristics. Although there is competition within TANU, other parties are not allowed to form. The party—and more particularly President Nyerere—has wide discretionary powers. Severe criticism of the regime may result in arrest or preventive detention. The media are expected to conform to general party policy, as are educational institutions. As the president himself has said, he has the potential power to be a dictator.

Not fitting into a neat or clear-cut category, the Tanzanian political system is flexible and changing. Party and government structures change as the policies of the leadership and the problems facing Tanzania change. In some periods, like the 1965 election period, emphasis was on participation and making the party more representative and responsive. In other periods, like the 1973 ujamaa villagization period, emphasis was on the mobilization and control of the population. The party serves as a directing and guiding institution. What has remained consistent throughout the independence period is the power, influence, and authority of the president.

Economic Goals

The economic goals enunciated by President Nyerere are conditioned by Tanzania's economic situation. Though Tanzania is a rural, agricultural

President Nyerere greets a contingent of Chinese military and technical advisers. Tanzania has received aid from both western and eastern nations. Keystone Press.

nation, the agricultural sector has been unproductive. The industrial sector remains small, suffering from low productivity and a shortage of trained manpower. Given these facts, development plans in Tanzania focus first on increasing agricultural productivity and, once this sector is sound, on increasing industrialization.

The transformation of agriculture centers on the formation of ujamaa villages. Cooperative villages are designed not only to increase agricultural productivity by making modern farming techniques more feasible and economical but also to improve the rural standard of living.

To date, the villagization schemes have had both successes and failures. Agricultural productivity has increased but not as rapidly as anticipated or hoped for. Climatic disasters, rising costs of energy and imported heavy machinery, and the inefficiency of government and party administrators all have slowed growth. In the late 1970s the government shifted policy by paying more attention to the industrial sector. The goal became one of achieving a balance between agricultural and industrial growth.

A Model for Development

The legitimate authority of President Nyerere provides Tanzania with a political stability relatively rare in the developing world. The question must be asked: What will happen when President Nyerere no longer holds office? The direction and control, and the ideological guidance that the president has exercised, cannot easily be passed to his successor. Political systems strongly influenced by one individual often face a severe succession crisis.

Tanzania's economic policy has changed and will probably continue to do so. Economic policy is made within the context of both internal and external variables. Levels of foreign aid may increase or decrease, while the price of imported goods (especially items like heavy machinery and oil) may continue to rise. Nations whose primary exports are agricultural are also often in the unenviable position of seeing the price of their exports fall as the price of imports rises.

Any evaluation of the success or failure of the Tanzanian political and economic experiments must be partial and tentative. Tanzania is a nation undergoing economic, political, cultural, and social change. It is unique partly because these changes are being evaluated continually. It is also unique because of the magnitude of the changes envisioned.

Does Tanzania provide a model for other developing nations? The answer to this question depends on the goals of a nation's leaders, on the economic circumstances, and on the characteristics of the population of that nation. There are few, if any, models that can be applied to all nations—developed or developing. What Tanzania may offer is one model applicable to nations in similar conditions.

▪ CHILE ▪

The political tensions and conflicts that traditionally mark Chilean political life have grown stronger and more pronounced since 1970. Constitutional remedies and solutions gave way to extra-constitutional solutions as the military increasingly intervened in politics. The struggle for control of the government turned violent and what had been one of Latin America's oldest democratic systems collapsed.

Chilean Political Traditions

Chilean politics have evolved over a 150-year period. The power of the traditional, landowning elites gradually merged with the rising power of new industrial and commercial classes. As the economy was transformed from largely agricultural to mixed agricultural/industrial, new groups and interests demanded participation and representation in the political process.

Social and economic changes produced political changes. Urbanization, industrialization, and increased literacy and educational opportunity during the twentieth century brought demands from the lower classes for better standards of living and greater political participation. New political parties developed to represent them.

The shift in political power and political control is shown most clearly in the period after World War II. The presidency passed from the conservative/traditional interests, to the moderate/liberal interests of the Christian Democrats in the 1960s, to the radical/socialist interests represented by Salvadore Allende in the early 1970s. During each transition the calls for social, economic, and political change became more sweeping. The victory of Eduardo Frei (1964–1970) and the Christian Democrats in the 1964 presidential election provided a mandate for gradual change. The victory of Salvadore Allende (1970–1973) and his leftist Popular Unity coalition provided a limited mandate for more radical and revolutionary change.

These political shifts occurred within the framework of the 1925 constitution, which established the political rules of the game, distributed power and described the relationships among the different branches of government. The constitution, developed in part as a response to the chaotic, fractionalized politics of the parliamentary period (1880–1925), replaced the parliamentary system with a more presidential/executive system. The broad powers of the president were balanced against the powers of the congressional legislative branch. In this highly centralized political system, presidents often found themselves in political conflict with the legislature.

In few periods of Chilean history was this conflict so sharp and bitter as during the Allende presidency. As a minority president, Salvadore Allende found that many of his proposals and policies were opposed strongly by the more moderate and conservative Congress. As the economic situation deteriorated in 1972 and 1973, the conflicts became more intense. When the traditional rules of the game were no longer enforceable, the political system was unable to handle the intensity and bitterness of the conflict. There were few grounds for compromise or for achieving a general consensus; confrontation was the norm.

In 1973 the military, which traditionally had played a relatively minor role in politics, intervened and violently ended the political confrontation. The military represented not only its own interests but also those of the traditional, conservative Chileans who feared Allende and his politics. The stated reasons for military intervention included the need to restore economic order and reverse the economic policies of Allende, to prevent Communist takeover of the government, and to end the political chaos and instability that had immobilized the government.

The Military Regime

The civilian regime, based on the 1925 constitution, was replaced by a more openly authoritarian regime that banned political parties, canceled elections, curtailed open political discussion, and imprisoned, exiled, or, in some cases, executed many of its political opponents. Political power now rests with the military junta under the direction of President (General) Augusto Pinochet. His support comes from the military, from the police and security establishments, and from widespread sections of the population that opposed and feared Allende. The powers of the president are broad and relatively unhampered by checks or limitations.

Partly in response to international and United Nations pressure and condemnation, President Pinochet held a plebiscite on military rule in 1978. The aims of the referendum were to prove the legitimacy of, and support for, the military regime and President Pinochet and to blunt criticism of Chile concerning its human rights policy. The electorate was allowed to vote "yes" or "no" to this statement:

In the face of international aggression unleashed against the Government of our homeland, I support President Pinochet in his defense of the dignity of Chile, and reaffirm the legitimacy of the Government of the republic to conduct, in a sovereign way, the process of institutionalization of the country.[2]

Seventy-five percent of the Chilean voters voted "yes" to the statement.

Not surprisingly, supporters of the current government viewed the vote as a strong endorsement. Equally not surprising, opponents questioned not only the vote itself but also the spirit and way in which the vote was conducted. They claimed that the vote did not present a fair test of support for the military and that election tactics and restrictions made it difficult to vote "no."

The Future of Chilean Politics

The 1978 plebiscite is a reminder of the sharp divisions within the Chilean population. Supporters and opponents of various political persuasions often resort to emotional pleas and protests. For many in Chile, the military represents political stability and traditional economic order. The revocation of most of Allende's economic policies is viewed as just and economically sound. Likewise, the restoration of political stability is viewed as an important contribution. The anarchy and crisis that plagued Chile in 1972 and 1973 was ample justification, from this perspective, for military intervention.

On the other hand, supporters of the Allende government feel that his platform was never given a fair hearing and that his policies were sabotaged by opponents. From this perspective, the economic crises of 1972 and 1973 were as much the fault of international (particularly United States) intervention and of conservative and moderate opposition and

---

[2] *New York Times,* January 5, 1978, p. 12.

intransigence as they were the fault of the Allende administration. The harsh treatment dealt members and supporters of the Allende government following the coup d'état reinforces these feelings. The economic policies of the military regime that have most affected the poor and lower-class supporters of Allende are viewed as little more than the re-establishment of the old order of privilege.

Finally, a third position may exist. Those in the middle fear the politics represented both by Allende and by the military. While many supported the military intervention as a "necessary evil," they oppose the continuation and institutionalization of military rule. Their ultimate goal is the re-establishment of a democratic polity but without the sharp divisions of the 1970–1973 period.

Chilean politics have changed dramatically in the recent past. The current regime appears prepared to institutionalize military rule and to prevent, at all costs, challenges to their authority. The Chilean example suggests the strains and limitations under which both democratic and developing systems exist. The attempted transformation of the political and economic systems produced conflicts that the political actors were unable to resolve. The new demands and interests emerging from the social and economic changes challenged both the authority of political actors and the legitimacy of the political system.

As changes occur, political systems and political actors must evolve and respond to these changes. New demands and interests continually present potential threats to the performance and continuance of the political system. In the Chilean case, potential threats became real in 1972 and 1973. The tenure of the military government may depend not only on their ability to control the coercive apparatus of the state but also on their responsiveness to the challenges facing them.

BIBLIOGRAPHY

For students who wish to study the politics of the eight nations in more detail, this brief bibliography will serve as a good starting point. The works cited were selected for a variety of reasons. Some were chosen because they discuss in more detail the issues described in the text. Others provide a historical background that will help in making present-day politics more understandable. Still others were selected because they contain extensive political or economic data. Where possible, we have listed works published relatively recently. Students needing information for the very recent past should consult newspapers and journals.

THE UNITED KINGDOM

Bagehot, Walter. *The English Constitution*. London: William Collins, 1963.

Barker, Anthony, and Michael Rush. *The Member of Parliament and His Information*. London: George Allen & Unwin, 1970.

Beer, Samuel H. *British Politics in the Collectivist Age*. New York: Random House, 1969.

Brennan, Tom. *Politics and Government in Britain: An Introductory Survey*. London: Cambridge University Press, 1972.

Butler, David E., and Donald Stokes. *Political Change in Britain: Factors Shaping Electoral Choice*. College ed. New York: St. Martin's Press, 1971.

Butt, Ronald. *The Power of Parliament*. London: Constable, 1969.

Cartwright, Timothy J. *Royal Commissions and Departmental Committees in Britain: A Case-Study in Institutional Adaptiveness and Public Participation in Government*. London: Hodder and Stoughton, 1975.

Craig, Frederick W. S. *Minor Parties at British Parliamentary Elections, 1885–1974*. London: Macmillan, 1975.

Mackintosh, John P. *The British Cabinet*. London: Methuen, 1969.

McKenzie, R. T. *British Political Parties*. New York: Praeger, 1964.

Penniman, Howard R., ed. *Britain at the Polls*. Washington, D.C.: American Enterprise Institute for Public Policy Research, 1974.

Punnett, R. M. *British Government and Politics*. New York: W. W. Norton, 1971.

Rose, Richard. *Governing Without Consensus*. Boston: Beacon, 1972.

———. *Politics in England*, 2nd ed. Boston: Little, Brown, 1974.

Toyne, Anthony. *An English-Reader's History of England.* London: Oxford University Press, 1971.

Walkland, S. A. *The Legislative Process in Great Britain.* London: George Allen & Unwin, 1968.

THE FEDERAL REPUBLIC OF GERMANY

Ashkenasi, Abraham. *Modern German Nationalism.* Cambridge, England: Schenkman, 1976.

Braunthal, Gerard. *The West German Legislative Process.* Ithaca, N.Y.: Cornell University Press, 1972.

Childs, David. *Germany Since 1918.* New York: Harper & Row, 1971.

Condradt, David P. *The German Polity.* New York: Longman, 1978.

Crawley, Aidan. *The Rise of Western Germany, 1945–1972.* London: Collins, 1973.

Dahrendorf, Ralf. *Society and Democracy in Germany.* Garden City, N.Y.: Doubleday, 1967.

Edinger, Lewis J. *Politics in West Germany,* 2nd ed. Boston: Little, Brown, 1977.

Grosser, Alfred. *Germany in Our Time.* New York: Praeger, 1971.

———. *The Federal Republic of Germany: A Concise History.* Translated by Nelson Aldrich. New York: Praeger, 1964.

Loewenberg, Gerhard. *Parliament in the German Political System.* Ithaca, N.Y.: Cornell University Press, 1966.

Mayntz, Renate, and Fritz W. Scharpf. *Policy-Making in the German Federal Bureaucracy.* Amsterdam: Elsevier, 1975.

Merkle, Peter W. *The Origin of the West German Republic.* New York: Oxford University Press, 1963.

Safran, William. *Veto-Group Politics: The Case of Health-Insurance Reform in West Germany.* San Francisco: Chandler, 1967.

Schoonmaker, Donald, ed. *German Politics.* Lexington, Mass.: D. C. Heath, 1971.

Stern, J. P. *The Führer and the People.* Berkeley: University of California Press, 1975.

Walton, Henry. *Germany.* London: Thames & Hudson, 1969.

FRANCE

Aron, Raymond. *The Elusive Revolution: Anatomy of a Student Revolt.* Trans. by Gordon Clough. New York: Praeger, 1969.

Blondel, Jean, and Godfrey Drexel, Jr. *The Government of France,* 3rd ed. New York: Crowell, 1968.

Brown, Bernard E. *Protest in Paris: Anatomy of a Revolt.* Morristown, N.J.: General Learning Corporation Press, 1974.

Ehrmann, Henry W. *Politics in France,* 3rd ed. Boston: Little, Brown, 1976.

Harrison, Martin, ed. *French Politics.* Lexington, Mass.: D. C. Heath, 1969.

Hoffman, Stanley. *Decline or Renewal: France since the 1930s.* New York: Viking Press, 1974.

Kesselman, Mark. *The Ambiguous Consensus: A Study of Local Government in France.* New York: Knopf, 1967.

Macridis, Roy C. *French Politics in Transition: The Years after De Gaulle.* Cambridge, Mass.: Winthrop, 1975.

Penniman, Howard R., ed. *France at the Polls: The Presidential Election of 1974.* Washington, D.C.: American Enterprise Institute for Public Policy Research, 1975.

Pierce, Roy. *French Politics and Political Institutions.* New York: Harper & Row, 1973.

Schonfeld, William R. *Obedience and Revolt: French Behavior Toward Authority.* Beverly Hills, Calif.: Sage, 1976.

Suleiman, Ezra N. *Politics, Power and Bureaucracy in France: The Administrative Elite.* Princeton, N.J.: Princeton University Press, 1974.

Waterman, Harvey. *Political Change in Contemporary France: The Politics of an Industrial Democracy.* Columbus, Ohio: Charles E. Merrill, 1969.

Williams, Philip M. *Crisis and Compromise: Politics in the Fourth Republic.* London: Longman, 1972.

———. *French Politicians and Elections, 1951–1969.* London: Cambridge University Press, 1970.

———. *The French Parliament: Politics in the Fifth Republic.* New York: Praeger, 1968.

THE SOVIET UNION

Armstrong, John A. *Ideology, Politics and Government in the Soviet Union.* New York: Praeger, 1974.

Auty, Robert, and Dimitri Obolensky, eds. *An Introduction to Russian History.* Cambridge, England: Cambridge University Press, 1976.

Barghoorn, Frederick. *Politics in the USSR,* 2nd ed. Boston: Little, Brown, 1972.

Brzezinski, Zbigniew, and Samuel Huntington. *Political Power: USA/USSR.* New York: Viking Press, 1964.

Brown, Archie, and Michael Kaser, eds. *The Soviet Union since the Fall of Khrushchev.* New York: The Free Press, 1975.

Crankshaw, Edward. *The Shadow of the Winter Palace.* New York: Viking Press, 1976.

Hammer, Darrell P. *U.S.S.R.: The Politics of Oligarchy.* Hinsdale, Ill.: The Dryden Press, 1974.

Hollander, Gayle Durham. *Soviet Political Indoctrination.* New York: Praeger, 1972.

Hough, Jerry F. *The Soviet Prefects: Local Party Organs in Industrial Decision-Making.* Cambridge, Mass.: Harvard University Press, 1969.

Juviler, Peter H. *Revolutionary Law and Order: Politics and Social Change in the USSR.* New York: The Free Press, 1976.

Matthews, Mervyn. *Class and Society in Soviet Russia.* London: Allen Lane, 1972.

Ploss, Sidney L., ed. *The Soviet Political Process: Aims, Techniques, and Examples of Analysis.* Waltham, Mass.: Ginn, 1971.

Rigby, T. H. *Communist Party Membership in the U.S.S.R., 1917–1967.* Princeton, N.J.: Princeton University Press, 1968.

Skilling, H. Gordon, and Franklyn Griffiths, eds. *Interest Groups in Soviet Politics.* Princeton, N.J.: Princeton University Press, 1971.

Smith, Hedrick. *The Russians.* New York: Ballantine, 1976.

Strong, John W., ed. *The Soviet Union Under Brezhnev and Kosygin.* New York: Van Nostrand, 1971.

Tatu, Michael. *Power in the Kremlin: From Khrushchev to Kosygin.* New York: Viking Press, 1970.

Tokes, Rudolf L., ed. *Dissent in the U.S.S.R.: Politics, Ideology, and People.* Baltimore, Md.: Johns Hopkins University Press, 1975.

Tucker, Robert C. *The Soviet Political Mind.* New York: Praeger, 1963.

NIGERIA

Arnold, Guy. *Modern Nigeria.* London: Longman, 1977.

Awolowo, Obafemi. *Awo: The Autobiography of Chief Obafemi Awolowo.* Cambridge: Cambridge University Press, 1960.

Azikiwe, Nnamdi. *My Odyssey, An Autobiography.* New York: Praeger, 1970.

Bello, Ahmadu. *My Life.* Cambridge: Cambridge University Press, 1962.

Bretton, Henry. *Power and Stability in Nigeria.* New York: Praeger, 1962.

Coleman, James S. *Nigeria, Background to Nationalism.* Berkeley: University of California Press, 1971.

Crowder, Michael. *A Short History of Nigeria.* New York: Praeger, 1966.

Dudley, Billy J. *Parties and Politics in Northern Nigeria.* London: Frank Cass, 1968.

Hodgkin, Thomas L. *Nigerian Perspectives.* London: Oxford University Press, 1960.

Kirk-Greene, A. H. M. *Crisis and Conflict in Nigeria, A Documentary Sourcebook 1966–1970. Vol. I. January 1966–July 1967.* London: Oxford University Press, 1971.

————. *Crisis and Conflict in Nigeria, A Documentary Sourcebook 1966–1970. Vol. II. August 1967–January 1970.* London: Oxford University Press, 1971.

Luckham, Robin. *The Nigerian Military: A Sociological Analysis of Authority and Revolt, 1960–1967.* Cambridge: Cambridge University Press, 1971.

Mackintosh, John P. *Nigerian Government and Politics.* Evanston, Ill.: Northwestern University Press, 1966.

Melson, Robert, and Howard Wolpe, eds. *Nigeria: Modernization and Politics of Communalism.* East Lansing: Michigan State University Press, 1971.

Nwabueze, Benjamin O. *Constitutionalism in the Emergent States.* Rutherford, N.J.: Fairleigh Dickinson University Press, 1973.

Post, K. W. J. *The Nigerian Federal Election of 1959: Politics and Administration in a Developing Political System.* London: Oxford University Press, 1963.

Post, K. W. J., and Michael Vickers. *Structure and Conflict in Nigeria, 1960–1965.* Madison: University of Wisconsin Press, 1973.

Sklar, Richard L. *Nigerian Political Parties, Power in an Emergent African Nation.* Princeton, N.J.: Princeton University Press, 1963.

Whitaker, C. S. Jr. *The Politics of Tradition, Continuity and Change in Northern Nigeria, 1946–1966.* Princeton, N.J.: Princeton University Press, 1970.

EGYPT

Baer, Gabriel. *Studies in the Social History of Modern Egypt.* Chicago: University of Chicago Press, 1969.

Berger, Morroe. *Bureaucracy and Society in Egypt, A Study of the Higher Civil Service.* Princeton, N.J.: Princeton University Press, 1957.

Dekmejian, R. Hrair. *Egypt Under Nasir.* Albany: State University of New York Press, 1971.

Issawi, Charles. *Egypt in Revolution: An Economic Analysis.* London: Oxford University Press, 1963.

Jankowski, James P. *Egypt's Young Rebels: "Young Egypt," 1933–1952.* Stanford, Calif.: Hoover Institution Press, 1975.

Kardouche, George. *The U.A.R. in Development.* New York: Praeger, 1966.

Lacouture, Jean, and Simone Lacouture. *Egypt in Transition.* New York: Criterion, 1958.

————. *Nasser.* New York: Alfred Knopf, 1973.

Little, Tom. *Modern Egypt.* London: Ernest Benn, 1967.

Mansfield, Peter. *Nasser's Egypt.* Baltimore: Penguin, 1965.

————. *The British in Egypt.* London: Weidenfeld and Nicholson, 1971.

Nasser, Gamal Abdul. *Egypt's Liberation: The Philosophy of the Revolution.* Washington, D.C.: Public Affairs Press, 1955.

O'Brien, Patrick. *The Revolution in Egypt's Economic System: From Private Enterprise to Socialism 1952–1965.* London: Oxford University Press, 1966.

Perlmutter, Amos. *Egypt the Praetorian State.* New Brunswick, N.J.: Transaction Books, 1974.

Vatikitotis, P. J. *Egypt Since the Revolution.* New York: Praeger, 1968.

Wendell, Charles. *The Evolution of the Egyptian National Image.* Berkeley: University of California Press, 1972.

TANZANIA

Bienen, Henry. *Tanzania: Party Transformation and Economic Development.* Expanded ed. Princeton, N.J.: Princeton University Press, 1970.

Cliffe, Lionel, ed. *One Party Democracy, The 1965 Tanzania General Elections.* Nairobi, Kenya: East African Publishing House, 1967.

Hatch, John Charles. *Tanzania: A Profile.* New York: Praeger, 1972.

————. *Two African Statesmen: Kaunda of Zambia and Nyerere of Tanzania.* Chicago: Regnery, 1976.

Hopkins, Raymond R. *Political Roles in a New State: Tanzania's First Decade.* New Haven, Conn.: Yale University Press, 1971.

Ingle, Clyde R. *From Village to State in Tanzania: The Politics of Rural Development.* Ithaca, N.Y.: Cornell University Press, 1972.

Kimambo, I. N., and A. J. Temu. *A History of Tanzania.* Evanston, Ill.: Northwestern University Press.

Maguire, G. Andrew. *Toward 'Uhuru' in Tanzania: The Politics of Participation.* London: Cambridge University Press, 1969.

Morrison, David R. *Education and Politics in Africa, The Tanzanian Case.* London: C. Hurst, 1976.

Nyerere, Julius K. *Freedom and Development/Uhuru Na Maendeleo.* London: Oxford University Press, 1973.

————. *Freedom and Socialism/Uhuru Na Ujamaa.* London: Oxford University Press, 1968.

————. *Man and Development/Binadamu Na Maendeleo.* London: Oxford University Press, 1974.

Potholm, Christian P. *Four African Political Systems.* Englewood Cliffs, N.J.: Prentice-Hall, 1970.

Samoff, Joel. *Local Politics and the Structure of Power.* Madison: University of Wisconsin Press, 1975.

Stephens, Hugh. *The Political Transformation of Tanganyika: 1920–1967.* New York: Praeger, 1968.

Tordoff, William. *Government and Politics in Tanzania.* Nairobi, Kenya: East African Publishing House, 1967.

Mabro, Robert, and Samir Radwan. *The Industrialization of Egypt 1939–1973: Policy and Performance.* Oxford: Clarendon, 1976.

CHILE

Burnett, Ben G. *Political Groups in Chile.* Austin: University of Texas Press, 1970.

Cleaves, Peter S. *Bureaucratic Politics and Administration in Chile.* Berkeley: University of California Press, 1974.

De Vylder, Stefan. *Allende's Chile: The Political Economy of the Rise and Fall of the Unidad Popular.* Cambridge: Cambridge University Press, 1976.

Gil, Federico G. *The Political System of Chile.* Boston: Houghton Mifflin, 1966.

Kaufman, Robert. *The Politics of Land Reform in Chile, 1950–1970.* Cambridge, Mass.: Harvard University Press, 1972.

Kinsbruner, Jay. *Chile: A Historical Interpretation.* New York: Harper & Row, 1973.

Loveman, Brian. *Struggle in the Countryside: Politics and Rural Labor in Chile, 1919–1973.* Bloomington: Indiana University Press, 1976.

Nunn, F. M. *The Military in Chilean History: Essays on Civil-Military Relations, 1810–1973.* Albuquerque: University of New Mexico Press, 1976.

O'Brien, Philip. *Allende's Chile.* New York: Praeger, 1976.

Petras, James. *Politics and Social Forces in Chilean Development.* Berkeley: University of California Press, 1969.

Roxborough, Ian, Philip O'Brien, and Jackie Roddick. *Chile: The State and Revolution.* New York: Holmes & Meier, 1977.

Sigmund, Paul E. *The Overthrow of Allende and the Politics of Chile, 1964–1976.* Pittsburgh: University of Pittsburgh Press, 1977.

Silvert, Kalman H. *Chile: Yesterday and Today.* Holt, Rinehart and Winston, 1965.

———, and Leonard Reissman. *Education, Class and Nation: The Experiences of Chile and Venezuela.* New York: Elsevier, 1976.

Valenzuela, Arturo, and J. Samuel Valenzuela, eds. *Chile: Politics and Society.* New Brunswick, N.J.: Transaction Books, 1976.

Zammit, J. Ann., ed. *The Chilean Road to Socialism.* Austin: University of Texas Press, 1973.

APPENDIXES

Using comparative data is both frustrating and dangerous. It is frustrating because we would always like to have more complete and more recent data with which to make our comparisons. It is dangerous because collecting data is an imprecise art.

Unfortunately, collecting data takes time, and the time lag from when the data are collected to when they are publicly reported is often a long one. Ideally, it also would be helpful to know who collected the data, why they collected them, what techniques were used in the collection process, and how great is the margin for error. Some data are clearly more reliable than others, just as some nations are more efficient and accurate than others in their collection and reporting. Politicians, administrators, and academics are not above using statistics and data to prove what they believe is true or would like to believe is true.

The data presented in the following appendixes provide an overview and summary of some of the more commonly collected and reported political, economic, social, and cultural indicators. The tables and charts scratch only the surface of available, reported data for the eight nations in the study. Those students interested in more detailed and complete data may wish to consult one or more of the following references:

Arthur S. Banks, ed., *Political Handbook of the World: 1977* (New York: McGraw-Hill, 1977).

John Paxton, ed., *The Statesman's Year-Book: 1977–1978* (New York: St. Martin's Press, 1977).

The Europa Year Book: 1977 World Survey (London: Europa Publications Limited, 1977). Published yearly.

Donald G. Morrison, Robert C. Mitchell, John N. Paden, and Hugh M. Stevenson, *Black Africa: A Comparative Handbook* (New York: The Free Press, 1972).

Charles Taylor and Michael Hudson, *World Handbook of Social and Political Indicators* (New Haven: Yale University Press, 1972).

APPENDIX A
Selected Population and Demographic Indicators in Eight Nations[a]

	United Kingdom	West Germany	France
Population	56,921,000	61,200,000	53,500,000
Land area (sq. miles)	94,226	95,987	211,207
Population of national capital	London 7,173,900	Bonn 283,260	Paris 2,299,830
Percentage of population living in urban areas	67.6	86.0	71
Population growth rate (in %)	+.05	−.2	+.7

[a] Population figures and growth rates are estimates from the mid-1970s. Most estimates are from 1976–1977.
Sources: Arthur S. Banks, ed., *Political Handbook of the World: 1977* (New York: McGraw-Hill, 1977); John Paxton, ed., *The Statesman's Year-Book: 1977–1978* (New York: St. Martin's Press, 1977);

APPENDIX B
Occupational Breakdown in Percentages of the Economically Active Populations in Eight Nations

Economic Sector	United Kingdom[a]	West Germany[b]	France[c]
Agriculture, Fishing	2.7	6.4	11.3
Mining	1.6	1.4	.8
Manufacturing	34.3	34.8	27.4
Electricity, Gas, Water	1.3	.9	.7
Construction	7.0	7.7	9.1
Wholesale, Retail, Commerce, Trade, Hotels	15.6	14.0	16.1
Transportation, Communication	6.6	5.7	5.3
Finance	5.8	5.1	5.4
Social Service	24.1	21.9	22.2
Other	.7	2.1	1.3

Source: Percentages computed on figures found in *The Europa Year Book: 1977 World Survey* (London: Europa Publications Limited, 1977).
[a] Percentages computed on 1971 data.   [b] Percentages computed on 1975 data.
[c] Percentages computed on 1974 data.

Soviet Union	Nigeria	Egypt	Tanzania	Chile
259,006,000	62,925,000	38,791,000	15,880,000	10,814,000
8,649,489	356,667	386,659	364,898	292,256
Moscow 7,734,000	Lagos 900,969	Cairo 5,500,000	Dar es Salaam 517,000	Santiago 1,759,087
60	16	38	5	74
+.9	+2.7	+2.2	+2.7	+1.8

The Europa Year Book: 1977 World Survey (London: Europa Publications Limited, 1977); Laurence Urdang, ed., The CBS News Almanac (Maplewood, N.J.: Hammond Almanac, 1976); The Demographic Yearbook: 1975 (New York: United Nations Publications,1976).

Soviet Union[c]	Nigeria[d]	Egypt[c]	Tanzania[e]	Chile[a]
22.6	62	47.3	91	19.5
1.7		—	—	1.9
25.2		15.3	2	23.5
.6		1.0	—	.5
8.9		2.6	1	8.3
5.9	14[f]	11.6	1.4	13.8
9.1		4.5	1.0	8.7
1.5[g]		1.0	—	—
23.1	24	16.5	3.6	23.5
1.4		1.0	1	.1

[d] Percentages computed on 1970 data.
[f] Industry.

[e] Percentages computed on 1967 data.
[g] Other manufacturing.

APPENDIX C

Major Ethnic or Identity Groups in Eight Nations (in percent)

United Kingdom		West Germany	
English	79	German	94
Scots	9	Guest workers	6
Welsh	5	(Turkish, Italian, other European)	
Irish	4		
Asian, African, and other	3		

France		Soviet Union	
French citizens	95	Russian	53
Peoples of Italian,	5	Ukranian	17
Spanish, Eastern European,		Belorussian	4
and North African descent		Uzbek	4
		Tatar	3
		Kazakh	3
		140 other ethnic groups	16

Nigeria		Egypt	
Hausa-Fulani	29	Egyptian	98 (approx.)
Yoruba	20	Greeks, Armenians,	2 (approx.)
Ibo	17	Jews, and others	
Tiv and Plateau	9		
Ibibio	6		
Kanuri	5		
Other	14		

Tanzania		Chile	
Nyamwesi Type	19	Spanish (Indian)	68
Interlacustrine Bantu	14	Spanish (European)	30
Northeast Coastal Bantu	11	Indian	2
Central Bantu Cluster	11		
Rift Cluster	10		
Rufiji Cluster	9		
Nyakyusa Cluster	6		
Rukwa Cluster	5		
Kenya Highland Cluster	5		
Other	10		

Sources: John Paxton, ed., *The Statesman's Year-Book: 1976–1977* (New York: St. Martin's Press, 1976); Donald G. Morrison, Robert C. Mitchell, John N. Paden, Hugh M. Stevenson, *Black Africa: A Comparative Handbook* (New York: The Free Press, 1972).

APPENDIX D

Major Religious Affiliations in Eight Nations (in percent)

United Kingdom

Anglican	55
Roman Catholic	10
Presbyterian	5
Jewish	.8
Other Protestant or none	29.2

West Germany

Protestant	49
Roman Catholic	45
Jewish	.1
Other or none	5.9

France

Roman Catholic	85
Protestant	2
Jewish	1
Muslim	1
Other or none	11

Soviet Union

Atheist	70
Russian Orthodox	18
Muslim	9
Other	3

Nigeria

Muslim	52
Christian	35
Traditional African	13

Egypt

Muslim	92
Orthodox and Protestant Copts	8

Tanzania

Muslim	23
Christian	40
Traditional African	37

Chile

Roman Catholic	90
Protestant	5
Jewish, Freethinkers, Agnostic, or other	5

Sources: John Paxton, ed., *The Statesman's Year-Book: 1976–1977* (New York: St. Martin's Press, 1976); Donald G. Morrison, Robert C. Mitchell, John N. Paden, Hugh M. Stevenson, *Black Africa: A Comparative Handbook* (New York: The Free Press, 1972).

APPENDIX E
Current National and Political Leaders in Eight Nations, 1979

United Kingdom

Sovereign	Queen Elizabeth II	Crowned June 2, 1953
Prime Minister	Margaret Thatcher	Conservative party, assumed office following May 1979 election

Federal Republic of Germany

Federal President	Walter Scheel	Elected by Federal Assembly on May 15, 1974
Federal Chancellor	Helmut Schmidt	Social Democratic party, assumed office on the resignation of Willy Brandt, May 1974

France

President	Valéry Giscard d'Estaing	Elected to office in May 1974
Premier	Raymond Barre	Appointed to office by the president in August 1976

Union of Soviet Socialist Republics

President of the Presidium of the Supreme Soviet	Leonid I. Brezhnev	Elected by the Supreme Soviet in June 1977
Chairman of the Council of Ministers	Alexei N. Kosygin	Assumed Office in October 1964
General Secretary of the Communist Party	Leonid I. Brezhnev	Elected by the Central Committee of the Communist Party in October 1964

Nigeria

Chairman of the Supreme Military Council, Head of the Federal Military Government	General Olusegun Obasanjo	Assumed office on the death of General Murtala Mohammed in an abortive coup d'état in January 1976

Egypt

President	Muhammad Anwar el-Sadat	Assumed office on the death of Gamal Abdul Nasser in September 1970; confirmed in office by referendum in October 1970
Vice President	Muhammad Hosni Mubarak	Appointed by the president in 1975
Prime Minister	Mustafa Khalil	Appointed by the president in 1978

United Republic of Tanzania

President	Julius K. Nyerere	Has served as head of state since independence in 1961. Most recently re-elected in uncontested election in 1975
First Vice President and Chairman of the Zanzibar Revolutionary Council	Aboud Jumbe	Assumed office following the assassination of Abeid Karume in 1972
Second Vice President and Prime Minister	Edward Sokinwe	Appointed to office by the president in February 1977

Republic of Chile

Chief of State	General Augusto Pinochet Ugarte	Assumed power following military coup d'état in September 1973

APPENDIX F-1
Summary of the Major Political Parties and Their Representation in Major Legislative Bodies in the United Kingdom, West Germany, France, and the Soviet Union

United Kingdom

Party	No. of Seats in the House of Commons as a result of the March 1979 election
Labour Party	268
Conservative Party	339
Liberal Party	11
Scottish Nationalist Party	2
Plaid Cymru (Welsh nationalists)	2
Ulster Unionist Party	10
Other	2

West Germany

Party	No. of Seats in the Bundestag as a result of the October 1976 election
Social Democratic Party	224
Christian Democratic Union/ Christian Social Union	254
Free Democratic Party	40

France

Party	No. of Seats in the National Assembly as a result of the April 1978 elections
Gaullists	148
Independent Republicans	137
Socialists (and allies)	103
Communist Party	86
Radicals	10

Soviet Union

Party	Number of seats in Soviet of the Union and Soviet of Nationalities
Communist Party of the Soviet Union	Approximately two-thirds to three-fourths of the 767 members in the Soviet of the Union and 750 members in the Soviet of Nationalities are party members. Most all candidates receive party scrutiny at some level.

APPENDIX F-2
**Summary of the Status of Political Parties
in Nigeria, Egypt, Tanzania, and Chile**

Nigeria

Over 80 political parties and organizations were banned following the January 1966 military coup d'état. In October 1978 new political parties were allowed to form in anticipation of the return to civilian rule in 1979. New parties must be national in membership and are not allowed to appeal to ethnic or sectional interests.

Egypt

Since 1976 political party activity re-emerged under the umbrella of the Arab Socialist Union. Factions representing political opinion on the right, center, and left formed. In August 1978 further re-alignments occurred. The National Democrat party, loyal to President Sadat, became the most important and powerful party. Other parties were the Socialist Labour party, the National Progressive party (opposition party), and the Liberal Socialist party.

Tanzania

In February 1977 the Tanzanian African National Union (the sole party on mainland Tanzania) and the Afro-Shirazi party (the sole party on the island of Zanzibar) officially merged to form Chama Cha Mapinduzi (Revolutionary party). This is the only legal party in Tanzania.

Chile

Following the September 1973 military intervention in Chile, political parties were either outlawed or recessed. Parties and coalitions of the left, like the Popular Unity, were outlawed. Parties of the more moderate center and the right, like the Christian Democrats, generally were recessed. No political party activity has been allowed since September 1973.

APPENDIX G
Estimated Literacy Rates in Eight Nations (in percent)

United Kingdom	99	Nigeria	33
West Germany	99	Egypt	30
France	99	Tanzania	18
Soviet Union	99	Chile	84

Source: Charles Taylor and Michael Hudson, *World Handbook of Social and Political Indicators* (New Haven: Yale University Press, 1972), pp. 232–234.

INDEX